FUNDAMENTALS OF CLINICAL SUPERVISION

SECOND EDITION

JANINE M. BERNARD

Fairfield University

RODNEY K. GOODYEAR

University of Southern California

ALLYN AND BACON

Boston   London   Toronto   Sydney   Tokyo   Singapore

Vice President, Publisher, Education: Nancy Forsyth
Senior Editor: Raymond Short
Editorial Assistant: Karin Huang
Marketing Manager: Kathy Hunter
Editorial Production Service: Raeia Maes, Maes Associates
Manufacturing Buyer: Suzanne Lareau
Cover Administrator: Jennifer Hart

Copyright © 1998, 1992 by Allyn & Bacon
A Viacom Company
160 Gould Street
Needham Heights, MA 02194

Internet: www.abacon.com
America Online: keyword: College Online

Library of Congress Cataloging-in-Publication Data

Bernard, Janine M.
    Fundamentals of clinical supervision / Janine M. Bernard, Rodney
K. Goodyear.—2nd ed.
      p. cm.
    Includes bibliographical references and index.
    ISBN 0-205-17531-7
    1. Psychotherapists—Supervision of. 2. Counselors—Supervision
of. 3. Clinical psychologists—Supervision of.   I. Goodyear,
Rodney K. II. Title.
RC480.5.B455 1998
362.2'0425'0683—dc21   97-31203
                                       CIP

Printed in the United States of America
10 9 8 7 6 5 4 3 2   02 01 00 99 98

CONTENTS

CHAPTER 4.   THE SUPERVISORY RELATIONSHIP: PROCESSES AND ISSUES   61

**CHAPTER 7.   SUPERVISION INTERVENTIONS: LIVE
SUPERVISION   131**

PREFACE

The years since we wrote the first edition of *Fundamentals of Clinical Supervision* have been productive for those interested in clinical supervision in the mental health disciplines. When we wrote the first edition, we described clinical supervision as in its adolescence. Clearly, the area has been launched and operates in its own right within each of the mental health professions.

The growth of clinical supervision has meant that this second edition could not be a simple update of the literature. Significant changes have taken place, and we have attempted to reflect these changes. We also, of course, wanted to improve the book in a variety of ways and hope that we have succeeded.

Some things are the same. We continued to resist writing a text that promotes any one approach to clinical supervision; we also continued to draw from the literature of the various mental health disciplines, rather than to write a book targeted for only one or two of the disciplines. That being said, we found that the fields of counseling and psychology continue to produce the majority of professional literature in clinical supervision, and this is reflected in the text. Marriage and family therapy and social work contributions also appear prominently; psychiatry much less so.

Finally, another goal that this edition shares with the first is our intent to offer a review of the clinical supervision field in a way that will be equally useful to the student of supervision and to the supervision practitioner as a professional resource. We intended that the book be both scholarly (accomplished through a comprehensive review of the literature) and pragmatic (accomplished through our choice of topics and manner of writing).

Chapter 1 defines supervision and differentiates it from other related professional activities, including training. It is intended to establish a foundation for the chapters that follow.

Chapter 2 is significantly different from the theoretical overview that we provided in the first edition. Although the broader context is still provided, the focus of the chapter is a more comprehensive presentation of some distinct models of clinical supervision. It is our opinion that the field justifies a closer look at distinct approaches and that this will be beneficial both to students and practitioners.

Chapters 3 and 4 represent both some reconfiguration of issues and information from the first edition and the presentation of concepts not represented in our earlier work. Both have to do with establishing and maintaining a supervision relationship and should be considered together for that purpose.

Chapter 3 is intended to be somewhat more generic than Chapter 4. The focus of Chapter 3 is on individual and developmental differences that play a role in all supervisory relationships. The material on developmental differences, personal style, and belief systems is all new to this edition. Because of the keen interest in supervisee development held by many researchers, the information in this area is vast and forms a complicated matrix. We have attempted to sort out the literature and draw what conclusions seemed justifiable.

Chapter 3 also includes what was presented separately in the first edition as "supervision in a multicultural context." Although literature pertaining to race, gender, and sexual orientation continues to be presented separately, we believe it is appropriate for these issues to be viewed as endemic to forming *any* supervision relationship and not treated in a way that isolates (and, therefore, marginalizes) them.

Chapter 4 builds on Chapter 3 by looking at unique relationship processes and issues that may occur during supervision. Not to recognize them can jeopardize effectiveness. On the other hand, to understand some of these processes and issues can provide supervisors with useful perspectives and tools.

As in the first edition, the following three chapters also might be seen as a unit in that they each cover a particular mode of supervision. Chapter 5 is a comprehensive review of the methods used for the individual case conference, ranging from self-report and the use of process notes to videotape usage and live observation. Chapter 6 focuses on group supervision and offers the reader a rationale for the use of group supervision, a review of the dynamics that determine the success of the group, and different models for use in supervision groups. Finally, Chapter 7 is devoted to live supervision, a method of supervision that is increasingly popular in training programs and, having its own unique advantages and challenges, does not fit within either individual or group supervision.

Chapters 8 and 9 address the professional responsibilities of clinical supervisors, with Chapter 10 highlighting some of the skills that make both professional and clinical responsibilities of supervisors possible. Chapter 8 is devoted to the crucial task of evaluation. Included in the chapter are favorable conditions for evaluation, criteria, the process of evaluation, and chronic issues. Chapter 9, dealing with ethical and legal issues, continues our theme of professional responsibility. Throughout this chapter, therapy dimensions that the supervisor must oversee and ethical and legal issues that are endemic to supervision are differentiated. Both are reviewed in detail, along with some of the leading legal precedents that determine accepted practice today. Finally, Chapter 10 takes a serious look at the management of clinical supervision. In this chapter we take the position that a supervisor who is clinically outstanding, but who ignores structure and the need to take time to plan supervision, will have only partial or random influence on supervisees. But when all the standards of professional competencies presented in these three chapters are employed *along with* advanced clinical skill as a supervisor, supervisees are likely to have an outstanding learning experience.

Chapter 11 introduces a topic new to this edition. In it, we first address developmental stages and processes of supervisors and then discuss issues and strategies in training supervisors.

Finally, Chapter 12 addresses supervision research. Specifically, it covers selected topics to address in supervision (other than those already suggested by the previous 11 chapters) and then addresses some methodological issues in conducting supervision research. A topic in this chapter new to this edition is treatment manuals and some of the issues they seem to present for supervisors.

Appendixes A and B represent documents from professional groups that have attempted to describe the parameters of clinical supervision. Appendix A offers the Standards for Counselor Supervision endorsed by the Association for Counselor Education and Supervision and the American Association for Counseling and Development (1990). These standards can serve as a checklist for the practice of clinical supervisors.

Appendix B follows with the ethical codes for the practice of supervision endorsed by the Association for Counselor Education and Supervision and the British Association for Counselling's Code of Ethics and Practice for Supervisors and Counsellors.

Appendix C is a compilation of selected instruments for evaluating the supervision process.

Finally, Appendix D is the complete manual for a two-day workshop in clinical supervision. This manual can be used for in-service training of novice or seasoned supervisors. (It has been used successfully with both populations.) Or the eight sessions can be infused into a more traditional course in clinical supervision as the experiential component.

Although admittedly sophomoric, many authors refer to their writing using a "child" metaphor. Borrowing from this legacy, we approached this project assuming that the second child would be easier than the first. On that count, we were wrong! For both of us, this was a first attempt at a revision and we found it uniquely challenging. Like a second child, however, the book is easily recognizable as a relative of the first, though distinctly different. Finally, the child metaphor is appropriate in that we have spent many, if not most, weekends over the past two years with this child. We have been fortunate to have real families that both appreciated the task we had set out for ourselves and had the good sense to tell us when to stop working and enjoy their marvelous company. Our biggest debt and our greatest thanks go to them.

In addition, we would like to express our sincerest appreciation to Patricia Wolleat for her comments that helped to kick off the second edition. We also wish to thank our professional colleagues, who devote a good bit of their own energies to studying, discussing, and doing clinical supervision, as well as our supervisees. Their work and their comments over the years have helped to direct our thinking and maintain our own enthusiasm about this important topic.

J.M.B.
R.K.G.

CHAPTER 1

The Importance, Scope, and Definition
of Clinical Supervision

For millennia, less experienced members of a profession have relied on more senior colleagues to teach them craft and tradition. This has been true in virtually all professions. The first few lines of the famous Hippocratic oath suggest just how old this practice is. At least as important, the oath also suggests the esteem with which educators and supervisors are often held.

> I SWEAR by Apollo the physician, and Aesculapius, and Health, and All-heal, and all the gods and goddesses, that, according to my ability and judgment, I will keep this Oath and this stipulation—to reckon him who taught me this Art equally dear to me as my parents, to share my substance with him, and relieve his necessities if required; to look upon his offspring in the same footing as my own brothers. . . . (Hippocrates, ca. 400 B.C.)

But whereas supervision has been performed through the ages, recognition that it is a discrete intervention with its own concepts and techniques is actually new, at least in the mental health professions. Yet, the literature on clinical supervision in the mental health professions is growing rapidly and is increasingly robust. This book is intended to provide mental health professionals who are or who would be supervisors with an overview of the more important issues, concepts, and techniques of this important intervention.

Two important premises guided our writing of this book. The first is that clinical supervision is an intervention in its own right. It is possible, therefore, to isolate and describe issues, theory, and technique that are unique to it. The second premise is that the several mental health professions are more alike than different in their practice of supervision and that there exists a corpus of knowledge about clinical supervision that is broader than what is found in the literature of any single one of these professions (e.g., psychology counseling; social work; family therapy; psychiatry; psychiatric nursing). This book, then, draws from an interdisciplinary literature to address the breadth of issues and content that seem to characterize clinical supervision in mental health. This chapter begins the book by considering the importance, scope, and definition of supervision.

CLINICAL SUPERVISION IN THE PREPARATION OF MENTAL HEALTH PROFESSIONALS

Mental health professionals receive relatively extensive education and training. The content and nature of that preparation differs somewhat according to the specific profession the person has entered. But, despite this, substantial between-profession overlap exists with respect to such core competencies as therapy, assessment, and clinical supervision. At its most basic level, this professional preparation centers on two general realms of knowledge (Schön, 1983).

— Formal theories and observations that have been confirmed, or are confirmable, by research
— The knowledge and accompanying skills that have accrued through the professional experiences of practitioners

These realms, which often are talked about, respectively, as "science" and "art," are both essential bases of knowledge. Each should complement

1

and inform the other. In fact, this assumed complementarity is at the heart of the scientist–practitioner model in which most psychologists are trained (O'Sullivan & Quevillon, 1992). Yet, because the two knowledge realms are differentially valued, to reach an optimal balance between the two is often difficult. That is, within the academy (i.e., the university), the first realm is too often regarded as that of *real* knowledge, whereas the latter is either ignored or even regarded with some disdain. The reverse prejudice is too often true among practitioners.

These prejudices are one barrier to students' appropriate integration of the two knowledge domains. Another is the fact that students are typically exposed to those domains sequentially. That is, they first learn formal theory in the classroom. They gain the practitioner-driven knowledge later when they actually begin to participate in the delivery of human services and to solicit the wisdom of other service providers.

Clinical supervision provides the crucible in which supervisees can blend these two knowledge types and begin to incorporate them as their own working knowledge. That is, supervision is teaching that occurs in the context of practice and provides a bridge between campus and clinic (Williams, 1995); the bridge by which supervisees begin to span the "large theory–practice gulf" to which Ronnestad and Skovholt (1993, p. 396) allude.

In fact, a necessary condition for supervisees to develop their professional competence is that they practice their skills in laboratory and clinical settings. Fortunately, supervisees generally have excitement about and commitment to this aspect of their training. Practicing these professional activities was their purpose in entering the field in the first place. But important as this practice is necessary, it is an insufficient basis for the supervisee to attain competence.

Beutler (1988) has discussed the "germ theory" of psychotherapy education that he suggested has been too prevalent in the past. That is, students and supervisees were expected to acquire—or "catch"—skills through exposure. But unless practice is accompanied by the systematic feedback and reflection that supervision provides, supervisees can be assured of gaining no more than the *illusion* that they are developing professional expertise. In fact, the skills and work habits they develop will likely be different from and even contrary to usual standards of practice. Sechrest pointedly addressed this matter in a 1995 e-mail posting to the Society for a Science of Clinical Psychology listserv: "As one wag has put it, 'You are only young once, but it is possible to be immature forever': By analogy, you are only inexperienced once, but it is possible to be incompetent forever."

It has been the experience of many of us who provide clinical training that the most troublesome supervisee often is the one with extensive unsupervised human service experience—obtained, for example, during work as a paraprofessional substance abuse counselor—who now has returned to school for more formal training. Such supervisees tend to have unwarranted confidence in their own idiosyncratic approaches.

Such supervisees are explained, in part, by Dawes (1994) who asserted that:

> *Two conditions are important for experiential learning: one, a clear understanding of what constitutes an incorrect response or error in judgment, and two, immediate, unambiguous and consistent feedback when such errors are made. In the mental health professions, neither of these conditions is satisfied.* (p. 111)

Dawes's assertions about the two conditions necessary for experiential learning are compelling. But, on the other hand, we believe his assertion that *neither* condition is met in the mental health professions is overstated. It is a premise of this entire book that supervision can satisfy these and other necessary conditions for learning.

It is true that in the case of many motor and performance skills it may not be necessary to have a "supervisor" (by whatever name) to attain a satisfactory level of competence. In these domains, simply to perform the task may provide sufficient feedback for skill mastery. Learning to type is one example of this; learning to drive an automobile is another (Dawes, 1994). When driving, the person who turns the steering wheel too abruptly receives immediate feedback from the vehicle; the same is true if the driver is too slow applying the brakes when approaching another vehicle. In these and other ways, experience behind the wheel gives the person an opportunity to obtain immediate and unambiguous feedback. Driving skills therefore are likely to develop and improve simply with the experience of driving.

But psychological practice skills are of a different type. In this domain, experience alone rarely provides *either* of the two conditions Dawes stipulates as necessary for experiential learning to occur. The practitioner's skills cannot be shaped by simple experience in the same automatic manner that occurs with the development of driving skills. She or he must receive intentional, clear feedback such as is available in supervision.

Hill, Charles, and Reed (1981) reported empirical data that seem to speak to this. In their study, previous counseling experience was found *not* to accelerate the clinical progress of students in a doctoral-level psychology program. And both Wiley and Ray (1986) and Reising and Daniels (1983) found that, though *supervised* counseling experiences correlated with the supervisory needs of supervisees at various developmental stages, unsupervised experience did not.

Confidence in one's abilities can exist independently of actual skills. It is, however, still a desired training goal. Therefore, Bradley and Olsen's (1980) findings concerning clinical psychology students' felt competence as psychotherapists are significant. Of all the variables they examined as possible correlates of felt competence (e.g., total number of hours of therapy conducted; amount of therapy coursework), only two were related to it: (1) the number of hours of formal supervision in which the students had participated and (2) the number of supervisors they had.

In short, supervision must accompany client-contact experiences if students in the mental health professions are to acquire the necessary practice skills and conceptual ability. As Breshears (1995)

noted, "arguments have been made about how long supervision should last and how much supervision is needed, but not over its necessity" (p. 692).

Recognition of supervision's importance is evident in the extent to which licensure, credentialing, and accreditation bodies require it of applicants. States stipulate amounts and types of supervision that licensure candidates are to accrue; this typically runs into the hundred or thousands of hours. The same is true of independent credentialing groups, such as the Academy of Certified Social Workers, the American Board of Professional Psychology, the National Board for Certified Counselors, and the American Association for Marriage and Family Therapists.

Licensing and credentialing groups, however, govern the individual professional. Accrediting bodies, on the other hand, govern the training programs that prepare practitioners, specifying the scope, content, and quality of training. Like the licensure and credentialing bodies, the accreditation groups stipulate amounts and conditions of supervision. The Council for the Accreditation of Counseling and Related Educational Programs (CACREP), for example, requires that a student receive a minimum of 1 hour per week individual and 1.5 hours of group supervision during practicum and internship (Council for the Accreditation of Counseling and Related Educational Programs, 1994).

State licensure laws ensure that this supervised training experience is not limited to the period in which the supervisee is enrolled in a formal degree program. These laws almost invariably stipulate a particular amount of supervised clinical experience that must be acquired postdegree. And aside from the legal aspects of fulfilling licensure requirements, many agencies require newly hired professionals to be supervised as a way of ensuring quality of care for their clients.

As well, it is important to note that many, if not most, postgraduate, credentialed practitioners *want* to continue some level and type of supervision. This was a finding of Borders and Usher's (1992) survey of National Certified Counselors, which complemented the findings of other studies (e.g.,

McCarthy, Kulakowski, & Kenfield, 1994; Wiley, 1994) of postdegree supervision practices.

And whereas supervision is essential in the preparation of competent mental health professionals, it is also essential as a means to protect the welfare of clients these supervisees see. This, as much as the training intent, is behind state requirements that postdegree practitioners who are not yet licensed receive supervision.

Occasionally, too, supervision is used as a method to "rehabilitate" impaired professionals (see, e.g., Frick, McCartney, & Lazarus, 1995). Whereas this overlaps with both the training and client-protective purposes of supervision, it really should be considered a third purpose of supervision.

Munson (1987) has noted that, in contrast to their colleagues in psychiatry, professionals in related disciplines such as psychology, counseling, social work, and family therapy have had to struggle to establish themselves as autonomous practitioners. He observed that "one autonomy-building strategy (although not always deliberate) has been to de-emphasize supervision. The logic is that one cannot be autonomous and be supervised" (p. 237). Perhaps he is right. But, if so, it is a strategy that is contrary to what seems necessary for supervisees; it is also contrary to state laws and other credentialing requirements.

Because supervision is such an essential aspect of professional training and because so much of it is required, it should not be surprising that it is one of the more frequent activities of mental health professionals. Two decades ago, Garfield and Kurtz (1976) found that supervision was fifth in a list of activities in which clinical psychologists engaged, ranking ahead of such activities as group therapy and research; more recently, Norcross, Prochaska, and Gallager (1989) tracked similar activities. Norcross, Prochaska, and Farber, however, found that clinical supervision was the *second* most frequently reported activity among members of APA's Division of Psychotherapy (barely edging out diagnosis and assessment). Similar results have been obtained in studies of counseling psychologists (e.g., Fitzgerald & Os-

ipow, 1986; Watkins, Lopez, Campbell, & Himmell, 1986). And Kadushin (1976) reported that, depending on their field of practice, between 12.6 and 20 percent of social workers had some supervisory responsibilities.

But this frequently used and essential intervention is distinct from any other. As we shall discuss, supervision has elements in common with such other interventions as teaching, therapy, and consultation, yet is unique from any of them. For this reason, its practitioners should receive specific preparation. Although earlier studies (Hess & Hess, 1983; McColley & Baker, 1982) found supervision training to be a relatively infrequent activity, it is our impression that the situation has improved. For example, both CACREP- and AAMFT-accredited doctoral programs now are required to offer a supervision course, and the new accreditation guidelines for The American Psychological Association stipulate supervision as a competence area; the Association for Counselor Education and Supervision (ACES) has endorsed Standards for Counseling Supervisors (see Appendix A) and the American Association for Marriage and Family Therapy has a supervisor membership category that requires specified training. Thus, whereas Ross and Goh (1993) found that only 11.2 percent of school psychologists reported coursework or training during their graduate programs in school psychology, this likely will change as the new accreditation guidelines are followed.

To the extent that supervisor training becomes a precondition for working as a supervisor, then Haley's (1993) following satirical comments will have increasingly less basis in fact:

> *Anyone who does therapy without a license is breaking the law. To gain the license, the therapist must listen to a supervisor and pay for the privilege. . . . The supervisor too must be certified, but fortunately, that does not require much. Showing success in teaching therapists how to induce change is not required. All that is needed is many hours of therapist and supervisor sitting and talking together. Any supervisor with a comfortable chair and healthy vocal chords can do that.* (p. 52)

One hindrance to the development of more universal training of supervisors has been that many mental health professionals apparently have believed that to be an effective therapist is the primary prerequisite to being a good supervisor. But to assume this is analogous to assuming that a good athlete inevitably will make a good coach (or, perhaps, a good sports announcer). We all can find instances in which that has not been the case. The great players tend not to become the great coaches, and vice versa. But, at the same time, most great coaches have "played the game," and some have played well. Carroll (1996), though, said, "It sounds a terrible choice, but given the option between a good counsellor who was a poor educator, or a poor counsellor who was a good educator, I would choose the latter as a supervisor" (p. 27).

It is the close, but not quite perfect, relationship between therapy and supervision that perpetuates the belief by some that supervision training is unnecessary. In fact, supervisors may lack specific training in supervision, but they find themselves *doing* it—and typically believe they are pretty good at it. In fact, this circumstance is directly analogous to a situation we discussed above in which the person who obtains therapy experience with inadequate supervision will develop a sense of professional competence, but likely will perform as a therapist in an idiosyncratic and uneven manner. Self-assessments of competence and actual competence are often independent of one another, for both therapists *and* supervisors.

Professionals who take on supervisory roles in this manner are more inclined to believe that if they have learned it without formal preparation their students and supervisees can as easily do so. Moreover, these faculty and field supervisors can serve as role models to supervisees, who then can receive mixed messages about the actual importance of supervision training. In this way, then, they hinder the implementation of more general training in supervision.

This book is for mental health professionals who are or intend to become clinical supervisors. It draws from the literature of the several mental health disciplines, for the practice of clinical supervision has more between-discipline similarities than differences. Certain essential processes and issues in supervision are common across all these disciplines. This book speaks to those commonalties.

Supervision Defined

To have "super vision" is a fantasy that many supervisors must entertain. In fact, it is possible for a supervisor to gain a clarity of perspective about counseling or therapy processes precisely because she or he is not one of the involved parties. In this way, the supervisor is able to work from a vantage point that is not afforded the therapist who is actually involved in the process.

Levenson (1984) spoke to this when he observed that, in the ordinary course of his work as a therapist, he spent a considerable time perplexed, confused, bored, and "at sea." But "when I supervise, all is clear to me!" (p. 153). He reported finding that theoretical and technical difficulties were surprisingly clear to him. Moreover, he maintained that people whom he supervised and who seemed confused most of the time they were supervisees reported that they attained a similar clarity when they were supervising. He speculated that this is "an odd, seductive aspect of the phenomenology of the supervisory process itself" (p. 154) that occurs at a different level of abstraction than therapy. Perhaps this is the perspective of the "Monday morning quarterback."

Despite this, though, the etymological definition of supervision is not "super vision." It is simply "to oversee" (Webster, 1966). This is what supervisors in virtually any profession do. This definition, though, misses the teaching and learning that occur in clinical supervision. It is important, then, to have a more precise and specific definition.

The working definitions of clinical supervision that various authors have offered differ considerably as a function of such factors as the author's discipline and training focus. Our intent in this book is to offer a definition that is specific enough to be helpful, but at the same time broad enough to encompass the multiples roles, disciplines, and settings associated with supervision. Before offering that definition, it might be useful to consider two definitions that have been offered.

Loganbill, Hardy, and Delworth (1982) defined supervision as "an intensive, interpersonally focused one-to-one relationship in which one person is designated to facilitate the development of therapeutic competence in the other person" (p. 4). In contrast to the definition of supervision as "to oversee," which was too broad and inclusive to be helpful, this definition suggested a focus more narrow and restrictive than that which we will maintain in this book. For example, in their consideration of supervision as something that occurs only in the context of a one-to-one relationship, Loganbill et al. (1982) overlook group supervision. However, clinical supervisors frequently employ that modality (Goodyear & Nelson, 1997).

Also, in declaring their goal to be the development of the supervisee's therapeutic competence, Loganbill et al. (1982) left no room for supervising such other psychological services as psychoeducation or career counseling. Although the larger portion of this book will focus on the supervision of psychotherapy, we believe many of the essential issues and processes remain the same in the supervision of other psychological interventions. Finally, the Loganbill et al. (1982) definition did not acknowledge explicitly the client-protective function of supervision.

Hart's (1982) definition more closely approximated that which we intend to consider, though he, too, seemed to suggest a one-to-one focus. He offered that supervision is "an ongoing educational process in which one person in the role of supervisor helps another person in the role of the supervisee acquire appropriate professional behavior through an examination of the trainee's professional activities" (p. 12).

For this book, we are offering the following working definition of supervision:

> *An intervention provided by a more senior member of a profession to a more junior member or members of that same profession. This relationship is evaluative, extends over time, and has the simultaneous purposes of enhancing the professional functioning of the more junior person(s), monitoring the quality of professional services offered to the client(s) she, he, or they see(s), and serving as a gatekeeper of those who are to enter the particular profession.*

This succinct definition merits further explication. It would be useful, therefore, to break it into component parts and then consider each part in greater detail. Prior to doing this, however, we wish to define briefly several of the terms we will use in this book.

Whereas many supervisors use the terms *trainee* and *supervisee* interchangeably, we believe *supervisee* is the more inclusive term. *Trainee* connotes a supervisee who is still enrolled in a formal training program; it seems less appropriate for postgraduate professionals who seek supervision. Therefore, in most cases we will use *supervisee.* Occasionally, when a more delimited term seems necessary, we will use either *trainee* or *therapist* (to designate postdegree supervisees) as appropriate.

We will use *counseling, therapy,* and *psychotherapy* interchangeably. Patterson (1986) has pointed out that distinctions among these terms are artificial and serve little function. Also, we will follow the convention suggested by Rogers (1951) of referring to the recipient of therapeutic services as a *client.*

Finally, we distinguish between *supervision* and *training.* Both are essential components in the imparting of therapeutic skills, and they often are treated together in reviews of literature (e.g., Matarazzo & Patterson, 1986). Training differs from supervision, however, in its more limited scope and its focus on specific skills (e.g., how to offer restatements of client affect and content). Also, such training often takes place in laboratory courses rather than with real clients.

We turn now to a more complete explication of our working definition of supervision. Each of the following sections will address a specific element of that definition.

Supervision Is a Distinct Intervention

Supervision is an intervention, just as are education, psychotherapy, and mental health consultation. Although there are substantial ways in which supervision overlaps with these other interventions, it is unique.

Education versus Supervision.   As with education, one goal of supervision is to teach; moreover, the role of the supervisee is that of a learner (cf. the title of the classic Ekstein and Wallerstein book, *The Teaching and Learning of Psychotherapy,* 1972). Moreover, education and supervision are alike in that there is an evaluative aspect to the intervention. Relatedly, each ultimately serves a gatekeeping function, regulating who is legitimized to enter the world of work in their chosen area.

In education, however, there typically is an explicit curriculum with teaching goals that are imposed uniformly on everyone. Certainly, education in this sense does occur in clinical preparation. In fact, training (e.g., to impart specific skills such as the ability to reflect feelings) is an example of this. Yet, even though the focus of supervision at its broadest level (e.g., to prepare competent practitioners) might seem to speak to common goals, the actual intervention is tailored to the needs of the individual supervisee and the supervisee's clients.

Counseling versus Supervision.   There are elements, too, of counseling or therapy in supervision. That is, supervisors often help supervisees to examine aspects of their behavior, thoughts, or feelings that are stimulated by a client, particularly as these may act as barriers to their work with the client. Any therapeutic intervention with supervisees, however, should *only* be in the service of helping supervisees become more effective with clients: To provide therapy that has broader goals is ethical misconduct.

There are other differences, too. For example, clients generally are free to enter therapy or not; when they do, they usually have a voice in choosing their therapists. Supervisees, on the other hand, are not given a choice about whether to receive supervision and often have no voice in who their supervisor is to be.

The single most important difference between therapy and supervision may reside in the evaluative responsibilities of the supervisor. Although few would maintain that counseling or therapy is or could be entirely value free, most therapists actively resist imposing their values on clients or otherwise making explicit evaluations of them. On the other hand, supervisees are evaluated against criteria that are imposed on them by others.

Consultation versus Supervision.   Mental health consultation is yet another intervention that overlaps with supervision. In fact, for more-senior professionals, supervision often evolves into consultation. That is, the experienced therapist might meet informally on an occasional basis with a colleague to get ideas about how to handle a particularly difficult client or to regain needed objectivity. We all encounter blind spots in ourselves, and it is to our benefit to obtain help in this manner.

But, despite the similarities, there are distinctions between consultation and supervision. Caplan (1970), for example, suggested several of these. One such distinction is that the parties in the consultation relationship are often not of the same professional discipline (e.g., a social worker might consult with a teacher about a child's problem). Another distinction is that consultation is more likely than supervision to be a one-time-only event.

Two consultation–supervision distinctions echo distinctions already made between therapy and supervision. One is that supervision is more likely imposed, whereas consultation typically is freely sought. More significantly, there is no evaluative role for the consultant—Caplan maintained that the relationship was between two equals—whereas evaluation is one of the defining attributes of supervision.

In summary, then, specific aspects of such related interventions as education, therapy, and consultation are also present as components of supervision. That is, certain skills of teachers, therapists, and consultants are common, too, in supervision. But, although there are common skills across these several interventions, the manner in which they are arrayed is unique in each. Martin (1990) made some useful observations about skills that have implications for thinking about supervision and its relationship to the related interventions of counseling, education, and consultation:

> *The word* skill *has a specific meaning. It is an ability that can be perfected by training and exercise of the ability itself, usually without much regard to the particular context in which it may be put to use. Thus, dribbling a basketball is a skill; so too is typing or enunciation of words and phrases in oral speech. Of course, matters are complicated somewhat by the fact that any skill typically can be subdivided into various subskills. Skills also can be combined with other skills, at a similar level and category, to comprise more inclusive skills. Nonetheless, there is much more to playing basketball, writing meaningful prose, or effective public speaking than dribbling, typing, or enunciating.* (p. 403)

To put this into a context relevant to this book, then, supervision should be thought of as an intervention that is comprised of multiple skills, many of which are common to other forms of intervention. Yet their *configuration* is such as to make supervision unique among psychological interventions. Moreover, there is at least one phenomenon, that of parallel or reciprocal processes (e.g., Doehrman, 1976; Searles, 1955), that is unique to supervision and distinguishes it from other interventions (parallel processes are discussed in Chapter 4).

Member of Same Profession

The widely acknowledged purpose of supervision is to facilitate supervisees' development of therapeutic and case management skills. Certainly, this is essential. Moreover, it is possible to accomplish this purpose when the supervisory dyad is comprised of members of two different disciplines (e.g., a marital and family therapist might supervise the work of a counselor). But, though this arrangement results in technical competence, it overlooks the socialization function that supervision serves. Supervisees are developing a sense of professional identity, and this is best acquired through association with more senior members of the supervisees' own professional discipline.

Ekstein and Wallerstein (1972) spoke to this when they noted that it would be possible for a training program to prepare its supervisees with all the basic psychotherapeutic skills, but still to fall short. Skill acquisition is not enough: "What would still be missing is a specific quality in the psychotherapist that makes him [or her] into a truly professional person, a quality we wish to refer to as his [or her] professional identity" (p. 65).

To socialize supervisees into a profession must be accomplished by supervisors serving as role models. It follows, then, that most of the supervisors with whom a supervisee works should be of the profession of which the supervisee intends to be a member. Social work students should receive supervision from social workers, psychology students should receive supervision from psychologists, and so on. Each of those professions is in some ways distinct, with its own history and philosophy; each also has functions more typical of it than for the others. Most state laws that govern the licensure of mental health professions stipulate that the licensure applicant have a certain portion of his or her supervised clinical hours from supervisors of a like profession. Ekstein and Wallerstein (1972) observed that this is normative. The major exception occurs with multidisciplinary training institutes that offer postgraduate preparation in a specific approach (e.g., psychoanalytic, Jungian, rational emotive, strategic, and so on).

In a cautionary tale of the adverse consequences of using members of one profession to supervise neophyte members of another profession, Albee (1970) invoked the metaphor of the cuckoo: The cuckoo is a bird that lays its eggs in the nests of other birds, who then raise the offspring as their own. His case in point was clinical psychology, which had used the Veterans Administration system as a primary base of training in the decades following World War II. From Albee's perspective, this was unfortunate, for the clinical psychology fledglings were put in the care of psychiatrists, who then socialized them into their way of viewing the world. Albee asserted that a consequence of this pervasive practice was that clinical psychology lost some of what was unique to it as its members incorporated the perspectives of psychiatry.

Supervision Is Evaluative

We have already mentioned several times that evaluation stands as one of supervision's hallmarks, distinguishing it from both counseling or therapy and consultation. Evaluation is implicit in the supervisors' mandate to safeguard clients, both those currently being seen by the supervisee and those who would be seen in the future by the trainee if the trainee were to finish the professional program.

Evaluation is also a tool that provides the supervisor with an important source of interpersonal influence. For example, although most supervisees have a very high degree of intrinsic motivation to learn and to use feedback to self-correct, evaluation can provide supervisees with an additional, extrinsic motivation to change or evolve.

But, despite its importance as a component of supervision, both supervisor and supervisee can experience evaluation with discomfort. Supervisors, for example, were trained first in the more nonevaluative role of counselor or therapist. Indeed, they may well have been attracted to the field because of this feature of counseling. The role of evaluator therefore can be not only new, but uncomfortable as well.

> The role of evaluator also affects the trainee's perception of the supervisor: Students are not only taught psychotherapy by their supervisors, they are also evaluated by them. The criteria for evaluating students' performances tend to be subjective and ambiguous, in large part because the skills being evaluated are highly complex, intensely personal, and difficult to measure. Students know that their psychological health, interpersonal skills, and therapeutic competence are being judged against unclear standards. . . . Supervisors are thus not only admired teachers but feared judges who have real power. (Doehrman, 1976, pp. 10–11)

Evaluation, then, is an important, integral component of supervision, but one that often is the source of problems for supervisors and super-

visees alike. Therefore, we have devoted an entire chapter of this book to the topic of evaluation. Although there is no way in which evaluation could (or should) be removed from supervision, there are ways to enhance its usefulness and to minimize problems attendant to it.

Supervision Extends over Time

A final element of our definition of supervision is that it is an intervention that extends over time. This distinguishes supervision from training, which might be brief, as for example in a brief workshop intended to impart a specific skill; it distinguishes supervision, too, from consultation, which might be very time limited as one professional seeks the help of another to gain or regain objectivity in his or her work with a client.

The fact that it is ongoing allows the supervisor–supervisee relationship to grow and develop. Indeed, many supervision theorists have focused particular importance on the growing, developing nature of this relationship. In recognition of this, we devote two chapters of this book to the supervisory relationship, including ways that it evolves and changes across time.

SUPERVISION GOALS

In our definition, we offer two goals for supervision. One concerns teaching and learning; the other concerns the monitoring of client welfare. Each is an essential goal. It is possible, however, for a given supervisor to more heavily emphasize one than the other. For example, a student working at a field placement might have both a university-based and an on-site supervisor. In this situation, it is possible for the university-based supervisor to give relatively greater emphasis to the teaching–learning goals of supervision and the on-site supervisor to give relatively greater emphasis to the client-monitoring aspects.

Feiner (1994) alluded to this dichotomy of goals when he suggested:

> Some supervisors assume that their most important ethical responsibility is to the student's patient. This would impel them to make the student a conduit for

their own expertise. Others make the assumption that their ultimate responsibility is to the development of the student. . . . Their concern is the possible lowering of the student's self-esteem when confronted by the supervisor and his rising fantasy that he should become a shoe salesman.

Enhancing Professional Functioning

We state the teaching–learning goal simply as "to enhance professional functioning." This is a pragmatic definition that meets our need to provide a succinct and generally applicable definition of supervision. It is silent about any performance criteria supervisees are to meet or even about the content of learning.

For any given supervisor, then, this goal is an insufficient basis for practice. We would suggest that supervision can be considered to have goals that vary both in their specificity and in their time orientation. That is, the supervisor might have some very precise and concrete goals to accomplish with the supervisee during their work together; the supervisor might even break these into subgoals. Typically, these derive from some combination of the supervisor's own theory or model and of the supervisor's sensitivity to the supervisee's particular developmental needs.

In addition, the supervisor almost certainly would want the supervisee to be developing skills and competencies necessary for eventual licensure or certification. This is a utilitarian goal that has the virtue of specificity. That is, supervisors generally know what competencies the supervisee will have to demonstrate for licensure, at least in his or her own state. Moreover, this is a logical target in that to attain licensure is the point at which the person makes the transition to an autonomously functioning professional and is no long legally mandated to be supervised.

Other longer-term goals for supervisees are more abstract. One is to move the supervisee along a continuum of expertise: She or he begins training as a novice, but gradually grows in expertise. This process, however, is an extended one. Fried (1991) offered the folk wisdom that it takes 10 years to become a really good psychotherapist. In fact, Hayes (1981) estimated that it requires about 10 years to become an expert in *any* skill domain; Ericcson and Lehmann (1996) referred to this as "the ten year rule of necessary preparation." Yet, for many professionals, time alone will be insufficient to attain expert status. Supervisors, then, should consider expertise an aspirational goal.

Another of these more abstract, longer-term goals is to help supervisees attain clinical wisdom. Williams (1995), in particular, made a strong argument in favor of this as a training goal. Although this is a multifaceted construct, a succinct working definition might be "the ability of a professional to make clinical decisions under conditions of uncertainty." Yet wisdom has proved inordinately difficult to operationalize (cf., Sternberg, 1990). Consider, for example, that wisdom traditionally has been regarded as an attribute of older people. Yet only *some* older people might be considered wise, and to obtain consensus about who among these are wise would be hard. Therefore, helping the supervisee to attain clinical wisdom is—as with the case of expertise—a long-term, aspirational goal for the supervisor. Perhaps it should be no surprise, then, that Smith, Staudinger, and Baltes (1994) found no relationship between clinical psychologists' ages and their demonstrated wisdom.

Monitoring Client Care

The teaching and learning purposes of supervision receive particular attention in the literature. Nevertheless, it is important that supervisors not lose sight of the fact that monitoring client care is an essential supervision goal. In fact, Loganbill, Hardy, and Delworth (1982) correctly maintained that this is the supervisor's *paramount* responsibility. Blocher (1983) stated it bluntly when he observed that clients "are not expendable laboratory animals to be blithely sacrificed in the name of training" (p. 29). And should a sense of professional responsibility be insufficient motivation to keep the supervisor focused on monitoring quality of client care, self-interest should; as we will discuss in Chapter 9, the concept of vicarious liability is that the supervisor can be held liable for any harm done by the supervisee under supervision.

It is useful to remember that the original purpose of clinical supervision was to monitor client care. Supervision in the mental health disciplines almost certainly began with social work supervision, which "dates from the nineteenth century Charity Organization Societies in which paid social work agents supervised the moral treatment of the poor by friendly visitors" (Harkness & Poertner, 1989, p. 115). The focus of this supervision was on the *client.*

Eisenberg (1956) noted that the first known call for supervision to focus on the professional rather than exclusively on the client was expressed by Zilphia Smith in 1901. This supervisory focus did not become the norm, however, until approximately the time of the depression of the 1930s when supervisors were influenced by the combination of large caseloads, Freud's new psychology, and a greater emphasis on the professional training of social workers (Harkness & Poertner, 1989).

But, despite its importance, the need to ensure quality of client care is one job demand with particular potential for causing dissonance in the supervisor. Most of the time, supervisors are able to perceive themselves as allies of their supervisees. Yet they also must be prepared, should they see harm being done to clients, to risk bruising the egos of their supervisees or, in extreme cases, even to steer the supervisee from the profession. From the perspective of supervisees, especially those with autonomy conflicts, this aspect of supervision can lead to what Kadushin (1976) spoke of as "snooper vision."

METAPHORS THAT IMPLICITLY DEFINE SUPERVISION

Most of us recognize metaphor as a phenomenon of speech and language. We all know it, for example, as an essential component of poetry. Yet metaphor operates at multiple levels of behavior and is not strictly limited to the verbal domain.

Mental health professionals, in fact, base much of their work on the assumption that a person's previous life experiences can and often do function metaphorically for current ones.

Such metaphoric functioning provides the mechanism by which transference and countertransference reactions occur. Sullivan (1953) used the term *parataxic distortion* to address the everyday counterpart of this. The essential idea is that person A, by virtue of some shared characteristics with person B, is responded to (affectively; behaviorally; cognitively) as if she or he *were* person B.

In other words, then, particular life experiences and patterns serve us as something of a template: our perceptions and responses to a new situation are organized and structured as they were in a previous similar situation. Because of their apparent similarities, we then respond to the new situation *as if* it were the earlier one.

Not only do mental health practitioners employ metaphor in their interventions, but they also draw on particular root metaphors or archetypes to define their professional roles. Kopp (1971), for example, drew from various sources to describe several basic metaphors that find their expression as roles that therapists adopt. Among these, for example, are the priest or shaman; the Zen master; and, Socrates, who saw himself as "midwife to the ideas of others." Kopp discussed, too, ways in which such stories for children as *The Wizard of Oz* (Baum, 1956) can serve as metaphors for psychotherapy.

There are, of course, many other metaphors to define the work of therapists. Common among these are therapist-as-healer, therapist-as-scientist, and the humanistic notion of the therapist-as-cotraveler-on-the-journey-of-life. The list of possible metaphors for a therapist is long.

If the roles and behaviors of clients and therapists are, in part, metaphoric expressions of other life experiences, this almost certainly must be the case for the supervisor and supervisee. Proctor (1991), for example, commented:

A number of my colleagues asked me what archetypes went into taking the trainer role; we immediately identified a number. There are the Guru, *or*

Wise Woman, *from whom wisdom is expected, and the* Earth Mother—*the all-provider, unconditional positive regarder. In contrast there is the* Clown *or* Jester—*enjoying performance, and cloaking his truth in riddles, without taking responsibility for how it is received. The* Patriarch *creates order and unselfconsciously wields power. The* Actor/Director *allocates roles and tasks and holds the Drama; the* Bureaucrat *demands compliance to the letter of the law. The* Whore *gives services for money, which can be indistinguishable from love, and re-engages with group after group. There is even the* Warrior—*valiant for truth; and of course the* Judge—*upholding standards and impartially assessing. The* Shepherd/Sheep-dog *gently and firmly rounds up and pens.* (p. 65)

During supervision workshops he has conducted, Michael Ellis has employed metaphors that characterize different facets of supervision. Among these are a parent teaching a child to ride a bike, a teacher–student relationship in a school setting, a shepherd and flock, an oasis in the desert, and (more ominously) going to the principal's office.

In short, then, roles from our previous life experiences are likely to affect how we approach and behave in supervision. Some are so ingrained that they operate outside our awareness. To the extent that these influences on the supervisory process remain unavailable for scrutiny, they may serve as contaminants. The following discussions of more frequently occurring metaphors are therefore in the service of making them available for consideration.

Supervisor–Supervisee as Parent–Child

Family metaphors seem to be particularly common in supervision. And the most basic of these is that of the parent–child relationship. Lower (1972), for example, employed this metaphor in alluding to the unconscious parent–child fantasies that he believed are stimulated by the supervisory situation itself.

Many theorists have, of course, employed this metaphor of parent–child relationship as a way to think about therapy. As it may apply to supervision, the metaphor simultaneously is both *less* and *more* appropriate than for therapy. It is less apt in

that personal growth is not a primary goal of the intervention, as it is in therapy, but rather is an instrumental goal that works in the service of making the supervisee a better therapist. It is more apt, on the other hand, in that supervision is an evaluative relationship just as parenting is—and therapy presumably is not.

Just knowing that they are being evaluated is often sufficient to trigger in supervisees an expectation of a guilt–punishment sequence that recapitulates early parent–child interactions. Supervisors can, through their actions, intensify such transference responses among supervisees, triggering perceptions of them as a "good" or "bad" parent. We have heard, for example, of instances in which supervisors posted publicly in the staff lounge the names of supervisees who had too many client "no-shows." The atmosphere created in situations such as this can easily establish supervisory staff as "feared parents."

Still another parallel between parent–child and supervisor–supervisee relationships is that status, knowledge, maturity, and power differences between the participants eventually will begin to disappear. The parties who today are supervisor and supervisee can expect that one day they might relate to one another as peers and colleagues.

The parent–child metaphor is suggested, too, in the frequent use of developmental metaphors to describe supervision. And Hillerbrand's (1989) suggestion that supervisors begin to consider the theorizing of Vygotsky (1978) also suggested this. The following description of Vygotsky's thinking really derives at the most basic level from the manner in which parents teach life tasks to their children:

[Vygotsky] *proposed that cognitive skills are acquired through social interaction. Unskilled persons learn cognitive skills by assuming more and more responsibility from experts during performance (what he called "expert scaffolding"). Novices first observe an expert's cognitive activity while the experts do most of the work. As novices begin to perform the skills, they receive feedback from the experts on their performance; as they learn to perform the skill correctly, they begin to assume more responsibility for the cognitive skill. Finally, novices assume the major responsibility for the cognitive skill, and experts become passive observers.* (Hillerbrand, p. 294)

Sibling and Master–Apprentice Metaphors

A second family metaphor that can pertain in supervision is that of older and younger sibling. For many supervisory dyads, this probably is more apt than the parent–child metaphor. The supervisor is farther along on the same path being traveled by the supervisee. As such, she or he is in a position to show the way in a nurturing, mentoring relationship. But, as with siblings, issues of competence can sometimes trigger competition over who is more skilled or more brilliant in understanding the client.

Yet another metaphor that has been used with some frequency is that of the relationship between master craftspersons and their apprentices. Such relationships have existed for thousands of years and are perpetuated in supervision. In these relationships, master craftspersons serve as mentors to the people who aspire to enter the occupation, showing them the skills, procedures, and culture of that occupation. In this manner, too, master craftspersons help to perpetuate the craft. Eventually, after what is usually a stipulated period of apprenticeship, their apprentices becomes peers of the craftspersons.

These metaphors, particularly those of parenting or sibling, occur at fundamental and often primitive levels. Because they influence in an immediate and felt way, they have special and probably ongoing influence on the supervisory relationship. Moreover, such metaphors probably operate outside the awareness of the supervisor.

Metaphors from Previous Professional Roles

If it is true that supervision is a unique intervention, then one might reasonably infer that there is a unique role characteristic of supervisors in general. In a broad sense, this is true, and we can identify at least two major components of this "generic" supervisory role. The first of these is the perspective from which the supervisor views his or her work;

the second pertains to the commonly endorsed expectation that the supervisor will give feedback to the supervisee.

This topic of supervisor roles is one to which we will give greater attention in Chapter 2, as we discuss social role models of supervision. There are, though, aspects of it that are important to cover at this point.

Liddle (1988) discussed the transition from therapist to supervisor as a role development process that involves several evolutionary steps. An essential early step is for the emerging supervisor to make a shift in focus. That is, the supervisor eventually must realize that the purpose of supervision is neither to treat the client indirectly through the supervisee nor to provide psychotherapy to the supervisee.

Borders (1989a) discussed this same step in the supervisor-to-be's professional evolution. She maintained that the supervisor-to-be must make a cognitive shift as he or she switches from the role of counselor or therapist. To illustrate how difficult this often is for new supervisors, she gave the example of a neophyte supervisor who persisted for some time in referring to his supervisee as "my client." Until he was able to correctly label the trainee's role in relation to himself, his perceptual set remained that of a therapist.

This shift, then, requires the supervisor to give up doing what might be called "therapy by proxy" or "therapy by remote control." We would note, however, that the pull to doing this may always remain present, even if unexpressed in practice. In part, this is reinforced by the supervisor's mandate always to function as a monitor of client care, vigilant about how the client is functioning. Similarly, the longer the person has functioned as a therapist, the harder it may be for the supervisor to make the necessary shift in perspective. It is interesting to note, for example, that Carl Rogers talked about having occasionally experienced the strong impulse to take over the therapy of a supervisee, likening himself to an old firehorse heeding the call (Hackney & Goodyear, 1984).

Borders (1989a), in fact, observed that untrained professionals do not necessarily make this shift on their own, simply as a result of experience as a supervisor. As a matter of fact, some "experienced" professionals seem to have more difficulty changing their thinking than do doctoral students and advanced master's students in supervision courses. One goal of this book, then, is to help provide the bridge that enables professionals to move from the professional role of counselor or therapist to that of supervisor.

CONCLUSION

The purpose of this chapter was to provide a foundation for thinking about supervision. We have discussed the importance of supervision and offered a working definition of it. During the latter portion of the chapter, we discussed roles supervisors enact. These and other issues will be considered at greater length in the chapters that follow.

We alluded early in the chapter to the two realms of knowledge (Schön, 1983) that are the basis of professional training: the theory and research that is the focus of university training and the knowledge derived from practitioners' experience. We asserted, too, that these actually are complementary knowledge domains (e.g., Holloway, 1994). Because of that conviction, material in this book is drawn from both realms of knowledge with the belief that each informs the other. That is, in the course of their work we draw both from theoretical and empirical literature and from literature that describes the insights and practices of supervisors themselves.

CHAPTER 2

Supervision Models and Theories

Kurt Lewin is known for asserting that "there is nothing so practical as a good theory" (Marrow, 1969). Theories enable us to make sense of and organize what otherwise might be overwhelming amounts of information and then to focus selectively on just a few things. For this reason, it would be nearly impossible for a practitioner to function without *some* theory.

Strupp and Hadley (1979) found, for example, that one of the college professors who served in their study as paraprofessional therapists worked from a model that explained male clients' problems in terms of the "girl troubles" they were having. This is "theory" of the most rudimentary sort, but it apparently was of service to him (as a matter of added significance, consider that the central finding of this study was that these untrained paraprofessionals achieved similar treatment outcomes as experienced clinical psychologists).

Interestingly, though, theories need not need actually be "true" to be useful. Levenson (1984), for example, discussed how people in the Middle Ages were convinced that to avoid malaria, they should build their houses on high land, make sure there was no stagnant water in or around the house, and close the windows at night. This generally is an effective strategy. The *theory* behind it, though, concerned avoiding evil effects from the humors and the night air, whereas the more contemporary theory is that anopheles mosquitoes serve as disease-carrying agents.

THEORY IN CLINICAL SUPERVISION

The particular focus of this chapter is on theories and models of clinical supervision. Most aspiring supervisors already appreciate the importance of theory in their work as therapists. Their next step is to extend that appreciation to the theories that might guide their supervisory work. As Hart (1982) has noted, "One can imitate an outstanding supervisor, but without theory or a conceptual model one does not really understand the process of supervision" (p. 27). Or, to put it another way, professionals differ from technicians in their use of a formal theory.

Qualities of a Good Theory

Before we discuss the actual theories or models of supervision, we want to offer some criteria by which to evaluate theory. Keeping these criteria in mind can be helpful in evaluating the overall merits of the particular models available to supervisors.

Six criteria seem particularly important. The first five were outlined by Patterson (1986) and are given minor elaboration here.

1. *Preciseness and clarity.* A theory should be understandable, free from ambiguities, and internally consistent.
2. *Parsimony or simplicity.* A theory should employ only the minimum number of assumptions and interrelationships among them that are necessary to explain the domain that is the focus of the theory. The importance of economy in theory construction also is known as Occam's razor (i.e., the "principle of parsimony"), after the fourteenth-century English epistemologist, William of Ockham.
3. *Comprehensiveness.* A theory should make use of the known data in the particular domain of interest.
4. *Operationality.* It should be possible to specify a theory's hypotheses and concepts in clear and measurable terms.

5. *Practicality.* We began this chapter by asserting the practicality of a good theory. This is an essential criterion by which to evaluate theory. Even if it is not actually "true" (as in our example of the night humors and malaria), the theory should be useful to practitioners.

6. *Falsifiability.* It is not possible to prove that any theory is correct or true. However, the theory should be formulated in such a manner that its propositions can be *disproved*. This is Popper's (1935/1959) criterion of falsifiability. Falsifiability has been the basis for critiquing the claim of certain therapeutic models that they deserve theory status. This is especially true of psychoanalysis, for some of its propositions have been set up so that they are virtually impossible to disprove (see, e.g., Popper, 1968).

Theories and Models in Supervision. These six criteria apply to scientific theories. Theories used by psychological practitioners, however, tend to be less formal and precise and therefore are more likely to fall short when assessed against one or more of these criteria. In a strict sense, therefore, most "theories" of therapy and of supervision more accurately should be described as models, which meet fewer of these six criteria, especially that of comprehensiveness. As a practical matter, though, it probably does not make a great deal of difference which term is used. Therefore, we will use both terms (almost) interchangeably.

Another important point to make concerns a bias in the literature that will affect our emphasis here. That is, most theorists and researchers have focused on supervision as an intervention that occurs in the context of a one-to-one relationship. As a result, most supervision theory has evolved independently of the advancements made in group and/or team supervision. As a consequence, we discuss group and team forms of supervision only tangentially in this chapter and more fully later in Chapters 6 and 7.

In the remainder of this chapter we review some of the theories and models available to guide supervisors. The organization recognizes that there are two broad categories of supervision models: those

based on psychotherapy theories and those developed specifically for supervision. Holloway (1992) suggested that this latter group generally can be subdivided into either developmental models or social role models. Then there are models that fit neither category. Accordingly, we have organized this discussion into four sections: (1) psychotherapy-based theories, (2) developmental models, (3) social role models, and (4) several of the eclectic or integrationist models.

PSYCHOTHERAPY THEORY-BASED SUPERVISION

The first category of supervision theory we address includes direct extensions of psychotherapy theories. Virtually all supervisors must be influenced to some extent by the theories they use as counselors or therapists. But it is our impression that it is possible to array supervisors on a continuum, ranging from those whose work is simply "flavored" by their therapy theory to those who base their work *totally* and *consistently* on their theory of counseling or psychotherapy (see, e.g., Bartlett, Goodyear, & Bradley, 1983; Hess, 1980; Watkins, 1997).

On one level, extrapolations of therapy theory to supervisory practice make excellent sense. As Shoben (1962) and others have argued, each counselor or therapist works from an implicit theory of human nature that must also influence how the therapist construes reality, including interpersonal behavior, normal personality development (or family development), and abnormal or dysfunctional development. It is reasonable to assume that this same theory of human nature is constant across roles and affects the professional's work as both therapist and supervisor (see, e.g., data from Friedlander & Ward, 1984; Goodyear, Abadie, & Efros, 1984; and Holloway, Freund, Gardner, Nelson, & Walker, 1989).

For these reasons, then, at least some of the content, focus, and process of supervision inevitably will be grounded in the supervisor's particular counseling model. For example, Putney, Worthington, and McCulloughy (1992) found that psychology interns perceived cognitive–behavioral supervisors to be in a consultant role and to focus on skills and strategies more than humanistic, psychodynamic, and existential supervisors. Supervisors who adhered to these latter models, though, were perceived as more likely to use the relationship model, to play the therapist role, and to focus on conceptualization. Guest and Beutler (1988) have shown that supervisory behaviors and conceptions affect the theoretical orientation that supervisees adopt.

It is inevitable, then, that supervisors will use therapy as at least one of the lenses through which they view supervision. But supervisors who use this as the *only* lens will miss important information about their supervisees and about the range and impact of interventions they might use to help those supervisees. Moreover, this single lens leads supervisors to think in therapeutic ways about their supervisees. As Worthington noted:

> In counseling, a client is often involved in stable personal interactions and personality and mood states. In supervision, the supervisee usually is not rigidly bound into the same personality dynamics across situations and further, at least in the beginning, the supervisee does not know how to counsel. Thus, supervision is better described by a teaching metaphor than by a counseling metaphor. (Personal communication, 1990)

For these and other reasons, supervisors gradually are giving up an exclusive reliance on therapy theories to inform their supervisory practice, especially as they have available to them models specific to supervision. But therapy-based models are still employed. Moreover, they have made important contributions to our understanding of supervision processes.

By many estimates, there are several hundred theories, or at least aspiring theories, of therapy. Supervision has been described from a number of those perspectives, including Adlerian (e.g., Kopp & Robles, 1989), reality (e.g., Smadi & Landreth, 1988), gestalt (Hoyt & Goulding, 1989), solution focused (Marek, Sandifer, Beach, Coward, & Protinsky, 1994), Jungian (Kugler, 1995), and in-

tegrative therapies (e.g., Tennen, 1988). In the interest of space, though, we will cover only five psychotherapy-based models of supervision. The first three—psychoanalytic, client centered, and cognitive–behavioral—reflect the more common theories employed by mental health practitioners. In addition, we address systemic models and narrative therapy, the latter being one of the newer models being embraced primarily by marital and family therapists.

Psychodynamic Supervision

Psychoanalytic conceptions of supervision have a long history. This is true not only because psychoanalysis preceded the other therapies, but also because it addressed supervision from its very inception (cf., Caligor, 1984). Frayn (1991) suggested that formal psychotherapy supervision was first instituted in the early 1920s by Max Eitingon at the Berlin Institute of Psychoanalysis. And Caligor (1984) noted that in 1922 the International Psychoanalytic Society, to standardize training, adopted formalized standards that stipulated formal coursework and the treatment of several patients under supervision.

During the 1930s, two competing views developed concerning the place of "control analysis," which was the psychoanalytic term for supervision. One group (the Budapest School) maintained that it should be a continuation of the supervisee's personal analysis (with the same analyst in each case) and focus on transference in the candidate's therapy and countertransference in his or her supervision. The other group (the Viennese School) maintained that the transference and countertransference issues should be addressed in the candidate's personal analysis, whereas supervision itself should emphasize didactic teaching.

Caligor suggested that, to the extent that there now is a generally accepted psychoanalytic perspective on supervision, it is the one articulated by Ekstein and Wallerstein (1972). These authors portrayed supervision as a teaching and learning process that gives particular emphasis to the relationships between and among patient, therapist, and supervisor and the processes that interplay among them. Its purpose is not to therapize but to teach, and the reason for working closely with the trainee is to have him or her learn how to understand the dynamics of resolving relational conflicts between supervisor and trainee (cf., Bordin, 1983; Mueller & Kell, 1972) for the benefit of future work with clients.

The supervisor teaches the trainee to be open to experience using a process that often mirrors therapy. Moldawsky (1980) explained that "anxiety in the patient induces anxiety in the therapist, and unless the therapist is open to the experience, he/she will defend against the anxiety by characterological or symptomatic defenses and will unconsciously encourage repression in the patient, rather than exposure" (p. 126). Moldawsky went on to say that the therapist ultimately must learn the "analytic attitude" (p. 126), which includes patience, trust in the analytic process, interest in the client, and respect for the power and tenacity of client resistance. An assumption of psychodynamic supervision is that the best way for the trainee to learn these qualities is by receiving the same in the supervisory relationship.

Moldawsky (1980) noted that as a supervisor he structured his remarks to trainees in a manner that was less intrusive into their personal lives than if they were themselves patients. Therefore, he might point to the trainee's resistance, but not search for the roots of the resistance in the trainee's past. The latter, he argued, should happen in analysis, not in supervision. This middle of the road position is probably more representative of present day psychodynamic supervision.

In the interest of space, we necessarily minimize the existing diversity within the psychoanalytic or psychodynamic arena. There are, in fact, multiple psychoanalytic or psychodynamic schools and therefore multiple perspectives on supervision. Moreover, there has been considerable evolution of psychodynamic conception and practice during the past century. Teitelbaum (1995) has reviewed some of these developments.

Because of both the diversity within the psychoanalytic perspective and the richness of its conceptualizations, it has provided a rich source of ideas and concepts that have been infused throughout supervision. The following two contributions, in particular, merit highlighting. They are only mentioned here, though, as we discuss each of them in Chapter 4.

Working Alliance Model.   Psychodynamic therapists and supervisors have long given attention to the therapeutic or working alliance. Bordin (1979) articulated a perspective on working alliances that he maintained could serve as something of a metamodel, transcending any particular model. He later (1983) extended that working alliance model to supervision.

Parallel Processes.   Parallel processes, the phenomenon in which dynamics of the client or of the client–therapist relationship are mirrored in the supervisee or in the supervisee–supervisor relationship (or vice versa), are now acknowledged across many types and models of supervision.

Identifying and elaborating on parallel processes, though, has been a contribution of psychoanalytically oriented supervisors. It was, for example, first described by Searles (1955), a psychoanalyst, who initially termed it the "reflection process." What arguably has been the most influential study of parallel processes (Doehrmann, 1976) was done in a psychoanalytic training context.

Person-centered Supervision

Supervision was a central and long-standing concern of Carl Rogers and has been for those who since have identified with the client-centered model. Rogers (1942; and also Covner, 1942a, b) was among the very first to report using electronically recorded interviews and transcripts for supervision purposes. Until then, supervision had been based entirely on self-reports of supervisees, as it often still is in psychoanalytically oriented supervision.

Rogers (1942) concluded from listening to these early recordings of therapy interviews that mere didactic training in (what then was called) nondirective methods was insufficient; only when students had direct access to the content of their interviews could they identify their natural tendencies to provide advice and otherwise control their sessions. This is consistent with Patterson's (1964) contention two decades later that client-centered supervision was an influencing process that incorporated elements of teaching and therapy, though it was neither.

More recently, Carl Rogers's own conception of supervision seemed to lean more toward therapy. In an interview with Goodyear, he stated:

> I think my major goal is to help the therapist to grow in self-confidence and to grow in understanding of himself or herself, and to grow in understanding the therapeutic process. And to that end, I find it very fruitful to explore any difficulties the therapist may feel he or she is having working with the client. Supervision for me becomes a modified form of the therapeutic interview. (Hackney & Goodyear, 1984, p. 283)

Later, when he was asked how he differentiated supervision from therapy, Rogers answered:

> I think there is no clean way. I think it does exist on a continuum. Sometimes therapists starting in to discuss some of the problems they're having with a client will look deeply into themselves and it's straight therapy. Sometimes it is more concerned with problems of the relationship and that is clearly supervision. But in that sense, too, I will follow the lead, in this case, the lead of the therapist. The one difference is I might feel more free to express how I might have done it than I would if I were dealing with a client. (p. 285)

It is clear from Rogers's words that his counseling theory informed his supervision in a relatively direct way. He believed the facilitative conditions (i.e., genuineness, empathy, warmth) were necessary for trainees and clients alike. Rice (1980) described person-centered supervision as relying on a theory of *process* in the context of *relationship*. The successful person-centered supervisor must have a profound trust that the trainee has within him or herself the ability and motivation to grow and explore both the therapy situation and the self. This mirrors the trust that the

therapist must have of clients (Rice, 1980). Patterson (1983), too, emphasized the similarity between the conditions and processes of therapy and those that occur during supervision.

Patterson and Rice both outlined the attitudes toward human nature and change and the attitude toward self that the supervisor must model for the trainee. First and foremost is the belief in the growth motivation and in the person's ability to differentiate and move toward self-actualization. The trainee who sees this as absurd will not be able to offer the kind of psychological environment necessary for their clients to change. Other blocks to successful use of this theory are a strong belief in the dynamic unconscious and/or a basic need to control and be directive. Finally, the therapist and supervisor must accept themselves and be able to "prize" each other and the clients with whom they work.

We conclude this section by noting that Rogers's work has exerted a central and enduring role on the training of mental health professionals. That is, others—especially Truax and Carkhuff (1967)—operationalized his facilitative conditions in such a way that they could be systematically taught. In these and other ways, Rogers and his followers taught us to listen and to communicate our understanding in a way that most of us had not experienced prior to our training as professional helpers. But person-centered supervision is more than listening and responding; it is believing in the phenomenological process to such an extent that the wisdom of giving advice or instruction becomes a moot issue. It is stepping into the experience of those we wish to influence. It is a mirror and a paradox.

Cognitive–Behavioral Supervision

Behavioral therapy and the rational and the cognitive therapies initially evolved somewhat independently of each other. The former has had a focus on observable behaviors and a reliance on conditioning (classical and operant) models of learning. The latter was concerned with modifying clients' cognitions, especially those that were manifest as "self-talk" (e.g., Beck, Rush, Shaw, &

Emery, 1979; Ellis, 1974; Mahoney, 1974, 1977; Meichenbaum, 1977). The convention, though, has become one of grouping these two types of therapy into the broader category of cognitive–behavioral models. Although much cognitive–behavioral treatment has been on the individual level (see, e.g., Barlow, 1993), there certainly have been applications to couples and families (e.g., Jacobsen, Everett, & Koerpal, 1986). In addition, the systemic therapies, especially strategic family therapy, have obvious cognitive–behavioral underpinnings.

Whether working with the individual or with a larger system, the behavioral supervisor, like the behavioral therapist, operates on the assumption that both adaptive and maladaptive behaviors are learned and maintained through their consequences (Russell et al., 1984). It is probably no surprise that behavioral supervisors have been more specific and more systematic than supervisors of other orientations in their presentation of the goals and processes of supervision.

Leddick and Bernard (1980) reported that Wolpe, Knopp, and Garfield (1966) were among the first to outline procedures for behavioral supervision. In fact, Wolpe gave considerable attention to supervision a few years later in a series of articles (1972a, b, c; 1973a, b, c, d).

During the past 25 years, a number of behavioral training or supervision models have been discussed (Boyd, 1978; Delaney, 1972; Jakubowski-Spector, Dustin, & George, 1971; Levine & Tilker, 1974; Linehan, 1980; Schmidt, 1979). Boyd (1978) suggested that most had in common an endorsement of some variation on the following four propositions:

1. *Proficient therapist performance is more a function of learned skills than a "personality fit." The purpose of supervision is to teach appropriate therapist behaviors and extinguish inappropriate behavior.*
2. *The therapist's professional role consists of identifiable tasks, each one requiring specific skills. Training and supervision should assist the trainee in developing these skills, applying and refining them.*

3. *Therapy skills are behaviorally definable and are responsive to learning theory, just as are other behaviors.*
4. *Supervision should employ the principles of learning theory within its procedures.* (p. 89)

The supervisory methods typically described by behavioral supervisors include establishing a trusting relationship, skill analysis and assessment, setting goals for the trainee, construction and implementation of strategies to accomplish goals, and follow-up evaluation and generalization of learning (Bradley, 1989). Additionally, Schmidt (1979) and others (Friedberg & Taylor, 1994; Perris, 1994) have discussed cognitive–behavioral approaches to supervision.

Perhaps illustrative of the more purely cognitive approaches is that of Liese and Beck (1997). Like Ellis and his associates (e.g., Ellis, 1989; Wessler & Ellis, 1983; Woods & Ellis, 1996), they emphasize challenging supervisee cognitions and misperceptions. They caution that three supervisory styles are particular barriers to effective cognitive therapy based supervision: the Mister Rogers Supervisor ("It is bad when someone's feelings get hurt"); Attila the Supervisor ("I need to be right all the time"); and the "How do you feel?" supervisor (who believes supervisees' feelings about clients are more important than their conceptualizations about them).

In summary, behavioral supervisors define the potential of the trainee as the potential to learn. Supervisors take at least part of the responsibility for learning to occur, for they are the experts who can guide the trainee into the correct learning environment. Perhaps more than most supervisors, they are concerned about the extent to which trainees demonstrate technical mastery and that their work have fidelity with the particular mode of treatment being taught (see our discussion in Chapter 12 of the supervision of manualized treatments, many of which are cognitive–behavioral).

Systemic Supervision

Systemic supervision is characterized by attention to the interlocking family and supervisory systems.

It is, then, virtually synonymous with family therapy supervision, which as been a family therapy specialty since at least the late 1960s (Liddle, Becker, & Diamond, 1997). Liddle et al. review the key publications and trends that have affected the development of this specialty, making clear that this has occurred independently of psychotherapy supervision:

> Family therapy supervision and psychotherapy supervision, paralleling the parent fields of family therapy and psychotherapy, have not interacted much throughout their respective histories. Like proverbial ships passing in the night, these kindred areas of thinking, research, and practice do not interrelate. For that matter, each barely acknowledges the existence of the other and they remain intellectual strangers.   (p. 400)

McDaniel, Weber, and McKeever (1983) reviewed the structural, strategic, Bowenian, and experiential schools of systemic family therapy and argued that supervision in these schools should be theoretically consistent. Therefore, if the goal of the therapy was to maintain a clear boundary between therapist and family (and between parents in the family and the children), then there should be a clear boundary between the supervisor and the therapist. Furthermore, if therapy focused on family of origin issues, the therapist must be encouraged to relate training to his or her own family of origin issues.

Some discussion has ensued regarding the appropriateness of theory-based supervision when the therapy upon which supervision is based is nonegalitarian, if not overtly manipulative. Strategic family therapy supervision has become a case in point. Many strategic directives are paradoxical in nature or, at the very least, do not rely on the insight of the recipient. Strategic supervisors have asked themselves, therefore, if strategic interventions are appropriate for trainees.

To date, at least as reflected in the scant literature on the topic, the answer seems to be yes. Storm and Heath (1982) reported that their supervisees expected their supervisors to use strategic interventions with them. But when supervisors were caught using such an approach, the supervisees' reactions were negative. In other words, supervisees were comfortable with the notion that they might need to be manipulated in order to learn, but they expected the manipulation to be very clever and subtle. This begs the question about what to do as supervisees gain in their own clinical skill.

Protinsky and Preli (1987) offered at least a partial solution to this dilemma. In their discussion of strategic supervision, they proposed that interventions (though admittedly manipulative) follow the development of the trainee. They offered seven examples of strategic supervisory interventions ranging from the use of paradox to "graduating to equality" (p. 22). The following example was described as the use of an aversive reframe. The therapist in the example has been working with a family made up of an acting out adolescent, a meek and submissive mother, and an arrogant and abrasive father. The therapist repeatedly has gotten caught in struggles with the father. The supervisor has pointed out the circular nature of the sequence (i.e., adolescent acts out, mother acts overwhelmed, father acts abrasive, therapist reacts to father); however, there has been no progress to this point.

In a postsession meeting the supervisor suddenly changed her position and framed the therapist's protection of the mother as positive. Who wouldn't protect a woman from such an abrasive man! She then left without discussing the case further. The trainee prided herself on her objectivity and at first complained how mistaken the supervisor was to the other trainees. She did not like to be perceived as protecting the mother and stated that she would never knowingly do such a thing. At the next session, however, she modified her behavior so that she could prove that she was objective. By reacting more positively toward the father and refraining from protecting the mother, the therapist was then able to use effective strategic interventions.

The use of paradoxical interventions, then, is one distinguishing feature of systemic supervision. However, it is important to acknowledge at least two other contributions that systemic supervisors have made to the field. (e.g., Liddle et al., 1997) One is attention to isomorphism, which concerns reciprocal relationships between the client–therapist and supervisor–supervisee interactions. As such, it has certain similarities to parallel processes; both of these phenomena are discussed in Chapter 4. The other contribution of systemic supervisors has been to the use of live supervision, which we discuss in Chapter 5.

Narrative Approaches to Supervision

A recent development in the human sciences has been the emergence of a world view that has been characterized as "postmodern," "postpostivist," or "social constructionism." The terms are not completely synonymous, but do have in common the position that reality and truth are contextual and exist as creations of the observer. Truth is a construction grounded in social interactions and informed by verbal behavior.

Much of this discussion has concerned the nature of science and inquiry (see, e.g., Gergen, 1982; also see Lazarus's (1993) critique of Gergen's position as *counterscience,* p. 675). Some mental health workers, however, have begun to apply this world view in the ways they conceptualize clients and their work with them. One such conceptualization has been characterized as a narrative approach (Parry & Doan, 1994; Polkinghorne, 1988). Therapists who work from this perspective assume that people are story tellers who develop a story about themselves that serves as a template both to organize past experience and to influence future behavior. This story is populated with characters who are chosen for—or who are influenced to perform—certain roles in that story.

The narrative approach seems an intellectual heir of Adler's ideas about life-style (Ansbacher & Ansbacher, 1956) and Berne's ideas about life scripts (1972). Family therapists (e.g., Hardy, 1993; Parry, 1991) have been especially, although not exclusively, interested in this approach (see, e.g., Gonccalves, 1994; Vogel, 1994).

Clients come to therapy with a story that they have developed about themselves over a lifetime.

The therapist's role is to help the person tell his or her story, while being careful not to "be violent" with the client by insisting that she or he accept a particular point of view. The therapist serves as a story editor. In this role, the therapist is careful to ask questions in the subjunctive ("as if") rather than the indicative ("this is the way it is") mode.

Whereas clients have a generally developed story of self that they seek to modify, the trainee is just beginning to develop his or her own story of self-as-professional. The supervisors' role, then, is both to assist the trainee in the editing of the client's story and to help the trainee develop his or her own professional story. Supervision is a process of revising stories that trainees (1) tell about their clients, (2) tell about themselves, and (3) tell about other therapists (Parry & Doan, 1994); Clifton, Doan, & Mitchell, 1990).

We should also note that the live supervision technique of reflection teams (e.g., Landis, 1994; Prest, Darden, & Keller, 1990) has been embraced as a modality of narrative therapists, even though it is not exclusive to that model. We discuss reflection teams in Chapter 7.

DEVELOPMENTAL APPROACHES TO SUPERVISION

The previous section discussed psychotherapy-based theories of supervision. But it is an indicator of supervision coming into its own that supervisors increasingly have available to them models that were developed independent of psychotherapy theory. The remainder of this chapter will be devoted to those models.

This particular section focuses on what are typically described as developmental models. Their primary focus is on how supervisees change as they gain training and supervised experience. But whereas the focus is on supervisees, these models all have implications for how supervisors might then work with the developing supervisee.

Holloway's (1987) comment a decade ago that "developmental models of supervision have become the Zeitgeist of supervision thinking and research" (p. 209) still rings true. By far the most visible theme in the tremendous growth in the supervision literature has been that of trainee development. This has been true in psychiatry, psychology, counseling, and social work (Worthington, 1984), though perhaps less so in marriage and family therapy (Everett & Koerpel, 1986).

Developmental concepts occasionally were employed by supervision theorists before the decade of the 1980s. For example, Fleming (1953) offered an early developmental way of thinking, and Hogan (1964) proposed his model a decade later; Littrell, Lee-Bordin, and Lorenz (1979) proposed theirs in the late 1970s. But the catalyst for what then became a veritable explosion of interest in developmental conceptions was the work of a small cadre at the University of Iowa. Stoltenberg (1981) conceived his developmental model when he still was an Iowa doctoral student, influenced by discussions with Delworth and with Loganbill. The next year, Delworth and Loganbill themselves coauthored a developmental model with another University of Iowa Counseling Center staff member (Loganbill, Hardy, & Delworth, 1982). Still later, Stoltenberg and Delworth (1987) collaborated to describe a blending and elaboration of these two early conceptions.

These articles by Stoltenberg (1981) and Loganbill et al. (1982), along with several other contemporary ones (e.g., Blocher, 1983; Littrell, Lee-Bordin, & Lorenz, 1979), struck a resonant chord in the supervision community. When Worthington (1987) reviewed the literature only a few years later, he was able to report that he had examined 16 models of counselor–trainee development; in a later expansion of that review, Watkins (1995) identified 6 more. Because their reviews were not exhaustive, it would be conservative to estimate that more than 22 different conceptions of counselor development exist. Almost all have implications for supervision, some more directly than others.

Chagnon and Russell (1995) point out that developmental conceptions of supervision are based on two basic assumptions. The first is that in the process of moving toward competence supervisees move through a series of stages that are qualitatively different from one another. The second is that each supervisee stage requires a qualitatively different supervisory environment if optimal supervisee satisfaction and growth are to occur.

Authors have differed about how to organize the developmental literature. Borders (1986) divided developmental models into: (1) those that focus on the role of the supervisor (e.g., Littrell, Lee-Bordin, & Lorenz, 1979); (2) those that focus on the dynamics of the trainee (e.g., Loganbill, Hardy, & Delworth, 1982); and (3) those that focus on the learning environment of supervision (e.g., Stoltenberg, 1981).

Russell et al. (1984) divided developmental models into two categories: (1) those in the Eriksonian tradition that offer definitive linear stages of development (e.g., Hogan, 1964; Stoltenberg, 1981; Littrell et al., 1979); and (2) those that propose a step-by-step process for conflict resolution or skill mastery, a process that will be repeated as the trainee faces more complicated issues (e.g., Ekstein & Wallerstein, 1972; Mueller & Kell, 1972; Loganbill et al., 1982).

Holloway (1987) divided developmental models into (1) those that have linked their origins to psychosocial developmental theory (Blocher, 1983; Loganbill et al., 1982; Stoltenberg, 1981) and (2) those that have not (Hogan, 1964; Littrell et al., 1979).

Finally, in an extremely comprehensive review of developmental models and the empirical studies spawned by these models, Worthington (1987) divided the literature into (1) models and studies that have addressed supervision of the developing counselor (e.g., Hill, Charles, & Reed, 1981; Stoltenberg, 1981; Loganbill et al., 1982) and (2) those that have taken the complementary tack of addressing supervision by the developing supervisor (e.g., Alonso, 1983; Hess, 1986).

In the next section we review several developmental models. We chose these particular models to illustrate both some of the apparent between-model commonalities and some of their differences. Also, whereas the first four are based on clinical observation, the last evolved from research findings.

The Littrell, Lee-Borden, and Lorenz Model

Littrell et al. (1979) proposed a four-stage model that attempted to match supervisor behavior to the developmental needs of the trainee. The first stage is characterized by relationship building, goal setting, and contracting. During the second stage, the supervisor vacillates between a counselor role and a teacher role as the trainee is faced with affective issues and skill deficits. The third stage requires that the supervisor adopt the more collegial role of consultant as the trainee gains confidence and expertise. The fourth and final stage is for the trainee to become a self-supervisor and take responsibility as the "principle designer of his or her learning" (p. 134). The supervisor, we assume, becomes a more distant consultant at this time.

The Stoltenberg Model

Stoltenberg (1981) defined four stages (levels) in his complexity model. He drew from Hogan's (1964) suggestions about stages through which trainees progress and overlaid that with the notion of conceptual level. For the latter, he drew from the work of Harvey, Hunt, and Schroeder (1961).

Stoltenberg described the trainee at each level, along with the supervision environment that would be optimal to meet that trainee's needs. *Level 1* depicts a trainee who is dependent on the supervisor, imitative, lacking in self- and other awareness, and limited by categorical thinking and little experience. The supervisory environment for this level should offer instruction, interpretation, support, and structure. Autonomy should be encouraged within the limits of the level. *Level 2* is characterized by a dependency–autonomy conflict. As awareness increases, there is a striving for independence, fluctuating motivation, more assertion, and less imitation. The environment should offer less structure and instruction. The supervisor should model high autonomy, support, and ambivalence, giving clarification only when asked.

Level 3 is one of conditional dependency. The trainee is more differentiated, motivated, insightful, and empathic. The supervisor should treat the trainee more as a peer and allow for his or her autonomy. There should be mutual sharing, exemplification, and confrontation. *Level 4* describes the "master counselor," who is not only skilled interpersonally and cognitively, but professionally. At this point, supervision, if continued, is collegial.

The Loganbill, Hardy, and Delworth Model

Loganbill et al. (1982) conceived what apparently was the first comprehensive model of counselor development to appear in the literature (Holloway, 1987). These authors drew from Chickering's (1969) developmental tasks of youth and redefined them into eight professional issues for helpers. For each issue, the trainee might be at one of three stages or in transition between stages.

> **The issues:** competence, emotional awareness, autonomy, identity, respect for individual differences, purpose and direction, personal motivation, and professional ethics
>
> **The stages:** *stagnation* (unawareness, dualistic thinking, extreme dependence); *confusion* (instability, conflict, fluctuation of feeling regarding ability of self and supervisor); and *integration* (calm reorganization, refreezing of attitudes, realistic view of self and supervisor)

Loganbill et al. suggested that the supervisor's role is to assess each trainee for each issue and to attempt to move the trainee to the next stage of development. The supervisor's repertoire of interventions include facilitating, confronting, conceptualizing, prescribing, and catalyzing (getting things moving). This is a complex model, though, probably too much so for the practicing supervisor who would be trying to track the trainee's progress through 24 different positions with respect to the model (8 issues times 3 stages).

The Stoltenberg and Delworth Model

Stoltenberg and Delworth (1987) revised Stoltenberg's (1981) earlier developmental model borrowing also from the Loganbill et al. (1982)

contribution. Stoltenberg and Delworth described three developmental levels of the trainee over eight dimensions (intervention skills, assessment techniques, interpersonal assessment, client conceptualization, individual differences, theoretical orientation, treatment goals and plans, and professional ethics). Three structures are proposed in the model to trace the progress of trainees through the levels on each of the dimensions. These structures are (1) the trainee's awareness of self and others, (2) motivation toward the development process, and (3) the amount of dependency or autonomy displayed by the trainee.

The Skovholt and Ronnestad Model

A shortcoming of most models has been that the counselor or therapist development they describe occurs primarily through the period of graduate training. By implication, then, professional development must stop shortly after counselors or therapists earn their professional degree. The work of Skovholt and Ronnestad (1992a, b; Ronnestad & Skovholt, 1993) is therefore important in its recognition that therapist development continues across the life-span.

Their work was grounded in interviews with 100 counselors and therapists who ranged in experience from the first year of graduate school to 40 years beyond graduate school. In qualitative analyses of those interviews, Skovholt and Ronnestad identified eight stages, each of which might be characterized along a number of dimensions (e.g., predominant affect, predominant sources of influence, role and working style, style of learning, determinants of effectiveness and satisfaction). As well, they identified 20 themes that were not specifically stage related, but that characterized therapist development across time. In the interest of space, we will illustrate each of the eight stages with a succinct summary of only two issues: central task and conceptual system used.

Persons at the first stage, *competence,* are untrained, though they may have experience working with clients; they may stay many years at this level. The central task: to use what one naturally

knows; the conceptual system is one of common sense. Then, in the first year of graduate school (*transition to professional training*), the central task is to assimilate information from a number of sources and to apply it in practice; the conceptual system is driven by an urgency in learning conceptual ideas and techniques. During the middle years of graduate school (*imitation of experts*), the trainee's central task is to imitate experts at the practical level, while also maintaining an openness to a diversity of ideas and positions; the trainee is developing a conceptual map of some sort, though typically it is not complex.

Conditional autonomy occurs during internship. Trainees have the central task of functioning as professionals; they have begun to develop a refined mastery of conceptual ideas and techniques. The next stage, *exploration,* coincides roughly with graduation and typically extends from 2 to 5 years. The central task of these professionals is to explore beyond the known; conceptually, the person will begin rejecting some previously embraced ideas and models.

The next stage, *integration,* typically lasts from 2 to 5 years, and professionals have the central task of developing authenticity, their conceptual system and working style are individualized and enable them to express their personalities in natural and productive ways. As a consequence, they most typically are eclectic or integrative.

The stage of *individuation* is the longest, lasting approximately 10 to 30 years. Its central task is highly individualized development toward an even deeper authenticity; the person's conceptual system is highly individualized and personalized. The final stage, *integrity,* may last from 1 to 10 years. The task is to become oneself and to prepare for retirement. The person's conceptual system is highly individualized and integrated.

There are relatively few variables that a researcher reasonably might address in any one study. Skovholt and Ronnestad focused primarily on therapists' development and secondarily on corresponding supervisor behaviors. Those supervisor behaviors are implied, but it is up to future researchers to flesh them out in greater detail.

Conclusions about Developmental Models

A developmental approach to supervision is intuitively appealing, for most of us believe we have become better with experience and training. We therefore are able to validate the general approach in a very personal way. This perspective also is hopeful in its assumptions.

Yet these attributes that make this approach attractive may blind their advocates to competing explanations of what goes on in supervision. Most empirical investigations of developmental models of supervision report "partial" or "some" support (e.g., Borders, 1989c; Krause & Allen, 1988; Reising & Daniels, 1983; Miars, Tracey, Ray, Cornfield, O'Farrell, & Gelso, 1983). A smaller number of studies (e.g., Fisher, 1989; Moy & Goodman, 1984) found no support for developmental theory. Perhaps the assumptions of developmental models are, as yet, only partially salient. In other words, perhaps there is a developmental process that we experience intuitively, but are still only in the beginnings stages of operationalizing.

Russell et al. (1984) criticized most developmental models as being too simplistic. They implied that the development of the professional helper involves a great deal more than these models would suggest. Holloway (1987) articulated a similar view and suggested that supervision is only one event going on in the trainee's professional and personal life, and perhaps not the most important. Empirically, therefore, Holloway proposed that it is too early to assume a predictable development paradigm.

> *Although researchers are interpreting their results as tentatively supporting a developmental model, lack of developmental-specific methodology, confinement to the supervisory experience as a source of information, predominant use of structured self-report questionnaires, and lack of evidence of distinct, sequential stages in trainee's growth reflect the prematurity of such claims.* (p. 215)

In subsequent publications (Holloway, 1988; Stoltenberg & Delworth, 1988), a dialogue has been established that will further our understanding of the cognitive constructs and behavioral and affective components of different levels of therapeutic competence, as well as the training prerequisites at each level.

In his excellent review of empirical studies based on developmental models, Worthington (1987) reached the following conclusions about developmental supervision:

— There is some support for general developmental models.
— In general, perceptions of supervisors and trainees have been broadly consistent with developmental theories.
— The behavior of supervisors changes as trainees gain experience.
— The supervision relationship changes as counselors gain experience.
— Supervisors do not become more competent as they gain experience.

In their review of the research that has been published since the Worthington (1987) review, Stoltenberg, McNeill, and Crethar (1994) concluded that "evidence appears solid for developmental changes across training levels" (p. 419). They also noted that, whereas experience alone is a relatively crude measure of "development," it has been used in most studies. For that reason, and given that most of this research had focused on a restricted range of experience (e.g., first practicum versus second practicum versus internship), Stoltenberg et al. found that "it is remarkable that so many differences have been found among trainees based on this categorization" (p. 419).

SOCIAL ROLE SUPERVISION MODELS

In Chapter 1 we discussed some root metaphors that might influence expectations and behaviors of supervisors and supervisees. These are metaphors based on enduring, ingrained role behaviors such as occur in parent–child, sibling, and mentor–apprenticeship relationships. Because these relationships are so very basic and indelible, they may affect supervision in ways that remain outside our awareness.

Another class of metaphors consists of the professional roles supervisors already have mastered in their professional work. It is logical, then, that these would become metaphors or templates for their work as supervisors. Ekstein and Wallerstein (1972) addressed this point in stating that

> *The one confronted with something new will try at first to reduce the new to the familiar. The psychotherapist who becomes a teacher of psychotherapy will frequently be tempted to fall back on skills that represent prior acquisitions. He will thus try to convert the teaching relationship into a therapeutic relationship.* (pp. 254–255)

This tendency of supervisors to draw on what already has been learned is complemented by the fact that it is possible to consider supervision a higher-order role that encompasses other professional roles. Douce (1989), for example, pointed out that "supervision is a separate skill similar to teaching—but different; similar to counseling—but different; and similar to consulting—but different" (p. 5). This reflects the point suggested in the title of Ekstein's (1964) article, "Supervision of psychotherapy: Is it teaching? Is it administration? Or is it therapy?"

But there are a number of determinants of the role or roles a supervisor will employ at any given point. It therefore is useful to consider the model Friedlander and Ward (1984) developed, which is depicted in Figure 2.1. Each of its concentric circles is successively less broad and encompassing; at the same time, each influences the level "below" it. Too, this model makes clear in a visual way that terms such as "role," "theory," "focus," and "technique" are *not* interchangeable. Not all authors have been clear about these distinctions.

In the Friedlander and Ward model, *assumptive world* refers to the person's past professional and life experience, training, values, cultural background, and general outlook on life. It influences the person's choice of *theoretical orientation* (e.g., behavioral, psychoanalytic, eclectic, feminist, etc.), which, in turn, influences his or her choice of *style or role.* Style or role determines *strategy–focus* which in turn influences choice of *format* (or *method;* e.g., live supervision, group supervision,

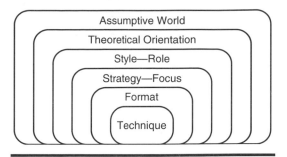

FIGURE 2.1 Interrelated Sources of Variability Among Supervisors.

From M. L. Friedlander & L. G. Ward (1984), Development and validation of the supervisory styles inventory, *Journal of Counseling Psychology, 31,* 541–557. Reprinted with permission.

etc.), which in turn influences choice of technique. In short, then, the model assumes the following path of causal influence: assumptive world → theoretical orientation → style–role → strategy–focus → format → technique.

One aspect of the Friedlander and Ward (1984) model was supported by Putney, Worthington, and McCulloughy (1992). That is, they found theoretical orientation to predict supervisor role.

Supervisors, though, typically employ only a relatively few roles. This is illustrated in Table 2.1, which depicts the supervisory roles suggested by several authors (Bernard, 1979; Carroll, 1996; Ekstein, 1964; Hess, 1981; Holloway, 1995; Williams, 1995). This selection of authors includes those who have been most influential. Moreover, these models are sufficient to convey the range of supervisor roles. It is clear from this table that the two roles of counselor–therapist and teacher were suggested by all these authors; also, all but one suggested the role of consultant. The next most frequently suggested role is that of evaluator or monitor. Holloway (1992) characterized the supervision models that have given particular focus to these roles as social role models. In the following sections, we will briefly summarize three of them. As will be clear, whereas the focus on roles is in each case foundational to the model, this is but one aspect of that model.

28   Chapter 2

TABLE 2.1 Supervisor Roles as Suggested by a Sample of Theorists

BERNARD (1979)	EKSTEIN (1964)	WILLIAMS (1995)	HESS (1981)	HOLLOWAY[a] (1995)	CARROLL[a] (1996)
			Lecturer		
				Relating	
Teacher	Teacher	Teacher	Teacher	Instructing–advising	Teaching
				Modeling	
Counselor	Therapist	Facilitator	Therapist	Supporting–and sharing	Counseling
Consultant		Consultant	Consultant	Consulting	Consulting
		Evaluator	Monitor–evaluator	Monitoring–evaluating	Monitoring Evaluating
			Case reviewer–master therapist		
	Administrator				Administrating

[a] Holloway (1995) suggested making the transformation from nouns (roles) to verbs (functions); Carroll (1996) followed that same convention.

The Discrimination Model

Bernard (1997) recently reported that the discrimination model was developed in the mid-1970s as a teaching tool. Having been assigned to teach a supervision course and "having recently received my doctorate, I was close enough to the experience of assuming the role of supervisor for the first time to understand my students' need for an aid to organize their initial supervision activities" (p. 310). The result of these efforts was "the simplest of maps to direct their teaching efforts" (p. 310). It is an eclectic model that attempts both parsimony and versatility.

The discrimination model (Bernard, 1979) attends to three separate foci for supervision, as well as three supervisor roles:

Foci: Supervisors might focus on trainees' *intervention* (formerly referred to as process) skills (what the trainee is doing in the session that is observable by the supervisor); trainees' *conceptualization* skills (how the trainee understands what is occurring in the session, identifies patterns, or chooses interventions—all covert processes); and trainees' *personalization* skills (how the trainee interfaces a personal style with therapy at the same time that he or she attempts to keep therapy uncontaminated by personal issues and countertransference responses).

Roles: Once supervisors have made a judgment about their trainees' abilities within each focus area, they must choose a role to accomplish their supervision goals. The available roles are those of *teacher, counselor,* or *consultant.*

As a consequence, the supervisor might be responding at any given moment in one of nine different ways (i.e., three roles by three foci). Table 2.2 illustrates how the model might operate in practice.

TABLE 2.2   The Discrimination Model

FOCUS OF SUPERVISION	SUPERVISOR ROLE		
	Teacher	*Counselor*	*Consultant*
Intervention	Supervisee would like to use systematic desensitization with a client but has never learned the technique	Supervisee is able to use a variety of intervention skills, but with one client uses question-asking as his primary style	Supervisee finds her clients reacting well to her humor and would like to know more ways to use humor in counseling
	Supervisor teaches the supervisee relaxation techniques, successive approximation, hierarchy building, and the desensitization process	Supervisor attempts to help supervisee determine the effect of this client on him which limits his use of skills in therapy sessions	Supervisor works with supervisee to identify different uses of humor in counseling and to practice these
Conceptualization	Supervisee is unable to recognize themes and patterns of client thought either during or following therapy sessions	Supervisee is unable to set realistic goals for her client who requests assertion training	Supervisee would like to use a different model for case conceptualization
	Supervisor uses session transcripts to teach supervisee to identify thematic client statements (e.g., blaming; dependence)	Supervisor helps supervisee relate her discomfort to her own inability to be assertive in several relationships	Supervisor discusses several models for supervisee to consider
Personalization	Supervisee is unaware her preference for a close seating arrangement intimidates the client	Supervisee is unaware that his female client is attracted to him sexually	Supervisee would like to feel more comfortable working with older clients
	Supervisor assigns the reading of literature summarizing proximity studies	Supervisor attempts to help the supervisee confront his own sexuality and his resistance to recognizing sexual cues from women	Supervisor and supervisee discuss developmental concerns of older people

Adapted from Bernard (1979), Supervisor training: A discrimination model, *Counselor Education and Supervision, 19,* 60–69.

The model is situation specific. In fact, it is called the discrimination model precisely because it implies that supervisors will tailor their responses to the particular supervisee's needs. This means the supervisor's roles and foci should change, not only across sessions, but also *within* session.

Supervisors should employ each focus as appropriate. The problems arise either when the supervisor adopts one focus at the expense of the supervisee's more salient needs or, relatedly, when the supervisor is rigid in using one particular focus. There are many reasons to choose a role, but the worst reason is habit or personal preference independent of the trainee's needs.

Theory and research concerning developmental approaches suggest that supervisors are more likely to employ the teaching role with novice supervisees and the consultant role with those who are more advanced. Also, supervisors of beginning trainees might expect to focus predominantly on intervention skills, whereas supervisors of more advanced students might expect to offer more balance across foci.

But these are general tendencies. An argument could be made (Bernard 1979, 1997) that the effective supervisor will be prepared to employ all roles and address all foci for supervisees at any level.

Our own professional experience has been that the discrimination model is useful in training and supervising supervisors. Nevertheless, it merits some critical examination, specifically as follows:

1. Because it addresses both roles and foci, this is more inclusive than most social role models. In fact, the discrimination model is rooted in a technical eclecticism. It frees the user to be broadly flexible in responding to the supervisee.

The fact is, though, that supervisors never can or will divorce themselves totally from the influence of their theoretical beliefs. Moreover, they often will invoke theory as a rationalization for what actually is personal idiosyncrasy. Gizynski (1978), for example, has observed that the supervisor can easily confuse his or her style as not a manifestation of personality characteristics, but

rather "as a distillation of his [or her] accumulated experience in clinical intervention" (p. 207). But whether theory or rationalization, the net result is to block the supervisor's flexibility demanded to fully use the discrimination model.

2. The discrimination model is concerned specifically with the *training* aspects of supervision. Therefore, it does not speak to the role of evaluator or monitor, which is important as a means to ensure quality of client care. But though that role is not spoken to in the model, its presence is assumed.

3. Russell et al. (1984) correctly noted that very little research has tested models of supervision that suggest supervisor roles. One strength of the discrimination model is that it may be the most researched of these models. During the past decade, a number of studies have either explicitly tested the discrimination model or employed it as a way to frame research questions (e.g., Ellis & Dell, 1986; Ellis, Dell, & Good, 1988; Glidden & Tracey, 1989; Goodyear, Abadie, & Efros, 1984; Goodyear & Robyak, 1982; Stenack & Dye, 1982; Yager, Wilson, Brewer, & Kinnetz, 1989). The model seems generally to have been supported in the various findings of these studies.

Interestingly, the role of consultant has remained somewhat elusive in these studies. For example, Goodyear, Abadie, and Efros (1984) found that a sample of experienced supervisors was able to differentiate among the supervision sessions of four major psychotherapy theorists according to their use of the teacher and counselor roles, but not the consultant role. Similarly, the counselor and teacher roles were validated, but the consultant role was not in a factor analytic study by Stenack and Dye (1982). In multidimensional scaling studies by Ellis and Dell (1986) and Glidden and Tracey (1989) the teaching and counseling roles were found to anchor opposite ends of a single dimension; the consultant role did not clearly emerge from their data. This is curious because the idea of the consultant role for supervisors is intuitively appealing, especially in work with more advanced supervisees (e.g., Gurk & Wicas, 1979). One possible explanation is that the consultant role is "fuzzier" than the others. Though it is frequently endorsed, there is not the common understanding of it that is true of the counselor and teacher roles.

The Hawkins and Shohet Model

Virtually all the models we have covered were developed by researchers and theorists and in the United States. But attention is being given worldwide to supervision. These include models by British (Carroll, 1996; Hawkins & Shohet, 1989) and Australian (Williams, 1995) theorists. In this section, we will cover the social role model of Hawkins and Shohet (1989).

The orienting metaphor for their work is that of the "good enough" supervisor, which we discuss in greater depth in Chapter 4. The essential concept is that the supervisor is there not only to offer support and reassurance, but also to contain the otherwise overwhelming affective responses the trainee might have.

Hawkins and Shohet (1989) have suggested that supervisors might focus on six different phenomena. Their model has been termed the "six-focused approach" (Williams, 1995) or, more colloquially and colorfully, the "six-eyed model of supervision." The six categories they suggest for identifying supervision focus are organized to recognize the two interlocking systems that occur in supervision: (1) the *therapy system* and (2) the *supervisory system.* Figure 2.2 depicts their model. The various foci are listed next. In parentheses at each description is Williams' (1995) descriptor for that same focus.

> **Focus 1:** *Reflection on the content of the therapy session* (therapist narrative). This concerns the actual phenomena of the therapy session, including clients' verbal and nonverbal behaviors, what clients choose to discuss and explore, and how session content might relate to content in previous sessions.
> **Focus 2:** *Exploration of the strategies and interventions used by the therapist* (therapist activity). This concerns the counselor's interventions with clients.
> **Focus 3:** *Exploration of the therapy process and relationship* (therapy process).

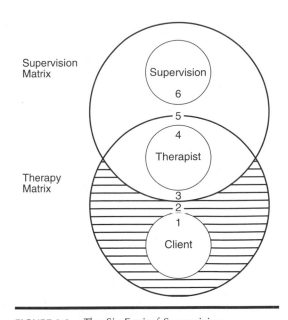

FIGURE 2.2   The Six Foci of Supervision

From P. Hawkins & R. Shohet (1989), *Supervision in the Helping Professions,* Open University Press, Philadelphia Reprinted with permission.

> **Focus 4:** *Focus on the therapist's countertransference* (supervisee state).
> **Focus 5:** *Focus on here-and-now process as a mirror or parallel of the there-and-then* (supervision process) What has been discussed by others as parallel processes.
> **Focus 6:** *Focus on the supervisor's countertransference* (supervisor experience).

In an unpublished manuscript, Michael Ellis suggested that, in making the decision about where to focus, supervisors should employ the following continuum: supervisor chooses focus → supervisor offers option of focus → supervisor helps counselor review options → counselor chooses focus. Ellis further suggested that the choice of focus should be determined by such matters as the contract with the supervisee; the developmental stage of the supervisee; the supervisee's theoretical orientation; identified learning needs from previous sessions; if the supervisee is a student; any tie-in to current course learning; the stage of the supervisee's work with the client; time constraints; and the mood of the moment.

Hawkins and Shohet's model, though, addresses more than these six foci. Those foci are of greatest salience to our discussion here in the context of social role theories. However, readers should understand that the full Hawkins and Shohet model has five factors: (1) the style or role of the supervisor (which encompasses the six foci); (2) the stage of development of the supervisee; (3) the counseling orientation of both the supervisor and trainee; (4) the supervisor–supervisee contract; and (5) the setting, or what we would call modality (individual, group, etc.).

The Holloway Model

It is clear from the number of times and contexts in which we cite her throughout this book that Holloway has been among the most prolific and influential supervision researchers and theorists. Hers (Holloway, 1995, 1997) is perhaps the most comprehensive of the available models. Holloway's full-blown model takes into account seven dimensions that have been identified in the empirical, conceptual, and practice literature on supervision. These dimensions—which exert mutual influence on each other—and interact as part of a complex process include the supervisory relationship itself (including phase, contract, and structure); characteristics of the supervisor; characteristics of the institution in which the supervision occurs; characteristics of the client; and characteristics of the trainee.

Because our focus here is on the social role models, we will note only the aspects of Holloway's model that concern functions and tasks. These are, respectively, the *how* and *what* of supervision.

Tasks: monitoring–evaluating; instructing–advising; modeling; consulting; supporting–sharing

functions: counseling skill; case conceptualization; professional role; emotional awareness; self-evaluation.

The consequence is a 5 (task) by 5 (function) matrix, with 25 resulting task–function combinations. A supervisor might, for example, engage in

monitoring–evaluating (the how) of the trainee's counseling skill (the what), or might engage in consulting concerning the trainee's emotional awareness, and so on. Holloway (1997) noted that "hypothetically a supervisor may engage in any [task] with any [function, but] . . . realistically there are probably some task and function matches that are more likely to occur in supervision" (p. 258). So that readers can more easily see the relationship between Holloway's model and others such as Bernard's (1979, 1997), they should understand that her functions correspond to what others have called foci; that her tasks are the verb form of the terms others have used to describe roles.

ECLECTIC AND INTEGRATIONIST MODELS

The three organizing categories we employed in this chapter address the primary models and theories being employed by supervision theorists and researchers. We should acknowledge, though, that some models do not fit neatly into any of those categories.*

The clearest example of models that belong here is that of eclectic or integrationist supervisions. It is likely, in fact, that most supervisors behave as eclectics or integrationists. Norcross and Napolitano (1986) used a culinary metaphor to suggest that, whereas "the eclectic selects among several dishes to constitute a meal, the integrationist creates new dishes by combining different ingredients" (p. 253).

Bernard's (1979; 1997) discrimination model is explicitly eclectic. An example of an integrationist perspective might be that of Webb's (1983) life model, which combines ego psychology and communications theory into a conceptual framework devised to understand the training needs for "competent" clinical practitioners. Another is Sharon's

---

* We would note here that, whereas Kagan's interpersonal process recall (Kagan, 1976, 1980; Kagan & Kratwohl, 1967; Kagan, Kratwohl, & Farquhar, 1965; Kagan, Kratwohl, & Miller, 1963; Kagan & Kagan, 1997) is often treated as a model, we have come to treat it instead as an approach (see Chapter 5). Also, whereas the use of parallel processes (see Chapter 4) are used by many supervisors as a primary approach, we do not believe they merit status as a model.

(1986) ABCX model based on work done by Hill (1958) and McCubbin and Patterson (1983). Sharon's conceptualization of the supervision process is complex (parts read like a geometry text), but worthwhile. ABCX stand for (1) event, (2) perception of event, (3) resources to meet the event, and (4) effective change.

But most supervisors eventually develop their own, unique, integrationist perspectives. Indeed, a central finding of Skovholt and Ronnestadt's (1992a, b) research was that to develop such an individualized perspective was a hallmark of the advanced practitioner. Norcross and Halgin (1997) suggested that, in developing an integrationist perspective, supervisors should attend to what they called *cardinal principles of integrative supervision.* Among their cardinal principles were to customize supervision to the individual student; conduct a needs assessment; construct explicit contracts; blend supervision methods; address with trainees their "relationships of choice"; operate from a coherent framework; match supervision to trainee variables; consider the therapy approach (in general, "the 'how' of supervision [method] should parallel the 'what' of supervision [content]," 1997, p. 210); consider the developmental level of the trainee, the cognitive style of the trainee, and the trainee's personal idiom; assess the trainee's therapeutic skills; evaluate the outcomes.

CONCLUSION

Supervisors traditionally have employed their theories of therapy to inform their work with supervisees. Because of supervision's close relationship to therapy, it is inevitable that this will occur. But it is a mark of the vitality of supervision as an area of practice and inquiry that increasingly there are models that have been developed specifically for supervision. Although our coverage of those models was necessarily scant, we hope it will help orient aspiring supervisors to literature that they can explore in more detail.

CHAPTER 3

The Supervisory Relationship
The Influence of Individual and Developmental Differences

Striking similarities exist between the process of counseling and the process of clinical supervision. Perhaps the most pronounced of these similarities is the centrality and role of interpersonal relationship in both processes. Just as a positive and productive relationship is critical to successful counseling, so too is a positive and productive relationship critical to successful supervision (Ronnestad & Skovholt, 1993; Worthen & McNeill, 1996). Understanding relationship variables that affect the supervisory relationship and having the skill to establish a productive supervisory relationship have been cited as requisite elements of supervision preparation and practice (Borders et al., 1991; Supervision Interest Network, 1990). In fact, when supervision participants are asked to identify critical incidents in supervision, the most frequently identified element is the supervisory relationship (Ellis, 1991).

This chapter will examine the effect that individual, cultural, and developmental differences can have on the supervisory relationship. By individual differences, we refer to those unique personal qualities that give form to one's identity, qualities such as self-presentation, self-comfort, and self-monitoring. They also include personal style, learning style, and belief systems. Cultural differences include cultural identities and the meanings attached to those identities. Developmental differences refer to one's placement along the continuum of counseling skill acquisition. Development is dynamic, and a number of attributes that are associated with it are transient. For example, many behaviors and

perceptions of the first-year student will be different when the student is in the second or third year of training. But developmental differences, though transient, are included in this chapter because, within time-limited supervisory contracts, trainees' developmental stages dictate certain relationship dimensions. (Chapter 4 focuses more directly on the interpersonal processes and issues that may occur between supervisors and supervisees.)

THE UNIQUENESS OF TWO PERSONS IN RELATIONSHIP

The supervisory relationship is a product of the uniqueness of two individuals, paired with the purposes of meeting for supervision and modified by the demands of the various contexts that are the subject or content of that experience. Knowing some of the personal variables that have been considered in the professional literature will arm the supervisors with additional tools to assist the trainee in achieving competence. Furthermore, because we have some evidence that personal compatibility between supervisor and trainee will affect evaluation (see Chapter 8), it is essential that the supervisor be aware of personal and interpersonal style variables to avoid biased reviews.

Personal characteristics have not received the same level of attention in the supervision literature as developmental differences, perhaps because of methodological challenges in studying personal style. Furthermore, unlike the literature of developmental supervision differences, personal style research and model development seem to be more scattered and disconnected. These limits aside, this section will consider what the literature has to report on personal characteristics such as *self-presentation, cognitive styles, and learning styles.*

Self-presentation

Self-presentation is a concept drawn from the social–psychological literature and refers to the trainee's interpersonal style. Self-presentation includes expressive behaviors that are habitual and automatic, having once served a deliberate function, but no longer exactly purposeful (Holloway, 1995). Self-presentation style is not always prominent in supervision; therefore, it is more likely to be problematic or advantageous under discrete conditions. And self-presentation is a dynamic that can be highly influenced by environmental or contextual variables.

There has been a good deal of attention in the professional literature to the supervisee's presentation of anxiety (Friedlander, Keller, Peca-Baker, & Olk, 1986; Jackson & Stricker, 1989). Anxiety has been reported to be inversely related to performance and to self-efficacy (Friedlander et al., 1986). These findings are particularly relevant when viewed within the context of earlier results reported by Friedlander and Snyder (1983) that confidence and high expectations of supervision were more predictive of success than level of training. Anxiety, while relatively normal for novice trainees, is most relevant when it undermines self-confidence and leads to an assumption that supervision will end in an ego-diminishing fashion. Viewed in this way, it becomes obvious how such initial anxiety can have the power to form a less than satisfactory supervisory relationship unless the anxiety is isolated and addressed directly in a way that might diffuse it. Studies have reported findings related to the presence or absence of anxiety in the supervisory relationship, including the relationship between competence and trainee willingness to experiment actively (Herzberg, 1994); the effect of tolerance for ambiguity, ego resiliency, and willingness to risk in decreasing anxiety (Rodenhauser, Rudisill, & Painter, 1989); and the role of lack of information in increasing anxiety (Jackson and Stricker, 1989). We will discuss anxiety in greater detail in Chapter 4.

Watkins (1995) drew from Bowlby's (1969) work to introduce the topic of attachment styles to the supervision literature. The three pathological styles of attachment he discussed—anxious attachment, compulsive self-reliance, and compulsive care giving—certainly are evident in groups of trainees. As the developmental literature becomes more sophisticated about attachment issues over the life-span, more will be known about how adult attachment styles can affect the formation of the supervisory relationship from both the trainee's and the supervisor's perspectives.

Finally, Haferkamp (1989) discussed self-monitoring as a self-presentation issue, suggesting that high-self-monitoring persons, being particularly sensitive about social appropriateness, are sensitive to others' behavior and use this to monitor their own behavior. Low-self-monitoring persons are more internally focused, relying on their own feelings, values, and attitudes to guide their behavior. As a result, low-self-monitoring individuals are more consistent from situation to situation. Referring to the work of Mill (1984), Haferkamp reported the interesting finding that, whereas low self-monitors were found to be more *emotionally* empathic, high self-monitors were more *cognitively* empathic. Haferkamp noted, therefore, that both types need to fine-tune their process skills.

Haverkamp (1994) found that low self-monitors scored low on conformity. A supervision issue can arise, then, if the trainee's style has components that are not conducive to counseling. Low self-monitors will be less likely to follow the lead of the supervisor if it is inconsistent with their self-perception. At the same time, Haverkamp suggested that low self-monitors would be more easily trained to conduct family or group therapy because they are less likely to be overly responsive to individual demands of a family or group member.

High self-monitors, on the other hand, because they are more open to the supervisor's lead, may become confused by too many cues. The need for direction often associated with novice trainees may be, in part, a response to the high self-monitors' need for suggestions. Finally, Haverkamp postulated that high self-monitors are more difficult to read because of their focus outside themselves. They also report their internal reality with far less accuracy than low self-monitors.

Thinking in terms of constructs such as self-monitoring can assist the supervisor to understand many individual responses from trainees. What looks like resistance can be reframed as cognitive dissonance for a low self-monitor. What seems like cognitive confusion can be understood to be the attempt of the high self-monitor to reflect too many divergent opinions. Haverkamp (1994) urges supervisors to evaluate the self-monitoring profile of trainees because of its relevance to supervision and the ease with which this construct can be measured using the Snyder Self-Monitoring Scale (Snyder, 1987; Snyder & Gangestad, 1986).

Cognitive or Learning Styles

Cognitive or learning styles concern a person's particular ways of processing information and different preferences in learning. These do not indicate differential ability. And, unlike conceptual levels, cognitive or learning styles are assumed to be nonhierarchical.

Most studies of cognitive style in supervision have used the Myers–Briggs Type Indicator (Myers, 1962; Myers & McCaulley, 1985) to distinguish trainees. Ing (1990) translated the learning style theories of Kolb (1984) and Gregorc (1979) to the supervisory experience. Taken together, these authors offer a relatively rich discussion of the importance of cognitive or learning style in establishing the supervisory relationship. We will begin by considering the implication of MBTI type.

The MBTI produces a profile that addresses the following differences:

— Focus of interest [*Extroversion* (E)], focusing on outer world of people and things, versus *Introversion* (I), directed toward the inner world of ideas)

— Information gathering [*Sensing* (S)], relying on facts and data, versus Intuiting (N), relying on intuition to understand meaning
— Involvement with information [*Feeling* (F)], focusing on subjective experience, versus Thinking (T), looking to objective analysis
— Information management [*Judging* (J)], attempting to regulate and control, versus Perceiving (P), looking to experience life and adapt to it

Although the study focused on communication disorders, Craig and Sleight (1990) found significant differences between supervisors and trainees. Supervisors were far more likely to have a profile of ENTJ, INTJ, or ESTJ. Not surprisingly, these same profiles have been found to be common among those drawn to college teaching. The most dramatic differences between supervisors and supervisees had to do with the T–F scale and the J–P scale.

Craig and Sleight (1990) addressed some of the implications of these findings. For example, a Thinking–Judging supervisor (i.e., the most common profile among supervisors in academic settings) will find a trainee who makes decisions based on subjective data to be frustrating. Similarly, the well-organized supervisor (J) may be critical of the supervisee whose paper work or general approach to learning seems too random. At the same time, FP trainees may in fact be more capable of achieving empathy with clients than their supervisors.

Another area of distinction is the N–S scale. Because the preference represented by this scale has to do with gathering of information, it can affect supervision in a number of ways. A Sensing trainee will be attempting to understand through a collection of facts; therefore, an intuitive insight from an N supervisor may only confuse and frustrate the supervisee who cannot track the origin of the suggestion (Craig & Sleight, 1990). Furthermore, students who were Intuitive rather than Sensing have been found to receive far more regard from supervisors and were evaluated as significantly more competent than Sensing trainees (Handley, 1982). (Despite these findings, Handley also reported that the cognitive style of the supervisor did not affect trainees' ratings of their relationship with their supervisors or their satisfaction with supervision.)

Swanson and O'Saben (1993) also found the MBTI to be relevant to supervision: Supervisees with a Thinking–Perceiving profile expressed a greater need for supervisors who were willing to struggle and argue with them, as well as to confront them about more personal aspects of behavior; supervisees who were Intuitive expressed a need for gentle confrontation and direct supervision of counseling sessions and lesser need for supervision that provided tangible intervention in crises or supervision that excluded personal issues; and Introvert trainees expressed a greater need for gentle confrontation and lesser need for direct supervision of sessions.

Moving from cognitive style to learning style, Ing (1990) took the four learning styles described by Kolb and Gregorc [converger, diverger, accommodator, and assimilator (Kolb, 1984; Gregorc, 1979)] and applied them to the supervision of child care workers. Her observations are highly pertinent to the supervision of counseling supervisees.

Convergers are comfortable in the arena of the abstract. They also like instruction to be concrete and orderly, are sequential in their thoughts and actions, prefer to work alone, and are strong in the area of visualization of tasks and issues. Convergers have difficulty with affective and behavioral learning environments. Any opportunity for convergers to work independently would enhance their learning. Ing suggested the use of case studies and other problem-solving approaches to assist the converger.

Divergers react positively to personalized feedback and shared feelings. Divergers are creative and do well with brainstorming activities. Not surprisingly, divergers prefer unstructured environments and seem to perform best if they can reflect on data that have been gathered before organizing them. Ing suggested that concrete suggestions and goal setting be avoided with divergers; rather, personal feedback, opportunity to apply learning, and discussions would be helpful with divergers. These

trainees would also need support to assist them with organization.

Accomodators are the most action-oriented learners. They thrive on involvement, on doing and completing tasks. They also like unstructured situations, but are less attuned to subtle nuances than are divergers. They are more spontaneous and measure success on how well something worked. These trainees may not learn efficiently with a lecture format and may benefit from immediate feedback, group supervision, and problem-solving processes.

Assimilators are the most abstract of the four types, favoring theoretical discussions and analytical approaches. Like convergers, they prefer sequential presentations from which they can glean the central themes. Ing suggested that assimilators be allowed to observe and reflect in order to learn. When feedback is offered to assimilators, they might need time to analyze and assimilate it into their cognitive schemata.

Because personal or interpersonal styles are relatively stable and enduring, it is essential that supervisors be inquisitive regarding the empirical findings that relate to these and supervision, as well as to be open to those who have theorized regarding this important aspect of supervision. Like all individual differences, whether cognitive, interpersonal, or cultural, the point is to be aware of one's own frame of reference and the other's so that areas of existing strength can be maximized and areas of weakness can receive supportive attention. Furthermore, supervisors may need to operate from other than their preferred style of thinking and acting if they intend to be of service to a variety of supervisees. The consideration of cognitive and learning style especially underscores the educational texture of supervision.

BELIEF SYSTEMS

There is perhaps nothing more individual to trainees than their belief systems. Similarly, there is perhaps nothing more intrinsically essential to the process of counseling and psychotherapy than the interplay between the world views of therapist and client. All the topics presented in this chapter affect one's beliefs about human nature and one-self or are affected by it. Belief systems are both the result and the bridge of our interactions with each other. Within psychotherapy, aspects of belief systems have been formulated into theoretical orientations.

Theoretical Orientation

There is a great deal of speculation and some evidence (e.g., Kennard, Stewart, & Gluck, 1987) that similarity of theoretical orientation between supervisor and supervisee is consequential for the relationship. Guest and Beutler (1988) presented data to suggest that several years after training early supervisory experiences can still exert an effect on the supervisee's theoretical position. Even so, when compared to other relationship factors, such as respect for the supervisee, theoretical orientation has been found to be the lesser influence (e.g., Schacht, Howe, & Berman, 1989; Wetcher, 1989). More recently, Putney, Worthington, and McCullough (1992) have shed some light on this issue.

As others (e.g., Holloway et al., 1989) have observed, Putney et al. (1992) found that the supervisor's theory is much more likely to drive supervision than is the supervisee's. In other words, most supervisors direct supervisees based on their vision of psychotherapy and change and do not attend to the differences between their vision and the supervisee's. In light of this finding, it is understandable that theoretical compatibility would benefit the supervisee. These authors concluded, however, that *perceived* similarity was more important than *actual* similarity. Furthermore, for pairs who shared theoretical assumptions, weak adherence to theory by the supervisor led to increased trainee autonomy.

Andrews' (1989) thoughtful and provocative work is highly relevant here. Andrews proposed that standard theoretical orientations reflect the personal visions of those authors who formulated them. Additionally, each vision has the potential for optimal or pathological functioning. Andrews goes on to argue for total theoretical integration (so that therapists may be tooled to react to the various vi-

sions presented by clients). Although Andrews does not mention supervision, his position begs the question of acknowledging individual vision in supervision as well as therapy. The important point here, however, is that theoretical orientation may be more a matter of individual difference than a cognitive construct that can be handed down from supervisor to supervisee. As the cultures of the helping professions become more attuned to individual differences, they must grapple with the consequences of these new awarenesses on the practice of therapy and supervision. Just as supervisors who ignore gender or racial considerations in their supervision lack credibility, we may have enough evidence to require that supervisors be sensitive to the visions of their supervisees and proceed accordingly. This would imply that supervisors no longer have the luxury of applying their own theoretical bias uniformly unless, of course, they supervise within a theoretically pure institute setting that has attracted trainees of similar visions. By no means does this presently represent the majority of psychotherapy supervision.

Spirituality

We were unable to identify a single published work devoted to spirituality as a legitimate supervision issue, despite the fact that there is growing interest in spirituality in the counseling and therapy literature, and studies that have surveyed therapists representing different disciplines have found the majority to consider spirituality an important mental health dimension (Grimm, 1994; Kelly, 1994, 1995; Pate & High, 1995; Shafranske & Malony, 1990). It would appear that, as is true of so many other issues, spirituality must become more visible in the counseling and therapy domain before it becomes salient as a supervision issue. For our present purposes, we simply assert the importance of spirituality in the development of the trainee, as a matter of individual difference and as a cultural matter. As such, spirituality must be included in the supervision agenda.

Like the concept of culture, spirituality poses the problem of definition. Some authors adhere to the more traditional view of the spiritual as having a direct connection to religion (e.g., Bergin, 1991; Kelly, 1995; Pate & Bondi, 1992); others offer a totally secular definition of spirituality (e.g., Hinterkopf, 1994). It becomes important, therefore, that any supervisor attempting to address spirituality in supervision begin by seeking an operational definition from the supervisee so that the dialogue may have meaning. Beyond definition, it would seem important for both supervisor and supervisee to be willing to share some personal beliefs because of the obvious implications these will have on choice and implementation of theoretical constructs. This is not a small task, especially in light of the history of both psychotherapy and religion–spirituality.

There is general agreement that at certain levels psychology gained its authority by being positioned as distinct (if not opposed) to the spiritual, not in accordance with it (Butler, 1990; Mack, 1994). In fact, some authors have proposed that psychology has replaced religion for many in the last generation, having become the "worldly competitor for influence over persons" (Grimm, 1994, p. 156). At the very least, religion and psychology have been very leery of each other since Freud. Butler (1990) stated that "Each vocation seemed so sure of its superior ability to engineer human development and change, and at the same time unwilling to admit to any common ground. The result was an underground rivalry" (p. 30). Butler went on to state that neither profession is a total answer to the challenges of lifelong development. Persons in either camp will be frustrated by mid-career without some appreciation of the other.

CULTURAL DIFFERENCES

The influence of cultural phenomena on the helping process has received particular attention in recent years. Pederson (1991) postulated that virtually all counseling is multicultural, because culture incorporates the influences of race, ethnicity, gender, sexual orientation, religion, class, and so on, on our thoughts, assumptions, and behaviors. Therefore, in Pederson's view, any discussion of individual differences must include a serious discussion of cultural differences.

We wish to note that the separation of these many developmental, interpersonal style, and cultural characteristics in this chapter is done for the purpose of closer scrutiny. In reality, however, cultural context, development, and interpersonal style all interact in a dynamic and continuous fashion. That being said, this particular section takes a closer look at supervision through a multicultural lens.

Virtually all our attention in the professional literature continues to revolve around disenfranchised groups. The danger of this focus is that it continues to allow persons who do not identify with any of these groups to diminish the importance of cultural constructs in their own lives (cf. Preli & Bernard, 1993). Although it is essential for supervisors to be minimally competent working with, for example, supervisees of different races, this must be so not only because some racial groups continue to struggle with disenfranchisement in our society, but because their cultural view is rich in its own right. This kind of awareness becomes salient only as supervisors become aware of the power of their own cultural assumptions to influence their thinking and their interactions with others. This leads our discussion to the necessity of multicultural training prior to the onset of supervision.

Several authors have asserted that entry-level training in multicultural issues must precede supervision if the latter is to be productive (e.g., Supervision Interest Network, 1990; Bernard, 1994; Fong & Lease, 1996; Priest, 1994). Recommended components of training usually include some sort of consciousness raising, the acquisition of cultural knowledge, experiential exercises, contact with diverse groups, and a practicum or internship with a diverse client population (McRae & Johnson, 1991; Parker, 1987; Parker, Bingham, & Fukuyama, 1985; Parker, Valley, & Geary, 1986; Ponterotto, Anderson, & Grieger, 1995; Ponterotto & Casas, 1987; Preli & Bernard, 1993; Sue, Akutsu, & Higashi, 1985). Training programs in the helping professions are far more likely to attend to consciousness raising than they were a decade ago, imparting cultural knowledge and addressing the basics of communication skills in working with different cultural groups. Programs still vary widely, however, with respect to the contact they provide trainees to different populations during practica and internships. As a result there is often much learning to be accomplished in supervision regarding the practice of counseling and therapy from a multicultural perspective. The cultural aspects of the supervision relationship can enhance this learning when addressed productively. It should be noted, however, that the triadic nature of supervision, along with the plethora of cultural dimensions, makes the process of multicultural supervision complex.

The multicultural supervision literature is still limited, and empirical contributions have been particularly sparse (Leong & Wagner, 1994). The thrust of the available literature continues to reflect the accurate assumption that more supervisors represent white, middle-class cultural perspectives than do their supervisees or their supervisees' clients. Although this is changing slowly, our professional knowledge to date reflects the limits of where we are in the evolution of our understanding of culture and the implications of culture on both therapy and supervision. Because race continues to be perhaps the most dramatic cultural marker in our society, we will begin by discussing supervision within and across racial groups. Before we do this, however, we want to address briefly the political nature of the helping professions and the culture of psychotherapy itself.

Political Nature of the Helping Professions

Another important notion to consider as part of our professional context is that the helping professions are sociopolitical in nature (Katz, 1985). By ignoring cultural differences, the dominant culture was able to ignore much injustice done to nondominant cultures. Supervision is as vulnerable to reflecting, say, the color blindness espoused by a culture-blind society as are other institutions (Peterson, 1991). Katz described this insensitivity as

an "invisible veil" that affects our interactions with others, often outside our awareness. This blind spot leaves supervisees and clients unacceptably vulnerable when diagnostic or evaluative conclusions are made that are culturally ignorant.

This leads to our proposition that supervisors cannot fully meet their responsibilities if they do not exercise political power. If we supervise from the standpoint of one cultural perspective to the detriment of a supervisee (or client) of another, we have committed an oppressive political act. Porter (1994) took a more affirming position regarding the political reality of supervision by stating that the final stage of multicultural supervision must be social action for clients, supervisees, supervisors, and institutions. To have a lesser vision significantly compromises the ability of supervisors to empower their supervisees.

The Psychotherapy Culture

Not only does counseling and psychotherapy continue to reflect the dominant culture in the United States, but it also makes up a culture in and of itself, "with its own belief systems, language, customs, governance, and norms" (Holiman & Lauver, 1987, p. 184). Holiman and Lauver made the excellent point that client-centered practice is perhaps far more difficult to achieve than is commonly assumed because of the counselor's enmeshment with the therapy culture. "To the extent that practitioners are acculturated within the counseling culture, their relationships with clients from outside of this culture are subject to barriers of cross-cultural understanding" (p. 185).

The simple assessment that someone is behaving defensively is an example of the therapy culture at work, in that this commonly used term is rooted in Freudian psychodynamic theory. If the supervisee has been successfully acculturated into the psychotherapy culture (and thus socialized into a particular helping profession), this may provide a bridge between supervisor and supervisee that might enhance the relationship. At the same time, a sharing of this professional culture may serve to assist supervisor and supervisee in denying the importance of far more encompassing differences between them.

Racial Issues within Multicultural Supervision

In his seminal work, Bradshaw (1982) addressed the implications of race in the supervisory relationship, asserting that race is a highly charged catalyst in our society, one that is bound to emerge, even if not addressed, in supervision. Helms and Piper (1994) magnified this assumption when they claimed that racial identity has evolved to occupy the greatest percentage of self-concept.

Bradshaw focused on situations where blacks and whites interact, a theme that has remained dominant in the supervision literature that addresses race (cf. Leong & Wagner, 1994). He noted that a black client seeing a white therapist who is supervised by a white supervisor is presently the most common multicultural occurrence in mental health practice. At the time of his writing, Bradshaw was visionary in alerting supervisors to be cautious that the white supervisor–white therapy dyad not ignore culture-based phenomena presented by black clients. In more recent years, the supervision literature has moved forward to recognize that supervisors who ignore culture within the supervisory relationship are far less likely to be prepared to successfully monitor therapy that is multicultural. This, of course, is even more the case as more and more supervisees represent diverse cultural groups.

Fong and Lease (1996) provided a comprehensive overview of the issues salient to the white supervisor attempting to provide culturally sensitive supervision to persons of a different race. They asserted that most of the challenges facing the white supervisor can be categorized by one of the following: (1) unintentional racism, (2) power dynamics, (3) trust and the supervisory alliance, and (4) communication issues. Basic to both unintentional racism and power dynamics, it seems to us, is the power and privilege of the supervisor to address the topic of race.

Kleintjes and Swartz (1996) interviewed a group of black clinical psychology trainees in a predominately white university in South Africa and found that, when race was not addressed by supervisors, trainees were reluctant to bring up the topic for any of six reasons: (1) they experienced the university as a "colorless zone" where, due to their strong antiapartheid stance, faculty deny any acknowledgment of race; (2) they feared being seen as using their blackness as an excuse for poor performance; (3) they feared being seen to be using their blackness as a defense against other issues; (4) they feared being seen as pathologically occupied with the issue of color and discrimination; (5) they were uncertain whether these issues were best shared or dealt with personally; and (6) they acknowledged their own personal insecurities as the reasons for not bringing up the issue of race. This list, which could just as easily have been acquired in the United States, reflects the lack of power felt by the supervisees interviewed.

Cook (1994) addressed power in two ways: the power inherent in the role of the supervisor and the power of being a member of the dominant culture in a sociopolitical context that is overtly and covertly racist. The latter is central to the concern of unintentional racism. Though inexcusable at this point in the evolution of the mental health professions, it is sadly conceivable that supervisors may remain ignorant of their racism due to their own racial identity development (Cook, 1994; Fong & Lease, 1996). Cook provided an extension of Helms's (1994) revised racial identity model to address potential supervisor dynamics for both whites and people of color (see Table 3.1). As Fong and Lease stated, supervisors are ill equipped to conduct multicultural supervision if they are below the immersion–emersion stages of development. Additionally, Cook addressed the development of the supervisor relative to the supervisee, describing progressive supervision as occurring when the supervisor's racial identity development is beyond the supervisee and regressive supervision when the supervisor's development lags behind. Because of the power inherent in the role of supervisor, it is that person's sophistication

TABLE 3.1 Summary of People of Color (POC) and White Racial Identity Ego Statuses
and Potential Approaches to Racial Issues in Supervision (PARI)

Conformity (POC)	Contact (White)

PARI: Ignores race of client, supervisee, and supervisor. Assumes theoretical approach generalizes to all individuals; focuses only on "common humanity."

Dissonance (POC)	Disintegration (White)

PARI: Acknowledges client's race as demographic or descriptive characteristic; lacks awareness of assumptions being made about the client based on race. Ignores supervisee's and supervisor's race.

Immersion/Emersion (POC)	Reintegration (White)

PARI: Recognizes own race as standard for "normal" behavior of client and "effective" performance of partner. Recognizes other-race clients, but cultural differences seen as deficits or forms of "resistance." Holds biases toward theoretical approaches that represent own cultural perspective.

Pseudo-Independence (White)

PARI: Discusses racial differences only if interacting with POC. Discusses cultural differences, based on generalized assumptions about various racial groups. Recognizes cultural biases of theories; lacks working knowledge of how to adapt theories to POC.

Immersion/Emersion (White)

PARI: Acknowledges race of client, supervisee, and supervisor, and their respective cultural assumptions and racial attitudes. Considers sociopolitical implications of race in therapy and supervision.

Internalization (POC)	Autonomy (White)

PARI: Integrates personal cultural values and therapeutic and supervision values. Acknowledges race of client, supervisee, and supervisor and the cultural and sociopolitical influences on the therapeutic and supervisory relationships. Names cultural conflicts in supervision interactions without internalizing racial prejudices of other-race supervision partner.

Integrative Awareness (POC)

PARI: Recognizes race as an aspect of each person's identity and potential variability in racial identity attitudes. Acknowledges cultural assumptions of supervision partners and negotiates cultural sensitive approaches to supervision and therapy. Serves as advocate for oppressed groups in interactions with agencies and training program.

From D. A. Cook (1994), Racial Identity in Supervision, *Counselor Education and Supervision, 34,*
140–141. © ACA. Reprinted with permission.

regarding racial implications that will drive supervision. Therefore, the helping professions can only begin to claim multicultural supervision when reaching this minimum stage of racial identity development becomes a prerequisite for assuming the role of supervisor (Bernard, 1994).

In a discussion about the black supervisor working with a white supervisee, Priest (1994) alluded to both trust and communication issues as hampering supervision, a point reiterated by Williams and Halgin (1995). Priest assumed that white supervisees would have negative outcome expectations when working with a black supervisor and that ignorance of different communication styles between the racial groups would lead to harmful miscommunication. Remington and DaCosta (1989) also focused on the black supervisor–white supervisee combination and particularly difficult moments than can occur in supervision, such as the supervisee counseling a racist client. Because of the trust and communication issues than can arise, Remington and DaCosta made the strong declaration that supervisors do not have time to wait for ethnocultural issues to "come up." They admonished that it is the supervisor's responsibility to attend to such concerns, thus setting the stage for a context in which all four of Fong and Lease's (1996) issues can be addressed. Remington and DaCosta also acknowledged the difficulty of supervising persons of a different race and suggested that supervisors not work in isolation but in conjunction with other supervisors, a suggestion we would underscore. It should be noted that, although the obstacles mentioned by these different authors are important, the white supervisee stands to gain a great deal when offered the opportunity to work under the supervision of a black supervisor (Vargas, 1989).

Batten (1990) discussed issues of communication and trust within cross-cultural supervision, but did so within the context of Australian society when a white supervisor worked with a Vietnamese supervisee. In addition to subtle communication differences similar to Priest's argument, Batten addressed substantial challenges when supervisor and supervisees do not share a common native language and have dramatically different cultural rules. Among her admonitions were that supervisors in such situations must be adept at dealing with frustration (e.g., when the therapy is conducted in a language they do not understand) and must be able to tolerate both curiosity and a sense of being unhelpful to the trainee. Paradoxically, this ability to expect less of oneself as a supervisor provides the cultural vigilance that will most likely lead to the most productive relationship possible within such a situation. Similar sentiments were expressed by Cheng (1993) in describing a supervision experience in Hong Kong, where he was directly confronted by Chinese therapeutic pessimism in both clients and supervisees. Only as he was able to adopt the posture of a student regarding cultural constraints was he able to be of real assistance to his supervisees.

Other authors have attempted to both highlight potential racial–ethnic areas of concern and offer plausible remedies. Zuniga (1987) reported a pilot project with Mexican-American supervisees in which supervision focused on ethnic identity, family history, acculturation, and racism experiences. When trainees vacillated between feelings of competence and inadequacy, these were processed within a cultural context. "As they talked about painful school experiences, they could comprehend how they had introjected the negative expectations of former teachers and school peers who assumed they would perform poorly because they were Mexican American" (p. 18). These insights were used not only for the interns' own growth but also as a vehicle for them to work with Mexican-American clients. On a positive note, supervision also focused on the strong survival attributes of these interns to negotiate their former hostile environments.

In an analysis of salient issues in cross-cultural supervision of Asian and Hispanic social workers by white supervisors, Ryan and Hendricks (1989) identified five differential characteristics that may become sources of conflict: (1) cognitive orientation, (2) motivational orientation, (3) communication styles, (4) value orientations, and (5) sensory orientation. In the first category, Ryan and Hendricks noted that supervisees of Japanese heritage might be more likely to trust nonverbal information than verbal analysis to solve a problem. This might put them at a disadvantage in a case conference. Representative of motivational orientation is the supervisor who might experience the Hispanic trainee as not paying enough attention to planning for therapy sessions, which is a behavior that might be linked to the traditional Hispanic belief that much of life is beyond one's control and planning does not change that basic premise.

The third category, communication styles, has received more attention elsewhere in the multicultural literature. Both Asian and male Hispanics, for different reasons, may be reticent to willingly admit to having trouble in their clinical work. Additionally, according to Ryan and Hendricks, Asian supervisees are likely to view excessive talking as indication of narcissism and attention seeking. This may be paired with a tendency to cut off the process of supervision and case conceptualization too soon. Reflecting the value orientation of humility, the authors reported one Asian intern who was told by her supervisor that she lacked self-confidence. She had to explain to him that she had often minimized her achievements so as not to appear boastful. In relationship to the relative value given to either hierarchical or egalitarian approaches, Ryan and Hendricks noted that both Asian and Hispanic societies embody a hierarchical structure. "In supervision, it is helpful to watch for nonverbal cues, such as facial expression or changes in body posture, in order to know if the supervisee is angry or disagreeing with the supervisor" (p. 36).

Finally, Ryan and Hendricks suggested that Asian supervisees are more visual, whereas Hispanics are more verbal. Hispanic supervisees might be resistant to writing out comprehensive case notes, whereas some Asian supervisees have difficulty with the auditory sense, making the audiotape a difficult vehicle for learning. Although Ryan and Hendricks's contribution of attempting to classify some of the inherent obstacles in cross-cultural supervision is significant, acculturation and intragroup differences may drastically minimize the utility of their observations.

Empirical Results. Most contributions to the multicultural supervision literature have been theoretical or anecdotal (cf. Leong & Wagner, 1994). It is important that these contributions be measured against the modest research efforts that have transpired to date.

VanderKolk (1974) apparently conducted the earliest study, investigating the relationship variables of personality, values, and race as these affected the anticipation of supervision with a white supervisor. No differences were found for personality or values. Black students, however, were more likely to anticipate that their supervisors would lack empathy, respect, and congruence than were white students. This study did not include a follow-up; its contribution was to help establish the salience of race as a key variable as relationships between supervisors and supervisees were being established.

Cook and Helms (1988) studied 225 Asian, black, Hispanic, or Native American supervisees to examine their satisfaction with cross-cultural supervision. Of the variables they considered, perceived supervisor liking and perceived conditional interest were found to contribute to greater satisfaction, with the perception that the supervisor liked them being the strongest factor by far. Regarding the second variable, the authors hypothesized that

supervisees may value conditional supervisory relationships as long as they perceive that the conditions occur in an atmosphere of caring. Perhaps in such a context supervisees are able to use the information communicated by the supervisor's conditions to help them figure out what is expected of them in this particular cross-cultural environment. (p. 273)

Overall, the supervisees tended to report a guarded relationship with their supervisors; additionally, Native-American and African-American supervisees were least satisfied with cross-cultural supervision and Asian-Americans were most satisfied. As Leong and Wagner (1994) later suggested, however, the lack of a white sample of supervisees makes these results difficult to interpret.

In a provocative examination of field instructors' and supervisees' working relationships within a cross-cultural context, McRoy, Freeman, Logan, and Blackmon (1986) found that actual problems were few, but that both supervisors and supervisees expected more problems than benefits in such relationships. Several black supervisors reported that white supervisees had questioned their competence and resisted their supervision. Hispanic supervisors also noted experiences that were related to a lack of acceptance of their authority by supervisees. Despite these responses, the actual number of supervisors (12, or 28 percent) and supervisees (7, or 16 percent) who reported having directly experienced a cross-cultural problem was quite low. When problems did occur, those supervisees who addressed the problem with their supervisors were satisfied with the outcome. Of the seven students who had experienced difficulty, however, only two chose to approach their supervisors about it. The others felt it was too threatening to do so because of the power differential in supervision. This study points to the vital issue of supervisor and supervisee expectations that influence cross-cultural encounters. It also reinforces the assertions by others (e.g., Cook, 1994; Vargas, 1989) that it is up to the supervisor to initiate cultural issues in a supervisory environment in which it is sufficiently safe to do so.

Hilton, Russell, and Salmi (1995) investigated the effects of supervisor support and race on counselor anxiety, perceived performance, satisfaction, and perceptions of the supervisory relationship. All supervisees were white; supervisors were either white or African-American. Whereas supervisor support emerged as a main effect, supervisor race did not. This kind of discrimination study, which weighs the effect of race against other relationship variables, is sorely needed in the supervision literature.

In a pilot study, Fukuyama (1994) elicited critical incidents from racial–ethnic minorities who had completed an APA internship. They were asked to offer positive and negative incidents and to describe organizational or environmental conditions that contributed to their professional development. Positive incidents fell into three categories: *openness and support* (e.g., not being stereotyped, supervisors demonstrating belief in their abilities), *culturally relevant supervision* (i.e., receiving supervision that addressed cultural implications both for the supervisee and for clients seen), and *opportunity to work in multicultural activities* (i.e., positively validating opportunities to contribute in ways that included cultural expertise).

Although very few trainees offered negative incidents, these were divided into two categories: *lack of supervisor cultural awareness* (e.g., interpreting culturally consistent behavior as a countertransference issue or using expressions that were offensive to the supervisee), and *questioning supervisee abilities* (e.g., not trusting the supervisee's interpretation of a client's behavior as culturally relevant when supervisee and client shared the same heritage). Trainees' suggestions offered by subjects to sensitize internship settings included providing more multicultural training, encouraging more discourse within supervision about cultural factors, and, conversely, cautioning

supervisors not to overestimate cultural diversity issues in an attempt to be "politically correct," an admonition emphasized by McNeill, Hom, and Perez (1995).

A review of the sparse literature would seem to indicate that, although racial diversity plays a role in supervision, other supervisor attributes are equally, if not more, important. The willingness of the supervisor to open the cultural door and walk through it with the supervisee is perhaps the single most powerful intervention for multicultural supervision. Whether one is a therapist or a supervisor, multicultural competence is not easily attained in a society that is phobic about race (Bernard, 1994; Porter, 1994). The will to attain such competence and the trust that can be engendered by such a commitment may be the most powerful operative variable within the supervisory relationship to move both supervisor and supervisee toward increased cultural competence.

Gender Issues within Multicultural Supervision

The status of women in our society has been a tenacious problem that has affected them economically and psychologically. Men have appeared to enjoy the benefits of gender bias, but more recent and discriminating research has shown that gender bias is problematic for both men and women (e.g., see Good & Mintz, 1990). Whereas racial and ethnic differences are more likely to be viewed as multicultural issues, gender may be resisted as such. Yet, as Gilbert and Rossman (1992) have reiterated, gender is a pervasive organizer in our culture, as can be supported by the proportion of men and women in various occupational areas. Furthermore, Gilbert and Rossman asserted that gender is a process, leading to "beliefs and stereotypes, and their concomitant behavioral expectations, [that] appear to influence individuals' behavior in response to certain situational cues" (p. 234). Because these differences seem more culturally determined than biologically determined, gender is legitimately included as a multicultural concern.

Turner (1993) stated that power shifts that are taking place in society will affect men and women in supervision, causing confusion and frustration. Rigazio-Digilio, Anderson, and Kunkler (1995), on the other hand, contended that gender-sensitive supervision was at a developmental impasse, relying on a limited set of theoretical orientations. Both of these viewpoints can probably be supported in most settings where male and female supervisees are being supervised by male or female supervisors. In this section we will attempt to navigate the supervision literature for its relevance to gender issues.

Like racial and ethnic issues, it is important that both supervisees and supervisors enter the supervision relationship having spent some time and energy addressing their own gender identities and assumptions and having been sensitized to the many ways that gender affects them in relationships, including relationships with clients (Stevens-Smith, 1995). Training should include a serious consideration of androgyny and the data that support the correlation of androgenous attitudes with successful interpersonal interactions (e.g., Fong, Borders, & Neimeyer, 1986).

Not only must trainees become sensitized to their own position along the traditional–androgenous continuum of gender attitudes and behaviors, but they must also become aware of how these interact with client issues. Moore and Nelson (1981) proposed a model for increasing awareness of sex role bias that is simple and would be easy to implement in most settings. They presented trainees with a minilecture about sex role issues. They then played videotaped vignettes (audiotapes could be used) of clients of different ages with counselors, all showing some gender bias on the part of the counselor. The trainees then were asked to identify the sex role bias in each vignette, address possible contingencies, and suggest alternative counselor behaviors. The matter of contingencies is crucial to such a process because it underlines the fact that sex role biases come from somewhere in the social makeup of the trainee. It is not just trainee responses that need to be changed; rather, it is the

attitudes underlying the behavior that are of utmost concern.

Finally, Ault-Riche (1988) and Nelson (1991) advised supervisors to remain vigilant regarding their own gender biases prior to engaging in supervision. Especially if, for example, a supervisor works mostly with female supervisees, issues of power, sensitivity to feedback, communication style, resolving conflict, and boundary issues are apt to emerge *for both supervisee and supervisor* when the supervisor switches to a male supervisee. This will be different, of course, depending on whether the supervisor is male or female. If any of these issues occurs in supervision without the supervisor's having addressed these possibilities prior to the onset of supervision, the process is bound to be ragged. Each relationship will be unique and will include unique challenges; however, the supervisor must be prepared to address cultural issues as they emerge, including those that involve gender. Without prior attention to this topic, this will probably not occur.

Some types of dilemmas involving gender are fairly predictable:

— A female supervisee does not think her male supervisor takes her seriously.
— A male supervisee states that he expected his female supervisor to be more supportive.
— A male supervisor finds his most talented supervisee to be the only female he is supervising. The male supervisees assume that the supervisor is sexually attracted to her.
— A female supervisor gives her male supervisee feedback that he is treating his female client in a sexist manner. The supervisee feels ganged up on and requests a male supervisor.

These are only a few of the complications around the issue of gender in the supervision process. The themes that seem to emerge with consistency, both in practice and in the supervision literature, have to do with the different voices of female versus male supervisors and supervisees, the different ways power is awarded and used depending on the supervisor's or supervisee's gender, and the implications of matching gender in supervision or not. To the extent possible, these themes will be addressed separately. At the same time, it is relevant to reiterate that all gender themes emerge as an interaction of legitimate cultural differences between males and females and the sexism still pervasive in society. Like racism and homophobia, sexism leads to a perversion of the supervision process and must be distinguished from the more benign challenge of appreciating gender differences (Bernard, 1994).

Different Voices.   Carol Gilligan (1982) is usually credited with the "voice" metaphor, suggesting that women and men are socialized to approach interpersonal relationships differently; women take on the voice of care, which focuses on "loving and being loved, listening and being listened to, responding and being responded to" (Brown & Gilligan, 1990, p. 8), and men take on the voice of justice, which focuses on "a vision of equality, reciprocity, and fairness between persons" (Brown & Gilligan, 1990, p. 8). Twohey and Volker (1993) argued that, because the supervisory role has more often been held by men, the voice of justice has been the predominant voice in supervision, emphasizing objective and scientific perspectives.

Twohey and Volker asserted that the Western tradition of splitting intellectual and emotional events has been perpetuated by diminishing the care voice in supervision, a less than adequate model for supervision. By contrast, when the voice of care is included, some of the most pertinent issues in the supervision relationship can be addressed openly and in the context of support. The balance encouraged by Twohey and Volker is one where gender differences are appreciated through a supervisory style that is androgenous, regardless of the gender of the supervisor. They implied, however, that trainees should experience supervision from both men and women in order to assure well-rounded supervision.

Bernstein (1993) and Ellis and Robbins (1993) stressed the error in assuming that male supervisors (and supervisees) consistently speak from the voice of justice and that female supervisors (and supervisees) represent primarily the voice of care. They noted that this assumption is not supported empirically, a position ardently emphasized by Osterberg (1996). Furthermore, Ellis and Robbins addressed both the gains and disadvantages of matching the supervisee's voice. In other words, although Twohey and Volker seemed to indicate that the care voice is unrepresented in supervision and should be attended to more consistently, Ellis and Robbins took a more strategic approach and suggested that the supervisor choose the voice that will either challenge or support the supervisee, depending on the supervision goal at the time. All the authors in this discourse, however, emphasize that supervisors must appreciate that both voices represent conceptual frameworks for understanding the supervisory relationship and, therefore, must both be within the supervisor's repertoire.

Although Bernstein (1993) and Ellis and Robbins (1993) put forth a convincing argument for androgenous supervision, current gender stereotypes may confound the outcome. Ault-Riche (1998), for example, noted that capable female supervisors are often misinterpreted as to whether they deliver the voice of care or justice. "Those supervisors who present as primarily nurturant are devalued for not being clear thinkers; those who present as primarily task-focused are experienced as dangerous" (p. 188). Ault-Riche's discussion implies that it would be naive for supervisors of either gender to think that their supervisees are not influenced by gender stereotypes. These stereotypes are, after all, the product of lifelong socialization. Whereas they can be modified by training and supervision, those modifications may occur only by increments. This, it seems to us, needs further empirical investigation.

The metaphors of care and justice have led to a great deal of speculation, only some of which has been supported with research. Paisley (1994) noted that, as a critical variable, gender needs to be considered at four levels: the client's problem, the gender perspective of the counselor or therapist, the interventions used, and the supervisory relationships in terms of gender. While we focus on the supervisory relationship and, to some extent, the gender perspective of the supervisee, we invite the reader to consider all four of Paisley's levels as having the power to alter the dynamics within supervision.

Differences between Male and Female Supervisors. The supervision literature regarding differences between male and female supervisors, as well as distinguishable reactions to supervisors because of their gender, draws both from conjecture and scientific investigation. Watson (1993), for example, warned that female supervisors might be more prone to find themselves in therapylike dual relationships with their supervisees as an extension of their inclination or desire to be nurturant. Similarly, Stoltenberg and Delworth (1987) advised supervisors to watch out for their female trainees who might overidentify with client affect and "wallow in the confusion," while male trainees might avoid affect and "escape the necessary ambivalence" by focusing on cognition primarily (p. 176). One could extend this admonition to supervisors. Female supervisors, for example, relying on their intuitive strength of connecting with others (Gilligan, 1982), might overidentify with their supervisees and appear confused at times. Male supervisors might arrive at their perceptions more quickly, but may be employing less data to do so. Female supervisors might also take feedback from supervisees more to heart (Reid, McDaniel, Donaldson, & Tollers, 1987) than would their male counterparts.

Granello (1996) suggested that, because supervision is largely a conversational process, findings regarding the different conversational styles of men and women are relevant. As examples, Granello surveyed authors and researchers who have noted that males are not socialized to be listeners (Hotelling & Forrest, 1985); that males have been found to respond differently in conversations when they are in positions of power, while women do not (Sagrestano, 1992); and that males have been found to execute 75 percent of all conversational interruptions (Kollock, Blumstein, & Schwartz, 1985).

Empirical support for gender differences related specifically to supervision is modest, the most examined gender-related issue being the execution of power within supervision. Aside from the power issue, there is no central focus to the empirical literature.

Petty and Odewahn (1983) reported a study conducted with 144 social workers and their supervisors. Male social workers responded negatively to female supervisors initiating structure and positively to male supervisors doing the same, thus reinforcing social stereotypes. Female social workers responded more positively to female supervisors initiating structure than to males doing so. All supervisors in the study (male and female) were found to be equally "considerate"; therefore, the results do not seem to indicate real interpersonal differences between genders.

More recently, Sells, Goodyear, Lichtenberg, and Polkinghorne (1997) studied gender-related differences for both supervisors and supervisees. These authors found that female supervisors had a greater relational focus than did male supervisors, spending more time in supervision focused on the trainee. Male supervisors, on the other hand, spent a significantly greater amount of time focused on the trainee's client. When male supervisors worked with male trainees, these trainees rated their technical skills higher; when female supervisors worked with female trainees, the latter rated their personal awareness higher. Perhaps the most important finding of the Sells et al. study (from the perspective of the supervisee) was that gender was not related to an evaluation of the impact of supervision by either supervisor or supervisee, nor was it related to the supervisor's evaluation of the supervisee. Warburton, Newberry, and Alexander (1989) also reported that male and females supervisees were found to be equally effective with clients.

On the other hand, in studies that considered the perceived competence of supervisors, female and male supervisors were viewed as equally competent (Allen, Szollos, & Williams, 1986; Schiavone & Jessell, 1988). Yet gender does play a part during evaluation. Warburton et al. reported that female supervisees tended to underestimate their accomplishments, while male supervisees overestimated them. Taken together, therefore, these studies may indicate that evaluation is minimally affected by gender. Some attention, however, may need to be given to the supervisee's gender as it relates to how evaluation is received.

The Use of Power within Supervision. Social or interpersonal power is a critical factor in supervision; power, or the capacity to influence the behavior of another person, is also endemic to gender relations. This combination makes it a consequential variable to be acknowledged within the supervision relationship (Turner, 1993; Watson, 1993).

Robyak, Goodyear, and Prange (1987) considered the topic of power and whether male and female supervisors were different in their use of power as it had been conceptualized by French and Raven (1959). They categorized power as either *expert* (the display of such resources as specialized knowledge and skills, confidence, and rationality), *referent* (derived from interpersonal attraction and based on trainees perceiving that they hold in common with supervisors relevant values, attitudes, opinions, and experiences), or *legitimate* (a consequence of perceived trustworthiness because the supervisor is a socially sanctioned provider of services who is not motivated by personal gain). Contrary to what one might expect, male supervisors reported greater preference for referent power than did female supervisors. Robyak et al. also found that referent power supervisors with relatively little experience preferred referent power. They noted that there is an inherent danger in using referent power in that initial similarities might dissipate as supervisees and supervisors get to know each other better. These differences might seem more extreme if the relationship is based on perceived similarities. Also, the evaluation process can become more complicated when supervisees have been given the impression that they share important characteristics with their supervisors.

Robyak et al. (1987) hypothesized that male supervisors might lean on referent power in an attempt to compensate for the male tendency to separate rather than to "attach" (Gilligan, 1982). One can hypothesize, similarly, that female supervisors might try to compensate by using a power base that does not overly depend on relationship.

In a similar study that focused on supervisee behavior (Goodyear, 1990), both supervisees and their supervisors perceived female supervisees as more likely to employ a personal–dependent influence style in a conflict situation with their supervisors. This was the only significant finding of the study that examined eight different influence strategies for supervisees of both genders interacting with supervisors of both genders. It is interesting to note that both male and female supervisors perceived the female supervisees similarly. Furthermore, when we compare this study to that done by Robyak et al. (1987), it seems that female supervisees behave in a more stereotypic manner than female supervisors.

Finally, Nelson and Holloway (1990) provided an intriguing look at messages and interaction patterns within supervision for the manipulation of power by gender. Using all gender and role combinations possible, Nelson and Holloway found that both male and female supervisors were less likely to encourage the assumption of power in female trainees than in male trainees; furthermore, female trainees deferred to the power of the supervisor significantly more often than did male trainees. As explained by the authors,

> *It appears that individuals in the expert role, regardless of gender, may assume more power in interaction with their female subordinates than with their male subordinates, either by withholding support for the female subordinates' attempts at exerting power or by simply exerting stronger influence with female subordinates. In the supervisory relationship the female trainee may respond to this stance on the part of her supervisor by declining opportunities to assert herself as an expert.* (p. 479)

Similarly, Sells et al. (1997) reported that when the supervisor was male the influence over the structure of supervision was attributed to the supervisor; and when the supervisor was female, the structure of the supervision session was more often attributed to the trainee.

Clearly, supervision is a relationship that includes a power dynamic that is endemic. Given the complexity of gender relationships, it is not surprising that power is manipulated differently in supervision for men and women. Holloway and Wolleat (1994) appealed to supervisors to make the supervisory relationship a context for the female supervisee to discover her own professional power. Similarly, Hipp and Munson (1995) advocated for feminist models of supervision to empower all supervisees. To date, these prescriptions seem to be justified.

Same-gender and Cross-gender Pairs in Supervision. Arguably, one way to reduce the negative effects of gender within supervision is to control for it, that is, to attempt to match supervisors and supervisees by gender. There is some evidence that, when given a choice, supervisees prefer to work with a supervisor of the same gender (McCarthy, Kulakowski, & Kenfield, 1994). Behling, Curtis, and Foster (1988) found that matched gender (specifically, female–female pairings) resulted in the greatest satisfaction with supervision, and the most negative combination for supervision in the field occurred when a female supervisee was supervised by a male supervisor; Worthington and Stern (1985) found, on the other hand, that the closest relationships occurred in male–male pairings. Thyer, Sower-Hoag, and Love (1988) similarly found that same-gender pairs produced the most favorable ratings of supervision, but the authors made the point that gender accounted for only 5 percent of the variance. Therefore, the argument for matching supervisee and supervisor by gender may be tenuous.

Other authors have concluded that it is worthwhile to consider the differential gains of same-gender and cross-gender supervision pairs (e.g., Ellis & Robbins, 1993; Hartman & Brieger, 1992; Turner & Fine, 1997). Although it is important that women, in particular, have an opportunity to work with female role models (Bruce, 1995), androge-

nous supervisors of both genders will be more advantageous to the supervisee than working exclusively with a person of one's own gender. In support of this assumption, Putney, Worthington, and McCullough (1992) found that cross-gender pairs resulted in increased autonomy for the supervisee. Developmentally, such an outcome might be critical for positive professional growth. In short, because of its social impact, it is understandable that gender is both complex and essential as a variable to be manipulated within supervision, as well as a topic calling for careful and open scrutiny.

Lesbian, Gay, and Bisexual Issues within Multicultural Supervision

As the mental health professions grapple with greater inclusion of cultural variables within supervision, they still lag behind in their attention to lesbian, gay, and bisexual (LGB) issues. The supervision literature available is largely theoretical or anecdotal (e.g., Buhrke, 1989; Buhrke & Douce, 1991; Gautney, 1994; Schrag, 1994; Woolley, 1991), though there is some evidence that LGB trainees have experienced discrimination during supervision (Pilkington & Cantor, 1996). Though limited in number, these resources can begin to assist the supervisor in approaching the supervisory relationship in a culturally sensitive manner.

Supervisees should enter supervision with at least initial skills in recognizing LGB identity development stages (including an ability to differentiate these from psychopathology), a readiness to assist clients in addressing intimacy issues within a gay or lesbian relationship, and a readiness to confront their own heterosexual assumptions (Buhrke & Douce, 1991). These are necessary training elements when supervisee and supervisor are heterosexual and the client is gay, lesbian, or bisexual. When either supervisor or supervisee is gay, lesbian, or bisexual, relationship complexity increases.

Using broad stokes, Buhrke (1989) outlined four possibilities concerning lesbian-related issues within supervision. She divided them into nonconflictual and conflictual situations within the client–supervisee–supervisor triad. Of the nonconflictual situations, the most productive was when neither supervisor nor supervisee was homophobic. Under these circumstances, the following examples are possible: the lesbian supervisor can serve as a positive role model for her supervisees, the lesbian supervisor can openly discuss with the supervisee the appropriateness of coming out to a particular client, and mutual attraction between supervisor and supervisee (and the need to avoid a dual relationship) can be discussed openly and professionally.

Ironically, the second nonconflictual situation was described by Buhrke as "the worst of possible supervisory scenarios" (p. 200). In this case both supervisor and supervisee are homophobic. Buhrke described mutual homophobia as blocking many productive interactions (including either supervisor or supervisee coming out). Because supervisor and supervisee will reinforce each other's biases, a lesbian client either will be underserved (i.e., references to lesbian life-style will be ignored) or will be badly served (e.g., her lesbianism will be viewed as pathological).

Buhrke (1989) similarly saw one conflict situation as potentially positive and one as far more problematic. When the supervisor is not homophobic but the supervisee is, there is the potential for the supervisee to deal with her attitudes under the tutelage of the supervisor. Buhrke noted, however, that the supervisor must make a careful judgment call regarding the degree of homophobia (or the milder form of homophobia, heterosexual bias) and the supervisee's ability to work productively with a lesbian client. When the supervisee is free from homophobia but the supervisor is not, the power differential may make it difficult for the former to "challenge the supervisor's irrational beliefs about homosexuality" (p. 202). Furthermore, the lesbian supervisee might feel the necessity to conceal her life-style preference, a tragic outcome given the context in which it occurs.

With Buhrke's (1989) contribution in mind, it is obvious that the homophobic supervisor is an especially powerful and potentially very destructive influence in the therapy system. Therefore,

any supervisor who is aware of negative attitudes toward LGB life-styles should seek the consultation of a colleague to deal with such attitudes. Short of that, the supervisor should help supervisees find additional supervision when the issue of a gay life-style emerges.

When the supervisor has a positive view of alternative life-styles, the supervisor can be an important role model for supervisees, gay and nongay alike (Schrag, 1994). Furthermore, when the supervisor takes such a posture, it is more likely that LGB supervisees will come out to the supervisor. As Schrag (1994) stated, "my openness models a method of moving from shame to self-empowerment, from abuse to compassion, and from secrecy to taking care of myself. These are pivotal for all therapists to acquire" (p. 7). Additionally, one lesbian supervisee who was "out" in supervision but who never received supervision specific to her sexual orientation, now regrets the conspiracy of silence between her and her supervisor:

> The advice I am about to give is strictly from the perspective of a lesbian supervisee to supervisors: Bring it up. Talk about it. Whether your supervisee or her clients are heterosexual or homosexual, sexual orientation is a relevant issue that may be avoided unless you attend to it. Take the responsibility, because you probably have less to risk than your supervisees. And if your supervisee is gay or lesbian, believe me, they are already thinking about it. (Gautney, 1994, p. 7)

In an excellent discussion of supervision issues particular to LGB supervisees, Buhrke and Douce (1991) considered transference and countertransference issues that might emerge when the supervisee counsels the same-gender coming-out client. Noting the strong emotions present throughout the coming-out process, it is quite likely that the client will experience attraction for the counselor, especially if that person is lesbian, gay, or bisexual. From the perspective of both gay and nongay supervisees, dealing with same-gender attraction is a topic that supervisors must be willing to address without negative bias. If supervisors shut down the supervisee by communicating distaste for the topic, the supervisee is far more vulnerable to handling the attraction inappropriately. Finally, Buhrke and Douce noted that LGB supervisees working with LGB clients or supervisors are perhaps more vulnerable to dual relationships than nongay supervisees and supervisors because of the advocacy required in working with disenfranchised populations, as well as the reality of overlapping social circles common to the LGB community. Buhrke and Douce advised that a strict definition of dual relationships may not be appropriate in this situation; at the same time, the supervisee will need assistance in determining appropriate boundaries that allow the supervisee to practice ethically and productively.

Working with LGBs, similar to working with other cultural groups, has implications for the institution in which the supervisor practices. Any personal effort will be frustrated if it is not part of the culture of the larger organizational context. Buhrke and Douce (1991) suggested institutional guidelines that could be summarized into four overall suggestions for improving the environment for LGBs: (1) respect the individual developmental path of each person, including the right to come out on one's own terms, if at all; (2) respect each person for all his or her gifts and do not stereotype the LGB person's contributions to his or her lifestyle choice; (3) do not look to the LGB member of the community to make the environment safe for LGBs; and (4) be sensitive to oppression and appreciate the strength evident in the person who has grown, in spite of oppression, to be a positive influence in her or his surroundings.

Because of the societal context within which our relationships occur, we expect those *across* gender or race to have certain aspects that are distinct from relationships *within* gender or race. Yet, the implications of developmental differences among supervisees and not cultural differences have received more empirical attention in the professional literature in recent years than any other supervision issue. We now turn to the issue of development.

DEVELOPMENTAL DIFFERENCES

The professional development of the supervisee is of paramount importance to the clinical supervisor.

In fact, it could be argued that the development of the supervisee is the *raison d'etre* of supervision. Development, however, has proved to be a multifaceted concept when applied to the acquisition of competence as a counselor or therapist. The empirical attention given to developmental concepts in recent years has provided supervisors with both information and tools to assess the developmental level of supervisees in order to provide appropriate supervision. Furthermore, empirical attention to developmental concerns may be considered as either the effect of the developmental status of the supervisee or the effect of supervision on the supervisee's development.

Experience Level

The supervisee's level of experience, a developmental status issue, has been one of the more broadly researched areas of development. Although there are a few exceptions (e.g., Friedlander & Snyder, 1983), the great majority of empirical studies has suggested that supervisees have different characteristics and different abilities based on the amount of supervised experience they have accrued (e.g., Borders, 1990; Cummings et al., 1990; Mallinckrodt & Nelson, 1991; McNeill, Stoltenberg, & Pierce, 1985; McNeill, Stoltenberg, & Romans, 1992; Olk & Friedlander, 1992; Swanson & O'Saben, 1993; Tracey et al., 1988; Tracey, Ellickson, & Sherry, 1989; Wiley & Ray, 1986; Winter & Holloway, 1991). Other reviewers of the empirical literature (Holloway, 1992, 1995; Stoltenberg, McNeill, & Crethar, 1994) also identified experience level as an important point of departure for understanding the developmental needs of the supervisee.

Ellis and Ladany (1997) echoed Holloway's (1992) earlier caution, however, that there are multiple problems in interpreting results of most developmental studies, one of these being the lack of longitudinal studies. In other words, without tracking the same supervisees over time, it is very difficult to discern whether the significant results of various studies depict true *development* or cohort effects. But even without this and other issues fully resolved, there is still ample empirical evidence to support an examination of the supervisee's experience level as one indicator of developmental level.

Most early experience–effect research involved students in training programs. Neophyte supervisees in their first practicum were compared to those at the end of their master's or doctoral program. More recently, studies have occasionally included postdoctoral supervisees. Additionally, models are beginning to emerge for advanced supervisees only (e.g., Braver, Graffin, & Holahan, 1990; Sawatzy, Jevne, & Clark, 1994) and for development of mental health professionals across the life-span (e.g., Ronnestad, 1992). These may spawn yet more informative longitudinal or cross-sectional research. Because of the variability of operational definitions across studies, we will be careful to stipulate the levels of experience used by the particular researchers we are discussing.

Researchers have examined the relationship between amount of training and supervisee behavior. Looking at the beginning practicum student, Borders (1990) found significant change in supervisee self-reports for self-awareness, dependency–autonomy, and theory–skills acquisition over one semester. McNeill, Stoltenberg, and Pierce (1985) obtained similar results when they compared beginning trainees to intermediate trainees. More recently, McNeill, Stoltenberg, and Romans (1992) offered validation for the Stoltenberg and Delworth (1987) Integrated Developmental Model (IDM) and revised the Supervisee Levels Questionnaire to reflect the three overriding structures espoused by IDM as central to counselor development (self–other awareness, motivation, and dependency–autonomy).

Studies comparing novice and experienced counselors have reported inconsistent results. Cummings et al. (1990) and Martin et al. (1989) found that experienced counselors were more efficient in their conceptualization, employing well-established cognitive schemata to conceptualize clients, while novice counselors seemed to require much more specific information about the clients to conceptualize the problem; they were more random in their information seeking, and their ultimate conceptualizations were less sophisticated. Hillerbrand & Claiborn (1990) arrived at somewhat different conclusions. They found no differences in cognitive processes used by experienced and novice counselors when asked to diagnose client cases of different complexity. What they did find was that confidence and clarity in presenting cases were greater for the more experienced counselors. Hillerbrand and Claiborn's findings might be explained by the fact that they defined novice as doctoral students with one to three semesters of practicum; experts were defined as professionals with at least 5 years postdoctoral experience.

Some researchers have looked at a broader continuum of experience. Tracey, Hays, Malone, and Herman (1988) studied counselor responses across three experience levels: beginning counselors (0 to 1 year of practicum), advanced counselors (graduate students with more than 1 year of practicum), and doctoral counselors (at least 2 years postdoctoral experience). Olk and Friedlander (1992) studied role conflict (encountering opposing expectations and role ambiguity (being unsure of supervisory expectations) for doctoral supervisees at the practicum, internship, and postdoctoral fellowship levels. These studies have noted differences between levels of experience on the following dimensions:

1. When supervisee interventions (i.e., dominance, approach–avoidance, focus on affect, immediacy, breadth versus specificity, meeting client demands, verbosity and confrontation) were compared across groups, doctoral-level counselors were less dominant (yet confronted more), were less verbose, and yielded less to client demands than nondoctoral-level counselors (Tracey et al., 1988).

2. Olk and Friedlander (1992) found that, across training levels, role ambiguity was more prevalent than role conflict. Role ambiguity diminishes as the supervisee gains experience. Conversely, although role conflict is observed less often, it is more likely to be an issue for the more experienced supervisee, who, perhaps, is chafing at the bit for more autonomy and a more integrated existence. Whereas role difficulties were few overall, Olk and Friedlander noted that, when present, they may have a negative impact on the supervisory relationship.

Interaction between Experience and Other Variables

One might consider experience to be the single critical variable in the development of supervisees. However, experience has often been found to be moderated by other variables. Occasionally, those other variables have been found to be more important than experience itself.

1. A study reported by Friedlander and Snyder (1983) involved three levels of trainees (one at the master's level and two at the doctoral level) and found that the more confident trainees at all levels who expected supervision to be highly worthwhile translated their posture into expecting more from their supervisors in every respect. Although it is uncommon for trainee experience to be found a nonsignificant variable, this study is important for the insight it provides into the importance of self-efficacy and positive expectations.

2. Winter and Holloway (1991) found that less experienced trainees were more likely to focus on client conceptualization, whereas more advanced trainees were more likely to focus on personal growth. Trainees with higher conceptual levels were more likely to request a focus on the development of counseling skills and to request feedback, thus indicating less concern about evaluation. Both level of experience and conceptual level, therefore, produced significant results in this study.

3. Borders, Fong, and Neimeyer (1986) found neither experience nor ego development to relate to perceptions of clients for trainees at three different levels within a master's program. Despite the nonsignificant findings, the authors noted that students at the higher ego levels "seemed to have a greater awareness of the interactive nature of the counselor–client relationship, perhaps thinking of their clients more often in terms of this process than did student at low ego levels" (p. 46).

4. Swanson and O'Saben (1993) reported that trainees' Myers–Briggs Type Indicator (MBTI) profile, amount of practicum experience (ranging from prepracticum to 15 completed semesters of practicum), and type of program (counseling psychology, clinical psychology, or counselor educa-

tion) all produced significant differences in terms of supervisee needs and expectations for supervision. Program membership was the least dramatic predictor of differences, and level of experience produced the greatest differences. Level of experience differences produced results similar to other experience studies, indicating that supervisees with less experience expected more supervisor involvement, direction, and support.

The picture that begins to emerge, then, is that, when all other things are equal, experience level is highly related to differences among supervisees. However, it is moderated by and interacts with a number of other variables. An interesting study by Tracey, Ellickson, and Sherry (1989) considered the interaction of level of experience (beginning or advanced counseling psychology doctoral students), reactance potential (an individual's need to resist imposed structure), supervision structure (low structure or high structure), and content of supervision (crisis or noncrisis), using Brehm's (1966) concept of reactance potential. The authors found that advanced trainees with high reactance preferred supervision with less structure than did advanced trainees with low reactance. In noncrisis situations (i.e., when all things were equal), beginning trainees preferred structured supervision, while more experienced trainees preferred less structure. However, in crisis situations, all trainees preferred structured supervision regardless of their level of experience or reactance.

This last finding is reinforced by Zarski, Sand-Pringle, Pannell, and Lindon (1995), who noted that supervision must be modified based on the severity of individual cases. For supervisees working with difficult or volatile situations (e.g., family violence), more structure may be needed for advanced trainees until they have attained a necessary level of comfort and competence. Similarly, when Wetchler and Vaughn (1991) surveyed marriage and family therapists at multiple levels, supervisor directiveness was the most frequently identified supervisor skill that therapists thought enhanced their development. This result may indicate that more advanced supervisees take more difficult cases to supervision, thus requiring more direction from the supervisor around these identified cases.

A final comment regarding experience is in order before we proceed. Although we have evidence that mental health professionals *change* with experience, the data do not support that all therapists *improve* with experience. Training is more predictive of expertise than is experience alone (Hill, Charles, & Reed, 1981), but neither training nor experience has received strong empirical support as relevant to therapeutic outcomes. Yet the changes observed within supervisees under supervision are promising. An inference one can draw is that experience obtained under close scrutiny and with specific feedback is necessary for learning to occur. The more direct methods of supervision that have been espoused in recent years, therefore, may account for some of the differences that have been observed among supervisees at different experience levels. Furthermore, differences that emerge as a result of close supervision may be more significant in terms of expertise.

Additional Developmental Variables

To this point, all the research we have considered has focused on level of experience as either the sole or primary independent variable. Some authors have also focused on discernible cognitive and ego developmental differences within groups of supervisees at the same level of training. The role ego development plays in in-session cognitions of supervisees and in the mastery of specific counseling skills was examined by Borders (1989) and (Borders & Fong, 1989). They reported (1) that ego development was more predictive of performance for first-semester EdS students than for more advanced students (late EdS or doctoral students) (Borders and Fong, 1989); and (2) Borders found only limited relationship between ego development and in-session cognitions. She did conclude that higher ego development functioning led to more nonjudgmental and objective reactions, while lower ego levels led to more frustration, impatience, or anger toward clients (Borders, 1989).

Other studies have examined the relationship between the conceptual level of functioning (CL) and supervisee behavior.

1. A meta-analysis of 24 studies (Holloway and Wampold, 1986) reported that low CLs who were provided with high structure and high CLs who were provided with low structure performed better than those supervisees who were mismatched in terms of environment. The matched environment, however, was found to be far more important for low CLs than for high CLs. Holloway and Wampold suggested that the issue is to provide the correct supervision environment so that supervisees of all CLs can use their energy to learn the necessary skills, rather than combating the frustration of either too much ambiguity or an atmosphere that feels constraining (Holloway and Wampold, 1986).

2. Birk and Mahalik (1996) examined the interaction between CL, anxiety, and supervision environment and reported that higher-CL supervisees were more self-confident about supervision and were able to focus better on the counseling process, while more anxious supervisees rated themselves as exhibiting lower developmental levels and needing more structure. Furthermore, the evaluative role of supervision did not seem to affect anxiety level; thus, the need for structure for anxious supervisees did not seem to be correlated with evaluation.

Drawing on Ivey's (1986, 1991) developmental therapy model, Rigazio-Digilio and Anderson (1994) have developed a Systemic Cognitive Developmental Supervision (SCDS) model for supervision. In it, they propose that (1) a relationship exists between the supervisee's primary orientation (e.g., sensorimotor, concrete) and identifiable supervisee strengths and challenges; (2) thus, cognitive levels are not hierarchical; and (3) *both* matched and unmatched supervisory environments are viable in that matching supervisory environment will support a supervisee's natural abilities, while mismating environment will challenge the supervisee toward new growth. Although the SCDS needs empirical verification, it offers supervisors a more comprehensive view of the possibilities in working with each supervisee.

Matching Supervision Environment with Developmental Level

Prior to considering the supervision environment that is suitable for a variety of developmental levels, we should note that most empirical investigations that have examined developmental concepts have employed a linear, unidirectional approach. Authors who have concerned themselves with the development of supervisees, however, have often suggested more cyclical models (e.g., Sawatzky, Jevne, & Clark, 1994; Stoltenberg & Delworth, 1987). It is likely that supervisees master particular aspects of the therapeutic process, thus reflecting more advanced developmental characteristics around these, while still faltering with other aspects of skill development. One group of supervisees, therefore, may represent several levels of development when measured on one variable; at the same time, if multiple variables are considered, each supervisee may offer a developmental profile in which the supervisee is more advanced on some variables than on others. If differing developmental levels require different supervision interventions, each supervisee may need a variety of interventions offered in a discriminant fashion. In this section we will examine the supervisory response to different developmental levels.

Much research interest has been shown in the relative importance of matching supervisee developmental level with the appropriate supervisory conditions, typically referred to as the "supervision environment." Researchers (Bear & Kivlighan, 1994; Borders & Usher, 1992; Dodenhoff, 1981; Fisher, 1989; Glidden & Tracey, 1992; Guest & Beutler, 1988; Heppner & Handley, 1982; Heppner & Roehlke, 1984; Holloway & Wampold, 1983; Krause & Allen, 1988; Miars et al., 1983; Rabinowitz, Heppner, & Roehlke, 1986; Reisling & Daniels, 1983; Stoltenberg, Pierce, & McNeill, 1987; Usher & Borders, 1993; Wetchler, 1989;

Wiley & Ray, 1986; Winter & Holloway, 1991; and Worthington & Stern, 1985) have investigated the following:

1. Whether supervisors intuitively provide the correct environment for supervisees
2. Whether the matching of environment to developmental level alters the perceptions of supervisees and/or supervisors about supervision
3. Whether the matching of environment to development level of supervisee significantly enhances supervisee learning

All three questions have received some support, although there certainly have been some mixed results when the literature is examined closely.

In general, studies have attempted to verify the Stoltenberg (1981) and Stoltenberg and Delworth (1987) models that were examined in Chapter 2. Whether the variable has been experience or some developmental construct (such as cognitive level), the assumption was that the supervisee should be offered significant structure, direction, and support early on to assure movement in a positive direction. As supervisees gain some experience, expertise, and confidence, they are ready to have some of the structure diminished, to be challenged with alternative conceptualizations of the cases they have been assigned, to be given technical guidance as needed, and to begin to look at personal issues that affect their work. Because each supervisee is different, supervision gets more complicated as supervisees progress and develop in their idiosyncratic ways. At the same time, variables that are independent of experience will be more apparent early in training when they are as yet unconfounded by the training experience itself. For these early stages under supervision, therefore, the issue may be largely one of assessment to determine the correct environment; for later stages, supervisors need to allow advanced supervisees enough freedom to bump into their own issues, yet ample guidance when the supervisee gets stuck on either a personal issue or a client issue. Furthermore, supervisors may need to be more resourceful when supervising the advanced trainee.

Although supervisors seem to offer different environments when supervisees' developmental differences are pronounced, empirical findings do not as yet support some of the finer distinctions made by developmental theorists. It is difficult to determine if the problem is in the design of particular studies or with the developmental models themselves (Ellis & Ladany, 1997). It is important to recall, however, that development is multifaceted, and the ability to address different levels of competence at any one point in the supervision process is difficult indeed.

Additionally, we do not know what stage of development might take precedence at any measuring point. For example, it may be that a supervisee is very advanced on several criteria but is in crisis regarding one particular aspect of personal functioning as a counselor or therapist. The supervisor may need to respond by being directive around this one issue, thereby altering the supervisory climate until the crisis is over. It is probably best if the supervisor consider both development and environment to be dynamic and fluid, requiring astute observation and flexibility, especially for all but the initial phases of training.

Supervisor Experience

Supervisor training and development is the focus of Chapter 11. Here we will only mention the importance of supervisor experience as it relates to forming a relationship with a supervisee.

Research suggests the following:

1. Supervisors of all levels (including no experience in supervision) might be able to assess supervisees using the first three levels of the Stoltenberg (1981) model. At the same time, supervisors of different levels of experience shared a difficulty in identifying supervisees at level 2 [perhaps supporting Stoltenberg's movement from a four- to a three-level model (Stoltenberg & Delworth, 1987; Chagnon and Russell, 1995)].

2. There is little behavioral distinction among supervisors with different levels of experience (Fisher, 1989).
3. With experience, supervisors are less likely to project negative personal attributes onto supervisees who are having difficulty in counseling sessions. Instead, they are more likely to view difficulties as behavioral or situational and therefore subject to change with proper supervision (Worthington, 1984).

From the limited data now available to us, it would seem that a common practice of matching the novice supervisor to the novice supervisee might be fraught with difficulty, especially if the supervisor is asked to work with the supervisee in a relatively autonomous fashion. Although Stoltenberg and Delworth (1987) supported this pairing as highly functional (see Chapter 11), other outcomes are possible. For example, novice supervisors might personalize their supervisee's weaknesses out of their own insecurity about what to do about them. If, as Rodenhauser (1994) described, supervisors new to the role spend most of their time attempting to attain a degree of comfort through an understanding of methods for structuring supervision, they may indeed parallel tendencies found in novice supervisees of delivering interventions in a manner that is both rigid and overstated. Though this would provide the supervisee the needed element of structure, it is unlikely that the structure will contain the necessary support and insight that are necessary for developmental progress. This, then, becomes a supervision of supervision issue and one that might be of concern to many training programs.

Thus far, we have been addressing experience levels (and implicitly, developmental levels) of supervisee and supervisor. Only recently (e.g., Stevens, Goodyear, & Robertson, in press) have the possible effects of supervisor training on supervisor development begun to be addressed. Findings to date support earlier research that supervisors did not become more competent or change their perceptions with experience (Ellis & Dell, 1986;

Marikis, Russell, & Dell, 1985; Zucker & Worthington, 1986). Stevens et al. found that training, on the other hand, affected supervision in positive and significant ways. Only as supervisor training becomes as standard as counselor training will there be reliable information on which to build supervisor developmental models.

IMPLICATIONS OF DEVELOPMENTAL DIFFERENCES FOR SUPERVISION

As supervisors approach a supervisory relationship, how do they weigh the different developmental contingencies we have addressed thus far? Some empirical findings are conflicting, yet there are definitely some themes that warrant serious attention. Because of the complexity of the issues, we offer the following as guidelines for the supervisor to consider.

Level of Experience

1. Experience obtained under supervision seems to be enough to stimulate development (Martin et al., 1989). Perhaps the scrutiny of supervision, despite the particular interventions used, causes the kind of self-scrutiny that allows the supervisee to improve. This assumption is supported by the fact that experience without supervision does not lead to the same kind of development (Hill, Charles, & Reed, 1981; Wiley & Ray, 1986). Because experience under supervision is a reliable indicator of development, the supervisor should begin the relationship with the expectation that different types of interventions will be required for supervisees at different experience levels.

2. With experience, the supervisee should exhibit an increase of (a) self-awareness of behavior and motivation within counseling sessions, (b) consistency in the execution of counseling interventions, and (c) autonomy (Borders, 1990; McNeill, Stoltenberg, & Romans, 1992). If these are not forthcoming, supervisors need to consider whether a particular supervisee should be advanced to the next level of training, if interventions that provide more direction should be reintroduced, or if other

important factors (e.g., conceptual level, personality, or cultural issues) need to be considered more carefully.

3. With experience, it is expected that supervisees will develop more sophisticated ways to conceptualize the counseling process and the issues their clients present and be less distracted by random specific information (Cummings et al., 1990). With an eye to the necessary development ahead of supervisees, then, supervisors would be well advised to spend time and energy with novice supervisees helping them to learn to organize client information into meaningful themes. To focus on personal issues with a novice supervisee (cf. Bernard, 1979) might be developmentally inappropriate (cf. Winter & Holloway, 1991) unless the personal issues are blocking the supervisee from grasping the conceptual information in counseling sessions.

4. Novice supervisees will be more rigid and less discriminating in their delivery of therapeutic interventions. An "exaggerated forcefulness" (Tracey et al., 1988) in the delivery of an intervention for a more advanced trainee may indicate that the supervisee is at the front end of a learning curve regarding that intervention. Modeling for supervisees who show such tendencies will be helpful regardless of the level of experience of the supervisee. A hallmark of more advanced supervisees is that they are more flexible and less dominant when delivering interventions such as confrontation. Therefore, a lack of flexibility or an introduction of dominance may indicate that a particular case is either personally threatening for the supervisee or is experienced by the supervisee as beyond his or her level of competence. The supervisor will need to determine if more direction is needed or if an invitation to address personal issues stimulated by the case is appropriate.

5. Seeing oneself as a counselor or therapist calls for a role assimilation that may represent a stretch for some supervisees. Role ambiguity is common for novice supervisees who are not familiar with the expectations of the training context (Olk & Friedlander, 1992). Supervisors should not skip this important area of confusion and should spend time exploring the implications of both the helper role and supervisee role. Role ambiguity is far less an issue for more advanced supervisees, but, for some, role conflict emerges as an issue, that is, the tension that occurs when supervisees are asked to behave differently in different contexts. A redefinition of supervisee might be called for that legitimizes the increased autonomy wanted by and often expected of advanced supervisees. Ronnestad and Skovholt (1993) also addressed the tension within supervision that could be expected in working with advanced trainees (e.g., due to style of supervision or theoretical differences). In life-span developmental terms, the tension at this stage might be the necessary ingredient for individuation from the supervisor and launching into professional practice.

6. Although research consistently suggests that the more advanced supervisee will want or require less structure in supervision, several variables can change this prediction, including a crisis situation (Tracey, Ellickson, & Sherry, 1989), a particularly difficult client population (Zarski et al., 1995), or a strong personality characteristic (Friedlander & Snyder, 1983). It is important to remember, therefore, that in most instances supervision of an advanced supervisee is more idiosyncratic than supervision of a novice supervisee.

7. The amount of experience accrued by supervisors does not seem to affect their ability to assess the development level of supervisees (Chagnon & Russell, 1995). Rather, the complication that is more likely to occur with novice supervisors supervising novice supervisees has to do with relationship issues; that is, both parties are distracted by their need to assimilate a new role and are less likely to be self-aware. Supervision of supervision should focus on this dynamic when novice supervisors are assigned to novice trainees.

Like the results found with supervisees, there is indication that supervisors do not develop with unsupervised experience. The fact that at least one study (Stevens, Goodyear, & Robertson, in press) has found training to be more critical than experience implies that there are indeed content areas

and skills that must be introduced to novice supervisors in order to stimulate a developmental process.

8. Early developmental psychologists made the mistake of assuming that development stopped with adulthood. Some of the training literature has made a similar error in assuming supervisee development ends when formal training ends. A lifespan approach indicates that supervision should benefit practitioners throughout their careers and that most studies to date have only tracked development through professional adolescence (cf. Kaslow, McCarthy, Rogers, & Summerville, 1992; Lipovsky, 1988). Furthermore, because of the truncated fashion with which supervisee development has been studied, the terms "advanced" and "expert" may be applied prematurely and far too uniformly to specific cohorts of supervisees.

Additional Developmental Issues

1. Stoltenberg (1981) and Blocher (1983) were among those who have suggested that—at least for novices—experience and conceptual level (CL) are highly correlated. Indeed, they suggested that it is possible to predict CL from experience. It is not surprising, then, that in terms of structure of supervision requirements CL seems to operate much like experience, low CLs requiring more structure than high CLs (Winter & Holloway, 1991). Additionally, the structure needs of low CLs seem more imperative than those of high CLs. As might be expected, high CLs appear more confident and ask for more feedback to improve counseling skills and thus are seemingly less concerned with evaluation. It is likely that the process of counseling is more exciting to high CLs because they are able to produce and weigh more options and choose the most appropriate intervention (Gordon, 1990; Holloway & Wampold, 1986).

Conceptual level of trainee, then, should affect supervision in several ways. If conceptual level remains relatively stable, clients should be carefully selected (i.e., relatively low CL to work with a relatively low CL supervisee) so that the trainee may, through supervision, model the kind of techniques that can help the client resolve his or her issues. Supervision interventions should assist the low-CL trainee in forming cognitive maps that can be used to assess client issues so the trainee can move on to solution strategies. Supervision interventions that challenge the trainee to conceptualize in highly abstract ways will be counterproductive for the low-CL supervisee.

2. Ego development has been found to discriminate among novice trainees more than for those with more experience (Borders & Fong, 1989). We can speculate that training eventually compensates for ego development, at least enough that differences are not significant. Because anger with clients and impatience were associated with low ego development for novice trainees (Borders, 1989), it is important that supervisors consider this possibility when they experience a trainee who seems unable to empathize with a client. A modified IPR technique, for example, may be helpful in allowing the trainee the psychological safety (i.e., outside the session) to develop empathic responses, especially if an understanding supervisor can assist the trainee in an empathic manner.

3. The developmental literature suggests that certain issues are simply premature for novice trainees, for example, theoretical identity (Borders, 1989). The assumption that practice must be grounded first in theoretical sophistication may seem intuitively correct, but pragmatically and experientially it is flawed. Initial counseling experiences may need to rely on almost universal helping behaviors while trainees begin the more lengthy road of identifying theoretical premises. The only other option is to foreclose the theoretical discussion by superimposing a theoretical model onto trainees (Bernard, 1992). Though tempting, this option may only complicate future developmental stages for the trainee.

4. Although the supervision literature has devoted an inordinate amount of attention to the developmental aspects of supervision, the criticism by Russell, Crimmings, and Lent (1984) seems still to hold: that developmental models are too simplistic to predict trainee behavior in any comprehensive and consistent way. Holloway (1987) put forth a similar view and suggested that supervision is only one event in the trainee's professional and personal life, and it is perhaps not the most important event. The supervisor, therefore, may want to reflect developmental principles, but should resist being driven by them.

CONCLUSION

This chapter surveyed a variety of topics relevant to the formation of a supervisory relationship. The developmental status of the supervisee may be determined by level of experience or by other variables, but, though a reliable predictor of supervisee needs and expectations in many circumstances, developmental level can be secondary to cognitive and interpersonal style. Likewise, belief systems and cultural variables are key to understanding the supervision relationship at its outset and throughout the supervision experience.

More than any other, the point of this chapter is that each supervisee presents to supervision a rich blend of experience, insight, and habit that will affect supervision with or without the supervisor's knowledge. In this respect, the topics covered in the chapter are only examples of the types of issues that might interest the supervisor in assessing where to begin with a supervisee. Broad themes of lifelong learning (developmental level), uniqueness (personal style, belief systems, and cultural identity), and oppression (disenfranchised groups) may adequately represent the important elements in this chapter as well as other critical issues for conducting successful supervision. Perhaps more than any other chapter, this discussion has underscored the part of supervision that is new with each supervisee, calling forth from the supervisor an openness to discovery in his or her work. In short, this chapter has attempted to explain what every supervisor knows: the experience with each supervisee is different.

CHAPTER 4

The Supervisory Relationship

Processes and Issues

Supervision occurs within the context of a relationship. In this way, it resembles a number of other psychosocial and medical interventions, especially counseling or psychotherapy. But whereas relationship (e.g, Rogers, 1957) and social psychological (e.g., Frank, 1973) factors might account for a substantial portion of client change in therapy independent of technique, supervision is an educational process in which the supervisee is learning new skills. If supervision were to consist *only* of the supervisor–supervisee relationship, the supervisee would be unlikely to develop many of the skills and conceptualizations necessary for practice.

Hess (1987) captured the essence of this situation when he asserted that whereas the supervisory relationship is part of supervision it is not *the* supervision. Nevertheless, it is arguably the most essential part.

The working definition Gelso and Carter (1985) offered for therapeutic relationships applies just as well to supervisory relationships: "the feelings and attitudes that counseling [and supervisory] participants have toward one another, and the manner in which these are expressed" (p. 159). But as this definition suggests, to discuss "the relationship" is misleading, for each supervisory dyad (or group) has its own unique rhythm, sequences, and content. Many factors can affect a relationship. We discussed some of these (e.g., gender, race–ethnicity, developmental stage) in Chapter 3. But there are many others as well. For example, Tracey, Ellickson, and Sherry (1989) showed that *client problem type* can affect supervisory relationships. In this case, they found that with a suicidal client supervisees at all experience levels preferred more structured supervision. Variables related to *setting* can

affect supervisory relationships (Albott, 1984). The *format* (individual versus group) and method (e.g., case notes versus live observation) undoubtedly affect the relationship as well.

Throughout this chapter, our writing is informed by the assumption that supervisory relationships—like *all* human relationships—are bidirectional and based on mutual influence (see, e.g., Claiborn & Lichtenberg, 1989; Heppner & Claiborn, 1989). Or, put another way, each person affects the other and exerts a major influence on the character, quality, and course of their relationship.

But, even though we assume relationships are based on mutual influence, there are specific instances in which it can be useful to examine the relationship in such a way that the influence of one person or the other is highlighted. Therefore, in several portions of this chapter, we will isolate supervisee and supervisor issues and phenomena for specific discussion. To employ a statistical metaphor, think of the supervisory relationship as having both main and interaction effects: Although the interaction effects typically are the more interesting and meaningful, main effects (e.g., the separate effect of the supervisee or supervisor) are sometimes essential to consider by themselves.

Space permits us to cover only some of the possible issues and factors that might affect supervisory relationships. They are covered in four sections. In the first section, we address relationship phenomena that arise from the fact that at least three people—client, therapist–supervisee, and supervisor—are ultimately involved in and affect the supervisory relationship system. In the second section, we address relationship issues that arise in the supervisee–supervisor relationship. In the third section, we address supervisee issues that affect the relationship. And, finally, in the fourth section, we address supervisor issues that affect the relationship.

SECTION ONE: SUPERVISION AS A THREE- (OR MORE) PERSON SYSTEM

Whereas the therapy relationship typically is a two-person system, the supervisory relationship is at least a three-person system comprised of client, therapist–supervisee, and supervisor. This multi-person system is one in which the number and types of relationships are more numerous—and correspondingly more complex—than in therapy. Lesser (1983) noted that "It is important to be aware that the supervisory room is crowded with all sorts of persons who create anxieties for both the supervisor and the supervisee. It is often more crowded than the analytic one" (p. 126).

We will discuss in this section two particular relationship issues that arise from the multiperson nature of the supervisory system. These are interpersonal triangles and parallel processes (or isomorphism). We will address each in turn.

Interpersonal Triangles

It seems customary, at least in our culture, to think of the dyad as the basic social unit. Bowen (e.g., 1978), however, did a great deal to sensitize mental health professionals—especially family therapists—to the notion that the interpersonal triangle actually may be the more fundamental unit of relationship.

Conceptualizing relationships in terms of triangles is not new. Caplow (1968) noted that since at least the 1890s there have been theorists who have maintained that triangles constitute a type of social geometry in which two members will tend to form a coalition against a third. An observer can predict the patterns of coalitions for any given triangle with some accuracy, based on that observer's knowledge of the relative power of the individuals involved in the triangle. Put another way, coalitions are a means to redistribute power.

In fact, Caplow (1968) maintained that the most distinctive feature of triadic social systems is "the transformation of strength into weakness and weakness into strength" (p. 3).

Caplow surveyed the variety of ways in which triangles occur during our day-to-day living, ranging from the nuclear family and its "Oedipal triangles" to the triangles that occur within governments (e.g., with liberal, moderate, and conservative groups) and even among nations. We all can think back to childhood relationships in which, of three friends, there was one dyad that was particularly close. During times of tension between these two, however, the less involved third member was drawn into an alliance with one of them against the other.

One especially interesting characteristic of triangles is that they seem to have a catalytic effect on participant behaviors. That is, although coalitions can occur between two members of a triangle without the third member present, his or her presence almost always modifies the relationship of the other two. Caplow offers as an illustrative example the common playground situation in which the presence of a mutual antagonist enhances the affection between two friends and their felt hostility toward the antagonist.

Bowen (1978) maintained that a coalition exists when two members discuss a third in privacy. We all have seen this in our families. Most of us have also experienced in work settings the situation where two colleagues meet to express to each other their concerns about the behavior of a third. Significantly, too, this describes the behavior of supervisors and supervisees with respect to the client.

In supervision the most obvious triangle is that of the client, the counselor, and the supervisor. This particular triangle does, however, have its own characteristics that constrain the possible coalitions. Two of these are the way in which power is arrayed (the least powerful member of this group is the client; the most powerful, the supervisor) and the fact that the supervisor and client rarely will have an ongoing face-to-face relationship with each other. Strategically oriented family therapists sometimes use these characteristics to their advantage in supervision. That is, the supervisor is deliberately set up in the oppressor role as a means both of enhancing the strength of the client–counselor bond and of steering the client toward a desired behavior. For example, the supervisee might be asked to say something like this to the client: "My supervisor is convinced that your problem is _____ and that I should be doing _____ about it. Just between us, though, I think she's off base. In fact, I think she's pretty insensitive to your issues."

Supervision, of course, occurs in a larger context, and many other possible triangles can come into play. For example, the supervisee might "triangle in" another supervisor (either present or past) by saying something like, "I'm feeling confused: You are saying this, but the supervisor I had last semester [or the supervisor I have in my other setting] has been telling me something really different." In this case, the coalition is between the supervisee and another supervisor who may not even realize he or she has become a member of this particular triangle. Because coalitions—even with a phantom member such as this—are used to redistribute power, it is easy to infer the supervisee's purpose in using this tactic (even though the supervisee might not be aware of that purpose).

The point of this is not to suggest that triangles are bad and, therefore, to be avoided. In fact, they cannot. Therefore, it is essential for the supervisor to understand them and their effects on supervision.

Parallel Processes and Isomorphism

Simply stated, parallel process refers to the common phenomenon of the *dynamics* in supervision replicating those that occurred or are occurring in the supervisee's therapy. Or as Friedlander, Siegel, and Brenock (1989) described the concept, "supervisees unconsciously present themselves to their supervisors as their clients have presented to them. The process reverses when the supervisee adopts attitudes and behaviors of the supervisor in relating to the client" (p. 149). Hawkins and Shohet (1989) explain it at a more basic, colloquial

level: "we do to others what has been done to us" (p. 96).

The concept of parallel process has its roots in psychodynamic supervision, specifically in the concepts or transference and countertransference (Friedman, 1983; Grey & Fiscalini, 1987; Schneider, 1992). Searles (1955) apparently was the first to write about the parallel process, referring to it as the "reflection process" between therapy and supervision (Schön, 1987, has continued this metaphor, by alluding to the emphasis on parallel processes in supervision as the use of a "hall of mirrors" to educate supervisees). Searles's concept has been expanded (e.g., Ekstein & Wallerstein, 1972; Mueller & Kell, 1972; Mueller, 1982) and has appeared as a key concept in virtually every major writing on the topic of supervision.

In recent years, the premise of parallel process has been adopted and expanded by systemic family therapists, especially those of the structural–strategic school. Haley (1976) apparently spearheaded this development (Liddle & Saba, 1983). Choosing the term "isomorphism," systemic supervisors have focused on the interrelational and structural similarities between therapy and supervision, rather than on the intrapsychic parallels.

For our purposes here, we will treat parallel process and isomorphism separately. Although we view them as two sides of the same coin, we believe the focus each offers is and should remain a separate contribution.

Parallel Processes. Mueller (1982) stated that parallel process cannot be denied any more than transference can be denied. Russell et al. (1984) suggested two ways that the parallel process framework can be useful in supervision:

> *First, as the supervisee becomes aware of the parallels in the relationships with the client and the supervisor, understanding of the client's psychological maladjustment is increased. Second, the supervisee's understanding of the therapeutic process grows in that the supervisee learns how to respond therapeutically to the client just as the supervisor has responded to the supervisee.* (p. 629)

Traditionally, it was assumed that parallel process was a *bottom-up* (or transference only) phenomenon. The supervisee would replay in the supervisory relationship a conflict from a therapeutic relationship. As Grey and Fiscalini (1987) noted, these conflicts most typically are intertwined concerns about authority and dependency. This replaying would be out of the supervisee's consciousness (Mueller & Kell, 1972). Explanations for the occurrence vary and include the following:

1. Supervisees should identify with clients and, therefore, produce reactions in their supervisors that they themselves felt in response to their clients (Russell et al., 1984).
2. The parallel chosen (unconsciously) by the supervisee reflects the initial impasse formed between the client and the supervisee (Mueller & Kell, 1972).
3. Through a natural screening process, the supervisee selects a part of the client's problem that parallels one that the supervisee shares (Mueller & Kell, 1972).
4. Through lack of skill, the supervisee is prone to those aspects of the client's problem that parallel the supervisee's specific learning problems in supervision (Ekstein & Wallerstein, 1972).

Ekstein and Wallerstein added that parallel process is a "never-ending surprise," based on the "irrational expectation that the teaching and learning of psychotherapy should consist primarily of rational elements" (p. 177). The flavor of this comment, however, is that the irrationality comes from the supervisee, which is not always the case. With Doehrman's (1976) research came the realization that parallel process was bi-directional and thereby involved countertransference as well as transference. The supervisor was as likely to initiate a dynamic that would then be played out in the supervisee's therapy as the reverse. Or, as Grey and Fiscalini (1987) noted, the parallel process has come to be seen as "a chain reaction that may occur in any interconnected series of interpersonal situations that are structurally and dynamically similar in significant respects" (p. 131). More recently, therefore, there has been more discussion of *top-down* parallel process. Regardless

of the direction, though, "the conduits for parallel processes are supervisees: they are members of both systems (though with different roles) and carry one system into the other" (Carroll, 1996, p. 107).

McNeill and Worthen (1989) reported some empirical support, albeit sparse, that parallel process does occur between therapy and supervision. Several studies of this phenomenon using some version of a case study format are those of Alpher (1991), Doehrman (1976), and Friedlander, Siegel, and Brenock (1989).

Parallel process, therefore, would seem to be an important conceptual approach to supervision, at least as one perspective for the supervisor to consider when supervision dynamics seem inconsistent with what was expected. "It is as though we work with a constant 'metaphor' in which the patient's problem in psychotherapy may be used to express the therapist's problem in supervision— and vice versa" (Ekstein & Wallerstein, 1958, p. 180).

Neufeldt, Iverson, and Juntunen (1995) pointed out that, whereas a supervisor might anticipate many interventions in advance, the opportunity to address parallel processes in a supervision session occurs serendipitously. Once a parallel process is noted, though, the supervisor has to decide what actions to take. Neufeldt et al. noted that, although psychodynamic supervisors are likely to point out or interpret parallel processes to more advanced supervisees as they observe them, this can be confusing to less advanced students. Moreover, as Carroll (1996) points out, simply to have awareness of a particular parallel process does not make it disappear.

Neufeldt et al. recommended instead that the supervisor respond less directly and serve as a model for the supervisee about how to respond to the client issues that the supervisee is mirroring in the supervisory sessions. For more intractable situations, Carroll (1996) recommends having the supervisee role play the client to gain a clearer perspective.

McNeill and Worthen (1989) cautioned that too much focus on the *process* of supervision might become tiresome for supervisees and that, in general, more advanced supervisees are most likely to benefit from a discussion of transference and countertransference. Finally, Vargas (1989) noted that when supervisor, therapist, and/or client represent different cultural backgrounds, parallel processes will reflect cross-cultural issues.

Friedman (1983) offered the following example of parallel process:

> [A] mother and child were being seen by the same student therapist for a diagnostic assessment. The student described the mother as being very unfocused and disorganized, so that she had a hard time keeping the mother on track. . . . Mother presented herself as very undifferentiated and presented members of her family in the same way, e.g., speaking of Michael, Jr. and Michael, Sr. as Michael. In mother's mind, all the children appeared to be unseparated so that when the student asked about the developmental history of M. Jr., the mother would speak of all the children in her undifferentiated way.
>
> The student in her supervisory hour, and this was after several earlier sessions with the mother, reported that even after she had seen M. Jr. twice she was unable to visualize the boy's face and could not recall any of his features. . . . The student found this very disconcerting. . . . The student had been so caught up in her counter-transference reaction to the mother that this well-organized, well-structured, competent student . . . experienced the child as being as undifferentiated as did the mother. (pp. 9–10)

McWilliams (1994) acknowledged that the fact that attitudes can be unconsciously induced by one person in another can sound mystical. For someone trained with the hard-nosed skepticism that sometimes characterizes the scientist–practitioner, this apparent mysticism can be particularly troublesome. McWilliams suggested, though, that these processes become more comprehensible when one realizes that in the earliest years of life most communication with others is nonverbal and that we then continue to employ this mode throughout life without necessarily understanding the extent to which we do so.

> People relating to babies figure out what they need largely on the basis of intuitive, emotional reactions. Nonverbal communication can be remarkably powerful, as anyone who has ever taken care of a

> newborn or been moved to tears, or fallen inexplicably in love can testify. (McWilliams, 1994, p. 34)

But if a too skeptical perception of parallel processes is one issue, the complementary issue is to invoke it too frequently and uncritically without considering alternative explanations for what may be occurring within the supervisory system. Schimel (1984), for example, acknowledged that the concept of "parallel processes" can be useful in supervision. But he also asserted that the concept can be invoked in an irresponsible and possibly trivial manner to frame in psychological terms a matter that actually is one of skill and competence.

> The basic observation is a simple one. The patient wants something from the therapist that is not forthcoming. He or she is displeased. This troubles the therapist, who, in turn, looks to the supervisor for help that may or may not be forthcoming. The therapist is displeased with the supervisor, who, in his turn, may be troubled and displeased with the supervisee and himself. This is a common situation. One has reason to expect, however, that with the increasing skill of the supervisee and the accumulating experience of the supervisor that this kind of situation will be recognized early and dealt with by putting it into an appropriate perspective. (p. 239)

Feiner (1994) is another who urged caution in putting too much credence in the parallel process as a supervision phenomenon:

> The supervisor is allegedly "put" (not deliberately) in the position of a proxy therapist with the supervisee playing the part of the patient. Although out-of-awareness, the enactment is not taken by sophisticated supervisors as a simple, mechanistic repetition, but as more likely representing some sort of homology. It's as though the student were saying, "Do it with me and I'll know what to do with my patients." But . . . while the issues that belong to the patient may seem similar to the issues that the therapist-as-student brings into supervision . . . the similarity is more apparent than real. It's sort of like the descriptions of a spouse by a patient. The image of the described other cannot be taken as objective truth. (pp. 61–62)

Feiner pointed out that one risk of a too heavy reliance on parallel process thinking is that it may ignore, obscure, or even deny the supervisor's or the supervisee's own contributions to the interactions occurring between them.

Isomorphism. Abroms (1977) offered the term "metatransference" and defined it in terms that are similar, if not identical, to parallel process. Furthermore, in discussing this phenomenon, Abroms came as close as anyone to blending the concepts of parallel process and isomorphism: "To think in terms of metatransference is to think in parallel structures at different levels of abstraction, that is, to recognize the multilevel, isomorphic mirroring of interactional processes" (p. 93). This may, therefore, be a useful bridge between the parallel process section and this one on isomorphism.

Because it is a technical word, it may be helpful to define isomorphism:

> The word "isomorphic" applies when two complex structures can be mapped on to each other, in such a way that to each part of one structure there is a corresponding part in the other structure, where "corresponding" means that the two parts play similar roles in their respective structures. This usage of the word "isomorphic" is derived from a more precise notion in mathematics. (Hofstadter, 1979, p. 49)

For systems therapists, isomorphism refers to the "recursive replication" (Liddle et al., 1984) that occurs between therapy and supervision. The focus is interrelational and not intrapsychic (Liddle, Becker, & Diamond, 1997). As Liddle and Saba (1983) suggested, the two fields (therapy and supervision) constantly influence and are influenced by each other; both are interpersonal systems with properties of all systems, including boundaries, hierarchies, and subsystems, each with its own distinct characteristics. There is no linear reality in this construct, only reverberations. Content is less important than the repeating patterns.

Because supervision is viewed as the isomorph of therapy, Liddle et al. (1984) suggested that the same rules apply to both, including the need to join with both clients and supervisees, the need for setting goals and thinking in stages, the importance of appreciating contextual sensitivity, and the charge of challenging realities. In other words, like

advocates of parallel process, those who adhere to the isomorphic relationship between therapy and supervision view it as dictating intervention and not as a descriptive construct solely. "It suggests that trainers would do well to understand and intentionally utilize with their supervisees the same basic principles of change employed in therapy" (Liddle et al., 1984, p. 141).

The supervisor who is aware of this process will watch for dynamics in supervision that reflect the initial assessment the supervisor has made about what is transpiring in therapy. In that way, the assessment is either verified or called into question. Because the client is usually a group (i.e., family), and many systemic supervisors prefer team supervision, the interactions are easily replicated. For example, an overwhelmed parent will appeal to the supervisee for help (while other family members sit expectantly), which will be followed by an overwhelmed supervisee appealing to the supervisor for help (while other team members sit expectantly).

When intervening into the therapeutic system (supervisee plus family), it is important that there be consistency down the hierarchy. For example, Haley (1987) recommended that if the goal is for the parents to be firm with their teenager the therapist must be firm with the parents. And, to complete the isomorph, the supervisor must be firm with the therapist. In this way, content and process are matched and communicate the same message throughout the interconnected systems.

Liddle and Saba (1983) argued that live supervision, by requiring risk taking and experiential behavior on the part of the therapist, parallels structural family therapy, where family members are actively put in direct contact with each other. Therefore, live supervision is an isomorphically correct form of supervision for structural family therapy. Knowing a good metaphor when they had one, Liddle and Saba (1982) described an introductory course in marriage and family therapy where the content and process of the course were designed to follow all the rules for the progression of family therapy. The authors noted that matching process and content right from the start of training makes for a much more powerful learning experience.

The following illustrates the isomorphic relationship between therapy and supervision:

> *Ted is seeing the Doyles for marriage counseling. There is a supervision team observing the session. The Doyles have been married for twenty years. They have no children. Mr. Doyle has fought depression through most of his adult life. Mrs. Doyle tells how hard it has been to help him, only to have her efforts go nowhere. She cries intermittently. It is obvious watching Ted that he is feeling this couple's plight. In the supervision room, there is virtually no movement. The team mirrors the sadness and despair of the couple. Halfway through the session, Ted excuses himself to consult with the team. . . . As Ted is seated, Bill turns to him and says, "Boy, what do you do for them at this point?" Ted shrugs and looks around for help.*

In addition to recognizing the isomorphic nature of what is transpiring, the supervisor must (1) determine how to approach the team, (2) predict Ted's role in the group, and (3) decide on an intervention that will not only help to stimulate Ted and the team, but will serve to initiate a direction for Ted to take with the Doyles.

SECTION TWO: SUPERVISION AS A TWO-PERSON SYSTEM— SUPERVISOR AND SUPERVISEE

Theory and research on the supervisor–supervisee relationship often have evolved as a direct extension of theory and research on client–therapist relationships. For example, during the early 1970s, Carkhuff's (1969) model became a dominant relationship paradigm, both for counseling and for supervision. Carkhuff's (e.g., 1969) assertion that the level and quality of the supervisor's interpersonal skills may establish a ceiling for the supervisee's own skills seemed for a time the "received view" in the field. This meant, for example, that the supervisee could be no more empathic, on average, with clients than the supervisee's supervisor was with him or her.

This hypothesis drove studies such as those of Pierce and Schauble (1970, 1971) and Lambert

(1974), which examined the extent to which supervisors' levels of empathy, regard, genuineness, and concreteness (i.e., facilitative conditions) influenced the development of those same conditions in their supervisees (for summaries of this and related research, see Lambert & Arnold, 1987; Matarazzo & Patterson, 1986; and Lambert & Ogles, 1997). Based on their review, Lambert and Ogles concluded that "there exists little empirical evidence supporting the necessity of a therapeutic climate for the acquisition of interpersonal skills . . . and it appears that learning these skills can occur without high levels of empathy, genuineness, and unconditional positive regard, as long as the supervisee perceives the supervisor is indeed trying to be helpful" (p. 426). In short, although Rogerian-defined relationship dimensions are too important to ignore, they seem to have greater salience in the practice of therapy than in the practice of supervision.

It also is interesting to consider that, as useful as the Rogerian-based relationship paradigm has been to the field generally, it has possibly reached the upper limits of its applicability. It may be time for a paradigm shift. This was the compelling argument of Gelso and Carter (1985), who found promise in Bordin's (1979) working alliance model.

Bordin suggested that the working alliance, or "collaboration to change" (p. 73), is common to all models of therapy. It is composed of three elements: the *bond* between therapist and client, the extent to which they agree on *goals,* and the extent to which they agree on *tasks.* He argued that real change in therapy or in supervision occurs during processes of weakening and then repair of the relationship or alliance.

Bordin's initial work concerned therapeutic relationships. Later, though, he (Bordin, 1983) extended his working alliance model to include supervision, which demands a "teaching–learning" alliance between supervisee and supervisor. This has provided researchers (e.g., Baker, 1990, Efstation, Patton, & Kardash, 1990) with a fresh way to think about supervisory relationships. The development of the Working Alliance Inventory

(Horvath & Greenberg, 1989) provided a useful tool for such studies.

Supervision research on alliances was further aided by Efstation, Patton, and Kardash's (1990) Supervisory Working Alliance Inventory (presented in Appendix C). The working alliance model has been the focus of several studies that have used it either as the specific focus of the study (Burke, 1992) or as a dependent variable that might be affected by specific supervision procedures (e.g., Bahrick, 1990; Bahrick, Russell, & Salmi, 1991; Kivlighan, Angelone, & Swafford, 1991), interpersonal processes (Adamson, 1993), or particular characteristics of supervisee and supervisor (Baker, 1990).

Working Alliance Bonds

Attachment theory is useful in understanding the bonding aspect of the working alliance model, for this theory is focused on the making and breaking of affectional bonds. Bowlby (1977), generally credited as attachment theory's primary developer, has stated that "Briefly put, attachment behavior is conceived as any form of behavior that results in a person attaining or retaining proximity to some other differentiated and preferred individual, who is usually conceived as stronger and/or wiser" (p. 203).

Watkins (1995a; Pistole & Watkins, 1995) suggested that supervision is an attachment process that involves the development and eventual loosening of an affectional bond. He argued, therefore, that attachment theory has useful implications for understanding supervisor–supervisee relationships.

Bowlby (1977, 1978) described two primary problematic attachment patterns or styles. One is *anxious attachment;* the other is *compulsive self-reliance.* A third, something of a variant on the second, is *compulsive care giving.* Bowlby argued that a person's style (i.e., the way he or she approaches and maintains relationships) is learned during childhood, based on experiences with parents and other care-givers. The style then persists throughout life in relationships with important others—regardless of the style's current appropriateness. It endures across people and situations.

A supervisee with an anxious attachment style is likely to be very dependent and even "clingy," constantly call the supervisor for help, wanting to be the supervisor's favorite, and resenting the supervisor for not needing him or her in a reciprocal way. A supervisee who is a compulsive caregiver is likely to "rescue" clients, working to immediately lessen their concerns and problems (often at the expense of letting them fully grapple with and find resolution to their issues); this supervisee also is likely to be uncomfortable and even anxious in the supervisory context where she or he is the recipient of the supervisor's help and support. And a compulsively self-reliant supervisee is likely to refuse, resist, or even resent the supervisor's attempts to help; to do as he or she wants in therapy (informing the supervisor later); and yet to really want the supervisor's approval desperately.

Watkins suggested that when supervisors encounter a supervisee with a pathological attachment style, they will feel caught up in something they may not initially understand. That is, they may be concerned about what they may have done to provoke the supervisee's responses, wonder about their competence, and feel exasperated. Watkins suggested that, for the relatively rare supervisee who actually does meet criterion for one of these three pathological attachment styles, psychotherapy is the appropriate intervention.

Watkins (1995a) noted that, even though they may have features of one or another of these three patterns, most supervisees have a sufficiently secure attachment style to allow supervision to occur in a satisfactory manner. Nevertheless, it is useful for supervisors to have these behavioral styles in mind as ways to conceptualize problematic bonding between them and their supervisees.

Working Alliance Goals

One contribution of the working alliance model has been to underscore the importance of expectations (i.e., what Bordin calls "goals") to the nature and quality of the supervisory relationship. Bahrick, Russell, and Salmi (1991) and Olk and Friedlander (1992) addressed expectations in supervision; Ellis, Anderson-Hanley, Dennin, Anderson, Chapin, and Polastri (1994) made supervisor–supervisee expectations an explicit focus of their work. They defined expectations as "a person's anticipatory beliefs about the nature (i.e., roles, behaviors, interactions, and tasks) or outcome of a particular event or outcome" (p. 3). Ellis et al. cited counseling and psychotherapy literature showing that *congruence* of expectations (i.e., shared goals) between or among people in a relationship is at least as important—and likely more important—than the expectations of any one individual.

Sometimes supervisor and supervisee have differing expectations because the supervisee simply is uninformed about the appropriate role(s) she or he is to assume as supervisee. To maximize the likelihood of supervisor–supervisee congruence in expectations for supervision, an initial negotiation or contracting should occur between them. When the supervisee simply does not know role options, as might be the case with a beginning supervisee, it is possible to educate him or her about expected behaviors and role through, for example, discussions and audio- or videotape modeling.

Although little research has been done to investigate the effectiveness of this educational procedure, generally referred to as "role induction," in supervision, its effectiveness with therapy clients has been demonstrated (see, e.g., Garfield, 1986; Kaul & Bednar, 1986). Bahrick, Russell, and Salmi (1991) developed a 10-minute audiotaped summary of Bernard's (1979) supervision model and administered it to 19 supervisees at one of several points in the semester. They found that after supervisees heard the tape they reported having a clearer conceptualization of supervision and being more willing to reveal concerns to their supervisors. This effect occurred regardless of when in the semester supervisees heard the tapes. In a more recent study, Ellis, Chapin, Dennin, and Anderson-Hanley (1996) found that a role induction they conducted significantly decreased supervisee anxiety compared to a control group.

Another useful supervision strategy is to assess participants' expectations. To that end, Ellis et al. (1994) have developed parallel, 52-item scales (one for supervisees and another for supervisors) to examine expectations for supervision. Tinsley and his associates (e.g., Tinsley, Workman, & Kass, 1980; Tinsley, Bowman, & Ray, 1988) have conducted programmatic research on client's expectations for counseling, and their instrument for assessing counselor–client expectations has been frequently employed in counseling research. The Ellis et al. (1994) scale has promise as a means of extending this work to the area of supervision. It should be of use not only to researchers, but also to supervision practitioners who then might check for potentially problematic expectation mismatches.

The Role of Conflict in Supervisory Relationships

Betcher and Zinberg (1988) asserted that supervisory and therapeutic relationships are similar in several important ways. One of those similarities is that participants have the capacity to undo the human errors that they make, especially with one another. This is a particularly important aspect of the supervisory relationship. In fact, a central thesis of Mueller and Kell's (1972) now classic supervision book, *Coping with Conflict,* was that in any relationship, whether personal or professional, conflict inevitably will occur between or among the parties. That conflict can stem from opposing goals the two parties entertain; often, though, it stems from a "mistake" that one party has made. The manner in which the parties resolve or fail to resolve that conflict will dictate whether the relationship continues to grow and develop or to stagnate (see, also, Loganbill, Hardy, & Delworth, 1982). This is similar to Bordin's (1983) assertion that it is the "weakening and repair" of the working alliance between two people that constitutes the basis of therapeutic change.

In fact, this weakening and repair often constitute supervision's most important process, for it allows learning to occur that generalizes beyond the specific supervisor–supervisee relationship. A metaphor we have heard to describe the effects of this process is that scarred tissue often is stronger than the original tissue.

Lesser (1983) addressed this matter, stating that

Sullivan's statement, "God keep me from a therapy that goes well!" can be extended to "Keep me from a supervisory relationship that goes well!" Going well may mean that there is more superficiality in the relationship, but less anxiety; a more comfortable atmosphere, but limited interpersonal engagement; a greater sense of certainty, but complexities are dissociated; more interpretations, but little structural change in the relatedness between the participants . . . disappointments and struggles have more likely been avoided, but the potential richness and joy of a significant relationship [are] lost. (p. 128)

Before going further, though, perhaps we should make it clear that supervisee–supervisor conflicts can arise from many sources, some more problematic than others. The type of conflict we have been addressing so far in this chapter is normative, for it arises from the processes of any two people who interact over time: Inevitably there will be times in *any* ongoing relationship when the parties will feel angry, hurt, surprised, and/or disappointed with one another. To resolve those conflicts and impasses is healthy and strengthens the relationship.

Another normative factor in supervisee–supervisor conflict concerns the supervisee's developmental level. In particular, Ronnestad and Skovholt (1993) suggested that tension and dissatisfaction with supervision may be at its greatest with the more advanced student. Like any adolescent, supervisees at this level vacillate between feelings of confidence and of insecurity. "The student has now actively assimilated information from many sources but still has not had enough time to accommodate and find her or his own way of behaving professionally" (p. 400). This is not, in itself, a matter for concern, particularly if the supervisor is able to understand and anticipate this particular developmental phenomenon.

But conflicts can also arise for more problematic reasons. For example, the conflict may arise from supervisee transference and/or from supervisor countertransference, as we discuss later in this chapter. Or conflict might also arise from a personality conflict between supervisee and supervisor that simply is not to be resolved. Mental health professionals generally acknowledge that therapists may not be expected to form an effective working relationship with every client they see: Why should we have a different expectation for supervision? In the (fortunately rare) cases of intractable personality conflicts, the responsible supervisor will transfer the supervisee to another supervisor or otherwise work to protect the supervisee's interests.

Finally, Robiner, Fuhrman, and Ritvedt (1993) made the point that to provide summative assessment (see Chapter 8 in this book) may often stimulate supervisee–supervisor conflict. They noted that, in particular, this process "exposes potential contradictions in the dual role of the supervisor as nurturant teacher and vigilant gatekeeper" (p. 4). This observation raises the important matter of role clarity and the importance of minimizing role conflicts.

Role Conflict and Role Ambiguity.   Robiner et al. (1993) were addressing role conflicts that occur during the supervisor's functioning. At least as important are the role conflicts and ambiguities that supervisees experience. Olk and Friedlander (1992) suggested that at various points the supervisee may be required to function in the roles of student, client, counselor, or colleague. Then, drawing from organizational psychology literature, they suggested *role ambiguity* or *role conflict* as two role-related problems that a supervisee might face.

Role ambiguity occurs when the supervisee is uncertain about role expectations the supervisor and/or agency has for him or her. We already have discussed role induction as one means to minimize role ambiguity. The most frequent means, though, is to engage in clear contracting with the supervisee about the nature and expectations of supervision.

Role conflict occurs (1) when the supervisees are required to engage in two or more roles that may require inconsistent behavior or (2) when the supervisees are required to engage in behavior that is incongruent with their personal judgment (see Ladany & Friedlander, 1995). For example, in the first case, supervisees may be required to reveal personal weaknesses and potential inadequacies while *also* needing to present themselves to the supervisor as competent so that they will pass the practicum. This might be understood as a conflict between the supervisee-as-client and supervisee-as-counselor. In the second case, the supervisor might give directives to behave in a manner that is inconsistent with the supervisee's ethical or theoretical beliefs. Here the conflict is between the roles of supervisee-as-student and supervisee-as-counselor.

To study these two types of supervisee role difficulties, Olk and Friedlander (1992) developed the Role Conflict and Role Ambiguity Inventory (RCRAI). Readers interested in using it in their own research or in monitoring supervisee role difficulties will find the RCRAI in Appendix C of this book.

Olk and Friedlander (1992) found that many supervisees did not report role difficulties. Those who did, however, were more likely to report work-related anxiety and dissatisfaction as well as dissatisfaction with supervision. In a subsequent study in which they used both the RCRAI and a version of the Working Alliance Inventory (WAI; Horvath & Greenberg, 1989), Ladany and Friedlander (1995) obtained two findings of potential importance to supervisors. One was that the greater the strength of the supervisor–supervisee emotional bond the less role conflict the supervisee experienced. This may suggest that the stronger their bond the more likely that supervisor and supervisee will work together to resolve their conflicts. An alternative possibility is that the less the role conflicts in the first place, the greater the emotional bonds. Olk and Friedlander also found that supervisees reported less role ambiguity when they perceived themselves to have been offered clear statements from their supervisors about their expectations for supervision.

Dual Relationships as a Specific Instance of Role Conflict.

Most mental health professionals are sensitive to the fact that dual relationships are problematic and to be avoided as much as possible. Yet, what is a dual relationship but one in which there is a role conflict or, to use Robiner's (1982) term, role diffusion?

Certain of these role conflicts–dual relationships are more obvious and therefore perhaps easier to anticipate and head off than others. For example, most mental health professionals recognize it is wrong for members of a supervisory dyad also to be romantic or sexual partners (e.g., Hall, 1988) or for students in a training program also to serve as clients to other members of that program (Patrick, 1989). In these cases, the conflict is between a supervision-appropriate role and one that is not supervision appropriate (dual relationships are discussed in Chapter 9).

Other role conflicts, particularly between roles that both are supervision appropriate but with competing or antagonistic goals, are more difficult to avoid, even by the best intentioned and most alert supervisor. For example, the supervisor who draws from a counselor role may intend to increase supervisees' development by encouraging them to be self-disclosing and open. At the same time, however, the supervisor also functions in the role of evaluator. It is conceivable, therefore, that material the supervisor gains by encouraging supervisees' self-disclosure may then lead the supervisor to conclude that the supervisee simply is not suited for this line of work. The consequent actions the supervisor may take in the role of evaluator can be antithetical to the supervisee's personal and professional development, the training goals of the intervention.

It is not possible, then, for supervisors to avoid role conflicts completely. They can, however, be alert to the adoption of extra-supervision roles (e.g., lover) that are *certain* to cause role conflict. They can also attenuate, to some extent, the effects of supervision-appropriate role conflicts by informing the supervisee at the outset of the relationship about the possibility of such conflicts and their consequences.

Power

Supervisory relationships are characterized by a power inequality. Power inequality exists in psychotherapy, of course. Several aspects of the therapeutic context contribute to it. For example, the person in a relationship who needs the other more (the client) typically has less power than the person who is needed (see, e.g., Strong, 1968); and the person who has permission to comment on the other's behavior also has the greater power.

These circumstances exist in supervision. But, in addition, the supervisor has evaluative responsibilities with respect to the supervisee, an additional type of power. Robiner (1982) pointed out that the power difference is a constant obstacle to gaining the mutual trust that is so important in supervision. He suggested that mutual respect is one important means of overcoming the impasse that this can present. The supervisor's position of power suggests that he or she must model that respect if both the supervisor and supervisee are to attain it. Because of the supervisor's position of greater power, there is more responsibility for the relationship. Supervisors aware of the hierarchically derived power they have in the supervisory relationship can use it to effective, positive ends. Not to be aware of it—or to deny it—can lead both to abuses and to the failure to use it effectively to offer support and protection to the supervisee.

But the social–psychological conception of power concerns the social "influence" of one person on another. This broadens the perspective of power, for all behavior is communication, and communication is an act of influence (Watzlawick & Beavin, 1976). This perspective allows for *mutual* influence—the supervisee can also influence the supervisor, even though the latter continues to have the greater possibility to influence the supervisee.

Social psychologists have long seen social power in these terms. Strong (1968) applied this to counseling by adopting the work of French and Raven (1959) to suggest the ways in which therapists employ social influence to affect client change. This and later work by Strong stimulated the development of a substantial research and conceptual literature that has been summarized by Heppner and Claiborn (1989). Within this broader area of research has been some that has focused on social influence processes in supervision (see, e.g., Claiborn, Etringer, & Hillerbrand, 1995; Dixon & Claiborn, 1987).

Penman (1980) developed a system of categorizing interpersonal interactions so that they were arrayed along the dimensions of *power* and *involvement*. Like the Strong, Hills, Kilmartin, DeVries, Lanier, Nelson, Strickland, and Meyer (1988) model, Penman's was based on Leary's (1957) model of interpersonal behavior. At least three studies (Abadie, 1985; Holloway, Freund, Gardner, Nelson, & Walker, 1989; Martin, Goodyear, & Newton, 1987) have employed Penman's system to analyze supervisory interactions. Only that of Holloway et al. (1989), however, has highlighted the results strongly in terms of the power and involvement dimensions of supervision.

Holloway (1995, 1997) has continued to expand her conceptions of how power and involvement interact. Her particular contribution has been to emphasize the importance of "involvement" or social bonding in determining the social power each party in the relationship has with respect to the other.

The Role of Trust
in Supervisory Relationships

Mutual trust between supervisee and supervisor is essential to effective supervision. Trust affects the behavior of all parties involved in the supervisory relationship, extending even to the client, who must have some implicit trust of the supervisor, even though they may never meet. The people in each of these three roles must overcome their feelings of vulnerability (Liddle, 1988).

But the vulnerabilities of supervisor and supervisee are of different types and felt intensities. For supervisees, the vulnerability concerns their personal feeling and even career paths. Supervisors have some level of personal vulnerability, but more a sense of professional vulnerability that stems from their responsibility to the welfare of the client.

Liddle (1988) suggested that an atmosphere of safety is a necessary condition to counteract the vulnerability. Trustworthiness, as discussed by Strong (1968), accrues to the counselor (or, here, the supervisor) as the other person is able to believe that this person is acting professionally and not in a way to exploit the relationship to meet his or her own needs. There is an old aphorism that "trust is efficient." That is, in interpersonal relationships, to trust means to relax vigilance, which consumes energy and even time. For both supervisee and supervisor, then, the challenge is to find an optimal level of trust.

One characteristic of trust is that it always exists in some degree: It is not an all or nothing phenomenon. Another characteristic of trust is that it is earned over the course of many interactions and interpersonal risks taken together—it is not something that can occur instantaneously.

For supervisees, the level of trust will influence the degree to which they will disclose what is occurring in interactions with the client. For the supervisor, trust can help avoid too much intrusion into and control over the supervisee's work. Yet to trust too much or inappropriately risks possible harm to the client or even the supervisee.

SECTION THREE: SUPERVISEE AS A SOURCE OF VARIANCE IN THE SUPERVISORY RELATIONSHIP

In the preceding section, our primary focus was on the supervisory dyad. In this section, we isolate the supervisee from that unit and consider his or her influence on that relationship. Whereas many supervisee variables and issues influence supervisory relationships, two seem particularly important. These are (1) supervisees' need to feel

and appear competent and (2) supervisees' experience of anxiety. These motivational (i.e., drive toward competence) and affective (i.e., anxiety) states are pervasive and color virtually all supervisory relationships.

It is the nature of supervision that supervisees are expected to be highly involved, but to have relatively little power, at least in comparison to that of their supervisors (Holloway, 1995). This situation affects the supervisee's levels of both anxiety and felt competence.

In this section we treat supervisee competence and supervisee anxiety as independent issues simply for the purpose of explication. In real life they are intertwined and each affects the other: The supervisees' need to feel and appear competent can elicit anxiety, *especially* during summative evaluations; the experience of anxiety, on the other hand, can affect not only how competent supervisees *appear* to be, but also how competent they *feel*. Friedlander, Keller, Peca-Baker, and Olk (1986), for example, found an inverse relationship between supervisees' levels of anxiety and of self-efficacy.

Supervisees' Need to Feel and Appear Competent

Bordin (1983) noted supervisees' strong need for felt competence. He stated that when he would contract with supervisees about goals they wished to accomplish during supervision he found that their overt request typically was for fairly limited and focused goals (e.g., "learning to deal more effectively with manipulative clients;" "becoming more aware of when my own need to nurture gets in my way of being therapeutic."). Yet the supervisees' unspoken agenda almost always seemed to be the wish for global feedback about their overall level of functioning.

At first, I thought that this goal would be satisfied by the feedback I was giving in connection with the more specifically stated ones. But I soon learned such feedback was not enough. Despite our reviews of what the therapist was doing or not doing and of its appropriateness and effectiveness, the supervisee seemed uncertain how I evaluated him or her. Only as I offered the remark that I saw him or her as typical of (or even above or below) those of his or her level of training and experience was that need satisfied.   (p. 39)

Developmental psychologists (e.g., White, 1959) have noted that we all need to feel competent and that this need becomes especially salient at a particular stage of childhood. Competence is similarly important to supervisees. And, just as is the case with children, its salience varies according to the supervisee's level of (professional) development. This is explicit in Loganbill, Hardy, and Delworth's (1982) developmental model. And Rabinowitz, Heppner, and Roehlke (1986) found that beginning practicum students, compared to intern-level supervisees, rated as significantly more important to them the issue, of *Believing that I have sufficient skills as a counselor or psychotherapist to be competent in working with my clients.*

Stoltenberg (1981) hypothesized that supervisees at level 2 (of a four-level model in which level 4 is the most advanced) move from the strong dependency that is characteristic of beginning-level supervisees to a dependency–autonomy conflict. Correspondingly, "there is a constant oscillation between being overconfident in newly learned counseling skills and being overwhelmed by the increasing responsibility" (p. 62). This is very similar to the struggle adolescents experiences as they enter that middle ground between childhood and adulthood. Kell and Mueller (1966) suggested that this struggle can be characterized as

an effort to stay on a highway which is bordered on one side by the beautiful and inviting "Omnipotence Mountains" and on the other side by terrifying "Impotence Cliff." Clients can and often do tempt counselors to climb to the mountain tops. Sometimes the counselor's own needs and dynamics can push him into mountain climbing. More often, the complex, subtle interaction of counselor and client dynamics together lead[s] to counselor trips into the rarified mountain air. Yet the attainment of a mountain top may stir uneasy and uncomfortable feelings. From a mountain top, what direction is there to go except

downward? The view to the bottom of the cliff below may be frightening and compelling. The trip down the mountain may well not stop at the highway. The momentum may carry our counselor on over the cliff where he [or she] will experience the crushing effects of inadequacy and immobilization. . . . It seems that either feeling state [omnipotence or impotence] carries the seeds of the other. . . . Rapid oscillation between the two kinds of feeling can occur in such a short time span as a five minute segment of an interview.   (pp. 124–125)

Skill Mastery, Scrutiny, and Felt Competence. Supervisees' sense of *felt* competence is linked to their *actual* competence. Orlinsky and Howard (1986) found in their review of psychotherapy outcome literature that in studies in which these variables were examined therapist self-confidence and client outcome were related two-thirds of the time. On the other hand, they found no instances of therapist "unsureness" being positively related to outcome.

But supervisees, especially newer supervisees, are often dismayed to find that their therapeutic skills become fragile and vulnerable to deterioration under conditions of observation. This certainly has implications for supervisors' behavior.

Schauer, Seymour, and Geen (1985) drew from social-psychological research to offer a hypothesis that seems intuitively true, even though it has not yet been empirically supported in the specific context of clinical supervision. Their hypothesis was that being observed will impair the performance of a person who has not fully mastered a skill; on the other hand, when that skill has been overlearned (i.e., highly developed through repeated practice), observing will facilitate that person's performance. In fact, data suggest both that inexperienced supervisees are more anxious than those who are more experienced and that videotape reviews of their work may stimulate supervisee anxiety (e.g., Gelso, 1974; Hale & Stoltenberg, 1988; Yenawine & Arbuckle, 1971).

An excellent example of this is the performance of Olympic athletes, individuals who have overlearned their particular athletic skill through thousands of hours of practice. Under conditions of competition and close scrutiny, their performance may attain record-breaking levels. In contrast, consider practicum students who are just beginning to achieve adequate levels of basic interviewing skills: When observed or monitored by a supervisor, their performance is vulnerable to deterioration.

Miller (1989) suggested that *automaticity* can explain this performance vulnerability. The concept of automaticity is that, through practice, counselor behaviors such as reflections of feeling or restatements that were techniques (i.e., behaviors that may not have felt entirely comfortable or natural) eventually become automatic and are performed without effort. As this automaticity begins to occur, the counselor needs to engage in less and less internal dialogue ("What response should I give now?" or even "If I were in a situation like that, how would I feel? What then should I do with that information?"). This automaticity therefore has the effect of freeing up the counselor to attend to other dynamics going on in the client–counselor interaction.

Until automaticity develops the skills in question can be especially fragile under conditions of observation. That is, the supervisee is still relying on fairly overt internal dialogue, which is then vulnerable to disruption. In many instances, to communicate this awareness of performance disruption to the supervisee can itself be an effective supervision intervention to lower supervisee anxiety.

In summary, then, supervisees need to feel competent. However, they often fluctuate between the extreme positions of feeling exceptionally competent and of feeling totally incompetent. Sometimes the very act of being observed interferes with competent behavior.

Another competence-related supervisee phenomenon is that of experiencing themselves as impostors (Harvey & Katz, 1985) who are vulnerable to being found out. This occurs when their level of actual competence exceeds that of their felt competence. Although they behave as therapists, they worry that they are acting a charade, that it will be only a matter of time before they are found out to be the impostors they believe themselves to be. Significantly, then, Kell and Mueller (1966) contended that supervision is "a process of mobilizing [the supervisee's] adequacy" (p. 18). As they experience feelings of adequacy or competence more consistently, they will experience their sense of being an imposter less and less.

Occasionally, though, supervisees will experience really difficult and even painful affective responses in the face of their own and the supervisor's demands for competency. They can, for example, experience occasional feelings of demoralization, perhaps even shame or guilt. In discussing such supervisee responses, Alonso and Rutan (1988) suggested supervisors enable the supervisee to examine "secret failures that [he or she] was too horrified to admit" (p. 580). For example, the supervisor might contribute to the supervisee's sense of dignity and security by offering consistent support and backing. Another is that supervisors take the risk of disclosing to supervisees embarrassing moments in their own work.

Supervisee Anxiety

Anxiety affects supervision in many ways and arises from multiple sources. Client, supervisee, and supervisor anxieties all can affect the supervisory relationship in nontrivial ways. And to make matters even more complex, anxiety experienced *anywhere* in the multiperson system that comprises supervision can affect the entire system.

A great deal of what occurs in supervision directly or indirectly concerns the containment and management of client anxiety. However, the client's experience of anxiety certainly can reverberate up, affecting the therapist and even the supervisor.

Although the supervisor's anxieties are not often discussed, they, too, are a factor in supervision. Lesser (1983) discussed possible sources of supervisor anxiety. Among them are the anxieties that arise in evaluation and the feelings of responsibility both to supervisees and to the public that they will serve if successful in training; criticism or praise, whether overt or covert, may elicit anxiety; anxiety can arise when a client is in crisis and the supervisor has some doubts, however small, about the supervisee's ability to handle it [that the supervisor is vicariously liable (see Chapter 9) certainly can amplify this feeling]; and anxieties can occur at times when the supervisor may feel no longer needed.

It is the supervisee's anxiety, however, that seems the most salient in our discussion of supervisory relationships. The supervisee is under continual scrutiny and evaluation, including self-evaluation. Also, the supervisee experiences anxiety on *two* fronts: in work with the client and in work with the supervisor. But, on either front, the supervisor's actions or lack thereof can affect the level and type of the supervisee's anxiety and ultimately that of the client as well. One of the really striking findings in Skovholt and Ronnestad's (1992a, b) qualitative study of therapists across the life-span was the intense anxiety experienced by graduate students. Interestingly, though, they were less able to access this anxiety from their graduate student informants than they were from more senior practitioners who were reflecting back on their experiences in graduate school.

Whereas anxiety is a fact of life for the supervisee, there is no simple or uniform way to characterize it. This is so because a supervisee's anxiety may arise from a number of sources and is moderated by such factors as the supervisee's maturity, experience level, personality, and relationships with clients and the supervisor. Another factor is the supervisees' typical status as students, for the achievement orientation, competitiveness, and evaluative nature of the academic climate tend to exacerbate anxiety.

Most discussions of the effects of anxiety on the supervisee have focused on its undesirable consequences. Dombeck and Brody (1995) have commented, for example, that, although all learning processes begin with observation, a person's capacity to observe is reduced during states of high anxiety. As a direct consequence, that person's capacity to learn is reduced. Friedlander et al. (1986) found, for example, the supervisees' performance was inversely related to their anxiety levels. And among the negative effects of anxiety that Schauer et al. (1985) found in their literature review was

that it activates speech productivity while disrupting its flow; reduces the accuracy of the therapist's perception of the client; decreases the therapist's recall of words and feelings expressed in a session; and elicits overelaboration or argumentative behavior from the therapist.

Eysenck and Calvo (1992) argued for what they referred to as "processing efficiency theory." They suggested that anxiety reduces the storage and processing capacity of the person's working memory system available for a concurrent task. However, the person then increases his or her on-task effort and activities designed to improve performance. A crucial distinction lies in the theory between *performance effectiveness* and *processing efficiency*. This model (and the data Eysenck and Calvo summarized to support it) suggests that anxiety characteristically impairs efficiency more than it does effectiveness.

Unfortunately, a focus on these and other consequences of anxiety could lead to the erroneous conclusion that supervisees' anxiety is always to be avoided or minimized. In fact, Rioch (in Rioch et al., 1976) is among those who have observed that, within limits, the more anxiety counselors are able to allow themselves, the more they will learn: anxiety is not always something to ward off. As counselors or therapists, we know that much of the time it is unhelpful to rush in with attempts to diminish a client's anxiety. The same rule pertains to supervisors' response to supervisee anxiety.

Despite questions Neiss (1988) recently raised about it, Yerkes and Dodson's (1908) inverted-U hypothesis remains a useful way to think of anxiety. This is one of psychology's most famous hypotheses. It is that anxiety is an arousal state that, in moderate amounts, serves to motivate the individual and to facilitate task performance; performance suffers, however, when the individual experiences either *too little* and *too much* anxiety: too little and one lacks sufficient motivation to perform; too much and one is debilitated. It is not difficult then to extrapolate this general law of human learning to supervision and conclude that there is an optimal level of anxiety for supervisees to experience.

If there is an optimal level of anxiety that it is necessary for supervisees to experience, then supervisors logically have the simultaneous goals of (1) helping to keep their supervisees from engaging in anxiety-avoidant behaviors and also of (2) helping to keep supervisee anxiety in bounds so that it works in the service of performance. Kell and Burow (1970) noted, for example, that they worked "not only to facilitate . . . an awareness of the anxiety associated with the seriousness of learning, but also to leaven and help control the anxious experience" (p. 184).

Supervision Styles and Supervisee Anxiety. But if supervisors have particular responsibility for helping to leaven and control the supervisee's anxiety, they should understand the ways in which their relationship may affect that anxiety. For example, Ellis et al. (1996) suggest that Zajonc's (1980) social facilitation theory is useful in understanding how the evaluative aspects of supervision may activate supervisee anxiety. This theory is that the arousal caused by having others present—in fact or in imagination—will enhance the performance of easy tasks and diminish the performance of more difficult tasks. Therefore, "the presence of the evaluative supervisor increases the supervisee's drive and anxiety, which activates well-learned responses (e.g., typical defense mechanisms) and inhibits the supervisee to engage in more complex learning tasks involved in supervision (e.g., examining the supervisee's reactions to the client)" (Ellis et al., 1996, p. 3).

But this process is relatively normative. There are particular supervisory styles that are likely to heighten supervisee anxiety beyond what might be expected as typical. Therefore, it is useful to consider the types of objectionable supervisory styles that Rosenblatt and Mayer (1975) identified from written narrative accounts by social work students. Three of those styles seemed to increase supervisee anxiety.

They called the first of those styles *amorphous supervision.* Supervisors using this style offer too little clarity about what they expect. They also offer the supervisee too little structure and/or guidance.

Anxiety is a natural response for anyone in a new situation. So, too, with supervisees entering a new supervisory relationship. Much of this anxiety will dissipate as supervisees orient to their new environment. Anxiety will be maintained, however, to the extent that supervisors fail to provide clear structure and expectations. This is the characteristic of amorphous supervision.

It is important to remember also that supervisees' experience level moderates the amount of structure they perceive themselves to need. That is, beginning supervisees perceive themselves as needing more structure than those who are more advanced (e.g., Heppner & Roehkle, 1984; McNeill, Stoltenberg, & Pierce, 1985; Reising & Daniels, 1983; Stoltenberg, Pierce, & McNeill, 1987; Tracey, Ellickson, & Sherry, 1989; Wiley & Ray, 1986). But across all levels of supervisee experience, ambiguity in the supervisory context apparently is a root cause of supervisee anxiety.

There are many ways the supervisor–supervisee relationship itself can be ambiguous. But *other* aspects of the training situation can be ambiguous as well. Hollingsworth and Witten (1983) suggested, for example, that a source of anxiety for some supervisees concerns their uncertainty about the roles they are expected to fill in their field placements (see, e.g., our discussion earlier in this chapter of the effects of role ambiguity). Yet another source of anxiety for supervisees is ambiguity about the criteria and procedures by which they will be evaluated.

Because these last two types of ambiguity can be anticipated by supervisors, it is easy enough for them to take steps to reduce it. For example, supervisors can orient supervisees to agency policies and role expectations prior to establishing them in their field placements. If the source of ambiguity should reside in misunderstandings or lack of clear communication between the training institution and the agency, dialogue between the two units should be initiated (see Chapter 10). As we discuss in Chapter 8, supervisors have an obligation to establish clearly the procedures and criteria of evaluation at the very outset of the supervision experience. Earlier in this chapter, we also mentioned role induction as a means to reduce ambiguity.

Rosenblatt and Mayer (1975) called their second objectionable style *unsupportive supervision*. Supervisors employing this style generally are cold, aloof, and perhaps even hostile. This is consistent with way supervisees in Hutt, Scott, and King's (1983) phenomenological study described "negative supervision" they had received.

Hutt et al. (1983) found that in this type of supervision the emotional tone was negative and the supervisee came to expect the supervisor to offer criticism, but no support. This caused supervisees to feel vulnerable and threatened. As a self-protective stance, they then would censor what they told the supervisor and would manage their anxiety through various forms of resistance.

The supervisor, in turn, would take no responsibility for his or her role in the impasse that occurred in the supervisory relationship. If the supervisee attempted to resolve the impasse by expressing negative reactions to the supervisor, the supervisee was met with a defensive or impassive reaction.

The following account by a respondent in the Rosenblatt and Mayer (1975) study is illustrative of these relationship dynamics:

> *After the first couple of sessions [my supervisor] began to grow increasingly critical and unsupportive, and as a result I became more anxious and insecure. . . . When we tried to talk about my clients, I would be so anxious that I couldn't think and would end up staring miserably at her, trying not to cry. My self-esteem hit rock bottom. I remember becoming almost sick with anxiety before a supervisory session because I was so sensitive to her criticism.*   (p. 186)

It is true, as Blocher (1983) asserted, that it is not possible to make supervision "idiot proof or bastard resistant" (p. 30). But perhaps, as formal training in supervision becomes more widespread, supervisors in general will become more sensitized to how they might function in more supportive ways with supervisees.

Kell, Morse, and Grater (undated) discussed their own supportive stance for supervisees, particularly new ones, in order to keep their anxiety from unduly hindering their work.

Perhaps above all, with every supervisee we attempt to give a great deal of permission, perhaps even our expectation that he [sic] will make errors. We hope to reduce for them the threat of failure and the need to strive for success, allowing him to admit that he knows little and thus might learn a lot.

Rosenblatt and Mayer called their third objectionable style *"therapeutic" supervision*. In this form of supervision, shortcomings in the supervisee's work are attributed to some deficiencies in his or her personality, which the supervisor then attempts to address in detail within supervision. Significantly, supervisees who were surveyed typically had no quarrel with being told that their work somehow was inappropriate. What they did find objectionable was, first, the causal attribution given by the supervisor (i.e., that the supervisee's behavior was a function of some personal deficit) and, second, the supervisor's attempt then to remedy it in supervision. Liddle (1988) seems to have been speaking of this type of supervision when he alluded to the supervisor who acts as a "deficit detective."

An example recounted by a student illustrates this style of supervision.

> *My supervisor wanted to know why I didn't get into a discussion of sexual matters more rapidly with my clients in cases where it would be appropriate. . . . My supervisor insisted that I held back because I did not want to reawaken memories of the loss of such activities due to my husband's recent death. Later on, whatever criticism she had of my work with clients, she managed to attribute to my personal circumstances. I did not object to her criticism of my performance, only to the reasons she gave for it. When I disagreed with her reasons, she said that I could not be objective—that I was being defensive. I still felt she was wrong, but how could I argue with her?*   (Rosenblatt & Mayer, 1975, p. 186)

A second such example is provided in an anecdote Goin and Kline (1976) took from their study of supervisor–supervisee interactions.

> *[The supervisee] was having difficulty understanding a case and saw the patient's dynamics differently than the supervisor did. The supervisor attributed these difficulties to the resident's psychological make up, saying "You keep responding to the*

patient as if he is anxious. What you don't hear is his anger. I realize you have a problem handling your own anger, so that must be interfering with your appreciation for what is going on." (p. 431)

Rosenblatt and Mayer (1975) concluded that students who receive this "therapeutic" form of supervision were more distraught than those who received any of the other objectionable types of supervision they had identified. In part this may be because, no matter how obviously wrong the supervisor's construction of the situation may seem to the supervisee, the supervisee may be left with the secret worry that the supervisor may be correct. To compound the matter, the problems being identified in this type of supervision typically are difficult to remedy and also tend to be central to the supervisee's sense of personal competence or adequacy.

Supervisees who attempt to challenge their supervisor's wrong attributions may find themselves in a double bind: Their objections may be construed as resistance, which itself then confirms the supervisor's belief about the supervisee. Remember, too, that one necessary condition for a double bind is that the recipient cannot easily exit the relationship in which it is occurring (Sluzki, Beavin, Tarnopolski, & Vernon, 1967). This condition characterizes supervision, which is hierarchical and the supervisee cannot readily leave it.

We conclude this section by speculating that the tendency to make such attributions is not limited to one particular type of supervisor. In fact, there are data to suggest that there may be reliable attributional differences between supervisors and supervisees. Dixon and Kruczek (1989), for example, found that supervisees were more likely to explain their behaviors with clients in terms of external, situational variables, whereas supervisors were more likely to perceive those same behaviors as being more within the supervisees' control and to reflect stable, dispositional aspects of the supervisees. But regardless of supervisors' accuracy in these instances, they should remain sensitive to the likelihood that these attributions, when offered as the primary supervision intervention, will most assuredly heighten supervisee anxiety, perhaps to a debilitating level.

All supervisees approach supervision expecting to be judged and, therefore, inevitably are anxious to some degree. The experience of positive supervision, however, is such that the supervisee's anxiety does not rise to such a level that the work of supervision is hindered. This occurs because the supervisor is able to offer an optimal balance between *support* (including structure) and *challenge* (see Blocher, 1979) [reflected also in the findings of Worthington and Roehlke (1979), whose factor analysis of supervisors' behaviors yielded two factors that they labeled *support* and *evaluation,* which certainly is a form of challenge].

We already have discussed the problems of the supervisor offering too little support. What we did not mention is that too *much* support robs the supervisee of initiative and the opportunity to try new behaviors. By the same token, the level of supervisor challenge needs to be optimized: too little and the supervisee will not have the external push to try new behaviors; too much and the supervisee may become overwhelmed and incapacitated.

In positive supervision, then, the supervisee is given permission to make mistakes and then not to experience them as failure. The supervisor is respectful of the supervisee, including the need for autonomy. The supervisor self-discloses to the supervisee and this, in turn, encourages appropriate self-disclosure from the supervisee. Evaluation of the supervisee occurs as a shared process between supervisor and supervisee.

Supervisees' Anxiety-avoidant Maneuvers: Impression Management.   In the preceding section we addressed supervisor styles that might heighten supervisee anxiety. We now turn to a closely related matter: how supervisees' anxiety may then affect their relationship with the supervisor.

One source of anxiety for virtually all of us arises from our concerns about how others are perceiving us (e.g., Schlenker & Leary, 1982). That is, we want to convey a certain impression, but worry about how well we are accomplishing it. Supervisees, however, deal not only with these "ordinary" concerns about creating a desired social impression, but also with the added concern of creating the impressions necessary to earn them satisfactory evaluations from their supervisors.

Social psychologists have discussed strategies people use to cope with these concerns as *impression management* (or *strategic self-presentation*). This is the person's attempt to project a certain image through physical appearance, overt behaviors, verbal descriptions of attributes and behaviors, and selective presentation of data about self and work. It is possible to use the perspective of the theater and think of *any* person's social behavior as performances that are being given to create a desired effect on others.

A person's motives for doing this include those of wanting (1) to maximize expected rewards while minimizing expected punishments (e.g., Schlenker, 1980), (2) to enhance self-esteem (e.g., Rosenberg, 1979), and (3) to promote a desired identity (e.g., Goffman, 1959; Schlenker, 1980). For supervisees, all these purposes are important.

Based on their review of the literature, Leary and Kowalski (1990) suggested that one aspect of impression management is *impression motivation*. A person's motivation to manage impressions can be influenced by a number of factors. One is the importance to the person of a particular goal (e.g., a supervisee is likely to want to present himself or herself as having the characteristics and skills that the supervisor will believe necessary to be an effective mental health professional). Another factor is whether the person is to be evaluated in some manner—a condition that *absolutely* applies to supervisees—and therefore would want to project a particular image. In a related vein, Leary and Kowalski cited studies showing that a person is more likely to want to impression manage with teachers and employers than with friends.

Still another factor in impression motivation is the person's desire to resolve discrepancies between his or her desired versus current image. People will use impression management strategies to gain respect and admiration after their social image has been damaged. For example, when individuals believe they have failed at an important task, they tend to behave in a more self-enhancing

manner in order to repair their image (Schlenker, 1980).

They also are likely to become more self-enhancing about their task performance after they have received negative evaluations of their work. Interestingly, though, only a couple of studies so far have examined directly supervisees' self-presentation motivations and impression construction strategies (Friedlander & Schwartz, 1985; Ward, Friedlander, Schoen, & Klein, 1985). It is important to note, however, that a number of supervision studies that have not been framed as ones in impression management actually have implications for that conception of supervisee behavior. Ladany, Hill, Corbett, and Nutt's (1996) recent study of issues that supervisees choose not to disclose to their supervisors is an excellent case in point.

The particular supervision modality the supervisor uses can be one factor that affects supervisee anxiety and therefore stimulates impression management strategies. Betcher and Zinberg (1988), for example, expressed concern that the use of audio or video recordings in supervision may, at least at times, constitute unwarranted invasions of the supervisee's privacy and therefore pose threats to his or her sense of safety. Although many supervisors believe those concerns are unwarranted, it certainly is true that to be observed, whether by audio or video recordings or by direct observation, stimulates anxiety and triggers coping mechanisms, especially among newer supervisees. As a consequence, supervisees often develop self-protective strategies.

Supervisees employ some of these strategies so often that one colleague (D. Stevens, personal communication, May 27, 1995) has suggested, somewhat tongue in cheek, that supervisees move through several stages in their use of tape recordings. These range from "I know that I am supposed to tape my sessions, but I am certain the client is not going to allow me to tape—it is just going to be too frightening for him or her" to "Well, my client has allowed me to tape, but I am worried about the effects this is having on the counseling process" to "I am sorry I don't have a tape today for our supervision session: The tape recorder malfunctioned."

Ronnestad and Skovholt (1993) came to similar conclusions, noting that "the anxious student may tend to discuss in supervision only clients who show good progress, choose themes in which he or she is functioning well, or choose a mode of presenting data that allows full control over what the supervisor learns" (p. 398). They suggest that the supervisor may therefore, in the beginning, allow the student to select or even distort data until some of that anxiety dissipates.

In summary, then, supervisors can profit from an awareness of impression management strategies and from knowing that supervisees are most likely to use them when they are feeling anxious about how they are being perceived (e.g., normatively, this occurs early in the supervisory relationship, during periods of evaluation, and after the supervisee has received critical feedback). To understand behaviors that the supervisor otherwise might label defensive or even manipulative as impression management can open up new response possibilities for the supervisor.

Supervisees' Anxiety-avoidant Maneuvers: Games.   Impression management is one supervisee response to anxiety. Impression management, though, suggests only one-sided behaviors. In other situations, where the supervisee's behaviors are matched by the supervisors' complementary behaviors, it is useful to think in terms of the psychological games that Berne (1964) first described.

Consider this example from McWilliams (1994):

> Therapists in training who approach supervision in a flood of self-criticism are often using a masochistic strategy to hedge their bets: If my supervisor thinks I made a major error with my client, I've already shown that I'm aware of it and have been punished enough; if not, I get reassured and exonerated. (p. 263)

If the supervisor does respond to this invitation to behave in a sympathetic manner and therefore mutes the criticism she or he otherwise would offer, this would seem to illustrate a classic inter-

personal game (and one that is observed frequently in supervision). A game, then, is understood as a series of transactions that are to some extent stylized and that emanate from interlocking or complementary roles the participants adopt. This assumes that each participant understands and accepts these roles with greater or lesser degrees of conscious awareness.

In fact, the concept of games is that supervisors and supervisees collude at some unspoken level to engage in behaviors that will minimize the anxiety experienced by either or both of them. It is inappropriate (and counterproductive), therefore, for the supervisor to scold or blame the supervisee for games in which both of them have participated. On the other hand, to confront *invitations* to engage in these games is warranted. For example, in the McWilliams (1994) example given, the supervisor might point out to the supervisee what seems his or her masochistic strategy (being careful, of course, not to play a complementary role by coming across as angry or otherwise "sadistic" toward the supervisee).

Kadushin (1968) identified a series of such games that occur in supervision. Many are summarized in Table 4.1.

We have found that most therapists and supervisors readily recognize one or more or these interaction patterns as something they have experienced themselves at one time or another as supervisor, supervisee, or both. We acknowledge also that, whereas anxiety management is basic to most of these games, these maneuvers also allow the supervisor and supervisee to meet other needs as well.

Note, too, that we are not offering here our suggestions for specific supervisor strategies to avoid or end these games. We believe that for the supervisor simply to have an awareness of these frequent interaction patterns can be sufficient to suggest alternative responses.

Supervisee Transference

Supervisee Need to Idealize Supervisor.   Supervisees' very early life experiences can affect their

TABLE 4.1   Summary of Selected Supervision "Games"

	PARTICIPANT ROLES	
Game	*Supervisee*	*Supervisor*
"Be nice to me because I am nice you."	Flatters the supervisor ("You are the best supervisor I've had"; "You're so perceptive.")	Colludes with the supervisee, accepting the praise; supervisor then finds it difficult to hold supervisee to legitimate demands.
"Evaluation is not for friends."	Takes coffee breaks with the supervisor, invites him or her to lunch, walks him or her to parking lot, and so on.	Begins redefining the relationship as friendship; finds it increasingly hard to monitor and impose limits on the "friend."
"If you knew Dostoyevsky like I know Dostoyevsky."	In discussing clients, makes allusions to how they remind him or her of certain literary characters—which the supervisor, of course, *must* remember; the content varies and often may focus on the latest therapy theorists (especially when the supervisor may not have read their work).	Colludes in the conspiracy not to expose ignorance about the subject matter; in the process, teacher–learner roles are covertly changed; power disparities are reduced.
"I have a little list."	Comes prepared with a list of questions (often carefully chosen to correspond to areas of the supervisor's greatest interest and/or expertise); each is presented, in turn, for the supervisor's response.	Given this opportunity to help the supervisee by demonstrating knowledge, supervisor responds to each question with a short lecture.
"Little old me."	Presents self as dependent on the supervisor's detailed prescription for how to proceed ("What would you do next?"; "Then what would you say?").	Responds as the capable parent; than can take pleasure in vicariously doing therapy with the client.
"I did like you told me."	Often—though not always—the outcome of the "little old me"; scrupulously follows supervisor's suggestions; then comes to report that it didn't work (confirms to self that supervisor can be of no help).	Responds defensively, but with feelings of inadequacy; forced to adopt a one-down position in relationship to the supervisee.
"It's all so confusing."	In the face of advice from the supervisor, mentions that in similar situations former supervisor(s) gave different advice; consequently, she or he is confused. (Note: When the supervisee has more than one supervisor at one time, each also can be played off the other this way.)	Responds by defending his or her approach against the competitor; finds sense of authority with the supervisee shaken.
"Heading them off at the pass."	Anticipating criticism of his or her work, opens the supervision by freely admitting mistakes, self-flagellating to excess.	Responds with reassurance and praise for what the supervisee did well; finds self uneasy about focusing on mistakes the supervisee already has pointed out and is so miserable about.
"Treat me; don't beat me."	Prefers to expose self rather than his or her work; therefore, raises personal problems that are affecting his or her work and invites the supervisor's help in solving them.	Trained initially as a therapist and still being motivated to help people in pain, supervisor crosses boundary between supervision and therapy; nature and extent of demands on supervisee change.
"I wonder why you really said that."	Disagrees with supervisor and expresses it; later, accepts the premise of the supervisor's response (that the disagreement was prompted by some underlying—hence, unknown—personal problem in his or her self).	Redefines honest disagreement (with the necessity that he or she defend position) as supervisee's psychological resistance—prompted by motives and needs outside his or her awareness.
"One good question deserves another."	Asks a question of the supervisor; later, does not challenge or confront the supervisor's response.	Responds to the supervisee's question with another (i.e., what he or she thinks about it). (Note: A further ploy in case a satisfactory answer is not forthcoming is the suggest they think about it and discuss it next session.)

*Material in this table was adapted from Kadushin (1968).

attachment styles (see, e.g., Watkins, 1995a), stages of separation–individuation (e.g., Watkins, 1990), and other ways of responding to relationships. It should be no surprise that these factors also may influence the supervisor–supervisee relationship.

Our perceptions of others and expectations we have of them are based on our own individual needs and interpersonal histories. It is common, for example, to meet someone and find ourselves immediately liking or disliking him or her on the basis of some similarity to another person we have known. Sullivan (1953) called this common phenomenon "parataxic distortion."

We expect that our clients might maintain distortions of this type in their relationships with us. We may be less likely, though, to remain sensitive to such distortions in supervisor–supervisee relationships (see, e.g., Fiscalini, 1985, for one discussion of those processes). Lane's (1986) psychodynamic discussion of supervision illustrates how the supervisee's life history can intrude on and affect the supervisory relationship:

> *The supervisor becomes the father who died or who left them or the mother who was never there for them, and is accused of taking something from them. This gives them the right of refusal to take in anything from the supervisor parent . . . the supervisor is made to feel as helpless and inadequate as the supervisee felt as a child.* (p. 71).

Allphin (1987), too, invokes a parenting metaphor, noting that supervisees often need to idealize their supervisors. To do so can fill an important need, especially at the very early stages of training. Specifically, it can be important for neophytes to have a relationship with someone who seems more competent and therefore capable of guiding their learning and development, someone to serve as a model. Supervisors should be aware of this supervisee need. Otherwise, it is easy to err in either of two ways in responding to it.

The first error is simply to lean into the good feelings that come with receiving adulation and to do nothing to dissipate it. This stance, though, can not only blind the supervisor to his or her mistakes, but it also disempowers the supervisee. The

second type of error is for the supervisor *not* to allow the supervisee to use him or her as a model to idealize. In this stance ("the two of us are, after all, just colleagues working together toward a common goal"), the supervisor is too quick to be self-disclosing and even self-effacing about his or her failures and problem areas.

In short, then, the supervisor should steer a careful course in responding to the supervisee's need to idealize. The need should be respected, but not encouraged to the point that the supervisee is cheated of the chance to develop his or her own sense of competence.

Alonso and Rutan (1988) commented that health care professionals often are in denial about their own neediness and helplessness, especially as they begin their careers. To the extent this is true, one implication for supervisors is that the supervisee should be helped to acknowledge this aspect of themselves. To accomplish this, the supervisor should be prepared neither to avoid, or worse, to shrink from any manifestations of the supervisee's neediness. As Kaslow and Deering (1994) point out, supervision progresses best when the supervisor provides a secure "holding environment" in which the supervisee can regress and progress as he or she needs.

Anxiety Reduction through Metaphor

We have already mentioned that supportive, appropriately structured supervisory styles can be useful in moderating supervisee anxiety. We also mentioned that minimizing supervisor and supervisee role conflicts can help in this regard. In addition to these more general steps, we would like to mention one very specific supervisory intervention to address supervisee anxiety, that is, the use of metaphors that capture the essence of the supervisee's situation (Barnat, 1977).

Barnat gives some that supervisors could employ. For example, "If you're acting, it will be dust and ashes in your mouth," or "You're a surfer on a board and the client is the wave" (p. 307).

One metaphor Barnat related occurred in response to an intake session he conducted with a female client in which there was mutual magnetism and that concluded with her asking him for his phone number; he found himself flustered and gave her the number. The event was discussed during supervision, along with the issues of control (or lack thereof) implicit in someone having your number. Then, when the supervisor asked, metaphorically, whether it would be possible to get his number back, Barnat reported experiencing this as a statement that he hadn't lost his adequacy in this situation; he only thought he had.

Of course, supervisors vary in their ability to generate metaphors spontaneously. Supervisors who find this process to be relatively easy will already have discovered metaphors' usefulness in therapy. For them to use metaphors in supervision will be an easy, natural extension of an existing skill. Other supervisors, though, should take heart from Linehan's (personal communication, October 1995) assertion that a metaphor need not be generated spontaneously. In her treatment program (Linehan, 1993), members of her treatment team all share metaphors that they use and, through this process, they have generated a large number that each member can employ. If the client has not heard that metaphor before, she or he will perceive it as spontaneous. The same principle likely is true in supervision. Supervisors, then, might find utility in sharing with one another those metaphors that they have found useful.

SECTION FOUR: SUPERVISOR AS A SOURCE OF VARIANCE IN THE SUPERVISORY RELATIONSHIP

In this section, we turn to the supervisor and some of the ways he or she influences the supervisory relationship. In particular, we focus on countertransference reactions the supervisor might have to the supervisee.

Supervisor Countertransference

By virtue of their role, supervisors have particular responsibilities to be sensitive to their super-visees' needs and to have a repertoire of effective responses. But simply because they are human, supervisors will experience some degree of distortion and bias in their responses to at least some of their supervisees. As Gizynski (1978) has noted, belief in supervisors' unwavering self-awareness is "a comforting but unwarranted assumption" (p. 203).

In their work with supervisees, supervisors are prone to the same types of blind spots and lapses of objectivity that therapists experience in their work with clients. It is important, then, to consider the matter of supervisor countertransference. The literature on this topic is relatively small, and empirical investigations of it are virtually nonexistent. Nevertheless, there seems general recognition that the phenomenon is important. For example, Ekstein and Wallerstein (1972) noted that the process of mutual evaluation and reevaluation that occurs in supervision does not occur on strictly an intellectual level. It will "be accompanied by interactions on every level, which would be described, were they to occur in a therapeutic context, as transference reactions of the one and countertransference reactions of the other" (p. 284).

Lower (1972) observed that "the learning alliance . . . is threatened continuously by resistances that derive from immature, neurotic, conflict-laden elements of the personality" (p. 70). Teitelbaum (1990) suggested the term "supertransference" to characterize the reactions of the supervisor to the supervisee and to the supervisee's treatment. However, because mental health professionals are already familiar with the concepts of transference and countertransference, it probably is better simply to retain those familiar terms in discussing supervision.

To identify their own countertransference reactions and, then, the possible sources is difficult enough for therapists. But this is more difficult for supervisors. Once a supervisor has recognized that his or her response to the supervisee might, indeed, be tainted by countertransference, he or she then needs to determine the extent to which this has its origins in the supervisory dyad alone versus in the client–therapist dyad. A particular characteristic of supervision is that what is occurring between the supervisor and supervisee may have "percolated up" from the client–therapist interactions as a parallel process. This adds an element not present in therapy, in which the therapist is reacting only to the dynamics present in the therapy room.

As an illustrative example of this point, consider the supervisor who experienced irritation in the face of the supervisee's self-presentation of confusion and indecision. Eventually, they both come to recognize that the supervisee was mirroring the confusion and indecision of the client. Although the supervisor's reaction was to the supervisee's behavior, its root cause was the client. This and similar examples make it clear why it is important that supervisors have available to them a colleague who can serve as a supervisor or consultant on at least an occasional basis.

Lower (1972) suggested that supervisors' countertransference might be categorized into four areas: (1) general personality characteristics, (2) inner conflicts reactivated by the supervision situation, (3) countertransference reactions to the individual supervisee, and (4) countertransference reactions to the supervisee's transference. These categories provide a useful way to examine the origins of supervisor countertransference.

Categories of Supervisor Countertransference

General Personality Characteristics. This type of countertransference stems from the supervisor's own characterological defenses, which then affect the supervisory relationship. Lower noted that one of the most common manifestations of this occurs in the supervisor's wish to foster the supervisee's identification with the supervisor at the expense of the therapeutic process; perhaps this extends even to having fantasies of developing a following among the supervisees. The result is to encourage the supervisee to be passive and dependent.

Another frequent manifestation of this occurs with the supervisor's tendency to overidentify with the student. Lower (1972) discussed this as motivated by the supervisor's wish to protect him-

self or herself in the supervisee. As a consequence, the supervisor becomes indulgent of the supervisee and does not offer clear feedback, particularly about problems the supervisee may be having.

Gizynski (1978) seemed to be speaking of the same phenomenon when he discussed the supervisor who is "personally possessive" of the supervisee. She saw it as especially manifesting itself in the supervisor's advocacy for the supervisee in relationship to other members of the agency or training program. The message—overt or covert—is that the supervisor is the one who really understands the supervisee. The supervisee therefore can discount feedback from other faculty or staff because they are unduly critical and/or in error. "Students become a narcissistic extension of the supervisor; loyalty issues tend to override expectations of clinical performance and the supervisor loses his [or her] objectivity in evaluation and freedom in teaching" (p. 206).

Inner Conflicts Reactivated by the Supervisory Situation. The second of Lower's category focused on supervisors' inner conflicts that are triggered by the supervision. Although some of the supervisor behaviors might resemble those of the first category, they have different origins.

Lower, who wrote from a psychoanalytic perspective, argued that many of the conflicts aroused in the supervisor are Oedipal in nature. This is so because the supervisor's role is essentially that of a parent; moreover, the many latent triangles among the supervisor, supervisee, client, agency, colleagues, and so on, can also reactivate Oedipal issues. There are many ways such reactivated conflicts can intrude in supervision. For example, the supervisor may attempt to be the good parent and attempt to offer more of a favorable supervisory environment than that which was offered the supervisor. Or, alternatively, the supervisor (parent) may behave sadistically to defend against an anticipated challenge from the supervisee (child).

The following list of other supervisor responses suggests the myriad ways supervisors' own inner conflicts can be manifest in supervision. Lower (1972) suggested that they may

1. Play favorites with the supervisees
2. Covertly encourage the supervisee to act out his or her own conflicts with other colleagues or encourage rebellion against the institution
3. Compete with other supervisors for supervisees' affection
4. Harbor exaggerated expectations of the supervisee that, when unmet or rejected by the supervisee, lead to frustration and perhaps even aggression
5. Have narcissistic needs to be admired that divert the supervisor from the appropriate tasks of supervision

Reactions to the Individual Supervisee   The types of supervisor countertransference discussed so far have been triggered by the supervisor's response to broader aspects of the supervisory situation. But there also may be aspects of the individual supervisee that stimulate supervisor countertransference. For example, if the supervisee seems brighter (or more socially successful, or financially better off, etc.) than the supervisor, this may elicit from the supervisor competitive impulses to engage in one-up behaviors. Alternatively, in the face of these same supervisee attributes, the supervisor might feel compelled to take a one-down position in relation to the apparently stronger supervisee. The supervisee who appears too normal or too healthy may be discounted as being shallow and unable to respond to the needs of clients.

Sexual or Romantic Attraction.   Sexual or romantic attraction is one type of supervisor countertransference reaction to the individual supervisee that merits specific mention. At the same time, though, we need to acknowledge that countertransference is not the only possible source of such attraction. Goodyear and Sinnett (1984) observed that one aspect of interpersonal attractiveness is shared interests and values, a condition that prevails among people within any particular occupation. Therefore, it is not surprising that supervisors and supervisees occasionally may find themselves drawn to one another.

But regardless of the source of the attraction and whether it fits the strict definition of transference and countertransference, it is important that the supervisor and supervisee not act on it while they are in their supervisory relationship. Whether the supervisor chooses to address his or her attraction directly with the supervisee, the supervisor should not attempt to deny it to himself or herself. Attending to it may be useful in understanding the supervisee or perhaps even the client.

Hall (1988b) discussed the problems posed by preexisting supervisor–supervisee sociosexual relationships (e.g., in spousal relationships). The transference and countertransference problems these supervision relationships pose are sufficient reason to avoid them. To illustrate, she offered a vignette in which a woman was supervising her husband. Hall noted two transference-related issues likely to emerge with this particular relationship. First, the wife, because of her relationship with her husband, might be inclined to be relaxed in her monitoring of his work, assuming he was doing a competent job, whether or not this was true. Second, the wife very likely would be reluctant to acknowledge or confront transference and countertransference issues in her husband's work; certainly the closeness of these issues to their *own* relationship would have some effect on the objectivity with which they were handled. Consider, for example, the situation in which the husband is experiencing feelings of attraction toward a client who also has attained life successes of which the wife–supervisor feels some envy.

Cultural Countertransference.   Another type of supervisor countertransference may reside in cultural differences between the supervisor and supervisee. Vargas (1989) differentiated between this type of countertransference and prejudice: "Whereas prejudice refers to an opinion for or against someone or something without adequate basis, the sources and consequences of cultural countertransference are far more insidious and are often repressed by the therapist" (p. 3). Although Vargas's discussion centered on *therapists'* countertransference reactions, we will extrapolate his ideas to a consideration of possible sources of supervisors' cultural countertransference.

Vargas (1989) noted that cultural countertransference reactions can originate in either of two ways. The first and more common instance occurs when the supervisor has limited experience with members of the supervisee's ethnic minority group. Vargas argues that a frequent supervisor response in this situation would engage in overgeneralization. For example, the supervisor might expect all Asian-American supervisees to find it difficult to engage in directly confrontive behaviors. Vargas maintains that this typically is a relatively easy consequence of cultural countertransference with which to deal. There are less direct consequences that are more problematic. For example, mental health professionals may deal with their own unresolved issues toward a particular minority group, including, perhaps, possible guilt feelings about societal oppression that group has experienced, by romanticizing that group. This provides the supervisor a mechanism to reduce possible ethnic tensions with the supervisee. Its manifestations in supervision might include perceiving most of the supervisee's behavior through the lens of culture, blinding the supervisor to supervisee issues and problems that actually are individual to the supervisee and that should be addressed in supervision.

The second source of cultural countertransference Vargas (1989) discussed stems from potent feelings associated with *non*minority people in the supervisor's past with whom the current minority supervisee is associated. Whereas the example Vargas gave illustrated a therapist's countertransference, it does suggest how similar dynamics might occur between supervisor and supervisee of different ethnic groups. He discussed the hypothetical situation of a white male therapist having

intensely negative feelings about the raw expression of anger as a result of his own unresolved experiences regarding his own anger at this father who left him and his mother when the therapist was very young. When confronted with a belligerent and sadistically taunting Black adolescent, the therapist experiences intense disgust and hostility toward the patient which the therapist considers as disturbing evidence of his prejudice. In reality, it is not prejudice in the true sense of the word, but rather a type of cultural countertransference misconstrued as prejudice.   (p. 4)

Countertransference to the Supervisee's Transference. Perhaps supervisors are at the greatest risk of experiencing countertransference reactions when the supervisee manifests transference responses to the supervisor. It is true that Ekstein and Wallerstein (1972) argued that supervisees do not actually experience transference reactions toward the supervisor in the same sense that clients do toward therapists. This is so because, in contrast to therapy, the supervisory relationship does not encourage regression, but instead encourages the supervisee to think independently; also, the supervisor and supervisee are in constant, task-focused dialogue.

Nevertheless, there is little question that supervisees distort their perceptions of the supervisor and that they behave in accordance with those distortions. The supervisor countertransference this elicits may be expressed in numerous ways. Lower (1972) offered an example of one such manifestation.

A resident had been working in psychotherapy with a . . . young woman for about six months when a new supervisor questioned his formulations and treatment goals and suggested that they follow the patient in supervision over a period of time. The resident responded as though the supervisor were intruding on his relationship with the patient and became more and more vague in his presentation of material. In reaction, the supervisor became increasingly active in suggesting what the therapist should pursue with the patient and at last asked to see the patient together with the resident in order to make his own assessment. Only after the supervisor began the interview by asking the patient "Well how are you and Doctor what's-his-name here getting along" did he recognize the Oedipal conflict within both himself and the resident that had interfered with the learning alliance.   (p. 74)

TERMINATING SUPERVISORY RELATIONSHIPS

Relationships have a temporal dimension in that they exist across time. As participants develop a history together, their relationship evolves. Holloway (1995) suggested that this process of relationship development across time is one of reducing uncertainty. That is, as people interact, they learn more about one another and also are able to make more accurate predictions about the behavior, particularly how the other will react to specific messages. Participants in a new relationship initially will rely on what Holloway called the "noninterpersonal" aspects, which include such cues as general social and cultural information. As the relationship develops, there then will be more reliance on the uniquess of the particular individuals involved in the relationship.

Although space constraints precluded us from addressing temporality at greater length, we do want to address one particular manifestation of it in the supervisory relationship. This is the process of termination.

Hoffman (1994) discussed common themes she observed to occur during the termination of supervisory relationships. One is the *experience of doubt,* at least by the supervisor. This is suggested by such questions as "Did I do enough? Did we accomplish anything? Was the supervision effective?" These concerns are complicated by the fact that the termination typically occurs at a point where the supervisory working relationship has stabilized and is working well.

Hoffman (1994) has discussed the importance of a review of goals and progress so that inevitable *disappointments* can be addressed by the supervisor and supervisee. Each party entered the relationship with particular expectations that were met with varying degrees of success. Some supervisory relationships are more satisfying, with fewer residual disappointments, than others. It is important, though, as part of any termination process to review expectations each party had going into it and then the degree to which those expectations were met.

The timing of termination typically will be dictated by the academic or training calendar or perhaps by the fact that the supervisee finally has accrued enough supervision hours to apply for licensure or some other credential. When termina-

tion occurs because of a training calendar, the supervisee typically will be terminating with clients as well. This is an isomorphism that adds complexity to the supervisor–supervisee termination. That complexity is further amplified by the fact that supervisory termination typically coincides with the summative evaluation that we discuss in Chapter 8.

It is important to recognize, though, that supervisees typically will work with a number of supervisors during the course of their training. Therefore, they will experience a series of relationships (versus, in therapy, *a* relationship) and, ultimately, a series of supervision terminations. The valence and intensity of these likely will vary across supervisory experiences.

In therapeutic relationships, termination generally means that the relationship is *over.* For the supervisor and supervisee, however, the relationship typically continues in one form or another. In fact, when some of the professional boundaries are removed, it may even deepen into a lifelong friendship. For example, one colleague had a former supervisor serve as best man at his wedding. This would be evidence of a problem and perhaps even unethical behavior in a terminated counselor–client relationship; however, this is not so in a training context where the ultimate goal is to make the supervisee "one of us."

CONCLUSION

In conclusion, supervisory relationships are affected by a number of interpersonal processes as well as by the professional demands of the training situation. Moreover, they are intimately related to and reverberate with the counseling relationships that are being supervised. This level of complexity likely accounts for much of the appeal of supervision.

Acker also spoke to this complexity when he commented that "the supervisory relationship is a relationship between unequals, the objective of which is equalization. This would seem to be an inherent contradiction, a paradox, and is the challenge in supervision" (Acker, 1992).

CHAPTER 5

Supervision Interventions
Individual Supervision

Having described some of the parameters of supervision and the supervisory relationship in the first four chapters, we are now prepared to consider more specifically the delivery of a variety of supervision interventions. This chapter on individual supervision is only one of three chapters that will look at methods of supervision. It will be followed by chapters on group supervision and live supervision.

Individual supervision is still considered the cornerstone of professional development. Although most supervisees will experience some form of group supervision in their training and some may have an opportunity to work within a live supervision paradigm, virtually all supervisees will experience individual supervision sessions. Whether these individual conferences will produce memories and insights that will linger long into the supervisee's career or will frustrate or perhaps even bore the supervisee has something to do with the supervisor's skill in choosing and using a variety of supervision methods. At this point in the history of the helping professions, there are many different approaches and techniques from which the supervisor can choose to conduct an individual case conference. This chapter will outline these assorted approaches and discuss their advantages and occasional disadvantages.

Although all the supervision interventions described in this chapter are appropriate for individual conferences, many of them also could be applied within a group supervision context. Chapter 6 on group supervision, however, focuses on strategies that rely on group dynamics for their implementation.

Finally, we will make one cautionary remark. When writing a textbook of this sort, each chapter becomes an artificial compartmentalization of one aspect of the whole. The gestalt, so to speak, is violated. Although this cannot be avoided, it seems particularly problematic as we consider methods and techniques of supervision. Of all the many aspects of clinical supervision, methods of supervision are the most vulnerable to abuse. That is, it is possible to conduct supervision using a great many different formats without stepping back to consider the bigger picture—a conceptual base, an evaluation plan, ethical constraints, and so on. We urge the reader, therefore, to view this chapter not in isolation but in the context of other concepts presented in this book.

INITIAL CRITERIA FOR CHOOSING SUPERVISION INTERVENTIONS

A supervisor's initial choice of method is influenced by a number of factors, both rational and irrational. The supervisor might believe that without an audiotape or videotape of counseling or therapy there is no real way to know what has transpired between supervisees and their clients. Or the supervisor might be adamant that self-report is the only form of supervision that provides a glimpse at the supervisee's internal reasoning. The list can, and indeed does, go on. Borders and Leddick (1987) listed six reasons for choosing different supervision methods: "The supervisee's learning goals, the supervisee's experience level and developmental issues, the supervisee's learning style, the supervisor's goals for the supervisee, the supervisor's theoretical orientation, and the supervisor's own learning goals for the supervisory experience" (p. 28).

Chapter 3 addressed many of the issues of individual differences among supervisees, including developmental level and learning style. Authors have often implied that developmental constraints and learning style dictate the amount of structure that is called for in working with specific supervisees. This chapter will offer some thoughts about the issue of structure in supervision. Beyond and in addition to such considerations are the supervisee's goals and the supervisor's goals for the process and outcome of supervision.

Supervision is best placed between training and consultation. In other words, the supervisee should come to supervision with some ability to articulate learning goals based on initial experiences in training, but cannot be expected to function autonomously with only occasional needs for consultation. Supervision methods, therefore, will need to take into account the supervisee's stated goals and known supervision needs, as well as how far down the training–supervision–consultation axis the supervisee has traveled. By and large, however, supervision methods will reflect the supervisor's vision of supervision more than the supervisee's, with the exception perhaps of the more advanced supervisee. The issue of vision, therefore, deserves attention before describing unique supervision modalities.

By supervisor vision we mean the convictions held by the supervisor about how supervisees become competent practitioners. Whether this vision is derived from the professional literature, personal experience, or some other cluster of factors is irrelevant to our discussion. Regardless of its origin or validity, the supervisor's vision will inspire the process of supervision. The supervisor may or may not be aware of having a vision of supervision, but the vision will influence greatly the supervisor's selection of models and the methods that derive from them.

As described earlier in Chapter 2, supervision has grown significantly in terms of the options available to the supervisor. While increased attention has been given in the recent past to highly active forms of supervision (e.g., live supervision), there is a new emergence of authors calling for supervision methods that will increase supervisees' thoughtfulness and ability to reflect on their work as they increase in skill (Dubin, 1991; Glickauf-Hughes & Campbell, 1991; Neufeldt, in press; Overholser, 1991; Skovholt & Ronnestad, 1992; Yerushalmi, 1992). Neufeldt (in press) pointed out that the supervisor may be in the position of deliberately ignoring such empirical findings as that which indicated that novice trainees prefer structured supervision interventions in order to encourage reflectivity in the supervisee. But if the supervisee is not only a novice but concrete in conceptual style, some structured intervention may be necessary to usher the supervisee into a process that may lead to reflectivity. Methods and techniques, therefore, must be malleable and conducive to reaching a variety of supervision goals. Technical eclecticism may be as important to supervisors as it has been perceived to be for therapists. Our point is that within the supervisor's vision there may be a variety of methods from which to choose. The supervisor's vision need not be compromised, but creative alternatives may be needed to accomplish immediate goals as well as goals that are more long range.

Finally and most specifically, an additional aid for the supervisor in determining what method to use in a given situation is to pinpoint the immediate function of supervision. There are three general functions of supervision interventions (Borders, Bernard, Dye, Fong, Henderson, & Nance, 1991): (1) assessing the learning needs of the supervisee; (2) changing, shaping, or supporting the supervisee's behavior; and (3) evaluating the performance of the supervisee. Although the majority of supervision falls within the second function, supervisors are continually reassessing their supervisee's learning needs and evaluating their progress. As these separate functions are being addressed, the supervisor might find that different methods fit the approach to one function better than others. For example, a supervisor might choose to watch a videotape of a supervisee in order to assess that person's skills, but rely on process notes to accomplish the second function of attempting to change, support, or redirect the supervisee's work.

STRUCTURED VERSUS UNSTRUCTURED INTERVENTIONS

Much of the literature addressing developmental issues, cognitive style of the supervisee, and a host of other topics refers to the relative need of structure in supervision. Rarely, however, do authors describe specifically what is meant by structure or the lack of it. Highly structured supervision can be viewed as an extension of training, while unstructured supervision can be viewed as approaching consultation. Although methods of supervision are often associated with a particular degree of structure, it is the supervisor's use of the method that will determine the level of structure. For example, Rigazio-Digilio and Anderson (1994) noted that a structured use of live supervision might entail the use of the bug-in-the-ear, thus coaching the supervisee through a therapy session, while a less structured form might rely on presession planning, midsession coaching, and postsession debriefing. (See Chapter 7 for a complete description of this process.) Similarly, individual supervision based on audiotape may be directed by the supervisor and follow the supervisor's instructional agenda, or the use of audiotape may be requested by the supervisee to reflect on a moment in a counseling session that had special meaning for the supervisee.

In short, structured interventions are supervisor directed and involve a reasonably high amount of supervision activity; unstructured interventions may be supervisor or supervisee directed and require more discipline on the part of the supervisor to allow learning to take place without directing it. For the supervisor who is impatient, who dislikes ambiguity, unstructured interventions will be more challenging; for the supervisor who has difficulty

planning ahead and organizing learning, structured interventions will be more challenging. The great majority of supervisees will benefit from both types of interventions at different junctures in their professional development.

METHODS, FORMS, AND TECHNIQUES OF SUPERVISION

With technology and computer capabilities becoming more sophisticated every day and with the helping professions exhibiting a heightened interest in supervision, different techniques, methods, and paradigms for conducting supervision continue to evolve at a rapid pace. Because of the dynamic nature of the field, therefore, we do not presume to present an inclusive list of supervision interventions. Rather, we hope to present an appreciation for the diversity of choices that have been spawned as clinical supervision continues to evolve, some rationale for using different methods, and the findings on their frequency of use and relative strengths and weaknesses as reported in the literature.

Borders (1992) identified one issue endemic to all supervision case conference situations, that being the challenge to think like a supervisor rather than a therapist. She contended that seasoned practitioners tend to continue to be fascinated by therapy issues, thus focusing on client issues rather than the learning and developmental needs of their supervisees. As part of a training package to help supervisors make the shift, Borders suggested that supervisors observe or listen to a trainee's counseling session and take notes on the content. The supervisors are then asked to peruse their notes, looking for the relative amount of attention they paid to supervisee behaviors versus the client's behaviors. In other words, have they focused on the supervisee's interventions or have they assumed their former practitioner stance and focused on the client? Other aids suggested by Borders include planning for supervision by considering learning goals for supervisees, writing case notes on supervision sessions that focus on supervisory goals and outcomes, and asking for feedback from supervisees to make certain that their supervision needs are being met. It may also be helpful for supervisors to keep in mind the supervisor intentions (e.g., assess, support, educate) listed by Strozier, Kivlighan, and Thoreson (1993) that clearly focus on the supervisor–supervisee relationship to assist novice supervisors in staying focused and to allow them a means to evaluate their supervision session afterward.

Once some of these issues of overall framework are resolved, the stage is set for the work of supervision. The remainder of this chapter has been designed to review some of the behaviors that accomplish that work, advancing from methods that allow least direct observation by the supervisor to those that allow the most. Therefore, self-report begins our list as a case conference format that relies on the supervisee's recollections of counseling or therapy as the source of information to be used for supervision.

Self-report

Although it is a simple form of supervision in one sense, we consider self-report to be a difficult method to perform well. In fact, some of the best and the worst supervision can be found within the domain of self-report. Under the best of conditions, supervisees will be challenged conceptually and personally and will learn a great deal. Many supervisors relying on self-report, however, have fallen into stagnation; supervision becomes pro forma, with little difference evident from session to session or from supervisee to supervisee.

The professional literature has given relatively little attention to self-report in the recent past, focusing much more in earnest on the technological forms of supervision. Self-report, however, continues to be a commonly used form of supervision, especially for postgraduate supervision (e.g., Goodyear & Nelson, 1997; Magnuson, 1995). At its best, self-report is an intense tutorial relationship in which the supervisee fine tunes both case conceptualization ability and personal knowledge

as each relates to therapist–client relationships. Self-report is generally viewed as far less appropriate for novice supervisees for reasons delineated by Holloway (1988) who doubted the wisdom of a supervision model that excludes direct observation, including the use of audio or videotape. Holloway stated that supervision without direct observation forfeits "the opportunity for (a) independent judgment regarding the client's problem, and (b) illustrating directly with the case in question how to draw inferences from client information" (p. 256). Holloway's point is well taken and underscores one of the key vulnerabilities of the self-report method: As a supervision strategy, it is only as good as the observational and conceptual abilities of the supervisee and the seasoned insightfulness of the supervisor. It seems, therefore, that self-report offers too many opportunities for failure if it represents the complete supervision plan. Campbell (1994) supported this contention on ethical and legal grounds. He referred to the study conducted by Muslin, Thurnblad, and Meschel (1981) in which more than 50 percent of the important issues evident in videotapes of therapy sessions of psychiatric trainees were not reported in supervision; furthermore, some degree of distortion characterized more than 50 percent of supervisees' reports. Campbell described such supervision as supervision in absentia and stated that

> As a result of their inexperience, trainees find it difficult to comprehend the problems of their clients. Because they do not observe trainees, supervisors find it difficult to correct their errors. Thus, trainees struggle with what they do not understand; and supervisors labor with what they cannot see. (p. 11)

A more recent study further indicted the memories of therapists when a group of licensed psychologists was asked to recall the molar (main) and molecular (supporting) ideas from specific segments of actual therapy sessions. Wynne, Susman, Ries, Birringer, and Katz (1994) reported only a 42 percent recall rate for molar ideas and 30 percent recall for molecular ideas. It seems reasonable to ask whether such a rate is adequate for the purposes of supervision, especially when the supervisee is relatively inexperienced.

Because self-report is the grandfather of supervision forms, there also is a tendency to return to it when other supervisory processes become tiring or tiresome. Hess and Hess (1983) reported that training in supervision did not necessarily translate to the use of methods other than self-report. In fact, studies that investigated the frequency of methods used in supervision continue to find self-report as a relatively dominant method and often the most frequently used method (Borders, Cashwell, & Rotter, 1995; Coll, 1995; Romans, Boswell, Carlozzi, & Ferguson, 1995; Wetchler, Piercy, & Sprenkle, 1989). When these same supervisees (and sometimes supervisors) were asked to identify the most valuable form of supervision, self-report dropped in its primacy (e.g., Wetchler, Piercy, & Sprenkle, 1989). Supporting the mixed reviews given to self-report, Rogers and McDonald (1995) found that when supervisors used more direct methods of supervision they evaluated their supervisees as less prepared for the job than when they used self-report. Such results reinforce the position that self-report is weakest when used with supervisees who have not reached a minimally acceptable level of professional competence.

Finally, an interesting investigation conducted by Wetchler and Vaughn (1992) honed in on the supervision method used during what, in retrospect, was identified as a critical supervisory incident that had a positive developmental impact on the supervisee. For both supervisors and supervisees, the method most frequently noted was an individual conference without reference to the use of any technology. Although this study may seem to contradict other findings, it may be viewed as underscoring our earlier statement that self-report includes some of the best as well as some of the weakest supervision experiences. When a situation is highly charged for the supervisee, it may take the more open-ended context of a conference based on self-report to help the supervisee to process the meaning of what is occurring. There are times that information does not enlighten but rather detracts from the issues. Knowing when this is the case takes both experience and a posture of keen attentiveness.

Process Notes

The above discussion of self-report did not assume the use of any form of systematic written documentation of the cases being presented in supervision or of therapeutic interventions. For supervisors who do not use more direct or active forms of supervision, case notes can provide a means of controlling the type of information offered in supervision.

Goldberg (1985) offered a helpful look at the advantages of process notes and audiotape and videotape as different information sources for supervision. He observed that an early obstacle to the development of clinical supervision was the controversy between those who prefer to base their supervision on the introspection allowed by process notes and those who prefer their supervision to be based on direct access to the supervisee's clinical work. Goldberg supported Borders and Leddick's (1987) belief that the method should be based on the immediate learning needs of the supervisee and that supervisors need to avoid fixed styles in their supervision.

Many of the advantages of using process notes, according to Goldberg (1985), are similar to the advantages discussed under self-report. (Goldberg used individual dynamic psychotherapy as his point of reference, in which process notes are the supervisee's written explanation of the content of the therapy session, the interactional processes that occurred between therapist and client, the therapist's feelings about the client, and the rationale and manner of intervention.) Goldberg argued, as have Olsen and Stern (1990), that process notes allow a wealth of information to enter the supervisory session and, therefore, allow the supervisor an opportunity to track the supervisee's cognitive processes in ways that more active forms of supervision disallow. Goldberg also found value in the experiential component between supervisor and supervisee who are free from the distraction of media, and he predicted more worthwhile modeling of therapeutic conditions to occur when process notes, as opposed to media, are the focus of supervision.

Goldberg acknowledged that the use of process notes as the exclusive method of supervision might be more advantageous for the advanced supervisee. He reported the work of Muslin, Singer, Meusea, and Leahy (1968), who compared process notes based on therapy sessions with actual recordings of the sessions and found "gross distortions and deletions of information at a variety of levels" (Goldberg, p. 7). As we have already stated, Muslin, Thurnblad, and Meschel (1981) found similar results in a later study. Therefore, for supervisees other than the most exceptional, process notes will compromise the accuracy of the information being presented. In fact, supervisors might be well advised to view process notes more as metaphors of counseling or therapy than as literal accounts of what transpired. Again, this type of view parallels the supervision goals usually associated with self-report.

Being reminded of the limits of process notes does not underestimate their value, especially when used in conjunction with other supervision methods. Even a brief outline to track a counseling session can help both novice and experienced supervisees order their thinking in meaningful ways, allowing them to use their supervision time more fully. Schwartz (1981) suggested a one-page worksheet that family therapy trainees complete after each session to include

> *(1) diagnosis and hypotheses (or changes in these) of the case based upon the previous session; (2) assessment of the previous session's goals, strategies and interventions; (3) goals (or changes in goals) for the case and for yourself based upon the previous session; (4) specific objectives (therapist's) for the next session; and (5) strategies for attaining therapist's objectives for next session.* (p. 90)

A similar process notes outline is offered in Table 5.1.

If the supervision goal is for the supervisee to learn to conceptualize the ecological reality of

---

TABLE 5.1 Progress Notes

1. What were your goals for this session?
2. Did anything happen *during* the session that caused you to reconsider your goals? How did you resolve this?
3. What was the major theme of the session? Was there any content that you consider critical?
4. Describe interpersonal dynamics between you and the client during the session.
5. How did individual differences between you and the client (e.g., gender, ethnicity or race, developmental level) affect the session?
6. How successful was the session? Were your initial goals achieved?
7. What did you learn (if anything) about the helping process from this session?
8. What are your plans and goals for the next session?
9. What specific questions do you have for your supervisor regarding your work with this client?

---

the client, then a more comprehensive, client- or system-centered outline can be followed. [see, e.g., Hackney & Cormier, 1996; Loganbill & Stoltenberg, 1983; Resnikoff, 1981)]. Such detailed, or intake, assessments are critical to supervision even if not formally required in a particular setting.

Audiotape

Although live observation and videotape have led to some of the more dramatic breakthroughs in the supervision process, the audiotape was the first to revolutionize our perceptions of what could be accomplished in supervision, and Rogers (1942) and Covner (1942a, b) are attributed with this development (Goodyear & Nelson, 1997). Without the facilities of a laboratory and without the funds, technological expertise, or necessary space to utilize videotape, the audiotape allowed supervisees to transport an accurate (albeit partial) recording of counseling or therapy to a supervisor who was not present at the time the session occurred. The audiotape is still one of the most widely used sources of information for supervisors who expect to have some sort of direct access to the work of their supervisees (e.g., Borders, Cashwell, & Rotter, 1995; Coll, 1995; Olsen & Stern, 1990).

When audiotape is first required of supervisees (especially if they have been relying on self-report or process notes), there is often some resistance that takes the form of "My clients won't be comfortable." This reaction is occasionally echoed at practicum or internship sites when a training institution asks for audiotapes of the supervisee's clinical work. Although client resistance to taping may be real and must be addressed in a sensitive and ethical manner, it is often not the client but the trainee who is experiencing the greatest amount of discomfort at the prospect of being scrutinized. In fact, the majority of clients are open to having their sessions audiotaped as long as they have an assurance that confidentiality will not be compromised and the supervisee's demeanor is not tense (implying danger) when presenting the topic of audiotaping.

Planning Supervision.   The least productive way to use an audiotape in supervision may be that which is depicted in the following vignette: The supervisee arrives with two or three audiotapes of recent counseling sessions, without having reviewed any of them privately. Because the supervisee has made no decision about which session to discuss during supervision, the supervisee spends several minutes telling the supervisor about the cases that are on tape. The supervisor eventually picks one tape, which the trainee must then rewind. The counseling session is played from the beginning until something strikes the supervisor as important.

Our point is simple: The process of supervision must be based on a plan, and it is the supervisor's responsibility to outline that plan. We do believe that spontaneity is important, but it is unlikely to emerge when the supervision process has no vitality. Listening to an audiotape for 20 minutes with a supervisee saying, "Gee, I guess the part I was talking about was further into the session than I realized" is one sure way to kill supervision vitality.

Audiotaped segments can be used in several ways. West, Bubenzer, Pinsoneault and Holeman (1993) noted that delayed review of audiotapes (and videotapes) is best used to facilitate the supervisee's perceptual–conceptual skills. Goldberg (1985) identified several teaching goals that can be accomplished using audiotape, including focusing on specific therapy techniques, helping the supervisee see the relationship between process and content, focusing on how things are said (paralanguage), and helping the supervisee differentiate between a conversational tone and a therapeutic one. Audiotape can also be used to provide an experiential moment for the supervisee if a segment of tape is chosen where it is obvious that the supervisee is struggling personally or interpersonally in the taped session.

During the initial phase of a supervision relationship, it may be advisable for the supervisor to listen to an entire therapy session prior to supervision in order to get an overview of the supervisee's ability and have control over what segment of tape will be chosen for supervision. It is important also to help the supervisee understand the rationale behind the choice of tape segment if this is not apparent. Preselected segments can be chosen for a variety of reasons:

1. To highlight the most productive part of the session
2. To highlight the most important part of the session
3. To highlight the part of the session where the supervisee is struggling the most
4. To underscore any number of content issues, including metaphors and recurring themes
5. To ask about a confusing part of the session, perhaps because paralanguage contradicts content
6. To focus attention on the point in the session where interpersonal or cross-cultural dynamics were either particularly therapeutic or particularly strained or where cultural encapsulation is evident (Cashwell, Looby, & Housley, 1997)

In other words, supervisors will almost always have in mind a teaching function when they preselect a section of audiotape for supervision.

This process should evolve, however, as the supervisee develops in conceptual ability and experience. Relatively quickly the supervisee can be preselecting the section of tape that will determine the direction of supervision. Often supervisees are just asked to choose a part of the session where they felt confused, lost, overwhelmed, or frustrated. The supervisor will then listen to the segment with them and proceed from there. If this format is used, the supervisee should be prepared to

- State the reason for selecting this part of the session for discussion in supervision
- Briefly state what transpired up to that point
- Explain what he or she was trying to accomplish at that point in the session
- Clearly state the specific help desired from the supervisor

Although a valid supervision format, the same format used repeatedly may make supervision become stagnant. When the supervisee is repeatedly asked to select a troublesome tape segment, for example, the supervision may become skewed toward problems in counseling sessions, with little opportunity for the supervisee to enjoy successes as a practitioner. Additionally, the supervisor has no way of knowing if there are more productive moments in therapy if difficult moments become the theme for supervision.

As an alternative method of using audiotapes, the supervisor might assign a theme for the next session and have the supervisee be responsible for producing the segment of tape. For example, the supervisor might suggest that reframing would be of great help for a particular client or family and that the supervisee should try to reframe as often as possible in the next session and choose the most successful of these attempts to present in the next supervision session. In addition to using supervision to sharpen a skill, this strategy also allows the supervisor to connect technique to a counseling situation and to get data on the supervisee's self-evaluation ability. The types of assignments that can direct the use of audiotape are potentially limitless and can

focus on the process of therapy, the conceptual issues in therapy, personal or interpersonal issues, and ethical dilemmas, among others; it can also reflect different supervisee developmental levels. In summary, careful preselection of an audiotape segment is perhaps most crucial in making the audiotape a powerful supervision tool.

Although the use of direct supervision methods is not usually associated with psychodynamic approaches to therapy, Aveline (1992) and Brandell (1992) have addressed the unique advantages of using audiotaped segments in supervision. In a particularly adroit description of the benefit of hearing a supervisee's session, Aveline stated

> I am stimulated by the way in which words are used, the metaphors deployed and the images evoked. Snatches of interaction often vividly illustrate the central dilemmas of a person's life. . . . The medium is particularly well placed to identify such phenomena as the patient filling all the space of [the] session with words so as to leave no room for the therapist to say anything for fear that what might be said will disrupt the inner equilibrium; the nervous laugh that as surely indicates that there is an issue of importance at hand as does the bird with trailing wing that the nest is nearby; the therapist whose words of encouragement are belied by his impatient tone or gesture; and the patient whose placatory dependence is shot through with hostility.   (p. 350)

Despite his convincing arguments in favor of the use of audiotaping for supervision, Aveline also cautioned that there are significant disadvantages. Primarily, Aveline argued that a tape recorder *always* has an effect on therapy, and its meaning to the client (and the therapist) must be explored. He cautioned that taping might even be abusive to a client who is in too weak a position to refute its use. Similarly, Aveline saw the possibility that taping could hurt the supervisory relationship if the exposure that the tape allowed led to humiliation for the therapist. In all cases, Aveline stressed that the supervisor must be willing to address the consequences that the audiotape has produced. "Taping is a supervisory aid; it is servant, not master" (Aveline, 1992, p. 351).

Brandell (1992) focused more on using audiotape to assist the supervisee in understanding the process of psychoanalytic psychotherapy. He described a format where a 5- to 10-minute excerpt from a therapy session is transcribed, and both supervisor and supervisee complete a checklist about the client's focal conflict. The checklist requires that decisions be made about the client's wishes, reactions, maladaptive solutions, and adaptive solutions. The completed checklists become the source for the instructional learning that will take place in supervision.

Dual-channel Supervision.   Yet another use of the audiotape deserving special attention is Smith's (1984) dual-channel supervision. Reacting to a need expressed by practicum students in counseling for direct supervision from the supervisor, Smith used stereophonic cassette recorders to combine live observation with audiotaped feedback. While observing sessions, Smith was able to react to moment-to-moment interactions between the counselor and client and record his feedback. After the session, the trainee could listen to the tape unobstructed by supervisor reactions by turning the balance control to the left channel or could listen to the tape with the supervisor's feedback by setting the balance control at the midpoint.

This use of audiotape has two distinct advantages: It forces the trainee to review the tape of the session in order to receive feedback, and it allows regularly scheduled supervision time to be focused on either conceptual issues or other more global themes because the more specific bits of feedback have been taken care of on tape. The major disadvantage of this approach is that it makes it difficult for the supervisor to roam among several concurrent counseling sessions (Smith, 1984). There is nothing, however, to prevent the supervisor from signing on and off of a session for a period to time. This would still allow for the advantages of this model. More recently, Hurt and Mattox (1990) suggested that dual-cassette recorders have some of the same advantages of dual-channel supervision but are much less costly. Basically, this method requires the supervisor to copy the trainee's tape onto a second tape and insert supervisory comments as warranted. The trainee's original tape is not altered as the second tape is being created.

While these forms of supervision may seem technologically driven, there is no question that we are only seeing the very tip of the iceberg regarding the use of technology in supervision (Casey, Bloom, & Moan, 1994). As communication mediums like the Internet settle into our consciousness, our assumptions about the appropriate contexts for supervision will no doubt be altered. Access will need to be weighed against continuity; the ethics of new ways to conduct therapy and supervision will need to be addressed. There is no question, however, that some of our present modus operandi may appear quaint in the foreseeable future.

The Written Critique of Audiotapes.   For those who are more visual than auditory, the supervisor can combine a written analysis of an audiotape with individual supervision. Many supervisors choose to listen to tapes between supervision sessions rather than during them. This is especially so during the beginning stages of supervision. Rather than taking notes to use in a subsequent supervision session, the supervisor writes an analysis of the session that can be given to the student. Word processors make this chore somewhat more palatable, and the exercise forces the supervisor to conceptualize the feedback before the supervision session. Additionally, the critiques automatically become a record of supervision; they allow the supervisee to review comments made by the supervisor; and they can become a way of coordinating supervision if other supervisors are involved (e.g., a site supervisor could be sent a copy of the critique prepared by the university supervisor). In fact, the critiques serve as excellent instructional material for the training of supervisors in the planning and giving of feedback. It must be noted, however, that such written feedback does not replace either individual or group supervision. In particular circumstances, however, such as long distances between supervisor and supervisee, mailing audiotapes and receiving written feedback have been used to supplement more personal supervision (Miller & Crago, 1989).

Videotape

Although the audiotape is still our back-up, the videotape has certainly taken center stage as the technology of choice in supervision (e.g., Romans, Boswell, Carlozzi, & Ferguson, 1995; Wetchler, Piercy, & Sprenkle, 1989). Those who use videotape are firm about its superiority over audiotape (e.g., Broder & Sloman, 1982; Stoltenberg & Delworth, 1987). We want to emphasize, however, that many of the process variables we mentioned for using audiotape could be used with videotape, as well as the reverse.

With no intention of insulting our readers, we will point out that the videotape has one major advantage, the addition of the picture, and two major disadvantages, its expense and its bulk (though better equipment continues to reduce the latter issue). To say that a picture is worth a thousand words is less trite when one sees a client that one has heard but not seen up to that time. A voice that is gruff matched with a persona that is gentle, a precise presentation of plot when the physical presentation is disorganization, the smiles, the nods, the looking away, the hand gestures—all comprise a wealth of information. When the client is a family, the phenomenon grows exponentially. In fact, experiencing an overload of data is one of the reasons that Goldberg (1985) and Hart (1982) suggested using videotape at later stages of supervision. Or as Rubinstein and Hammond (1982) aptly put it, "[p]aradoxically, the greatest limitation of videotape may result from what it best provides the supervisor—a wealth of material about the recorded session" (p. 161).

The bulk of the videotape (camera, recorder, and monitor) makes it more likely to be used in group supervision, but there are notable exceptions to this (e.g., interpersonal process recall). Regardless of the numbers involved, videotape supervision will take more room than working with audiotape.

If one does supervision within the confines of a small private office, feedback based on videotape may have to be foregone. Another drawback of using videotape is that a higher level of comfort with technology is required than with audiotape. If someone throws the wrong switch, the supervisor who does not like to tinker may be unduly frustrated by using videotape.

According to Munson (1983), the associations trainees may make between videotaped supervision and commercial television can present yet another problem. Because television connotes entertainment, Munson saw the dual problem of observers not finding others' sessions entertaining enough and trainees feeling they must "perform" on videotape, thereby suffering from excessive "performance anxiety." The supervisor's role, according to Munson, includes structuring supervision so that observers are stimulated cognitively (usually by means of a specific task related to the videotaped segment), while at the same time attempting to safeguard the integrity of the trainee on tape. Munson's admonition has been supported by more recent empirical findings that videotape review of counseling sessions caused a shift from positive mood at the end of a counseling session to a lowered mood after videotape review for therapists and therapists-in-training (Hill et al., 1994). It seems, therefore, that the obvious advantage of videotape can become a liability and must be monitored carefully by the supervisor. As one supervisee put it, "[v]ideotape is a little like some hotel room mirrors; the reflection is *too* accurate."

Despite all these valid cautions regarding the use of videotape in supervision, there is no question that our knowledge base and experiential alternatives have increased greatly as a result of this technology. With videotape, supervisees can literally see themselves in the role of helper, thus allowing them to be an observer of their work, which is not possible with audiotape (Sternitzke, Dixon, & Ponterotto, 1988; Whiffen, 1982).

In an excellent discussion of the use of videotape in the supervision of marriage and family therapy, Breunlin, Karrer, McGuire, & Cimmarusti (1988) argued that videotape supervision should be focused on the interaction between trainee and clients, as well as on the far more subtle internal processes experienced by the trainee during both the therapy session and the supervision session. To focus on one to the exclusion of the other would be an error, according to Breunlin et al. Furthermore, they stated that therapists can never be objective observers of their own roles separate from the family (or individual) client, as this is an interactional impossibility. Breunlin et al., therefore, recommended six guidelines for working with both the cold accuracy of the videotape and the dynamic reality experienced by the supervisee (pp. 199–204). These guidelines, when followed, help to alleviate some of the dangers noted by Munson (1983) and Hill et al. (1994). (We should note that the guidelines outlined by Breunlin et al. also apply to other methods of supervision.)

1. *Focus videotape supervision by setting realistic goals for the supervised therapy session.* This has two advantages: It reduces the sense of information overload by narrowing down the field to those interventions that are connected to goals, and it increases the possibility that the supervisee will emerge from the session moderately satisfied because realistic goals are attainable. As Breunlin et al. expressed it, "[m]oderate satisfaction minimizes dread and the anxiety that distorts internal process, and also motivates the therapist to want to review the tape" (p. 200).

2. *Relate internal process across contexts.* The point here is that what the therapist experiences in the session is important to discuss in supervision. Furthermore, Breunlin et al. emphasized that supervisors should allow therapists to disclose their perceptions first, rather than supervisors offering their observations. Most important, however, is the issue of validating the internal processes of the therapist, rather than forfeiting such a discussion in favor of "strategy review." Interpersonal process recall (Kagan, 1976, 1980), as described later in this chapter, is an excellent model for meeting this guideline.

3. *Select tape segments that focus on remedial performance.* By this, the authors mean that the focus of corrective feedback should be on performance that the therapist has the ability to change. In other words, focusing on aspects of the therapist's personal style or on skills that are too complex for immediate attainment will be nonproductive.

4. *Use supervisor comments to create a moderate evaluation of performance.* The authors relied on the research of Fuller and Manning (1973) to arrive at this guideline. The latter found that a moderate discrepancy between performance and the target goal is optimal for learning. Therefore, the supervisor must find videotape segments that are neither exemplary nor too far from the stated goal. We can begin to appreciate the kind of supervisor commitment that is required to use the suggestions of Breunlin et al.

5. *Refine goals moderately.* This guideline underscores the fact that videotape review must be seen in the larger context of supervisee development. Sometimes the multitude of possibilities that a review can generate are irrespective of the skill level of the therapist. Additionally, Breunlin et al. remind us that what appears easy when viewing a session can be far more difficult to pull off in therapy. Moderation, therefore, must remain the constant focus for the supervisor.

6. *Maintain a moderate level of arousal.* The authors posited that attending to the first five guidelines will take care of the sixth. The supervisor, however, must always be cautious to see that the supervisee is stimulated to grow without becoming overly threatened. Therefore, the supervisor, as always, must be alert to multiple levels of experience.

Also addressing supervisee internal processes, Rubinstein and Hammond (1982) maintained that the supervisor who uses videotape must have a healthy respect for its power. There is no hiding from the stark reality of one's picture and voice being projected into the supervision room. Therefore, Rubinstein and Hammond cautioned that videotape should not be used unless there is a relatively good relationship between supervisor and supervisee. We would concur up to a point but also postulate that a good relationship can be formed in the process of using videotape sensitively. In addition, the supervisee will be far less camera shy if videotape was used in training prior to supervision. Rubinstein and Hammond made one fine suggestion that supervisors appear on videotape prior to having their supervisees do the same. This can serve many purposes, but especially attractive is dispelling the myth that supervisors conduct perfect therapy sessions. As all supervisors know, the insight and cleverness that are evidenced in supervision are rarely matched in one's own therapy.

Finally, Rubinstein and Hammond suggested that the use of the videotape remain technologically simple. They are not in favor of split screens, superimposed images, or other such equipment capabilities, believing that it detracts from the lifelike experience of watching the taped session. In stark contrast to this opinion is the work done by Froehle (1984), who used a computer to track physiological data on the therapist while in the process of conducting interpersonal process recall. Of course, decisions about using videotape reflect the supervisor's fascination, or lack thereof, with technology, as well as the supervision goals. And yet, as we stated earlier, supervisor comfort and technological expertise may need to increase as the present technological revolution continues (Casey, Bloom, and Moan, 1994). Each supervisor ultimately will find a viable comfort level with technological advances, but the supervisor would still be wise to remember Rubinstein and Hammond's caution lest technology and its multiple uses become the center of supervision.

Interpersonal Process Recall (IPR). Perhaps the most widely known supervision model using videotape is interpersonal process recall (Kagan, 1976, 1980; Kagan & Kratwohl, 1967; Kagan, Kratwohl, & Farquhar, 1965; Kagan, Kratwohl, & Miller, 1963; Kagan & Kagan, 1997). As a result of a national survey of counselor education programs, Borders and Leddick (1988) found that IPR was one of only two clearly delineated methods of supervision taught in supervision courses, the other

being live supervision. IPR began as a therapy model and occasionally is still used as such; for our purposes here, however, our discussion will be confined to the use of IPR in supervision. Kagan (1980) asserted that there are many psychological barriers to complete communication and that these operate in counseling and therapy as they do in other daily interactions. Primary among these is the strongly socialized habit of behaving diplomatically. As a result, much of what a supervisee thinks, intuits, and feels during counseling and therapy is disregarded almost automatically because allowing such perceptions to surface would confront the predisposition to be diplomatic.

The purpose of IPR, then, is to give the supervisee a safe haven for these internal reactions. Kagan (1980) strongly maintained that all persons are "the best authority of their own dynamics and the best interpreter of their own experience" (pp. 279–280). Starting with this assumption, therefore, the supervisor's role becomes that of a facilitator to stimulate the awareness of the supervisee beyond the point at which it operated during the therapy session.

The process of IPR is relatively simple. The supervisor and trainee view a prerecorded videotape of a counseling session together. At any point at which either person believes that something of importance is happening on tape, especially something that is not being addressed in the counseling session, the videotape is stopped (dual controls are helpful, but it is easy enough to signal the person holding the controls to stop the tape). If the trainee stops the tape, the trainee will speak first, saying, for example "I was getting really frustrated here. I didn't know what she wanted. We had been over all of this before. I thought it was resolved last week but here it is again." At this point, it is essential that the supervisor not adopt a teaching role and instruct the trainee about what might have been done. Rather, the supervisor needs to allow the trainee the psychological space to investigate internal processes to some resolution. At the same time, the good facilitator, or "inquirer," as Kagan preferred to call it, can ask direct questions that are assertive, perhaps even confrontive. Some possibilities for the above example are: What do you wish you had said to her? How do you think she might have reacted if you said those things to her? What kept you from saying what you wanted to say? If you had the opportunity now, how might you tell her what you are thinking and feeling? Once it is felt that the dynamics for the chosen segment of tape have been sufficiently reexamined, the tape is allowed to continue. Table 5.2 lists a variety of lead statements that reflect different supervision goals. Specifically, leads are listed that inspire affective exploration, check out unstated agendas, encourage cognitive examination, get at images, or help search out expectations.

As one can certainly discern, this process is slow. Only a portion of a therapy session can be reviewed in this manner unless supervision is extended significantly. Therefore, choosing the most interpersonally weighted or most metaphorically meaningful segment of videotape will be most productive for supervision purposes.

One caution is advisable: Because IPR often puts interpersonal dynamics under a microscope, it is possible that they will be magnified to the extent of distortion (Bernard, 1981). In other words, what is a perfectly functional helping relationship can come to look somehow dysfunctional when overexposed, and as all persons in the helping professions know, some relationship dynamics are best left underexposed. We need not be in perfect sync with all our clients to be of help to them. The clinical skill comes in determining which interactions are important and which are not. IPR has no internal reasoning; therefore, it is up to the supervisor and supervisee to decide which interactions warrant exploration and which do not. Because the supervisee is usually more reticent than the supervisor, the supervisor will most often be left to make such decisions. Answering the following two questions may be useful in selecting segments for IPR: From what I can observe, does this interaction seem to be interrupting the flow of counseling? From what I know of the trainee, would focusing on this interaction aid in his or her development as a mental health professional? Ap-

pendix D describes the inclusion of IPR in a training package for clinical supervisors.

The Reflective Process. Goodyear and Nelson (1997) described efforts to develop reflectivity in supervisees as an elaboration on some of the tenets of IPR. Neufeldt, Karno, and Nelson (1996) provided the following description of the reflective process:

> *The reflective process itself is a search for understanding of the phenomena of the counseling session, with attention to therapist actions, emotions, and thoughts, as well as to the interaction between the therapist and the client. The intent to understand what has occurred, active inquiry, openness to that understanding, and vulnerability and risk-taking, rather than defensive self-protection, characterize the stance of the reflective supervisee. Supervisees use theory, their prior personal and professional experience, and their experience of themselves in the counseling session as sources of understanding. If they are to contribute to future development, reflections must be profound rather than superficial and must be meaningful to the supervisees. To complete the sequence, reflectivity in supervision leads to changes in perception, changes in counseling practice, and an increased capacity to make meaning of experiences.* (p. 8)

As was discussed in Chapter 3, Neufeldt et al. (1996) noted that supervisee personality and cognitive capacities, as well as the supervision environment, must be considered when attempting to move the supervisee toward reflectivity. Inspired by the work of Skovholt and Ronnestad (1992), who determined the importance of continuous professional reflection, Neufeldt (1994) and Neufeldt, Iversen, and Juntunen (1995) developed strategies for encouraging supervisee reflectivity for beginning counselors. Neufeldt (1994, 1995) described supervisor strategies, using videotape review, that encourage supervisees to examine their counseling sessions in light of present thoughts about the dynamics within the sessions (e.g., feelings about observed behaviors on the part of the client toward their responses), as well as the meaning of those observations (e.g., whether their counseling interventions reflect their beliefs

TABLE 5.2 Supervisor Leads for Use with Interpersonal Process Recall

Leads That Inspire Affective Exploration
How did that make you feel?
How did that make you feel about him or her?
Do you remember what you were feeling?
Were you aware of any feelings?
What do those feeling mean to you?
Does that feeling have any special meaning to you?
Is it a familiar feeling?
What did you do (or decide to do) about that feeling you had?
Did you want to express that feeling at any time?
Did you have any fantasies of taking any risk?

Leads That Check out Unstated Agendas
What would you have liked to have said to her or him at this point?
What's happening here?
What did you feel like doing?
How were you feeling about your role as counseling at this point?
What had that meant to you?
If you had more time, where would you have liked to have gone?

Leads That Encourage Cognitive Examination
What were you thinking at that time?
What thoughts were you having about the other person at that time?
Something going on there?
Anything going on there?
Had you any ideas about what you wanted to do with that?
Did you fantasize taking any risks?
Were you able to say it the way you wanted to?
Did you want to say anything else then?
Did you have any plan of where you wanted the session to go next?
Did you think the other person knew what you wanted?
What kind of image were you aware of projecting?
Is that the image you wanted to project?
Can you recall what effect the setting had on you or the interaction?
Can you recall what effect you thought the setting had on the other person?
Did the equipment affect you in any way?
(If reaction to the recorder) What did you want, or not want, the recorder to hear from you?

Leads That Get at Images
Were you having any fantasies at that moment?

Were any pictures, images, or memories flashing through your mind then?
What was going on in your mind at that time? Did it remind you of anything?
Did you think you had "been there before"? Is that familiar to you?
Where had that put you in the past?

Leads That Explore Mutual Perceptions between Client and Counselor
What did you think she or he was feeling about you?
How do you think she or he was seeing you at that point?
Do you think she or he was aware of your feelings? Your thoughts?
What message do you think she or he was trying to give you?
Did you feel that he or she had any expectations of you at that point?
What did you think she or he wanted you to think or feel or do?
Do you think your description of the interaction would coincide with her or his description?
Was she or he giving you any cues as to how she or he was feeling?
How do you think she or he felt about talking about this problem?
How do you think she or he felt about continuing to talk with you at this point?

Leads That Help Search out Expectations
What did you want her or him to tell you?
What did you want to hear?
What would you have liked from her or him?
Were you expecting anything of her or him at that point?
Did you want her or him to see you in some particular way? How?
What do you think her or his perceptions were of you?
What message did you want to give her or him?
Was there anything in particular you wanted her or him to say or do or think?
Was she or he "with you"? How did her or his responses hit you?
What did you really want to tell her or him at this moment? What prevented you from doing so?
What did you want her or him to do?
Did you want her or him to do something that would have made it easier for you?
What would that have been?

about how people change). Unlike IPR, supervisor strategies used in this endeavor include some directive responses. Neufeldt (1994) and Neufeldt et al. (1995) described the supervisor strategies as an embellishment on the original 17 strategies suggested by Stenack and Dye (1982), all of which reflect Bernard's (1979) discrimination model, as well as offering 9 additional advanced strategies. Table 5.3 lists all 26 supervisor strategies that en-

courage supervisee reflectivity and are fully examined in Neufeldt, Iversen, and Juntunen (1995).

Live Observation

Live observation is a frequent form of supervision in many training programs; it is used less frequently in the field because of scheduling difficulties and structural constraints. We differentiate between live

TABLE 5.3   Supervisor Strategies That Encourage Supervisee Reflectivity

Basic Strategies: Teaching Functions
  1. Evaluate observed counseling session interactions.
  2. Ask counselor to provide a hypothesis about the client.
  3. Identify appropriate interventions.
  4. Teach, demonstrate, or model intervention strategies.
  5. Explain the rationale behind specific strategies and/or interventions.
  6. Interpret significant events in the counseling session.

Basic Strategies: Counseling Functions
  7. Explore trainee feelings during the counseling session.
  8. Explore trainee feelings during the supervision session.
  9. Explore trainee feelings concerning specific techniques and/or interventions.
 10. Facilitate trainee self-explorations of confidence and/or worries in the counseling session.
 11. Help the trainee define personal competencies and areas for growth.
 12. Provide opportunities for trainees to process their own affect and/or worries in the counseling session.

Basic Strategies: Consulting Functions
 13. Provide alternative interventions and/or conceptualizing for trainee use.
 14. Encourage trainee brainstorming of strategies and/or interventions.
 15. Encourage trainee discussion of client problems, motivations, etc.
 16. Solicit and attempt to satisfy trainee needs during the session.
 17. Allow the trainee to structure the supervision session.

Advance Strategies: Combined Functions
 18. Assist the trainee to conceptualize a case.
 19. Explore the trainee's feelings to facilitate understanding to the client.
 20. Present a developmental challenge.
 21. Use parallel process to model appropriate strategies for dealing with clients.
 22. Explore the trainee's intentions in a session.
 23. Explore the trainee–client boundary issues.
 24. Help the trainee to process feelings of distress aroused by the client.
 25. Assist the trainee to identify and use cues in the client's and therapist's behavior.
 26. Reframe trainee ideas and behaviors in a positive manner and build on them.

From S. A. Neufeldt (1994), Use of a manual to train supervisors, *Counselor Education and Supervision, 33*(4), 327–336. Copyright © 1994 by the American Counseling Association. Reprinted by permission.

observation and live supervision, the former being a method of observing the supervisee but not interacting with the supervisee during the session (except in case of emergency) and the latter being a combination of observation and active supervision during the session. Because the involvement of the supervisor in live supervision represents a paradigm shift from all other supervisory methods, we treat it separately in Chapter 7.

Live observation offers several advantages over all other forms of supervision, with the exception of live supervision. First, there is a high safeguard for client welfare when live observation is employed because the supervisor is immediately available to intervene in case of emergency. A second advantage of live observation is that it affords the supervisor a more complete picture of clients and supervisees than is attainable through the use of audiotape or videotape. When using the latter, for example, the camera position is often fixed throughout a session, giving only side views of both client and supervisee or focusing on the client exclusively. Supervisors who have used both live observation and taping can certainly attest to the more firsthand experience that live observation provides.

A third, and perhaps most utilized, advantage of live observation is that it offers the utmost flexibility regarding the timing of the case conference. Should the supervisor choose to conduct supervision immediately after the counseling session, the supervisee has the maximum amount of time available to use supervision in preparing for the next counseling session. Certainly, the use of live observation will reduce the chances of a most frustrating situation where the supervisor is watching a videotape of a session only to be told that the supervisee has seen the client again since the video was made. It is difficult to make supervision fresh when the therapy session is stale. Because the timing of a supervision session affects all individual supervision, we will address this topic separately.

One advantage of live observation must be monitored carefully. When other trainees are present in the observation room, there is an opportunity to offer instruction based on the session that is tran-

spiring. This instruction can become very objective and candid, and the supervisor might point out dynamics that he or she might not consider helpful to mention to the counselor. This, of course, will affect the level of trust among all the members of the supervisory group. Whenever other supervisees are present during an observation, a protocol must be established, such as that all comments will be shared with the counselor either in individual or group supervision.

Timing of Supervision

Regardless of the methods used to produce the material for the case conference, an additional matter, the timing of the conference, must be considered. Little has been said in the professional literature about the timing of supervision except to warn that supervision that is scheduled for convenience only (e.g., every Tuesday at 10:00 for 1 hour) may invite legal liability if there are no provisions for the occasion when the supervisee experiences a more pressing need for supervision (Cohen, 1979; Disney & Stephens, 1994).

Couchon and Bernard (1984) conducted a study that examined how several variables were influenced by the timing of supervision. Among the variables that were considered were supervisor and counselor behavior in supervision, follow-through from supervision to counseling, client and counselor satisfaction with counseling, and counselor satisfaction with supervision. Three treatments were introduced: supervision within 4 hours prior to an upcoming counseling session, supervision the day before a specified counseling session, and supervision occurring more than 2 days before a specified counseling session.

Some provocative results emerged from this study. Perhaps the most surprising result was that the timing of supervision seemed to affect supervisor behavior in the supervision session more so than counselor behavior. Supervision the day before a specified counseling session was very content oriented. Perhaps because the counseling session was still 1 day away, supervisors felt the permission to offer several alternative strategies for counselors to consider. The supervisor was more likely to adopt an instructional mode and, therefore, was doing more of the work in the supervision session. We do not know how much the supervisee actually learned in these supervision sessions, but follow-through to the subsequent counseling session was low. In other words, strategies discussed and approved by the supervisor in the supervision session were not acted on in counseling to any significant degree. We can hypothesize that because information was so voluminous in supervision the counselor was not able to prioritize or translate supervisory information into counseling strategies.

Supervision conducted within 4 hours of a subsequent session was quite different. With the press of the upcoming session, the supervisor was far less likely to offer content and, instead, adopted a more consultative role. Fewer strategies were discussed, more of the strategies were offered by the counselor than by the supervisor, and those that were suggested met with more supervisor approval. Furthermore, there was far more follow-through from supervision to counseling for this treatment condition. Therefore, we can view supervision immediately before counseling to be more of a work session for the counselor with support from the supervisor as needed.

The third timing of supervision, more or less midway between counseling sessions, had no strong effects. Because other counseling sessions with other clients intervened and there was no immediate pressure to prepare for an upcoming session, the supervision conference was simply more diffuse in its content and follow-through.

The Couchon and Bernard study highlighted the importance of timing as a process variable in supervision. Depending on the developmental and learning needs of the supervisee, different timing of supervision might be appropriate. For example,

a counselor who conceptualizes well but who implements ideas poorly might benefit more from supervision immediately before counseling. On the other hand, a counselor who performs well but who lacks conceptual ability might benefit from supervision conducted the day before counseling. (Couchon & Bernard, 1984, p. 18)

Contrary to the assumptions of many supervisors, the counselors in the Couchon and Bernard study were equally satisfied with supervision of when supervision was offered. (Timing also did not affect client or counselor satisfaction with counseling.) It should be noted, however, that an important time for supervision, immediately after counseling, was not studied. We hypothesize that if there is a time that would get an elevated satisfaction rating it would be immediately after counseling when the supervisee might benefit from support and reinforcement. This hypothesis is supported in part by Smith (1984), who found that practicum students evaluated postsession supervisor feedback as most effective among several choices. But postsession was not clearly defined and may or may not have occurred immediately after counseling. Additionally, regardless of supervisee satisfaction, the amount and kind of learning resulting from this timing of supervision is unknown.

Supervision Formats: Frequency of Use

Several investigators in the fields of counseling, psychology, and marriage and family therapy have sought to establish the types of supervision formats that are used in a variety of contexts (Borders, Cashwell, & Rotter, 1995; Coll, 1995; Freeman & McHenry, 1996; Nichols, Nichols, & Hardy, 1990; Romans, Boswell, Carlozzi, & Ferguson, 1995; Wetchler, Piercy, & Sprenkle, 1989). It must be noted that the parameters of each study are distinct; thus, comparing the results across studies cannot be done in any definitive manner. Yet the variety of studies across several disciplines, describing methods used both within and beyond training, established the leading supervision formats. Within individual supervision, self-report was the most common in the field, while supervision using videotape replay was the strongest within training programs. Live supervision and audiotape replay were also found to rate highly in particular studies and to rank third and fourth overall. In all the studies that included cotherapy as a form of supervision, this format ranked last with the exception of Freeman and McHenry (1996), where one form of live supervision (bug-in-the-ear) ranked lowest (while other forms of live supervision ranked second in frequency). Finally, it was difficult to discern when studies collapsed the use of process notes with self-report; therefore, the former is not considered separately. It would seem that if one goal of supervision is to prepare the supervisee to successfully use supervision in the future (certainly a goal of training programs) exposure to several different supervision formats would expedite that goal.

Supervisor Goals during Supervision

For the most part, our discussion thus far has focused on the methods used by the supervisor to obtain the data that will be used in supervision, as well as the timing of the supervision conference. Although important, these issues do not automatically translate into a productive supervision session. The supervisor also must produce behaviors that will match supervisory intentions (Strozier, Kivlighan, & Thoreson, 1993). Interpersonal process recall, for example, uses videotape as the method for obtaining supervision data, but the technique is intended to increase supervisee reflectivity regarding the interpersonal dynamics that were present during the session being reviewed. If the supervisor had concerns about the supervisee's ability to be reflective, this technique should be avoided—at least for the present.

As part of their developmental model (described in Chapter 2), Loganbill, Hardy and Delworth (1982) described five supervisor techniques–strategies that would assist supervisees to get beyond stagnation or confusion and move toward integration for any of Chickering's (1969) eight vectors addressed by Loganbill et al. in their model. These interventions are not limited to a specific format for supervision (e.g., the use of audiotape).

1. *Facilitative interventions* are as much a set of assumptions and attitudes as direct interventions. They are supervisee centered and help promote the natural developmental process. Inherent in this cat-

egory is the belief that with support and reflective activity the supervisee can learn and change.

2. *Confrontive interventions* are a type of intervention that "brings together two things for examination and comparison" (p. 33). The discrepancy can be internal to the supervisee, for example, a conflict between feelings and behavior, or it can be a discrepancy between the supervisee and an external actuality, for example, the supervisor seeing client dynamics in a way very different from how they have been perceived by the supervisee.

3. *Conceptual interventions* occur whenever the supervisor is asking the supervisee to think analytically or theoretically. Loganbill et al. cautioned the supervisor to take learning styles into consideration because some supervisees grasp theory through experience, whereas others need a theoretical grounding prior to experience.

4. *Prescriptive interventions* take the form of coaching the supervisee to either perform certain behaviors or to delete certain behaviors. This is the most direct intervention category described by Loganbill et al. Therefore, they warned that prescriptive interventions could thwart supervisee development if used too liberally or when a more conservative approach might be substituted. (We will find a similar caution in our discussion of live supervision in Chapter 7.) Client welfare is a frequent rationale for using prescriptive interventions.

5. *Catalytic interventions* include those supervisor statements that are "designed to get things moving" (p. 35). Although the authors noted that in one sense all supervision interventions are catalytic, they also argued that catalytic interventions are qualitatively different from each of the other four. When a supervisor uses a catalytic intervention, the supervisor is seizing the moment to bring additional meaning to the supervisory process. Loganbill et al. offered two examples of catalytic interventions: helping the supervisee to appreciate realistic client potential for change and, thereby, setting appropriate goals (a buffer, the authors asserted, from burnout) and encouraging the supervisee to experiment with new roles in the therapeutic relationship.

To summarize, the process of developmental supervision using the Loganbill et al. (1982) model begins by assessing the supervisee on eight dimensions as either stagnate, confused, or integrated. Then the supervisor relies on combinations of the five supervisor intervention categories to bring the supervisee to integration on as many dimensions as possible. The source of supervision information on which the supervisor relies would depend on the issue, some needing direct observation, others being more contemplative in nature.

Johnson and Moses (1988) followed Loganbill et al. by relying on Chickering's vectors as the criteria for supervisee development. Rather than the five interventions proposed by Loganbill et al., however, Johnson and Moses reduced supervisor input to either *challenge* or *support*. If the supervisor offers too little challenge, the supervisee might slip into stagnation (borrowing from the Loganbill et al. model); with too much challenge and too little support, the supervisee may get discouraged or defensive. The choice between challenge and support was seen by Johnson and Moses as the most critical decision the supervisor makes. Once this decision is made, Johnson and Moses referred to the Bernard (1979) schema of roles (teacher, consultant, counselor) as being the primary choices for the supervisor to help the supervisee attain the desired growth. Although Johnson and Moses did not imply that either support or challenge interventions should constitute the majority of supervisor interventions, McCarthy, Kulakowski, and Kenfield (1994) found that the most frequent supervisor technique was the offering of support and encouragement, while confrontation and the assignment of homework were rarely used. Between these two extremes were techniques such as interpretation, self-disclosure, and reflection of content and feelings.

In summary, then, supervision techniques are much the same as those used in counseling or therapy. The differences lie in the parameters of the relationship, including the central role that evaluation plays in the relationship.

Instruction

Instruction could be viewed as a supervision format, as is usually the case during initial stages of training in the helping professions. Additionally, however, instruction can be a supervisor technique within other formats of supervision at times when the supervisor determines that it represents the most efficient and productive strategy. The most obvious example of this is when the supervisee is ready to learn more advanced skills that were not considered essential for the novice supervisee, but that are highly useful once the supervisee is prepared to learn them. Paradoxical interventions are one example of sophisticated skills that would probably require additional instruction once a supervisee is more advanced.

Instructional needs usually are determined by the client load carried by a supervisee. Hawthorne (1987) argued that all of a trainee's field experiences can be put to an educational purpose. But even if one prefers less of a teaching role in supervision, a typical client load will certainly lead the trainee to a need for new counseling strategies. With laboratory courses being hard pressed to cover the basics, it is most likely (and desirable) that more instruction is conducted once clinical work commences.

Microtraining (Daniels, Rigazio-Digilio, & Ivey, 1997; Ivey, 1971; Ivey & Authier, 1978) is most widely utilized in training programs as a systematic approach to teaching therapeutic skills. As described by Forsyth and Ivey (1980), the four steps of microtraining are quite straightforward:

1. *Teach one skill at a time.* When done as part of supervision, the trainee must understand that the skill about to be learned will later be placed in the context of treatment objectives. In other words, one skill may be a small part of the entire therapeutic intervention, but, nonetheless, is important to be executed adroitly. Furthermore, if the skill is complex (e.g., systematic desensitization), each part of the skill will be taught separately, pulling it all together at the end.

2. *Present the skill.* Modeling is an important part of microtraining and can consist of a live demonstration by the supervisor or a taped enactment of the target skill. Explaining the skill verbally is not an adequate presentation.

3. *Practice the skill.* Again, it is not sufficient for the trainee to see the skill performed and then to be expected to accomplish it competently in the next counseling session. The trainee must be allowed to practice the skill in the supervisory context. Better yet, the trainee's efforts should be videotaped or audiotaped so that the power of self-modeling (Hosford, 1981) can be integrated into the instruction. Practicing the skill will necessitate a sequence of role plays and/or reverse role plays. If done in individual supervision, this means that the supervisor must be willing to invest in each part of the role play and that the supervisee must be sufficiently comfortable with the supervisor to put their relationship aside for the sake of the practice session. It is because of this latter complication that supervisors may choose to steer away from microtraining in individual supervision, preferring it as a group supervision model.

4. *Allow for mastery.* The most common mistake made in instruction of clinical skills is to allow the trainee to terminate practice prior to mastery. Of course, in this context, mastery is a relative term and means a level at which both the supervisor and supervisee are comfortable that the skill will contribute to a successful therapeutic intervention. Only when mastery has been achieved should the supervisee be asked to use the skill in treatment. If mastery is not accomplished, it can either mean that enough time has not been given to the instructional task, the modeling was insufficient, or the skill is beyond the capacity of the trainee at this time. As noted by Breunlin et al. (1988), the latter would be the more serious supervision error because it may move the trainee from a moderate amount of anxiety to a level that can block learning.

Lambert and Arnold (1987) substituted *feedback* for *mastery* as the fourth element for efficient learning. It makes sense that the clarity and accuracy of supervisor feedback as the supervisee practices a skill are essential for learning. Additionally, a combination of feedback and practice most assuredly presents the supervisee with the greatest opportunity for mastery. As part of the training laboratory outlined in Appendix D, there are additional guidelines for using microtraining in supervision and in the training of supervisors.

Putting It All Together

Reviewing each supervision format is a bit like reviewing theories of psychotherapy. While within the context of considering a particular format, it may seem attractive and worthwhile. Like psychotherapy, however, the use of supervision formats and techniques requires an acceptable level of expertise and a sound rationale that is compatible with the supervisor's vision. This takes both experience with the format and the specific techniques within the format and planning for the activity of supervision. Technical eclecticism among supervisors is desirable because it allows the supervisor to help a variety of supervisees attain a variety of supervision goals.

At the beginning of the chapter, we discussed initial criteria for choosing an intervention. Here we will attempt to draw on the information in this chapter, as well as broader topics, to form a list of questions to ask when selecting format and technique within individual supervision.

1. *How will this method of supervision be received?* No format is appropriate if the supervisee cannot become more expert within the format. At times this may be a developmental issue only. For example, a supervisee may be too novice and/or too concrete to be able to benefit from the advantages of self-report. Occasionally, a particular method of supervision may simply be a bad fit for the supervisee as an individual. Not only developmental level and learning styles, but temperament and cultural norms will determine the receptivity to particular supervision delivery systems.

2. *Am I being true to my beliefs about how one learns to be a mental health practitioner?* As stated earlier, if the supervisor believes that reflectivity is the cornerstone of becoming an expert therapist, then the supervision modality must achieve reflectivity. In such cases, supervisee behaviors will be viewed in the context of the larger dynamics of interpersonal process and meaning, not the other way around. Other supervisors will assume that supervisees will become more competent with a series of successes and will therefore focus more on therapeutic interventions. The larger point is that if the supervisor doesn't accept the outcome of a supervision method as crucial to the supervisee's development the method will most likely be used in a perfunctory manner.

3. *Am I considering the three functions of supervision?* Using a different method to assess from one used to promote supervisee development may make the supervision process clearer to the supervisee. Furthermore, a change of method can help the supervisor maintain boundaries between different supervisor roles.

4. *Am I considering the timing and/or relative structure of my supervision?* Busy professional schedules often dictate the timing of supervision. But for the supervisee who is floundering, timing may be a relatively easy and potentially important variable to assist a breakthrough in learning. Similarly, the relative use of structure may be manipulated to allow a different and potentially potent learning opportunity for the supervisee.

5. *Are administrative constraints real or am I not advocating with a strong enough voice?* It is not uncommon to hear that a piece of media equipment is too expensive or that a method of supervision is too time consuming for a particular setting. Yet a strong supervision program can energize a setting so that what is accomplished is more efficient and of higher quality. Supervisors must advocate for the kind and level of supervision that they believe must be present. As models to supervisees, it is imperative that supervisors work in ways that are productive and credible.

6. *What does this particular supervisee need to learn next? Am I using the best method for that purpose?* Sometimes a new method is called for because the supervisor needs to alter the system;

other times, the supervisor must realize that the method being used is simply not accomplishing the desired outcome. One supervisor reported that, after spending several frustrating weeks in supervision with the supervisee making little progress conceptualizing client issues, the supervisor began to assign homework that required that the supervisee come to the conference with three different avenues to take with each client to be discussed, one of which had to be unconventional. This assignment seemed to energize the counselor and she started to make significant gains in her area of weakness.

What the supervisee needs may also challenge the comfort level of the supervisor. It may be more comfortable to remain supportive when the supervisee needs to be challenged. It may be more natural to continue a highly structured approach to supervision when the supervisee is ready for the supervisor to be more of a consultant in approach. If supervision is fairly standard from supervisee to supervisee, the supervisor should question whether it is the supervisor that needs to be stretched.

7. *Am I skilled in the use of this particular method or technique?* Ultimately, supervision will fall flat if the method is used poorly. IPR is a good example of a technique that can easily deteriorate if the supervisor is not skilled at asking probing questions without loading them with the supervisor's opinion. As we stated earlier, self-report can be a highly charged method of supervision, but only when the supervisor is expert and knows how to use the method to challenge the supervisee.

8. *Have I considered ethical safeguards?* Supervision is based on the premise that the supervisee is not yet expert enough to handle a wide range of clients autonomously. An important criterion for choosing a method of supervision, therefore, must be some judgement about the level of competence of the supervisee. This is one reason why self-report is considered foolhardy for novice counselors. The ethics of supervision include the supervisor's responsibility to the supervisee. Supervision that does not assist the supervisee in learning the helping process could be considered unethical.

9. *Is it time to try something new?* Even if the supervisor is adamant about the centrality of one aspect of therapeutic practice (e.g., establishing an empathic relationship with the client), there are different ways to help the supervisee reach the goal. For example, Sterling and Bugental (1993) suggested using role play to help the supervisee make phenomenological gains; Stone and Amundson (1989) suggested the technique of metaphoric case drawing to assist in conceptualization. The training literature is replete with examples of specific techniques to arrive at a variety of areas of competence. Trying something new is targeted as much on the supervisor as the supervisee. The goal is to stay fresh or to use a new method or technique to stimulate new and sometimes unexpected learning.

10. *Can I document the success of my method?* It would be nice if supervisors had hard data to support their work with each supervisee. In the absence of such data, it is still important that the supervisor glean a sense of accomplishment from the method or techniques being used. Each method chosen translates to alternative methods rejected. Therefore, supervisors must seek some justification for the continuation of a particular approach to supervision. At the very least, supervisors should seek feedback from supervisees about what they experienced as most helpful to their learning.

11. *Am I willing confront my own assumptions?* Good supervisors can revisit familiar tenets with new scrutiny. No vision is complete. No supervision method has been found to be indispensable. Supervision at its best is a healthy balance of authority and humility. Supervisors who opt for confusion over stagnation model the essence of professional growth for their supervisees.

CONCLUSION

As the supervisor conducts individual supervision, many options are available regarding the form that supervision will take. Much of this will be determined by prior experience, interest in experimenting with different methods, and perceived supervisee need. All methods carry with them opportunities and opportunities bypassed. The quality of supervision we offer is intimately related to the decisions we make about methods. But presently there is not sufficient empirical evidence to either encourage or reject the use of any of the available methods. Clearly, supervisors need not only to expand their repertoire, but also to systematically study their methods and techniques, to examine both the process and the meaning of what they do (Holloway & Carroll, 1996). In this way they can best serve both their supervisees and their profession.

CHAPTER 6

Supervision Interventions
Group Supervision

Historically, most supervisors have considered individual supervision the cornerstone for training. Yet a great deal of supervision also takes place in a group format. It is our impression, for example, that virtually all university training programs employ group supervision at one point or another during their clinical courses. CACREP standards (Council, 1994), in fact, *require* group supervision.

Group supervision is also central in internship and other training settings as several studies have indicated. Riva and Cornish (1995) found that 65 percent of predoctoral psychology internship sites reported using group supervision. And supervisors in two recent studies reported that, whereas they used individual supervision most frequently, group supervision was a close second. Supervisors surveyed in one of the studies (Goodyear & Nelson, 1997) were based in university counseling centers; those surveyed in the other were family therapy supervisors (Wetchler, Piercy, & Sprenkle, 1989). That such similar findings were obtained across both supervisory orientation and setting suggests the general validity of the belief that group supervision is, indeed, widely practiced.

The purpose of this chapter is to provide an overview of group supervision. In so doing, we hope to dispel the myth that individual supervision is the inherently superior modality (cf. McCarthy, DeBell, Kanuha, & McLeod, 1988). For this chapter we will draw from the limited empirical literature that exists and supplement it liberally with available conceptual and practice-based writings.

The assumptions that guide this chapter are aptly summarized by the following three propositions that Cartwright and Zander (1968) offered:

1. *groups mobilize powerful forces that produce effects of utmost importance to individuals;*
2. *groups may produce both good and bad consequences;*
3. *a correct understanding of group dynamics… permits the possibility that desirable consequences from groups can be deliberately enhanced.* (p. 23)

GROUP SUPERVISION DEFINED

Holloway and Johnston (1985) defined group supervision as a process "in which supervisors oversee a supervisee's professional development in a group of peers" (p. 333). Our own, somewhat more extended definition, is that

group supervision is the regular meeting of a group of supervisees with a designated supervisor, for the purpose of furthering their understanding of themselves as clinicians, of the clients with whom they work, and/or of service delivery in general, and who are aided in this endeavor by their interaction with each other in the context of group process.

This definition of group supervision is consistent with Cartwright and Zander's (1968) definition of a group as "a collection of individuals who have relations to one another that make them interdependent to some significant degree" (p. 46).

There apparently has been no research on the best size for a supervision group. Aronson (1990) suggested that "the optimal size seems to be 5 or 6 if one is to devote sufficient attention to each person, especially if each participant is treating a sizable caseload" (p. 91). Chaiklin and Munson

111

(1983) recommended 6 to 12 members, whereas Schreiber and Frank (1983) suggested at least 7, both sets of authors suggested that to involve fewer supervisees is to risk disruption because of absences and drop-outs.

These optimal sizes are often difficult, though, to achieve in practice. Riva and Cornish (1995) found in their survey of psychology internship sites that the typical supervision group consisted of between three and five supervisees, which would correspond to the number of interns on site. In university training programs, on the other hand, practicum groups typically range in size up to ten members. This often is guided by course enrollment constraints of the particular university in which a given practicum is offered.

ADVANTAGES AND LIMITATIONS OF SUPERVISING IN GROUPS

Advantages of Group Supervision

Holloway and Johnston (1985) criticized the fact that the practice of group supervision so far outstrips the research available to support it. Their concern had merit then, and apparently does now, as Prieto's (1996) recent review of the literature confirmed. But despite the dearth of hard evidence concerning group supervision, its practitioners offer compelling reasons for using this format. Therefore, it would seem ill-advised to forego the use of group supervision while we wait for data concerning its processes and outcomes.

Following are 10 frequently suggested advantages of group supervision. For related discussions of the advantages of group supervision, the reader might consult Carroll (1996), Hawkins and Shohet (1989) or Hayes (1989); also Riva and Cornish (1995).

1. *Economies of time, money, and expertise:* A common observation among supervisors is that group supervision offers many of the same economies that group counseling or therapy affords. In particular, these include economies of time, money, and expertise (Hawkins & Shohet, 1989). Because this is perhaps the most obvious advantage of group

supervision, we want to emphasize that these economies are being obtained even as *other* important advantages are obtained as well.

2. *Minimized supervisee dependence:* Advocates for group supervision often argue that its use can help avoid or at least minimize supervisee dependence (Getzel & Salmon, 1985; Parihar, 1983). In addition, group supervision can diminish the hierarchical issues between supervisor and supervisee by encouraging more input from other supervisees in case analysis (Allen, 1976; Cohen, Gross, & Turner, 1976).

3. *Opportunities for vicarious learning:* To observe peers' successes and failures as they conceptualize and intervene in particular ways can provide an important vicarious learning. Significantly, Hillerbrand (1987) cited data that suggest that novices who observe peers performing a skill are more likely to exhibit skill improvement and increased self-efficacy than those who *instead* viewed an expert. Moreover, what is learned from peers will likely not be strictly limited to the professional realm, but include personal learnings as well. That is, to observe and then discuss other group members' experiences and feelings can serve as a valuable means to normalize them (Hawkins & Shohet, 1989) for all members of the group.

4. *Supervisee exposure to a broader range of clients:* During group supervision, supervisees are exposed to and learn about the clients with whom the other group members are working. In this manner, they all are able to learn about a broader range of clients than if they were working only in dyadic supervision.

5. *Feedback for the supervisee: greater quantity and diversity:* Another justification for using group supervision is that supervisees can offer each other a variety of perspectives that no one supervisor could provide. Hawkins and Shohet (1989) suggested that a group enhances the range of life experiences and other individual differences available to those who give feedback to the supervisee. Such individual differences will include age, gender, sexual orientation, race, and culture. This, in turn, increases the likelihood that at least one person will have empathy for both (1) the supervisee and (2) the client.

This similarly expands the range of expertise within the group. For example, in our group supervision, we have often encouraged a supervisee of a particular background to serve as consultant to the group when the discussion concerns treatment of a client of that background (e.g., a Korean-American supervisee who provided the group with information about Korean cultural norms when the focus had been on one supervisee's work with a Korean-American client).

Although supervisors must remain vigilant against the tendency of one person's representing a cultural group, some recognition of group identity can encourage a discussion of the importance of culture for both therapy and supervision. Therefore, the supervisor must be skilled in using peer consultants to open the group to new considerations, but not close down the group in deference to an "expert."

6. *Feedback for the supervisee: greater quality:* Hillerbrand (1987) drew from the cognitive science literature on the development of expertise (for a recent review of that literature, see Ericcson & Lehmann, 1996) to discuss unique strengths of group supervision. The expertise literature suggests that as people become expert in *any* domain their knowledge becomes more "proceduralized." That is, problem solving will occur at an increasingly automatic level and outside their awareness. Therefore, "although experts are able to perform cognitive skills, they . . . are generally poor at post hoc descriptions of their actual cognitive processes" (p. 294). Novices (i.e., fellow supervisees) are more likely to employ language that is more understandable to other novices than that of the supervisor–expert. Moreover, they may be better able to decode nonverbal cues used by other novices to indicate confusion.

Starling, Baker, and Campbell (1996) reported a qualitative study in which four participants in group supervision were interviewed both at the midpoint and at the end of the semester. Among their several findings was that feedback from peers was an especially important aspect of the group experience. Therefore, contrary to the opinions of many seasoned supervisors, the individual supervision modality may offer the supervisee a less valuable experience, at least with respect to quality of feedback.

7. *A more comprehensive picture of the supervisee:* The group supervision format enriches the ways the supervisor perceives and ultimately evaluates the supervisee. A particular supervisee might, for example, seem blocked when discussing his or her own work and yet still be an intelligent and insightful contributor to group discussions. To be able to see this can allow the supervisor to view the supervisee's difficulties in a different way (e.g., as a function of fear; isomorphism; etc.) than might be the case if individual supervision were the exclusive modality.

In other words, group supervision allows us to see our supervisees perform in a relatively ego protected environment, at least when another supervisee's clinical work is the focus. In addition, supervisees can experience positive feedback from their colleagues when the insights they offer to the group are particularly astute.

Hawkins and Shohet (1989) suggested that the supervisor is able to gain important information observing reactions the supervisees are having to material being discussed, to one another, and to the supervisor. Expanding on this point, Counselman and Gumpert (1993) argued that parallel processes can be *especially* transparent in groups: "Group member reactions such as boredom, anger, anxiety, and excessive helpfulness can serve as important clues to the case dynamics" (p. 26). Moreover, they suggested that the feedback about these processes by a number of peers is often more potent than similar feedback delivered by a single supervisor.

Also, Aronson (1990) suggested an advantage of group supervision that seems at least conceptually related here. He suggested that the group format can be useful in moderating any potentially destructive countertransference reactions the supervisor might develop.

8. *Facilitated risk taking:* One of the more interesting phenomena documented in the group dynamics literature is that of the "risky shift." This is a situation in which "group interaction will eventuate in increased risk-taking relative to the average of the prior decisions of the group members working separately" (Wallach, Kogan, & Bem, 1962, p. 76).

This attribute of groups can be useful to help encourage particular supervisees to take actions they otherwise might not have done. This could, for example, include using some particular technique or perhaps taking an interpersonal risk of some sort. Of course, the moderating influence of the supervisor is important here, to ensure that the supervisees do not undertake actions that are beyond their skill levels or that will endanger the client in some way.

9. *Greater opportunity to use action techniques:* Supervisors who employ action techniques will find the group especially useful (Hawkins & Shohet, 1989; Williams, 1995). Williams, whose particular emphasis has been on the use of psychodrama, provided an illustration of how he has used an action approach:

> *If one is going to conduct a supervision group using action, it is desirable to establish an "action culture" as soon as possible . . . to take the awe out of the method, to make it seem ordinary. [For example, in an initial session, the supervisor might] ask the supervisee [Tina] to imagine a line in the room, one end of which represents 0 and the other 10. Let us suppose that one of Tina's selected training needs is "more strength in hypothesizing about cases," and she stands at a "3" on her present strength. The supervisor interviews her as she stands on that spot to find out what "3" means in terms of hypothesizing strength. She then is asked where she will be (rather than "would like to be") at the end of the year. Let us say that she goes to a "7," wavers, and ends up at "6." Again, the supervisor interviews her as if she is that "6 person." . . . After a couple of demonstrations, the supervisor might ask those who have already been interviewed to interview the remainder of the group using [this] physical scaling. . . . This brings into operation one of the most important guidelines for group supervision: Use the group.* (Williams, 1995, pp. 215–216).

10. *Mirroring the supervisees' intervention (specific to the supervision of group therapists):* A final advantage of group supervision pertains specifically to the supervision of one treatment modality: that of group counseling or therapy. By having a supervision format that mirrors that of the treatment being supervised, supervisees and the supervisor alike have the opportunity to benefit (Hart, 1982; Hawkins & Shohet, 1989). For example, parallel processes and isomorphism are more likely to be observed; supervisees can apply group process learnings from their supervision group to their counseling groups.

Limitations of Group Supervision

There is an important caveat to these suggested advantages of group supervision. That is, regardless of these strengths of the modality, we have not found any authors suggesting that it actually should *replace* individual supervision. Working with supervisees as a group consistently has been viewed as a complement to individual supervision or as a format to follow individual supervision in the course of training and, most often, beyond training.

Moreover, there are some drawbacks to group supervision that we should acknowledge. The following list is adapted from suggestions made by Carroll (1996), supplemented by other sources and our own observations:

1. *The group format may not allow individuals to get what they need:* This can occur for several reasons.

a. Supervisees with heavy caseloads may not get all the supervision time they need.

b. In groups that are heterogeneous with respect to the skill levels of group members, the more skilled members may end up not getting what they need.

c. The learning available to each group member in group supervision may be too diffuse to be worthwhile (Hamlin & Timberlake, 1982).

d. An overpowering group member might rob others of their instructional needs, or the structure itself might fit the majority of members, but offer virtually nothing to a distinct minority of the members (Parihar, 1983).

2. *Confidentiality concerns:* In group supervision, there must be concerns about confidentiality of both (a) the clients who are the focus of attention and (b) the supervisees in the group. In both cases, confidentiality is less secure in groups.

3. *The group format is not isomorphic with that of individual counseling:* Because of this, the group is less likely to mirror some of the individual processes that occur in that counseling format. This is a significant concern given that most group supervision concerns counseling that is occurring in an individual format.

4. *Certain group phenomena can impede learning:* Between-member competition and scapegoating are among the phenomena that, if unchecked, can interfere with learning and in some cases even result in deleterious effects to one or more of the supervisees.

5. *The group may focus too much time on issues not of particular relevance to or interest for the other group members:* As Aronson (1990) pointed out, though, it is the supervisor's responsibility to ensure that all members feel that they are getting something from the group.

BETWEEN-SUPERVISEE ISSUES AND PROCESSES

Of the many possible interpersonal processes that occur during group supervision, we believe two merit particular attention: between-supervisee competition and between-supervisee support. We will address each briefly.

Competition

In Chapter 4 we discussed supervisees' needs both to feel and to seem competent. This supervisee need is present in all supervision formats. In group supervision, though, it can help to fuel between-supervisee competition, especially over which particular supervisee will be perceived as the "best" or perhaps the supervisor's "favorite."

Some level of between-supervisee competition is inevitable. In fact, when it is appropriately channeled, it can be useful in stimulating group members to stretch to be the best they can. The supervisor, though, has an important role in containing and channeling that competition.

In some educational contexts, educators actually encourage an openly competitive atmosphere. Aronson (1990) pointed out that one of the clearest examples occurs in some law schools: Because legal practice is adversarial, to encourage the development of combative skills is to prepare the students for practice. Aronson, though, was blunt when he asserted that "this model is totally inappropriate for the training of psychotherapists" (p. 89).

Competition must be acknowledged in order for group members to put it into proper perspective. The following is one supervisor's intervention that was intended both to make between-supervisee competition an open issue and to diffuse its negative effects:

> *Could it be that the seminar is skirting around the question of who is the best therapist here? That is no doubt a hot potato, and what is even more hot is the question of who is the worst therapist. . . . The issue of competition can contribute to the work of the group if everyone tries to do the best he* [sic] *can. It may also interfere if people become too afraid of being rejected or envied.* (Rioch et al., 1976, p. 24)

Support

Reed (1990) suggested that many students anticipate the group supervision that occurs as part of practicum as "a boot camp for counselors" and that when they complete it, "they would know they were no longer students; they were beginning counselors" (p. 3). This suggests, of course, group supervision's importance. But in invoking a military metaphor Reed implicitly suggests that the experience may be harrowing and perhaps even abusive. Perhaps this is true in some few instances. We believe, however, that most supervisees actually will find group supervision to offer a *greater* amount of support than does individual supervision.

Nicholas (1989) suggested that in the early stages of a supervision group the supervisor must provide "nurturant" energy. But as group members begin to invest emotionally in the group and in each other, primary responsibility for this nurturant energy shifts from the supervisor to the group members. This process corresponds with the development of group cohesiveness, which Yalom (1985) asserted is the group equivalent of empathy.

These processes, then, lead to an atmosphere of support between and among group members. And as support levels increase, so too do levels of between-member trust and therefore the extent to which supervisees are willing to become vulnerable with one another and to reveal their mistakes and weaknesses. All this contributes to the increasing value of the supervisory group to members.

Support might be understood to counterbalance between-member competitiveness. In fact, competition typically is more manifest in the early stages of the group, but then becomes moderated as group cohesiveness and mutual support develop.

One interesting phenomenon we have observed on several occasions concerns the situation in which a particular member of the supervision group clearly is faltering badly and the group rallies to protect that person. This protectiveness takes the form of giving softened and nurturing feedback and often even worrying that the supervisor may be behaving in an unduly harsh manner with this group member (despite objective evidence to the contrary).

MORE GENERAL TASKS OF THE SUPERVISOR: CHALLENGING AND SUPPORTING

Blocher (1983) argued that an effective supervisor will offer a balance of *challenge* and *support.* Challenge can have several forms, including supervisor confrontation and also the encouragement to stretch to try out new behaviors. Support, too, can have multiple forms, including encouragement and positive feedback. The supervisor is to offer enough challenge to help propel supervisees forward to try new behaviors, but not so much that they feel overwhelmed. At the same time, the supervisor is to provide support while the supervisees attempt to meet the challenges with which they have been presented, but not so much support that the supervisor infantilizes the

supervisees or conveys the belief that they are too fragile or inept to handle honest feedback or work tasks.

To offer this balance of challenge and support is an ongoing task of supervisors. Its particular form, though, will likely change in group supervision according to the stage of the group's development, as will its salience to supervisees. For example, one important earlier challenge is aimed at the group itself. This is for the supervisor to have group members take on shared responsibility for the group by, for example, only "filling in the gaps," rather than being the sole feedback provider. To the extent that the supervisor successfully models a balanced delivery of challenge and support, the group will adopt and begin responding to effective norms.

Some practitioners employ the intrapsychic concept that group members, individually and collectively, reenact earlier relationships with their primary group, the family (Bion, 1961). This suggests particular ways to understand group behavior. Cooper and Gustafson (1985) have asserted, for example, that "When adults' group behavior unfolds, it is all too apparent that a group character is emerging which dramatizes (in the here and now) patterned roles, sets of expectations, and tests all deriving from family group experiences" (p. 7).

Because of these patterns that supervisees have adopted from their earlier family interactions, the quality and form of at least some of their within-group behavior might be understood as responses that occur outside their awareness. These include difficulties of handing inordinate authority over oneself to the supervisor out of unconscious respect for one's parents. This speaks to old family loyalties. Old family sacrifices also color interactions. These might, for example, cause a supervisee to react negatively to any feedback of a personal nature that comes from an authority figure because the supervisee suffered an excessive amount of humiliation within his or her family of origin.

To summarize, then, optimizing the balance between challenge and support is a responsibility of supervisors in *any* format. Format, though, does affect the manifestions of these supervisor conditions. For example, group supervisors can capitalize on the support available through a cohesive work group; their challenges might include the demands, implicit or otherwise, for supervisees to face the group the following week by having accomplished some particular task. Also, old behaviors supervisees learn in their families of origin can affect the extent to which they see a given supervisor behavior as challenging or supportive.

But at least two other factors affect the forms of challenge and support available to the group supervisor. One is the conceptual model of the supervisor, which is illustrated by the discussion in the paragraphs immediately above. The other is the developmental stage of the particular supervision group. For example, the supervisor's responsibility for providing support and ensuring safety is very different in the earliest weeks of a supervision group than in the middle stages.

MORE SPECIFIC TASKS AND FOCI OF THE SUPERVISOR

Considerable overlap exists in the ways the various authors have conceptualized group supervision, though differences do exist. We will address here some of those similarities and differences. The astute reader will note that these several writings mirror what we covered in Chapter 2 with regard to appropriate supervisory foci. Bernard's (1979) discrimination model and Hawkins and Shohet's "six eyes" model both seem germane here, though the group context adds an additional dimension as well.

Sansbury (1982) suggested the following four group supervision tasks:

1. *teaching interventions directed at the entire group;*
2. *presenting specific case-oriented information, suggestions or feedback;*
3. *focusing on affective responses of a particular supervisee as the feelings pertain to the client;*
4. *processing the group's interaction and development, which can be used to facilitate supervisee exploration, openness and responses.* (p. 54)

Getzel and Salmon (1985) differed from Sansbury in that they suggested the focus should be on the relationship between the supervisee and client. In addition, they included as legitimate foci (1) the

supervision group's interpersonal relationships, (2) supervisor–supervisee relationships, and (3) supervisee relationships to the organizations (either training programs or mental health settings) in which they practiced.

In their review of the group supervision literature, Holloway and Johnston (1985) found support for three group foci: (1) didactic, (2) case conceptualization, and (3) interpersonal process. They pointed out that groups devoted exclusively to an interpersonal process focus had been more common during an earlier era for training programs. Such an approach is perceived as much less credible now.

In their own reviews, Wilbur, Roberts-Wilbur, Morris, Betz, & Hart (1991) and Wilbur, Roberts-Wilbur, Hart, Morris, & Betz (1994) identified three categories of supervision groups: the task process group modality, which seems to be a combination of didactic and case conceptualization material; the psychoprocess modality, which seems to parallel the intrapsychic growth expected in the interpersonal process group; and the socioprocess modality, which parallels the interpersonal relationship growth expected in the interpersonal process group.

Kruger, Cherniss, Maher, and Leichtman (1988) conducted a multiple-case study of four supervision groups with paraprofessionals. They identified the main activity of groups as problem solving and divided this activity into clarifying problems, designing counseling programs, action planning, and evaluating, all of which could be subsumed under case conceptualization. Additionally, Kruger et al. identified "counselor problems" as a nonproblem-solving activity, a category defined as "verbal behavior that helped the team (group) understand or reduce team members' social or affective problems" (p. 336). This final focus again seems akin to interpersonal process activity, blending both individual and group development.

Shulman (1982) conceptualized the supervision of staff groups (in a work setting) as falling into four categories. The first two of the categories (staff meetings and in-service training) are marginally related to our conception of supervision. His last two categories, though, were case consultation and group supervision. He differentiated between the two by referring to the former as focusing on the client and the latter as focusing on supervisee growth.

Shulman saw these as discrete categories because the former may occur even for the seasoned professional who may need consultation for a particular client, whereas the latter assumes less experienced supervisees who are developing in their professional identity. Furthermore, whereas the case consultation group remains fairly faithful to the task of case analysis, the group supervision groups can focus on a variety of topics central to supervisee development, including "job management skills and professional practice skills, impact skills, and learning skills" (p. 224).

Table 6.1 depicts these authors' conceptualization of group supervision. We have identified five discrete categories (didactic presentations, case conceptualization, supervisee individual development, group development, and organization issues) and one less discrete category (supervisee–supervisor issues), which legitimately might be subsumed under group development. This chapter will give particular attention to case conceptualization, supervisee individual development, and group development. Didactic presentations and organizational issues will not be a specific focus since they are not as generic to group supervision as it has developed in recent years.

Before we conclude this section, we want to at least mention Balint groups (Balint, 1985; Norell,

1991), which are employed worldwide in the training of novice physicians. Balint groups were developed from a psychodynamic model and initially had the primary purpose of teaching novice physicians to respond empathically to their patients. In this country, though, they have become more didactic in their format, have broader goals, and most frequently are found in family practice residencies. Brock and Stock (1990) found in their survey of family practice residencies that most such groups meet weekly for 2 to 3 years and follow a format of having the novice physicians spontaneously present cases from memory. As a group, the surveyed supervisors indicated that their two primary objectives for Balint groups were (1) to provide support for the residents and (2) to help residents resolve professional role conflicts.

It is interesting that professionals in different domains may engage in very similar work, yet have no substantial commerce with one another. This is the case with respect to Balint groups, for many mental health professionals are unfamiliar with them. It is possible, though, that there may be aspects of this supervision tradition from which we in mental health might draw.

GROUP STAGES AND PROCESSES

Groups of all types have relatively predictable stages through which they move. Based on a review of the literature, Tuckman (1965) proposed and then later refined (Tuckman & Jensen, 1977)

TABLE 6.1   Group Supervision Activities

	Didactic Presentations	Case Conference	Individual Development	Group Development	Organizational Issues	Supervisor– Supervisee Issues
Sansbury (1982)	×	×	×	×		
Getzel & Salmon (1985)			×	×	×	×
Holloway & Johnston (1985)	×	×	×	×		
Wilbur et al. (1994)	×	×	×	×		
Kruger et al. (1988)		×	×	×		
Shulman (1982)	×	×	×	×		

what has become perhaps the most recognized model of group development. Specifically, the model suggests that groups proceed through five stages, each with characteristic goals for the members:

— *Forming:* members work to become comfortable with one another.
— *Storming:* members work to resolve issues of power; in a supervisory context, this is the stage at which between-member competitiveness is likely to be in its most direct and obvious form.
— *Norming:* members work to set norms for appropriate within-group behavior. Norms concern what is expected of those who are participating in the group (Hayes, 1989). Although these may develop and function outside group members' conscious awareness, they still exert powerful influences on behavior. Sanctions for their violation can be strong. Supervisors have a particular responsibility both (1) to be aware of emerging norms and (2) to shape them by, for example, modeling behaviors that should become normative (e.g., starting the group on time) and helping the members to identify the norms that are developing. In the next section our discussion of establishing ground rules and structure really addresses this stage.
— *Performing:* this is the stage at which members tackle work-related tasks. It is the group's most productive stage.
— *Adjourning:* members work on saying goodbye to one another.

Although all types of groups will move through these stages, different types of groups will move through them differently and with varying levels of intensity. Therefore, whereas it is important that group supervisors be sensitive to these stages, they should also keep in mind that supervision is a *task-oriented* rather than a therapy experience and that movement through the stages will reflect this.

Keith, Connell, and Whitaker (1992) suggested that therapy groups begin with the therapist adopting a *maternal* role. That is, the therapist invites the group members to be comfortable, is nurturing,

and is solicitous of their feelings. The leader gradually shifts to a *paternal* role as she or he begins setting limits on topics and making demands on group members. Then, as the members' emotional investment in the group increases, the therapist gradually turns more and more of the leadership over to them. Supervision groups, though, are different. Keith et al. noted that the supervision group

passes through similar stages, but the maternal and paternal periods are usually brief. And to the extent the supervisor is either maternal or paternal, the parenting model is that of parent and older teenager; that is, it is very limited, acknowledging the freedom and maturity of the second generation. . . . The early 4 to 6 sessions require guidance; like learning to drive a car. Then the teacher becomes less active . . . (the driving instructor chooses to move to the back seat).   (p. 98)

This observation would suggest, then, that the supervision group should be well into the performing stage by the fourth to the sixth session.

Following are several supervision tasks and responsibilities to get the supervision group to the important performing stage. The supervisor's handling of these tasks will affect the way in which the particular group handles the phases of development listed above.

Screening Group Members

One of the very early responsibilities of the supervisor is to screen the members who will comprise the group. In many cases, the supervisor will have relatively little discretion in this matter (e.g., in the case of teaching a university-based practicum or field placement). Nevertheless, there are some issues concerning screening that merit attention. Perhaps the most important of these concerns the extent to which a group could or should be *homogeneous* or *heterogeneous* with respect to such matters as supervisee ability, experience level, theoretical orientation, and characteristics of field site.

For novices, there seems to be a case for relative homogeneity among the group members. When supervisees are more or less in the same boat, they are likely to have greater empathy for one another and to more easily accomplish trust building. Furthermore, in a homogeneous group, one's relative strength can be more readily appreciated because experience level does not cloud individual talent. It may be the case, for example, that one supervisee is more likely to take a risk by using a novel intervention, whereas another will lead the group in conceptualization ability. Although an awareness of the relative strengths of the group members can feed the competitiveness we already have discussed, it can also enhance supervisees' self-awareness. The supervisor's responsibility is to have supervisees identify their baseline strengths and build from there.

Supervisees are more likely to find themselves in heterogeneous supervision groups after they have obtained some experiences in a work setting. Chaiklin and Munson (1983) noted that it is the more experienced supervisees who lose when the group is mixed. Parihar (1983) also found heterogeneity to be a disadvantage in that different experience levels meant very different expectations that supervisees brought to supervision. Therefore, the group supervisor would be bound to make compromises in a mixed group, leading to some level of dissatisfaction with the experience. Allen (1976) echoed these concerns and suggested that heterogeneity is a major drawback for supervision groups in mental health settings.

Wendorf, Wendorf, and Bond (1985) were more positive about the heterogeneous group, arguing that it is more realistic and allows different group members to adopt more responsible roles as they are ready. In the meantime, more experienced clinicians can be taking appropriate leadership positions and modeling higher-level functioning for those who are less experienced. Getzel and Salmon (1985) also asserted that too much homogeneity would stifle the exact benefits hoped for in group supervision, including spontaneity. Furthermore, they pointed out that homogeneity of cultural background can produce an undesirable situation, especially if the clientele being served is culturally diverse. Finally, homogeneity of experience but not of perspective was recommended by Schreiber and Frank (1983) for

experienced clinicians in private practice pursuing peer supervision. In discussing their position, the authors stated that

> *Our sense was that at a more advanced state in career development these differences (in perspective and expertise) are welcomed and perceived as edifying. By this time each of us was secure enough about our skills to feel comfortable with a peer having another approach in which she was expert.* (p. 31)

Because homogeneity versus heterogeneity is an unresolved issue for group supervision, the supervisor must consider the makeup of the group carefully and attempt to compensate for the disadvantages of either situation through group structure and ground rules.

Establishing Ground Rules and Structure

Although group structure and ground rules may seem a mundane topic, they can significantly influence the group process. In fact, to determine these ground rules is a particular focus of the *norming* stage of the group: If the supervisor does not exert leadership in setting these rules, the group members will. This, in turn, will affect group behavior in the *performing* stage.

Helping the group to establish effective group norms can minimize the risk of having some supervisees establish norms that are counterproductive to an effective supervision experience. For example, the wrong norms might allow the group to become a place for some supervisees to ventilate their miseries, expressing sensitive material in order to keep sympathies of the other members high, but their feedback low. Especially in groups of helping professionals who have a vocation or calling to take care of others, this can be a successful trainee maneuver, at least initially.

This illustrates only one of a number of possibly counterproductive norms that might be established if the supervisor does not take an active role in influencing norm development. In fact, by imposing an optimal level of structure, the supervisor not only influences the development of norms, but helps provide group members with the sense of safety that is needed to risk exposing their clinical work—and themselves—to their peers. Yet the key word here is optimal, for if structure is too rigid, it can create its own tension by stifling spontaneity and fitting some members far better than others. The supervisor, therefore, needs not only to create an initial structure, but monitor its effect on the group and be prepared to alter or abandon part of the group's structure based on group feedback (in fact, to request feedback is *itself* a structural matter).

The following sections on meeting place(s), frequency of meetings, attendance, and manner of case presentation all are matters of ground rules and structure. We will discuss each in turn. Although we are attempting to convey what we understand to be conventional clinical wisdom with respect to these matters, we realize that not all supervisors would be in complete agreement on these points. What is important, though, is that supervisors be clear about how they intend to handle these several matters and then to convey that clearly to group members.

Meeting Place(s).   Whether the group meets on common ground (e.g., the work site) or rotates meeting place (e.g., one meeting at each member's home) will affect the feelings group members have about each other and accelerate or delay cohesion. Because of the need to mirror the structure of therapy, it probably is important as much as possible in establishing meeting places to maintain appropriate boundaries with respect to such matters as meeting time, professionalism of the setting and members' demeanor, and so on.

Frequency of Meetings.   How often the group meets will also affect group process: meeting once a month, for instance, might make it difficult to arrive at a viable atmosphere, although meeting twice a week might be untenable for some members and cause resentment. Marks and Hixon (1986) found that groups that met weekly (as opposed to biweekly) provided their members with the most growth, including "an increased willingness to deal with feelings associated with the treatment process, and a marked decrease in anxiety

due to an increase in trust" (p. 422). By contrast, groups that met biweekly remained more cognitive and formal.

Attendance.   Regular attendance is an especially important ground rule to adopt and enforce. Absences affect the group in multiple ways, including the sense of cohesion members feel as well as the energy and vitality experienced during the meeting. Moreover, group members essentially are committing to be there for one another. As well, members will attach meaning to absences of other supervisees. For example, the supervisee who does not come the week after she presents a difficult case will cause others to worry that their feedback might have been too confrontive. This will not only affect the group session with the missing member, but, if not addressed in the group, will affect the quality of feedback given to this member when she returns.

Manner of Case Presentation.   Another matter involving structure is the means by which cases will be presented (which was a major focus of Chapter 5). Ground rules concerning case presentations are essential if the group is to serve any consistent purpose. A ground rule of openness and respect can be achieved at the outset if the supervisor states his or her expectations regarding confidentiality, responsibility of each member, and level of participation of each group member and protects members from undue peer pressure or intimidation. Many of the ground rules for group supervision have to do with how clinical material will be presented and processed. For example, Munson (1983) offered the following guidelines for case presentations:

1. The supervisor should present a case first.
2. The supervisee should be granted time to prepare the case for presentation.
3. The presentation should be based on written or audiovisual material.
4. The presentation should be built around questions to be answered.
5. The presentation should be organized and focused.

6. The presentation should progress from client dynamics to supervisee dynamics. (p. 104)

Munson also outlined ground rules for supervisors, suggesting that the following be *avoided:* (1) presentation of several cases in a short session, (2) presentation of a specific problem rather than the case in context, (3) presentation of additional problems in a single case, (4) therapist dynamics preceding case dynamics during discussion, and (5) intervention expectations beyond the capabilities of therapist (p. 104).

Perhaps the most common ground rules for group supervision have to do with the offering of feedback to each other as a result of case presentation. These ground rules can be suggested by the supervisor, but they should receive some level of group consensus. Table 6.2 is one such set of guidelines that helps the group members to organize their thoughts and provide feedback in a focused way. Note that is organized so that the supervisee who is presenting a case will speak first, using the first five items to guide that presentation. Subsequent items are to guide group members' observations and comments.

Wilbur and Wilbur (1983; also, Wilbur, Roberts-Wilbur, Hart, Morris, & Betz, 1994) have devised a structure that distracts supervisees from some of their more personal issues and seems, in our experience, to work very well with groups that approach

---

TABLE 6.2   Guidelines for Using a Case Conference Format

The Supervisee: Presenting to Group
1. Of what content, events, and processes were you most aware in today's session (perhaps playing selected tape segments to illustrate)? [description]
2. What do you believe is the most likely explanation for the content (events or processes)? [inference]
3. What feelings were you experiencing toward the client during the session? Also, were you aware of any thoughts or fantasies about the client during the session?
4. What feelings and thoughts do you believe the client was having with you during the session?
5. State the specific feedback that you particularly want from the group.

Group Members
1. Note what the *counselor* did.
   a. What were things you liked about the counselor's approach? (No one likes to hear criticism right off the bat.)
   b. What seemed to be the client's reaction to the counselor's behavior?
   c. What would you have added to the session?
   d. What things did the counselor do that might have been done in a different way?
   e. Were there any things in the session done by the counselor that you think were unhelpful? If so, what were they? What do you believe should have been done instead?
2. Note what the *client* did.
   a. What do you think of this client's concerns?
   b. What feelings did this client elicit in you?
   c. What themes were evident?
   d. Were you confused by any inconsistencies?
   e. Did the client's input seem to make things clearer?
3. Note what the *session* accomplished.
   a. Given what you know about this client, were appropriate process or outcome goals accomplished during this session?
   b. What would you say was the major accomplishment of this session?
   c. What would you say was the major flaw of this session?
4. If this were your client, what would be reasonable and productive goals for the next session? How would you accomplish these goals?

the task of case conferences in an overly cautious fashion. The structured group supervision model (SGS) is presented in Table 6.3.

Supervision during the Performing Stage

By the time the group reaches the performing stage, much of the especially important work of group supervision will already have occurred. If this work has been effective, group members will have taken on appropriate levels of shared responsibility for the group and for one another. Individually, they will have begun to trust and will be energized by a commitment to explore and examine their own therapeutic efforts. Supervisees present cases that show them stretching the upper limits of their skill, rather than cases that are too clear or too impossible to elicit critical comments.

One supervisory behavior that might be expected to change as a function of group stage is the proportion of speech activity exhibited by the supervisor versus the group members. That is, it is reasonable to assume that, with increased cohesion and the movement into a performing mode, the supervisees will speak a greater proportion of the time (and the supervisor, consequently, will speak less) than earlier in the group. Unfortunately, we are aware of only two studies that concern this.

TABLE 6.3   Steps of the Structured Group Supervision Model

Step 1: Plea for Help. The supervisee states what assistance is being requested from the supervision group. The supervisee provides group with summary information relating to the request for assistance. Information may be in the form of audio or videotaped material, a written summary, or verbal communication. Following the presentation of the summary information, supervisee makes Plea for Help statement, e.g., "I need your help with. . . ."

Step 2: Question Period. The supervision group members ask the supervisee questions about the information presented in Step 1. This step allows group members to obtain additional information or clarify any misperceptions concerning the summary information. One at a time, in an orderly manner, group members ask one question at a time of the supervisee. The process is repeated until there are no more questions.

Step 3: Feedback/Consultation. Group supervision members respond to the information provided in Steps 1 and 2 by stating how they would handle the supervisee's issue, problem, client, etc. During this step, the supervisee remains silent but may take notes regarding the comments or suggestions. When giving feedback, group members again proceed one at a time stating how they would handle the supervisee's dilemma. First person is used, e.g., "If this were my client, I would. . . ." The process is repeated until there is no additional feedback.

Pause or Break. There is a 10 to 15 minute break between Steps 3 and 4. Group members should not converse with the supervisee during this break. This is time for the supervisee to reflect on the group's feedback and to prepare for Step 4.

Step 4: Response Statement. The group members remain silent and the supervisee, in round-robin fashion, respond to each group member's feedback. The supervisee tells group members which of their statements were helpful, which were not helpful, and why they were beneficial or not.

Optional Step 5: Discussion. The supervisor may conduct a discussion of the four-step process, summarize, react feedback offered, process group dynamics, etc.

From M. P. Wilbur, J. Roberts-Wilbur, G. M. Hart, J. R. Morris, and R. L. Betz (1994). Structured group supervision (SGS): A pilot study. *Counselor Education and Supervision, 33,* 262–279. Alexandria, VA: American Counseling Association. Copyright © (1994). Reprinted by permission.

Kruger et al. (1988) conducted a multiple-case study of four supervision groups. Two were led by more experienced supervisors; two, by novices. They found that the overall speech activity of supervisees was greater with the more experienced supervisors ($M = 49.4$ percent) than with the less experienced supervisors ($M = 44.04$). Unfortunately, they did not report data in such a way to allow inferences about trends of speech activity across sessions. It is important to note, as well, that these were supervision groups with paraprofessional counselors.

Ravets, Goodyear, and Halon (1994) conducted an intensive case study of two supervision groups: one, for practicum students, was co-led by a faculty supervisor and a teaching assistant; the other, for more advanced supervisees, was run by a single supervisor in an agency setting. In the first group the combined supervisors' feedback accounted for an average of 21 percent of the speech acts across 10 sessions (range from 12 percent to 31 percent). In the other group, the supervisor's average proportion of speech activity was 33.6 percent (range from 18 percent to 55 percent). There were no apparent trends in speech activity as a function of group stage. Apparently, this is one of the areas in group supervision that merits more research attention.

But having helped the group arrive at this performing stage, the supervisor will continue to have issues and tasks to address, albeit of a somewhat different form than in the earlier stages. The sensitive supervisor will be watching for signs of "nonwork" occurring and will change direction, ask the group for feedback, or offer the group some process feedback if this occurs. On the other hand, the supervisor must understand the importance of a recycling of issues if, in fact, they are being understood and confronted at new levels. What might feel like an old theme revisited might be a theme that finally is understood.

Borders (1989) has suggested a model in which the supervisor is to be both a *moderator* and a *process commentator*. As moderator, the supervisor keeps the group on task, choreographs the experience, and summarizes feedback. As process

commentator, the supervisor attends to immediate group dynamics. For both roles, Borders emphasized the need for the supervisor to be cognizant of the developmental level of supervisees (e.g., novice counselors needing more direction and structure or more advanced supervisees being able to take on more responsibility). The model, therefore, requires a good deal of supervisor flexibility.

Indeed, the success of this approach depends on the supervisor's artistry in recognizing a needed and appropriate intervention, assigning tasks to particular peer group members, and orchestrating the feedback. Often working at several levels, the supervisor helps a productive learning experience to unfold. (pp. 5–6)

Borders (1989c) also has suggested a structured group exercise that can breathe life into group processes when they become stagnate. She relies on videotape for the presentation of cases and requires supervisees to *present specific questions* about the client or the session and to *ask for specific feedback.* Other group members are then assigned one of four tasks to direct their observation of the videotape segment, depending on the issues raised by the supervisee.

The *first task* is to engage in focused observation. A peer might be asked to focus on the use of one type of skill (e.g., confrontation) or one aspect of the session, such as the relationship between the counselor and client. Borders pointed out that a particular observation task can be used to develop specific skills of the observer. For example, the observer who has a tendency to quicken the pace of his or her sessions might be asked to observe the pace of the videotaped session.

The *second task* is role taking. An observer might be asked, for example, to take the role of the counselor, of the client, or even of some significant person in the client's life (e.g., a parent or a spouse). For family sessions, the assignment could be to represent the family member who refuses to come to therapy. After the videotape has been shown, the observer gives feedback from the perspective of the person he or she represents.

The *third task* is to observe the session from a particular theoretical orientation. One observer could be assigned this task or several observers could be looking at a session from different theoretical perspectives. For example, one supervisee could be asked to observe another supervisee's counseling session from a systemic perspective; another, from a cognitive–behavioral perspective. Not only does this exercise help supervisees apply theory to practice, but it also helps bring forth underlying assumptions about problem formation and resolution.

The *fourth task* is for an observer to watch the session with the assignment of developing a descriptive metaphor. Borders reported that this approach has been particularly helpful when the issue is the interpersonal dynamics between the client and counselor or the counselor feeling "stuck." For example, an observer might be asked to think of a road map and describe the direction counseling is taking or to view the counselor–client relationship within the context of a movie and describe each person's part in the drama.

Finally, when the group is in the performing stage, individual differences should be more salient. Because there is more group cohesion, there is less need for group conformity. For example, each person's brand of humor should be more evident at this stage, as should personal philosophies of life and of helping. When a supervision group is working well, there are no stars (including the supervisor) and no dunces. Rather, each supervisee is known for his or her particular talents, idiosyncratic way of viewing clients, and personal supervision goals. Everyone has something to gain from the group and something to offer to the group.

Some groups may never get fully to this performing stage; and probably all groups have some periods of "nonwork" throughout their life-span. Shulman (1982) argued that the supervision group's "culture" is an important concept to keep in mind. The culture is the gestalt that makes the group feel different from all other groups; these are the norms and rules the group has adopted. Many of these are outside members' conscious awareness, but powerful nevertheless. One such rule might be, "Give feedback, but don't make anyone angry." Although benign enough in the initial stages of group supervision, if such a rule were to persevere as more powerful that the injunction to be honest, it would adversely affect the work of the group.

It is rewarding when nonproductive aspects of the supervision group's culture are called into question by supervisees. But if this does not occur, it is ultimately up to the supervisor to be aware of and to confront the limitations brought about by certain aspects of the group's culture.

Supervision during the Adjourning Stage

It is likely that the majority of supervision groups are time limited. However, some are ongoing groups. Therefore, it is appropriate to discuss each type of group separately in terms of their termination processes.

The Time-limited Group.   The time frames for many supervisory relationships are determined by a training calendar. Often this corresponds to a semester or to an internship cycle or rotation.

For practicum and internship groups, then, the supervision experience can be one of weeks, rather than months or years. Especially when the life of the supervision group is across a single semester, the ending of the group may feel premature to almost everyone. In addition, toward the conclusion of the semester, there will be a sense of urgency in managing the termination of each supervisee's client load that may override any consideration of the closure issues in the group itself.

It would be a mistake, though, to end a supervision group without allowing the group to process this phase. Moreover, because the endings of the therapeutic relationships coincide with the ending of the supervisory group, the parallels become a useful tool and provide important material to process.

Virtually all brief therapy models have a particular structure, an emphasis on a treatment plan, and a particular emphasis on the termination. In a sense, this is a model that applies to supervision, whether dyadic or in a group, as well. The goals of the supervision group should be specific enough to be noticed when they have been achieved so that supervisees can feel a sense of accomplishment upon ending. At the same time, the supervisor needs to help supervisees put their learning into context to alleviate any panic at ending the supervision experience. We are referring to the naive assumption that most supervisees have upon entering supervision that they will feel totally competent upon its completion. We know, of course, that training is only the beginning of the practitioner's learning of his or her trade (for this reason, supervision among experienced practitioners is becoming more and more prevalent). It is important to discuss this reality in closing out group supervision. Equally important is giving each supervisee some direction regarding the learning to be accomplished in the immediate future. This may need to be done individually, although certainly some supervision groups will have developed sufficiently to handle this task in the group context.

The point is that a time-limited experience inherently limits opportunity to learn. Therefore, supervisees must be evaluated knowing that the amount of time given to them most likely has been insufficient for their needs and that it is essential for them to leave the supervision experience with a plan for self-improvement. A part of this plan for each supervisee will most likely be the securing of additional supervision. An important culminating experience, therefore, would be to crystallize what can be learned from supervision and how one goes about securing this type of supervision for oneself.

One aspect of time-limited supervision that can be frustrating for the supervisor is the nearly universal tendency of supervisees to begin withdrawing from the group when the end is in sight. Supervisees who are simultaneously approaching closure with their clients will complain that their clients have stopped "working." Often these same supervisees will be unaware that they are working less with each other in the supervision group. The need for psychological distance in order to cope with the loss of both people and a valuable process

is important to address in the group as supervisees handle multiple closure experiences.

The Ongoing Supervision Group.   A danger of the ongoing supervision group is that it might fizzle out, rather than end. Just like a relationship that fizzles out, the group that terminates in this fashion is left with more unfinished business and perhaps an inadequate understanding of what caused the ending to occur. In order to avoid this, it is advisable to schedule an ending from the outset of the group. Like all social systems, groups need markers in order to appreciate their development. An ending can provide this kind of marker, even if the group reconstitutes itself immediately with no change of membership.

The kind of ending we are suggesting may be an appointed time when the group reviews the assumptions and decisions that were made in the pregroup phase. It is a time when as many things as possible become negotiable, including ground rules and the process of supervision itself. It is a time for supervisees to evaluate their individual development and their level of commitment and contribution to the goals of the group. It is a time for the supervisor to evaluate the amount of responsibility that has been shared with group members, the process that has been in place, and the feasibility of continuance.

There are several ways that endings can be added to the life of a group. One way is to freeze membership for a certain amount of time, say one year, at which time some members might leave and others might enter. The change of membership gives the group a chance to start over in a sense. Another way is for the process of the group itself to change. For example, a supervisor might decide that it is time for the group to change from a supervisor-led group to a peer supervision group. This juncture could be planned as an ending. Time can also be manipulated to produce a marker. A break of 4 to 6 weeks could be planned to occur every 6 months in order to encourage an evaluation and renegotiation period prior to or immediately after the break. Each group will find its own way to end once the importance of ending is appreciated.

Thus far, our discussion pertains to most supervision groups. We would like to devote the rest of this chapter, however, to a special kind of group, the peer supervision group.

PEER GROUP SUPERVISION

In Chapter 1 we differentiated supervision from consultation, noting that the former included evaluation and was an ongoing, hierarchical relationship. The practice of peer supervision, though, is neither hierarchical nor does it include formal evaluation. In this sense, it is more like consultation than supervision. But, at the same time, it is ongoing, and group members feel more accountable to each other than they might in a consulting relationship. It is difficult, therefore, to properly categorize it as being either supervision or consultation.

But, however categorized, peer supervision seems to be a growing phenomenon and an important ingredient to the vitality of the mental health professions. Therefore, we determined that it was an important topic for us to cover.

Anyone who has been in the helping professions for a while has heard colleagues talk about the problem of isolation and the fear of practitioner burnout, along with the fear of becoming stale. In more recent years, professional organizations have highlighted the need for continuing supervision, often incorporating the expectation of posttraining supervision into certification requirements. But there comes a time when one has met the profession's designated criteria, and one is far more likely to be the supervisor than the supervisee. For an increasing number of professionals, the alternative to receiving no additional supervision has come in the form of peer group supervision.

Although peer supervision has received only modest coverage in the professional literature, Lewis, Greenburg, & Hatch (1988) found, at least among psychologists in private practice, that 23 percent of a national sample were currently members of peer supervision groups, 24 percent had belonged to such a group in the past, and 61 percent expressed a desire to belong to a group if one

were available. Among the reasons for joining peer groups (in rank order by importance) were (1) suggestions for problem cases, (2) discussing ethical professional issues, (3) countering isolation, (4) sharing information, (5) exploring problematic feelings and attitudes toward clients, (6) learning and mastering therapeutic techniques, (7) support for stress in private practice, (8) countering burnout, and (9) exposure to other theoretical approaches.

Wiley (1994) reported a survey of members of the American Psychological Association's Division of Counseling Psychology who were in private practice. She found that the proportion of those who reported participating either weekly or biweekly in peer supervision groups were as follows:

- Those who were 3 to 7 years postdoctorate, 25 percent
- Those who were 8 to 15 years postdoctorate, 38 percent
- Those 16 or more years postdoctorate, 32 percent

The sizes of her samples were small, but they are generally consistent with the Lewis et al. findings. Moreover, they are relatively consistent over time, even for very experienced practitioners.

Peer supervision groups can either develop from supervisor-led groups to peer groups or can be conceived as peer supervision groups from the outset. In either case, at the point that peers attempt to offer each other supervision (or consultation, as some authors prefer to designate it), certain conditions must exist if the process is to be successful. Chaiklin and Munson (1983) noted that a sincere desire to improve one's clinical skills is, of course, the primary condition for peer supervision. They also favored the model of a peer group beginning with a supervisor whose role is to work himself or herself out of a job. For practitioners working in mental health settings, the second major condition is administrative backing (Chaiklin & Munson, 1983; Marks & Hixon, 1986). If peer supervision is not viewed as valuable and cost effective by administrators, and if this is not communicated by the provision of space and time to conduct supervision meetings, the within-agency peer group will certainly falter.

The independent peer group (i.e., outside any employment setting) has probably the greatest potential for compatibility among its members because such a group tends to be formed by professionals who already know and respect each other. For the peer group formed within an institution, there may be some history to overcome among some of the members, such as political entanglements, competitiveness, or personality issues (Hamlin & Timberlake, 1982). In addition, lack of homogeneity of experience is far more likely for the within-agency group, which means that the group will most likely veer either toward the more experienced or least experienced members, to the potential frustration of the other members of the group. Regardless of the initial compatibility of the peer group, however, the group stages outlined by Tuckman and Jensen (1977) will still occur and need attention. It is a common error of professionals who are already comfortable with one another to forego the planning stage for the group until issues begin to arise. Another potential for all supervision groups, but more so with peer groups, is differential contact among its members outside supervision. Ground rules may need to be outlined regarding any processing of supervision outside the group so as not to drain off energy that legitimately belongs within the group.

The Process of Peer Supervision Groups

Peer supervision groups tend to be more informal than other types of supervision groups (Lewis et al., 1988). This might be considered an error, at least in the beginning. Without the direction of a designated leader, structure can give the group some measure of stability as it is finding its particular rhythm.

Part of the structure must be, in fact, a plan for handling the leadership of the group. Although leaderless by definition, peer groups have realized that ignoring the issue of leadership gives rise to competitiveness (Schreiber & Frank, 1983). Therefore, most groups rotate the leadership role, with one person directing each meeting. The leader may concern himself or herself with group leadership issues only or may also be asked to take responsibility for secretarial issues arising as a result of the meeting, including communicating with absent members about the next meeting, keeping records of supervision meetings and actions taken, and the like.

The process also includes a plan for case presentation. Typically, one or two cases are the maximum that can be reasonably discussed at one meeting. Marks and Hixon (1986) suggested that the presenter come prepared with two or three questions about the case to direct the group's discussion. They also suggested that a process observer be appointed (different from either the presenter or the designated leader). This person would give feedback at the end of the supervision meeting about the group process that he or she observed, including "a statement regarding the group's ability to stay task-oriented, its adherence to ground rules, what group building may have occurred and the participation level of the group members" (p. 421).

Advantages and Disadvantages of Peer Supervision Groups

Those practitioners who participate in peer supervision groups tend to be very favorable about them. There is every reason to assume, therefore, that the numbers of peer supervision groups will grow. Among the advantages ascribed to peer supervision groups are the following (Hamlin & Timberlake, 1982; Lewis et al., 1988; Marks & Hixon, 1986; Schreiber & Frank, 1983; Wendorf et al., 1985):

1. They help clinicians to remain reflective about their work and offer clinicians options beyond their individual frameworks.
2. They offer the type of environment that is especially attractive to adult learners.
3. They provide a forum for the reexamination of familiar experiences (e.g., early terminations or working with one particular ethnic group).

4. They provide a peer review process that maintains high standards for practice, thus reducing the risk of ethical violations.

5. They provide a forum for transmitting new information, thus providing continuing education for members.

6. They provide the continuity necessary for serious consultation.

7. They can provide some of the therapeutic factors often attributed to group process, including reassurance, validation, and a sense of belonging. As a result, they can reduce the potential for burnout.

8. They enable clinicians to become more aware of countertransference issues and parallel process.

9. Because feedback is offered by peers, rather than an expert, supervision is less likely to be compromised by conflicts with authority figures.

The major limitation reported by members of peer supervision groups came from within-agency groups (Marks & Hixon, 1986). Because group members might form their own coalitions, interagency communication might not be facilitated. Also, when group members must work with each other outside the group, they may be reticent to self-disclose and are less trustful in the group. Finally, the structure of the group may be inflexible in dealing with crisis situations that are bound to occasionally occur in agencies. Allen (1976) mentioned one additional disadvantage of peer groups: they may limit the amount of individual supervision sought by the group members. However, Marks and Hixon (1986) found that peer group supervision strengthened individual supervision by "pointing out its gaps" (p. 423).

Group supervision is a cost-effective form of supervision that offers the supervisee the benefits of peer relationships, exposure to a greater number of cases, and vicarious as well as direct learning. There is little doubt that group supervision will continue to be an important supplement to individual supervision. Therefore, we would be well advised to give this vital form of supervision more

empirical attention at the same time that we develop and test group supervision models.

A PROCEDURE FOR SUPERVISEE ASSESSMENT AND FEEDBACK

Advances in computer and software technology have made sophisticated statistical procedures user friendly and accessible to many clinical supervisors who previously have perceived them as too daunting to use. The Windows-based versions of the more popular statistical packages such as SPSS (Statistical Package for the Social Sciences) have made it relatively easy to understand and use statistical procedures. The user does not have to write programming commands, but only to "point and click." Such advances have the potential to affect supervisory practices in important ways.

One statistical procedure many supervisors may find valuable is *multidimensional scaling* (MDS). MDS provides a means for obtaining a picture of how the supervisees in a supervision group perceive one another. Such a picture can be an important form of feedback for the supervisees; it also can provide valuable additional data to the supervisor who is attempting to develop evaluative (formative or summative) impressions of the supervisee.

MDS is "designed to detect the hidden structure of similarity judgments" (Stalans, 1995, p. 138). This structure then is plotted in two- (or more) dimensional space. It is analogous to creating the group's map of the location of the various members in relationship to one another.

MDS is based on a series of comparisons of the perceived relatedness or proximities between pairs of concepts. For our purposes, the supervisees in the supervision group are the concepts on which we are focusing. For the purpose of simplicity and brevity, let us assume that a particular supervision group had five students: Joe, Sally, Celeste, Estella, and Will. As Figure 6.1 indicates, whereas the group members perceived Joe, Sally, and Estella as relatively similar to one another, they perceived Celeste and Will as different both from the larger group and from each other. Based on what

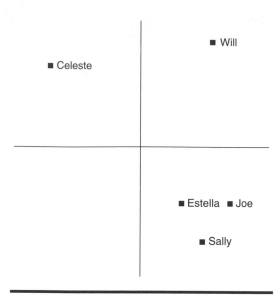

FIGURE 6.1   Hypothetical MDS Array of Supervision Group Members.

the supervisor knows of the characteristics of these students, she or he can attach meaning to the particular configuration.

The group members are the source of data for the MDS analyses. There are both metric and parametric MDS analyses, each of which requires a different type of data. However, to conduct the metric analyses, a supervisor might use a form that will allow a comparison of each group member with each of the others. Each of these between-member pairings would be rated on, say, a seven-point scale where one end is anchored with "not at all similar" and the other end with "extremely similar." Each group member would complete his or her own version of the rating form. These would provide results such as those depicted in Figure 6.1. To obtain a result of this sort, the supervisor would need to request a two-dimensional solution from the MDS program.

Group supervisors might be interested, too, in a public-domain computer program, Circumgrids (Chambers & Grice, 1986), that yields somewhat similar data (note that, at the time of this writing, interested supervisors can download copies of this program from the Internet; simply use one of the World Wide Web's search engines to search for Circumgrids). This procedure, based on Kelly's repertoire grid technique, gives a printout that is plotted similarly to the MDS output described above. But, whereas the MDS procedure is based on either group or individual data, the output for the Circumgrids program is for a *single* supervisee's perceptions of the relationships among group members. Therefore, a group with, say, seven members would yield seven different arrays.

Data entry in this case is different as well. Here, the supervisee enters data directly via the computer keyboard. The supervisor can set up the task for each person. The program is designed to depict distance between or among "personal constructs." In this case, the supervisees in the group are the personal constructs.

CONCLUSION

We established at the outset of this chapter that group supervision is practiced widely. The obvious economies of time and money are but several of the unique advantages of this format. Supervisors tend to report their conviction that group supervision is effective.

This widespread use of groups for supervision has not been matched, though, by commensurate levels of research attention. This will be important in order to validate and extend the substantial clinically based knowledge of group features, processes, and outcomes that already exists. In the meantime, though, the group format is simply too important for supervisors to set aside while we wait. Moreover, most supervisors report that they find it fun!

CHAPTER 7

Supervision Interventions
Live Supervision

In Chapters 5 and 6 we reviewed the supervision interventions that typically transpire in individual case conferences and in the context of group supervision. That material addressed supervision as it is practiced by the majority of mental health professionals. A significant minority of supervisors, however, rely on and often prefer the use of live supervision interventions. Live supervision is especially popular in training programs where facilities are more conducive to its application.

Live supervision represents a paradigmatic shift from either individual supervision or group supervision; therefore, it cannot be considered a subgroup of either. This shift essentially consists of two components: (1) The distinction between therapy and supervision seems less pronounced than in traditional supervision, and (2) the role of the supervisor is significantly changed to include both coaching and cotherapist dimensions. As a result of these essential differences, the process of live supervision and its advantages and drawbacks are different from other forms of supervision. This chapter will address the evolution of live supervision, describe its process both with and without a team, note the advantages and disadvantages for both forms of live supervision, and address the empirical findings about its effectiveness that are available.

Until recently, live supervision was considered the "hallmark of family therapy" (Nichols, 1984, p. 89). Although marriage and family therapy training programs still rely heavily on live supervision (Nichols, Nichols, & Hardy, 1990), its popularity has grown among the other mental health professions (Bubenzer, West, & Gold, 1991; Kivlighan, Angelone, & Swafford, 1991). Live supervision began as an intensive method for working with an individual trainee (or perhaps two trainees working as cotherapists). In more recent years, the team form of live supervision has gained in momentum. The team is a group of therapists or trainees, with or without a supervisor, who work together on their cases. Because of the significantly different dynamics between live supervision without a team and team supervision, we will begin with the former and address team supervision later in the chapter. Furthermore, because "the literature suggests that the one-way mirror may be as basic to family therapy as the couch was to psychoanalysis" (Lewis & Rohrbaugh, 1989, p. 323), our discussion will follow suit and assume, in most cases, that the client is a family. Finally, we will not attempt to make clear distinctions between training or supervision (with the supervisee as the focus) and intervention (with the family system as the focus), even though we are aware that such distinctions sometimes are made in the literature on live supervision. It could easily be argued that the distinction between training and service delivery is artificial and more a matter of supervisor priority. Live supervision has brought the dual levels of supervision more into focus by attending to both levels more or less concurrently. McCollum (1995) reflected this phenomenon when he stated that "live supervision is not so much a matter of mirrors and wires as it is a matter of blending together different points of view" (p. 4). Within the live supervision paradigm, those views represent client, therapist, supervisor, and, perhaps, team members.

Live supervision was initiated by Jay Haley and Salvadore Minuchin (Simon, 1982) in the late 1960s as a result of a rather singular project. At the time, both were invested in treating poor families but were not enamored with the idea of trying to teach middle-class therapists what it was like to be poor. Therefore, they decided to recruit people from poor communities with no more than a high school education and train them to work with other poor families. Because of the real need to protect the families being treated, Haley and Minuchin devised a live supervision model in which they could guide these inexperienced and untrained therapists as they worked. The result? In Haley's words: "Actually they did very well. We worked with them in live supervision, 40 hours a week for two years. Nobody has ever been trained that intensely" (Simon, 1982, p. 29).

Live supervision combines direct observation of the therapy session with some method that enables the supervisor to communicate with and thereby influence the work of the supervisee. Therefore, the supervisor is simultaneously in charge of both training the therapist and controlling the course and, ultimately, the outcome of therapy (Lewis, 1988). Because of the dual agenda of both observing and interacting with the supervisee, much has been written about the technology of live supervision, especially about different methods for communicating with the supervisee. We will begin, therefore, by reviewing the different technologies used to communicate with the supervisee(s); we will also consider the messages that are given by the supervisor during live supervision, as well as the function of presession and postsession deliberations. Once we have explored how live supervision is conducted, we will back up to consider some of the guidelines for the use of live supervision.

METHODS OF LIVE SUPERVISION

Bubenzer, Mahrle, and West (1987) listed six methods used to conduct live supervision: *bug-in-the-ear, monitoring, in vivo, walk-in, phone-in,* and *consultation.* We will explain each of these briefly, as well as *using computer technology* to communicate with the therapist (Klitzke & Lombardo, 1991; Neukrug, 1991).

Bug-in-the-Ear

The bug-in-the-ear (BITE) consists of a wireless earphone that is worn by the supervisee through which the supervisor can coach the supervisee during the therapy session. It has three major advantages: First, it allows the supervisor to make minor adjustments (e.g., "Get them to talk to each other") or to briefly reinforce the therapist (e.g., "Excellent") without interrupting the flow of the therapy session. In fact, much of what can be communicated through BITE might not warrant a more formal interruption of the session. Second, it has been established that BITE works as a behavioral strategy on the part of the supervisor to increase trainee behaviors through such reinforcement (Gallant, Thyer, & Bailey, 1991). Third, BITE protects the therapy relationship more fully than other live supervision technologies because clients are unaware which comments are the direct suggestion of the supervisor (Alderfer, 1983, as cited in Gallant & Thyer, 1989).

The disadvantages of BITE emerge from its advantages: Because BITE is seemingly so nonintrusive, it can be overused by the supervisor and can be a distraction to the supervisee who is trying to track the family as well as take in advice from the supervisor. Similarly, there is a danger of "echo therapy" (Byng-Hall, 1982, as cited in Adamek, 1994), where the trainee simply parrots the words of the supervisor with little or no assimilation of the therapeutic implications of what is being said, thus encouraging trainee dependence. Finally, it is a less crisp form of live supervision that can produce awkward moments. For example, the trainee who is attempting to listen to a supervision comment might need to interrupt the family in order to focus on the supervisory input. Furthermore, because family members do not know when the supervisee is receiving input, the device itself can produce ambivalent feelings because of the secrecy it symbolizes.

Monitoring

The second form of live supervision, monitoring, is used minimally. Monitoring is the process whereby the supervisor observes the session and intervenes directly into the session if the therapist is in difficulty (Minuchin & Fishman, 1981). By implication, therefore, monitoring can be either a way to safeguard client welfare (in which case it is really not live supervision per se, but something that many supervisors might do if they felt a sense of urgency) or a form of live supervision that is less sensitive to the dynamics between therapist and family. Conversely, an advantage of monitoring, assuming that the supervisor takes over when entering the room, is that it allows the supervisor to directly experience the family dynamics. A final advantage of monitoring is that it allows the trainee to benefit from the modeling provided by the supervisor working with the family.

For more experienced therapists, supervisors can be called into an ongoing case as a consultant–supervisor (Richman, Aitken, & Prather, 1990). The supervisor is briefed ahead of time about the case and the difficulties the therapist is having. The supervisor then conducts a session with the therapist present, typically referring particularly to the impasse that is being faced in therapy. Richman et al. remarked that using supervision in this way models and normalizes appropriate help-seeking behavior for the clients, as well as providing a helpful interruption to the therapy system that has been established.

In Vivo

In vivo has some similarity to monitoring in that it allows clients to see the supervisor in operation. Rather than taking over for the therapist, however, the supervisor consults with the therapist in view of the clients. With in vivo supervision, there is an assumption that the family deserves to have access to all information, including a discussion of interventions. Seen from a different angle, the conversation between supervisor and therapist can itself constitute an intervention by heightening the family's awareness of particular dynamics, especially when dynamics are therapeutically reframed for the benefit of the family. In vivo supervision has some similarity to some forms of

team supervision, which will be discussed later in the chapter.

The Walk-in

A final intervention that has similar characteristics to the two previous ones is the walk-in. The supervisor enters the room at some deliberate moment, interacts with both the therapist and the clients, and then leaves. The walk-in does not imply an emergency, nor does it imply the kind of collegiality that is evident with in vivo supervision. A walk-in, therefore, can be used to redirect therapy and to establish certain dynamics between the supervisor and the family or the therapist and the family. As a result, it can be viewed as more of a therapy intervention than either monitoring or in vivo supervision. All three methods of supervision that involve having the supervisor enter the therapy room are more intrusive in the therapy relationship than the methods that follow.

Phones-ins and Consultation Breaks

The most common forms of live supervision are phone-ins or consultation breaks. These methods are similar in that they both interrupt therapy for the therapist to receive input from the supervisor. There is little opportunity for the therapist to react to the intervention, however, when it is phoned in using an intercom system. In the consultation break, the therapist leaves the therapy room to consult with the supervisor (when the supervisor alerts the therapist by, for example, knocking on the door; when the therapist feels the need to consult; or at a predetermined point in the therapy hour). The therapist then has an opportunity to clarify what the supervisor is suggesting prior to returning to the therapy room.

Using Computers for Live Supervision

Referred to as "a bug-in-the-eye" by Klitzke and Lombardo (1991), this alternative to BITE uses a monitor in the therapy room in a fashion similar to how teleprompters are used in broadcast journalism. Rather than speaking into the ear of the supervisee, supervisors can unobtrusively make suggestions by typing them from a keyboard in the observation room to be read on the monitor placed behind the client.

Proponents of this method argue that it retains all the advantages while eliminating the disadvantages of BITE. Because the supervisee controls when it is an opportune time to read the supervisor's message, the supervisee feels less distracted by the method. Supposedly, this translates to a smooth session from the client's perspective. Neukrug (1991) added that the ability to save supervisor feedback on a disk in order to print it out for the supervisee is an additional advantage that allows the supervisee to review the feedback (along with an audiotape or videotape of the session) or the supervisor and supervisee to discuss the feedback at length in supervision.

Some supervisors are firmly committed to one method of live supervision. For example, Todtman, Bobele, and Strano (1988) implied that the phone is the most desirable method because it is culturally familiar to the client system. They also commented that it is less intrusive than a supervisor walking into the therapy room, but stops therapy nonetheless, avoiding the confusion that can occur when using the bug-in-the-ear. Others feel equally strongly about the advantages of consultation breaks during the session. Most of the literature on live supervision, however, underplays the method used for live supervision, focusing instead on guidelines for the intervention or directive, parameters that must be respected when using live supervision, the acculturation of supervisees to live supervision, and supervisee issues while working within the live supervision framework.

THE LIVE SUPERVISION INTERVENTION

Supervisor to supervisee communications during live supervision are typically referred to as the *supervisory intervention* or *supervisor directives*. For our purposes here, the terms are interchangeable. We will discuss interventions delivered by means of the bug-in-the-ear, phone-ins, and consultation breaks, as these are commonly used

methods of live supervision. Consultation breaks are a commonly used intervention when a team is involved in live supervision. Consultation within the context of team supervision will be discussed later in the chapter.

Prior to intervening, the supervisor should ask: (1) Is redirection necessarily called for in the session? (2) Might the therapist redirect the session without intervention? (3) Will the therapist be able to carry out the intervention successfully? (4) Is the focus on the needs of the therapist and the client or on the supervisor's desire to do cotherapy? (Frankel & Piercy, 1990; Heath, 1982; Liddle & Schwartz, 1983.) Additionally, the supervisor must consider the strengths and limitations of the intervention modality to be used.

Bug-in-the-Ear Interventions

There is no question that this form of sending a supervision directive is the most limited for reasons we have already discussed. In particular situations and for specific reasons, however, BITE may still be the intervention method of choice. BITE is especially recommended for novice supervisees (Adamek, 1994) when relatively frequent, yet brief, suggestions are warranted. The new supervisee would also benefit from the reinforcing potential of BITE (e.g., "Nice question") that might be lost using other methods of supervision. It stands to reason that the use of BITE implies that the supervisor will not be attempting to focus on other than the most basic executive skills during the therapy session. Additionally, it follows that if BITE is the method of delivering interventions, the major part of supervision must occur either before or after the session. Finally, because BITE is inherently distracting, the supervisor must be sensitive to its effect for each supervisee. There may be instances, for example, when the use of BITE has no benefits at all because of the reactivity of the supervisee and the supervisee's inability to conduct a coherent session while receiving information through BITE.

It might be appropriate to use BITE for a more advanced supervisee if the supervisee had a specific goal for a particular session. For example, if a supervisee had been consistently sidetracked by a particular client, the supervisor could alert the supervisee when this was occurring in the session using BITE. As this example demonstrates, BITE interventions take the form of coaching whether they are delivered to novice supervisees or more experienced therapists.

Telephone Interventions

Unlike BITE, telephone interventions have the advantage of stopping the therapy session. This allows the supervisee to listen to the directive without having to attempt to pay attention to the client at the same time. The phone-in has another advantage in that the client is alerted simultaneously that the therapist is being advised and will be prepared for a change in direction in the session. Furthermore, because the client knows that the therapist is receiving feedback, the directive can be the intervention itself. For example, if the supervisor believes that a member of the family is getting lost, the therapist might be advised to continue the session with "My supervisor thinks that we women (referring to her and the mother) have been doing all the talking and we're not letting John (the father) have a say. My supervisor would like to hear what you think is going on between your wife and your son."

Keeney (1990) went one step further and suggested that the supervisor occasionally phone the client rather than the therapist. Such an intervention takes the form of suggesting ways that the client can assist the therapist in achieving stated therapeutic goals. Keeney defended this technique as establishing a contextual structure that "enables supervisors to help clients awaken the therapist's creativity and imagination" (p. 51).

As is the case for all live supervision interventions, telephone directives should be used conservatively; furthermore, they should be brief, concise, and generally action oriented (Haley, 1987; Lewis & Rohrbaugh, 1989; Rickert & Turner, 1978; Wright, 1986). Depending on the developmental level of the supervisee, a verbatim directive might be given (e.g., "Ask the mother 'What is your worst fear about Thomas if he continues with his present

crowd?' "), or, for the more advanced trainee, a more flexible directive might be given (e.g., "Reframe Mom's behavior as concern") (Rickert & Turner, 1978; Wright, 1986). Other generally accepted guidelines when phoning in interventions include (Frankel & Piercy, 1990; Lewis & Rohrbaugh, 1989; Wright, 1986) avoiding process statements (or keeping them very brief) and refraining from complex directives; not exceeding two instructions per phone-in; being sensitive to the timing of the intervention and avoiding interventions during the first 10 minutes of the therapy session; limiting phone-ins to a maximum of five per therapy session; and communicating that it is the supervisee's call when a suggestion can be worked into the session (unless the supervisor has clearly stipulated a time for the intervention).

Wright asserted additionally that it is sometimes strategically wise to begin an intervention with positive reinforcement of what has transpired in the session up to the present. In other words, taking the time to say "You're really doing a terrific job keeping Dad from taking over" might be worth the time and increase the supervisee's investment in carrying out future interventions. This advice was supported by research that found that supervisees experienced phone-ins that included support components as "most effective"; conversely, supervisees were twice as likely as their supervisors to judge phone-in interventions without support as "least effective" (Frankel, 1990). Supportive statements were also found to stimulate isomorphic outcomes in the therapy relationship. When supervisors were effectively supportive, supervisees were more likely to become more supportive with clients; when supervisors' support was not effective, supervisees' support tended to deteriorate (Frankel, 1990; Frankel & Piercy, 1990). Such a strong isomorphic relationship between supervision and therapy was not found for other types of interventions. Unfortunately, Frankel (1990) found that supervisors using phone-ins employed supportive interventions only about one-third as often as they used directive behaviors.

In summary, the phone-in is the optimal live supervision method when the message is relatively brief, uncomplicated, and action oriented, rather than addressing more complicated process issues. When the supervisee needs more clarification than can be provided with a phone directive, the supervisee should leave the room for a consultation break (Haley, 1987).

Consultation Break Interventions

Even if a phone system is available to the supervisor, a consultation break may be the method of choice. In addition to the supervisee's need for clarification, consultation will be preferred if it is the opinion of the supervisor that

1. the intervention will be lengthy and the supervisee will need some extra time to absorb it (Rickert & Turner, 1978);
2. the supervisee will need a rationale for the intervention, which is not accomplished well using the phone-in (Rickert & Turner, 1978);
3. the supervisee will profit from the opportunity to react to the intervention, perhaps to be sure that it is understood or compatible with how the supervisee is experiencing the family; and
4. it will be important to check out some impressions with the supervisee as part of forming the intervention.

When consultation is used, it is essential that the supervisor be attentive to the amount of time the conference takes away from therapy. There is a momentum to the therapy session that is diluted by a live supervision conference. This momentum must be considered as part of the formula for successful live supervision. If the therapist remains out of the therapy room too long, the intervention that is carried back to the client might be moot. A partial exception to this admonition is if the client system has been forewarned that a lengthy consultation is part of the therapy hour. In fact, when strategic family therapy is being implemented, the consultation may take place somewhere near the halfway mark of the therapy hour, and the supervisee might return to the session only to deliver the final directive, usually in the form of a homework assignment.

The practice of live supervision in the form of consultation breaks can lead to a respect for a break

from the intensity of the therapy hour. Some therapists will take a break during their therapy sessions even when there is no one to consult. As many practitioners know, a moment or two away from the dynamics of the therapy system can lead to highly therapeutic insights.

Finally, Heppner et al. (1994) studied supervisor inventions delivered during individual therapy sessions. Using a walk-in mode, supervisors were instructed to intervene when the therapy session seemed to lack direction, when the therapist seemed stuck, or when the supervisors were concerned for the client's welfare. Supervisors intervened between one and three times a session. An analysis of the interventions found that six dimensions were identifiable, each being bidirectional (pp. 230–232):

1. *Directing–instructing versus deepening.* At one end of this dimension, the supervisor offered the supervisee explicit suggestions or direction. The opposite pole of this dimension found the supervisor offering minor adjustment to deepen an already well moving emotional process occurring in the session.

2. *Cognitive clarification versus emotional encouragement.* On one side, the supervisor focused on the content of the session or a task and attempted to help the therapist come to a better understanding of what was transpiring. The opposite side for this dimension was described as supervisors attempting to get supervisees to express the feelings they were having in the session, especially as they related to the client.

3. *Confronting versus encouraging the client.* At one end, the supervisor was identifying how the client was impeding the supervisee and how this could be altered; on the opposite end of this dimension, the supervisor engaged in attempting to make the client more comfortable and willing to take risks.

4. *Didactic–distant versus emotionally involved.* At one end of this dimension, the supervisor seemed to be taking a detached, expert stance, while at the other end the supervisor seemed emotionally involved with both supervisee and client and appeared highly invested in the outcome of therapy.

5. *Joining versus challenging the trainee.* For this dimension, it was the relationship between supervisor and trainee that seemed to vary from reinforcing the trainee and attempting to help the client understand what the trainee was trying to accomplish to the supervisor challenging the trainee to examine his or her approach and perhaps consider a different approach.

6. *Providing direction versus resignation.* On one end of the continuum, the supervisor was highly invested in the session and worked hard to get the process to move forward, while on the other end the supervisor communicated that there was little that could be done from the supervisor's standpoint to move the session forward.

In reviewing these six dimensions, Heppner et al. determined that to analyze an intervention one needed to consider the content or goal of the intervention, the relational context of the intervention, and the immediate effects of the intervention on the supervisor. Especially for live supervision approaches in which the supervisor and client interact, these three interfacing, yet distinct, components, and the six dimensions identified by Heppner et al. should be considered as interventions are formed and executed. Because live supervision is, in fact, without rehearsal, this expectation is formidable.

The Heppner et al. study can also be used to evaluate live supervision after the fact, especially if the supervisor is dissatisfied with the outcome of a live supervision session. If, for example, most interventions challenged the supervisee (dimension 5), Frankel's (1990) research indicated that more support of the supervisee must be included in the interventions, especially if the outcome of the session is clients who feel less support. (A research question yet to be addressed is the differential effect of supervisor support of the therapist versus supervisor support of the client. When the supervisor is supportive of the client but challenging of the supervisee, does this make clients feel supported or ambivalent?)

In summary, during-session interventions are far more complex than they may appear. A good directive must be succinct and add clarity, not confusion, to the supervisee's deliberations. Even consultation breaks must be efficient in their use of therapy time and will focus primarily on the supervisee's executive skills (West, Bubenzer, Pinsoneault, & Holeman, 1993). For the supervisee to have an opportunity to develop perceptual and cognitive skills, presession and postsession conferences are requisite.

PRESESSION PLANNING AND POSTSESSION DEBRIEFING

Although the interaction between the supervisor and the therapy system is the core of live supervision, what comes before and after are the underpinnings of the successful implementation of the model. Especially because of the level of activity involved in live supervision, there is a necessity for groundwork to be done in order for the activity during the session to remain meaningful.

As one might suppose, the goal of the presession is to prepare the trainee for the upcoming therapy session. There will be some speculation about what the family might bring to this session. The supervisor will have two goals in the presession: to prepare the trainee for the upcoming session and to focus on the trainee's own learning goals as they pertain to the upcoming session. Piercy stated that he wants his trainees to show evidence of having a "theoretical map" and then to be able to "tie it to a practical understanding of how to bring about change" (West, Bubenzer, & Zarski, 1989, p. 27). Additionally, trainees are often asked to attempt a particular technique (e.g., to raise the intensity of the interactions between family members), or they may be asked if they have something particular that they would like the supervisor to observe. In other words, it is important that both the supervisee and the supervisor complete the presession with some clarity about their roles for the therapy session.

On the other hand, Okun argued that family therapy "cannot be organized like a lesson plan" (West et al., 1989, p. 27). Families will force both trainees and supervisors to be spontaneous even if they are adequately prepared for the session. The developmental level of the trainee must be reflected in presession planning just as it is in the therapy session. The supervisor will be more active with the novice trainee in terms of both helping to provide a conceptual overview and planning for immediate interventions. Once the trainee has gained in experience, it is expected that the supervisor will take a more consultative position (West et al., 1989; West et al., 1993).

The postsession debriefing allows the trainee and the supervisor to discuss what transpired in the session. Because they were both involved in the therapy but held different vantage points, this is an important time to share perceptions, review the effectiveness of interventions, offer feedback, and address any unfinished business from the session as a precursor to planning the next session.

If homework has been assigned to the family, this is also a time to consider ways in which the family might respond to the assignment and to begin to consider future interventions based on the family's response. In other words, the successful postsession will leave the trainee with some food for thought to consider prior to the next presession (West et al., 1989).

Although the presession conference is an important coaching session, the postsession debriefing is the optimal time for the conceptual growth of the supervisee. This conference, therefore, should not be rushed. If there is no opportunity for the conference immediately after the therapy session, it should be scheduled at another time, but far enough prior to the next therapy session so that it does not feel like another presession conference. Couchon and Bernard (1984) found that supervisor behaviors are significantly influenced by the timing of a supervision session in relation to the next counseling session for the supervisee. In other words, when a supervisee is facing an upcoming session, the supervisor will become far more directive in order to help the supervisee prepare, even if the last session has not been previously critiqued with the supervisee. Therefore, the postsession must occur at a time when the next session with the same client is not imminent and when there is ample time to move beyond intervention issues to larger conceptual and relationship issues.

Now that the overall process of live supervision has been described, we turn our attention to conditions for the effective use of live supervision.

IMPLEMENTING LIVE SUPERVISION

In his seminal article, Montalvo (1973) listed six guidelines for live supervision that continue to be relevant today.

1. *Supervisor and supervisee agree that a supervisor can either call the supervisee out or that the latter can come out for feedback when he [sic] wishes.*
2. *Supervisor and supervisee, before settling down to work, agree on defined limits within which both will operate. [For example, the supervisor outlines under what condition, if any, the supervisee can reject the supervisor's intervention.]*
3. *The supervisor endeavors not to inhibit the supervisee's freedom of exploration and operation too much, but, if he does so, the supervisee is expected to tell him.*
4. *The mechanism for establishing direction is routine talks before and after the session. [Montalvo felt strongly that the family should not be privy to these discussions and that efforts to "democratize" the therapy process have not proven useful. To date, there is no uniform opinion among family therapy theorists about this issue.]*
5. *The supervisor tries to find procedures that best fit the supervisee's style and preferred way of working.*
6. *The beginner should understand that at the start he may feel as if he is under remote control.* (pp. 343–345)

These guidelines reflect Montalvo's structural family therapy bias. The wisdom of the guidelines, however, lies in both their clarity regarding the supervision hierarchy and their respect for the integrity, if not the ego, of the supervisee. Insufficient attention to one of these issues can result in an unsatisfactory experience with live supervision.

More recently, Elizur (1990) revisited baseline conditions for live supervision. Because Elizur perceives live supervision to be an inherently anxiety provoking model, his first admonition was that the use of live supervision should be agreed to by each supervisee within an explicit supervision contract. Elizur also emphasized that the supervisee must trust that the supervisor has the welfare of the clients at heart and will not let harm come to the clients. Additionally, supervisors must be supportive of trainees as they struggle to enlarge their intervention repertoire by gauging their level of expertise and allowing them to attempt new interventions, while appreciating the stress inherent in such a process. McCollum (1995) addressed the supervisor's own stress in these moments by posing a question: "How do I keep my own anxiety under control and curb my own oldest-brother wish to take over and make things 'right' versus letting the [supervisee] and clients stew with their troubles?" (p. 4).

Bubenzer et al. (1987) made four suggestions to help desensitize supervisees to live supervision. Using phone-ins as their method, they suggested that supervisors first show new supervisees videotapes of family sessions during which the phone rings and the session is interrupted. By doing this, trainees are able to observe how clients react when the phone rings and how things proceed afterward. This is often one of the first concerns for new trainees. Second, new supervisees are allowed to be observers while live supervision is being conducted with other counselors. They are encouraged to ask the supervisor any questions as things proceed. Third, hypothetical cases are presented to the trainees for them to practice the consecutive stages of pretreatment (or presession planning), counseling during session, and posttreatment (or postsession debriefing). At that time the possible use of phone-ins is discussed. Finally, again through role play of hypothetical cases, the supervisees conduct sessions, following through on their plans and experience phone-ins during the session as previously discussed. With the amount of anxiety that can surround supervision of any type, the idea of allowing a trial run as described by Bubenzer et al. makes intuitive sense and has been implemented elsewhere (e.g., Neukrug, 1991).

Once the therapist becomes used to the idea of the inevitability of being interrupted during ther-

apy and knows what form that will take, the pressure is on the supervisor to be concise and helpful. Berger and Dammann (1982) offered two astute observations about the supervisor's reality versus the supervisee's reality during live supervision. Because of the one-way mirror separating them, the supervisor "will see patterns more quickly and will be better able to think about them—to think meta to them—than the therapist will" (p. 338). Second, "the supervisor will lack accurate information as to the intensity of the family affect. This becomes readily apparent if the supervisor enters the room to talk with the family" (pp. 338–339).

There are outgrowths to each of these perceptual differences. Because of the advantage the supervisor enjoys by being behind the one-way mirror, a common reaction for the therapist, according to Berger and Dammann, is to "feel stupid" (p. 338) once something is called to the therapist's attention. The reason, of course, that the trainee feels stupid is because what is pointed out seems painfully obvious but is something that eluded the trainee during the therapy session. The wise supervisor will prepare supervisees for this reaction and allow them opportunities to experience firsthand the cleverness that comes from being at a safe distance from the therapy interaction.

Regarding the intensity issue, the supervisee might rightfully feel that the supervisor does not understand the family if the supervisor is underestimating the intensity of family affect. It is for this reason, that is, the direct contact with the family experienced primarily by the supervisee, that Berger and Dammann supported others who believed that, except for an emergency, "the supervisor proposes and the therapist disposes" (p. 339).

Gershenson and Cohen (1978) also noted that the relationship between trainee and supervisor can begin on rocky ground because of the vulnerability felt by the trainee. This vulnerability can be experienced as anxiety and resistance, persecutory fantasies, and anger. It could be conjectured that at this stage the trainee is reacting to the unfair advantage of the supervisor (behind the one-way mirror) along with extreme embarrassment at the mediocrity of his or her own performance. Fortunately, this initial stage seems to be short-lived for most trainees. According to Gershenson and Cohen, a second stage follows characterized by high emotional investment in the process and perceiving the supervisor as a supporter rather than as critic. We can assume that this stage also represents a heightened dependence on the supervisor. Finally, a third stage emerges in which "the directions of our supervisor became less important as techniques to be implemented and instead served as a stimulus to our own thinking . . . [we] reached a point at which we were able to initiate our own therapeutic strategies" (p. 229).

ADVANTAGES AND DISADVANTAGES

Advantages

The advocates of live supervision have been ardent (Bubenzer, West, & Gold, 1991). The well-documented advantage of live supervision is that, through this form of coaching by a more experienced clinician, there is a much greater likelihood that therapy will go well. There is also an assumption and some empirical evidence (Kivlighan, Angelone, & Swafford, 1991; Landis & Young, 1994; Storm, 1994) that the supervisee will learn more efficiently and, perhaps, more profoundly as a result of these successful therapy sessions. To return to our coaching metaphor, it is better to be coached and to win the game than to be playing independently and suffer defeat.

In addition to the training function of live supervision, there is a built-in safeguard for client welfare. Because the supervisor is immediately accessible, clients are protected more directly. This also allows trainees to work with more challenging cases, which might be too difficult for them if another form of supervision were being used (Cormier & Bernard, 1982). Of course, the difficulty of the case must be considered carefully. Too difficult a therapy case will mean that the trainee is simply the voice of the supervisor and little more. The supervisor must be astute regarding the developmental level of the trainee and determine what

cases are within the trainee's grasp. A similar advantage to live supervision is that the trainee is more likely to risk more in conducting therapy because of the knowledge that the supervisor is there to help with interventions (Berger & Dammann, 1982). Furthermore, because of the direct involvement of the highly skilled supervisor, clients assigned to trainees will receive better treatment (Rickert & Turner, 1978).

Another set of advantages related to live supervision has to do with the trainee's relationship with the supervisor. Because the supervisor will often share responsibility for interventions, the supervisor is far more vulnerable than in other forms of supervision. Especially if a verbatim directive is given, the supervisor cannot come back later and say, "You misunderstood the intent of my comment." This kind of sharing of responsibility, when it occurs, will reduce the distance between supervisor and trainee. Not all supervisors, however, value an egalitarian relationship with their supervisees (e.g., Montalvo, 1973); this is a topic that has particular relevance for team supervision and will be considered later in the chapter.

The use of live supervision also affords supervisees the opportunity to appreciate the extent to which therapists become entrenched in the family system, because they experience a jarring removal from the family system when called for a consultation break. Proponents of live supervision believe that such entrenchment is inevitable (if not desirable if therapists are to understand the parameters of the family), but only live supervision offers an opportunity for the trainee to understand these dynamics experientially.

Finally, the trainee's view of the process of therapy will also be affected by live supervision as therapy will unfold far more systematically due to the input from the supervisor. When the supervisor gives a rationale for an intervention, predicts reactions, and proves to be right, the therapist experiences firsthand the predictability of patterns once they have been comprehended. This is an exciting moment for the therapist; fortunately, it is balanced by those moments when clients react unpredictably, thus ensuring our sense of fallibility as helpers.

Disadvantages

The most noted disadvantages of live supervision are the time it demands of supervisors (Bubenzer, West, & Gold, 1991) (although the efficiency with which supervisees are trained has been reported to offset this initial time commitment), the cost of facilities, the problem of scheduling cases to accommodate all those who are to be involved, and the potential reactions of clients and trainees to this unorthodox form of supervising (e.g., Anonymous, 1995). Additionally, Schwartz, Liddle, and Breunlin (1988) returned to one of Montalvo's (1973) initial concerns and alerted supervisors to the tendency of "robotization" in using live supervision. Unless the supervisor is highly systematic in giving the trainee more and more autonomy, live supervision can produce clinicians who show little initiative or creativity during therapy and who conceptualize inadequately. This potential disadvantage of live supervision has been echoed by others (e.g., Adamek, 1994; Kaplan, 1987; Montalvo, 1973; Rickert & Turner, 1978; Storm, 1997; Wright, 1986). Schwartz et al. (1988) noted that both critics and proponents of live supervision are concerned about how live supervision underplays the therapist's own observations and intuitions in favor of the supervisor's.

In addition to the danger of the supervisor dominating therapy through live supervision, there is some danger that the supervisor will suggest "dramatic, yet inappropriate, interventions" (Goodman, 1985, p. 48). In other words, Goodman acknowledged the very human possibility of the supervisor being tempted to show off in front of trainees. Even if an intervention is appropriate, the supervisor must determine whether it is one that the trainee can carry off successfully. If not, the supervisor is trying to do therapy through the supervisee, rather than conducting live supervision.

Additionally, if live supervision is the only method used within a training program, it may not adequately prepare trainees for working in the far more isolated world of the mental health professions. In other words, even if the supervisor is attentive to trainee developmental levels, live supervision represents a paradigmatic shift not only from other supervision forms, but also from the typical autonomy of therapists' responsibility. Again, this disadvantage is serious only when all of one's training has been completed within the context of live supervision.

Related to the above, there is virtually no evidence in the professional literature that skills learned within a live supervision context generalize to other counseling situations (Gallant, Thyer, & Bailey, 1991; Kivlighan, Angelone, & Swafford, 1991). This is a serious gap in our knowledge for both trainee welfare and client welfare, especially in cases where supervision is limited to the live supervision modality.

TEAM SUPERVISION

To this point we have focused on the supervisor–therapist relationship in live supervision. More and more, however, live supervision has become synonymous with team supervision, that is, live supervision with other trainees (in addition to the supervisor) behind the one-way mirror. Although team therapy was originally developed by seasoned practitioners (peers) as a means to study and improve their trade, it has become increasingly popular as a method of training even novice practitioners (e.g., Haley, 1987; Heppner et al., 1994; Landis & Young, 1994). Team supervision can also take on a variety of forms. Defining the two most common forms, Roberts (1983) differentiated between supervisor-guided live supervision, in which the supervisor is the only or primary person from the team who offers direction to the trainee, and the collaborative team model (also described by Sperling et al., 1986), in which, although the supervisor offers initial direction, team members are encouraged to take more and more responsibility for the direction of therapy as time goes on. For our purposes here, we believe that supervisor-guided live supervision, as described by Roberts, differs very little from live supervision as it has been presented thus far in this chapter, the only difference being that observers have an opportunity to learn vicariously while the supervisor is working with the supervisee. Therefore, we will focus our attention on the collaborative team model, where team members are actively involved in the progress of therapy and in the development of the supervisee.

Briefly described, the process of team supervision has a group of trainees present with the supervisor behind the one-way mirror during the therapy session. Typically, one trainee will serve as the therapist for a case while the rest of the group works as team members along with the supervisor. As with supervisor-only live supervision, the technology most frequently used in team supervision is the phone. The other common method of communication is consultation in the observation room.

Therefore, while the therapist is working with the family, the team is observing interactions, metacommunication, and so on, to arrive at some sort of decision regarding the direction therapy should go. The observation room is as busy, if not busier, than the therapy room. The team members have the luxury of being one step removed, allowing them to see the entire therapeutic system, including the therapist. The assumption is that this more objective posture will aid the conceptualization process, as will the synergy of ideas as the family is deliberated. Team supervision also allows the supervisor to do a great deal of teaching while therapy is being conducted and to culminate an important clinical lesson with a timely intervention sent to the family through the therapist. Team supervision, therefore, becomes therapy, supervision, and classroom all in one.

In order to facilitate the activity and efficiency of the team, it is sometimes helpful to assign specific tasks to different team members (West, Bubenzer, & Zarski, 1989). These tasks can be assigned by the supervisor or, if the therapist is looking for specific feedback, by the therapist. For example, the therapist trainee who is concerned about her ability to maintain appropriate boundaries within the session might ask one team member to observe only this aspect of the session.

Bernstein, Brown, & Ferrier (1984) presented a model describing what they considered essential roles in team supervision: the *therapist,* the person who will sit with the family during the session and will remain attuned to the mechanics of running the session; the *taskmaster,* the member of the team assigned to direct the conference and keep the team from deviating from the previously agreed on structure for analyzing the information being produced by the family, while ensuring an atmosphere conducive to creativity and spontaneity; and the *historian,* the person responsible for maintaining the threads of continuity across and within treatment sessions.

The supervisor can organize the team to accomplish any number of goals. One member could be asked to observe one member of the family or one relationship (e.g., father–child) or to track one theme, such as what happens in the family when feelings are introduced. Such assignments allow the supervisor to teach the importance of particular dynamics for progress in therapy. Furthermore, the supervisor can assign tasks to specific team members that represent their unique training goals. For instance, the team member who has a difficult time joining with children in therapy sessions can be asked to observe another trainee's joining style with children. The team, therefore, offers not only the advantage of in-session assistance but also numerous and rich possibilities for learning and post-session feedback.

The Reflecting Team

In his seminal work, Anderson (1987) described a novel team approach to working with families. His reflecting team represented a way to demystify the team approach to therapy for the family. Rather than leaving the family to their conjectures when the therapist joined the team for consultation, Anderson proposed that light and sound be switched from the therapy room to the observation room and the family and therapist listen to the team reflect on what they have heard during the session to that point. Anderson suggested that the team's reflections could either be sought by the therapist (e.g., "I wonder if the team has any ideas that might be helpful at this point") or could be offered by the team (e.g., "We have some ideas that might be useful to your conversation"). As a therapy model, the reflecting team approach is embedded in the work of Bateson (1972) and others, and the team's deliberations are carefully formed to reflect communication patterns within the family's repertoire. Because our interest in the reflecting team is as a supervision model, we will not focus on this aspect of the model.

By having the team's deliberations observed by the family, a certain egalitarianism was added to the live supervision model that seemed to be an advantage in accomplishing therapeutic goals. Rather than receiving one central message delivered by a spokesperson for the team, the family was able to hear the deliberations themselves and draw from them as they might. Reflections could represent competing, yet equally sound alternatives that allowed the family to reflect on others' impressions of their options. The input from the team, therefore, was far richer from the family's perspective.

For the team, the reflecting team model made all deliberations public. Because there could be no throwaway comments within this model, team members were more attentive as observers and more disciplined in their reflections. Guidelines for framing comments became more important than they were with confidential consultation breaks.

Anderson suggested that there be three team members who would participate in the model (not counting the therapist who stayed with the family). This way, a third person could react to the deliberations of the other two. If the team was larger than this, Anderson advised that additional members be observers only, participating if called on by the team. Additionally, Anderson noted that persons could change rooms if it was not possible to reverse lights and sound with a facility. In the original discussion of reflecting teams, trainees were mentioned only tangentially. Anderson stated that

trainees were invited to participate as reflecting team members as they felt ready, and most became increasingly active with experience.

Since Anderson's introduction of the reflecting team approach, the model has received attention as a supervision model (e.g., Shilts, Rudes, & Madigan, 1993; Roberts, 1997; Young et al., 1989). Young et al. (1989) offered a strong rationale for the reflecting team based on the disadvantages of the more standard live supervision team. The latter, according to Young et al. were at least four in number: First, regardless of the espoused support of the team, the trainee in the room filling the role of therapist felt anxious and on the spot, not only with the family but in relation to the observing team. The reflecting team spreads out the spotlight. The therapist is no longer the sole representative of this team of experts. The experts can speak for themselves and may look no more impressive than the therapist. Second, trainees found it very difficult to disengage from the family, join the team in any meaningful way, and reengage with the family in the short times available for consultations. With the reflecting team, the therapist stays with the family, both physically and systemically. The therapist hears the team's thoughts as the family does and is in a position to facilitate the family's response to the team's comments from the vantage point of a neutral position. Similarly, the message delivered back to the family in traditional team approaches was often construed under time pressures and with uneven contributions from team members. With the reflecting team, the reflections themselves become the intervention and, therefore, need only arrive as far as they can logically in the time allotted. The value is in the musings themselves as team members attempt to view the family's situation from different angles. Also, because of the structure of the team, the likelihood that one member will dominate is greatly diminished. Finally, Young et al. cited the relationship between clients and the team as a problem that the reflecting team addresses. In the more traditional model, the team becomes a cause for suspicion, "spies" from on high, persons of dubious motives.

This apprehension is erased when clients hear the team members firsthand, not with slick interventions to transmit, but with their spontaneous interactions on the family's behalf.

Because the contributions of all members are part of the process, Young et al. suggested guidelines for all deliberations:

1. *All remarks or comments are made in terms of positive connotations and genuine respect for family members.*
2. *Ideas and speculations are put in terms of the family's belief's, not the team member's beliefs.*
3. *The team's beliefs about the family's belief's are couched in "possibilities," or "maybes."*
4. *As a result, as many sides as can be seen of a situation are argued, by different team members.*
5. *Team members should enjoy trust and respect for each other.*   (p. 70)

Young et al. sought feedback from supervisors, trainees, and clients about the use of the reflecting team. Supervisors expressed initial nervousness that team members would say negative unhelpful things (as they had done in confidential team meetings). When this did not occur, they found themselves trusting the process more and, ultimately, feeling liberated. Trainees felt rudderless at the thought of the process, but found the experience itself to be affirming. Of 20 responses received from clients, 18 found the reflecting team to be either extremely helpful or moderately helpful; the remaining 2 were unsure of their reactions. In a separate study of clients' reaction to the reflecting team, Smith, Yoshioka, and Winton (1993) found that clients also reacted positively to the reflecting team's ability to offer them multiple perspectives. Smith et al. ascertained that these multiple perspectives were most helpful "when they contained dialectic tensions. Clients who are confronted with two or more credible explanations of the same event benefitted from teams able to articulate the differences between positions and hence their dialectic" (p. 40).

In spite of the many strengths claimed about reflecting teams as a therapy model and a method of supervision, there are some cautions. Is the egalitarianism it espouses an evolution of training and supervision (Hardy, 1993) or is it a model that fuses therapy and supervision to a point that supervision is compromised? Does the model diffuse individual contributions in its focus on the collective? Does the therapist lose the feeling of control over the outcome of therapy (Young et al.)? In spite of these concerns, it seems that the reflecting team will continue to contribute to our understanding of live supervision.

Other Novel Forms of Team Supervision

As many practitioners have discovered, once the traditional mold of therapy has been broken, the possibilities for reconstructing both therapy and supervision, and a combination of the two, are innumerable. There have been several variations on the theme of the therapeutic team, each carrying with it new assumptions and parameters for both therapy and supervision.

For example, Olson and Pegg (1979) described what they referred to as direct open supervision (DOS). In their model the team is present in the therapy room and is used in therapy as needed. For example, Olson and Pegg described one case where the husband and wife would do battle whenever they tried to negotiate. Two team members were asked to role play one of their arguments and to then model some negotiating behaviors. Following this, the couple gave feedback about what they thought they could use from the role play and what would not work for them. At the end of the session, the team processed what transpired in the therapy session with the family present. Like the reflecting team, no private deliberations are allowed in this model. Whatever team members and the supervisor have to say to each other is heard by the family.

An even busier model than DOS is the "Pick-a-Dali Circus (PDC) (Landau & Stanton, 1983; Stanton & Stanton, 1986) in which all team members (including the therapist) are asked to play a variety of roles in order to highlight family dynamics and push the family toward resolution. "In many ways, PDC is like theater of the absurd. Team members respond singularly, in couples or small groups, or in unison in an ongoing, flowing way during the session. They may physically situate themselves at different places in the room, change their position, leave the room alone or in groups to observe through a one-way mirror, and so on, in accordance with the therapeutic stratagem of the moment" (Stanton & Stanton, 1986, p. 171). We assume that careful preparation and a highly regarded supervisor are necessary elements for the successful implementation of PDC, lest therapy does become theater of the absurd.

Finally, Brodsky and Myers (1986) presented a model similar to those that have already been described, but designed for individual clients. Again, the entire team is present in the room for what the authors described as in vivo rotation. A client contracts for 13 weekly sessions. For the first 4 to 6 sessions, the supervisor conducts therapy with the trainees observing, followed by each trainee taking a turn in the therapist role for the next several weeks. The supervisor again assumes the role of therapist for the final session.

Each session follows three phases. During the first, the therapist works with the client for 45 minutes. Next, the therapist joins the observers (in view of the client) for a 30-minute discussion of what has transpired in therapy, including client dynamics and therapist technique. The therapist then rejoins the client for 15 minutes, and they process the issues raised by the observation group. At no time are observers allowed to intervene directly with the client. Although the authors reported substantial benefits from the use of the in vivo rotation, they admitted that it is not for everyone.

Because it is not possible to cover adequately all the dynamics to be considered for these various team models, we will use as our reference for the rest of the chapter the standard model where the team and supervisor are positioned behind the one-way mirror with the therapist and client group in the therapy room.

Team Dynamics

With the variety of opportunities offered by team supervision, it is perhaps not surprising that a team approach involves some initial issues and complications not typically associated with other forms of supervision. The most central of these is the cohesion of the group that will form the team. Wendorf (1984) suggested that before the team attempts to work as a unit in offering therapy they come together as a group through a careful examination of group process. In order to help the team understand each member's needs and agendas, Wendorf recommended that the group alternate between meetings with a supervisor and meetings with peers only. His experience has been that team members will relate to each other differently depending on whether the supervisor is present and that prior to doing therapy the team needs to know as much as possible about each member.

As might be expected, Wendorf's recommendations are not universally accepted. Theoretical compatibility among team members has been viewed as another essential ingredient for success (Cade, Speed, & Seligman, 1986). Although another type of supervision group might be enhanced by participants coming from widely varying assumptions about therapy, this would be far less so with a therapeutic team. Because there is a limited amount of time within a session for the team to confer and recommend an intervention, there needs to be enough theoretical compatibility to allow the team to work efficiently. Furthermore, the supervisee cannot be expected to integrate different theoretical assumptions within such a complex supervision process. (Later in this chapter we will present an opposing view as argued by Markowski and Cain, 1983.)

In-session (Midsession) Dynamics. The therapist's right to accept or reject the intervention (i.e., supervision) is a chronic supervisory issue and one that is exacerbated with a team. Unlike the situation with a solitary supervisor, where a trainee might be asked to carry out an intervention even though not totally committed to it, the dynamic is more complicated when a group of peers is primarily responsible for the intervention. Even if the supervisor is supportive of the team's direction, it is more important for the trainee to be in agreement with the directive than it is when no team exists. If not, the therapist will eventually feel manipulated by his or her peers, and team dynamics might eventually override the goal of providing exemplary therapy.

Heath (1982) asserted that it is the supervisor's responsibility to choreograph the input from the team to the therapist and to be sure that the intervention is compatible with the therapist's style, "unless the style has become part of the problem" (p. 192). Heath also acknowledged that prior to the in-session conference, the supervisor may be confronted with competitiveness among team members, an understandable phenomenon when the role of therapist is curtailed in favor of the team approach to therapy and training.

A final issue that should receive attention prior to the actual therapy session is which and how many team members will be allowed to formulate interventions for the therapist. When consultation is the method used, this is less of an issue, especially if there is a designated taskmaster to translate the group discussion into an intervention. However, when directives are phoned in or the therapist is called into the consultation room to receive the directive rather than to confer with the team, will several members of the team be allowed to be involved in the interchange or just one? This may seem like a minor issue, but it is probably one of the most critical process issues for a team if relations between the therapist and the team are to remain intact. Once again, it is up to the supervisor to monitor the activity level of the observation room and the readiness of individual team members to participate in a more direct fashion.

Pre- and Postsessions. Because of the complexity and intensity of team supervision during the therapy session, it is vital for planning sessions and debriefing sessions to occur. Liddle and Schwartz (1983) maintained that the presession conference should address family, trainee, relationship, and teaching considerations. If the team goes into the session knowing pretty well what is to be accomplished with the family and what the trainee will be working on personally, the during-session

consultations should serve the function of "mid-course corrections to the general session plan" (p. 478). Additionally, giving time in the presession to team dynamics, taking time to convey a respect for the position and perspective of the therapist, and addressing how this particular session dovetails with overall training goals will prepare the team for the intensity and activity of team supervision.

The postsession conference is equally important. Regardless of the amount of planning that has occurred, team members, especially the therapist, will have a need to debrief. Furthermore, Adams (1995) reported that trainees ask their best questions during the postsession. Heath (1982) suggested that the supervisor allow the therapist to suggest a format for the discussion. In addition to a general discussion of the session, including a discussion of hypotheses and goals, the postsession should include some feedback to the therapist and feedback to the team (Heath, 1982). Heath also maintained that emotional reactions on the part of different team members can be appropriate to address if they enhance the process, but that criticism be offered only if paired with alternative action. In a similar vein, Cade et al. (1986) stated that

> [t]he therapist will often need time to "disengage" mentally and emotionally from the family before feeling able to consider what the team has to offer. The advantages of multiple perspectives can become a disadvantage if the therapist becomes swamped with ideas, particularly where these are conflicting ideas arising out of conflicting frameworks. (pp. 112–113)

Once more immediate session issues have been processed, the supervisor should help the team address the session that just occurred as it fits in the larger context of training (Adams, 1995; Liddle & Schwartz, 1983) and direct team members' thinking for the next scheduled presession.

Advantages and Disadvantages of Team Supervision

Advantages. We stated earlier that advocates of live supervision tend to be enthusiastic in their support. This is true of working with the team model of live supervision as well. Among the advantages enumerated are the following (Cade et al., 1986; Elizur, 1990; Hardy, 1993; Landis & Young, 1994; Quinn, Atkinson, & Hood, 1985; Speed, Seligman, Kingston, & Cade, 1982; Sperling et al., 1985):

1. Team work appears to be highly satisfying. "Family therapy is always difficult, sometimes nerve-wracking and sometimes depressing; working in teams can be creative, highly supportive, challenging and very often fun" (Speed et al., 1982, p. 283).

2. When a crisis occurs within a case, the therapist can attend to the immediate needs of the client while the team wrestles with conceptualizing the case.

3. As with other forms of group supervision, the therapeutic team reinforces the value of case consultation. Because the team must brainstorm during the session, the criticism that live supervision is primarily a model for executive skill development is canceled.

4. The model requires that team members work on their feet, thus training them to arrive at therapeutic interventions more quickly.

5. The team model automatically multiplies the numbers of interesting cases with which each team member has the opportunity to work.

6. The team itself can be used to enhance therapeutic goals. For example, a team split can be used as the intervention (Sperling et al., 1985), where the team is said to be in disagreement behind the mirror and sends in two opposing courses of action. This allows the therapist to stay in a neutral position and help the family look at alternatives while acknowledging that there is more than one valid way to proceed.

7. A group of therapists is more likely to take greater risks and operate at a more creative level than an individual therapist. For highly intransigent cases, creative approaches to intervention are called for if the client system is to improve.

8. When the supervisor is clearly directing the team and the team is stuck, the supervisor must assess whether he or she is part of the problem (Elizur, 1990). As a result, supervisors are less insulated from their own blind spots and team members benefit from realizing that challenge is part of therapy regardless of the expertness of the therapist.

9. Because the team will present different cultural backgrounds, the therapy process is more likely to reflect a sensitivity to culture, as will training (Hardy, 1993).

Disadvantages. Although the team model is intriguing and dynamic, there are certain disadvantages and pitfalls to be considered and for the supervisor to avoid (Cade et al., 1986; Wendorf, Wendorf, & Bond, 1985):

1. Because of the intensity of the team's efforts, the group can find itself engaged in unproductive interactions with members unable to extricate themselves (Todd, 1997).

2. It is very difficult for competitive team members to resist using the therapy sessions to prove their conceptual superiority. This not only means that team members are competing with each other instead of supporting each other, but it also means that sometimes interventions sent in to families are unduly complicated or clever and not necessarily the most productive for accomplishing therapeutic goals.

3. Because of the high level of group cohesiveness that typically is associated with therapeutic teams, members can become overprotective and fail to challenge each other. For peer team groups, members might drop from the team rather than pursue a different line of thinking.

4. If a team is a subunit of an agency or a training program, the members of the team can pose a threat to other staff members. "A mystique can develop around what a particular team is 'up to.' Other staff feel 'put down' or patronized when in discussion with team members who can somehow convey that they are in possession of 'the truth' " (Cade et al., 1986, pp. 114–115). At the very least, team members will share a common experience not available to others, thus promoting an atmosphere of an "in" group and an "out" group.

5. For a team that has a long span of time to work together, there is a danger of becoming the "other family." We believe, as did Cade et al., that every group has a limited creative life-span, at least without the impetus of new members or a change of context. Supervisors need to be sensitive to systemic dynamics within teams as well as within client groups.

6. For some cases, the team approach is more intensive than is needed and may distort client dynamics through unnecessary scrutiny. One way to compensate for this pitfall is to vary one's approaches to supervision. We think the Quinn et al. (1985) "stuck-case clinic" is an excellent approach to team supervision. Rather than having the team consider all cases (and thereby running the risk of overkill for some cases), each team member is charged with bringing his or her most difficult case to the team. As a result, the team's time is spent efficiently, and the risk of client distortion is diminished.

7. Finally, it seems to us that team supervision is as much a closed system as some other forms of supervision. By this we mean that there is definitely some self-selection among those supervisors who choose team supervision as their method of choice. They might, for example, be somewhat more theatrical than other supervisors, or perhaps they enjoy therapy more than supervision. Regardless, training programs that wed themselves entirely to team supervision might be discriminating against some of their trainees unknowingly—trainees who are equally talented but more traditional in their approach to therapy. Supervisors should be challenged to vary their approaches to supervision, just as trainees are challenged to vary their approaches to therapy.

RESEARCH RESULTS AND QUESTIONS

Live supervision has been found to be effective in training supervisees in initial counseling techniques (Gallant, Thyer, & Bailey, 1991; Heppner et al. 1993; Kivlighan, Angelone, & Swafford, 1991; Klitzke & Lombardo, 1991) and marriage and family therapy skills (e.g., Fenell, Hovestadt, & Harvey, 1986). To date, however, in spite of the

ardor of those supervisors who prefer a live supervision model, there is no evidence that live supervision is better than, or weaker than, any other method of supervision.

Because live supervision breaks many normative canons of psychotherapy having to do with privacy and the centrality of relationship to therapy, there has been a good deal of interest in the reaction of clients and trainees to the model. Piercy, Sprenkle, and Constantine (1986) conducted a follow-up study of both groups and found that almost one-third (32 percent) of trainees would have preferred no observers to their therapy, and family members reported discomfort with the model in certain situations. Although comfort level was impeded, it is important to note that for these therapists and families the outcome of therapy did not seem to be affected by their negative feelings. Liddle, Davidson, and Barrett (1988) found that novice supervisees were most sensitive to evaluation issues during live supervision while more experienced therapists focused on power and control issues. Reactions of both groups, however, minimized with continued use of live supervision, a result supported by Wong's (1997) subsequent research. Finally, Smith, Yoshioka, and Winton (1993) conducted a qualitative study to determine client reactions to reflective teams. Clients were asked about their reactions at three different times during therapy (fourth week, seventh week, and eighth week), and questions became more sophisticated as the clients gained more experience with the model. The results indicated that clients had a reasonable grasp of the process, found much of the process to be beneficial, and were able to articulate some limitations (e.g., feeling overwhelmed by the additional team members, the team going off on its own tangent, and the abruptness experienced when a session had some emotional content and the team interrupted).

Another issue that has received empirical attention is the relative frequency of use of live supervision. McKenzie, Atkinson, Quinn, and Heath (1986) conducted a national survey of AAMFT-approved supervisors to determine what form of supervision they used most and what form they believed to be most productive. The results showed some discrepancies. From the supervisors' perspective, the most effective form of supervision was live supervision with immediate feedback. But the most frequently used method of supervision was listening to an audiotape, followed by relying on written process notes. Different forms of live supervision ranked seventh through tenth in frequency, even though only 33 percent of the sample reported not using live supervision at all. Furthermore, only 8.5 percent of the respondents thought that process notes were an effective form of supervision, despite the high rate of usage. Nichols, Nichols, and Hardy (1990) found similar results, with approximately two-thirds of approved supervisors using live supervision nationally.

Lewis and Rohrbaugh (1989) conducted a similar study in one state (Virginia) and surveyed all family therapists who were members of AAMFT. Their study found only one-third of family therapists who supervise using a live supervision model. Lewis and Rohrbaugh correctly cautioned that Virginia might not be representative of the rest of the country. Also, the former study surveyed only approved supervisors, while the Virginia study included AAMFT clinical members and associate members who were offering supervision as part of their professional duties. It could be hypothesized, therefore, that approved supervisors use live supervision more frequently. One consideration that neither study addressed was the number of supervisors who were in training settings versus those who were in mental health delivery settings. We believe this to be an important missing datum, especially if, as we assume, live supervision is far more prevalent in training settings.

As live supervision has become less novel to the mental health professions and as its overall tenability as a supervision model has been established, there has been more interest in understanding the discrete contributions of different aspects of the model. We have already reported the work of Frankel (1990) and Frankel and Piercy (1990) that investigated types of supervisor directives and their different effects. Kivlighan, Angelone, and Swafford (1991) conducted a similar study that focused on supervisee intentions rather than supervisor in-

tentions. Supervisees in this study were learning an interpersonal–dynamic approach to individual psychotherapy. Kivlighan et al. were interested in the difference between supervisees exposed to live supervision versus those using videotaped supervision. The dependent variable was the intention motivating each therapist response. Overall, the intentions for those in the live supervision treatment were consistent with the interpersonal approach to therapy (i.e., more support and relationship intentions). Therefore, the authors concluded that the live supervision approach allowed supervisees to learn more quickly. In addition to types of intentions, the authors hypothesized that live supervision would lead to stronger working alliances with clients and to therapy sessions that were *deeper* and *rougher* (Stiles, Shapiro, & Firth-Cozens, 1988). The working alliance was considered stronger by clients for the live supervision condition than for the videotape condition, and sessions were viewed as rougher. Sessions were not experienced as deeper, however, a characteristic typically associated with interpersonal–dynamic therapy.

The Kivlighan et al. result that live supervision may have compromised the depth of interpersonal therapy session leads to the first of several questions we believe need to be posed regarding live supervision.

1. Thus far, most live supervision experience and observation have been done with supervisees conducting family therapy. Although live supervision has become popular outside of family therapy, we know very little about its utility across theoretical approaches (Bubenzer, West, & Gold, 1991). The requisite interruptions of therapy when conducting live supervision may discourage levels of interpersonal depth required of some therapies.

2. As more authors argue for an increased egalitarianism within live supervision (e.g., Hardy, 1993; Woodside, 1994), the relationship between such a movement and the ability of the supervisor to evaluate supervisees must be measured. Additionally, a recent qualitative study determined that supervisees receiving live supervision found a unique combination of a nonegalitarian supervisory hierarchy (involving instruction and support) paired with adequate autonomy to be the most helpful to them (Wark, 1995).

3. There has been virtually no study of the generalizability or continuity of the behaviors exhibited in live supervision (Gallant et al., 1991; Kivlighan et al., 1991).

4. Hardy (1993) proposed that live supervision may change dramatically to reflect changes in our understanding of cultural variables, especially as they relate to power. To date, these variables have not been isolated within live supervision research.

5. Finally, with the exception that BITE is best used with more novice trainees, the developmental level of the trainee has received little empirical attention within live supervision research. Especially in terms of team activity, the developmental needs and abilities of supervisees are unknown.

LIVE SUPERVISION IN DIFFERENT CONTEXTS

To date, live supervision is more prevalent in training settings than in work settings. In part, this reflects both the facilities requirements and the break with tradition that live supervision represents. For professionals trained within a live supervision model, one consequence might be a disenchantment in the supervision offered beyond training. Conversely, if live supervision remains only realistic within a training context, academic programs might eventually be criticized for not providing their students with supervision that will translate to future work sites.

Although live supervision has been a topic in the professional literature for over 20 years, there are still very few references in the literature to this type of activity other than to those settings that were developed as specialized marriage and family therapy clinics, such as the Ackerman Institute or the Philadelphia Guidance Clinic. We will report the experiences of two public agencies that introduced live supervision to their operation, one agency subscribing to a systemic framework and one committed to diverse conceptual frameworks.

We might assume that live supervision is easier to implement if the staff already operates within a systemic framework. Based on Lewis's (1988) discussion, it seems that this assumption is valid. Lewis described the infusion of live supervision into a rural public mental health and substance abuse agency. Although the problems of the clients varied greatly, the staff and agency had adopted a systemic orientation. It is possible, therefore, that several staff members had experienced live supervision prior to their employment. Lewis reported no resistance to the live supervision paradigm, either from clinical staff, administration, or clients. He does, however, make a distinction between live supervision and live consultation, the latter being the use of a team, but with no evaluative responsibility.

Markowski and Cain (1983), on the other hand, reported the introduction of live supervision to a community mental health center staffed by clinicians of various theoretical persuasions. The goal of the mental health center was to increase the skill of a group of core staff in marriage and family therapy. Therefore, an outside consultant was hired to conduct live (team) supervision one-half day per week for the purpose of helping this core staff acquire sufficient competence to function without the consultant. An additional incentive for the staff was meeting the criteria for state certification as marriage and family therapists. For this eclectic staff, it was critical that the consultant be supportive of different clinical orientations so that the integrity of the staff members involved was protected.

Markowski and Cain reported that the bug-in-the-ear was an unsatisfactory method for their teams (two were formed) and that consultation breaks became the method of choice. We assume that the range of theoretical positions of the team required the kind of give and take that is possible during consultations, but not using BITE. In time, Markowski and Cain also found that team members became more sensitive to their differences and were better able to suggest interventions that fit the therapist's own style and therapeutic assumptions. Therefore, it might be argued that, in this case, live supervision made the members of a diverse staff more respectful of their individual contributions, rather than clones of the supervisor, as some authors have feared.

Although a positive experience, Markowski and Cain recounted difficulties, too, especially as they related to record keeping, the necessity of separation of services, and the acceptance of the individual illness model by third-party insurers. The authors concluded that, if there is respect and administrative support for such a program, "both the individual and the systems models can co-exist in productive harmony" (p. 44).

CONCLUSION

The introduction of live supervision to the mental health professions represents a blending of skills training and the more contemplative forms of clinical supervision. Its primary advantage is the closing of the gap between the supervisee's experience and the supervisor's review of that experience; the assumed outcome of this advantage is accelerated learning. The disadvantages of the model revolve around the time commitment required of the supervisor, the need for specific facilities, and the intrusion into the therapy relationship. Team approaches to live supervision offer additional training possibilities, as well as additional challenges and potential disadvantages. The reflecting team moves live supervision to a point that it may as likely be called live consultation (Lewis, 1988).

In recent years, live supervision has moved from its identity as a family therapy training model exclusively to increased use within the other mental health professions. Empirical investigation of live supervision has commenced and shows promise of ultimately assisting clinical supervisors in determining the optimal conditions for the use of live supervision, as well as its most necessary components.

CHAPTER 8

Evaluation

Evaluation could be viewed as the nucleus of clinical supervision. The history of supervision is that supervisors have taught and encouraged, but also monitored, those who enter the helping professions. The ethical and legal issues surrounding supervision are primarily embedded in the evaluation function. Many of the more direct methods for conducting clinical supervision have developed, in part, as a response to a need to evaluate more accurately.

As central as it is to proper functioning of clinical supervision, most supervisors are troubled by evaluation, at least occasionally. Some view it as a necessary evil; a few see it as antithetical to the helping professions (Cohen, 1987). Part of the problem is that clinical supervisors were first trained as therapists and their values often lie within that domain. Therapists are taught to accept their clients' limitations and to respect their clients' goals. Like good parents, good therapists learn to respect the boundary between clients' ambitions for themselves and therapists' ambitions for them. Good therapists distinguish between advocacy and responsibility. The good therapist is a facilitator of another's change and is not a decision maker about what change is necessary.

Many of the working conditions within supervision reflect those for therapy. Yet there is an essential, paradigmatic difference: The supervisor might want to use the trainee's progress as the critical criterion for evaluation, but responsibility to the profession and to the trainee's future clients would preclude this. The supervisor is charged to evaluate the trainee based on some external set of criteria. These criteria must meet institutional standards, but also reflect national standards of practice (Robiner, Fuhrman, Ristvedt, Bobbitt, & Schirvar, 1994). An essential assumption underlying evaluation is that the criteria chosen or derived from professional standards reflect competent practice. Herein lies the first major obstacle in conducting sound evaluation.

Robiner, Fuhrman and Ristvedt (1993) described clinical competence as a "moving target with an elusive criterion" (p. 5). Although the accrediting and state regulatory bodies of the helping professions prescribe knowledge and skill standards, the research continues to undermine the assumption that particular types of knowledge, skill, or level of experience determine client outcome (Herman, 1993). Rather, reviews of the outcome literature have produced mixed results (e.g., Pinsof & Wynne, 1995; Shaw & Dobson, 1988), and some continue to support the notion that nonspecific factors such as the therapist's personal characteristics might be more predictive of successful outcome with clients (Herman, 1993; Orlinsky, Grawe, & Parks, 1994; Shaw & Dobson, 1988). Because of this, helping professionals have not yet determined the educational experiences that yield competent practitioners nor have they developed performance measures that distinguish competent from incompetent practitioners (Robiner et al., 1993).

Of course, the confrontive conclusion that much of training may be irrelevant makes highly credentialed professionals defensive, including most clinical supervisors. Intuitively, most professionals believe, even in the absence of definitive data, that experience matters and that there is specific knowledge and skill that professionals must have. As a logical outgrowth of this belief, clinical supervisors assume they are responsible for monitoring trainees' development of knowledge and skill. The helping professions may need better research to indicate which aspects of training are especially important; in the meantime, it is safe to assume that supervisors will continue to evaluate supervisees based on their own knowledge of what is understood in their professional community to constitute acceptable standards of practice.

Given the consistent finding that personal characteristics of therapists are highly predictive of success (Herman, 1993; Sakinofsky, 1979), it may be of some comfort to clinical supervisors that the personal characteristics of trainees and supervisors alike have always been considered relevant to supervision, as is evidenced in this text by the amount of space given to issues like the supervision relationship, to individual differences, and to ethics as personal morality. These, however, do not cancel out the responsible supervisor's concern that, for the present, evaluation is grounded in accumulated professional wisdom more than in science. Moreover, this is a time when the call for more rigorous evaluations has increased due to legal accountability and the escalating sophistication of therapy modalities (Glenn & Serovich; 1994; Hahn & Molnar, 1991). As a result, Kadushin's (1985) reflection on the supervisor's plight continues to be highly relevant:

> [M]any supervisors question the legitimacy of evaluation and lack a sense of entitlement. They do not think they should or can judge another. Further, they are oppressed by conflicting, ambiguous evidence of performance and by imprecise, vague standards available for judging performance. Not feeling "without sin," they are reluctant to cast the first stone.   (p. 338)

These two factors then, the incompatibility of evaluation with their professional identity as therapists and the dearth of relevant outcome studies to determine the salient ingredients of therapeutic competence, can combine to cause considerable dissonance when supervisors are required to evaluate. Supervisors have two choices for managing

this dissonance: They can throw up their hands and minimize the function of evaluation in their supervision or they can work to counteract both dissonance-causing factors by thoughtful planning, structuring, intervening, and communicating. The rest of this chapter can be viewed as an outline of topics for consideration by those who will face evaluation head on and complete its requirements to the best of their ability, even in light of imperfect or incomplete criteria, within a social context that exhibits greater demands for accountability. To do this, supervisors must model a posture of inquiry even as they attempt to monitor and guide.

The first step for the supervisor is to plan a clear distinction between *formative* and *summative* evaluation (Levy, 1983). Robiner, Fuhrman and Ristvedt (1993) described formative assessment as the process of facilitating skill acquisition and professional growth through direct feedback. As such, they contended that formative evaluation causes little discomfort for clinical supervisors. Formative evaluation indeed represents the bulk of the supervisor's work with the trainee and does not feel like evaluation because it stresses process and progress, rather than outcome. Nevertheless, it is important to remember that there is an evaluative message in all supervision (Kadushin, 1976). When supervisors tell trainees that an intervention was successful, they are evaluating. When supervisors say nothing, trainees will either decide that their performance was exemplary or too awful to discuss. In other words, by virtue of the nature of the relationship, evaluation is a constant variable in supervision. Some of the supervisor's evaluative comments are sent (encoded) by the supervisor to the trainee; others are received (decoded) by the trainee and may or may not be an accurate understanding of the supervisor's assessments. Because we are always communicating, an evaluative message can always be inferred.

Summative evaluation, on the other hand, is what many of us mean when we discuss evaluation and causes far more stress for both supervisors and supervisees. This is the moment of truth when the supervisor steps back, takes stock, and decides how the trainee measures up. To do this supervisors must first decide on the criteria against which they are measuring trainees. Furthermore, the trainee should possess the same yardstick.

In truth, summative evaluations are trying because they are often disconnected from what has come before in the supervision relationship. Either because of lack of organization or lack of a clear set of standards, the supervisor may conduct summative evaluation in a vague or biased way. A supervisor who is helpful and articulate during the formative contacts can appear rushed and insecure at a summative conference. Robiner et al. (1993) asserted that because of the trepidation or ambivalence caused by summative assessment a generalized disdain for evaluation may result "despite its central importance in the supervisory process" (p. 4). Because summative evaluations are those that direct major administrative decisions, such disdain is highly problematic. The chief antidote to summative disdain is the amount of time and care invested in the formative evaluation process. But before any evaluation begins, the difficult task of identifying criteria must be addressed.

CRITERIA FOR EVALUATION

It goes without saying that criteria for evaluation become a problematic area when there is virtually no research to determine what is essential for supervisees to learn under supervision. Ironically, although the professions lack clear empirical direction about the necessary conditions for competence, the increasing fear of litigation has forced professionals to begin to grapple with definitions of impairment. Impairment for psychologists has been defined as a serious deficit in the areas of knowledge and application of professional standards, to include ethics, relevant mental health law, and professional behavior; competency in areas such as conceptualization, diagnosis and assessment, and appropriate interventions; and personal functioning, to include awareness of self,

the use of supervision, and management of personal stress (Lamb, Presser, Pfost, Baum, Jackson, & Jarvis, 1987; Lamb, Cochran, & Jackson, 1991).

Overholser and Fine (1990) have pursued examples of what they described as subtle cases of clinical incompetence, thus attempting to establish a more sophisticated boundary between competence and impairment. They cited five areas of investigation: factual knowledge, generic clinical skills, orientation-specific technical skills, clinical judgment, and interpersonal attributes. It would be expected that the other mental health professions would construe similar areas of concern. For example, one study that tracked criteria for competence in marriage and family therapy (Perlesz, Stolk, & Firestone, 1990) used perceptual skills (ability to make pertinent and accurate observations), conceptual skills (the process of attributing meaning to observations), and executive–intervention skills (ability to respond within sessions in a deliberate manner), as well as demonstrated personal development, as the targeted criteria. With the growing sensitivity to cultural variables in therapy, multicultural competence is increasingly identified as a criterion for therapy competence (Larson et al., 1992).

Frame and Stevens-Smith (1995) have made a serious attempt to operationalize those factors referred to as personal characteristics for purposes of evaluation. Based on a review of the literature, Frame and Stevens-Smith identified nine trainee functions that have been cited as relevant for success as professional counselors. The essential functions included students being open, flexible, positive, and cooperative; willing to accept and use feedback; aware of impact on others; and the ability to deal with conflict, accept personal responsibility, and express feelings effectively and appropriately. Frame and Stevens-Smith suggested that these functions be published for student consumption and that students be evaluated on these functions on a regular basis.

Accrediting bodies have become central in defining criteria, though they tend to avoid any reference to personal characteristics except in terms of admissions and termination policy. All the mental health professions have accrediting bodies that establish standards for the education of persons entering the profession. These standards include core areas of knowledge and often specialized curricular areas, as well as stipulations for clinical training. These standards, then, become the criteria for evaluation, at least for pre-degree candidates. Additionally, standards tend to increase in number over time, whether because of the increased complexity of mental health delivery (Hahn & Molnar, 1991) or because it is human nature to add rather than subtract when it comes to criteria (Mohl, Sadler, & Miller, 1994). For better or worse, professional standards are used by both training institutions and state regulatory bodies to evaluate persons entering specific mental health professions and are therefore legitimate compilations of criteria for evaluation. It should be noted, however, that even when criteria are specified expected competency *levels* often remain illusive to both supervisees and supervisors (Magnuson, 1995).

Mohl et al. (1994) described an alternative path for arriving at criteria. They surveyed a psychiatric residency faculty to determine training priorities by asking what components the faculty was willing to spend their time evaluating. Although this faculty did not represent clinical supervisors, the process used by these authors is one worth considering. The faculty was asked what it believed could be evaluated in the academic context, what could be evaluated within clinical supervision, what items should be combined, and what items should be eliminated.

The results suggested that the faculty found fundamental skills (e.g., making a differential diagnosis) were most essential. The faculty was also interested in evaluating such trainee attitudes as empathy. The areas that received less support were those associated with specialized areas of practice (e.g., diagnosis of childhood disorders). It seems that this type of process could be used by any training program or delivery system to capture what influential parties consider essential areas of evaluation. Trainees will ultimately progress or regress

based on their performance against a setting's valued criteria. The more these are fleshed out, the better.

Another approach to arriving at criteria is to conduct a systemic investigation of what supervisors tend to focus on during supervision sessions (e.g., Carey & Lanning, 1993; Lanning & Freeman, 1994). By tracking the behavior of supervisors, a list of criteria will eventually develop. Basically, this process adheres to a "trust what I do, not what I say" assumption.

Finally, a method for arriving at criteria for evaluation is to conduct a job analysis of knowledge and skills used and deemed important by mental health practitioners (e.g., Fitzgerald & Osipow, 1986; NBCC, 1993). The limitation of job analyses, however, is that "they inform us of *what is* rather than what *should* or *could be*. Matters such as these are more readily addressed when criteria are defined on the basis of conceptual models of training" (Goodyear, 1994, p. 3).

Robiner, Fuhrman, and Ristvedt (1993) reported the result of APA's Joint Council on Professional Education in Psychology (Stigall et al., 1990) attempt to delineate exit criteria for psychology doctoral internships. The eight areas of competence identified by the council are effective interpersonal functioning; ability to make sound professional judgments; ability to extend and expand basic assessment and intervention techniques to meet the needs of different settings, problems, and populations; ability to apply ethical and legal principles to practice; ability to assess and intervene appropriately with clients manifesting diverse characteristics; development of a primary professional identity as a psychologist; awareness of personal strengths and limitations and the need for continued supervision, consultation, and education; and preparedness to enter residency training and to choose appropriate advanced training. In addition to these, the Joint Council recommended that personal characteristics such as psychological health and awareness of self be considered as entry-level criteria for admission to professional training programs. Although generic in nature, these criteria most definitely offer a place to begin for outlining more specific behaviors for evaluation and can easily be translated to other mental health professions.

The difficulty of establishing criteria for evaluation and the equally difficult task of measuring them is a professional reality. We do not presume to offer a definitive list of criteria. Rather, we stress that, regardless of what criteria the supervisor identifies, the summative evaluation should relate directly to these same criteria. It is not unheard of for supervisors to find themselves hunting for an evaluation form at the end of the supervisory relationship as if the form had no relationship to the formative evaluation that preceded. On the contrary, whatever is to be used at the end of supervision to summarize the trainee's progress should be introduced early in supervision, should serve as teaching–learning objectives, and should be used throughout supervision as the basis for intermittent feedback.

FAVORABLE CONDITIONS FOR EVALUATION

A major problem with evaluation in the helping professions is that it hits so close to home. Therapy is a very human activity; therefore, to be lacking in therapeutic skills can be perceived as being a human failure. For this reason and because of the vulnerability accompanying any evaluation process, it is important that supervisors do all that is possible to create favorable conditions when evaluating. Favorable conditions not only make evaluation more palatable, but directly influence the content of supervision. As Ekstein and Wallerstein (1972) noted, when the context of supervision is favorable, the trainee stops asking "How can I avoid criticism?" and starts asking "How can I make the most of this supervision time?"

Several authors have addressed the conditions that make evaluation a more positive experience. The following list of conditions draws from our own thoughts as well as the work of Borders et al. (1991), Ekstein and Wallerstein (1972), Fox (1983), Fried,

Tiegs, and Bellamy (1992), Kadushin (1985), Mathews (1986), and Olsen and Stern (1990):

1. Supervisors must remember that supervision is an unequal relationship. No amount of empathy will erase the fact that supervisors' reactions to supervisees will have consequences for them, some of which may be negative. Being sensitive to the position of the trainee will make supervisors more compassionate evaluators.

2. Clarity adds to a positive context. Supervisors need to state clearly their administrative as well as clinical roles. Who will be privy to the feedback supervisors give trainees? Will the supervisor be making decisions regarding the trainee's continuation in a graduate program or job? If not, what is the supervisor's relationship to the persons who make those decisions? For example, most graduate programs conduct periodic student reviews. At these reviews the evaluation by the clinical supervisor is often weighed more heavily than other evaluations. Students should be aware, at the very least, that their performance in the clinical component of the program will be discussed by the total faculty at some point in the future. Clarity can also be communicated by structure. Supervisors must provide structure appropriate to the developmental level of the supervisee. Congenial supervisors who allow supervisees to flounder will eventually forfeit any goodwill they initially may have earned.

3. Supervisees' defensiveness should be addressed openly (Costa, 1994). Supervision makes trainees feel naked, at least initially. It is natural, if not desirable, that they attempt to defend themselves. Some will defend by trying to outguess the supervisor. Others will appear vulnerable and helpless. The truth is that all supervisees are vulnerable, and supervisors need to be sensitive to this fact and not hold their vulnerability against them. Rather, supervisors can introduce appropriate and inappropriate defensive tactics as a legitimate topic for discussion. "Games" frequently played by trainees (Bauman, 1972; Kadushin, 1968) can be described. If asked, trainees can usually tell what type of defense they are most likely to use. If the supervisor follows such a disclosure with "What should I do when you play 'I'm no good'?", the beginnings of an honest, working relationship have been established.

4. Along with defensiveness, individual differences should be addressed openly. Evaluation may well be affected by differences of background, gender, race, and so forth, particularly if these differences are not understood to be relevant to supervision. Furthermore, competence in therapy includes the ability to communicate in ways that are culturally flexible. The first cultural context to be addressed, therefore, is the supervision context.

5. Evaluation procedures should be spelled out in advance. Whatever process has been decided on, it should be known by the trainee. Differences between formative and summative evaluation should be explained. Among the procedural topics that should be included are the projected length of the supervisory relationship, the preferred methods of supervision and how these will be used, any additional sources that will be used to determine the trainee's progress, the frequency of supervision conferences, and how the evaluation will be conducted and used.

6. Evaluation should be a mutual and continuous process. The trainee should be actively involved in determining what is to be learned. In a sense, the supervisor is there to serve the trainee, and this contractual dimension should not get lost. Also, the formative aspect of evaluation should be the most active. Although both parties know that there must be a taking stock down the road, the process of learning and the evaluation of the learning should not feel static.

7. There should be enough flexibility that short-term intrusions will not jeopardize the quality of a trainee's summative evaluation. Kadushin (1985) made the excellent observation that outside obligations sometimes will interfere with a trainee's performance. Therefore, supervisors' evaluations should take this into account. Especially in a profession that attracts second-career adults, it is important that supervisors balance their expectations with the knowledge that, for

trainees as well as for themselves, children have crises, elderly parents can need care, and spouses lose or change jobs. Life does not always accommodate supervisees' career aspirations. In a Type A world, we all need to learn that the best laid plans are vulnerable to the unexpected.

Supervisors model an important attitude when they are accepting of life's impositions on their supervisees. It is equally important to leave enough space in a training schedule to accommodate life's (predictable) lack of predictability. There are times when the best advice a supervisor can give a trainee is that the trainee should postpone internship (or that extra project) until his or her personal life regains some semblance of normality. Learning to appreciate the balance between professional demands and personal demands is an important lesson for all of us in the helping professions. Of course, these comments do not fit the supervisee whose life is perpetually in crisis. That is a different evaluation issue.

8. Evaluation must occur within a strong administrative structure. Whether in an educational or work setting, supervisors must know that their evaluations will stick. Nothing is as frustrating and damaging as when a supervisor risks the consequences of a negative evaluation only to have this overturned by a superior in the organization. When this happens, more often than not, one of two things has happened. Either due process was not followed, or the supervisor did not have a clear sense of administrative support beforehand. In other words, the supervisor assumed that he or she would be backed up without bothering to check. Or the supervisor did not have the political savvy to inform his or her superiors prior to the evaluation, both to warn them and to make sure the process would be supported.

Whether the supervisor is correct in the evaluation can be a moot issue if the trainee's rights were not protected, or appeared not to be protected, during the evaluation process. It is as important that the system be as trustworthy in the supervisee's eyes as from the supervisor's perspective. If the history of the system is that evaluation is arbitrary or capricious, supervisees will risk less and will be more defensive overall in their interactions with supervisors.

Finally, even if the system has integrity, the supervisee must be confidant that the individual who supervises can be trusted. Supervisees must know that there is a place to go if they think an evaluation is unfair or incomplete. On university campuses, the grievance committee is usually the administrative body of choice once the head of the department has been consulted; in employment settings, the supervisor's immediate superior would be the appropriate person. If there is no such protective body or person, it is up to the supervisor to establish some sort of safeguard for the supervisee. Supervision objectives will be greatly handicapped if anyone in the system feels trapped. A strong administrative structure offers the same kind of security to supervisees that a strong and reasonable parental system offers children. We do not mean to treat supervisees like children, but we do believe that it is appropriate for the organization to acknowledge their subordinate positions and build in appropriate safeguards.

9. Premature evaluations of supervisees should be avoided. Whether a supervisor is working with one trainee or several, it is important to resist overreacting to the person who shows unusual potential or the person who seems to be faltering. We are not implying that one should withhold feedback or be dishonest. Rather, we believe that supervisors often react too quickly and by evaluating too quickly can do serious disservice to talented supervisees, as well as to those who need more grounding to begin their better work. If supervision occurs in a group, morale is hurt when it becomes obvious that early distinctions have been made among trainees. On the contrary, when the group is challenged to ensure that everyone achieves competence, the atmosphere is energetic, supportive, and competitive in the best sense.

Some trainees will enter supervision expecting to be recognized and treated as stars. It is the supervisor, however, who makes such a designation happen by relying on initial impressions and forgetting that some therapy skills can only be assessed accurately over the long term. Whether a trainee wears well will be terribly important to the trainee's future colleagues, supervisors, and clients. This cannot be determined in a few weeks, regardless of the strength of the trainee's entry behavior.

10. Supervisees need to witness the professional development of their supervisors. As a supervisor, the best way to do this is to invite feedback and use it. Trainees feel empowered if they sense that they have something valuable to offer their supervisor. Additionally, the supervisor's involvement and sharing of continuing education activities model for trainees the need for continuing expansion in the work of therapy. For supervisors to present new ideas that they are struggling with gives a much more accurate picture of the profession than for them to play the part of the all-knowing guru. Also, presenting some tentativeness in thinking will remind the supervisor to be tentative about the work of trainees. Supervisors must constantly remind themselves that they do not deal in a profession of facts, but of concepts.

11. Supervisors must always keep an eye to the relationship, which interacts with all aspects of supervision. Evaluation becomes especially difficult when the relationship has become too close or is strained. In fact, it is the reality of evaluation that behooves the supervisor to maintain both a positive and supportive relationship with the trainee—yet one that is professional, not personal. If relationships are strained for whatever reason, supervisors must ask themselves if they can evaluate objectively enough. (No evaluation is totally objective; the goal is to keep objective standards in mind while considering subjective impressions.) This point was underscored by Ladany, Hill, Corbett, and Nutt (1996), who found that negative reactions to the supervisor, personal issues, clinical mistakes, and evaluation concerns were the top four categories of supervisee nondisclosures in supervision. A weak relationship between supervisor and supervisee, then, can cause the supervisee to withhold essential supervision information.

Some personalities clash, and the best intentions do not make the initial dislike for the trainee or supervisor disappear. The trainee should not bear the brunt of this kind of situation. Whenever supervision is conducted, there should be some thought given to the possibility of strong incompatibility, and at least a sketchy plan should be in place for how to resolve such a problem. In short, it is the supervisee's right to trust the supervisor. A relationship without trust will be one of avoidance and mixed messages, which is poor material to culminate in an accurate evaluation.

12. No one who does not enjoy supervising should supervise. For this final condition, we go back to the point we made at the beginning of this chapter: Evaluation is difficult, even for those supervisors who love the challenge of supervision. For the supervisor who is supervising for any lesser reason, evaluation may feel like too great a burden. When this is the case, the supervisor will shortchange the trainee and give perfunctory evaluations or will avoid the task, especially if the evaluation could be confrontive. Supervisors always have many other responsibilities to use as rationalizations for keeping a trainee at arm's length. It is not difficult to find a helping professional who can attest to the frustration of getting little or no constructive feedback from a supervisor. Whenever a trainee is denied appropriate supervision and evaluation, the professional community is diminished.

Although the conditions listed above will not compensate for weak criteria or a poor process, they assure a sensitivity to the supervisee's rights and a realization of the seriousness of the contract between supervisor and supervisee. Seriousness, however, is an attribute that Sanville (1989) encouraged supervisors to keep in check. Viewing play as a primary source of creative curiosity, imagination, and openness to surprise, Sanville advanced playfulness in supervision as a favorable condition. She described effective playfulness as including

(1) a sense of freedom and choice, of the activity's being voluntary, (2) a sense of the encounter as a sort of "interlude from real life" in which the emotions of therapeutic sessions can be recollected in relative tranquility, (3) a sense that it is not only all right to entertain feelings of confusion and uncertainty, but that the "courage not to comprehend" (Reik, 1948) is a necessary prelude to developing new outlooks, (4) a sense of safety to counterbalance the felt risks of anticipated failures or successes and (5) safety to question even the most sacrosanct professional ideas. (p. 161)

THE PROCESS OF EVALUATION

We have discussed the important task of choosing criteria and have made brief reference to using some sort of evaluation instrument to make a final judgment regarding the supervisee's level of competence. These, respectively, comprise the beginning and the end of evaluation. *Process* defines how supervisors conduct their business between these two markers and how they incorporate the issue of evaluation from the beginning of supervision to its completion. In other words, the process of evaluation is not separate from the process of clinical supervision, but is embedded within it. The evaluation process also includes the means by which supervisors obtain the data they use to make their assessments, a topic more completely addressed in Chapters 5, 6, and 7. For our discussion here, the process of evaluation will be considered as having six elements, most of which interact throughout the supervision experience: negotiating a supervision–evaluation contract, choosing evaluation methods and supervision interventions, choosing evaluation instrument(s), communicating formative feedback, encouraging self-assessment, and conducting formal summative evaluation sessions.

The Supervision–Evaluation Contract

When students register for a course, they receive a syllabus identifying requirements, course objectives, an outline of activities or topics to be discussed, and the instructor's plan for evaluation. Whether clinical experience is gained within a course structure, each supervisee should be provided with a plan that parallels a syllabus. Unlike most course syllabi, however, the supervision contract should be individualized. Described as goal-directed supervision, Talen and Schindler (1993) asserted that supervisee-initiated goals set the stage for a collaborative relationship with the supervisor. Mead (1990) suggested that ample time be given during this process to considering discrepancies between the trainee's goals and those set for the trainee by the supervisor. Mead advised that some goals identified by the trainee may be a residue from past experiences in supervision and may need thorough discussion and modification. A conference regarding a supervision contract serves a purpose for new trainees also in that it helps them to understand the difference between clinical supervision and other learning experiences. Although plans can vary, all supervision contracts should establish training goals, describe criteria for evaluation, establish supervision methods that will be used, describe the length and frequency of supervision contacts, and establish how a summative evaluation will be achieved. The relationship of formative feedback to summative feedback should also be explained to the supervisee.

To proceed in a manner that is consistent with goal-directed supervision, each supervisory conference can and perhaps should end with a plan of action for goal attainment and a time frame for completion of the plan (Kadushin, 1985). In the same way, each conference should begin with an update on progress toward the goals set in the previous session. Middleman and Rhodes (1985) suggested that formative evaluation occur often enough for changes to be suggested with time to implement them before the summative evaluation. In other words, evaluation should be dynamic and relevant throughout the supervision experience, not just at the beginning and end.

The time when the absence of such a dynamic process becomes a conspicuous issue is in the unfortunate circumstance of a negative final evaluation. We discuss the due process rights of supervisees who are considered incompetent at the time of summative evaluation in Chapter 9. The time to consider this unfortunate possibility is in the beginning of the evaluative process, not at the end. Lamb et al. (1987) suggested that information given to new supervisees include agency and/or training program expectations; agency and/or program responsibilities in assisting supervisees to meet expectations; and evaluation procedures, including time frame, content of evaluations, use of verbal and written feedback, evaluation forms, and opportunities for supervisee feedback. Finally, Lamb et al. advised that due process procedures be reviewed with supervisees.

There is some admonition in the professional literature (e.g., Meyer, 1980) about overly fastidious evaluation procedures, especially when they are devised with the impaired student in mind. Miller and Rickard (1983) offered a middle of the road posture regarding procedures, warning that too elaborate a process can be burdensome and time consuming and can build inflexibility into the system, which they believed can work against trainees as often as it works for them. They favored having a simple, but precise, evaluation process for all students (not just those who are in trouble) and refraining from trying to articulate a procedure for problems that are unlikely to arise. Miller and Rickard referred to J. L. Bernard's (1975) four evaluation steps, which they used to evaluate clinical psychology students:

1. *Incoming students should be presented with written material fully describing conditions under which a student may be terminated, including personal unsuitability for the profession.*
2. *All students should be routinely evaluated at least once a year, and this evaluation should include a section on personal functioning.*
3. *If inadequacies are identified, the student is so advised, a remediation plan with a time line should be put in place, and the student should be made aware of the consequences of failure to remedy.*
4. *If sufficient remediation is not accomplished in the time designated, the student should be given time to prepare a case; then this should be presented to the faculty and the faculty then make a decision. If the student is terminated, all of the above should be summarized in writing to the student.*   (p. 832)

A final note about the supervision contract, and one that was confirmed by Talen and Schindler (1993), is the compatibility between this activity and the developmental needs of relatively inexperienced supervisees (Stoltenberg & Delworth, 1987). The structure offered through the process of establishing learning goals supplies the supervisee with a concrete anchor to help weather the onslaught of clinical sessions with all their unknowns.

Choosing Supervision Methods for Evaluation

Each method of supervision—process notes, self-report, audio- or videotapes of therapy sessions, or live supervision—influences evaluation differently. Live supervision can pose a particular problem if the supervisor is considered a part of the team of observers because the authority of the supervisor might be compromised. Haley (1987), however, suggested that the supervisor keep the hierarchy clear and not allow the role of supervisor to be diffused by live supervision. Some supervisors rely heavily on group supervision and may even encourage some form of peer evaluation among trainees. This approach provides markedly different information than that gathered from, for example, self-report. When the ultimate responsibility to evaluate is paramount in the supervisor's awareness, the supervisor will seek supplemental data if they are needed to arrive at a balanced evaluation.

Supervisees can be at a disadvantage when the form of supervision changes from one setting to the next. For example, Collins and Bogo (1986) have observed that early training experiences (on campus) tend to use a good amount of technology, while field supervision is more likely to be based on self-report and case notes. Therefore, they found that supervision in the field was far more reflective in nature than that on campus, which focused more on skills. Perhaps supervisors need not only to inform their students about the forms of supervision they use, but also to educate them about the forms they do not use.

Of paramount importance is that supervisors realize that supervision interventions have both instructional and evaluation consequences. A supervisor may favor one form of gathering supervision material (e.g., audiotape), but the supervisor must realize that each method is a lens through which to view the work of the supervisee. Some lenses provide the sharper image of one aspect of the supervisee's work, but a wide angle will allow the supervisor a different perspective from which to evaluate. Therefore, multiple methods are the surest way to get an accurate picture of the supervisee's strengths and weaknesses (Harris, 1994).

Choosing Evaluation Instruments

There are nearly as many evaluation instruments as there are training programs in the helping professions. Supervisors tend to develop and use Likert-type measures during summative conferences. Depending on how well that measure reflects criteria that already have been selected by the supervisor and communicated to the supervisee, the measure may help supervisees to appreciate their progress toward predetermined goals. When evaluation measures have not been integrated into the supervision experience, their use can be superficial or frustrating from the standpoint of the supervisee.

Homegrown evaluation measures are primarily a communication tool. Because most use Likert scales, supervisors use them to quantify their assessments of supervisees. Quantification, however, may need some explanation. For example, the supervisor must decide what is adequate (numerically speaking) for the supervisee to be given a positive evaluation. Additionally, it should be clear what level of performance is below standards and what level would be considered as meeting the highest standards. If a trainee comes into supervision with superior ability in several areas, the Likert scale ratings should reflect this. Some supervisors use scales differently, deciding that no supervisee should receive a score higher than a certain number (e.g., 5 out of a possible 7) until the supervisory experience is at least half complete. If this is the supervisor's policy, it is important that the supervisee know this. When the supervisor uses a scale in this way, however, the supervisor bypasses the issue of level of accomplishment. Hahn and Molnar (1991) developed a 7-point Likert scale with adequate description at each level to be of use to the supervision process (see Table 8.1), especially for summative evaluation.

Supervisees can also be encouraged to use Likert-type formats to communicate with their

TABLE 8.1   Intern Rating Scale

Please rate intern using the following 7-point scale:

Level 1   Performs inadequately for an intern in this area. Requires frequent and close supervision and monitoring of basic and advanced tasks in this area.

Level 2   Requires supervision and monitoring in carrying out routine tasks in this area and requires significant supervision and close monitoring in carrying out advanced tasks in this area.

Level 3   Requires some supervision and monitoring in carrying out routine tasks in this area. Requires guidance, training, education, and ongoing supervision for developing advanced skills in this area.

Level 4   Displays mastery of routine tasks in this area. Requires ongoing supervision for performance of advanced skills in this area. The intern occasionally, spontaneously demonstrates advanced skills in this area.

Level 5   Displays master of routine tasks in this area. Requires periodic supervision for refinement of advanced skills in this area.

Level 6   Displays mastery of routine tasks in this area. Could continue to benefit from some supervision on advanced and/or nonroutine tasks in this area.

Level 7   Performs at the independent practice level in this area and is capable of teaching others in this area. Performs without the general need of supervision, but consults when appropriate.

From W. K. Hahn and S. Molnar (1991), Intern evaluation in university counseling centers: Process, problems, and recommendations, *The Counseling Psychologist, 19,* 414–430. Copyright © 1991 by the Division of Counseling Psychology. Reprinted by permission.

supervisors. Marek, Sandifer, Beach, Coward, and Protinsky (1994) suggested asking supervisees to scale themselves from 1 to 10 on three different issues: satisfaction with therapy, level of confidence in achieving their goals, and their level of willingness to do so. By having supervisees make such judgments, communication between supervisor and supervisee is enhanced around these key aspects of supervisee development. In addition to challenging supervisees to reflect about their therapy sessions, Marek et al. suggested using scaling to encourage open communication about the supervision process itself.

> *The supervisor can also utilize these questions in connection to other issues brought forth by the supervisee and/or to assess how the supervisee's needs are being met in the present context. For example, "Where are you on the scale right now in terms of the case related issues you brought in to supervision today?" "What happened to allow you to move from a seven (7) to an eight (8)?" "What would it look like if you were at an eight and a half (8½)?" "What would you be doing differently?"* (p. 62)

A scientist–practitioner model would indicate that evaluation measures be more than a communication tool. There are very few measures, however, that have received any psychometric scrutiny. Another problem with many instruments is that they have too narrow a focus. Two assessment measures that are more comprehensive and credible than most are the Oetting/Michaels Anchored Rating for Therapists or OMART (Oetting & Michaels, 1982) and the Minnesota Supervisory Inventory (Robiner et al., 1991, 1994). Both of these measures are lengthier than the typical evaluation instruments used in supervision and might be viewed as unduly tedious because of this. For supervisors who insist that summative evaluations be comprehensive and reflect a training reality larger than their own context, however, these instruments represent a good place to begin.

Most evaluation measures are paper and pencil instruments that reflect a traditional view of assessment. There is, however, some research activity in the development of new evaluation tools (e.g.,

Lambert & Meier, 1992) that take advantage of computer technology and may offer ways to standardize therapist evaluation. Modern advancement notwithstanding, the traditional evaluation tool continues to be almost universal.

Finally, and again congruent with a scientist–practitioner posture, supervisors may seek client input or client outcome data for the sake of formative or summative evaluation of supervisees (Galassi & Brooks, 1992). The Session Evaluation Questionnaire developed by Stiles and Snow (1984), for example, is a brief evaluation tool that can be used after each therapy session to obtain impressions from both supervisees and clients regarding session depth (i.e., felt power and value) and smoothness (i.e., comfort and pleasantness) using pairs of bipolar adjective scales. These quantitative scales can be supplemented with open-ended sentence stems such as "I believe the *most* helpful things that happened in today's counseling session were . . . ," "I believe that the *least* helpful things that happened in today's counseling session were . . . ," and "In my next counseling session I would like. . . ." With the high level of control available in many training programs, various types of data, including that derived from single-case designs, can become part of the evaluation strategy (Galassi & Brooks, 1992; White, Rosenthal, & Fleuridas, 1993).

Increasingly, there are more and better choices for clinical supervisors when selecting evaluation instruments. What each supervisor must determine is whether a particular instrument is consistent with the supervisor's criteria, when and how to introduce the instrument to the supervisee, and how to use the instrument as an evaluation *intervention,* rather than being simply a completed form to be filed and forgotten.

Communicating Formative Feedback

When supervisees reflect on their supervision, what comes to mind most often is the quality and quantity of the feedback they received. Giving feedback is a central activity of clinical supervision and the core of evaluation (Hahn & Molnar,

1991). Curiously, researchers have given little specific attention to feedback within supervision. The study of Friedlander, Siegel, and Brenock (1989) is a notable exception. These authors first offered a working definition of feedback as

> *A statement, with an explicit or implicit evaluation component that refers to attitudes, ideas, emotions, or behaviors of the trainee or to aspects of the trainee–client relationship or the trainee–supervisor relationship. Feedback does not include questions or observations that lack an explicit or implied evaluation of the trainee on the part of the supervisor.* (p. 151)

Using this definition, they trained three raters to high levels of agreement (median interjudge agreement rate of 0.92) about the presence or absence of feedback in a particular supervisor speaking turn. These raters then examined each speaking turn of one supervisor across nine supervision sessions (ranging from 45 to 60 minutes in length) with one supervisee. They identified only 14 speaking turns as containing feedback. Eight speaking turns occurred in the last two sessions; sessions 3, 4, and 6 had no feedback whatsoever.

The Friedlander et al. (1989) study was an intensive case study. Therefore, the results might be idiosyncratic to the particular dyad they studied and may not apply to supervision in general. Yet supervisees who responded in Kadushin's (1992a) national survey also reported receiving far too little direct feedback in supervision, especially feedback that was critical. Therefore, it seems reasonable to ask the question of how frequently constructive feedback—as most supervisors understand it—actually is provided in supervision.

The feedback described by Friedlander et al. is linear, from supervisor to supervisee. Another view of feedback is the interactional (e.g., see Claiborn & Lichtenberg, 1989), which allows us to think of feedback as ongoing and constant between the supervisor and the supervisee. Two premises are basic to understanding the interactional perspective. The first is that you cannot not communicate. This premise has been suggested as an axiom of communication by Watzlawick, Beavin, and Jackson (1967). It means, for example, that even the act of ignoring another person is feedback to that person, communicating a message such as "Leave me alone" or, perhaps, "You are not important enough for me to talk with."

The second premise essential to understanding the interactional perspective is that any communication to another person contains both a message about the relationship between the two parties and a message about some particular content (Watzlawick et al., 1967). For example, within the context of supervision, the content may be about a particular, difficult moment in the supervisee's session with a client; the message about the relationship, however, might be "I enjoy working with you" or "This relationship is very tenuous." If the feedback about the relationship is negative or more pronounced than the content, it will be more difficult for the supervisee to hear the content in the way that the supervisor would like. It is for this reason that the relationship between supervisor and supervisees receives so much attention in the professional literature (see Chapters 3 and 4). Finally, it is imperative to remember that the supervisor is not only delivering both levels of feedback, but receiving both levels and reacting to these. The idea of supervisor feedback, therefore, is deceptively simple when compared to the actual interactive process.

This more sophisticated model of feedback notwithstanding, most supervisors conceptualize feedback as communicating to the supervisee an evaluation of particular behaviors as either on target or off, as either progressing toward competence or diverging in a different direction. The clarity of supervisors' communications is of paramount importance. Each message will either affirm, challenge, discourage, confuse, or anger a supervisee. If the meta-message is different from the stated message, the result will be an unclear communication. The most serious communication problem is when the message is dishonest, either intentionally or unintentionally. This typically happens when the supervisor is involved in denial and does not want to face up to the fact that the trainee is not meeting expectations. As a result,

the supervisor is not prepared to address the critical issues.

The interaction of supervisor discomfort and lack of communication clarity is why evaluation is often considered the supervisor's weak suit (Bernard, 1981). Borders and Leddick (1987) suggested that feedback to trainees focus on specific behavior and delineate alternative behavior. They also addressed the importance of the supervisor's willingness to confront and pointed out that confrontations challenge strengths rather than weaknesses. But, as Munson (1993) asserted, there will be times when the supervisor must criticize the trainee. Borrowing from the work of Weisinger and Lobsenz (1981), Munson outlined 20 suggestions for supervisors to consider when delivering criticism. Among these, Munson urged supervisors to focus only on behaviors that can be changed and to be specific in their criticism; to offer criticism as opinion, not fact; to work to separate personal feelings about the supervisee from the need to criticize; and to steer away from accusatory comments or ultimatums. Similar guidance is offered by Harris (1994).

Hawkins and Shohet (1989) have suggested that supervisors use a particular mnemonic to help remember how to give their supervisees good feedback. That mnemonic is CORBS, which stands for *Clear, Owned, Regular, Balanced,* and *Specific.*

> *Clear   Try to be clear about what the feedback is that you want to give. Being vague and faltering will increase anxiety in the receiver and not be understood.*

> *Owned   The feedback you give is your own perception and not an ultimate truth. It therefore says as much about you as it does about the person who receives it. It helps the receiver if this is stated or implied in the feedback, e.g., "I find you . . . " rather than "You are. . . ."*

> *Regular   If the feedback is given regularly it is more likely to be useful. If this does not happen, there is a danger that grievances are saved until they are delivered in one large package. Try to give the feedback as close to the event as possible and early enough for the person to do something about it, i.e., do not wait until someone is leaving to tell them how they could have done the job better.*

Balance It is good to balance negative and positive feedback and, if you find that the feedback you give to any individual is always either positive or negative, this probably means that your view is distorted in some way. This does not mean that each piece of critical feedback must always be accompanied by something positive, but rather a balance should be created over time.

Specific Generalized feedback is hard to learn from. Phrases like, "You are irritating" can only lead to hurt and anger. "It irritates me when you forget to record the telephone message" gives the receiver some information which he or she can choose to use or ignore. (pp. 83–84)

Poertner (1986) suggested that supervisor feedback be clear enough either to automatically reinforce trainees or give them direction for improvement. Directionality, therefore, is an important concept and one that the supervisor should attend to. It might be a good idea for the supervisor to ask before each supervision conference, "Do I like the direction in which things are going? If not, how do I help the trainee change direction?"

Returning to the issue of clarity, there can be many reasons for unclear or inaccurate communications. The supervisor can be uncomfortable with the power that comes with the role of evaluator; the supervisor may be unprepared for the conference; the supervisor might be intimidated by the trainee, professionally or personally; or the supervisor might have too little experience in giving negative feedback, for example, to do so kindly and clearly. Regardless of the reasons, the consequences for the trainee are the same: incomplete or inaccurate information, leaving the trainee ill-equipped to alter the course of his or her efforts.

Example. Dana has been supervising Nicole for two months. Until now she has attempted to focus on Nicole's strengths while gently suggesting other strategies for Nicole to consider. Nicole has found supervision to be a very positive experience thus far. Unfortunately, in Dana's opinion, Nicole has not picked up on Dana's suggestions and, therefore, has not progressed at all in her counseling. Of particular concern is Nicole's work with one client, Shirley. During the sessions that Dana has observed, Shirley regularly brings up her difficulties with her husband. Shirley is upset with his relationship with his ex-wife; the husband thinks that she is overly jealous. Nicole seems to keep the entire issue at arm's length and usually finds another topic to focus on.

DANA: I wanted to spend some time talking about Shirley's issues with her husband. These seem to keep coming up. What do you think is going on there?

NICOLE: I think Shirley's self-esteem is low and so she is insecure about her husband and his ex-wife. She doesn't like it that he has to deal with her around his kids. His behavior seems certainly reasonable to me.

DANA: I don't think there's any question that Shirley's self-esteem is low. I agree with you. But she keeps bringing up her husband and I don't see you doing much with that in the session. Is there a reason you avoid addressing that issue?

NICOLE: I just didn't see it as the real problem. Besides, Dr. *M* said that we can't deal with a marital issue if only one spouse is in the room.

DANA: OK. So you've been avoiding it because of Dr. *M*'s advice. Is there any way you can view the problem that would allow you to focus on Shirley and not the interaction between her and her husband?

NICOLE: And still deal with her jealousy about her husband?

DANA: Right.

NICOLE: I could ask her how she feels about her husband, but I already know that.

DANA: Yes, I think you do. What about her thought processes?

NICOLE: I'm not sure what you mean.

DANA: Well, that's important, of course. But I've noticed that you pretty much focus on the client's feelings in all of your counseling. I think you're doing well there, but I don't think it's a complete enough approach. You need to figure out some way to address the client's thoughts if you're going to help Shirley any more than you have. And remember. Addressing her thoughts will lead you to more of her internal life, including more of her feelings.

NICOLE: So, you don't think I'm helping Shirley?

DANA: I think you've gone about as far as you can go with the approach you've taken. But the issue is bigger than your work with Shirley. In order for you to become a better counselor, I think you need to start looking at how you address cognitive issues. I'd like to focus on that for a while.

NICOLE: OK.

From the perspective of formative evaluation, we might ask how successful was this segment between Dana and Nicole? Was Dana's intent clear? Did she hear all of Nicole's messages? Did she react adequately to Nicole's feedback? What was the content of Dana's communication? The message about the relationship? What was the content of Nicole's communication? The message about the relationship? In the past, Nicole has not picked up on Dana's suggestions. Has Dana done anything to ensure that Nicole has heard her this time? Finally, Talen and Schindler's (1993) study found that an attitude of trust and positive regard from the supervisor, validating supervisees' strengths, and accepting them at their present skill level were considered to be the most important supervision strategies from the perspective of supervisees. With this in mind, has this session compromised the supervision relationship between Dana and Nicole? How might the session have been conducted differently?

Encouraging Self-assessment

Assisting supervisees to evaluate their own work has been identified as an important aspect of supervision (Bernstein & Lecomte, 1979; Borders et al., 1991; Munson, 1983; Perlesz et al., 1990). It is our opinion that self-assessment is overused by supervisors and underused by therapists; therefore, we will focus on the latter in this section. Blodgett, Schmidt, and Scudder (1987) noted that little is being done to help clinicians and supervisors learn to self-evaluate. Assuming that their criticism is at least partially justified, the error in training is emphasized by the work of Dowling (1984), who found evidence that graduate student trainees were both accurate self-evaluators and good peer evaluators, a finding consistent with Hillerbrand's (1989) observations. Therefore, it would seem wise, if not an ethical imperative, for clinical supervisors to train their supervisees to self-evaluate.

From the vantage point of the clinical supervisor, the goal is to incorporate self-assessment into the larger framework of evaluation. Kadushin (1985) argued that supervisory evaluation, in and of itself, makes learning conspicuous to the trainee and helps to set a pattern of self-evaluation. Ekstein and Wallerstein (1972) were more cautious, reminding the supervisor that asking trainees to self-evaluate will stimulate all their past experiences of being selected, rejected, praised, and so on. We challenge this caution in that self-evaluation, we believe, takes some of the parental-like authority away from the supervisor, rather than adding to it. If negative feelings are going to be experienced as a result of evaluation, these will be there regardless of whether the trainee is given an opportunity to contribute to the assessment.

Yogev (1982) raised another important interpersonal issue of the supervisor's reaction to the trainee's self-assessment. She warned the supervisor not to put trainees in a no-win situation by asking for their evaluation and then holding it against them. For example, if a trainee admits feeling overwhelmed and intimidated by the training experience, the supervisor should not later criticize the trainee for being weak and dependent. Therefore, if supervisors ask for candid disclosure as part of a self-assessment, they must be ready to handle respectfully what transpires.

There are several highly productive ways that the trainee can be involved in self-assessment while in the context of supervision. The most obvious is for the supervisor to communicate an expectation that the trainee will do some sort of self-assessment prior to each supervision session. It has been our experience that unless the supervisor follows through on this expectation most trainees will falter in their intentions to self-assess.

A useful self-evaluating activity is to ask the trainee to periodically review a segment of a therapy session in greater depth for response patterns (Collins & Bogo, 1986). If the trainee can identify nonproductive patterns, this exercise can be instrumental in breaking nontherapeutic habits.

Involving the supervisee in self-assessment throughout supervision prepares the supervisee to be involved in the summative evaluation process. It is a sign of distinct success of supervision when supervisees can end the supervision contract with a relatively accurate assessment of their strengths and weakness and articulate their goals for further professional development.

The rationale for emphasizing self-assessment, however, is that it ultimately has utility beyond the formal training context. In other words, part of the responsibility of clinical supervisors is to assist supervisees in establishing a habit of self-scrutiny that will follow them into their professional careers. Although supervision is always warranted in the early years of practice, it is not always forthcoming—at least not always at an optimal level. Skill in self-assessment, therefore, can be crucial for practice (e.g., see Elks & Kirkhart, 1993).

Closely related to self-assessment is peer evaluation; it also is similar in that it is underused with trainees. When peers are asked to work together for each other's benefit, the skill-level differences within the group are diminished and a group cohesiveness is established. We have found that peers can be invaluable reviewers for each other, and it is consistently both humbling and inspiring when peers make observations that are absolutely correct and have been overlooked by the supervisor. But it is important to structure peer feedback. Often feedback is given verbally in group supervision, but we have found that the type of feedback that comes spontaneously, although valuable, is generally inferior to the type of feedback that is given in writing when a peer is asked to review an audio or videotape between supervision sessions. When, in addition, the reviewer is evaluated by the supervi-

sor for the critique, thoughtful and highly useful reviews are most often the result. It has been our experience that the more supervisors share the responsibility for trainee development with the trainee group, the better the students perform and the more positive the overall experience is.

Communicating Summative Evaluations

Although the word summative might imply a single final evaluation, summative evaluations usually occur at least twice during a typical supervisory relationship. In academic settings, there is usually a mid-semester and a final summative evaluation. For off-campus internships and work settings, the summative evaluations are given at the halfway mark and at the end or as annual reviews, respectively. If all has gone well within supervision, a final summative review should contain no surprises for the supervisee. In other words, the summative review should be the culmination of evaluation, not the beginning of it. The initial summative review is perhaps the more important because it is at this point that the supervisor will learn if the supervisee has understood the implications of formative assessments. If so, the summative evaluation will provide an opportunity to take stock and to plan a productive sequel to the supervision that has transpired to this point—a second supervision contract, so to speak. If formative assessment has been resisted by the supervisee, the first summative evaluation must be specific regarding the progress that is required for the supervisee to remain in good standing and must be conducted early enough for the supervisee to have a reasonable opportunity to achieve success. In all cases, summative evaluations should be conducted face to face and should also be put in writing (Belar et al., 1993).

Even when a correct process has been established for summative evaluations, their ultimate success depends on the communication skill of the supervisor. Unfortunately, supervisor training often gives short shrift to the process of conducting summative evaluation sessions. What follows are two segments taken from actual summative evaluation conferences conducted by supervisors-in-training with counselors-in-training. Both supervisor and counselor are female in each case. In the first segment, the pair begins by reviewing the Evaluation of Counselor Behaviors form (see Appendix C) that the supervisor completed prior to the session. The person referred to as Dr. P. is the counselor's faculty instructor.

S: Uh, I would put this more here, I think, and more here. Now you have to do another one of these? *(Referring to evaluation form on self)*

C: Are you asking me or telling me?

S: I'm asking.

C: I don't know.

S: Well the, you must not have to if you don't know. *(laughs)*

C: I've not. . . .

S: Have you not heard the news? *(laughs)*

C: I haven't seen it in my mailbox or anything. Of course, that doesn't mean that when I make contact with Dr. P., that he won't say that it has to be done.

S: And I think, you know, again, I did this here. I may go back and circle . . . if you see anything that you don't agree with, just go ahead and question it. I think you know how I look at it. I see you just having started to work.

C: Oh, I. . . .

S: You know, you may not like that. I just think since that one big leap, when you started to consciously try to do things differently. . . .

C: I can't even visualize 10 years down the line having you say that everything is excellent. I don't know. To me, you're asking for close to perfection.

S: It would be hard for me to get there *(laughs).* I wouldn't want to be evaluated.

C: So much that comes to me comes through experience.

S: Yeah. I suppose, you know, maybe it's the teacher part of me . . . whenever I see the word "always," I just can't . . . we're in trouble.

C: Yeah.

S: Even for me *(laughs).*

C: I understand. You know, as I look at this, it looks like a positive evaluation because of what you've said so far.

S: Um, well, you have a lot of 2's and 1's, but "good" to me is good. Letter grade wise, I don't know. I can't tell you. Part of me says, because of what has gone on the whole semester, you know, and part of me says, "Okay. What are you doing now?" So, you know, I don't assign grades. It won't be an A. I'm not too sure. I'd say probably a C+ to B– in that area.

C: But there are no pluses or minuses in the grading schedule.

S: That's right.

C: To me, a C is a failure and I'm assuming that you are not. . . .

S: I don't think I look at it as a failure. I think that maybe, you know, when you do course work and things like that, maybe you could look at it that way. But I don't look at it as a failure because failure is an F.

C: Um hum.

S: If I were to have to assess a grade by skill level, it probably would be close to a C/D. But in looking from the beginning, you know, you've come a long way. But that isn't for me to assess. That's for Dr. P. to assess and I don't know how he will do it. I definitely think that there has been a lot of improvement.

C: And to me, it seems like it's been such a short time.

S: Yes, a very short time.

It is not difficult to see that there are several communication problems in this example. Actually, four things have contributed to the ambiguity presented here: (1) the supervisor's personal style of communication is clouded. She does not finish many of her statements. She is not crisp. She would do well to practice the delivery of her feedback for clarity. (2) The process is ambiguous. Either Dr. P. has not been clear regarding procedures or neither supervisor nor counselor has attended to these details. The result is that the supervisor does not seem to know her role in the evaluation process. Another possibility is that, because of her discomfort, she is playing down her role and referring the counselor to Dr. P. for the difficult task of final evaluation. From the conversation as it stands, we cannot know which of these is the case. (3) Criteria for evaluation also seem to be ambiguous to the supervisor. She vacillates from references to skill level and references to progress. It is obvious that she is not clear about how Dr. P. will weigh each of these two factors. (4) The supervisor seems to be uncomfortable with the responsibility of evaluation, especially in this case where the practicum seems to be ending on a down note. We do not know if the supervisor has not prepared adequately for this conference or whether any amount of preparation would have countered her personal discomfort. The result is a series of mixed messages:

1. "You're not a very good counselor." / " 'C' isn't a bad grade."
2. "You've come a long way." / "You still aren't very good."
3. "I'm trying to be fair." / "I wouldn't want to be in your shoes."
4. "I'm recommending between a C+ and a B." / "I don't assign grades."

In our second summative session, the supervisor and counselor have had a better working relationship and the results are more positive.

S: I came up with some agenda items, things I thought we needed to touch base on. You can add to this agenda if you'd like. The concern that you expressed previously about the deadlines, wrapping up, dealing with your clients, and then talking about termination–continuation issues. Kind of finishing up, so that it concludes not only your client situations, but practicum. Again, the other issue I have down is evaluation. I am not sure how he (Dr. P.). . . . Did he mention that in class today? How he's going to handle that? Do you have a conference with him?

C: There will be the conference next Monday with the three of us and then it seems to me that the other was kind of nebulous as to if we had another conference with him about you. Is that what you mean?

S: No, no. I meant about you. See, I was not aware that we were meeting on Monday *(laughs)*.

C: Yes, yes.

S: O.K. *(laughs)*. What time did he say?

C: We had to choose a time and I chose 2:00 next Monday afternoon.

S: Oh, O.K. I wondered.

C: He sent around a piece of paper so that we could sign up for Monday or Tuesday.

S: Well, that's nice to be aware of. Surprise!

C: Yeah.

S: *(Laughs)*

C: So it will be the three of us for evaluation.

S: So I thought, depending upon if you had any concern about that, that maybe we can discuss that ahead of time. I don't know if we need to here today or not or whatever, but that was something that I had as a possibility at least.

C: There are other things that are more urgent.

S: Yes *(laughs)*.

C: That's next week.

C: Uh huh.

(Supervisor and counselor then talk about a particularly difficult case. The following occurs later in the same session.)

C: You've been very supportive. I really appreciate your feedback that you give me. A lot of good supportive feedback. It's not all the positive. There's been good constructive criticism you give too. I appreciate that.

S: You perceive that there has been enough of a balance?

C: Um, you've been heavier on the positive, but maybe it's just because I've done such a good job *(laughs)*.

S: *(Laughs)* I'm laughing because you're laughing.

C: You very nicely have couched the constructive criticism, preceding it with a lot of positive. "I like the way you did this, and then when you said this, it was very good, and then this was good and now you, probably if you had said this, perhaps you would have. . . ." You preceded criticism with about two or three positive things, which helps, helps the ego. I've appreciated that a lot.

S: Good.

C: Um, you know, I just, I think that we have learned a lot just being in the sessions, all the counselors, that we have learned from mistakes, and that there are times when we just haven't seen our mistakes. I think it's good to have them pointed out and I think you have done it very nicely. I appreciate that.

S: Kind of while we are on the subject, is there something that you can pinpoint at all that you feel that you've learned the most from practicum? Not necessarily from your clients, just anything in general. Is there something that sticks out in your mind that you have learned a lot from?

C: Um, well, with my two clients who were the most difficult, I feel that with both of them, I needed to be more forceful, and so, that's a lesson learned, that I'm not doing people a favor by letting them ramble on and on. That oftentimes I would do people a favor by stopping them and saying, "Now let's back up a little. Let's focus a little bit more." I haven't been quite assertive enough and I think I've learned that about myself *(counselor continues).*

S: I've seen you do continually more intervening and trying different things, being aware of this and trying to do things about it. Do you feel like, as you go away from here, you'll be able to take away something so that you can do that when you get into situations like this again?

C: Yeah, I've really learned that, and I do feel that I am doing it more.

S: Oh, yes, I think so.

The most dramatic difference between this pair and the previous pair is the quality of the relationship. Apparently, this has been a positive experience for both supervisor and counselor. There may or may not be some lack of comfort for the supervisor with evaluation in that what might have been a summative conference became a preconference by their mutual choice. But the important characteristic of their interaction, as it appears here, is that they seem to be current with each other. Evidently, there has been enough formative communication along the way that each person appears to know where she stands. Notice, however, that the same administrative problem that appeared in the first ex-

ample appears here, too. Again, we see that communication between the instructor and the supervisor has not occurred and this leaves the supervisor at a disadvantage in the conference. Because both of these sessions transpired in the same training program, we could come to the conclusion that the doctoral supervisors need more support from the faculty in the form of clearer guidelines about their role in the evaluation process and clearer communication down the administrative hierarchy.

Thus far we have discussed summative evaluations as they relate to the instructional needs of the supervisee. The process of arriving at the summative evaluation can also be a valuable learning experience for the supervisor. Too often this is an activity done alone. There is great value, however, in the use of additional evaluators to arrive at summative assessments. The following evaluation format was used in a counseling center where doctoral students served as the supervisors for master's level counselors: One doctoral student was assigned to three master's level students. Most semesters, there were 12 counselors and 4 supervisors. In addition to working closely with the supervisees, each doctoral student was required to observe (usually through a two-way mirror) three other counselors at least twice during the semester. The doctoral students did not have to share their observations with the counselors; their charge was simply to have some knowledge of the counselor's ability. Additionally, weekly supervision-of-supervision conferences were held, which included listening to taped supervision sessions between the doctoral supervisors and their three supervisees. When it was time to evaluate the counselors, the faculty instructors for both groups (supervisors and counselors), the center coordinator (who read all counselors' intake and termination reports), and the group of doctoral supervisors met together. Therefore, the work of each counselor was known by at least four people, and all were encouraged to voice their opinion.

These evaluation meetings provided both a learning experience for supervisors and the opportunity to arrive at consensus evaluations of the counselors. One of the most obvious dynamics in these meetings was the investment each supervisor had in the three supervisees. There were times when the supervisor would get noticeably defensive if the supervisor's counselors were seen as weaker than some others. Such reactions were always processed, and awareness was increased that the supervisory relationship can be a powerful one and can cloud a supervisor's ability to be objective.

A secondary issue was whether the supervisor felt responsible for the counselor's level of performance. Sometimes it was thought that the supervisor might have been partially responsible, but most times this was not the case. The most important lesson, however, was appreciating that different views could be held about the same supervisee, even when objective criteria were in place.

ADDITIONAL EVALUATION ISSUES

At the beginning of this chapter, we mentioned that evaluation is a difficult task because of the personal nature of the skills being evaluated. Having relatively clear criteria, good evaluation instruments, and a credible process goes far to diminish the difficulty of evaluation. But the therapeutic process is not sterile and neither is the evaluation process. What is called for when supervisors evaluate is a judgment based on as much objective data as possible. But the judgment will still include a subjective element.

The Subjective Element

Clinical supervisors all work hard to be fair and reasonable in their evaluations. Without some awareness of the pitfalls to objective evaluation, however, supervisors are at a disadvantage for attaining that goal. But supervisors must also be continually aware that the subjective element cannot and should not be totally eliminated. There is something intrinsically intuitive about psychotherapy, and this is equally true for clinical supervision. Supervisors are in a position to supervise because they have had more fine tuning of their intuitions. Evaluation is a delicate blend of subjective judgment and objective criteria. But sometimes our *personal subjectivity* contami-

nates our *professional subjectivity,* and evaluation becomes less intuitive and more biased. No clinical supervisor is above this dilemma. Being aware of the possibility, however, may help the supervisor draft a checklist of personal vulnerabilities and potential blind spots to review when evaluating.

Each clinical supervisor will have a separate list of subjective obstacles to navigate when facing the task of evaluation. Our list is only a partial delineation of some of the more common problems, ones that we have experienced or that have received attention in the professional literature.

Similarity. There is an assumption that has spawned a good deal of empirical investigation that attraction (which includes the concept of similarity) influences the therapeutic process and, likewise, the supervision process (Turban & Jones, 1988). Kaplan (1983), however, reported that findings were mixed when personality characteristics and value systems of supervisors and supervisees were the focus of research efforts. Royal and Golden (1981), on the other hand, found that attitude similarity between supervisor and employee had a significant influence on the evaluation of the employee's intelligence, personal adjustment, competence, quality of work, quantity of work, and motivation, among other things.

Similarity with one's supervisor is probably more of an advantage than a disadvantage. But there are times when this is not so. If the supervisor is suffering from a poor self-image, this may spill over to the trainee. From another vantage point, dissimilarity is an advantage for the trainee if the lack of similarity has a power valence. For example, if the supervisor is young and relatively inexperienced and the trainee is older and has more life experience, such dissimilarity might translate to a better evaluation than if the supervisor were the same age as the trainee. There is evidence also that females rate males higher in competence; therefore, a female supervisor might rate a male trainee higher than a male supervisor would (Goodyear, 1990). (Goodyear cited several of those studies, but in his own study found no evidence of gender bias in trainee evaluations.)

There is a situation-specific form of similarity that the supervisor should consider. When life has dealt two people the same hand, or at least some of the same cards, this tends to create a bond between them. Both supervisor and trainee might have recently been through a divorce, might have children of the same age, or might each have an alcoholic sibling. Depending on each person's comfort level about these life situations, such similarity can be an advantage or a disadvantage. Regardless, they must be considered.

Ultimately, the issue seems to be one of liking rather than similarity only. Turban, Jones, and Rozelle (1990) found that liked supervisees received more psychological support during supervision than disliked supervisees, supervisors extended more effort in working with liked supervisees, and supervisors evaluated liked supervisees more favorably than disliked supervisees. It is difficult to determine whether liking leads to inflated performance evaluation or if better performing supervisees are more liked; perhaps both are true. The fact that liking affects the interactions between supervisor and supervisee long before summative evaluation, however, makes this a variable to which supervisors should be alerted.

Familiarity. "He's difficult to get to know, but he wears well." How many of us have had negative first impressions of people who we now hold in high esteem? Not all of a person's qualities are apparent in the short run, and sometimes it takes a significant amount of time (in graduate training terms) to arrive at what later would look like a balanced view of the trainee's strengths and weaknesses. In conjunction with this, when affection for someone has grown over time, it can become more and more difficult to evaluate objectively. In fact, one can come to like Charlie so much that one might have to ask "How would I react if Marco did that instead of Charlie?" to have any hope of arriving at a fair judgment.

There is some empirical evidence to support the case that familiarity affects evaluation. Fried,

Tiegs, and Bellamy (1992) established that supervisors are reluctant to evaluate at all unless a supervisee has been under supervision for a certain amount of time (which is subjectively determined). Blodgett, Schmidt, and Scudder (1987) found that supervisors rated the same trainees differently depending on how long they knew the trainees. If a supervisor had had the trainee in a class prior to the supervision experience, the supervisor was more likely to evaluate the trainee more positively. Blodgett et al. noted that the trainees who had received their undergraduate and graduate training at the same institution had a distinct advantage in this particular study. The authors warned that it would be unwise, however, to assume that familiarity always works to the trainee's advantage. Our experience would support this admonition. Just as some trainees wear well, others do not. Entry behavior can be deceiving or at least highly inconclusive.

A corollary to the issue of familiarity is the perseverance of first impressions (Sternitzke, Dixon, & Ponterotto, 1988). Although we have already stated that our first impressions are not always our last, it is important to mention that first impressions can be long-lasting. If supervisors attribute dispositional characteristics to their trainees early in their relationship, it may require an inordinate amount of evidence for the trainee to reverse the supervisor's opinion. In this case, the trainee may be familiar to the supervisor, but the trainee might be far from known.

Priorities. Each supervisor has an individual set of priorities when judging the skill of a trainee. Most often, supervisors are not cognizant that their priorities are partially subjective and that an equally qualified supervisor might have a somewhat different list of priorities. All perception is selective, and we process more quickly what is familiar to us (Atwood, 1986) or what we value more.

We have some evidence (Bernard, 1982) that, when viewing the same therapy session, supervisors rate the trainee differently on the same criteria, depending on the value attributed to each criterion by the different supervisors. During a pilot investigation, supervisors were first analyzed using the discrimination model (Bernard, 1979) to discern if they had a primary focus; that is, did they tend to approach supervision from an intervention, conceptual, or personal skill perspective regardless of the therapy session they observed? (See Appendix D, Session 7.) In a majority of cases, a primary focus was identified. During the second stage of this investigation, the supervisors were asked to view two videotapes and to evaluate each trainee using a Likert scale for 15 items equally divided among the three focus areas. Again, a sizable number (although not statistically significant) of supervisors rated each trainee lower on their primary focus than on the other two categories. For example, when observing trainee A, supervisor A with an intervention focus rated trainee A lower on intervention skills than on conceptual skills and personalization skills, while supervisor B with a conceptual focus rated trainee A lower on conceptual skills than on intervention skills and personalization skills. This formula was substantiated for all three focus possibilities. In other words, the trainee was rated relative to the supervisor's bias and independently of a more objective set of criteria. Yet all supervisors thought they were being objective and, in several cases, were not aware of having a focus bias or priority. These results are supported by attribution theory as explained by Sternitzke et al. (1988). Building on the work of Ross (1977), they identified egocentric bias as a common problem for supervisors when observing trainee behavior and explained the nature of the bias as follows:

> One's estimate of deviance and normalcy is egocentrically biased in accord with one's own behavioral choices, because observers tend to think about what they would have done in a similar situation and then compare their hypothesized behavior with the actor's actual behavior. If the observers believe they would have acted differently, then there is an increased tendency for them to view the actor's [behavior] as deviant. If the observers believe they would have acted in a similar fashion, then their tendencies are to view the actor's behavior as normal. (p. 9)

Evidence of an egocentric bias is more reason to share the responsibility of evaluation whenever possible, rather than keep it as a private activity.

Rating Idiosyncracies.   Robiner et al. (1993) addressed idiosyncratic tendencies for individual supervisors to demonstrate a leniency bias, a strictness bias, or a central-tendency bias. A leniency bias, that is, the tendency to evaluate more favorably than objective data might warrant, may result from any of four sources: (1) measurement issues, such as a lack of clear criteria; (2) legal and administrative issues, such as a concern about a grievance procedure; (3) interpersonal issues, such as experiencing the anguish about damaging a supervisee's career; or (4) supervisor issues, such as having limited supervision experience. In all, Robiner et al. (1993) list 23 potential bases for a lenient evaluation (see Table 8.2)

Strictness bias is the tendency to rate supervisees more severely than warranted. This kind of bias would seem to be the most difficult for the supervisee. Ward, Friedlander, Schoen, and Klein (1985) suggested that such ratings can lead to excessive defensiveness on the part of the supervisee or attempts to manipulate the supervisor to gain more positive ratings. Robiner et al. (1993) proposed that critical ratings could lead to assumptions about training programs (e.g., weaker applicants being admitted), but are more likely to suggest problems within the supervisor (e.g., unrealistic standards or displaced personal frustration).

The central-tendency bias is the tendency to rate supervisees uniformly average. When this is the supervisor's bias, supervisees are denied feedback that would allow them to address deficits seriously or to appreciate that their performance was well above average. According to Robiner et al., "Central-tendency bias potentially is more misinformative than leniency bias or strictness bias, insofar as training directors cannot correct [supervisors'] neutral rating for positive slant or negative slant" (p. 8).

Although there are several different types of subjective variables that can influence evaluation, there may be a single action that can serve to counter their

TABLE 8.2   Factors Contributing to Leniency–Inflation in Faculty Evaluations of Interns

Definition and Measurement Issues

1. Lack of clear criteria and objective measures of competence/incompetence in psychology.
2. Lack of clear criteria and objective measures of impairment/distress in psychology.
3. Supervisor awareness of subjectivity inherent in evaluation.
4. Apprehension about defending evaluations due to lack of clear criteria and objective measures.

Legal and Administrative Issues

5. Concern that negative evaluations may result in administrative inquiry, audit, grievance, or litigation.
6. Lack of awareness of internship or institutional policies and procedures involved in negative evaluations.
7. Social and political dynamics: feared or perceived lack of support from institutions, directors of training, and colleagues for providing negative evaluations.
8. Concern that failing to "pass" an intern may result in loss of future training funds or training slots or the need to find additional funds to extend the intern's training.
9. Concern that failing to "pass" an intern may result in adverse publicity that could affect institutional reputation and the number of internship applicants.

Interpersonal Issues

10. Fear of diminishing rapport or provoking hostility from supervisees.
11. Fear of eliciting backlash from current or future trainees.
12. Anguish about damaging a supervisee's career or complicating or terminating their graduate training.

Supervisor Issues

13. Supervisors' wish to avoid scrutiny of their own behavior, competence, ethics, expectations, or judgment of their clinical and supervisory practices.
14. Limited supervisory experience with impaired or incompetent trainees.
15. Inability to impart negative evaluations (e.g., deficit in assertive communication skills).
16. Indifference to personal responsibility for upholding the standards of the profession.
17. Discomfort with "gatekeeper" role.
18. Identification with supervisee's problems.
19. Inadequate attention to supervisee's performance or problems.
20. Supervisors' presumption of supervisee competence (e.g., overreliance on selection procedures).
21. Minimization of incompetence or impairment in supervisees.
22. Inappropriate optimism that problems will resolve without intervention.
23. Preference to avoid the substantial energy and time commitment necessary to address or remediate deficient trainees.

effect: consultation. Supervision will be less vulnerable to subjective confounding when others are brought into the process. Supervisors are more likely to involve other opinions when there is a supervision crisis, especially if it has ethical or legal implications. The wise supervisor, though, involves others in the evaluation process when things are seemingly at their smoothest. Not only is this good practice, but it also affords the supervisor ongoing professional development that will assist the supervisor in becoming a better evaluator.

Consequences of Evaluation

Like most activities of any importance, the process of evaluation contains some risks. There have been false positives and false negatives in the evaluation experience of most clinical supervisors. Possibly because supervisors all know that they have evaluated incorrectly in the past, the consequences of their evaluations can loom before them like an unforgiving superego. Supervisors know that a positive evaluation may mean that a trainee will be competitive in the job market or an employee will be promoted, while a negative evaluation may result in a student's being dropped from a training program or an employee's being the first to go. It is because of supervisors' awareness of the consequences of evaluation that they find themselves doing some extra soul searching over the evaluations of the strongest and weakest supervisees.

But even for the average evaluation, there are consequences. Levy (1983) referred to the "costs" of evaluation as the inordinate time it requires of the supervisor, the anxiety it causes the trainee, and the stress it puts on the supervisory relationship. Levy noted that if the individual supervisee were all that was at stake the costs might be inordinately high. But when the larger picture is considered, including the integrity of the program or organization and the welfare of future clients, then the costs are in line with the benefits.

In a highly pragmatic discussion, Kadushin (1985) mentioned the administrative consequences for the supervisor when a negative evaluation is necessary. If in a work environment an employee is let go because of an evaluation, the supervisor will often be the person to feel the brunt of the extra workload until a replacement can be found. Even in a training program, a negative evaluation will typically mean more extensive documentation, the possibility of an appeal process, or, at the very least, a lengthy interview with the trainee involved. It is understandable, although not acceptable, that some supervisors shy away from negative evaluations in their work in order to avoid these unattractive consequences. Such shortsightedness, however, does not acknowledge the much more significant consequences when evaluations are not done properly.

Chronic Issues with Evaluation

We hope that this chapter has aided the supervisor in defining parameters for evaluation and in clarifying some of the issues involved in the task of evaluation. Some problems, however, are chronic and cannot be eliminated through adherence to a model, use of an evaluation tool, or communicating in a certain way. As we conclude this chapter, we pose some of the issues that we believe still enter the awareness of the conscientious clinical supervisor and are only partially resolved by some of the guidelines we have proposed to this point.

1. What should be the relationship of admissions, retention, hiring, and so on, to evaluation? Should the same people be involved in administrative decisions and clinical supervision? To what extent should evaluation be used to correct admissions or hiring errors? What are the consequences when evaluation is used in this way? (Cohen, 1987, argued that "supervisors who disengage themselves from the agency's evaluation process are violating their commitment to the supervisee's welfare," p. 195. Cohen included the role of "advocate" as an appropriate responsibility of the clinical supervisor, especially when a talented clinician is in some political trouble with the agency.)

2. How do we work around theoretical differences between supervisor and trainee (Milne, 1989)? Should the trainee be asked to adopt the supervisor's theoretical bias for the duration of supervision? Can a supervisor of a different theoretical orientation evaluate a trainee adequately?

3. Should peer evaluation ever be used for administrative purposes? If it is, what are the practical and ethical consequences of such a practice?

4. How do we determine how much of a trainee's development is the result of supervision? How does this affect evaluation?

5. Have supervisors trained their supervisees in all the skills that they later evaluate? Have they articulated adequately (to themselves) their overall goals for their trainees? Have they communicated these goals to their trainees?

6. Are supervisee evaluations based primarily on the competence of the supervisee or do they reflect more accurately the working relationship between the supervisor and the supervisee (Borders & Fong, 1991)? Lazar and Mosek (1993) found that the latter was more predictive of evaluation scores than the former. Without outside consultation, how can supervisors be confident that they have separated the two?

7. To what extent are training programs supervising and evaluating in a manner that fits external reality, including client needs and certification–licensure requirements? In other words, does training reflect the employment demands trainees will eventually face? Also, are supervisors sensitive to the fact that their trainees may or may not be eligible for a variety of professional certifications or licenses, and are they training and evaluating appropriately?

This is only a partial list of the issues related to evaluation that make the process more complicated. They must, however, be addressed, at least as limitations to the evaluation process, if clinical supervisors are to be cognizant and to approach fairness in their evaluations.

CONCLUSION

Evaluation poses the most extreme paradox for the clinical supervisor. It is at the same time the most disconcerting responsibility, the most challenging, and the most important. There are, however, conceptual and structural aids to help supervisors in this process that can increase confidence and competence and contribute to a productive evaluation process experience for the supervisee.

CHAPTER 9

Ethical and Legal Considerations

It is perhaps a sign of the times that ethics is an increasingly visible topic in the literature of the mental health professions. The passage of the first code of ethics specific to clinical supervision in the United States (Supervision Interest Network, 1993) has advanced an awareness of the responsibilities and expectations of the supervisory role distinct from other professional roles. Awareness of this responsibility, however, has not necessarily meant consensus about each tenet. The mental health disciplines continue to search for answers to troubling ethical dilemmas and to identify the appropriate posture supervisors must take in a variety of situations. In this chapter, we will present the areas most critical and relevant to the ethical practice of supervision.

In addition to their increased attention to ethics, the mental health professions have also become highly reactive to legal matters. This plight is not unique to mental health. Litigiousness has become a characteristic of United States society, one that all professions must address. Furthermore, counseling and psychotherapy are sought by a wider range of consumers than in generations past, thus making it a more public enterprise. With increased exposure has come increased accountability. If the practice of therapy was ever placid, it is no longer. One result is that, although suits against mental health professionals are still relatively rare, the fear of litigation has operationalized much of practice.

Even if ethics and legal matters are often related, each has a distinct purpose. Ethical codes are conceptually broad in nature, few in number, and open to interpretation by the practitioner (in most cases). Although they are sometimes perceived as strictures to be used to avoid professional liability, they are devised for a loftier purpose, that is, a call to ethical excellence. Ethical standards are a statement from a particular profession to the general public regarding what they stand for.

The law, on the other hand, is specific in nature and is introduced when a particular act (or series of acts) has been perceived to have endangered or harmed those whom the profession serves. Furthermore, the law is not concerned with the highest standards of professional practice when judging someone, but only in minimally acceptable behavior. As Woody (1984) stated, "the practitioner need not be superior but must possess and exercise the knowledge and skill of a member of the profession in good standing" (p. 393).

The reader might assume, therefore, that, because ethical codes are more stringent, to avoid litigation in one's supervision practice is simply a matter of behaving ethically. Unfortunately, it's not that simple. A moral act can at times subject one to retaliatory litigation. The opposite tendency seems to be the more prevalent, however, of an overly exclusive focus on legal tenets to the detriment of ethical deliberations. As Pope and Vasquez (1991) admonished, this tendency "can discourage ethical awareness and sensitivity. It is crucial to realize that ethical behavior is more than simply avoiding violation of legal standards and that one's ethical and legal duties may, in certain instances, be in conflict" (p. 48). At the same time, Meyer, Landis, and Hays (1988) advised that ethical standards can become legally binding for two reasons: (1) they may be used by the courts to determine professional duty, and (2) they are indirectly influential because they guide the thinking of others in the field who may be asked to testify.

It seems then that ethical standards and legal matters have a symbiotic rather than a perfectly symmetrical relationship. In this chapter, we first will discuss legal issues and then ethical issues.

MAJOR LEGAL ISSUES FOR CLINICAL SUPERVISORS

Malpractice

Malpractice is defined as "harm to another individual due to negligence consisting of the breach of a professional duty or standard of care. If, for example, a mental health professional fails to follow acceptable standards of practice and harm to clients results, the professional is liable for the harm caused" (Disney & Stephens, 1994, p. 7). Therapists' (and supervisors') vulnerability is directly linked to their assumption of professional roles. When they take the role of therapist or supervisor, they are expected to know and follow the law, as well as the profession's ethical standards. Some professionals are aghast at the legal profession's intrusion into the human services professions (Woody, 1984). And yet malpractice suits have resulted from faulty self-regulation systems within these professions (Bierig, 1983). Recent research seems to support therapists' great difficulty in judging each other's competence (Haas, Malouf, & Mayerson, 1986) and their reluctance to report known ethical violations of peers (J. L. Bernard & Jara, 1986) or peers who are impaired (Wood et al., 1985).

There are sociological factors that contribute as well to the increase of lawsuits against helping professionals. Cohen's (1979) claim seems even more relevant today that the three primary factors for the increase are (1) a general decline in the respect afforded helping professionals by clients and society at large, (2) increased awareness of consumer rights in general, and (3) highly publicized malpractice suits where settlements were enormous, leading to the conclusion that a lawsuit may be a means to obtain easy money. As the reader will note, all these factors increase the likelihood of potential lawsuits (however spurious) against the practitioner (however ethical).

There are four elements that must be proved in order for a plaintiff to succeed in a malpractice claim (Corey, Corey, & Callanan, 1993): (1) a professional relationship with the therapist (or supervisor) must have been established; (2) the therapist's (or supervisor's) conduct must have been improper or negligent and have fallen below the acceptable standard of care; (3) the client (or supervisee) must have suffered harm or injury, which must be demonstrated; and (4) a causal relationship must be established between the injury and the negligence or improper conduct. We are not aware of any suits brought against supervisors by trainees for inadequate supervision. It is more likely that supervisors would be involved in legal action as a codefendant in a malpractice suit (Snider, 1985) based on the alleged inadequate performance of the supervisee.

Although "failure to warn" accounts for a very small number of legal claims (Meyer, Landis, & Hays, 1988), the Tarasoff case has made this issue highly visible. The Tarasoff case also involved a clinical supervisor and thus introduces the concept of vicarious liability or *respondeat superior* (literally, "let the master answer"). Following the discussion regarding the duty to warn, therefore, will be a review of the salient direct and vicarious liability issues.

The Duty to Warn

The duty to warn is a prime example of a legal precedent becoming a direct influence on ethical codes. The duty to warn stems from the famous Tarasoff case (*Tarasoff* v. *Regents of the University of California,* 1976). In this landmark case, a university therapist believed that his client (Poddar) was dangerous and might do harm to a woman who had rejected Poddar's romantic advances (Tatiana Tarasoff). Because Poddar refused voluntary hospitalization, the therapist notified police to have him taken to a state hospital for involuntary hospitalization. The police spoke to Poddar and decided that he was not dangerous. *On the advice of his supervisor, who feared a lawsuit for breach of confidence* (Meyer et al., 1988), the therapist did not pursue the matter further. Poddar did not return to therapy. Two months later Poddar killed Tarasoff. Although most mental health professionals believe that the Tarasoffs won this case based on the duty to warn, actually the court only determined that they could file a suit on those grounds. Rather, the case was settled out of court (Meyer et al., 1988). In spite of this ambiguous outcome, the duty to warn has become a legal standard for all mental health professionals and has become the law in several states. It remains an important case for supervisors as well as therapists, because the supervisor was implicated in the case.

It is imperative then for supervisors to inform supervisees of conditions under which it would be appropriate to implement the duty to inform an intended victim (Munson, 1991). The question of determining dangerousness obviously is embedded in this decision. The practitioner and supervisor are not expected to see the unforeseeable; rather, there is an expectation that sound judgment and reasonable or due care were taken regarding the determination of dangerousness. For this reason, Schutz (1982) and other authorities on such legal matters make the point emphatically that consultation with others and documentation of treatment are vital in any questionable case.

In other situations, there is some indication that the client might be dangerous, but no potential victim has been named. In fact, there might not be a particular person in danger, but, rather, the client's hostility might be nonspecific. At present, ethical standards and legal experts seem to lean in favor of client privilege unless there is clear evidence that the client is immediately dangerous (Fulero, 1988; Schutz, 1982; Woody, 1984). In other words, therapists and supervisors are not expected to, nor should they, read between the lines when working with clients. Many clients make idle threats when they are frustrated. It is the job of mental health practitioners to make a reasonable evaluation of those threats. In fact, in the eyes of the law, it is more important that reasonable evaluation be made than that the prediction be accurate.

Direct Liability and Vicarious Liability

Direct liability would be argued when the actions of the supervisor were themselves the cause of harm. For example, if the supervisor did not perform supervision adequate for a novice counselor or if the supervisor suggested (and documented) an intervention that was determined to be the cause of harm (e.g., suggesting that a client use "tough love" strategies with a child that ended in physical harm to the child).

Vicarious liability, on the other hand, represents possibly the worst nightmare for the clinical supervisor, that is, being held liable for the actions of the supervisee when these were not suggested or even known by the supervisor. In such cases, the supervisor becomes liable by virtue of the relationship with the supervisee. Therefore, the supervisor generally is only held liable "for the negligent acts of supervisees if these acts are performed in the course and scope of the supervisory relationship" (Disney & Stephens, 1994, p. 15). Factors Disney and Stephens included that might be used to establish whether an action fell within the scope of the supervisory relationship are

1. *The supervisor's power to control the supervisee (e.g., is the supervisor the employer or responsible for evaluation);*
2. *the supervisee's duty to perform the act (e.g., doing therapy with assigned clients);*
3. *the time, place, and purpose of the act (e.g., was it done during counseling or away from the place of counseling?);*
4. *the motivation of the supervisee (e.g., was the supervisee attempting to be helpful?); and*
5. *whether the supervisor could have reasonably expected the supervisee to commit the act.* (pp. 15–16)

Disney and Stephens (1994) observed that should the supervisor be found guilty based on vicarious responsibility then the supervisor, if found not to be negligent in subsequent court proceedings, could recover damages from the supervisee.

Snider (1985) offered four guidelines to supervisors to reduce the likelihood of being named as a codefendant in a malpractice suit. First, maintain a trusting relationship with supervisees. Within a context of mutual trust and respect, supervisees will be far more likely to voice their concerns about their clients, themselves, and each other. Second, keep up to date regarding legal issues that affect mental health settings and the professional in general. Additionally, supervisors need to have a healthy respect for the complexity of the law and recognize the need for competent legal aid. Third, if the supervisor is the administrative head of an agency, it is essential that the supervisor retain the services of an attorney who specializes in malpractice litigation. If this is not the supervisor's decision, the supervisor should be sure that the organization has appropriate legal support. Fourth, supervisors should have adequate liability insurance and should be sure that their supervisees also carry liability insurance. Although this final precaution does not reduce the chances of being sued, it does, obviously, minimize the damage that could accrue from such an unfortunate experience.

Regrettably, there is little comfort to offer the timid supervisor who is afraid of the tremendous responsibility and potential legal liability inherent in supervision. Short of refusing to supervise, we believe protection for the supervisor lies in the same concepts of reasonable care and sound judgment that protect therapists. This includes an awareness of and command of the concepts and skills presented in this book. It also includes a commitment to investing the time and energy to supervise adequately and to document all supervisory contacts.

MAJOR ETHICAL ISSUES FOR CLINICAL SUPERVISORS

The following are the major ethical themes of which clinical supervisors should be cognizant. We will present the implications of these themes for the practice of supervision based on our understanding and on a review of the literature. We will limit our discussion to issues that have distinct and additional responsibilities for supervisors and, therefore, will not discuss topics such as research. At the same time, several ethical issues have implications for both the supervisory relationship and the therapy relationship that the supervisor oversees. We will attempt to address each dimension separately.

Due Process

Due process is a legal term for a procedure that ensures that notice and hearing must be given before an important right can be removed (Disney & Stephens, 1994). In the human services, due process has surfaced as an issue mostly around the proper route to take if a client needs to be committed to a mental health hospital (Ponterotto, 1987; Schutz, 1982). Most hospitals are aware of their due process duties, and professionals who work with volatile populations are also aware of correct procedures.

Supervisees have due process rights, too, and these are more likely to be overlooked. The ethical codes of the mental health professions give some attention to supervision, but their primary purpose is still in detailing ethical behavior for the provider of therapy (cf., AAMFT, 1991; ACA, 1995; APA, 1992; NASW, 1990). It is not surprising, therefore, that the Ethical Guidelines for Counseling Supervisors (Supervision Interest Network, 1993) address the issue of due process concerning supervisees most directly (see Appendix B). In addition to advising the supervisor regarding assessment and evaluation and the implications of supervisee impairment, section 2.14 states:

> *Supervisors should incorporate the principles of informed consent and participation; clarity of requirements, expectations, roles and rules; and due process and appeal into the establishment of policies and procedures of their institution, program, courses, and individual supervisory relationships. Mechanisms for due process appeal of individual supervisory actions should be established and made available to all supervisees.*

The most blatant violation of Guideline 2.14 occurs when a supervisee is given a negative final evaluation or dismissed from a training program or job without having had either prior warning that his or her performance was inadequate or a reasonable amount of time to improve. Ladany, Hill, Corbett, and Nutt (1996) found that being denied adequate performance evaluation was the most frequently cited supervisor violation reported by supervisees in their study. This ethical dilemma seems to originate, at least in part, from an avoidance of evaluation by training programs and clinical sites. Perhaps as a consequence, both tend to take a reactive posture to the issue of supervisee impairment (i.e., performing at an inadequate level for any number of reasons). They place their emphasis on screening for admission (Bradey & Post, 1991) with the unrealistic expectation that accepted students will uniformly complete training successfully. A national study of APA internship sites found that, by and large, supervisors appeared to be "waiting for the ax to fall" regarding impaired interns (Boxley, Drew, & Rangel, 1986). As a result, these sites also "appear not to have established formal guidelines in dealing with impaired trainees and, as a result, student due process procedures are missing in many of (the) internship experiences" (p. 52). A more recent study surveying social work training programs found similar results, leading the authors to comment that the gatekeeping assumption of training programs is at odds with the absence of policies for nonacademic termination of students (Koerin & Miller, 1995).

Some supervisors are unclear about what constitutes impairment. Lamb, Cochran, and Jackson (1991) identified the three broad aspects of professional functioning that constitute competence as professional development, knowledge and skill, and personal suitability for a mental health role. From these they established the following areas of possible impairment: "(a) an inability or unwillingness to acquire and integrate professional standards into one's repertoire of professional behavior; (b) an inability to acquire professional skills and reach an accepted level of competency; and (c) an inability to control personal stress, psychological dysfunction, or emotional reactions that may affect professional functioning" (p. 292). A

serious manifestation of any of these broad areas could be adequate grounds for dismissal. In order to be ethical and legally sound, supervisors must employ a process that is neither arbitrary nor capricious (Disney & Stephens, 1994). Lamb et al. (1991) outlined four important due process steps that ensure both supervisee protection and institutional credibility.

1. *Reconnaissance and identification.* This phase encompasses that period of time when the supervisee is seeing clients under supervision and areas of strength or vulnerability are observed. Lamb et al. suggested that supervisors meet regularly to consult with each other as these evaluations are occurring. They differentiated expected or remedial supervisee problems from impairment by using the following list from Lamb et al. (1987) to identify the latter:

a. The intern does not acknowledge, understand, or address the problematic behavior when it is identified.
b. The problematic behavior is not merely a reflection of a skill deficit that can be rectified by academic or didactic training.
c. The quality of service delivered by the intern is consistently negatively affected.
d. The problematic behavior is not restricted to one area of professional functioning.
e. The problematic behavior has potential for ethical or legal ramifications if not addressed.
f. A disproportionate amount of attention by training personnel is required.
g. The intern's behavior does not change as a function of feedback, remediation efforts, or time.
h. The intern's behavior negatively affects the public image of the agency. (Lamb et al., 1991, p. 292)

2. *Discussion and consultation.* Once an intern has been identified as displaying the possibility of impairment, Lamb et al. suggested that extreme care be taken to protect both the intern and the staff through extensive discussion among all relevant personnel. Furthermore, all former impressions and interventions should be reviewed. Finally, supervisors need to make a qualitative decision about the seriousness of the situation and review their documentation of the process up to this point.

3. *Implementation and review.* If more serious action is called for, this is the point at which it will occur. Probation or even termination may be the decision of the staff. (It is also possible that after careful scrutiny of their own behavior and consultation the staff will find a less dramatic intervention that is appropriate.) If probation is the avenue of choice, Lamb et al. suggested that a letter be sent to the intern that should state the following:

a. Identify the specific behaviors or areas of professional functioning that are of concern.

b. Directly relate these behaviors to the written evaluations (e.g., not showing up for counseling sessions as an example of inadequate professional functioning).

c. Provide several specific ways that these deficiencies can be remediated (e.g., from additional training to personal therapy).

d. Identify a specific probation period after which the performance of the intern will be reviewed (long enough for reasonable changes, but not so long that further action cannot be taken).

e. Stipulate, if appropriate, how the intern's functioning in the agency will change during the probation period (e.g., additional time in supervision).

f. Reiterate the due process procedures available to challenge the decision. (Lamb et al., 1991, p. 293)

Lamb et al. advised that a probation period be an active time of ongoing feedback to the intern and frequent consultation and documentation among staff. Finally, Lamb et al. are equally compendious if the decision is to terminate, advising that all implications be reviewed before action is taken, that the intern receive a letter reiterating the probation conditions and the reasons for dismissal, and that the intern be provided with an opportunity to appeal. Only then should the dismissal occur.

4. *Anticipating and responding to organizational reaction.* Lamb et al. (1991) wisely concluded that removing an impaired intern is not only an action that will call for support of that intern, but a systemic intervention as well. All levels of the system should be considered, including clients of the intern, supervisors who were pivotal in the decision, administration, and other staff and interns. Although the intern's rights to privacy must be protected, all persons who will be aware of the decision will have a reaction, and there should be some mechanism for that reaction to be addressed.

A review of the process suggested by Lamb et al. (1991) again indicates the strong positive relationship that can exist between ethical standards and legal mandates. When due process is followed, the supervisee in question is guaranteed a respectful review of a situation and the expert opinions of professionals, in addition to that of the person initiating the complaint. By following such a procedure, the institution is equally protected from the accusation that its action was capricious or arbitrary.

Although most supervisees do not challenge violations of due process rights, several authors have documented those cases where litigation followed such violations (e.g., Disney & Stephens, 1994; Knoff & Prout, 1985; Meyer, 1980). Disney and Stephens (1994) advised that, strictly speaking, due process rights are only protected within public institutions. Therefore, private institutions of higher learning and/or mental health sites that do not receive significant public funding would not be held legally accountable regarding due process procedures unless they were stipulated in the institution's official published materials. For this reason alone, due process is considered an ethical mandate for supervisors, regardless of legal implications.

Meyer (1980) distinguished between impairment based on conduct and that based on academic issues, stating that the former require a more stringent adherence to due process standards because they are inherently judgmental in nature, thus calling for more protection for the supervisee. Frame and Stevens-Smith (1995) proposed the development of a policy statement to emphasize the importance of personal characteristics and to use for ongoing evaluation of students during their training program. Students' due process rights are protected by the publication of the policy statement and the availability of the evaluations done for each student. When students are found to be in jeopardy, Frame and Stevens-Smith utilized a procedure very similar to that described by Lamb et al. (1991).

For academic dismissals, Meyer (1980) contended that court decisions indicate that formal hearings are not necessary. In general, it was Meyer's assertion that extensive and detailed procedures are not necessary to be legally defensible. In other words, those procedures suggested by Lamb et al. (1991) may represent more caution than is necessary. The issue, we believe, is to find the right balance in light of court decisions, the well-being of the supervisee, and the well-being of the system. More is not always better in terms of documented procedures; at the same time, inadequate care to due process can be a glaring omission once a crisis occurs.

Example: Hannah is in a master's program in mental health counseling. She has completed 10 courses in the program and is currently in practicum. Hannah has received a great deal of formative feedback throughout the practicum indicating that she had many areas that needed improvement. At the conclusion of the practicum, Hannah's instructor assigns Hannah a grade of F for the course. At this time, Hannah is informed that a failing grade in the practicum is grounds for dismissal from the program. Hannah is told that she may retake the practicum one time, but that the faculty are not optimistic that she will improve enough to receive a B or better, a condition for her continuing in the program. Although Hannah knew that she was not doing as well in the practicum as some others, she had no awareness that she was in danger of being terminated from the program until the final evaluation.

It is likely that Hannah will take the advice of the faculty and will discontinue the training program at this time. However, have her due process rights been protected? How vulnerable is her practicum instructor and the program if she should decide to challenge their decision? Even if Hannah does not appeal, what are the potential systemic implications of such a process? Even though there is no ill will evident in the action of the faculty and no indication that their decision was capricious or arbitrary, did the process they followed adequately protect the student and was it legally defensible?

Informed Consent

The concept of informed consent has been handed down to us from the medical profession. Within this context, informed consent requires physicians to inform patients about medical procedures that could be potentially harmful to them. Patients should also be apprised of any risks to a recommended treatment and of the alternative treatments available. The failure of physicians to inform their patients constitutes malpractice and leaves the physician vulnerable to liability should injuries occur as a result of treatment. The doctrine of informed consent has been extended to other health service providers, including those in the mental health fields (Disney & Stephens, 1994).

There is perhaps no ethical standard as far-reaching as that of informed consent for the practice of psychotherapy. This is underscored by Woody (1984), who asserted that informed consent is the best defense against a charge of malpractice for the practitioner. For the supervisor, there are really three levels of responsibility: (1) the supervisor must determine that clients have been informed by the supervisee regarding the parameters of therapy, (2) the supervisor must also be sure that clients are aware of the parameters of supervision that will affect them, and (3) the supervisor must provide the supervisee with the opportunity for informed consent. We will discuss each of these separately.

Informed Consent with Clients.   It is essential that clients understand and agree to the procedures of therapy prior to its beginning. This is not to imply that there will be no ambiguity in therapy or even that the therapist should be able to predict everything that will happen during the course of therapy. But it does imply that some assessment must occur that will be shared with clients, that goals will be determined, and that the general course of therapy will be outlined for the clients' approval. If it is determined later that a redirection of therapy would be beneficial, this process should be repeated.

Partly because of theoretical orientation, some therapists have resisted this process. But even less directive forms of therapy can and should be explained to clients prior to their commitment to the process. As Woody (1984) stated,

> *[t]he professional should be the last person to object to a requirement of informed consent. If anything, the professional should reach to the maximum allowed by public policy to ensure that the service recipient does, in fact, understand and consent to the treatment. To do otherwise is to court a disciplinary action for unethical conduct and/or a legal suit for malpractice.*   (p. 376)

According to Haas (1991), there are seven categories of information that, if revealed, would constitute necessary and sufficient informed consent. The first four apply to the therapeutic relationship. Haas began with the information most directly related to the medical precedent, that of the risks and benefits of treatment. In both cases, only what is reasonable need to be covered. The risks may be mild, such as embarrassment if others should learn that one is receiving counseling (Disney & Stephens, 1994), or they may be serious, such as the risk of terminating a marriage if one begins to address chronic relationship issues. Likewise, the potential benefits of therapy should be discussed. Margolin (1982) expressed a concern that the intervention of taking an optimistic posture advocated by some of the family therapy literature as a method of mobilizing family energy might in some cases be a violation of the spirit of describing benefits *reasonably* to be expected from therapy. This concern can also be raised for other therapies.

Haas's (1991) third category encompassed the logistics of treatment, including the length of sessions, cost, opportunity for telephone consultations, and the like. With the growing emphasis on managed care in the mental health service area, the limits of treatment in terms of numbers of sessions is a new critical area that must be covered by the supervisee (Haas & Cummings, 1991). Similarly, if the supervisee is a student assigned to a site for a limited amount of time (say, one semester), this information is important to convey for purposes of informed consent.

The fourth category described by Haas (1991) includes information about the type of therapy clients will be offered. If one is behaviorally oriented and will require homework, if the supervisee is in training as a marriage and family therapist and will require additional family members to be present, if one's approach to working with particular issues includes the use of group work, such stipulations should be explained at the outset of therapy. Disney and Stephens (1994) suggested that preferred alternatives to the type of treatment being suggested, as well as the risks of receiving no treatment at all, should be explained at this time as well.

Several authors have expressed a concern about informed consent within some of the marriage and family therapy paradigms (Corey, 1986; Green & Hansen, 1986; Hines & Hare-Mustin, 1978; Huber, 1994; Keith-Spiegel & Koocher, 1985; Margolin, 1982; Willbach, 1989). One of the issues raised most frequently by these authors is that of coercion if one or more family members do not want to be involved in therapy. This issue is of concern not only for adults, but for children, especially teenagers who are at an ambiguous stage as to their legal right of consent. Additionally, Huber (1994) reviewed the possibility of uneven outcomes for different family members as a consequence of family and marital therapies as an informed consent issue.

Finally, "manipulating a family for therapeutic reasons" ranked as number 12 of 39 frequently encountered ethical dilemmas for family therapists (Green & Hansen, 1986). It must be acknowledged, therefore, that such interventions have been perceived as troublesome at least by some family therapists, especially in terms of informed consent (Huber, 1994).

> *Example: Julian is a trainee in a mental health agency. He has been seeing Ellen for four months in individual counseling. It has become apparent that Ellen and her husband need marriage counseling. Julian has been trained in marriage and family therapy. He very much wants to follow this case to its conclusion. Without discussing alternatives, he suggests that Ellen bring her husband to the next session. Ellen says that she is relieved that he is willing to work with them. She was afraid that Julian would refer them to another therapist. Having Julian work with both her and her husband is exactly what she was hoping for.*

In this example, we must ask if Ellen has been given the opportunity of informed consent. Has her husband? Is there information about the therapy process that Julian should have offered to help both Ellen and her husband make the best decision for their present situation? At the very least, Julian has erred in not discussing alternatives. Julian's supervisor must now help Julian backtrack. If the supervisor had any inkling that marital therapy might be indicated, the supervisor was negligent for not coaching Julian regarding the client's informed consent rights, as well as her husband's.

Informed Consent Regarding Supervision. The client must not only be aware of therapeutic procedures, but also of supervision procedures. Whether sessions will be taped or observed, who will be involved in supervision (one person or a team of persons), how close will be the supervision, all these need to be communicated to the client.

Haas's (1991) final three categories regarding informed consent are related to supervision. The fifth area of information for which clients should be apprised are emergency procedures that are in

place. Because the supervisor should always be involved in an emergency situation, we have placed this category here. Clients should know if direct access to the therapist is available in case of emergency. Will the supervisor be available to the client? This leads to the next category of confidentiality. Most supervisees are apprised of their obligation to inform clients when confidentiality will be breached for reasons other than supervision, for example, if there was an indication that the client might do harm to another. However, the issue of confidentiality is equally relevant to the supervisory relationship. According to Disney and Stephens (1994), "supervisees place themselves in a position to be sued for invasion of privacy and breach of confidentiality if they do not inform their clients that they will be discussing sessions with their supervisor" (p. 50). Most training programs use written forms to alert clients of the conditions of supervision. It may be wise for the supervisor to meet with clients personally before the outset of therapy for a number of reasons: (1) by meeting the supervisor directly, the client usually is more comfortable with the prospect of supervision, (2) it gives the supervisor an opportunity to model for trainees the kind of direct, open communication that is needed to ensure informed consent, and (3) by not going through the trainee to communicate with clients, it is one less way that the supervisor could be vicariously responsible should the trainee not be clear or thorough.

The last area of information to be given to clients has to do with qualifications of the provider (Haas, 1991). As several authors have noted (e.g., Disney & Stephens, 1994; Harrar, VandeCreek, & Knapp, 1990; Knapp & VandeCreek, 1997; Pope & Vasquez, 1991), it is vitally important for ethical and legal reasons that clients understand when they are in therapy with a supervisee who is in training. Any attempt to obscure the status of a supervisee may expose both supervisee and supervisor to civil suits alleging fraud, misrepresentation, deceit, and lack of informed consent.

Even when clients are aware that their therapist is under supervision, informed consent can be compromised when trainees downplay the parameters of supervision. Situations occur when supervisees use ambiguous language like, "If it's alright with you, I'll be audiotaping our session," when what they mean is, "I am required to audiotape our sessions if I am to work with you." This leaves the trainee in the awkward position of setting an unwise precedent or of having to backpedal to explain the true conditions of therapy and supervision.

Example: Beth is a social worker who counsels battered women. She is well trained to do initial interviews with women in crisis, and her supervisor is confident in Beth's abilities to carry out these interviews without taping them. Additionally, there is the obvious concern that the use of audiotape would be insensitive to women who are frightened and vulnerable during the interview. The conditions of supervision, however, require Beth to audiotape all subsequent sessions.

Janell was one of Beth's interviewees. After the initial session, Janell decided that she was ready to receive counseling regarding her abusive marriage. She explained to Beth that she was afraid of her husband's reaction to counseling, so she made her first appointment for a day when she knew he would be out of town.

When Janell arrived for counseling, Beth discussed the conditions of counseling, including the requirement that she audiotape sessions for supervision. Janell became quite upset and told Beth that she never would have agreed to counseling if she had known that the sessions would not be held in strictest confidence. Beth attempted to explain that would still be the case, but Janell left and did not return.

How do you react to Beth's method of handling this situation? Were Janell's informed consent rights violated? What alternatives did Beth have that would protect both her and her client?

Informed Consent with Trainees. It goes without saying that it is as important that trainees be as well informed as clients. Trainees should enter the supervisory experience knowing the conditions that dictate their success or advancement. It also

should be clear to them what their responsibilities are and what the supervisor's are. Consider the following examples:

Ronald makes an appointment to see his academic advisor to discuss his internship now that he is near the end of his training program. He plans to do his internship in a local mental health agency. His advisor tells Ronald that the faculty recently evaluated students and that he was viewed as not having the capacity to be successful in clinical work. It was suggested that he pursue an internship in a "softer" area such as career counseling. Ronald states that he has no interest in career counseling. Ronald's advisor states that such an internship site is the only type that will be approved for him.

Ruth has been assigned to a local mental health hospital for her internship to work with patients who are preparing to be discharged. It is her first day at the site and she is meeting with her site supervisor. He gives her a form to fill out, which asks for information regarding her student malpractice insurance. When Ruth tells her supervisor that she does not carry such insurance, he advises her that it is their policy not to accept any student who does not have insurance. The supervisor also expresses some surprise, because this has always been the hospital's policy and Ruth is not the first student to be assigned to them from her training program.

Latoya is in her doctoral internship, working with very difficult clients. In supervision she shares that one client in particular has been "getting to her," most likely because some of the client's situation is so similar to Latoya's past. Latoya's supervisor immediately suggests that Latoya receive counseling regarding this issue. When Latoya says that she believes her past therapy was sufficient and that she would prefer to view the situation as a supervision one, her supervisor states that she will only continue to work with Latoya if she commits to counseling.

Pauline is in her first month of employment at a residential center for troubled youth. Most of her assignments have been what she considers "babysitting" rather than any serious work with her charges. When she talks to her supervisor about this, she is informed that she will not be assigned a case load for the first 6 months and only then if she is perceived as "ready." This is news to Pauline. She is frustrated because she turned down another job where she could have begun to work with kids immediately. Pauline is upset further because her husband has been notified by his firm that he will be transferred in 9 months to another location. Had Pauline known the conditions of her present position, she would not have accepted the job.

In each situation, how egregious is the violation of the supervisee's right to informed consent? To what extent do institutional materials cover issues of consent? How might each situation have been handled to better address the rights of the supervisee?

Whiston and Emerson (1989) addressed the informed consent violation if supervisors refer their trainees for therapy as a condition for continuing in a training program when their trainees were not aware of this possibility from the outset of training. In other words, if there is a possibility that personal counseling will be recommended for any trainees in a given program, all trainees should be cognizant of this practice upon entering the program. Similarly, Patrick (1989) warned against allowing trainees in a program to volunteer to be clients for a laboratory course if these trainees are not aware that exposing some types of personal information might lead to a change of status in that program.

These are only a few of the many types of information that trainees should be alerted to by their supervisors before they encounter any consequences. Others include the choice of supervisor, the form of supervision, the time that will be allotted for supervision, the expectations of the supervisor, the theoretical orientation of the supervisor, and the type of documentation required for supervision (Cohen, 1987; McCarthy et al., 1995; Pope & Vasquez, 1991). Simply put, the surprises in store for the trainee should be due to the learning process itself and the complexity of human problems and not to oversights on the part of the supervisor.

As a final comment about informed consent, we refer to Stout's (1987) injunction that supervisors

and supervisors-in-training also be forewarned about the parameters of supervision. "Supervisors, as such, should be allowed the prerogative of informed consent, that is, they need to be fully aware of the heavy responsibility, accountability, and even culpability involved in supervision" (p. 96).

Dual Relationships

Ethical standards of all mental health disciplines strongly advise that dual relationships, or engaging in relationships in addition to the professional relationship, between therapists and clients be avoided. Probably the most flagrant type of dual relationships are sexual relationships between therapists and clients, which are condemned. In most states, sexual intercourse with a client is grounds for the automatic revocation of licensure or certification. It is the responsibility of the supervisor to be certain that supervisees understand the definition of a dual relationship and avoid all such relationships with clients.

Dual relationships between supervisors and supervisees have proved to be a much more difficult issue to resolve and have been a topic of much debate in the professional literature. Problematic dual relationships with supervisees include intimate relationships, therapeutic relationships, and social relationships. Most authors concede that supervisors tend to have more than one professional relationship with a supervisee (e.g., supervisee and research assistant); these have typically not been viewed as problematic. What makes a dual relationship unethical is (1) the likelihood that it will impair the supervisor's judgment and (2) the risk to the supervisee of exploitation (Hall, 1988b).

By far the dual relationship that has received the most attention is sexual involvement between supervisor and supervisee. Prior to reviewing all types of dual relationships between supervisors and supervisees, we will review briefly a number of studies that have attempted to grasp how widespread is the issue. One nationwide survey (Pope, Levenson, & Schover, 1979) found that 10 percent of psychologists admitted to having sexual contact, as students, with their educators, and 13 percent reported having had a sexual relationship with their students now that they were educators. As might be expected, more female trainees reported having had sexual contact with their educators than male trainees. Furthermore, for those women who had graduated closer to the time of the study, the incidence was much higher (25 percent) compared to women who had graduated 20 years earlier (5 percent). Bartell and Rubin (1990), in their review of this important study, noted that of those women who had sexual relationships as students a striking 23 percent had similar relationships as educators. By contrast, only 6 percent of those educators who had not had such relationships as students had sexual relationships as educators. Bartell and Rubin, therefore, believed that there is an important modeling effect that may contribute to the perpetuation of unethical behavior in supervision.

A recent study using a similar definition of sexual contact as studies done in psychology found a lower rate (6 percent) of sexual intimacy between counselor educators and their students (Miller & Larrabee, 1995). Thoreson et al. (1993) surveyed male counselors and found that 16.9 percent admitted having sexual contact within professional relationships, with the majority occurring after the professional relationship had ended, a rate more similar to those involving psychologists. Two other studies involving clinical psychologists (Robinson & Reid, 1985; Glaser & Thorpe, 1986) found similar results to Pope et al. (1979). Additionally, Glaser and Thorpe investigated the issue of coercion. Of those individuals who reported sexual contact, the majority felt that they had not been coerced (72 percent). However, 51 percent saw some degree of coercion in retrospect. When asked their current opinion of sexual contact between educators and students, 95 percent considered it to be unethical and harmful. Thus, it seems that sexual relationships are condemned more easily in the abstract than when the situation actually arises (Bartell & Rubin, 1990). Finally, Tabachnick, Keith-Spiegel, and Pope (1991) conducted a survey to poll psychology educators and found that 11 percent of a national sample reported having sexual intimacies with students.

Whether 6 percent or 16 percent, the tangible outcomes of statistics such as these take the form of ethical complaints and professional sanction. Pope and Vasquez (1991) reported that in recent years the largest percentage (23 percent) of ethical complaints against psychologists to the APA Ethics Committee involved dual relationships, including sexual intimacies with clients. Similarly, the largest percentage (36 percent) of disciplinary actions taken by licensing boards against psychologists involved dual relationships, including sexual intimacies with clients. Dual relationships, therefore, must be viewed as the greatest ethical challenge in the helping professions. Unfortunately, the problem finds at least some of its roots within the training environment. (While these studies included all faculty in training programs, some of whom most certainly were not clinical supervisors, there is no reason to assume that supervisors are excluded from these data.)

All relevant ethical codes for the mental health professions make some reference to dual relationships between supervisors and supervisees. Sonne (1994) criticized the most recent APA Code of Ethics for neither defining a multiple relationship nor describing the conditions by which a dual relationship becomes unethical. It seems that this criticism could be directed at other codes as well. The ACES Supervision Interest Network Ethical Guidelines for Counseling Supervisors gives the most attention to dual relationships (2.09–2.11) and reflects the bias of the professional literature that all dual relationships should be avoided (see Appendix B).

Sexual Involvement Between Supervisor and Supervisee.   Sexual issues between supervisors and supervisees have been addressed in several ways in the professional literature and will be separated here for discussion.

Sexual Attraction.   In one study (Rodolfa et al., 1994), one-quarter of interns in postdoctoral internship sites reported feeling sexually attracted to their clinical supervisors. Ellis and Douce (1994) identified sexual attraction as one of eight recurring issues in supervision. Ladany et al. (1996) found that both counselor–client attraction issues and supervisee–supervisor attraction issues were among the topics that trainees were unwilling to disclose in supervision (9 percent of study participants for each category). As has also been noted by others (e.g., Vasquez, 1988; Pope & Vasquez, 1991), Ellis and Douce criticized training programs for not teaching trainees how to handle sexual attraction openly and ethically and to view it as a relatively normative part of both supervision and therapy dynamics. The authors further admonished that acting on sexual attraction in supervision results in "calamity."

Sexual Harassment.   Unlike sexual attraction, sexual harassment is an aberration of the supervision process and is never acceptable. Those supervisors who expect or request sexual favors or who take sexual liberties with their trainees are clearly in violation of all ethical codes for the helping professions. They have abused the power afforded them due to their professional status and serve as poor role models for future therapists (Corey et al., 1993). It is never acceptable for supervisors to put their own needs and wants in the foreground to the detriment of the professional development needs of the supervisee (Peterson, 1993). Sexual harassment can be insidious and subtle, leaving the victims doubting themselves (Anonymous, 1991) and/or manipulated into the role of caretaker (Peterson, 1993).

Consensual (but Hidden) Sexual Relationships. Results of national studies would indicate that the majority of sexual relationships between supervisor and supervisees falls in this category. By necessity, the word "consensual" is used broadly. As reported earlier, in retrospect, many persons believe there was more coercion involved in a sexual relationship than they thought

at the time. Furthermore, as Brodsky (1980) asserted, when "one person in a relationship has a position of power over the other, there is no true consent for the acceptance of a personal relationship" (p. 516). The frequency of these relationships, however, would indicate adequate levels of consensus at the time, even if in retrospect the situation could also be described as sexual coercion. The bulk of literature that depicts sexual dual relationships as inherently unethical seems to be directed at these liaisons (e.g., Bonosky, 1995; Bowman, Hatley, & Bowman, 1995; Larrabee & Miller, 1993; Miller & Larrabee, 1995; Slimp & Burian, 1994). In the most measured of commentary, Bartell and Rubin (1990) advised that "[s]exual involvement may further a human relationship, but it does so at the expense of the professional relationship" (p. 446).

Intimate Romantic Relationships.   There is virtually no distinction in the majority of the professional literature between those dual relationships that occur within supervision and those that *begin* there. By contrast, Lazarus (1995) asserted that the American Psychiatric Association, while discouraging all sexual involvement between supervisors and trainees, "realized that romantic relationships often develop in professional settings and that it in no way intended to stifle them" (p. 66). Sexual relationships that grow from positive, caring feelings on the part of both participants are more troublesome to label as clearly inappropriate. In fact, most of us know at least one dual-career couple whose relationship began while one or both was in training, some of whom had unequal professional status when they became involved with one another. When adults are working closely together in the intense world of therapy, it is understandable that intimate relationships might emerge. The question, therefore, is not how to prevent such relationships from occurring, but how to assure that such a relationship poses no ethical compromise for the supervisor or trainee and no negative consequence for the trainee's clients.

We would suggest the following to handle a dual relationship that emerges within the context of supervision: (1) If at all possible, a trainee should receive a new supervisor if an intimate relationship has evolved. This should be done in a manner that will not negatively affect clients being served or the professional growth of the trainee. If there is a rational reason for not replacing the present supervisor (e.g., the supervisor is the only Gestaltist on the staff and the student aspires to be a Gestalt therapist), then an additional supervisor should be involved to monitor the supervisory relationship. (2) There may be occasions when there is no possibility for removal of the supervisor or for an additional supervisor to be involved. In this case, we would suggest that both supervisor and trainee take great pains to document their work together. Having audio- or video-recorded examples of the trainee's work will be important when it is time to evaluate. Usually, it is not difficult to get a second opinion about a supervisee's abilities. The topics covered in supervision and their resolution should all be recorded. In addition, the supervisor should request consultation with colleagues more liberally than would be the case ordinarily. Finally, we would suggest that if group supervision is one of the models being used that the group be made aware of the personal relationship between supervisor and trainee (if they don't know already!). By bringing up the issue openly and asking the group to give them feedback if any preferential treatment is observed, the couple reduces the possibility that the relationship will be insidious to the group.

The above notwithstanding, it must be noted that such dual relationships are still dangerous and difficult to manage. It is enough to negotiate personal power in a new relationship without adding on the dimension of unequal professional power. If the relationship ends, the trainee is at a distinct disadvantage if the professional relationship must continue. It is also very typical for new couples to become insulated from the outside world and to see things in a way very protective of cach other. It is the rare person who can keep such dynamics from interfering with professional growth and service delivery. At the same time, if professional associations had more discourse regarding the appropriate behavior of legitimate relationships, those relationships that are illicit would be more apparent *to the supervisee.* The reluctance on the part of the supervisor to make an intimacy known to appropriate professionals would certainly be an indication that such a liaison is an abuse of power rather than an authentic intimate relationship.

Because of the practical difficulties and the ethical dubiousness of intimate relationships within supervision, preexisting couples should avoid using each other as supervisors. With the increasing availability of supervision, including distance-learning modalities, a more objective supervisor should be within reach.

Nonsexual Dual Relationships.   Goodyear and Sinnett (1984) argued that it is inevitable that supervisors and their supervisees will have dual relationships, an opinion shared by others (Aponte, 1994; Clarkson, 1994; Cornell, 1994; Ryder & Hepworth, 1990). Unlike therapy relationships, persons who work together will share other experiences with each other. Faculty and students in graduate programs often become close through formal and informal contacts. In addition, the same person who serves as a trainee's therapy supervisor could be a member of the same trainee's doctoral research committee, an instructor for another course, or the supervisor for an assistantship. In an agency or school, it sometimes happens that someone under supervision is the same person the supervisor learned to count on in a crisis or is someone with a personal style that allows the supervisor to be more candid than he or she is with other professional peers. Some of these relationships are very gratifying, and we would not choose to avoid them. It seems to us, therefore, that we should approach this matter, as Aponte (1994) suggested, by attempting to differentiate between dual relationships that abuse power, exploit supervisees, or harm the supervisee and those that occur within the positive context of a maturing professional relationship.

Lloyd (1992) charged that some professional writings have created "dual relationship phobia" while attempting to caution supervisors about unethical relationships. He was critical of those who have elevated their hypervigilance to the status of ethical standards rather than charging educators and supervisors to exercise their responsibility as decision makers and resolvers of conflict. Lloyd's comments seemed particularly salient when considering social contact and/or additional professional roles with supervisees

One area for which there is particular agreement in the field, however, is the inappropriateness of doing therapy with one's supervisee. Because supervision can stimulate personal issues in the supervisee, it is likely that a supervisor will be faced with the challenge of determining where supervision ends and therapy begins (Whiston & Emerson, 1989; Wise, Lowery, & Silvergrade, 1989). Pragmatically, Cornell (1994) determined that the confrontive interventions often called for in supervision might contradict or threaten a therapeutic relationship with a supervisee, thus advising against creating such a dichotomy. A study of the ethical choices required by psychologists (Pope, Tabachnick, & Keith-Spiegel, 1988) found this issue of offering some semblance of therapy to supervisees to be more problematic than other, clearer situations.

In spite of some confusion, most authors (e.g., Burns & Holloway, 1989; Green & Hansen, 1989; Kitchener, 1988; Patrick, 1989; Stout, 1987; Whiston & Emerson, 1989; Wise et al., 1989) recommend that supervisors be clear from the outset of supervision that personal issues might be activated in supervision and, if these issues are found to be substantial, that the supervisee will be asked to work through them with another professional. Furthermore, it is important to stress that this ethical question is not a novel one for supervisors. Green and Hansen (1989) reported that the trainee's personal issues was one the six most important ethical dilemmas cited by AAMFT clinical members. The collective wisdom of those authors who have grappled with this issue was that supervisors have the responsibility to help supervisees identify their issues, especially as they interfere with their work as therapists, but "after the supervisor identified the personal issues, the trainees must then be given the responsibility for resolving those issues" (Whiston & Emerson, 1989, p. 322).

Dual relationships appear to exist on a behavioral continuum (Dickey, Housley, & Guest, 1993) from extremely inappropriate and unethical behavior, such as sexual contact as a result of sexual harassment, to behavior that could easily be construed as part of the mentoring process, such as taking a few students to a social occasion at a professional meeting. Neither end of the continuum causes much difficulty among clinical supervisors. However, many situations in the middle represent "the murky pool of ambiguity" (Peterson, 1993, p. 1). Peterson cautioned that dual relationship challenges abound in supervisory relationships and cannot be regulated out of existence. We will consider the parameters of ethical decision making at the end of this chapter.

Example: Vanessa has been a marriage and family therapist at an agency for 6 months. Gary, one of the other three therapists in the agency and the only other single therapist, is her clinical supervisor. It will take Vanessa 2 years under supervision to accrue the experience she needs to be eligible to sit for the state licensing examination for her LMFT. One evening Gary calls Vanessa to inquire whether she would like to go to a day-long workshop with him. The speaker for the workshop specializes in a kind of therapy in which Vanessa has expressed interest. Vanessa accepts and the workshop turns out to be an excellent professional experience. On the way home, Vanessa and Gary stop for dinner. Vanessa picks up the tab to thank Gary for including her.

The following day Vanessa is sharing some of the experiences of the workshop with Camille, another therapist at the agency. When Camille asks, "Isn't Gary your supervisor?" Vanessa feels defensive and misunderstood. Later that day, Vanessa decides to go to her agency director and ask his opinion of the situation. He tells her not to be concerned about it and that Camille "worries about everything." During her next supervision session, Vanessa chooses not to mention either conversation to Gary.

Is Gary in danger of violating the principle of avoiding dual relationships? Has he already violated this principle? Was Camille's reaction appropriate? The agency director's? How do you evaluate Vanessa's choice to talk to her agency director? To not apprise Gary of the conversations with Camille and the agency director?

Example: Derek is a professor of clinical psychology. He is a gay male whose research is exclusively in the area of developmental issues for gay youth. When a candidate for admission lists a gay support group as a counseling activity, Derek insists that he be interviewed, although his academic record was not as strong as some other candidates. Louis is interviewed and Derek is his sole supporter. Although the admissions committee is a bit uncomfortable with their decision, they decide to admit Louis and they assign him to Derek for advising. Derek calls Louis immediately to suggest that he be involved in Derek's research. Louis, who informs Derek that he is gay, is ecstatic.

Does this situation describe the early stages of a dual relationship or a legitimate example of professional mentoring? Would the situation have been different if Louis had applied to this academic program for the distinct purpose of working with Derek? Are there other ethical issues that the faculty should be considering? What would have been your opinion if you were on the admissions committee? Would you feel differently if the faculty member in question were the sole woman on the faculty and the student was one of the few female applicants for the year?

Example: Sharon is a good therapist. In her work with Jeanne, her supervisor, she has been very open and unguarded. Sharon had a very troubled past and she has struggled hard to get where she is. A couple of times Sharon has shared some of her personal pain with Jeanne during intense supervision sessions. Sharon and Jeanne feel very close to each other. In the past couple of weeks, Sharon has not looked well. She's jumpy and short with Jeanne. When Jeanne pursues this change in behavior, Sharon begins to cry

and tells Jeanne that she has recently returned to an old cocaine habit. She begs Jeanne not to share her secret, promising that she will discontinue using the drug. She also asks that she be allowed to continue seeing clients.

How is power being negotiated in this example? How does each person stand to be damaged by this dual relationship? Has Jeanne been inappropriate up to this point? What should Jeanne do at this point to be ethical?

Example: Margaret is a school counselor who has been assigned a trainee from the local university for the academic year. As she observes Noah work with elementary school children, she is increasingly impressed with his skills. She asks him to work with Peter, a nine-year-old, who has not adjusted well to his parents' recent divorce. Again, she is impressed with Noah's skill, his warmth and understanding, and, ultimately, with the success he has in working with Peter. Margaret is a single parent who is concerned about her nine-year-old son. She decides to ask Noah to see him. Noah is complimented by her confidence in him. Margaret's son attends a different school, but she arranges to have Noah see him after school hours.

How is Noah vulnerable in this example? How is Margaret's son vulnerable? If Noah had had second thoughts about this situation, what are his recourses for resolution?

Competence

We all remember the feelings we had when we saw our first client. We might have doubted the sanity of our supervisor to trust an incompetent with someone who had a problem. And if we were observed for that session, it was even worse. (One of us recalls a nightmare where I am electrocuted by my audiorecorder as I try to record my first counseling session!) For most of us, those feelings waned with time, helped by encouraging feedback from our supervisors and the accumulation of experience. The feelings also lessened as we grew to appreciate that therapy is at least part art and probably a combination of many things, only some of which we control. Finally, the feelings diminished through the authenticity of the relationships we shared with our clients and the positive results of those relationships. The issue of our own competence became less and less bothersome to us. Eventually, we felt good enough about our own abilities that we agreed to supervise the work of another. Now we are involved in the developmental process at two levels: we are overseer of the initial steps taken by our supervisees while we continue to develop ourselves, and at times we can appreciate how far we have come by observing the tentative work of those under our charge.

There is something very self-assuring about having some experience and being able to see from where one has come. There also is something seductive, and even dangerous, about being in such a position: supervisors can forget to question their competence. This is not to imply that it is admirable to remain professionally insecure, but that it is vital for supervisors to remember that the issue of competence is one of the most central questions in the process of clinical supervision. Supervisors must remain competent not only as therapists, but also as judges of another's abilities, while being competent in many facets of supervision itself. In fact, the whole issue of competence, both for supervisors and supervisees, is central to the most pressing ethical responsibility of all, that of monitoring client welfare (Sherry, 1991).

Monitoring Supervisee Competence. By definition, the supervisee is not yet competent to practice independently. But if supervisees are to improve as practitioners, they must be challenged. Attending to the best interests of both client and supervisee *simultaneously* is the greatest clinical and ethical challenge of supervision (Sherry, 1991). Furthermore, monitoring supervisee competence begins with the assumption that the supervisor is a seasoned clinician.

The first of 11 core areas promulgated by ACES in the *Standards for Counseling Supervisors* (Supervision Interest Network, 1990) requires that the supervisor be an effective counselor. It goes without saying that the supervisor must be more advanced than the trainee in all areas that the trainee is practicing. This relates not only to the generic practice of psychotherapy, but to specific clinical problems as well. Most supervisors realize that they cannot be all things to all people. Yet they are tempted to forget this bit of wisdom when a trainee wants to gain some experience in an area that the supervisor is unfamiliar with. The helping professions, for better or worse, have become a field with many specialties. There are times when it can be a difficult decision whether the supervisor's skills are sufficient to supervise in a particular area. Supervisors would be wise to have a clear sense of the kinds of cases that they would either not supervise or would supervise only under certain conditions [e.g., for a limited number of sessions, for the purposes of referral, or, as suggested by Hall (1988a) and Sherry (1991), with the aid of a consultant]. Examples of specialties that some supervisors might choose to shy away from include substance abuse, sexual or physical abuse, eating disorders, or certain personality disorders.

Rinas and Clyne-Jackson (1988) defined competence as including ample relevant experience. They criticized some faculty in training programs for placing too heavy an emphasis on theory because they lack practical experience of their own. These authors asserted that such instruction may leave students inadequately prepared for the ethical and clinical complexities that arise in actual practice. A study done with psychiatric residents supported this contention (Rodenhauser, 1992). When directors of residency programs in psychiatry were asked to characterize practices and problems in their programs, issues of skill diversity of the faculty, theoretical flexibility, and overall competence emerged.

As the field has become more aware of the importance of cultural factors in therapy, experts in ethical issues have included competence in cultural matters as a significant area to be monitored by supervisors (Sherry, 1991; Vasquez, 1992). Again, such competence must first be acquired by the supervisor in order for the supervisor to assist the supervisee to work with persons representing diverse groups, as well as for the supervisor to be successful on this dimension in supervisory relationships.

Although it is essential that the supervisor be a competent clinician, the greater energy in supervision is in the oversight responsibility of the trainee's competence. Supervisors must be assured that the supervisee is generally capable, as well as specifically capable regarding any given situation. The only way that supervisors can have confidence in their judgments is by using direct forms of supervision, at least on an intermittent basis. Finally, Vasquez (1992) noted that part of the responsibility of the supervisor is to help the supervisee become a self-evaluator. In other words, if one of the ethical mandates of all helping professions is to practice only within one's competence, supervisees must become able to make such determinations for themselves.

Chapter 8 on evaluation offered assistance to the supervisor for monitoring supervisee competence.

Competence in the Practice of Supervision. As the knowledge and skill base for clinical supervision have increased, it will become more compulsory that supervisors be competent in the practice of supervision *above and beyond their competence as a therapist.* (See Appendix A for the ACES *Standards for Counseling Supervisors*). Although there are examples of professions already demanding such competence for clinical supervisors (e.g., AAMFT), this expectation is not yet uniform. Borders and Cashwell (1992) surveyed legislation regarding supervisor criteria and conduct of supervision for counselor licensure applicants and found that few state boards recognized the need for specialized training in supervision. Furthermore, they found state boards to be more attentive to the conduct of supervision than to criteria for supervisors. Unfortunately, regulatory bodies do not always reflect the highest standards of practice as described in the professional literature. Frick, McCartney, and Lazarus (1995) found that of the 10 supervisors charged by the American Psychiatric Association

Ethics Committee to supervise sexually exploitative psychiatrists none had any formal training in ethics supervision. Additionally, only one of the 10 supervisors had been given any information about the ethics charges and findings of the committee for the psychiatrist under supervision.

If, as Rinas and Clyne-Jackson (1988) charged, training program faculty are too academic in their approach to supervision, it is sometimes the case that field supervisors are too caught up in their immediate context and do not stay abreast of changes in national standards for practice. Navin, Beamish, and Johanson (1995) studied the ethics practice of field supervisors and compared them to the ACES *Ethical Guidelines for Counseling Supervisors* (Supervision Interest Network, 1993). Whether the problem was standards that are too lofty or field settings that lack adequate regulation, these authors found a good bit of disparity between standards and practice, at least for the supervision of practitioners at the master's level. Disney and Stephens (1994) noted that national standards (such as those for counseling supervisors) may represent the ideal and that liability is more likely to be determined using state standards. However, the court may refer to such standards as a guide. It would be an error, therefore, to assume that national standards are irrelevant for local practice.

Remaining Competent. Many seasoned professionals become complacent with their degree of competence and wean themselves from the professional literature and/or attendance at professional meetings or workshops (Campbell, 1994). When licenses or certifications do not require continuing education, this separation from the evolution of mental health practice can be complete (Overholser & Fine, 1990). Although most professionals would probably agree with the necessity of continuing education for all practitioners, and for supervisors in particular, the task itself can be enormous. Not only should supervisors be current in their own professional specialties, but they should also be aware of the substantial developments that are being made in the area of clinical supervision. Some would add that supervisors should be at least minimally aware of specialties that dovetail with their own. And, as has already been stated, awareness in current developments to assist an understanding of the impact of cultural phenomena in both therapy and supervision is also required.

In addition to continuing education, a liberal use of consultation with professional peers is important to prevent the kind of isolation that diminishes competence (Sherry, 1991). Supervision is a serious activity and one with unforeseen challenges. It is important that a supervisor has a network of colleagues, a place to go, for consultation so that the demands of supervision can be met adequately.

Being able to consult with a colleague seems especially important when trying to balance the client's therapy needs with the supervisee's training needs (Upchurch, 1985). There can be a rather narrow band of case complexity that will challenge the trainee without jeopardizing the client. Furthermore, interactions with another supervisor can increase a supervisor's skills in ways that may not have been predicted.

> *Example:* Dwayne has been a licensed psychologist in private practice for over 20 years. His therapeutic approach is primarily psychodynamic. Dwayne receives a call from a small group practice consisting of mental health counselors and marriage and family therapists. They are looking for a psychologist who wants to contract with them for supervision. Their interest is mostly that the psychologist be able to evaluate certain clients for possible referral to a psychologist or a psychiatrist. Dwayne has never supervised anyone and is ready for a new challenge. He makes an appointment to meet with the staff of the practice group.

What are the competency issues embedded in this example? If Dwayne decides to take this group on, what does he need to consider to be ethically sound? What conditions for supervision are advisable? As you understand it, is this arrangement legally defensible?

Confidentiality

Confidentiality is the ethical principle given the most attention in most training programs. In addition to liability concerns, we believe this is so because confidentiality represents the essence of therapy (a safe place where secrets and hidden fears can be exposed) and because much of our professional status comes from being the bearer of such secrets. We earn our clients' respect and the respect of others by the posture we take toward confidentiality. There was a time when confidentiality was a sacred obligation. In recent years, however, confidentiality has become the step-sibling to safety and judicial judgment. As a result, the issues surrounding confidentiality have become more complicated. In a recent study, Pope and Vetter (1992) surveyed over 1,300 psychologists about incidents that they found ethically troubling. Of the 703 incidents reported, the greatest number (128) fell into the category of confidentiality. Therefore, it seems that the most sacred trust in mental health practice is also the most vulnerable to insult. And as with all therapeutic components, the implications for supervision are more complex still.

Before we consider the legal realities regarding confidentiality, we would like to outline those dimensions that the supervisor must safeguard. First, the supervisor must be sure that the trainee keeps confidential all client information except for the purposes of supervision. Because supervision allows for a third-party discussion of the therapy situation, the trainee must be reminded that this type of discourse cannot be repeated elsewhere. In group supervision, the supervisor must reiterate this point and take the extra precaution of having cases presented using first names only and with as few demographic details as possible (Strein & Hershenson, 1991). When videotape or live supervision is employed with additional trainees present, the only recourse for the supervisor is to emphasize and reemphasize the importance of confidentiality. When students are asked to tape their sessions, they must be reminded that they have in their possession confidential "documents." Notes on clients should use code numbers rather than names and be guarded with great care.

In addition to having some assurance that trainees are meeting the requirement of confidentiality, the supervisor must be sure that trainees view the information received in supervision as confidential and not as akin to something read in a text of case studies. There is a certain discipline required to view someone else's clients as one's own as far as privacy is concerned.

Finally, there is the trainee's right to privacy and the supervisor's responsibility to keep information confidential. It is inevitable that supervision will be an opportunity for the supervisor to hear something about the trainee that would not be discovered in a less personal learning situation. For example, the trainee might share some painful aspect of childhood as it relates to a client. The divulging of such information might come from the trainee's concern that personal history should not detract from therapy and with the request that the supervisor monitor the case more closely. We can all imagine several situations in which such an encounter could take place; the topics could range from family secrets and sexual orientation to prejudicial attitudes that the trainee believes must be divulged. Prior to such an occurrence, the supervisee should understand the circumstances for revealing information obtained in supervision. Knowing that evaluative information from supervision may be passed along to faculty and that any particular issue that troubles the supervisor may be discussed with faculty colleagues allows the supervisee to make an informed decision about what to reveal in supervision (Sherry, 1991).

There is still some occasional confusion in the helping professions regarding the distinctions between confidentiality, privacy, and privileged communication. Confidentiality is defined by Siegel (1979) as follows: "Confidentiality involves professional ethics rather than any legalism and indicates an explicit promise or contract to reveal nothing about an individual except under conditions agreed to by the source or subject" (p. 251). Privacy is the other side of confidentiality. It is the client's right not to have private information divulged without informed consent, including the information gained in therapy. Privileged communication, on the other hand, is a legal concept and is the result of state statue. It refers to the right of clients not to have their con-

fidential communications used in open court without their consent. Therefore, "although all privileged communications are confidential communications, some confidential communications may not be privileged" (Disney & Stephens, 1994, p. 26).

Although these three terms are vital in therapy and supervision, they are not absolute. In fact, knowing the limits of each is as serious a responsibility for the clinician as honoring their intent. It is ultimately an individual decision when the therapist or supervisor will decide to overturn the client's (or supervisee's) right of privacy and break confidentiality. However, there are a number of cases where either legal precedent, state law, or a value of a higher order dictates such a direction. Those typically included as exceptions to privilege are reported by Corey et al. (1993) and are as follows:

1. When the therapist is appointed by the court
2. When there is a suicidal risk
3. When the client initiates a malpractice suit against the therapist (or supervisor)
4. When a client's (or supervisee's) mental health is questioned as part of a civil action
5. When the client is a child (under age 16) and is a victim of a crime
6. When information is mandated by the court
7. When clients need hospitalization for a psychological disorder
8. When clients express the intent to commit a crime or when they are accurately assessed as being dangerous to others or to themselves

Because privileged communication is a legal matter, it is always wise to receive legal counsel when confidential information is demanded. Outside court proceedings many situations fall into gray areas.

The trend in the helping professions seems to be toward a more guarded view of confidentiality. This professional obligation seems to be increasingly vulnerable to legal interpretation. It is considered wise, therefore, to make a discussion of confidentiality and its limits a common practice in therapy and supervision.

Marketplace Issues

As more states pass legislation to regulate all the mental health professions, the need for clinical supervisors to supervise entry-level professionals is increasing. At the same time, changes in mental health delivery systems require that supervisors stay informed so as to keep supervisees informed and to avoid any business arrangements that would prove to be unethical and/or illegal.

A common practice of the past involved the supervisor "signing off" for supervisees, often not because supervision was taking place but because the supervisor's credentials allowed for third-party payment while the supervisee's did not. This practice is, of course, unethical and illegal. But other marketplace issues are more ambiguous ethically. For example, should a supervisor accept payment from a supervisee for supervision that will lead to certification or licensure? Under what conditions might this be acceptable? If one is a supervisor for someone outside one's place of employment, what kinds of protections are necessary for the clients of the supervisee? The supervisee? The supervisor? With the introduction of managed care, new duties regarding informed consent are likely, as well as a careful selection of appropriate providers of care (Appelbaum, 1993). In short, the marketplace is changing dramatically as a result of legislation and changes in health care systems. It is the ethical and legal responsibility of clinical supervisors to stay abreast of relevant developments and to assure that supervisees' practice is consistent with ethical mandates and with the law.

ETHICAL DECISION MAKING

As we already have conveyed, the relationship between ethics and the law can be perceived to be a very close one. This is not only true for the human services, but also for society at large. The great danger of this perception is the pairing of what is "right" with "what I can get away with," leaving only "what I can't get away with" as "wrong." Knowing full well that most unethical behavior is not confronted, the practitioner becomes more likely to lose sight of the moral constants. The potential consequence is that the helping professions become another example of the law dictating professional ethics.

The only reasonable alternative to this approach is putting ethics in the foreground, in both training and practice, for therapists and clinical supervisors. Thinking regarding ethical issues should be proactive and not reactive. Waiting for ethical issues to emerge in supervision seems to set up the conditions for crisis training, not ethics training. The point is that ethical practice is a way of professional existence, not a command of a body of knowledge. Anything short of this is an inadequate position for the clinical supervisor.

One aid to ethical development is for training programs to use experiential learning and/or case analysis (cf. Storm & Haug, 1997). Many ethical mishaps result from acts of omission, not intentional malice (Bernard, 1981). Such omissions are more likely if professionals have not had an opportunity to experience the ins and outs of a similar situation. The use of simulation and behavioral rehearsal is an excellent way to safely allow both trainees and supervisors to face difficult situations, try alternate resolutions, and evaluate their outcomes.

Kitchener (1984) suggested that ethical codes are inadequate for deliberation and that, instead, ethical principles must be considered when ethical dilemmas surface. Because principles are more foundational in nature, they are relevant when ethical codes are vague, contradictory, or perhaps overly prescriptive for a unique situation. The principles Kitchener advocated are *autonomy* (both being responsible for one's behavior and having freedom of choice), *beneficence* (contributing to the well-being of others), *nonmaleficence* ("above all, do no harm"), *justice* (fairness in dealings with all people), and *fidelity* (the promotion of honesty and fulfilling commitments and contracts). These five principles, then, would provide the backdrop for the use of any ethical code for a specific situation. Tarvydas (1995) noted that much of our influence on supervisees may lie in our ability to model these principles. Additionally, Corey et al. (1993) proposed that Kitchener's principles be considered within the cultural context for each ethical situation. In other words, a cultural lens is essential to interpret principles ethically for any unique situation.

Finally, ethical decision making includes a cognitive process, a map to follow, from the presentation of the ethical dilemma to its resolution. Corey et al. (1993) suggested the following steps:

1. Identify the problem or dilemma.
2. Identify the potential issues involved.
3. Review relevant ethical guidelines.
4. Obtain consultation.
5. Consider possible and probable courses of action.
6. Enumerate the consequences of various decisions.
7. Decide what appears to be the best course of action.   (pp. 11–12)

CONCLUSION

As gatekeepers of the profession, clinical supervisors will continue to be heavily involved with ethical standards for practice. The most instrumental approach to this responsibility is to be well informed and personally and professionally sanguine. Both are accomplished by continually putting ethics in the foreground of discussion, contemplation, and practice. In this case, perhaps more than any other, supervisors' primary responsibility is to model what they aspire to teach.

CHAPTER 10

Managing Clinical Supervision

Traditionally, roles and responsibilities held by supervisors have been described as either administrative or clinical. Although there is almost always some overlap and, indeed, some supervisors fulfill both clinical and administrative duties for the same supervisees, these terms have helped to differentiate supervisory functions within an organization. The clinical supervisor has a dual investment in the quality of services offered to clients and the professional development of the trainee; the administrative supervisor, while concerned about service delivery, must also focus on matters such as organizational structure, personnel concerns, and fiscal issues, to name just a few. The administrative supervisor will, by necessity, need to view any particular piece of datum in the larger context (Falvey, 1987); the clinical supervisor will be more likely to focus on the uniqueness of the case at hand. In fact, the argument has been made that the tasks demanded of each role are divergent enough to make them essentially incompatible (Erera & Lazar, 1994).

Our position is that there is a strong and necessary component to clinical supervision that is managerial in nature, thus requiring skills that are similar to those used by administrative supervisors. One would have a difficult time accepting the information presented in either the chapter on ethics and legal issues or the chapter on clinical evaluation without recognizing that these issues must be managed adequately within the supervisory relationship. Therefore, our goal in this chapter is to address some of the most essential managerial aspects of clinical supervision.

We have chosen the word "managerial" in order to avoid the word "administrative." Borders et al. (1991) used the term "executive" to refer to the same set of behaviors and skills. All of these terms imply some choreography of an organizational system to achieve clinical supervision goals.

There are at least three matters that complicate a discussion of the managerial tasks of clinical supervision. The first is a bias among many mental health practitioners (clinical supervisors included) that managerial matters are tiresome, a necessary evil that detracts from, rather than enhances, one's clinical supervision. This bias is supported, in part, by Kadushin (1985), who found that the most highly ranked stress reported by clinical supervisors was "dissatisfaction with administrative 'housekeeping'" (p. 321). More recently, Kadushin (1992a, b) sampled a large number of social work supervisors and supervisees about supervisor strengths and shortcomings. Both supervisors and supervisees identified enacting managerial responsibilities as the major shortcoming of supervisors. Comments from both groups included the themes of communication, advocacy, time management, and planning. Although the supervisors were frank in delineating their shortcomings, it was the supervisees' comments that demonstrate the potential damage when managerial tasks are not attended to: "I never have his full attention," "My supervisor is wishy-washy . . . and doesn't support staff," "morale is very low," "He shows a chronic inability to structure a conference so as to avoid interruptions," "There is a lack of periodic feedback . . ." (Kadushin, 1992a, pp. 15–17). Kadushin (1992b) further reported that it was managerial failure that affected their work with clients that most distressed supervisees. Therefore, the managerial aspect of clinical supervision was viewed as distinct from other managerial duties. In short, the supervisees surveyed by Kadushin gave support to the notion that a lack of managerial skill can cancel out the supervisor's fine clinical skill. Supervisees can only benefit from knowledge and expertise that is transferred in an organized and consistent fashion.

From the two Kadushin studies, it would seem then that managerial tasks are avoided because they are stressful. We may surmise from this that supervisors are less prepared to accomplish these tasks than they are the purely clinical tasks of mentoring junior therapists. A vicious cycle follows where the clinical supervisor gives lower priority to those elements of clinical supervision that smack of management because these chores are inherently stressful, in part because the supervisor is not adequately prepared to succeed in their execution, thus leaving the supervisee frustrated with the supervisor around these issues and adding to the stress experienced by the supervisor when facing these same issues in the future.

The second complicating matter is an assumption that clinical perceptiveness and managerial competence are rarely found in the same individual. This is similar to the assumption about absentminded professors, that they can be brilliant in their field but have little ability to negotiate the real world. Although there is some basis for most stereotypes, we believe that in many instances a lack of organization is the result of systemic properties, rather than a deficit of inherent individual ability. In other words, if the managerial aspects of clinical supervision are isolated for the purpose of strengthening these skills, such scrutiny will lead to increased managerial competence among clinical supervisors. If the organization accepts the myth that clinical skill and managerial skill are incompatible, little change will occur.

The third complicating factor to our discussion is the reality that in some organizations there is no distinction between clinical supervision and administrative supervision. Supervisors are asked to wear one blended hat without the luxury of a clear focus in either direction. Several authors have commented on the inherent challenges of blending administrative and clinical supervision (Ercra & Lazar, 1994; Hardcastle, 1991; Henderson, 1994; Rodway, 1991). We acknowledge this dilemma as a real one and hope that having some clarity on the types of managerial activities that directly affect clinical supervision will somehow help the blended supervisor to be more deliberate in all activities.

With these complications in mind, we will begin by commenting on the importance of understanding an organizational context for clinical as well as administrative supervisors. We will then argue for the importance of managerial competence for the delivery of clinical supervision. Then we will consider the difference when supervision is offered within one system (organization) versus when two systems are involved. This will be followed by an examination of managerial competency in both university settings and field settings with the hope of eliminating any mystery about what constitutes an organized approach to supervision. Finally, we will suggest additional guidelines through which a clinical supervisor can attain managerial competence.

UNDERSTANDING ORGANIZATIONAL CONTEXT

The clinical supervisor cannot manage without some rudimentary understanding of the organizational context, or culture, within which the supervisor must function. Sparks and Loucks-Horsley (1989) outlined necessary organizational conditions for the professional development of teaching staff. Applying these to clinical supervision, they are as follows:

1. *The staff has a common set of goals.* It is essential that the organization value clinical supervision, rather than the person of the supervisor attempting to carry this torch. When it is the goal of the organization that clinical supervision be conducted well, more resources will be devoted to the planning and implementation of supervision.

2. *The administration models a norm of collegiality.* The tasks, challenges, and crises inevitably accompanying clinical supervision demand a backdrop of support, open communication, and collegiality from top administration to the supervisee. Although the evaluation of the supervisee implies a hierarchy, the organization must demonstrate an essential openness that assures that each person will be respected and treated as a valuable member of the team.

3. *The organization promotes professional development.* The goals of clinical supervision can only succeed when others are being challenged to develop professionally as well. A climate where seasoned staff are completing their duties in a pro forma manner is anathema to challenging supervisees to take advantage of various opportunities to challenge themselves.

4. *Progress towards goals is monitored actively, rather than waiting for outcome evaluation.* The confident, vital organization monitors itself frequently to be sure that it is on track. Obstacles are identified and handled as an organizational challenge, rather than allowing a situation to deteriorate and to be judged as showing a lack of competence of particular staff members.

5. *Support for clinical supervision is appropriately generous.* As important as shared goals and a collegial atmosphere are, they are not enough to support the goals of clinical supervision. Rather, the organization must be appropriately generous with its resources, time perhaps being the most precious of these. As Kadushin (1992a) discovered, both supervisors and supervisees felt that supervisors did not have the time to fulfill their duties appropriately. Organizations must not be penny wise and dollar foolish regarding the role of clinical supervision.

Although these descriptions of organizational context might be incomplete, they give the clinical supervisor a place to start in judging whether an organization is prepared to support the functions of clinical supervision. Additionally, they can provide a handle for the supervisor in determining what feels wrong in an organization when attempting to meet supervisory responsibilities. Congress (1992) noted that ethical decision making is controlled by agency culture rather than individual direction. The supervisor who has not attempted to evaluate organizational context may be unprepared for a discrepancy between a supervision goal and the culture within which supervision is occurring. Most likely, it is the supervision, not the culture, that will be compromised when there is such an occurrence.

IMPORTANCE OF
MANAGERIAL COMPETENCE

Even though there are many references to the importance of being organized in one's delivery of clinical supervision, there are very few direct data supporting the importance of managerial competence for clinical supervisors (Holloway, 1995). A distinct exception to this is a study conducted by Eisikovits et al. (1986) that looked at the relationship of eight factors—one of which was managerial competence of supervisors—to both service delivery and work environment.

Conducted in Israel with social workers, the study concluded that the managerial skill factor was correlated with pressure on professionals to be actively involved with the functioning of the agency; viewing the work environment as being highly task oriented; perceiving the agency as emphasizing order, organization, and planning in-service provision; and perceiving the agency as encouraging free expression on the client's part. In addition, these components were interrelated with one another. One surprise of the study was that, although managerial skill was shown to affect both work environment and service delivery positively, it's greatest effect was on the latter.

> *It seems that workers associate the process and components of supervision more with the ecology of service provision than with the ecology of the agency as a work place. Yet, when they do relate the professional development and administrative aspects of supervision to the work environment of the agency, they associate them with an agency's climate which allows them to be autonomous and task-oriented, and thereby enhanced their personal development;. . . . This may suggest that supervisors who emphasize the workers' professional development and who are administratively competent contribute to the workers' sense of mastery and competence in their work and to their perception of the agency as involving them as a group in its everyday functioning.* (Eisikovits et al., 1986, p. 54)

As a result of their findings, Eisikovits et al. recommended enhancing the administrative–managerial skills of clinical supervisors. They also recommended more research on this topic.

Despite the dearth of studies looking specifically at the managerial component of clinical supervision, several authors have asserted that practitioner burnout may indeed be related not only to service demands, but also to a poor administrative structure (Brashears, 1995; Kaslow & Rice, 1985; Malouf, Haas, & Farah, 1983; Murphy & Pardeck, 1986; Stoltenberg & Delworth, 1987). Murphy and Pardeck noted that either authoritarian or laissez-faire styles of management (supervision) add to burnout and that burnout may be more organizational than psychological. Echoing Eisikovits et al. (1986), they recommended that practitioners be involved in program planning, supervision not be viewed as oppressive by nature, and "a lack of planning is not understood to be the only method for encouraging individualism" (Murphy & Pardeck, 1986, p. 40). Brashears (1995) similarly noted that when the administrative tasks of supervision are viewed as too distinct from service delivery this false dichotomy contributed to job stress, burnout, and turnover.

Finally, a study conducted by Russell, Lankford, and Grinnell (1983) suggested that the present situation in the helping professions is in great need of correction. When one large agency was surveyed, 21 of 44 clinical supervisors were perceived as exemplifying an "impoverished" management style, indicating a low concern for people and for production.

We wish to underscore the concept that burnout may be organizational as well as, if not rather than, psychological. From the supervisee's perspective, it makes intuitive sense to us that the best of supervisory relationships or the finest of clinical insights can be sabotaged by weak managerial skills [as was indicated by some of the near desperate comments made by supervisees in Kadushin's (1992a) study]. This can be seen in training situations or in work situations when supervisees are no longer patient or tolerant of inconveniences or frustrations caused by the supervisor who can-

not maintain some level of mastery of the supervisory plan. Supervisees often realize that a lack of managerial skill not only leaves them vulnerable, but also leaves the client and agency vulnerable. When messages are inconsistent, communication erratic, procedures unclear or not adhered to, and conferences rushed, the entire experience of service delivery under supervision becomes tainted. Because of lack of experience, trainees or new employees are hard pressed to distinguish their feelings about service delivery from their feelings about supervision. Supervisors must realize, therefore, that signs of frustration or burnout may be feedback *to* the supervisor rather than *about* the supervisee.

To focus on burnout is to focus on the negative effects of managerial incompetence. Managerial competence, however, enhances positive experience or, as Lowy (1983) stated, "[T]he learning and teaching transactions in supervision require an organizational structure in order to become implementable" (p. 60). The educational literature is replete with studies confirming the need for structure in the learning process. Often, educational theory tends to be ignored in the helping professions. Yet there is evidence that the process of acquiring clinical skill follows predictable developmental sequences. Sound educational advice, therefore, calls for a stable background (administrative structure) to ground the trainee who is being asked to take risks and meet challenges in the clinical arena.

Finally, we maintain the importance of managerial competence because certain supervisory functions are inextricably tied to such competence. Specifically, evaluation of supervisees and maintaining an operation that meets minimal ethical standards require managerial skill. Because a deficit in these areas can become threatening to supervisors and supervisees alike, we hope that the importance of managerial competence becomes self-evident. But with the minimal attention given to this topic in the clinical supervision literature, it is understandable that these skills remain underdeveloped.

Once we have accepted the importance of the managerial component of clinical supervision, we begin to appreciate the importance of context to supervision. No part of supervision is more immediately affected by the environment than the part that attempts to organize the experience. The organizational context will form the experience even before supervision begins. As we stated earlier, every organization is maintained by a certain set of structural guidelines within which supervision must occur. Therefore, we will look at those systems and how the two major settings for supervision, university and field, require different managerial expertise of the clinical supervisor. But first we will consider the differences when one system is involved in clinical supervision versus when two systems are involved.

TRAINING SYSTEMS

One System

Although graduate training usually requires that the trainee work within at least two different systems, an increasing amount of supervision occurs within one system. Many agencies (used generically to include schools, hospitals, pastoral settings, and the like) incorporate ongoing supervision for postgraduate employees or new employees, often as prerequisites to attaining licensure. Similarly, some institutions of higher education run counseling centers or other training clinics on campus so that students receive clinical supervision and didactic education within more or less the same system (Myers, 1994). Universities often prefer such a setup for the very reasons that we will discuss in this chapter: It is much easier to negotiate one system than it is to react to two. Furthermore, because many of these university centers have training as a primary mission, the supervision needs of staff are not lost in the hustle and bustle of service delivery. The organizational context includes the supervisory function as essential.

University settings that include counseling centers or training clinics are usually viewed enviably by supervisors working in contexts with less of an emphasis on supervision. As was noted by Beavers (1986), such settings are usually less hurried, supervisees can expect individual attention, facilities are usually more than adequate, and supervisors are typically well grounded theoretically. At the same time, the challenges for these training institutions have been noted by several authors and include the essential issue of balancing training responsibilities with the responsibilities of service delivery (Bernard, 1994; Myers & Hutchinson, 1994); identifying, or perhaps recruiting, appropriate clients and matching clients with supervisees (Leddick, 1994; Scanlon & Gold, 1996); managing client expectations (Leddick, 1994); bridging the gap between the academic calendar and client needs (Scanlon & Gold, 1996); and clarifying the roles of professional staff, especially when a tiered system exists, that is, master's-level students supervised by doctoral students who are themselves supervised by faculty supervisors (Dye, 1994; Scanlon & Gold, 1996; West, Bubenzer, & Delmonico, 1994).

There is a downside to being supervised in a training facility. Beavers (1986) noted that, even though the staff may attempt to recruit a wide range of clients, it is most often the case that university settings offer a rather narrow and limited client population. Additionally, university supervisors may have less clinical experience than supervisors found in off-campus settings and are not as "street savvy." In other words, university settings may confront the supervisee with fewer dilemmas resulting from administrative protocol, but this can be reframed as offering the supervisee fewer experiences in negotiating complex systems to achieve service delivery and professional development goals.

As we shall see, as demanding as keeping both service delivery needs and training needs addressed within one system, the complexity of the task grows exponentially when more than one system is involved.

Two Systems: University and Field Site

Often, two systems are involved in the training of an individual supervisee. This, of course, is by design. Departments of social work and psychiatry were perhaps the first to realize the importance of field instruction to supplement academic instruction. Counseling, psychology, and marriage and family therapy, as well as a host of other health professions, also require the student to successfully complete a supervised field experience while still in a degree program. The site supervisor typically accepts the trainee because the supervisor enjoys influencing trainees regarding real client issues and agency circumstances (Holloway & Roehlke, 1987). Often the site supervisor would also like to influence the training program in terms of the preparation offered to trainees prior to field experience. Therefore, both systems have an investment in one another that is both practical and educational. Yet the differences between these two systems and their separate goals often are not acknowledged in a way that allows the principals to work them through. Additionally, adequate communication between the two systems is often wanting (Holtzman & Raskin, 1988; Olsen & Stern, 1990; Shapiro, 1988; Skolnik, 1988). We will address goals and communication separately.

Goals.   Dodds (1986) delineated the major difference between the training institution and the service delivery agency as a difference in population to be served. As depicted in Figure 10.1, the training institution is invested in education and training of its students, whereas the the mental health agency is primarily invested in the delivery

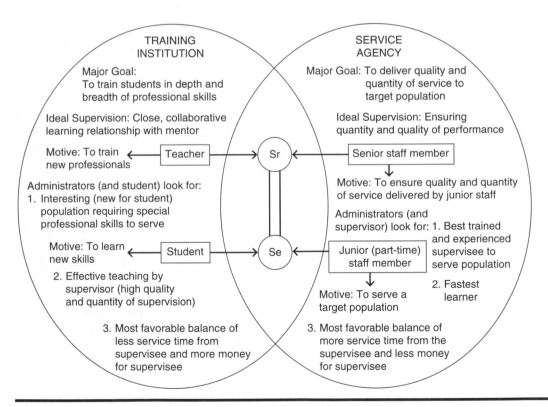

FIGURE 10.1   Overlapping Systems of a Training Institution and a Service Agency
(Sr, supervisor: Se, supervisee)

From J. B. Dodds, (1986), Supervision of psychology trainees in field placements, *Professional Psychology: Research and Practice, 17*(4), 296–300. Copyright © (1986) by the American Psychological Association. Reprinted by permission.

of quantity and quality services to a target population. Dodds warned, however, that to stereotype each system by these goals is to lose sight of each unit's investment in the other's mission. That notwithstanding, the basic goals of each system will determine the motives of that system's primary supervisor and the supervisor's managerial goals. As Figure 10.1 illustrates, the persons who have the responsibility for interfacing these two systems are the university and site supervisors involved. But if they default on this responsibility due to time constraints, disinterest, or the absence of managerial acumen, it is left to the supervisee to interface the two systems. When difficulties emerge, this leaves the least powerful individual (organizationally) to negotiate and attempt to find a resolution.

The first step in mastering the interface between the two systems is in understanding that there will be complications whenever two systems are simultaneously involved with a trainee because of each unit's systemic properties, including their different goals and even different calendars. Once that fact is accepted, supervisors can begin to predict issues that may arise. A primary strategy for reducing problems either within each system or especially between them is to increase the quantity and quality of communication.

Communication. The university supervisor is often very clear about what kinds of communication are expected from the site supervisor; however, a reciprocity of information often is lacking. Shapiro (1988) reported a high burnout rate for site supervisors when there was a significant discrepancy between what was initially communicated to them regarding expectations and the actual demands of supervision, which superseded those expectations. Another error both sides make is to keep information too limited in its focus. For example, there can be ample information about the placement expectations themselves from both sides. But university programs do not keep their field site current with program growth or curriculum changes (Malouf, Haas, & Farah, 1983), and agencies do not let university programs know

when administrative, fiscal, or programmatic changes are being planned or implemented. The result of such incomplete communication can be conflict that could have been avoided or two systems growing less and less relevant to each other without being aware of it. We will consider the types of communications that are desirable between university and site later in this chapter.

THE ESSENTIAL INGREDIENT: A SUPERVISION PLAN

Before we focus on the specific managerial duties of the supervisor, it is important that we give our attention to the primary task of all clinical supervisors—arriving at a cohesive supervision plan. One of the greatest misconceptions of those not in managerial positions is that administration is made up of filling out forms and making on-the-spot decisions. Random power and paper work come to be identified with the managerial function of any organization. On the contrary, the essential ingredients of managerial competence and the source of all sustained influence are planning and foresight (Covey, Merrill, & Merrill, 1994). Beyond these is the discipline to implement the plan in a methodical fashion, which, admittedly, often includes the creation of some paper work. It is interesting to note, however, that Eisikovits et al. (1986) found that highly competent supervisors did not attempt to control supervisees through unusual demands for written accountability. Rather, it can be assumed that competency includes the skills of efficiency and precision and that this is passed on through one's expectations of others. Henderson (1994) concurred, yet noted that it is indeed challenging for supervisors to establish a system that safeguards both supervisees and clients, yet is not perceived as burdensome by staff.

The primary responsibility of the clinical supervisor, therefore, is to plan an efficient training experience that will culminate in the emergence of a capable and realistic practitioner, while safeguarding client welfare. This goal will be frustrated if supervision is random or repetitive throughout the trainee's program or internship. The antithesis of planning occurs when a supervisor accepts a trainee, sets weekly appointments with the trainee, and lets things just happen or when a university instructor places students in field sites and then conducts weekly group supervision sessions that are based on self-report and little else. In both of these instances, there is no evidence of an awareness of trainees' developmental needs or of the desirability of some variety of learning modes. This is supervision as you go, not planned supervision.

Leddick and Dye (1987) reported that trainees often equate supervisor effectiveness with a comprehensive supervisory plan. "Trainees expect to learn from a variety of modalities including didactic presentations, feedback and evaluation, individual and group supervision, observing the supervisor as therapist, group discussion of cases and issues and peer observation" (p. 149). This sentiment is echoed by a growing number of training programs as they experiment with different methods of supervision. For example, Liddle et al. (1984) discussed a multimodal approach to training supervisors that included live supervision of supervision, a seminar to examine supervision issues, and individual meetings between the trainer and supervisor in training to discuss developmental concerns.

Focusing on supervision modalities, however, does not present a complete plan. Hardcastle (1991) reviewed the four functions of agency supervision, all of which have implications for clinical supervision:

1. *Teaching, training, and consultation.* This is the aspect of clinical supervision that is most easily identifiable and usually most rewarding to supervisors. It includes case conferences where knowledge is transferred, the supervisee is tutored through either challenge or support, and clinical expertise is central.

2. *Monitoring and accountability.* Hardcastle found that this function was the most time consuming of the four. Such clinical supervision activities included observing the supervisee, monitoring supervisee development, overseeing written documentation of counseling, screening clients, and ensuring client welfare. This function may also include reporting the outcome of clinical services to higher administration.

3. *Work design and coordination.* It is noteworthy that Hardcastle found this function to be one to which supervisors devoted the least amount of time. It is the time spent here, however, that allows for a sophisticated supervision program to exist. Without taking the time to design supervision activities and to work out the logistics, supervision in busy settings can continue to resemble the tail wagging the dog. Beyond designing supervision from beginning to end, supervisors must also coordinate supervision with their other agency responsibilities and with the responsibilities of others.

4. *Communication and linkage within agency and with external resources.* Clinical supervisors may not perceive themselves as "middle management," but they usually relate to feelings of being in the middle. Communication and linkage often become a very time draining task. Supervisors become troubleshooters for their supervisees; conversely, they also serve as the voice of the administration to supervisees. Furthermore, when client concerns translate to a need for referral or collaboration with external bodies, the supervisor inevitably is involved.

Rich (1993) proposed a similar, though somewhat different, typology to describe the major functions of clinical supervisors (see Table 10.1). Among the four functions proposed by Rich is that of staff socialization, a critical but often unaddressed supervisor function that includes directing supervisees toward professional values and addressing issues such as agency culture. Table 10.1 depicts Rich's four functions, subfunctions, and activities assigned to each.

Both the Hardcastle (1991) and Rich (1993) descriptions of the different aspects of supervision can provide an outline for what must be included in the management of clinical supervision. A supervision plan, therefore, will address all areas delineated, allocating time, resources, and personnel to cover each. The driving force will be a vision of what must transpire for supervisees to achieve competence. From there, the clinical supervisor

TABLE 10.1   A Four-Function Typology of Clinical Supervision

FUNCTION	SUBFUNCTIONS	ACTIVITIES WITHIN FUNCTION
Facilitation: Fostering a work environment that encourages creative thinking, autonomy, and communication and increases staff confidence	Team building	Facilitate the development of a mutually supportive and interpersonally effective staff group
	Goal clarification	Clarify and articulate organizational goals with respect to service delivery and individual client cases
	Problem Solving	Encourage staff to explore and develop methods for problem-solving issues and cases they may face
	Injection of new ideas	Foster the development of innovative thinking, introduce new ideas, and encourage the testing and adoption of new ideas
Staff development: Development of training or teaching environment in which skill learning is encouraged and opportunities for skill development and growth are provided	Skill building	Provide training opportunities for professional skill development in areas directly pertinent to staff clinical work
	Building employee knowledge base	Provide material and information about cases, methods, resources, the profession, etc., to build professional staff knowledge
	Developing employee behaviors	Help staff adjust to new ideas and methods and support the development and retention of new techniques and behaviors
	Employee self-awareness	Help staff recognize personal feelings, values, strengths, and limitations and assist in personal and professional growth
Staff socialization: Integrating and socializing new and existing direct care staff into expected and desired set of organizational and professional values, ethics, standards and culture	Organizing employee experiences	Interpret and organize staff past experiences in order to help them use these as the basis for future professional work
	Inculcating standards	Develop in staff an awareness of expected organizational and professional standards and ethics
	Orientation and integration	Introduce and integrate new staff into the professional and personal culture or the organization, the profession, and other staff
	Monitoring employee attitudes	Monitor staff attitudes toward work, clients, and other staff and correct attitudes that are incongruent with expectations
Service delivery: Assuring the ethical and competent delivery of client services in accordance with organizational and professional standards	Evaluating client services	Monitor and review the nature of client services, the level of staff skills, and the nature of staff–client interactions
	Improving client services	Develop a program of clinical services capable of meeting client needs
	Involvement in client services	Direct provision of client services in order to model desired clinical skills and to provide additional services where needed
	Protecting client welfare	Ensure that client rights are in no way compromised legally, ethically, or emotionally by staff involvement

From P. Rich (1993), The form, function, and content of clinical supervision: An integrated model, *The Clinical Supervisor, 11*(1), 150–151. Copyright (1993) by the Haworth Press, Inc., 10 Alice Street, Binghamton, NY. Reprinted by permission.

must create the context within which learning can occur. This context must be ideological and structural. It is our impression that clinical supervisors to date have been much stronger in the former than the latter, the latter receiving emphasis in both descriptions of supervisor functions. With the recent emergence of a variety of supervision models and techniques, it is even more important that supervisors be organized and appreciative of the central role that managerial ability plays within supervision.

The remainder of this chapter will outline some of the issues that can either enhance or detract from the goal of offering clinical supervision that is managed well. In and of itself, well-organized supervision is not necessarily good supervision.

But if clinical supervisors have addressed the categories that follow, they can have some confidence that supervisory efforts will not be undermined by a crumbling structural base.

THE UNIVERSITY SUPERVISOR

Our focus in this section will be those tasks specific to the university supervisor as overseer of trainees in field placements. We do not address those aspects of clinical supervision that occur on campus in prepracticum or other training contexts. Nor do we address the role of the university supervisor when the university *is* the site. These responsibilities will be covered in the later section on the site supervisor. Because our discussion will pertain only to local field placements, we will not be examining the concerns when students (usually doctoral students) relocate to complete an internship. Finally, we remind the reader that only the managerial aspect of clinical supervision will be covered here. Therefore, we will not be addressing the clinical supervision that may be offered on campus while a trainee is out in the field.

Preparing Students

Unless a training program has the luxury of a full-time (or even part-time) director of training or field placement coordinator, the first problem to hit university supervisors is coordinating an advising system that will determine when students will be eligible and available to take either a practicum or internship and determine if there are ample supervisory resources to cover the number of requests in any given semester. All too often, students discuss such matters with their academic advisors, but the procedure to get this information to the practicum or internship instructor is less than tightly managed. Sometimes this is no problem, but often it creates an atmosphere of rushed placements or compromises in placement. When matters are rushed, the field supervisor may think that the university program is slightly out of control and may feel less accountable to the university and the student as a result. At the very least, both student and campus supervisor begin the ex-

perience with nerves jangled and matters slightly off center when practicum and internship do not enjoy some organizational planning prior to their beginning.

A second issue is how much lead time a student should allow in finding an appropriate field placement. This will be determined by the following:

1. *The amount of local competition for field sites.* If there are other universities nearby or if other programs within the university are seeking the same sites, the student must start out earlier than if the market is wide open.
2. *The specificity of the student's interests.* If the student has a very specific interest not represented in a variety of sites (e.g., hospice work), then more lead time will be required.
3. *The policy of the specific agency.* Some agencies will only accept interns during a certain time period or may require a résumé and more than one interview, all of which are time consuming. To be assured enough time to find a site, the student should assume that there will be some hurdles to negotiate in the selection process.
4. *The relationship established between the university and a particular site.* Some sites not only want, but expect, students every semester. Because of their past dealings with the university, they require only minimal contact with the student prior to starting the field experience.

Selecting Sites

There is a good deal in the professional literature to assist doctoral students in selecting an appropriate internship (e.g., Brill, Wolkin, & McKeel, 1987; Gloria & Robinson, 1994; Grace, 1985; Stewart & Stewart, 1996), with little attention given to this topic for the more common placement of premaster's-level mental health trainees. In some academic programs it is the training director or the faculty supervisor who makes the initial contact with a potential field site. In other programs it is the student who makes the first contact. In either case, the faculty supervisor must assume a role in helping the student determine the appropriateness of a particular site based on three categories of variables: program factors, student factors, and agency factors.

Program factors are those baseline conditions that must be met before a site can be deemed as meeting training goals. For example, the program may require that students not only see a variety of clients, but have continuity in their work. Therefore, a crisis center that revolves around single-client contacts would not be an appropriate placement. Or the program may require that audiotaping be allowed for the purposes of campus supervision. This may be a nonnegotiable item for some sites and one that eliminates them.

Student factors can be introduced either by the student or observed by the supervisor. It has been suggested elsewhere (Brownstein, 1981; Wilson, 1981) that comprehensive surveys of the student be undertaken to determine the appropriateness of a particular site. Certainly, the student's career goals must be the most important variable in finding an appropriate site. Many other conditions can be survived if the site will increase the student's chances of pursuing a desired career path. Other student characteristics would include whether the student is a self-starter or someone who needs a more structured atmosphere and whether the student has the background or interest to work with a variety of ethnic or economic groups. The student's schedule may also be a limiting factor. If the student is working in addition to attending graduate school, the site might have to be one that serves clients in the evening or on weekends. Finally, the student's readiness for the demands of a site must be of paramount importance. Developmentally, a desired site may not be appropriate because of the difficulty of the clinical cases or the unavailability of close supervision that would ensure client protection. Site selection, therefore, often includes advising about realistic career options, at least at the entry level.

Agency factors are the third consideration and include the atmosphere of the work environment (Stoltenberg & Delworth, 1987), the interest of the agency to work with students, the variety of opportunities within the agency, and the theoretical orientation of the supervisor, to name a few. The

agency factors may or may not be known by the campus supervisor or the student if the site has not been used before. Therefore, the student should be assisted in determining a list of things to look for when making contact with the site.

Raskin (1985) surveyed 12 accredited social work programs to determine the importance of different variables in choosing placement sites. Although Raskin supported Wilson (1981) in her belief that student needs should be primary in the selection process, Raskin found that this was not the case, as can be seen in Table 10.2. In fact, when all factors were ranked, student concerns rated lowest in their impact on the placement decision, while school factors and environmental factors rated highest. This could be construed as the reality of the situation when many students compete for few good placements, and this, of course, is true in many geographical locations. It is disheartening, however, to note that the educational needs of the student rated 13 of 15 in importance when university field directors were seeking sites for their students. It would seem that this represents a breakdown in program goals. The solution might be a process that is more methodical in taking student factors into account as field placements are considered.

Hamilton and Else (1983) outlined 18 dimensions, shown in Table 10.3, that might be considered in making decisions regarding the appropriateness of a field placement site. It is doubtful that many sites will be optimal on all 18 dimensions, but such an outline could serve to raise students' awareness of which items are most important to them.

Communication with the Site

It is up to the university supervisor to communicate the program's expectations to the site supervisor, not the student's. Under the best of circumstances, this is done both in writing and in person. Personal contact allows the university supervisor to determine whether there is any resistance to meeting the program's requirements. It has been our experience that student trainees are typically not good judges of a site when the site is ambivalent about meeting program requirements.

TABLE 10.2   Fifteen Variables Ranked as Most Important by Field Directors

FACTOR	VARIABLE	RANK WITHIN FACTOR	MEAN[a]	RANK ALL VARIABLES
School	Quality of agencies and field instructors available	1	1.75	(3)
	Availability of agencies	2	2.33	(5)
	Availability of supervision	3	2.68	(6)
Field instructor	Interest in supervising	1	1.47	(1)
	Previous supervision	2	3.60	(9)
	Degree	3	4.90	(12)
Environmental	Professional support system	1	1.58	(2)
	Number of agencies available	2	2.08	(4)
	Supplemental opportunity	3	3.00	(7)
Agency	Provides social work supervision	1	3.41	(10)
	Type of experience agency provides	2	4.33	(8)
	Educational commitment	3	6.00	(14)
Student	Placement preference	1	4.70	(11)
	Educational needs	2	5.70	(13)
	Transportation	3	6.60	(15)

From M. S. Raskin, (1985), Field placement decision: Art, science or guesswork? *The Clinical Supervisor, 3*(3), 55–67. Copyright (1985) by The Haworth Press, Inc., 10 Alice Street, Binghamton, NY. Reprinted by permission.

[a]Based on responses from a 7-point Likert scale ranging from Always (1) taken into consideration as a placement variable to Never (7) taken into consideration as a placement variable.

Perhaps they are too eager to find an appropriate site to be discriminating. Even when they do discern ambivalence, they are in a vulnerable position regarding the site and are uncertain about asserting themselves with potential site supervisors. Clearly, this is something the university supervisor can and should do.

Once a site has been chosen, it is important that the campus supervisor stay in touch with the site supervisor. A phone call a couple of weeks after the student has been placed is a good idea to be sure that things are going reasonably well. Additionally, there should be a plan for formal contacts in order to evaluate the student's progress. These can be done in person at the site or through written evaluations from the site. The site supervisor should know, however, when these will occur and what form they will take.

Leonardelli and Gratz (1985) addressed another important occasion for communication between campus and site, and that is when there is some conflict between the student and the site. Although it is important for students to have experience in resolving conflict, the power differential between them and their site supervisors may make this difficult in some cases. In such instances, the campus supervisor has a legitimate role to play. Leonardelli and Gratz outlined three sources of conflict for which it is appropriate for the campus supervisor to become involved.

1. *Inconsistency in performance expectations.* An example of this type of conflict is if the student understood that he or she would be spending the majority of time at the site in direct service and finds, instead, that the site supervisor expects a sizable amount of time to be spent in meetings, outreach activities, written work, and the like.

2. *Incompatibility between expectations and reality of the facility.* Recently, one of our students

TABLE 10.3   Eighteen Dimensions to Aid in Choosing Appropriate Social Work Field Placements

Learning Opportunities
1. Administrative Structure and Location
   (a) agency
   (b) teaching
   (c) service
   (d) campus
2. Field of Practice or Social Problem Area
   (a) one field of practice or social problem area
   (b) multiple fields of practice or social problem areas
3. Theoretical Orientation of the Agency
   (a) one theoretical perspective
   (b) two or more theoretical perspectives
4. Methods of Practice
   (a) one practice method
   (b) one primary, other secondary methods of practice
   (c) multiple practice methods with relatively equal emphasis (generalist orientation)
5. Interdisciplinary Potential
   (a) social workers only
   (b) limited interdisciplinary exchange
   (c) extensive interdisciplinary teamwork
6. Primary Service Area
   (a) rural
   (b) small city
   (c) metropolitan area: inner city
   (d) metropolitan area: suburban
7. Diversity of Population Served
   (a) service assignments exclusively or primarily with people of one group, e.g., age, class, race, sex, religion
   (b) service assignments with people of diverse groups
8. Breadth of Service Assignments
   (a) one unit of one agency
   (b) several service or program units of one agency
   (c) primary assignment in one agency with supplementary assignments in other agencies
9. Potential for Student Innovation
   (a) work only with existing client groups using existing service approaches
   (b) develop alternative service approaches and/or extend services to new constituencies

Field Instruction[a]
10. Sources of Field Instruction
   (a) single (exclusive) field instructor
   (b) primary instructor plus secondary (supplementary) instructors
11. Number of Students Jointly in Placement
   (a) one
   (b) two to five
   (c) teaching unit of six to twelve students
12. Teaching Format
   (a) individual conferences
   (b) group sessions
   (c) both individual and group

Continued

TABLE 10.3 Continued

13. Teaching Methods
    (a) direct (during service) instruction (supervision) only
    (b) postservice instruction only
    (c) both direct and postservice instruction

Field Instructor

14. Theoretical Orientation of Field Instructor
    (a) one theoretical perspective
    (b) one primary theoretical perspective with understandings and techniques from other perspectives integrated into practice
    (c) several theoretical perspectives
15. Education and Experience as Practitioner
    (a) BA in social work with limited or extensive specialized training, professional experience, professional standing
    (b) MSW plus limited or extensive specialized training, professional experience, professional standing
    (c) degree in another discipline plus social work experience or orientation with limited or extensive specialized training, professional experience, professional standing
16. Education and Experience as Field Instructor
    (a) no formal education in field instruction and limited experience as an instructor
    (b) no formal education in field instruction and extensive experience as an instructor
    (c) formal seminar in field instruction and limited experience
    (d) formal seminar in field instruction and extensive experience
17. Field Instructors Employer
    (a) agency
    (b) educational institution
18. Time Committed to Field Instruction
    (a) full-time
    (b) part-time

From N. Hamilton and J. F. Else (1983), Designing field education: Philosophy, Structure and Process. Courtesy of Charles C Thomas, Publisher, Springfield, Illinois.

[a]The word supervisor can be substituted for instruction wherever it appears.

experienced this kind of conflict. She was placed in a community center that offered a program for high-risk children. She was advised that she would be working with the parents while the children were in group therapy. Parent involvement, however, was very low, and the student spent the majority of her time assisting in play therapy, not one of her career goals. In a review of unsuccessful field placements, Holtzman and Raskin (1988) found that a major contributing factor to their failure was "limited exploration and monitoring by the school of the learning opportunities in different agencies" (p. 131). Obviously, the faculty supervisor cannot be held accountable if an agency misrepresents itself, but it is probably more common that the faculty's investigation prior to the placement of the student is incomplete.

3. *Inconsistency between expectations of the educational facility and the field site.* A prime example of this would be when the educational facility expected that clinical supervision would occur primarily on the site, but the site expected the reverse.

In conflict situations, Leonardelli and Gratz asserted that the campus supervisor should attempt to mediate and find the best compromise between the site and the trainee, with either party potentially being asked to adjust to the other.

The final types of communication that should occur between campus and site are informational and educational. When sites have become regular placements for students from a particular program, there should be an effort to keep the site abreast of changes within the program or even with the everyday workings of the program. Meetings on campus of site supervisors can be planned for this purpose, or gestures as simple as sending copies of the minutes of program staff meetings could accomplish this goal. This type of communication not only aids students, but also enhances the overall relationship between the program and field sites.

Finally, training programs should attempt to communicate new developments in the area of supervision to their site supervisors. Although site supervisors have a wealth of practical knowledge, traditionally they have not stayed as current as university types in terms of the research on supervision, new models and techniques, and the supervision literature in general. Therefore, in-service training for site supervisors or seminars in which both campus and site supervisors share their ideas and experiences comprise a special kind of communication activity (Beck et al., 1989; Brown & Otto, 1986).

Agreements of Understanding

Supervision contracts or agreements of understanding are often drawn up between supervisors and trainees (Munson, 1993). Yet, as Munson pointed out, it is very difficult for the trainee to demand that the agency keep its end of the bargain. Through the involvement of the training program (by requiring that a contract be completed that outlines responsibilities of the trainee, the site supervisor, and the training institution), however, accountability is increased for all concerned. Osborn and Davis (1996) argued that contracts not only help to clarify the supervision relationship, but can also be used to promote ethical practice by itemizing important ethical standards (e.g., informed consent) and their implementation within supervision. Osborn and Davis suggested that supervision contracts include the following:

1. *Purpose, goals, and objectives.* This category includes the obvious purpose of safeguarding clients, as well as promoting trainee development. Putting this in writing, however, is an important ritual for both supervisor and trainee. Additionally, the more immediate goal of, for example, completing the clinical requirements for a training program is listed as well.

2. *Context of services.* The contract must include where and when supervision will take place, what method of monitoring will be in place, and what supervision modalities will be used. We would add a description of the clientele to be served to this item.

3. *Method of evaluation.* Both formative and summative evaluation methods and schedules should be included. Any instrument that will be used for evaluation should be given to the trainee at this time.

4. *Duties and responsibilities of supervisor and supervisee.* In this section, both persons outline the behaviors that they are committed to in order that supervision evolve successfully. For the supervisor, this may include challenging the trainee to consider different treatment methods; for the trainee, this may include coming to each supervision session with a preset videotaped sample of one's use of a particular technique. We would include the duties and responsibilities of the training program supervisor in this section of the contract.

5. *Procedural considerations.* Part of the contract must address issues such as emergency procedures and the format for record keeping required by the agency. Osborn and Davis also advised that the contract include a procedure that is to be followed if either party feels that a conflict within supervision has not been resolved.

6. *Supervisor's scope of practice.* Finally, Osborn and Davis suggested that the supervisor's experience and clinical credentials be listed to "make explicit to themselves and their supervisees their professional competence" (p. 130).

Although contracts of this kind must be considered legally nonbinding agreements, they raise everyone's consciousness about what is to transpire and how things are to evolve. Furthermore, they can decrease the amount of discomfort when confrontation is justified because one party is not living up to the agreement.

Quality Control

In terms of meeting program expectations, it is only reasonable that the university supervisor, as the invested party, monitor quality control (Rosenblum & Raphael, 1987; York, 1985). This is done throughout the field experience by means of personal contact with the site, careful reading of student documentation of site activities, and individual or group supervision on campus during which sites are discussed.

A special kind of quality control issue is to assure that standards that are tied to accreditation, certification, or licensure are met. Among the items that might need to be monitored are the credentials of the site supervisor, the type of supervision conducted (individual or group), the amount of supervision offered, the ratio between service delivery hours and supervision, and the ratio between service delivery and other related professional activities. While a trainee is enrolled in an academic training program, it is the responsibility of the university supervisor to know that standards are being met or to reject a field placement if it is not able to meet standards.

It should be noted that quality control may not be as straightforward as one might assume. As Beavers (1986) illustrated, the advantage to the trainee of gaining clinical experience in the field is directly related to its untidiness; in other words, mental health delivery systems are imperfect organizations, and the trainee who learns to navigate in such organizations is better prepared to enter the job market. The challenge for university training programs is to weigh each organizational deficit with the opportunities afforded trainees. Is it better for the trainee to be provided with a steady flow of diverse clients or to have closely monitored supervision? Is it better for the trainee to work within one strong framework or to be challenged to work from a variety of perspectives? Is it more important to bow to accreditation standards or to go with one's judgement of an exemplary experience? It is these kinds of questions that must constantly be raised and resolved as quality control is examined. It must be understood, however, that all but the most unique field placements represent some compromise for the training program.

Evaluation

Finally, it is the prerogative and responsibility of the university supervisor to develop an evaluation plan and to conduct all summative evaluations. The extent to which the site is being asked to evaluate the supervisee must be clearly communicated (Olsen & Stern, 1990). As Rosenblum and Raphael (1987) noted, however, site supervisors typically dread evaluating university students. Kadushin (1992b) offered empirical support that evaluation was among supervisors' least favorite responsibilities. When the site supervisor's experience with a trainee has been positive, evaluation tends to be glowing; when the trainee has not met expectations, the evaluation is sometimes avoided. It is our belief that site supervisors, because their relationship with trainees are short term and because their relationships with the universities are rarely mandated, should not be asked to carry out discriminating summative evaluations. For example, the site supervisor should not be asked to grade the student except to give a pass or fail recommendation. On the other hand, it is important for site supervisors to give feedback, to both the trainee and university supervisor. But the task of translating feedback into a final evaluation is clearly the charge of the program faculty. (Evaluation procedures were delineated in Chapter 8.)

THE FIELD SITE SUPERVISOR

Although it is clear that the campus supervisor does not relinquish all responsibility to the site supervisor during a practicum or internship, there are some managerial tasks that can only be accomplished by the site supervisor. These will be the focus of this section.

The Interview

It is the goal of the university supervisor to place all students; it is the goal of the site supervisor to make a judgment about the individual student's fit with the goals and work of the agency. Although background information is sometimes requested, the basis for the decision is usually the placement interview. It is essential that the site supervisor have a grasp of the attributes that are necessary for the student to take full advantage of the placement. If the site supervisor espouses a distinct model of therapy, this must be communicated clearly to the prospective supervisee (Olsen & Stern, 1990). It is equally essential that the supervisor be able to perceive what a time-limited experience in the agency will be like and communicate this realistically to the candidate.

Trainees should receive feedback about this interview whether or not the site accepts them. Hearing the supervisor's perception of why one was seen as appropriate is a good beginning for a working relationship with the site supervisor. When the trainee is not accepted, it is important to know if the decision was made based on a negative evaluation of the student's competence or because of a perceived lack of fit. If the feedback is not given directly to the student, it should at least be given to the campus supervisor.

The interview may serve as a metaphor for the agency. In other words, if the agency is unstructured and requires a great deal of creativity from staff, the interview should mirror this situation. If, on the other hand, the agency is highly structured with clear guidelines for each staff member's role, the interview should be handled similarly. This type of consistency serves two purposes: it becomes a first-level orientation for the student to the agency and its expectations, and it allows the site supervisor the opportunity to gain relevant data about the student on which to base a decision.

Orientation

Because of the relatively short duration of both practicum and internship situations, the trainee must be oriented to the organization and service delivery issues as efficiently as possible. There are some lessons that only a learn-as-you-go approach can accomplish. But many more things can be learned through an orientation. Unfortunately, many trainees feel that they are just getting a handle on procedures and policy issues as they wrap up their field experience. At least some of this can be attributed to an inadequate orientation process.

If an agency accepts trainees on a regular basis, the site supervisor would be wise to develop a trainee manual covering the major agency policies that must be mastered. (A good resource for such a manual is the trainees who are at the end of their field experience; they can usually be quite precise about what information would have made their adaptation easier.) If written orientation materials are not available, the site supervisor might schedule more intensive supervision the first week or so to cover orientation matters with the trainee. The supervisor would be wise to use simulations of situations and ask the trainee to provide the correct procedure to be followed in order to determine if the policies are clear.

Malouf et al. (1983) devised a questionnaire to reflect information they considered important to cover in orientation to APA-accredited internships. Their questionnaire includes items about policies, fees, referrals, procedures, supervision, case management, and ethical and legal matters. As the following three questions extracted from the Malouf et al. questionnaire demonstrate, orientation should cover not only nuts and bolts issues, but also dilemmas that are more subtle. (We have retained their item numbers.)

> 5. *What do you need to do when seeing a client for the first time? What information do you need to obtain? What paperwork do you need to do, etc.?*
> 10. *What do you do if you think one of your clients may need to be hospitalized?*

16. With whom can you ethically discuss your clients? Can you use your clients at the agency as examples in university classes, either identified by name or anonymously? (p. 626)

Reducing Burnout

A good administrative structure can help to reduce burnout among supervisees. The site supervisor has considerable control over the atmosphere within which the trainee (and all supervisees) work. The trainee is not likely to refer to an initial experience as one of burnout, but trainees have often referred to being overwhelmed and too busy to be able to integrate the experience (Kaslow & Rice, 1985). Stoltenberg and Delworth (1987) suggested that supervisors attempt to mold the setting to the developmental needs of the trainee, including determining number of direct service hours, amount of supervision, and contact between the training program and the site. In other words, there should be a sense of being weaned from the training program while being oriented into a professional setting. Too quick an emersion may be counterproductive for the trainee.

Supervisors who work with trainees often realize that *all* employees need to have their work environment managed. All mental health practitioners need time to regroup and consult if they are to remain vital in their direct service responsibilities. Structuring time so that supervisees have a variety of activities and the opportunity for collegial support in their day will raise not only the quality of the work environment, but also the quality of service delivery (Falvey, 1987). Protecting supervisees from overload communicates a respect for the practitioner and also respect for the work that needs to be done, work that should be done by persons who can perform at their optimum level.

Finally, the issue of supervisor burnout is relevant to this discussion. Managing from a perspective that protects supervisees must encompass a respect for the supervisor's multiple responsibilities as well. In their survey of clinical supervisors, Nichols, Nichols, and Hardy (1990) found that supervisors were less invested in doing supervision than supervisors were a decade earlier. Though the reasons for this decline in interest were not reported, the demands of supervision in organizations that do not provide adequate resources for this demanding role must be considered as a reasonable hypothesis. It seems imperative, therefore, that supervisors take themselves into consideration when developing a plan for supervision, a plan that allows them the time and support they need to conduct clinical supervision, in a manner that adds to the quality of their work environment.

Communication

Just as it is critical for the university supervisor to keep the site supervisor abreast of programmatic developments, it is equally important for the site supervisor to keep the university current. Political, organizational, and fiscal developments may affect trainees both in their field experiences and employment search. When campus supervisors are kept current about what is going in their sites, they are better able to advise students about the professions they are entering.

An invaluable contribution site supervisors can make to training programs is to communicate their opinion of the training the students have received prior to their field placement. Once a site supervisor has overseen several trainees from the same program, the supervisor is in a position to see thematic strengths and weaknesses. In order to do this, however, site supervisors must have a structure that allows them to view the trainee in a variety of ways so that this type of appraisal can be accomplished in a valid and consistent manner.

Finally, as specified by Hardcastle (1991), the site supervisor must organize communication within the agency to benefit the trainee. It happens occasionally that a trainee has contact only with the supervisor and feels isolated from the rest of the agency. In some instances, trainees are made to feel disloyal if they happen to ask some advice from another employee other than their supervisors. This always leads to a negative outcome. The supervisor should have a plan as to how the trainee will be integrated into the agency, including attendance at staff meetings and joint projects with other staff members.

Supervisor as Agency Representative

One function that the site supervisor is less likely to acknowledge as a managerial task is to serve as a liaison or advocate between supervisees and agency administration. (Even if the supervisor wears two hats, when in the role of clinical supervisor, the supervisor must communicate administrative issues to supervisees.) This function is often carried out in an informal manner, sharing bits and pieces of both spoken and unspoken rules, agency politics, and so on. When done in an informal fashion, however, the trainee is more likely to get incomplete information and/or become triangulated in organizational power struggles. It is far better for the interface between service delivery and organizational realities to be covered in supervision in a deliberate way. Perhaps part of each supervision session could be reserved for organizational issues, not as a gripe session but as a learning process. Munson (1993) stated that interns sometimes avoid certain interventions because they perceive them as being contrary to organizational policy. Whether or not the trainee is correct, this is an important area of discussion for the trainee and supervisor.

Another liaison function of the site supervisor is to structure some way that other agency personnel can give input about the performance of the trainee. Again, it is too common for this to occur informally and therefore inconsistently. The site supervisor can devise a short form and ask colleagues to complete it once or twice during the field placement. This kind of overture can have several positive effects.

1. It lessens the trainee's isolation by involving additional personnel in the trainee's experience.
2. It can provide the trainee with additional feedback from different perspectives or role positions.
3. It can confirm or confront the supervisor's own evaluation of the trainee.

TASKS COMMON TO ALL CLINICAL SUPERVISORS

Thus far, we have discriminated between managerial tasks relevant to university supervisors and those relevant to site supervisors. As the reader might have assumed, however, there are several tasks common to all clinical supervisors, and we will consider these now.

Time Management

Supervisors are busy people. Whether at the university or in the human service agency, there are many obligations that compete with supervision. Because supervision is an enjoyable role for many professionals, they often take it on when they really have little extra time. Time management, therefore, becomes a crucial skill, one that needs to be exercised and modeled for trainees who themselves are juggling several roles. Falvey (1987) listed several simple time-management strategies for administrative supervisors, which include coordinating activities to maximize one's productivity (e.g., tackling difficult tasks when one's energy is high), avoiding escapists behaviors (e.g., doing an unpleasant task first thing in the morning, rather than allowing it to bear on one's mind all day), and dividing difficult tasks so that they do not appear overwhelming.

Perhaps the most central time management skill is the ability to set priorities and keep to them. It is virtually impossible to end one's workday with absolutely no work left over for the following day. Rather, supervisors who can manage time have addressed the most important concerns immediately and have learned to pace themselves in accomplishing less pressing tasks. For some supervisors, it is a seemingly natural ability to take control of one's schedule; for others, it is a constant struggle that can be supplemented by time-management strategies suggested in the literature. Covey et al. (1994) warned against falling into an urgency mentality; that is, what is immediate is always treated as urgent, even when it is not. They also cautioned against using time-management strategies to fit an unreasonable amount of activity into one's schedule. In other words, time management can become part of the problem, not the solution. Regardless of how the supervisor accomplishes the goal of finding and protecting time for supervision, the supervisor must realize that making time must be a deliberate choice and is not something that will take care of itself.

Assuming that one has found an adequate amount of time to dedicate to supervision, the issue of timing emerges. When is it best to supervise? How often should supervisees be monitored? Does it matter? We discussed the supervision issues embedded in the timing of supervision in Chapter 5. Based on these, the supervisor should attempt to devise the most productive supervision schedule for the supervisee.

Choosing Supervision Methods

Chapters 5, 6, and 7 outlined a variety of ways in which the process of supervision can be conducted. Deciding on the form that supervision will take and implementing the desired process can be a managerial task of significant proportion. For example, the supervisor might decide that using interpersonal process recall (Kagan, 1976; Kagan & Kagan, 1997) would be desirable with a particular supervisee because of difficulties the supervisee is having with one of her clients. Using the technique, however, will require that videotape equipment be made available and that arrangements are made for videotaping the next therapy session. It is understandable, though regrettable, that supervisors often default on their supervision plans because the method that supervision should take becomes logistically too complicated. If the supervisor is convinced that a particular process (e.g., IPR or live supervision) is essential for the supervisee's learning, it is incumbent on the supervisor to work out the logistical details. When supervisors continue to put aside their teaching instincts because of the time and care they require, the quality of supervision eventually deteriorates. Perhaps there is no managerial responsibility so essential to clinical supervision as the choreogra-phy required to ensure that the method of supervision match the learning needs of supervisees.

Record Keeping

In a litigious era the process of record keeping has gained in importance for helping professionals of all disciplines. Schutz (1982) identified record keeping as one of five areas in therapy management that relates to the risk of liability suits. Others have concurred that good client records serve as a desirable defense against litigation (Snider, 1987; Soisson, VandeCreek, & Knapp, 1987).

Whether supervising from campus or on site, it is the supervisor's responsibility to be sure that client records are complete. Most agencies and university professors have established record-keeping procedures that have evolved over time. But with an ever changing professional and legal climate, the wise supervisor reviews the record-keeping system occasionally to be sure that it is current with national trends. Among the items that should be considered for inclusion in client records are the following (Mitchell, 1991; Schultz, 1982):

1. Written and signed informed consents for all treatment, as well as signed informed consent for all transmissions of confidential information
2. Treatment contracts, if used
3. Notes on all treatment contacts made, either in person or by telephone, including descriptions of significant events and interventions made
4. Notes on all contacts or consultation with significant others, including correspondence
5. A complete history and symptom picture leading to diagnosis, with regular review and revision of the diagnosis, as well as treatment direction based on diagnosis
6. A record of all prescriptions and current drug use profile
7. Any instructions, suggestions, or directives made to the client that he or she failed to follow through on
8. Records relevant to supervision, including permission to tape sessions, and consultations

sought by either supervisee or supervisor regarding a case

9. A record of termination and an aftercare plan (Beis, 1984)

Most supervisors are far more careful about client records than about supervision records. Yet, as the Tarasoff case pointed out (*Tarasoff* v. *Regents of the University of California,* 1974), supervision records can be equally important in a liability suit. On a more optimistic note, supervision records discipline supervisors to pause and consider their supervision with each supervisee, offering moments of insight that would not otherwise occur. Therefore, for legal and instructional reasons, supervisors must keep accurate and complete supervision records.

Munson's (1993) suggested outline for supervision records is as follows:

1. The supervisory contract, if used or required by the agency
2. A brief statement of supervisee experience, training, and learning needs
3. A summary of all performance evaluations
4. Notation of all supervisory sessions
5. Canceled or missed sessions
6. Notation of cases discussed and significant decisions
7. Significant problems encountered in the supervision and how they were resolved, or whether they remain unresolved and why (p. 220)

Bridge and Bascue (1990) stressed the importance of consistency in documentation, as well as the inclusion of both treatment and training recommendations. Figure 10.2 depicts the outline suggested by Bridge and Bascue for record keeping. Falvey, Caldwell, and Cohen (1996) have developed the Focused Risk Management Supervisory System (FoRMSS) in response to the legal liability of supervisors for the well-being of their supervisees' clients, as well as the challenge of offering ethical and comprehensive supervision in light of the trend toward brief managed care. Although FoRMSS is a complete documentation system, the

Supervisory Record Form is reprinted here (see Figure 10.3) and is the central method for tracking supervision as well as monitoring client well-being. Not only does the form require an updated case review, but it also requires the supervisor to record recommendations in several categories, including training recommendations for the supervisee. Finally, and most critical for risk management, the supervisor is alerted to review several ethical, clinical, and supervisory topics to ensure that these complicating issues are not neglected in supervision. If the supervisor is concerned about any issues listed in the shaded area, he or she documents whatever action is taken and this becomes part of the supervision record. FoRMSS represents a new standard for supervision record keeping and benefits the entire therapy system by keeping supervision focused on its multiple levels from a variety of angles.

Planning Ahead

We have come full circle and end where we began with a discussion about planning. The exemplary supervisor has a blueprint of what the well-trained practitioner looks like and how supervision can contribute to developing that picture in a systematic way. The best supervisors have planned ahead for situations that may or may not occur, but which demand that a process be in place (Rinas & Clyne-Jackson, 1988). It is frustrating, if not frightening, for a trainee to face an emergency with a client, for example, the need to hospitalize, and have no idea how the situation is to be handled. Emergency procedures should be in document form, given to the trainee during orientation, and placed in a convenient place for reference should an emergency occur.

Another time when planning ahead is crucial is when the supervisor will be away. For example, it is not unusual for all clinical supervisors in a training program to attend the same conference, leaving a university-based clinic either in the hands of doctoral students or fill-in supervisors. With the rush to prepare the paper that will be presented at the conference or the arrangements that

SUPERVISORY RECORD FORM

Date: _____

Supervisee: _____

Session No.:_____

IDENTIFYING INFORMATION

CASE: SUPERVISEE CONCERN:

_____   _____
_____   _____
_____   _____
_____   _____
_____   _____
_____   _____
_____   _____
_____   _____

SUPERVISORY GOALS: _____
_____
_____

SUPERVISORY ACTIVITY   SUPERVISORY RECOMMENDATIONS

1. Supporting Documents   1. Treatment:_____
   a. Case Record:_____   _____
   b. Audiovisual Record:_____   _____
   c. Other:_____   _____
2. Theoretical Issues:_____   _____
   _____   2. Training: _____
   _____   _____
   _____   _____
Process Observations: _____   _____
   _____   _____
   _____   _____
4. Therapist Self-awareness:_____   3. Other Comments:_____
   _____   _____
   _____   _____
5. Treatment Evaluation:_____   _____
   _____   _____
   _____   _____

FIGURE 10.2

From P. J. Bridge, and L. O. Bascue, (1990), Documentation of psychotherapy supervision, *Psychotherapy in Private Practice, 8* 82. Copyright © (1990) by The Haworth Press, Inc., 10 Alice Street, Binghamton, NY. Reprinted by permission.

SUPERVISORY RECORD FORM

Date: _____ Supervisee: _____ Client ID: _____ Review Method: _____

Updated Case Review:

_____

_____

Interventions/Outcomes:

_____

_____

Progress Toward Goals:

_____

Supervisee Concerns:

_____

_____

SUPERVISOR RECOMMENDATIONS

Treatment Interventions

_____

_____

Referrals (also recorded on case summary):

_____

Discussion (theoretical bases, case conceptualizations, clinical judgment, etc.):

_____

_____

_____

_____

Process Observations:

_____

Training Recommendations:

_____

_____

SUPERVISOR RISK MANAGEMENT

___ Informed Consent	___ Records Security	___ Sexual Misconduct	___ Vol/Invol Hospitalization
___ Confidentiality	___ Risk of Sign. Harm	___ Discharge/Termination	___ 3rd Party/UR Review
___ Parental Consent	___ Duty to Warn	___ Supervisee Expertise	___ Institutional Conflict
___ Dual Relationship	___ Medical Symptoms	___ Supervisor Expertise	___ Substance Abuse
___ Record Keeping	___ Child Abuse/Neglect	___ Info Release Request	_____

Action Taken: _____

_____

FIGURE 10.3

From J. E. Falvey, C. F. Caldwell, and C. R. Cohen (1996), *The Focused Risk Management Supervisory System (FoRMSS)*. Copyright © (1996) J. E. Falvey, C. F. Caldwell, and C. R. Cohen, Reprinted by permission.

must be made to cover one's classes, it often happens that a colleague from another department is asked to cover supervision with little or no information about the operations of the clinic, the status of any worrisome clients, or information about the student staff. This could easily be a case where the lack of managerial foresight takes on the characteristics of questionable ethical practice.

By planning ahead we do not mean to suggest that the supervisor compulsively worry about every possible way things may go wrong. "The sky is falling" is not a productive supervisory posture. Rather, we urge supervisors to take reasonable care regarding their responsibilities and, especially, to give themselves the time to plan well and to put their plans into action.

WORKING TOWARD MANAGERIAL COMPETENCE

Short of receiving training in management and/or administrative supervision, what can the clinical supervisor do to achieve managerial competence? This chapter has presented many of the goals that the clinical supervisor might set for himself or herself. The following are five simple guidelines that can be of use as one sets out to achieve these goals.

Get Support.   Before clinical supervisors commit themselves to the substantial task of supervising either on or off a university campus, they should be sure that they have administrative support for their activity. Beck et al. (1989) found that clinical supervision was compromised if the agency director did not support having trainees on site. This position was reiterated by Holloway and Roehlke (1987) regarding APA-accredited internship sites. Likewise, an academic program director must appreciate the time it takes to develop good field sites, to organize the operation of practicum and internship, and to serve as an ongoing liaison with sites. If, as Skolnik (1988) and others have suggested, the faculty supervisor also offers to train site supervisors, the responsibilities can begin to grow exponentially. The greater the support offered by superiors, the more that can be accomplished and the better the quality of the supervision. If support is limited, the clinical supervisor must decide if minimal standards can be met. If not, the supervisor must decline an offer to supervise on ethical grounds.

Know Yourself.   As simple as it sounds, there seems to be a relatively high degree of unawareness among clinical supervisors about their ability to organize themselves and those under their supervision. Perhaps supervisors assume that they already have the skills of a competent manager and therefore resist admitting that this is an area in which they need to grow. Perhaps the expectation that they already have all the skills they need to do the job comes from others around them, leaving them little room to be tentative. Regardless of the source, a cycle of false assumptions, followed by denial, can keep a clinical supervisor operating at a less than satisfactory level regarding the managerial responsibilities of the supervisor's position.

Organization comes far more naturally to some than to others. When supervisors believe that they fall in the latter category, they should find a member of their staff or a professional colleague who they believe can help develop a plan or, more likely, help implement a plan. The beginning of implementation is a critical juncture that calls for different abilities than those required for arriving at the original plan. This is the point at which many clinical supervisors could use assistance.

Gather Data.   There is nothing particularly virtuous about reinventing the wheel. As supervisors approach the task of organizing a training program or the clinical operation of an agency, they might contact other training programs or agencies and ask for samples of policy statements, supervision forms, and other materials relevant to their tasks. When a specific issue arises, consulting with colleagues and determining how they have managed the issue is a sound strategy. Isolating oneself is a common supervisor flaw, both in terms of clinical work and managerial tasks. Supervisors have a tremendous amount to learn from each other, and they need to model for their supervisees the ability to consult with others as part of good clinical practice.

The professional literature is another source for data collection. There is less about the management of clinical supervision in the literature than there might be, but the careful reader will gather important information from the research on supervision and from others' investigations and descriptions of the process of supervision and management in general.

Get Feedback. Any new procedure should be considered a pilot study of sorts. A managerial strategy may work well from the supervisor's vantage point but be untenable for supervisees. The competent supervisor knows how to manipulate procedures to work for people and the program, not the other way around. Part of this competence is demonstrated by seeking the opinions of others. The result is a managerial style that is always being fine tuned without continually starting over from scratch.

Go Slowly. One way to avoid having to scrap one plan for another (and thereby keeping those under supervision in a state of turmoil) is for supervisors to give themselves permission to build their managerial plan slowly. No one who is supervising for the first time will be totally organized in the first year. Rather, one should begin with those aspects of supervision that are most critical for ethical and safe practice and eventually pay heed to items that add to convenience and expediency of communi-

cation, among other things. For persons new to supervision, a significant amount of time shadowing a more experienced supervisor might serve as an excellent impetus to developing one's own supervision plan, thus serving as an efficient strategy in the long run. In addition to being practical, going slowly encourages the supervisor to home in immediately on those things that are absolutely essential to any supervisory operation. Discriminating between issues that are essential and those that are desirable is the beginning and the core of managerial competence.

CONCLUSION

Although management issues tend to fall to the bottom of the list of driving forces for clinical supervisors, the manner in which they are handled may be more predictive of long-term productivity than clinical expertise. Additionally, our management of professional responsibilities may be the closest indication we have of overriding principles that affect our clinical supervision in profound ways. Managerial tasks are tedious only when they are viewed as distractors. When viewed as building blocks for the essential work of supervision, managerial challenges can tap the energy typically reserved for clinical and instructional activities. Paradoxically, the energy invested in the management of clinical supervision may produce the greatest payoff in terms of protecting time and providing a context for exemplary supervisory practice.

CHAPTER 11

Supervisor Development and Training

Almost all mental health professionals eventually will supervise. Typically, they are eager to become supervisors, for they not only gain status, but obtain many other rewards as well. These include the pleasures of influencing the work of another, as well as the stimulation and impact that trainees can have them. As Alonso (1983) said, "It's exciting to make order out of chaos, to watch the contagious excitement of our students, and to share in the intimate pleasure of contact over emotional growth and expansion; it's fun to watch someone move from student to colleague, and watch the better parts of ourselves move into posterity" (p. 28). An important question, then, is how mental health professionals will prepare themselves for this important and almost inevitable role.

Traditionally, the supervisor-to-be's previous experience as a counselor or therapist has sufficed as "preparation." That is, mental health professionals seem generally to have assumed that they might become supervisors by (1) extrapolating their therapeutic skills to the supervisory context and (2) drawing from the lessons they learned by participating as trainees themselves.

We already have emphasized that extrapolating from work as therapist is insufficient to prepare one to become a supervisor (e.g., a good athlete does not necessarily then become a good coach). With regard to extrapolating from work as a trainee, Bonney (1994) asserted that it is roughly equivalent to learning how to be a therapist by participating as a client and then by modeling the therapist's behavior. Neither of these extrapolations is a sufficient basis for becoming a supervisor. The premise of this chapter is that supervision can and should be taught with at least the seriousness we give other psychological interventions.

Hoffman (1994) characterized the traditional lack of formal training for supervisors as the mental health professions' "dirty little secret" (p. 25). Like others (e.g., Pope & Vasquez, 1991; Stoltenberg & Delworth, 1987), she suggested that supervisors who practice without having been trained as supervisors are doing so unethically. For example, Principle A of the American Psychological Association's (1992) ethical code is very explicit about the importance of providing only services for which the person has been trained. Stoltenberg and Delworth asked, "In what other professional area would we allow trainees or professionals to practice without training?" (p. 160). Pope and Vasquez (1991) made this same point when they asserted that "[I]t would be no more ethical to 'improvise' supervision if one lacked education, training, and supervised experience than if one were to improvise hypnotherapy, systematic desensitization, or administration of a Hallstead–Retan Neuropsychological Test Battery without adequate preparation" (p. 171).

In a trenchant satire on what he perceived as the current state of supervisor practice, Haley (1993) suggested that

Just by being in a supervisory job means that one is considered knowledgeable. If a supervisor can find employment in a well-known institution, even a banal comment will be received as profound. A dumb statement in a wise context, such as Harvard University, can be admired, as many dumb supervisors there have found. It helps if the supervisor implies that he, or she, is descended from a distinguished line of supervisors. The famous, even legendary, supervisors who have been observed in weekend workshops can be defined as former teachers and referred to by first names. . . . [In addition], two vision mannerisms are helpful: one, the faraway look that implies one is considering all aspects of the larger situation; two, the keen, incisive look which shows the student that one is alert and quickly grasping the essentials. When a nervous student is worried about the fate of the client in his or her hands, the supervisor can win respect and even adulation just by being there and looking wise. The faraway look and thoughtful silence can, at times, cause the trainee to become impatient enough to come up with an idea. The supervisor can accept the trainee's views, perhaps implying that he [sic] had that in mind. (p. 42)

We interpret this statement as implicitly corroborating our position that supervisors need to be trained for their work.

Fortunately, practitioners in the several mental health professions now increasingly acknowledge how important it is for supervisors to receive formal training. This is encouraged also by the increasing emphasis that accreditation bodies now give to supervision training. For these and other reasons, then, it is reasonable to conclude that there is growing momentum for training programs to include and enhance formal supervisor training.

Supervisors and would-be supervisors are the primary audience for this book. But in this particular chapter, we *also* speak to those who train and supervise supervisors. We have organized the chapter in two parts. The first addresses conceptual and empirical literature on the development of supervisors. The second discusses training and supervising supervisors. Following the convention suggested by Hoffman (1990, 1994), we will use the acronym SIT to refer to the "supervisor in training."

SUPERVISOR DEVELOPMENT MODELS

Shechter (1990) noted that to become a supervisor is one additional step in professional development. It is, though, a large step that involves shifts in identity and felt responsibility. In many ways, these shifts are as substantial as those experienced by the person who moves into the professional world of the counselor or therapist for the first time. Moreover, the shift is not a one-time, single event, for as new supervisors gain experience,

they will continue to change, not only in skills, but also in perceptions of self and role.

Several theorists have described these relatively normative changes in terms of developmental stages, similar in type to the counselor developmental models we discussed in Chapter 2. That is, each of these posited stages is characterized by particular attitudes, cognitions, and relationships to both the trainees with whom the SITs work and to their own supervisor(s). These stages are sufficiently important that we will begin this chapter by summarizing them.

Conceptions of supervisor development are relatively recent. We suspect this is a function of two trends:

1. The counselor development models on which these were patterned are themselves relatively recent, most having been developed in only the past 15 years (see Chapter 2). Supervisor development models have largely been adaptations of counselor development models because they are similar in their emphases on shifts in professional identity and skills that occur with experience and training.

2. Interest in supervision as a distinct intervention meriting its own research and practice has been relatively recent.

Whereas at least 22 counselor development models have been proposed (cf., Watkins, 1995c; Worthington, 1987), so far, only a few models of supervisor development have been proposed. Table 11.1 summarizes the available models in a very brief and telegraphic style. It is useful to see, for example, that all have employed either a three- or four-stage model. We describe these four models in more detail in the section that follows.

Alonso's Model

Alonso (1983) proposed one of the earliest supervisor development models. It was influenced both by (1) psychodynamic and (2) life-span developmental perspectives. Because of the latter perspective, her model encompasses the person's entire professional life as a supervisor. This is in contrast to the several other supervisor development

TABLE 11.1 Summary of Supervisor Development Stages Suggested by Supervisor Developmental Theorists

ALONSO	HESS	RODENHAUSER	STOLTENBERG AND DELWORTH	WATKINS
Novice	Beginning	Emulation Conceptualization	Level I	Role shock Role recovery and transition
	Exploration		Level II	
		Incorporation		Role consolidation
	Confirmation of supervisor identity	Consolidation	Level III	Role mastery
			Level III integrated	
Midcareer				
Late career				

From Alonso (1983), Hess (1986, 1987), Rodenhauser (1994), Stoltenberg and Delworth (1987), Watkins (1990; 1993)

models, which each suggest three or four stages that might *all* be traversed in a matter of only a few years, perhaps a decade or less.

At each stage, the development of the supervisor is influenced by three different themes. These are (1) self and identity, (2) relationship between supervisor and therapist, and (3) relationship between the supervisor and the administrative structure within which the supervisor works.

During the *novice* stage, supervisors are nurturing a dream about what they might become, but also are confronted with developing a sense of self-as-supervisor. They also must cope with the anxiety that comes from needing to deal with narcissistic developmental needs (e.g., for validation, for approval, and for role models) that emerge in response to the need to defend themselves as novices once again after already having achieved some sense of mastery as therapists. These issues are exacerbated by the fact that their trainees typically are about the same age and are themselves career novices who are taking on new levels of responsibility.

In the *midcareer* stage, supervisors generally conform to Levinson's (1978) description of the ideal mentor. That is, they are moving from a focus on self to more of a focus on others.

Late career supervisors are often faced with the need to maintain self-esteem in the face of our culture's tendency to devalue older people. But, at the same time, they are in a position to enjoy the status of "village elder," using the supervisory role as a medium to exhibit their wisdom and expertise. This role provides an opportunity to work through conflicts regarding integrity versus despair.

Alonso may be unique among the supervisor developmental theorists in the attention she gave the role of institutional context. She noted that, because supervision usually takes place in the context of an institutional structure, this inevitably will affect the supervisor. For example, novice supervisors are likely to feel a greater need to be recognized by the institution and therefore may respond to trainees more harshly and critically than their more advanced colleagues. Conversely, because of their own still unresolved issues as former trainees, they might overidentify with their own trainees when they struggle with institutional rules and procedures. Mid-life supervisors, secure in their place in the structure, are able to see situations from both sides and to negotiate any differences that occur between agency and trainee. The late-life supervisor has a long-term perspective and can serve as a "voice for optimism and calm, having seen a multitude of crises rise and abate, often with benevolent results" (p. 32).

Hess's Model

Hess (1986, 1987) suggested that supervisor development occurs across three stages. In the *beginning* stage, the person changes roles (e.g., from trainee to supervisor) and reference groups (i.e., from novices to more experienced clinicians). This shift into new terrain with all its attendant ambiguity about roles and technique renders the supervisors vulnerable to self-consciousness and sensitivity to peer and trainee criticism. They compensate by employing a concrete structure in supervision and by focusing on the client and the teaching technique.

As supervisors gain experience, they develop both competence and confidence, along with a corresponding internalized belief in the professional value of supervision as an intervention. This characterizes the second or *exploration* stage. Hess suggested, though, that supervisors at this stage are prone to two particular response sets that can be problematic. One is to be too restrictive in their supervisory roles; the other is to become too intrusive with the trainee, addressing issues that are unrelated to the trainee's work as a therapist. The trainee is likely to respond to either of these with resistance.

When supervisors reach the third stage, *confirmation of supervisor identity,* they find more of their gratification and professional pride in their trainees' successes and, consequently, feel less dependent on receiving validation from others that they are "good supervisors." They are able to respond more to the trainee's learning agenda and actually to *be* in the relationship with the trainee, rather than dealing with the relationship at a cognitive level. Their sense of professional identity is strong and established.

Rodenhauser's Model

Rodenhauser observed that the newest supervisors will emulate their previous role models (*emula-*

tion stage). This identification establishes an essential foundation on which to begin developing competence and identity as a supervisor. Gradually, though, new supervisors will encounter the limits of emulation and then begin to search for their own methods and guidelines (*conceptualization stage*). Much of this search typically will occur in discussions with peers. This process of interacting with peers has the additional advantage of establishing alliances that reduce supervisors' likelihood of overidentifying with their supervisees.

The *incorporation stage* occurs as supervisors begin to develop an increasing awareness of the importance of the supervisory relationship. This awareness comes with increased sensitivity to the impact of their personal style on supervisees and, ultimately, on the supervisee–client relationship. Concommitant to this is supervisors' heightened awareness of individual differences (gender, race, and culture, etc.) that affect the supervisory triad.

Finally, in the *consolidation stage,* supervisors consolidate their learning and experience. One aspect of this stage is an increasing ability to use the supervisee's countertransference reactions in supervision, but also to balance this against the supervisees' need for privacy. Without deliberate effort, the supervisor at this stage is able to continually monitor parallel processes for instructional cues.

Stoltenberg and Delworth's Model

Stoltenberg and Delworth (1987) suggested that supervisors move through a series of stages analogous to those they had suggested in their counselor development model. In fact, they assume a sort of interlocking of counselor development and supervisor development stages. That is, they assert that the level I supervisor first should have reached the stage of at least a late level 2 counselor (see Chapter 2 for our summary and discussion of these counselor stages).

Level I supervisors, like level 1 counselor trainees, feel characteristically anxious and are eager to do the "right thing." They frequently behave in a mechanistic and structured way with trainees, are likely to assume an "expert" stance, and often are eager to push their own theoretical orientation and techniques on trainees. In turn, they are relatively dependent on their own supervisors for support.

SITs at level I are often very effective when they are responsible for supervising beginning counselor trainees—who *want* the structure and "expertness" the beginning supervisor will tend to offer. Stoltenberg and Delworth (1987) suggested, in fact, that level I supervisors who also are at level 2 in terms of their development as counselors frequently will be "far better" (p. 155) as supervisors than as counselors.

Level II is characterized by confusion and conflict. Fortunately, this tends to be a short-lived stage. SITs now understand supervision to be more complex and difficult than they originally had understood it would be. They may tend to focus heavily on the trainee, with a consequent risk of losing objectivity and, with it, the ability to guide and confront. But at the same time, SITs at this level may vary in their motivation to be supervisors, with the consequence that they may then blame trainees for their own problems as supervisor and become angry and withdraw. Stoltenberg and Delworth noted that level II SITs need their own supervisors to be expert and consistent with them.

Stoltenberg and Delworth suggested that most supervisors do reach level III. This level is characterized by a consistent motivation toward the supervisor role, which they approach as but one of the many they have as professionals. Supervisors at this level function with relative autonomy, though they may seek consultation or even regular supervision as needed. They are able to engage in honest and relatively accurate self-appraisals.

Level III integrated supervisors might be called "master supervisors." They can work well with trainees at any level of development and are unlikely to have strong preferences about trainee level. In their agencies, they often are in the role of supervising less advanced supervisors.

Hawkins and Shohet (1989) suggested that the essence of the Stoltenberg and Delworth's (1987) stages might be reduced to simple descriptors (note that, although they were discussing stages of counselor development, those stages seem to pertain reasonably well to supervisors, too; we have adapted their terminology accordingly):

Level I	self-centered	"Can I make it in this work?"
Level II	trainee centered	"Can I help this trainee make it?"
Level III	process centered	"How are we relating together?"
Level IV	process-in-context centered	"How do processes interpenetrate?"

Watkins's Model

In a series of articles, Watkins (Watkins, 1993, 1994, 1995b, c, d, e; Watkins, Schneider, Haynes, & Nieberding, 1995) reviewed the several conceptions of developmental stages through which supervisors progress. He (Watkins, 1993) suggested a model of supervisor development that is based on counselor development models originated by Hogan (1964) and enhanced by Stoltenberg (1981). Because of that very direct lineage, Watkins called his the *supervision complexity model* (SCM; Watkins, 1990; Watkins, 1993).

Watkins's basic concept is that development occurs as a response to increased challenge along several dimensions as the supervisor gains experience. Although there are many potential developmental issues across the stages, Watkins suggested four as being "central to much developmental thought." These principal developmental issues are

— Competency versus incompetency
— Autonomy versus dependency
— Identity versus identity diffusion
— Self-awareness versus unawareness

Watkins hypothesized that these issues become more complex as the supervisor moves through four developmental stages. Table 11.2 depicts

TABLE 11.2   Elaboration of the Supervisor Complexity Model: Optimal Supervision Environments by Supervisor Trainee Developmental Stages

Aspects of Supervision	Supervisor Trainee Developmental Stages			
	1	2	3	4
Role of supervisor	Provide secure "hold" for trainee, grounds and stabilizes him or her, more often directs, instructs, and teaches the trainee, provides tight structure for supervision relationship, assumes supportive guide–teacher role.	Continues to "hold" trainee, but loosens stance, still directs and teaches, but less so, stimulates expansion of trainee's awareness, assumes supportive guide–facilitator role.	Assumes supportive guide–collegial consultant role, focuses trainee increasingly on personal–professional issues, serves in more of a teaching–instructional resource capacity.	Assumes collaborative–collegial consultant role, helps trainee when therapy supervision problems arise, serves to challenge trainee in his–her theoretical approach and supervisory style.
Affective focus of supervision	Supervisor, in order to accommodate trainee's role shock and feelings of being much taken aback with his or her new role, avoids deep affective analysis, keeps focus more on trainee's surface, readily available, nonthreatening emotional experience, open to hearing about trainee's struggles with role.	Supervisor explores trainee's feelings more so and in more depth, discusses process issues more directly with the trainee, instructs trainee in better recognizing and dealing with process issues.	Very direct, intensive analysis of transference, countertransference, and parallel process phenomena, very direct, intensive analysis of one's personal issues and how they affect supervisory effectiveness.	If desired by trainee, even more direct, intensive, and exclusive process analysis could be done at this stage.
Cognitive–skills focus of supervision	Focus of teaching the trainee conceptual and intervention skills, helping the trainee to use skills she or he already possesses.	Continues to teach trainee skills as needed but strives more so to facilitate independent thought and action, encourages and supports trainee in developing her or his own conceptualizations and interventions.	Supervisor strives to complement the much better developed conceptual–intervention base that trainee now possesses, functions as cognitive–skills resource.	Supervisor offers alternative, conceptual ideas about specific cases that trainee presents. Intensively challenges all aspects of trainee's conceptual–intervention plan, helps trainee hone rationale for therapy supervision behavior.
Dependency in supervision	Greatest dependency on supervisor for structure, direction, instruction, and support.	Greater independence, less intense reliance on supervisor, lessened need for structure, direction, and instruction in supervision.	Greater, more elaborated sense of independence, usually able to function quite well on their own, uses supervisor to help him–her further develop in specific problem areas (e.g., responding to process more consistently).	Completely independent in functioning; no dependence on supervisor whatsoever.
Role of support–confrontation	Need for support from supervisor is greatest at this stage, use of confrontation should be none to minimal.	Support still important, but need for it is less intense; mild and even moderate confrontations can be used effectively.	Support ever present, but can be mixed even more so with confrontations.	Collegial supportive relationship, highest level of confrontation possible.

Source: C.E. Watkins, Jr. *American Journal of Psychotherapy*, Vol. 48, No. 3, 417–431, Summer, 1994.

Watkin's conception of how these issues are manifested at each of these four stages.

Stage 1, *role shock* is marked by "the impostor phenomenon" (Watkins, 1990). That is, new supervisors must struggle with "impostor feelings," just as they struggled before with issues of professional competence and authority as counselors or therapists. Watkins described the supervisor at this stage as "playing the role of supervisor." Supervisors are more likely to experience general, unresolved conflict at this stage than at any other time. They typically employ a concrete, rules-oriented approach, with little attention to the processes occurring between supervisor and supervisee. Novice supervisors are likely either to withdraw from trainees or to impose a too rigid structure.

Supervisors at stage 2, that of *role recovery and transition,* are beginning to develop a supervisory identity, along with self-confidence and a more realistic perception of strengths and weaknesses. Nevertheless, supervisors at this level are prone to wide fluctuations in self-appraisals, vacillating rapidly from feeling good about their performance to then feeling bad. Their tolerance of ambiguity is greater, as is their ability to recognize supervisory processes such as transference and countertransference (though their ability to address them is not yet at a commensurate level).

Supervisors at stage 3, *role consolidation,* are increasingly consistent in their thinking and acting as supervisors and in both self-confidence and accuracy of self-appraisal. They have begun to feel generally qualified for their role and, in fact, have begun to solidify a consistent and definably supervisory role. They are less controlling and leading with trainees and instead are more encouraging and supportive. Transference and countertransference issues no longer pose a significant threat. These and similar process issues become considerations during supervision.

Supervisors at stage 4, *role mastery,* have developed a consistent, solid sense of confidence as well as an integrated and well-elaborated sense of identity. Their supervisory style is well integrated, theoretically consistent, and personalized. They approach the crises and tasks of supervision in an open, adaptable manner that allows for differences between supervisees, while remaining theoretically consistent across all supervisory experiences.

Conclusions Regarding Supervisory Development Models

A decade ago, Worthington (1987) concluded from his review of the literature that empirical research on ways that supervisors change with experience was "at a rudimentary level" (p. 206) and that relatively few researchers had yet made this a focus of their research. As a consequence, there was little understanding of how supervisors' conceptual abilities or cognitive styles might change as they gain experience.

Most of the supervisor development models summarized in this chapter have been published since Worthington's article appeared. But as Russell and Petrie (1994) reminded us, they are in their formative stages and consequently are not yet supported by empirical data. Their conclusions about those models were as follows:

1. *There is considerable similarity among the theories of supervisor development. The theoretical models presented offer slightly different perspectives; however, all appear to describe a general process through which supervisors move from a new role in which they are overwhelmed, self-conscious, anxious, and insecure to an integrated identity where they feel comfortable, secure, and competent. Given these similar descriptions, there appears to be at least clinical, if not empirical support. What currently is needed, however, is model testing and not further model building.*

2. *The models of supervisor development provide preliminary guidelines for creating effective supervisory dyads in training environments. To develop the most effective training environments (i.e., supervisory dyads) for supervisees, training directors should pay attention to not only the developmental level of the supervisee, but also the level of the supervisor.*

3. *These models provide guidelines for developing training environments for supervisors. Awareness of the supervisor's developmental level may be helpful in guiding supervisor trainers in their interactions with their student supervisors.*

4. *These models provide directions and hypotheses for research on supervisor development. Although research examining supervisor developmental models has been virtually nonexistent, these models allow for specific hypotheses concerning supervisors' behaviors, thinking styles, emotions, and perceptions to be proposed and tested.* (pp. 34–35)

TRAINING AND SUPERVISING SUPERVISORS

Supervisor training can be offered in a number of formats and be intended for audiences of different types. It might be provided, for example, as a workshop or series of workshops for practitioners who already are working as supervisors. Alternatively, it might be provided as one or more formal university courses for graduate students.

We recognize that these training formats and target audiences inevitably will affect what is taught and how. Nevertheless, we believe all effective supervision training should have both *didactic* and *experiential* training components. Also, just as is the case of training in counseling or therapy, it should be designed as a series of graded experiences across time so that learners can have the opportunity to get consistent feedback based on practice.

Our discussion of supervisor training is written with university-based supervision courses specifically in mind. We believe, however, that the concepts pertain much more broadly and that they therefore generalize readily to other supervision training formats as well (and refer readers to the supervision workshop that is summarized in Appendix D). In line with this goal of offering more generalizable principles, we do not intend here to provide a detailed syllabus for a supervision course.

Minimum Qualifications for SITs

Before offering training, it first is necessary to know *who* should be targeted. In some cases, the training will be for practitioners who already are functioning as supervisors. In other cases, however, the SIT will never have supervised (this is especially likely in graduate training programs). In this latter case, decisions must be made about who

is qualified for that training. There seems no real consensus in the field about this matter.

State licensing boards often stipulate minimum amounts of experience required for someone to assume the legally sanctioned role of supervisor. Usually, this is stated in terms of the number of postlicensure years of experience.

Some professional associations and accrediting bodies also speak to the matter of necessary background. For example, the Association for Counselor Education and Supervision (ACES) has developed standards for counselor supervisors (see Appendix B) that suggest the supervisor should have postgraduate credentialing and licensure as a counselor, along with graduate courses and continuing education workshops in supervision. Similarly, the British Association of Counselling's Code of Ethics and Practice stipulate that the person "normally" should be an experienced and practicing counselor or therapist (see Appendix B).

It certainly makes sense that those who are to function autonomously as supervisors should be licensed in their own discipline. After all, supervision involves not only the professional development of the trainee, but *also* the protection of the client's well-being. For this latter role, a professional license would seem the minimal professional credential.

On the other hand, it is possible for a particular supervisor to have the more limited responsibility of helping the trainee to develop as a therapist. There are three frequent circumstances in which this might occur:

1. The supervisor is university based and supervising a trainee who is working in a field setting where his or her work is monitored by an on-site supervisor who will take responsibility for client welfare.

2. The supervisor is working as part of a vertical supervision team and has the relatively circumscribed role of helping the trainee to develop as a therapist. The supervisor's own supervisor would offer the necessary monitoring of client welfare. This occurs, for example, in situations where the person, in the practicum component of a graduate-level supervision course, supervises a beginning practicum student; it also occurs during internship when the intern supervises practicum students.

3. The supervisor might be a fellow student (or perhaps a fellow counselor) who is functioning as a peer supervisor (see, e.g., Benshoff, 1993). Bernard (1992), in fact, described one university's training program for master's-level students to serve as peer supervisors. Although this practice is useful both to the peer supervisor and to the person receiving that supervision, she did note that—in contrast to the training of doctoral students as supervisors—this practice posed several dual-relationship dilemmas that require particular attention by the faculty supervisor. These included (a) being careful about how the peer supervisor is involved in the summative evaluation process, (b) being more guarded during supervision-of-supervision in commenting on the performance of practicum students than might be acceptable if the supervision-of-supervision was with doctoral student SITs, and (c) difficulties of the peer supervisors and trainees sharing the same off-campus placements.

Any one of these three circumstances would allow nonlicensed professionals, including graduate students, to serve as supervisors. Common sense would dictate, however, that SITs would have *some* experience as counselors or therapists and that the level of this experience would exceed that of trainees they are to supervise. Ellis and Douce (1994) suggested that the SIT have 1 to 2 years of supervised practicum training as a counselor; Russell and Petrie (1994) suggested at least 1 year of practicum. To have at least this level of supervised experience is not only a matter of having the requisite skills, but also of having reached an appropriate level of professional identity, experience, and professional maturity (see, for example, our discussion above of the Stoltenberg and Delworth supervisory development model).

SIT Assessment: The First Step in Training

The first step in conducting *any* intervention should be to conduct some form of assessment. Because training supervisors is itself an intervention, the first step should be to conduct an assessment of the

intended trainees. This assessment can be for the trainer's information (e.g., to help the trainee more precisely address training needs). But it can also have an important benefit for the trainees themselves. In fact, such a self-assessment for trainees may stimulate reflections about their own experiences and actually then become an important initial part of their training (cf. Bonney, 1994; Borders & Leddick, 1987; Hawkins & Shohet, 1989; and Hoffman, 1990, 1994).

SITs enter supervisor training with life and professional experiences that are often substantial. An essential first step on the road to becoming a supervisor is therefore to take stock of this prior experience and to consider the ways it might generalize into this new role of supervisor. Hawkins and Shohet (1989), for example, developed a flow chart to depict what they believed the relationships to be among the multiple learning tasks of the beginning supervisor. This chart, depicted in our Figure 11.1, suggests that the first step should be the SIT's self-assessment.

Bonney reported asking SITs to remember and discuss their own first clinical experiences with clients and then to consider ways in which those feelings might resemble their current feelings about beginning to supervise. Borders and Leddick (1987) had new supervisors begin by constructing a "résumé" of their past supervision-relevant experiences. Their purpose was to stimulate a systematic review of the multiple relevant experiences the SIT will have had as counselor, teacher, consultant, researcher, and peer supervisor. They reason that each contributes to the SIT's new role of supervisor. The Borders and Leddick instrument, which we have reprinted in Table 11.3, is intended to begin the SIT's self-assessment of those skills. As they complete it, even the greenest supervision novices are likely to experience some feeling of affirmation.

Hoffman (1990) described a self-assessment procedure for SITs that complements that of Borders and Leddick. She asked them to complete a Supervision Life Line (SLL), which lists their past experiences of being supervised. For this task, they draw a vertical line down which they arrange their previous supervised experience in chronological order.

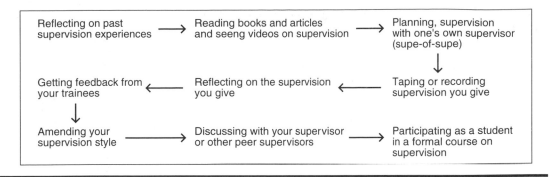

FIGURE 11.1   Supervision Learning Cycle

From P. Hawkins and R. Shohet (1989). *Supervision in the Helping Professions,* Milton Keyes, UK: Open University Press. Copyright © (1989) by Open University Press. Reprinted by permission.

The SITs are directed to list each of their experiences as a trainee, with the first one at the top, the next directly below it, and so on. For *each* experience, the SIT is directed to jot on the left side of the vertical line demographic information about that former supervisor. These include the supervisor's professional discipline, gender, age, and years of experience. On the right side of the line, directly opposite to this listing of supervisor demographics, SITs are to note the year of that particular supervision and its duration (e.g., "1995, 6 months") and to rate the value of that experience to their professional development (using a scale of 1 to 10, where 1 = *worst* and 10 = *best).*

Once SITs have done this, Hoffman suggested assigning them two follow-up tasks:

1. *To flesh out the various supervisory experiences in narrative form:* For example, she asked them to describe for each listed experience the client population that was served, the theoretical orientation that seemed to influence the supervisor's approach to supervision, the supervisor's approach to supervising, the most salient learnings from that supervisory experience, the aspects of that experience that were particularly easy and particularly difficult and, finally, anything that was felt to be missing from that supervisory experience.

2. *To write a discussion of what they have learned from both the SLL and the narrative material they wrote about it:* This discussion would include such observations as their conclusions re-garding their preferred styles of learning, differences in how they appreciated didactic versus experiential learning at various stages in their development, lessons from the way(s) conflict was handled during supervision, the various barriers to learning they encountered, and their preferences with respect to such supervisor attributes as age, gender, and discipline.

Hoffman then concluded this exercise with a discussion among group members about what they had learned from it and how this might be useful to them as they begin adopting the role of supervisor themselves.

The Didactic Component of Supervisor Training

The specifics of what is offered in the didactic portion of supervisory training are dictated by a number of factors, including instructors' characteristics (especially their professional discipline and theoretical orientation) and the characteristics of the particular institution or context in which training is offered. Nevertheless, those who train supervisors will be guided by a desire to cover essential areas.

Borders, Bernard, Dye, Fong, Henderson, and Nance (1991) suggested that supervisor training should address the following seven core areas:

1. Models of supervision
2. Counselor development

TABLE 11.3 Supervisor–Trainee Self-assessment of Supervision-related Knowledge and Skills

For each of the following items, circle the appropriate point on a continuum in which 1 = "very expert" and 7 = "very nonexpert"

Teaching Skills

Ability to identify learning needs of supervisee	1	2	3	4	5	6	7
Ability to identify learning style of supervisee	1	2	3	4	5	6	7
Ability to write learning goals and objectives	1	2	3	4	5	6	7
Ability to devise instructional strategies to accommodate needs and learning style of supervisee	1	2	3	4	5	6	7
Ability to present material in a didactic manner	1	2	3	4	5	6	7
Ability to present material in an experiential manner (e.g., to demonstrate or model)	1	2	3	4	5	6	7
Ability to explain the rationale for an intervention	1	2	3	4	5	6	7
Ability to evaluate supervisee's learning	1	2	3	4	5	6	7
Comfort in authority role	1	2	3	4	5	6	7
Ability to give constructive feedback to supervisee	1	2	3	4	5	6	7
Other_____	1	2	3	4	5	6	7

Counseling Skills

Ability to establish rapport, a working relationship with supervisee	1	2	3	4	5	6	7
Facilitative skills (e.g., warmth, primary empathy, genuineness, concreteness, etc.)	1	2	3	4	5	6	7
Challenging skills (e.g., self-disclosure, advanced empathy, confrontation, immediacy)	1	2	3	4	5	6	7
Expertise in counseling techniques (specify)	1	2	3	4	5	6	7
Expertise with particular clients and issues (e.g., suicide, career)	1	2	3	4	5	6	7
Ability to identify themes, patterns of behavior	1	2	3	4	5	6	7
Ability to model counseling skills	1	2	3	4	5	6	7
Ability to respond with flexibility	1	2	3	4	5	6	7
Ability to integrate data about supervisee into comprehensive "case conceptualization"	1	2	3	4	5	6	7
Other_____	1	2	3	4	5	6	7

Consultation Skills

Ability to objectively assess problem situation	1	2	3	4	5	6	7
Ability to provide alternative interventions and/or conceptualizations of problem or client	1	2	3	4	5	6	7
Ability to facilitate supervisee brainstorming of alternatives, options, solutions	1	2	3	4	5	6	7
Ability to encourage supervisee to make own choices, take responsibility for decisions concerning client and counseling	1	2	3	4	5	6	7
Ability to function in more peerlike, collegial relationship with supervisee	1	2	3	4	5	6	7
Other_____	1	2	3	4	5	6	7

Continued

TABLE 11.3   Continued

Research Skills							
Ability to make accurate and reliable observations (of client and of supervisee)	1	2	3	4	5	6	7
Ability to state testable hypothesis (e.g., is supervisee avoiding confrontation? Would role playing be an effective supervision intervention?)	1	2	3	4	5	6	7
Ability to gather data relevant to testing hypotheses	1	2	3	4	5	6	7
Ability to evaluate hypothesis	1	2	3	4	5	6	7
Ability to incorporate new data, restate and retest hypothesis	1	2	3	4	5	6	7
Ability to identify confounding variables affecting change (e.g., supervisees' personal issues)	1	2	3	4	5	6	7
Ability to critically examine and incorporate new research into supervision (e.g., on counselor–client dynamics, assessment, counseling intervention, supervision intervention)	1	2	3	4	5	6	7
Other_____	1	2	3	4	5	6	7

Adapted with permission from L. D. Borders and G. R. Leddick (1987), *Handbook of Counseling Supervision,* Association for Counselor Education and Supervision, Alexandria, VA.

3. Supervision methods and techniques
4. Supervisory relationship
5. Ethical, legal, and professional regulatory issues
6. Evaluation
7. Executive skills

Borders et al. also suggested three sets of learning objectives for each of these seven areas: (1) self-awareness, (2) theoretical and conceptual knowledge, and (3) skills and techniques. The result is therefore a 7 by 3 matrix with 21 types of learning objectives, which the authors then supplement with a list of more than 200 specific learning objectives. Russell and Petrie (1994) characterized this as the "most extensive set of recommendations for supervisor training" (p. 38), but then also suggested that the model "falls victim to its own complexity" (p. 38).

Russell and Petrie responded to the Borders et al. (1991) proposal by suggesting three essential areas for supervision training:

1. *Theoretical models of supervision:* They suggested that this be covered both with available

books on supervision and with videotapes demonstrating supervision from several approaches. They recommend, for example, Goodyear's (1982) videotape series that illustrates supervision from five different theoretical perspectives: Albert Ellis (rational–emotive), Carl Rogers (client centered), Erving Polster (Gestalt), Rudolph Ekstein (psychodynamic), and Norman Kagan (interpersonal process recall).

2. *Supervision research:* To familiarize students with the empirical literature, Russell and Petrie suggested two complementary strategies: (a) to assign students to read specific empirical articles that examine research issues in supervision; among these are selected research reviews and critiques (e.g., Avis & Sprenkle, 1990; Ellis, 1991; Ellis et al., 1996; Holloway, 1984; Holloway & Neufeldt, 1995; Lambert & Ogles, 1997); and (b) to develop a research proposal as their primary written product for the course. In doctoral programs and those master's degree programs that require a thesis, this paper might prove a springboard for some students' dissertation or thesis.

3. *Ethical and professional issues:* A review of ethical and legal issues that affect their work is important, especially as this is the first time students have been responsible for both the client *and* the trainee. Moreover, Russell and Petrie pointed out that there is a broader training opportunity in reviewing ethical and legal issues at this level. That is, it is a chance to revisit the issues at a time when the trainees are developmentally ready to consider them in a less rule bound and more critical manner than when they were first exposed to those issues earlier in training.

The number of supervision texts and books seems to be growing at an accelerating rate, and the supervision trainer now has available a substantial literature from which to draw. As an aid in locating appropriate training materials, we have compiled a list of most clinical supervision books that have been published during the past 25 years. These are summarized in Table 11.4. Many address a particular perspective or model (e.g., Ekstein & Wallerstein, 1972; Holloway, 1995; Kugler, 1995; Mueller & Kell, 1972; Sharpe, 1995; Stoltenberg & Delworth, 1987); others (e.g., Hess, 1980; Watkins, in press) are intended to give more general coverage to the domain of supervision, going "broad" rather than "deep." Other factors include discipline, such as social work (e.g., Holloway & Brager, 1989; Munson, 1993; Kadushin, 1992), psychiatry (e.g., Greben & Ruskin, 1994), and marital and family therapy (e.g., Liddle, Breulin, & Schwartz, 1988; Todd & Storm, 1997). It is also useful to note that there now is international attention to supervision, so this list includes books from Britain (e.g., Carroll, 1996; Dryden & Thorne, 1991, Hawkins & Shohet, 1989; Page & Wosket, 1994) and Australia (e.g., Williams, 1995).

Our own bias is that to assign one or more texts for a supervision course provides important but insufficient coverage of the material. Students should read not only research articles (studies, critiques, articles on methodology) such as Russell and Petrie recommend, but they should also be exposed to original work, including articles that are in some way "supervision classics" (two examples are Searles, 1955, and Stoltenberg, 1981).

Supervisory Skills: Laboratory Skills Training

It is now common in almost all graduate training programs for mental health professionals to offer a *laboratory skills* or *prepracticum* experience in basic counseling or therapeutic techniques. This usefully prepares the trainee for providing therapy to real clients in an actual treatment setting. By analogue, it is useful to provide SITs with some specific skills training prior to their actual work with counselor trainees.

In our own supervision training, we prefer to begin skills training by having SITs work in groups of about three to develop skits in which they depict "absolutely awful" supervision. This and the discussions that follow can have an ice-breaking role for a new group (and usually it is fun, for the nature of the task is really non-threatening). But in addition, it begins to define for the group what supervision *should not be*. To define what something is *not* is a developmental step for beginning to define what it should or might be.

To begin developing skills that the SITs will use in work with trainees, we provide them with early exposure to Kagan's IPR technique (see Chapter 5 for a description). In his workshops, Kagan would often discuss the "inquirer" role as one that would enable someone to function even as a "supervisor paraprofessional." That is, like the supervisor role that Williams (1995) advocates, the supervisor is to ask simple questions from a position of naive curiosity.

Session 4 in Bernard's Structured Workshop in Clinical Supervision (Appendix D) discusses IPR skills training. To that discussion we would add here that during this initial training (1) it is important that the person role playing the trainee (a) be given permission to stop the tape whenever she or he wants, but (b) be encouraged to do so relatively frequently for this training purpose; and (2) it is useful for the person role playing the supervisor to be given a list of IPR-type inquiries (e.g., a copy of our Table 5.4) and to be told that she or he should feel free to take time to study the list to find an appropriate inquiry; speed and smoothness are

TABLE 11.4   Supervision Books: 1972–1998

1972

Ekstein, R., & Wallerstein, R. (1972). *The teaching and learning of psychotherapy* (2nd Ed.). New York: International Universities Press.

Mueller, W. J., & Kell, B. L. (1972). *Coping with conflict: Supervising counselors and therapists.* New York: Appleton-Century-Crofts.

Seligman, M., & Baldwin, N. F. (Eds.) (1972). *Counselor education and supervision: Readings in theory, practice, and research.* Springfield, IL: Charles C Thomas.

1975

Mattinson, J. (1975). *The reflection process in casework supervision.* London: Tavistock Institute of Human Relations.

1976

Rioch, M. J., Coulter, W. R., & Weinberger, D. M. (1976). *Dialogues for therapists: Dynamics of learning and supervision.* San Francisco: Jossey-Bass.

1977

Kaslow, F. W., & Associates (1977). *Supervision, consultation, and staff training in the helping professions.* San Francisco: Jossey-Bass.

1979

Kadushin, A. (1979). *Supervision in social work.* New York: Columbia University Press.

Munson, C. E. (Ed.) (1979). *Social work supervision: Classic statements and critical issues.* New York: Free Press.

1980

Hess, A. K. (Ed.) (1980). *Psychotherapy supervision: Theory, research, and practice.* New York: Wiley.

1981

Wallerstein, R. S. (1981). *Becoming a psychoanalyst: A study of psychoanalytic supervision.* New York: International Universities Press.

1982

Blumenfield, M. (Ed.) (1982). *Applied supervision in psychotherapy.* New York: Grune & Stratton.

Hart, G. (1982). *The process of clinical supervision.* Baltimore, MD: University Park Press.

1983

Munson, C. E. (1983). *An introduction to clinical social work supervision.* New York: Haworth Press.

1984

Caligor, L., Bromberg, P. M., & Meltzer, J. D. (Eds.) (1984). *Clinical perspectives on the supervision of psychoanalysis and psychotherapy.* New York: Plenum Press.

Munson, C. E. (Ed.) (1984). *Family of origin applications in clinical supervision.* New York: Haworth Press.

1985

Alonso, A. (1985). *The quiet profession: Supervisors of psychotherapy.* New York: Macmillan.

Kadushin, A. (1985). *Supervision in social work* (2nd Ed.). New York: Columbia University Press.

1986

Piercy, F. P. (Ed.) (1986). *Family therapy education and supervision.* New York: Haworth Press.

1987

Borders, D. L., & Leddick, G. R. (1987). *Handbook of counseling supervision.* Alexandria, VA: Association for Counselor Education and Supervision.

Estadt, B., Compton, J. R., & Blanchette, M. (1987). *The art of clinical supervision: A pastoral counseling perspective.* New York: Paulist Press.

Stoltenberg, C., & Delworth, U. (1987). *Supervising counselors and therapists.* San Francisco: Jossey-Bass.

1988

Liddle, H. A., Breulin, D. C., & Schwartz, R. C. (Eds.) (1988). *Handbook of family therapy training and supervision.* New York: Guilford Press.

1989

Bradley, L. J., & Boyd, J. D. (Eds.) (1989). *Counselor supervision: Principles, process, and practice* (2nd Ed.). Muncie, IN: Accelerated Development, Inc.

Hawkins, P., & Shohet, R. (1989). *Supervision in the helping professions.* Milton Keynes, U. K.: Open University Press.

Continued

TABLE 11.4   Continued

Holloway, S., & Brager, G. (1989). *Supervising in the human services: The politics of practice.* New York: The Free Press.

1990

Hoffman, L. W. (1990). *Old scapes, new maps: A training program for psychotherapy supervisors.* Cambridge, MA: Milusik Press.

Lane, R. C. (Ed.) (1990). *Psychoanalytic approaches to supervision.* New York: Brunner/Mazel.

Mead, E. (1990). *Effective supervision: A task-oriented model for the mental health professions.* New York: Brunner/Mazel.

1991

Dryden, W., & Thorne, B. (Eds.) (1991). *Training and supervision for counselling in action.* Newbury Park, CA: Sage.

1992

Bernard, J. M., & Goodyear, R. K. (1992). *Fundamentals of clinical supervision.* Boston: Allyn & Bacon.

Kadushin, A. (1992). *Supervision in social work* (3rd Ed.). New York: Columbia University Press.

Skovholt, T. M., & Ronnestad, M. H. (1992). *The evolving professional self: Stages and themes in therapist and counselor development.* Chichester, England: Wiley.

1993

Munson, C. E. (1993). *Clinical social work supervision* (2nd Ed.). New York: Haworth Press.

Powell, D. J. (1993). *Clinical supervision in alcohol and drug abuse counseling: Principles, models, methods.* New York: Lexington Books.

1994

Feltham, C., & Dryden., W (Eds.) (1994). *Developing counsellor supervision.* Thousand Oaks, CA: Sage.

Greben, S. E., & Ruskin, R. (Eds.) (1994). *Clinical perspectives on psychotherapy supervision.* Washington, DC: American Psychiatric Press.

Page, S., & Wosket, V. (1994). *Supervising the counsellor: A cyclical model.* London: Routledge.

1995

Holloway, E. (1995). *Clinical supervision: A systems approach.* Thousand Oaks, CA: Sage.

Jacobs, D., David, P., & Meyer, D. J. (1995). *The supervisory encounter: A guide for teachers of psychodynamic psychotherapy and psychoanalysis.* New Haven, CT: Yale University Press.

Kugler, P. (1995). *Jungian perspectives on clinical supervision.* Einsiedeln, Switzerland: Daimon.

Neufeldt, S. A., Iverson, J. N., & Juntunen, C. L. (1995). *Supervision strategies for the first practicum.* Alexandria, VA: American Counseling Association.

Sharpe, M. (1995). *The third eye: Supervision of analytic groups.* New York: Routledge.

Taibbi, R. (1995). *Clinical supervision: A four-stage process of growth and discovery.* Milwaukee, WI: Families International.

Williams, A. (1995). *Visual and active supervision: Roles, focus, technique.* New York: W. W. Norton.

1996

Carroll, M. (1996). *Counseling supervision: Theory, skills, and practice.* London: Cassell.

Haber, R. (1996). *Dimensions of psychotherapy supervision: Maps and means.* New York: W. W. Norton.

1997

Gordan, K., Smith, T. B. S. (1997). *Psychotherapy supervision in education, clinical practice, and institutions.* Northvale, NJ: Jason Aronson.

Todd, T. C., & Storm, C. L. (Eds.) (1997). *The complete systemic supervisor: Context, philosophy and pragmatics.* Boston: Allyn and Bacon.

Watkins, C. E., Jr. (Ed.) (1997). *Handbook of psychotherapy supervision.* New York: Wiley.

1998

Bernard, J. M., & Goodyear, R. K. (1998). *Fundamentals of clinical supervision* (2nd Ed.). Boston: Allyn & Bacon.

This table lists *most* supervision books published during this period. We make no claims that it is inclusive.

not issues at this early stage in learning the technique.

Early training in IPR techniques empowers the SIT, who is now equipped with some skills on which to fall back. Moreover, it helps the trainee to screen out the teacher role, which often is difficult for beginning SITs to do.

Richardson and Bradley (1984) drew from the microcounseling model that Allen (1967) originally had developed to suggest a "microsupervision" model for the training of supervisors. As Bernard (Appendix D) suggests, this provides an excellent complement to the IPR model in that it emphasizes the teacher role.

Session 5 of Bernard's structured workshop is devoted to microskill training; she provides a discussion of training procedures. In addition, it is useful to think in terms of the three stages Richardson and Bradley suggested were operative in "microsupervision" training:

1. *Assessment:* to assess the SIT's skills and skill deficits and then to rank the deficits in a hierarchy
2. *Modeling:* to use videotape for modeling of each supervisory skill to be taught via microsupervision
3. *Transfer:* to transfer the skill to real practice settings via supervision role plays and self-evaluations of performance

These supervisory skills, though, should be accompanied by shifts in the ways the SITs think of themselves. Specifically, they need to make the cognitive shift from thinking like a counselor to thinking like a supervisor. As SITs gain experience and training in supervision, this shift will occur [one simple indicator is when SITs no longer inadvertently refer to their trainees as "my client(s)"]. Borders (1992), though, has suggested some strategies to help this occur.

One simple strategy is to have SITs review and take notes on a trainee tape as if they were going to meet with that counselor for supervision during the following hour. After watching (or listening to) 10 to 15 minutes of the tape, SITs are stopped and asked to review their notes. They are to count the number of statements about the *client* and about the *trainee.*

Typically, participants report few if any statements about the counselor. This has been especially true of experienced clinicians in inservice workshops. Then they are reminded that they will be meeting with the counselor, *not the client, during the next hour. What are they going to do during the* supervision *session to help the* counselor? *They are to keep this question utmost in their minds as they review the remainder of the session.* (Borders, 1992, p. 139)

A second strategy that Borders suggests is to encourage SITs to employ deliberate educational planning for their supervision sessions. This is guided by two types of data: (1) SITs' own assessment of trainees' strengths and weaknesses, based on a review of one or more of the trainees' counseling tapes and (2) the three to five learning goals for the supervisory experience that SITs have trainees develop during the initial supervisory session. SITs are then to use both trainees' learning goals and their own assessment of the trainees' work to guide the feedback they give the trainee.

Supervision-of-Supervision

Thirty years ago Hansen and Stevic (1967) argued for the development of practica in supervision. There was at that time virtually nothing of that sort for SITs. Fortunately, this is changing. In the section that follows we will discuss the practicum component of supervision training. This practicum experience sometimes is referred to informally as "supe-of-supe" (i.e., supervision-of-supervision).

The institutional context will determine the point at which SITs actually begin their practicum experience. For example, if their training is occurring in a university that offers a sequence of two or more supervision courses, the practicum component usually will begin after at least a term of didactic and laboratory skills preparation. On the other hand, if there is only a single course, the practicum might begin much earlier and coincide with the didactic portion. Still another scenario is an internship training site where the practicum experience might begin very early, perhaps after an orienting workshop or two.

The techniques and format for supe-of-supe could reasonably be any that are used in the supervision of counseling or therapy. Moreover, there have been discussions of some very innovative techniques and formats for supe-of-supe, including videotape review of the supe-of-supe (Wilcoxon, 1992), live supe-of-supe (Constantine, Piercy, & Sprenkle, 1984), and even role reversals in which the SIT then supervises his or her own supervisor (Fine & Fennell, 1985).

We speculate, however, that group may be the most frequent modality, for supe-of-supe is often a component of a graduate-level course where there also is simultaneous seminar-type didactic coverage of supervision-relevant material. Group also has other learning advantages, as Frayn (1991) makes clear in his discussion of the 13-year history of a supe-of-supe group for psychiatrists.

Ellis and Douce (1994) summarized one model of group supe-of-supe that they report having conducted (at the time they wrote the article) over 13 years with approximately 35 groups and 175 SITs. In their model, the supe-of-supe group meets 2 hours weekly and typically consists of five to eight SITs and two trainers. During each session (1) the first 30 to 60 minutes is spent with monitoring the supervisory work of the various group members and then (2) one SIT presents a supervisory case, supplementing that presentation with the playing of audio and/or vidotapes. Each SIT presents in this manner at least twice during the term.

The developmental models we discussed earlier should provide some guidance for the structuring of these supervisory experiences. In fact, there seems to be some general agreement among the several models about the needs of the beginning-level SIT (i.e., the one most typically to be seen in a supervisor training course or workshop). That is, very much like the novice counselor, the novice supervisor will want direction and structure—some guidelines about how to proceed.

Note that this is consistent with what we know about learning skills in *any* new domain. Consider, for example, Anderson's (1996) ACT cog-

nitive science model in which he proposes that novices rely heavily on *declarative knowledge,* that is, rules for behaving that they have learned from instructors and from their readings. As they practice skills that they apply in this manner, though, they are begin to develop *proceduralized knowledge,* that is, the ability to apply skills automatically, without having to think consciously about each step in their execution. As proceduralized knowledge begins to develop, novices can stop looking to rigid rules to guide their behavior.

Watkins (1994) made several suggestions for meeting the needs of novice supervisors, including:

(1) very closely monitoring the cases the trainee works with (which can . . . contribute to a feeling of being held, secured, and stabilized in the supervision relationship; "I am not alone in this"); (2) having a "setness" about the supervision of the supervisor trainee (i.e., having regularly scheduled meeting times that are clearly set as to place, time, frequency, and duration, which further grounds and stabilizes the supervision context); and (3) having a policy established about supervisory crises (i.e., if something comes up that the supervisor trainee feels unable to handle and which seemingly demands immediate attention, how can he/she then go about talking with the supervisor?), with which both the supervisor trainee and his/her supervisor feel comfortable. (p. 422)

Another step in providing structure and prescriptions for the beginning SIT should concern what to do during the first session(s) with a newly assigned trainee. Both Bonney (1994) and Borders and Leddick (1987) suggested that this first session be scheduled, if possible, before the trainee actually begins to see clients (if this is not possible, the session should address clients only in general terms).

The primary foci of this session should be at least a beginning of a mutual understanding of the nature and process of supervision, immediate and long range goals of each, their theoretical or philosophical orientations and the supervisee's relevant past experiences. A discussion of role expectations and a beginning of mutual role definitions would also be helpful. If all this proves to be overwhelming for one interview some of it may be delayed until a later time. (Bonney, 1994, p. 32)

Hoffman (1994) suggested that supervision might be thought of as having three phases: (1) beginning, (2) middle, and (3) end. This is a useful way to think not only about supervision itself, but also about the supe-of-supe. Each stage suggests certain natural tasks. We already have discussed some of the tasks of the beginning stage.

The Middle Phase. This is the longest of the stages and the one during which most of the work of both supervision and supe-of-supe will occur. Ellis and Douce (1994) suggested eight issues that commonly occur during supe-of-supe. Five of them are especially prominent during this middle stage.

1. *Balancing responsibility:* In their earlier professional roles, the SITs have had to be concerned with the welfare of their clients. As they move into the role of supervisor, that responsibility continues, but now with the sometimes frustrating fact that they do not themselves have the direct access to the client that they are used to having. Moreover, as supervisors, they now have the additional responsibility of facilitating the counselor trainee's development. Sometimes these responsibilities can be at odds, or at least seem to be. Ellis and Douce (1994) observed that attaining a balance between these responsibilities is often an especially difficult matter for the new supervisor to resolve. Ellis and Douce suggested a two-pronged intervention to address this. One is to assign and then discuss relevant literature (ethical, legal, and professional role related). The other is to suggest that the SIT use an IPR technique with his or her trainee.

2. *Parallel process:* SITs are most likely to encounter and find themselves responding to parallel processes (e.g., Ekstein & Wallerstein, 1972; Mueller & Kell, 1972) during this, the middle phase. We have already discussed these and the related concept of isomorphism in Chapter 4. What we would add here to that previous discussion is that supe-of-supe adds yet *another* level through which parallel processes may reverberate: Whereas in supervision the supervisor must be aware of reverberations of processes between the client–counselor and the supervisor–trainee relationships, in supe-of-supe those processes might

find expression at the additional level of the SIT and his or her supervisor. As Ellis and Douce (1994) pointed out, it is during supe-of-supe that parallel processes are most likely to be noticed. Noticing the patterns at this level gives a unique opportunity not only for teaching, but also for modification of that pattern.

3. *Power struggles:* A basic rule in counseling is that therapists should avoid overtly attempting to assert their wills against those of the client (e.g., there is the clinical wisdom to "go with the resistance"). There are characteristics of supervision, though, that make power struggles more likely to occur than in therapy. These include the fact the relationship is evaluative, that it has a teaching function, and that the supervisor ultimately is responsible for ensuring that the client's welfare is protected (and therefore is likely occasionally to slip into a therapy-by-remote-control mode when they believe they know what is best for the client). Compounding these already present characteristics is that beginning SITs are more likely than their more advanced colleagues to behave in a structured, controlling manner, while also remaining especially sensitive to any perceived threats to their authority.

Ellis and Douce noted that when these factors blossom into full-blown power struggles the counselor may "go on strike." This can occur through the more subtle means of regularly coming late to supervision sessions, of being inattentive, or of not following through on the supervisor's suggestions; in more extreme versions, the trainee may simply adopt a "make me" stance.

IPR can be an especially useful tool in helping to work through these power struggles. That is, IPR can be used during the supe-of-supe sessions to help the SIT get perspective. In turn, the SIT can use IPR with his or her trainee as a means to shift to a consultant role and away from the teacher role that would be more likely to elicit power struggles (Bernard, 1989).

4. *Individual differences:* Ellis and Douce suggested that attention to individual differences (which, in this context, include race, culture, gender, sexual orientation, and religion) is important during supe-of-supe. There are opportunities for

SITs to help their trainees address these issues in counseling; there are also opportunities to address them as they are salient in supervision. Although these differences may not have profound differences in the relationship(s), they remain important. For that reason, Ellis and Douce suggested that supervision trainers have particular responsibility for ensuring that individual differences are addressed during supe-of-supe.

5. *Sexual attraction:* Sexual attraction, either between counselor and client or between trainee and supervisor, is likely to occur during supe-of-supe. Such attraction can pose particular challenges for the SIT and/or the supervisor trainer. This problem is compounded by the fact that sexual attraction remains somewhat taboo, and therefore the involved professionals may feel uncomfortable addressing it openly when it occurs.

Ellis and Douce suggested that the supervisor trainer has a particular obligation to watch for instances of sexual attraction and then to address them openly. That is, sexual attraction is natural: in surveys, Pope, Spiegel, & Tabachnik (1986) found 95 percent of men and 76 percent of women psychologists reported having felt sexually attracted to a client; Pope, Tabachnik, and Spiegel (1987) found that 91 percent of psychologists reported this experience. However, although SITs generally are clear that sexual contact between either counselor and client or supervisor and trainee is unethical, they often are given too little training in the management of these naturally occurring feelings.

The End Phase.   Two primary issues confront the SIT during the End Phase of supervision. One is dealing with termination issues (certainly dealing with the termination of the SIT–trainee relationship, but often also helping the trainee to deal with termination issues as they are occurring with clients); the other is to address the matter of providing a summative evaluation of the trainee (Chapter 8).

The one addition we would make to those earlier discussions is our assertion that it is important that the SIT have had *some* role in evaluating the trainee and that the trainee be fully apprised of this role and its nature from the very beginning. This

gives what might be called ecological validity to their supervisory experience. That is, supervision occurs in an evaluative context; without that element, the supervisor has not had the opportunity to address the issues that arise around that.

Of course, the SIT is also terminating supe-of-supe at this stage, while also dealing with his or her own evaluation issues. These processes then provide an opportunity for the SIT to reflect on and integrate the experiences she or he has had as a novice supervisor. One way we have fostered this process has been to require that SITs end the term by making a formal presentation that summarizes their work across the term with at least one trainee. This is a chance, then, to review the course of their work together, including (1) interventions that worked and did not, (2) the nature of any conflicts that occurred and how they were resolved, (3) transference and countertransferences that seemed to have affected their work, and (4) any parallel processes that might have affected the work.

In so doing, SITs have the chance to get summative feedback from the trainer, as well as other group members. But, in addition, they can reflect on feedback their trainees have given them. That feedback should have been available in several forms.

1. During the summative evaluation of the trainee, the SIT should have solicited feedback about aspects of the supervision experience that were especially useful or not.

2. The SIT should have looked for informal ways to obtain feedback during the course of the relationship. For example, the regular use of an IPR technique is one means by which the SIT might get ongoing feedback.

3. We also believe it is important for the SIT to have used paper and pencil measures to obtain from the trainee regular and systematic feedback (after every session if possible). This is consistent with a scientist–practitioner orientation and has at least the following benefits:

   a. Obtaining repeated measures from trainees by using one or more specific questionnaires allows SITs to obtain feedback that is systematic and that can be compared across sessions. That is, they can look back over the supervisory experience with these data in hand and essentially regard it as $n = 1$ research. For example, which session(s) was rated especially high and what was occurring during that session? Which session(s) was rated low and why? (In fact, we encourage this process by asking that the SIT, during the end-of-term summary presentations, provide session evaluation data, plotted across sessions if possible, with discussions of possible supervisory processes that might explain these data trends.)

b. It may be more comfortable for both trainee and SIT to have the trainee give constructive feedback in written form than in a face to face meeting.

c. By making the solicitation of feedback a regular expectation, it can diffuse potential conflicts that otherwise might arise as the trainee "sits on" grievances or other bad feelings.

d. As SITs might receive negative feedback, it allows them the opportunity to reflect on it in private (as well as in supe-of-supe) and to consider what they will do with that constructive feedback (e.g., Williams, 1994).

There are a number of possible measures that SITs might use to obtain feedback from trainees. Williams (1994), for example, has developed the Supervision Feedback Form. Using Likert-type items, the SFF asks trainees to respond to (1) the extent to which certain aspects of the supervisory environment were present (e.g., the extent to which supervision was relaxed, empowering, clear, supportive, collaborative, and so on) and (2) the extent to which supervision was useful in meeting certain training goals (e.g., developing confidence, developing interventions, and conceptualizing cases). Other possible measures certainly could include the Supervisory Styles Inventory (Friedlander & Ward, 1984; see Appendix C) or the Session Evaluation Questionnaire (e.g., Stiles & Snow, 1984).

CONCLUSION

We began this chapter with the observation that most mental health professionals eventually will work as supervisors. This is a professional role that requires formal training. We then summarized literature on the professional development of supervisors. We also discussed the sequence and important elements in the training of supervisors.

Implict, though perhaps not as strongly stated as it might have been, is the important impact becoming a supervisor can have on the mental health professional who moves into that role. For example, it can be very empowering to advanced students who are affirmed that they really *do* have professional wisdom to pass on to other students. Moreover, the very act of supervising can help SITs gain new perspectives on their work as therapists.

Hawkins and Shohet (1989) pointed out that Ronald Winnicott's, (the psychoanalyst) concept of the "good-enough mother" provides a useful analogy for supervisors: that they should aspire to be "good-enough supervisors." By this, Hawkins and Shohet meant that the supervisor should be able to meet the trainee's needs, even in those times when the trainee is responding with wariness, avoidance, or even anger. Certainly, this concept of the "good-enough supervisor" logically extends the developmental metaphors we have used in this chapter and throughout the book. However, it also suggests that the supervisor will have received adequate preparation for this role. We hope this chapter will serve to sensitize supervisor trainers to some of the issues involved in that training.

CHAPTER 12

Supervision Research Issues, Directions, and Methods

We often hear of the singular breakthrough in science. But science more often is incremental and relies on the gradual accretion of new findings that will supplement and extend older ones. Paradigm shifts (cf. Kuhn, 1970) may refocus researchers' emphases and the concepts they use, but do not alter the sometimes tedious, step-by-step process of science that occurs through ongoing research programs. When this characteristic of science is considered in the context of the brief history of supervision research it really is remarkable that such a solid empirical foundation for supervision practice has already begun to develop.

The relatively short history of counseling and psychotherapy research dates only from approximately the end of World War II (Garfield, 1983). Supervision research has an even shorter history. It was only a couple of decades ago that Kell, Morse, and Grater (undated) asserted that "[t]he training of counselors and psychotherapists can perhaps be described by the old epigram, 'the blind leading the blind.' It is an attempt to teach, using methods about which we know practically nothing, a process about which we know far too little." Harkness and Poertner (1989) reported that the first published study of social work supervision appeared in 1958. It was at about that time also when *Counselor Education and Supervision* was founded (1961) to provide a journal outlet for articles on counselor training and supervision (that journal, along with the *Journal of Counseling Psychology* and *Professional Psychology: Research and Practice,* is consistently among the several journals where supervision research is most likely to be found).

Many researchers have conducted an occasional study of supervision during the past several decades. A number of them have been doctoral students who focus their dissertations on a topic very central to their academic lives at the time they are choosing a research topic. Perhaps only a score of researchers, though, are engaged in programmatic investigations of supervision. This seems generally consistent with Price's (1963) law, which is that

> *if* k *is the number of persons active in a discipline, then the square root of this number approximates the size of that subset who produced half of the contributions. Thus, about 250 composers are responsible for the music played in the classical repertoire. The square root of this number is 15.8. It turns out that a mere 16 composers put their names on half of all the pieces performed and recorded.* (Simonton, 1994)

But the cumulative effort both of this core group of supervision researchers and of those more occasional researchers has resulted in a healthy forward momentum to the science of supervision for which Holloway and Hosford (1983) called. Moreover, as researchers develop instrumentation (e.g., Friedlander & Ward, 1984; Ellis, Anderson-Hanley, Dennin, Anderson, Chapin, & Polstri, 1994; Ellis & Ladany, in press; McNeill, Stoltenberg, & Romans, 1992; Watkins, Schneider, Haynes, & Nieberding, 1995) and models (see Chapter 2) unique to supervision, this science increasingly is becoming independent of psychotherapy theory and research. Because this assertion relates directly to the very purpose of this chapter, we will digress briefly to address some of the issues involved.

Supervision models traditionally developed as extensions of therapy theories (e.g., Bartlett, Goodyear, & Bradley, 1983; Hess, 1980; Watkins, 1997; also, we discuss this in Chapter 2 of this book). On one level this type of extrapolation makes excellent sense, for Shoben (1962) and others have argued that each counselor or therapist works from an implicit theory of human nature that must also influence how the therapist construes reality (e.g., through epistemology) and interpersonal behavior. It is reasonable to assume that this same theory of human nature is present whether the professional is offering therapy, supervision, or some other intervention (e.g., see data from Friedlander & Ward, 1984; Goodyear, Abadie, & Efros, 1984; and, Holloway, Freund, Gardner, Nelson, & Walker, 1989). It is also true that much of the content of supervision (e.g., the teaching of specific counseling technique) inevitably is grounded in particular counseling models. For example, attention to trainee–client and supervisor–trainee working alliances derives from psychodynamic counseling models; skills in using an empty chair technique follow from a Gestalt therapy perspective. Lambert and Arnold (1987), in fact, made the strong assertion that research on the effects of supervision "will not progress faster than knowledge about the effective ingredients of psychotherapy" (p. 222).

Therapy models influence how supervisors conceptualize supervision. But, from the other direction, supervisees' models of counseling or therapy are influenced by their supervisors' therapy model, as Guest and Beutler (1988) demonstrated. Putney, Worthington, and McCulloughy (1992) also showed that supervisors' and supervisees' theories of therapy interacted in several ways, exerting a substantial effect on how the two perceived one another's roles and competence.

Despite these clear linkages between supervision and therapy, there are substantial drawbacks to using therapy models as the primary basis for conceptualizing supervision (Russell, Crimmings, & Lent, 1984). For example, fully articulated theories that are specific to supervision will not be developed as long as supervision remains anchored in theories of therapy. Also, therapy theorists have failed too often either to translate their hypotheses into testable propositions or to operationalize their constructs.

In short, despite the adverse consequences, it is natural for supervisors to use therapy as the lens through which they view supervision. But the tendency to use it as the *exclusive* lens has disadvantages and likely will weaken as (1) supervision research grows in both volume and sophistication and (2) formal training for supervisors becomes more universal.

Some of this growing volume of research on supervision has been summarized in critiques and reviews. Ellis, Ladany, Krengel, and Schult (1996) note that there have been at least 32 reviews of empirically based studies of supervision. Anyone seriously interested in conducting supervision research should begin by reading some of those available commentaries (e.g., Borders, 1989a; Ellis et al., 1996; Holloway, 1984, 1992; Holloway & Hosford, 1983; Lambert, 1980; Lambert & Arnold, 1987; Lambert & Ogles, 1997; Russell et al., 1984; Wampold & Holloway, 1997; Worthington, 1987).

In Chapter 1, we cited Schön's (1983) belief that professional training is a process of inculcating in trainees two distinct realms of knowledge: formal theories and observations that have been confirmed, or are confirmable, by research; and knowledge that has been accrued from the professional experience of practitioners. Because of our scientist–practitioner orientation, we have drawn from both realms in writing this book. We hope, then, that readers will have found at least some research questions to intrigue them as they read the first 11 chapters. In fact, the placement of this chapter at the end of the book reflects our hope that at this point readers will have been stimulated to think about which supervision-related questions still seem in need of empirical answers.

We will divide the remainder of this chapter into two parts. In the first part, we will single out some selected supervision issues that seem to merit particular research. In the second part, we will discuss methodological issues in the conduct of supervision research.

ISSUES AND DIRECTIONS FOR SUPERVISION RESEARCH

One of the exciting aspects of choosing supervision as a domain of inquiry is that there is no shortage of topics to pursue. We are tempted to offer here a list of research issues that we believe merit attention. But, as we have just noted, we hope readers will already have begun developing their own lists of research questions during their reading of earlier chapters. To illustrate this point, the four following areas from other chapters are important, yet have been the focus of almost no research:

— Personal characteristics of supervisors and of trainees exert important influences on the supervisory process (Wampold & Holloway, 1997). Yet investigations have focused on only a few types of individual differences, mostly concerned with some personality attributes, such as reactance (e.g., Tracey, Ellickson, & Sherry, 1989). But, as we indicated in Chapter 3, there are very few studies of the roles that either gender or race and culture play in supervision processes and outcomes.
— Most processes and outcomes of supervision-of-supervision, discussed in Chapter 11, remain unexplored. Supervision itself is a complex system that encompasses both the subsystems of the therapist–client and the supervisor–supervisee; supervision-of-supervision is even more complex and adds the relationship between the supervisor and the supervisor's supervisor as a third subsystem. Among the many questions that might be examined, then, are those that concern the possible effects of one of these subsystems on any of the others. For example, how are parallel processes manifest within this expanded system?
— The research literature concerning modalities used in family therapy training and supervision remains small. For example, processes and outcomes of live supervision, discussed in Chapter 7, have been investigated in only a very few studies so far (e.g., Heppner et al., 1994; Kivlighan et

al., 1991). There are many potentially rich issues that might be explored in this area. One of those, for example, concerns what client thought and affects are directed at the unseen people behind the one-way glass and how that might affect therapeutic processes.
— Group supervision, as we discussed in Chapter 6, has almost no empirical bases, which is especially surprising given the extent to which this modality is used.

But instead of expanding this list into a long catalog of topics, we want to use this space to discuss three issues not addressed earlier in the book, but which seem especially important for supervision researchers to consider. The first of these, the increased interest in manualized treatments, concerns an important professional practice issue. The other two concern more basic psychological science concepts that have the potential to inform our knowledge of supervisory practice. These are, respectively, social psychological models and concepts from cognitive science.

Manualized Treatments, Training, and Supervision

During the past decade, the movement to managed care of health services has affected mental health professionals in a number of ways. One has been an increased attention to the use of treatment protocols, or manuals, to standardize interventions. This trend has important implications for supervision and training. However, only a few authors (e.g., Lambert & Ogles, 1997; Multon, Kivlighan, & Gold, 1996; Stein & Lambert, 1995) so far have begun to address the topic.

Although manualized treatments fit the agenda of managed care companies, they actually evolved from the work of scientifically grounded mental health professionals. The manuals themselves were secondary to these professionals' interest in promoting treatments that had demonstrated effectiveness. These treatments are now generally manualized for reasons we will discuss.

Participants at a conference sponsored by the American Association of Applied and Preventive

Psychology (Hayes, Follette, Dawes, & Grady, 1995) invoked the practices of the U.S. Food and Drug Administration (FDA) to suggest how psychotherapeutic treatments might be regulated. That is, the FDA requires pharmaceuticals to meet stringent criteria with respect to both efficacy and possible deleterious effects. By extension, psychological treatments should receive similar scrutiny and meet related criteria for effectiveness and safety. This sentiment, in fact, has been evident in the movement to document, endorse, and publicize those psychological treatments for which clear empirical support exists (e.g., Task Force on Promotion and Dissemination of Psychological Procedures, 1995–1996).

Most advocates of what now are called empirically validated treatments (EVTs or, in Britain, evidence-based medicine; see Roth & Fonagy, 1996) do not disavow the nonspecific effects or common factors that underlie all therapies, factors such as therapist warmth and caring (Rogers, 1957) and the social–psychological factors Frank (1973) described. It *is* their strong position, though, that some treatments have demonstrated specific effects with particular disorders.

EVT advocates therefore dispute research reviews and metaanalyses that conclude that all psychological treatments obtain virtually equivalent effects (e.g., Smith & Glass, 1979). To illustrate with what may be an extreme example, penile squeeze technique is a specific treatment for men experiencing premature ejaculation, one that has demonstrated efficacy beyond the warmth and empathy that the therapist can offer. It is the position of EVT advocates that such specific treatments of demonstrated effectiveness are available for a number of disorders. Therefore, they dispute the "dodo bird verdict" that Luborsky, Singer, and Luborsky (1975) (and even earlier, Rosenzweig, 1936) suggested, based on their conclusion that different models of therapy achieved no demonstrably different levels of effectiveness (from *Alice in Wonderland:* "all have won and all shall have prizes").

The analogy between pharmaceutical treatments and psychotherapy extends also to how treatments are tested. The FDA requires that new drugs be evaluated during trials that are based on a protocol that stipulates criteria both for selecting patients and for how treatment is delivered (e.g., dosages and the like). In this way, there can be greater assurance of the internal validity of the study and of that study's congruence with similar studies. If the drug is shown eventually to be effective, physicians who prescribe it can then know clearly the circumstances under which this has been so.

Similar protocols are utilized increasingly in psychological treatment. As Weiss and Marmar (1993) note, virtually all psychological treatment studies funded by the Alcohol, Drug Abuse, and Mental Health Administration since the mid-1980s have been required to use such protocols (i.e., treatment manuals). Like the protocols for research on pharmacological efficacy, these stipulate the appropriate clientele for treatment, and then spell out in some specificity the treatment that is to be delivered. In 1984, Luborksy and DeRubeis declared this use of treatment manuals to be a "small revolution." Wilson (1996) has depicted manuals in terms of an appropriate interface between science and practice, that is, as the clinical application of research findings.

Many of the treatment manuals were developed for cognitive or cognitive–behavioral treatments (e.g., Beck, Rush, Shaw, & Emery, 1979; Craske & Barlow, 1990); Barlow (1993) is a compendium of treatment manuals for 12 different disorders. But, in fact, almost any coherent treatment model can be articulated in protocol form. Manuals now exist for a range of treatments, including psychodynamic (e.g., Luborksky, 1984) and interpersonal models (e.g., Klerman, Rounsaville, & Chevron, 1984). There even has been one attempt to manualize the practice of supervision (Neufeldt, Iverson, & Juntunen, 1995).

Most manualized treatments are suited for specific disorders. Opponents of the use of treatment manuals and EVTs argue, however, that this does *not* reflect the real-life work of most practitioners. Instead, clients typically present with multiple problems for which no single treatment is clearly indicated. Garfield (1996) raised other criticisms as well. These included possible limitations in the existing research concerning which judgments are made about what should be considered empirically validated or not, variability in client and therapist attributes that might affect treatment, and the important role that common factors play in psychotherapy. Moreover, as a recent metaanalytic study demonstrated (Wampold, Mondin, Moody, Stich, Benson, & Ahn, in press), the dodo bird hypothethis continues to have the weight of evidence behind it. The rush toward identifying EVTs may eventually prove to have been unwarranted.

But despite these caveats, the use of psychotherapy treatment manuals has increased enormously during the past decade. In a recent survey, for example, the majority of directors of clinical training and of APA-accredited internships reported providing students with supervised clinical experience that was based on manualized treatments (Crits-Christoph, Chambless, Frank, Brody, & Karp, 1995), which parallels the recently adopted APA accreditation guidelines, which emphasize the importance of students gaining exposure to "empirically supported treatments."

Supervisors need to be sensitive to this trend and its possible implications for this work. Moras (1993) suggested, for example, that manuals can be particularly effective with inexperienced trainees, because "First, a well-specified manual is a systematic, focused, and goal-oriented base for teaching. Second, a well-specified manual provides a common conceptual frame of reference for the supervisor–trainee's work" (p. 583).

Dobson and Shaw (1993) suggest a multistep sequence for manual-based training and supervision of therapists. Trainees should receive, in the following order, assigned readings on model's theory and technique, an intensive workshop on that model and its techniques, and, finally, practice of the techniques with less difficult clients.

Supervision becomes mandatory at this last training stage. The supervisor must be an expert in that model and in the manual that drives it. Videotaped or at least audiotaped samples of the trainee's work are essential, for an important goal is to bring the trainee to a criterion level of adherence to the protocol, to monitor and ensure fidelity of the trainee's behavior to that specified in the protocol (Moncher & Prinz, 1991).

There are pitfalls, though, for both trainees and supervisors. For the supervisor, the pitfall is to become merely a "police officer" who ensures that the trainee adheres to the manual. To do so would not only restrict what might be offered the trainee, but also have negative effects on the supervisor relationship.

For trainees, one pitfall is to respond to a client who presents with a matter that is pressing, but does not otherwise fit the protocol. The ideal is perhaps to find a middle course between the mechanical application of the manual and totally "winging it."

Another trainee challenge is to adhere to the techniques and procedures of the manualized treatment without cost to the quality of their relationship to the client. Henry, Strupp, Butler, Schact, and Binder (1993) found, for example, that the use of a manual was successful in changing therapists' technical interventions, but that it had unexpected, negative effects on the therapists' relationships with their clients. Specifically, these therapists became less optimistic, more authoritative and defensive, and less approving and supportive. Fortunately, Multon et al. (1996) since have found that—using the same time-limited dynamic therapy model that was the focus of Henry et al.—trainees were able to obtain stronger working alliances with their clients even as they demonstrated increasing adherence to the manual's interviewing style. Multon et al. speculated that, whereas trainees in the Henry et al. study were more experienced therapists, those in their study were relative novices who would not be as likely to experience disruption in interpersonal functioning as they learn a new technique. But this matter requires continued attention in both practice and research.

Lambert and Ogles (1988; 1997) raised several other concerns that are salient to supervision practitioners and researchers. For example, they note that "because treatment manuals have not been used in studies investigating their effectiveness in supervising and training graduate level students, it is not known if training in the specific manualized techniques can be a beneficial tool for training facilities" (1997, p. 433). Another issue they suggest requires further exploration is the comparative effectiveness of the trainee receiving supervision based on the manual versus simply reading it: "Perhaps supervision is the more important aspect of training with manuals and the manuals are really not any different from any other book on psychotherapy theory" (msp. 15).

In summary, the use of treatment manuals almost certainly will continue to affect supervision and the way it is delivered. Yet a great deal remains to be learned about the specific implications for supervisory practice. This area is fertile research ground.

Social Influence Models

Supervision occurs in a social context. For that reason, there is utility in looking to social psychology for hypotheses and concepts to employ in supervision theory and research. A decade ago, Dixon and Claiborn (1987) reviewed literature that concerned social psychological approaches to supervision. Claiborn, Etringer, and Hillerbrand (1995) and Stoltenberg, McNeill, and Crethar (1995) have been among those who have continued to invoke social psychological constructs for understanding supervision.

Literature applying social psychological concepts concerning interpersonal influence and attitude change to counseling and psychotherapy is more than three decades old. Heppner and Claiborn (1989) suggested that "formal articulation of the social influence point of view probably began with the publication of Frank's (1961) *Persuasion and Healing*" (p. 365). Further articulation of that point of view occurred in such other works as that of Goldstein, Heller, and Sechrest (1966) and Strong (1968). In fact, Strong's article, presenting a two-stage model of change, probably was most directly instrumental in stimulating what now has become a substantial literature.

In Strong's view, we as individuals give interpersonal power (or influence) to those in our lives whom we perceive to have resources necessary to meet our needs of one kind or another. These are the people with whom we form relationships of a personal or professional nature. By the same token, though, any relationship is reciprocal, and therefore we are also exerting influence on others even as they influence us. In short, any relationship is one of mutual influence.

In his original work, Strong (1968) drew from French and Raven (1959) to suggest that in counseling the basis of this influence resides in three basic resources that clients (or trainees) will seek from therapists (or supervisors). A therapist or supervisor will have interpersonal influence to the extent that he or she is perceived by the client or trainee as having *expertness, attractivenes* (i.e., perceived similarity in values, goals, etc.), and *trustworthiness*. Applying Strong's two-stage social influence model to supervision, we can understand that the supervisor's first task is to establish himself or herself as a credible resource (i.e., possessed of expertness, attractiveness, and trustworthiness). Once the trainee has come to perceive the supervisor as credible, the supervisor's second task is to begin attempts to influence the supervisee to make changes (skill, conceptual, etc.).

We have noted repeatedly throughout the book that one aspect of supervision that distinguishes it from counseling or therapy is its evaluative aspects. This suggests that French and Raven's (1959) *coercive power,* which was not invoked in Strong's (1968) original formulations of counseling, might be a source of supervisor influence. This has not been examined in supervision research.

The first decade of research on this basic model was summarized in separate reviews by Corrigan et al. (1980) and Heppner and Dixon (1981). More recently, Heppner and Claiborn (1989) reviewed the second decade of that research, and Dixon and Claiborn (1987) reviewed research on social influence processes in supervision.

The primary focus of most of this book has been on the *supervisor's* responsibility in the supervisory process. Perhaps an unfortunate consequence has been to imply a one-way process in which supervisors influence trainees, but not necessarily vice versa. Extensions of Strong's model (e.g., Strong & Claiborn, 1982; Strong & Matross, 1973) that recognize the bidirectional nature of social processes have been relatively overlooked. Just as the supervisor influences the trainee, the trainee *also* influences the supervisor.

The concept of strategic self-presentation bears directly on this issue of bidirectional influence. According to this concept, a person will modify his or her behavior to elicit a particular behavior from another person (Claiborn & Lichtenberg, 1989). Because of the threat of evaluation, supervisees' attempts to influence supervisors' impressions of them are likely of particular importance. Supervisees therefore engage in what social psychologists call *impression management* or *strategic self-presentation*. We discussed this in Chapter 3 as a relationship process. It remains an important potential source of research ideas.

Social–psychological applications to practice continue to be suggested. One current conception of social influence that is generating interest among some supervision researchers is that of Petty and Cacioppo's (1986) elaboration likelihood model (ELM). This model suggests that influence can occur through two information-processing routes: either *central* (involving an effortful elaboration of information) or *peripheral* (greater reliance on cues or on simple rules) routes for information processing. Influence that occurs through the central route is considered more enduring and has more effect on subsequent behaviors.

However, the route by which persuasion occurs depends on the *source* (e.g., credibility and attractiveness), *message variables* (i.e., the subjective strength of the arguments supporting a position), and *recipient characteristics* (e.g., degree of motivation to process the message). When people are motivated and able to consider messages that they perceive to have compelling arguments, they can then be influenced via a central route; otherwise, influence might occur through more peripheral means, such as the perceived expertness of the communicator. McNeil and Stoltenberg (1989) reviewed studies that have attempted to test the ELM framework within counseling. Both Claiborn et al. (1995) and Stoltenberg et al. (1995) have discussed the promise of the ELM model for research in supervision. Also of interest is that Stoltenberg et al. have attempted to incorporate what we already know about supervisee development into the ELM.

Blocher (1987) and Martin (1988) both distinguished between theories that are scientific and guide inquiry and those that are personal or process oriented and guide practice. Heppner and Claiborn (1989) asserted that the social influence model is of the former type, intended to guide scientific inquiry. Perhaps, as a result, many practitioners would find it "experience far" (Gelso, 1985), that is, foreign to their usual ways of understanding. This does not, however, negate its potential for leading eventually to findings with practical implications. In fact, the social influence area will likely remain a fertile source for hypotheses about supervision.

Information Processing, Cognition, and Supervision

Social-psychological and cognitive science models overlap considerably, as the foregoing discussion of the ELM illustrated. Whereas the context is social and the intent is one of influence and change, cognition and information processessing are essential components. Nevertheless, there is utility in separating these two domains for the purposes of discussion. In this section of the chapter, then, we will address issues of cognition that are relevant to understanding supervision processes and that have the potential to inform supervision research.

Stone (1988) noted that cognitive researchers "have been chastised for employing trivial tasks and inadequate models in describing human cognition" (p. 2). He argued that, because supervision overcomes these objections, it provides an ideal vehicle for cognitive search.

Supervision provides a domain involving such non-trivial factors as human context, affective experience, and personal beliefs, requiring more complex models of cognition; while a cognitive approach offers an appealing and heuristic alternative conceptualization of trainee experience. (p. 3)

There are at least three different lines of cognitive research that might have implications for supervision. Although they inevitably intertwine, we will treat them independently. They concern (1) cognitive structure and style, (2) attributions and self-efficacy, and (3) discrete cognitions (supervisors and supervisees).

Cognitive Structures and Styles: How People Process Information. When we were writing the first edition of this book, we asked Puncky Heppner what areas he thought should be considered important for future supervision research. He suggested the following research question:

> *How does supervision affect the supervisee's ability to arrange information cognitively about counseling? In particular, how does the supervisee begin to conceptualize clients differently or more effectively, diagnose clients, learn intervention strategies, and so on?* (Heppner, personal communication, 1989)

In raising these questions, Heppner was speaking to the issue of cognitive schemata. To understand current research on social cognition, consider that we are constantly bombarded with overwhelming amounts of information about our social environments. At any given moment, we have available to us far more information than we can register, much less process. Consequently, we attend selectively to that information. The selective encoding, representing, and recalling of information are guided by internal cognitive structures, or *schemata,* that provide us with some efficiency in our processing of information (e.g., see, Heppner & Krauskopf, 1987; Markus, 1977).

Martin (1985), in particular, has helped us to understand cognitive schemas. He and his colleagues have provided us with concepts and methods that have been employed in a number of recent studies (e.g., Martin, Slemon, Hiebert, Hallberg, & Cummings, 1989).

Cognitive Developmental Models. The notion of cognitive schemata is central to the cognitive developmental theorists such as Harvey, Hunt, and Schroeder (1961), Piaget (Piaget & Inhelder, 1969), Perry (1970), and Loevinger (1976). Cognitive developmental models, however, should be considered a subcategory because of their central assumption that there is a predictable pattern in how people attend to and process information. In general, these models all maintain that people progress from concrete, simple, and externally focused ways of processing information to ways that are more abstract, complex, and internally focused.

In counseling and supervision literature, the cognitive developmental model that has been employed most often is Harvey et al.'s (1961) conceptual systems theory (CST). A central tenet of this system is that optimal learning and performance depend on the degree of matching between the learner and the environment. The key personal variable in this model is that of conceptual level (CL), which usually is considered to exist on a continuum from low (concrete) to high (abstract). Note that CL is unreliably related to intelligence.

> *As individuals progress in their acquisition of abstract functioning, they increase the availability of multiple alternatives in evaluation and behavior, responding more relativistically and less dichotomously. [The] developmental hierarchy is often depicted on a concrete–abstract continuum. The concrete types, referred to as low CL, exhibit conceptual simplicity and external, dependent orientations to interpersonal affairs. The abstract types, referred to as high CL, demonstrate conceptual complexity and internal, interdependent orientations.* (Holloway & Wampold, 1986, p. 310)

That model has been used as a means to match classroom environments and students. It would predict, for example, that low-CL students would learn best in a more structured environment (e.g., one in which an instructor had a detailed syllabus that logically flowed from one topic to another; in class, the instructor would stay close to the outline, discourage tangents away from it, and minimize ambiguous material). High-CL students, on the other hand, would function better in less structured environments.

Holloway and Wampold (1986) noted that during the 1970s researchers began to apply CST to counselor training and the counseling process and that it was Stone and his associates (e.g., Berg & Stone, 1980; Stein & Stone, 1978) who were most involved in these early studies. But other researchers have conducted research in this domain as well. Holloway and Wolleat (1980), for example, found that higher-CL trainees produced more effective clinical hypotheses. Employing Loevinger's related model of ego development, Borders, Fong, and Neimeyer (1986) found that trainees at lower ego levels were more likely to describe their clients in simplistic concrete terms, whereas those at higher levels used more sophisticated, interactive descriptions. Holloway and Wampold (1986) reviewed the findings concerning the CST model; although their focus was primarily on counseling studies, many of their conclusions generalize to supervision.

Stoltenberg (1981) grounded his developmental model of supervision (see Chapter 2) in CST. According to this model, beginning supervisees are more likely to function at low conceptual levels and, therefore, demand more structured learning environments. As they progress in their training, supervisees move to higher conceptual levels and, therefore, require corresponding training environments. Blocher's (1983) model of supervision is also based on cognitive developmental models, including that of Harvey et al. (1961).

Holloway (1987) has offered a thoughtful critique of the actual congruence between the CST model and those of Stoltenberg and Blocher, who drew different conclusions about the implications of cognitive development for an optimal training environment. Whereas Stoltenberg maintained that the environment should be deliberately *matched* with the supervisee's level of cognitive functioning, Blocher argued for an intentional *mismatch* intended to force the supervisee to grow to a higher level of functioning. Quarto and Tracey (1989) have suggested that research designed to compare these contrasting assumptions should be examined.

Essential to the conduct of such research, though, is having effective measures of conceptual level. To date, researchers have used measures such as that of Harvey et al. (1961) or of Loevinger (1976). Blocher, Christensen, Hale-Friske, Neren, Spencer, and Fowlkes (1985) developed a cognitive development measure specific to supervision that appears to have promise.

Tetlock has offered a related construct, *integrative complexity,* which concerns a person's information processing and problem solving in almost any area of life. It is quite similar to conceptual complexity in how it is manifest. An important difference, though, is that, whereas the latter speaks to a person's characteristic level of functioning, integrative complexity may fluctuate across situations (e.g., see Tetlock & Hannum, 1984). To date, it apparently has been used in only a single supervision study, which examined its role in multicultural case conceptualization (Ladany, Inman, Constantine, & Hofheinz, 1997).

A recent study by Tetlock and Tyler (1996) demonstrated that conceptual and integrative complexity can differ considerably within the same individual. In this case, their data were policy statements by Winston Churchill and opponents from the 1930s, but apparently the same would be true of almost any person in almost any context. Some interesting research questions for supervision researchers might concern how trainees' integrative complexity changes in different situations (e.g., during a client emergency versus a more typical counseling situation or while being observed live or in anticipation of being evaluated) and across time.

Attributions and Self-efficacy.   Attributions just as easily could have been discussed in our section concerning social–psychological issues. We include it here, though, reasoning that the issue of this entire section on cognition is one of *how* people process information: attributions are conclusions drawn from that information.

One important finding of attributional research in supervision is that the perspective of the observer determines the types of attributions he or she will make about another's behaviors. For example, Dixon and Kruczek (1989) found in an analogue study that supervisors were more likely to attribute effects of therapy to the therapist's *actions.* Therapists, on the other hand, were more likely to attribute those effects to environmental factors. This is based on what is known in social psychology as the *fundamental attribution error* (Jones, 1979), or the actor–observer hypothesis: whereas I am likely to explain my own behaviors in terms of my responsiveness to environmental events, others who observe my behavior are likely to explain it in terms of my personality traits.

In another study based on this hypothesis, Worthington (1984a) found that the experience level of supervisors affected attributions they made of supervisees' behaviors. Specifically, he found that supervisors with greater experience were *less* likely to explain their supervisees' behaviors in terms of enduring traits (such as empathy, genuineness, etc.). Presumably, these more experienced therapists were seeing the world more through the eyes of their supervisees and therefore exhibiting empathy.

Self-efficacy beliefs (e.g., Bandura, 1982, 1986), a specific type of attribution, have particular implications for supervision. Self-efficacy can be understood as a person's certainty that he or she can execute a particular behavior successfully. Bandura hypothesized that behavior and behavior change are mediated by expectations of personal efficacy. Such expectations determine whether a behavior will be initiated, how much effort will be expended, and how long the behavior will be sustained in the face of obstacles. According to the model, a person's self-efficacy regarding a particular behavior is influenced by four basic factors: (1) actually having done the behavior, (2) vicariously observing another person perform the behavior, (3) being persuaded by an influential other that one can perform the behavior, and (4) physiological responses in the face of performing the behaviors (e.g., bodily concomitants of anxiety, which usually have an inhibiting effect on self-efficacy). In fact, a person with higher self-efficacy would respond to anxiety as a challenge rather than as a debilitating affect.

Self-efficacy has been a variable in several supervision studies (Friedlander, Keller, Peca-Baker, & Olk, 1986; Johnson & Seem, 1989; Johnson, Baker, Kopalo, Kiselica, & Thompson, 1989). For example, Efstation, Patton, and Kar-

dash (1990) found that scores on the supervisory working alliance measure correlated with a measure of trainee self-efficacy. Larson and Daniels (in press) have recently reviewed that literature; Larson (in press) has provided a supervision model in which self-efficacy is central.

The model seems promising as both an independent and a dependent variable for additional supervision research. For example, to what extent— and in what ways—does self-efficacy influence supervisee performance? In what way does the self-efficacy of a trainee change over time (e.g., is it linear or does it show some other pattern of development)? In what ways do certain supervisory styles affect supervisee self-efficacy? What links exist between supervisees' self-efficacy and their affective experience of supervision and the therapy in which they are participating?

Research of this sort depends, of course, on having adequate instruments to measure the particular construct. Fortunately, researchers have available to them at least several trainee self-efficacy scales. These include those of Friedlander and Snyder (1983), Johnson and Seems (1989), and Larson et al. (1992).

Discrete Cognitions in Counseling and Supervision. Perhaps corresponding to the rise of cognitive–behavioral models, mental health professionals and educators have become particularly interested in what people think as they engage in their activities. This interest has extended to supervision, with some promising lines of research. With the knowledge gained from this research, we will be in a better position to understand, employ, and even design supervisory interventions.

There are a number of ways to assess cognitions (e.g., see Merluzzi, Glass, & Genest, 1981). Among the better known of these is the thought-listing procedure of Cacioppo and Petty (1981). In this procedure, respondents are asked to record their thoughts about some event (e.g., an upcoming therapy session or a supervision session in which they have just participated). Cacioppo and Petty suggested that these thoughts then be classified on the three dimensions of *polarity* (favorable, neutral, or unfavorable), *origin* (internal or external), and *target*. Tarico, Van Zelzen, and Altmaier (1986) since have demonstrated that respondents themselves can rate the thoughts on these dimensions with no sacrifice of reliability or validity (as compared to using trained raters).

Related to thought listing is the thinking aloud technique (Genest & Turk, 1981), and Dole et al. (1984) developed a recall procedure that was an adaptation of Kagan's (1980) interpersonal process recall, designed to elicit and score the therapist's actual internal dialogue. Supervisee studies that have used one or another of these cognitive assessment procedures include those of Friedlander et al. (1986), Kurpius, Benjamin, and Morran (1985), and Borders (1989d). A recent variation has been to examine intentions, which are a specific type of cognition. For example, Kivlighan (1989) examined changes in counselor intentions as a function of training, and Strozier, Kivlighan, and Thoreson (1993) studied the role of supervisor intentions in supervisory processes.

One procedure that has not yet been used in supervision research, despite its apparent utility for this purpose, is what Davison, Navarre, and Vogel (1995) call the "Articulated Thoughts in Simulated Situations (ATSS)" procedure for use in cognitive assessment. Supervisors will recognize similarities to the recall process of IPR (e.g., Kagan, 1980), though the ATSS procedure offers greater constraints on the participant in ways that enhance reliability.

METHODOLOGICAL CONSIDERATIONS IN SUPERVISION RESEARCH

We anticipate that readers of this book will vary widely in their sophistication about research in general and supervision research specifically. Many will be graduate students who may be considering supervision as a thesis or dissertation topic. Others will be supervision practitioners whose interest is more focused on the implications of that research for their work as supervisors. We have written the

following section on methodology in supervision in a way that we hope balances the need to be simultaneously accessible and useful to readers across a spectrum of research sophistication.

Perhaps we should begin this section, though, by asserting that all studies in the behavioral sciences have limitations. Gelso (1979) vividly captured this issue in his discussion of the "bubble hypothesis":

> *A few years ago, a graduate student in a seminar I teach on counseling and psychotherapy research . . . proposed that the conduct of science was analogous to the placement of a sticker on a car windshield. During the placement, a bubble would appear. The owner presses the bubble in an attempt to eliminate it, but it reappears in another place. The only way to get rid of it is to eliminate the entire sticker. The student termed this phenomenon the "bubble hypothesis" . . . the idea behind it is obvious, ubiquitous—and all too infrequently in the awareness of students and researchers.* (p. 12)

Thus, a researcher might employ a very rigorous design to achieve high internal validity, but at the expense of external validity (generalizability). To redesign the study to have greater external validity, the researcher likely would have to sacrifice internal validity. Gelso discussed this tension as one between *rigor* and *relevance*. There is no perfect study.

But the fact that all investigations have limitations does not excuse the researcher from doing all he or she can to minimize them. In fact, Holloway and Hosford (1983) reported that several reviewers of supervision research literature had found such pervasive design shortcomings as

> *(a) nonrandom assignment and experimental groups, (b) inadequate sample size, (c) global and imprecisely defined variables, (d) lack of specificity in design procedures and treatment conditions, (e) invalid and/or unreliable scales of measurement, (f) criterion measures that do not accurately represent actual supervisory behaviors, and (g) unjustified generalization from findings of analogue studies. In fact, the majority of research in counselor supervision*

threatens the integrity of basic principles of internal, external, and construct validity. (p. 74)

Other reviewers of supervision research (e.g., Ellis, Ladany, Krengel, & Schult, 1996) have reached similar conclusions. In the following sections, we will address some of the methodological issues supervision researchers face.

Research Strategies for a Science of Supervision

Holloway and Hosford (1983) asserted that, in accordance with the progressive nature of science, supervision research should proceed through three stages: (1) one of descriptive observation in which a phenomenon is observed in its natural environment; (2) one in which important, specific variables are identified and relationships between and among them are clarified; and (3) one in which a theory is developed, based on the empirically derived evidence about variables and their interrelationships. This stage model provides a convenient framework for organizing the next two sections of the chapter.

Descriptive Research: Stage 1. Much of stage 1 research in supervision (i.e., descriptive observation) has been accomplished via extrapolations from counseling and psychotherapy and from the clinical (i.e., nonsystematic and subjective) observations of supervision practitioners. Increasingly, however, a body of literature has begun to evolve that provides essential descriptive data for this first stage of supervision science.

No one methodological approach is uniquely suited for providing these descriptive data. We believe, in fact, that it is essential to encourage methodological diversity. Invoking a metaphor to comment on this issue, Harmon (1989) noted that when a car does not run, the problem can be explained "by either a mechanic or a physicist without either of them necessarily understanding what the other was talking about. The point to be made here is that neither level of abstraction is wrong, it just depends on what your needs are" (p. 87).

With this metaphor in mind, we offer summaries of four research strategies that seem to have particular utility for describing supervision processes. Although all would be consistent with what Mahrer (1988) called a "discovery oriented" approach, they each give a somewhat different perspective of supervision. Each has potential to offer hypotheses to drive later research that is of a more experimental or quasi-experimental nature.

1. *Qualitative research.* Studies of this type can provide a rich source of information about the subjective experiences of supervisors and supervisees. Whereas many researchers have regarded such inquiry as unacceptably "soft," these attitudes are changing in favor of an increased appreciation for methodological diversity (e.g., Hoshmand, 1989). As a consequence, the number of qualitative studies of supervision has been growing. The phenomenological study of Hutt, Scott, and King (1983) is one early example of qualitative research. Doehrman's (1976) study of parallel processes also had qualitative elements to it.

One of the more ambitious qualitative studies was that of Skovholt and Ronnestad (1992a, b). Their data were obtained during interviews with 100 practitioners at levels of professional development that ranged from beginning graduate students to practitioners with more than 40 years of experience. Based on these interview data, Skovholt and Ronnestad developed a stage model of development that provided an important extension to counselor development theory. They also extracted 20 themes of counselor development from their participants' narratives.

Another example of qualitative research is Smith, Winton, and Yoshioka's (1992) consideration of a reflection team's experiences, beliefs, and aspirations, as represented in their responses to questions about their clinical practice. More recently, Neufeldt, Karno, and Nelson (1996) conducted a qualitative analysis of how prominent supervision experts conceptualized supervisee reflectivity. In the same journal issue, Worthen and McNeill (1996) reported a phenomenological investigation of what four men and four women supervisees regarded as "good" supervision events. It seems, then, that qualitative studies of supervision slowly are growing in number.

Recently, several computer programs have been developed to assist qualitative researchers to identify structure and meaning in text and narrative. One of the better known of these has the intriguing acronym, NUDIST ("Nonnumerical Unstructured Data Indexing Searching and Theorizing"; e.g., see Gorely, Gordon, & Ford, 1994). New tools such as these seem to have much to offer supervision researchers, both to make their work easier and to demonstrate intercoder reliabilities in ways that previously were not possible. No supervision studies using this type of software have yet been reported.

2. *Case study research.* A case study is a useful vehicle to address the first, descriptive, stage of science, for it provides "a holistic methodology for studying how multiple variables interact to affect the process and outcome of psychotherapy for an individual" (Hill, 1989, p. 17). Early case studies (e.g., Freud's cases of Dora and of Ratman), although perhaps clinically useful, were retrospective accounts by the therapist. For that reason and because there was no corroborating evidence, they inevitably were limited by the subjectivity and omissions of the person who recounted the case.

Doehrman's (1976) multiple-case study of parallel processes constituted a methodological improvement in supervision research. She employed structured interviews and an observer's perspective to gather and interpret data. Further rigor has been possible through innovations Hill and her colleagues have made to case studies in counseling research (e.g., Hill, Carter, & O'Farrell, 1983). By employing multiple measures that include psychometric data, the evaluations of trained raters, and the observations of the involved parties, she brought rigor to the case study. That approach to case studies has much to offer supervision researchers and has been employed in several studies (e.g., Alpher, 1991; Friedlander, Siegel, & Brenock, 1989: Martin et al., 1987; Strozier et al., 1993).

The videotape series Goodyear (1982) developed has allowed for between-supervisor comparisons that actually are multiple-case studies (e.g., Abadie, 1985; Friedlander & Ward, 1984; Harris & Goodyear, 1990; Holloway et al., 1989). These have in common a focus on supervisor–supervisee interactions and employ the research strategy covered in the next section.

3. *Interactional research.* Because supervision is largely a verbal endeavor, there is merit in examining the verbal discourse between the supervisor and supervisee and, perhaps, between the supervisee and client. Studies of this nature have been conducted for some time (e.g., Dodenhoff, 1981; Lambert, 1974; Pierce & Schauble, 1970). The sophistication with which supervisor–supervisee interactions have been analyzed, however, has increased considerably during the past decade, largely through the research program of Holloway and her colleagues (e.g., Holloway, 1982; Nelson & Holloway, 1990). Tracey and Sherry (1993) are among others who have conducted interactional research in supervision.

Interactional research can provide important information about patterns of interaction that occur between supervisors and supervisees. One limitation, though, is that they are concerned with moment-to-moment interactions, and these patterns cannot easily be linked to other behaviors that occur at later points. Moreover, the use of interactional analyses in naturalistic settings results in correlational data that preclude the making of causal inferences. Despite these and other limitations, however, interactional research is a very promising way to begin addressing the descriptive stage of science. A useful overview of interactional research methods can be found in Lichtenberg and Heck (1986), Wampold (1986), and Claiborn and Lichtenberg (1989).

4. *An events paradigm.* A fourth approach has been suggested by Stiles, Shapiro, and Elliott (1986) as the "events paradigm." Heppner and Claiborn (1989) summarize it as follows:

The events paradigm has three components: first, the identification of a specific context for examining the process of interest. . . . second, the manipulation of specific interventions to set the process in motion (such as different interpretation styles or levels of discrepancy); and, third, the measurement of effects (that is, attitude change in the direction of the interpretation). All of this can be done in a single session or series of sessions in ongoing counseling. The approach is based on the ideas that sessions themselves have outcomes and that the processes leading to them ought to be the focus of process research. (p. 375)

In short, then, a specific behavior occurs within the session and it elicits a particular kind of response from the other person. Such a bracketed sequence of behavior constitutes an event. To the extent that predictability in this sequence can be observed across different sessions and across different participants, we have learned something new about supervision processes.

These, then, are four of the possible methods for conducting the descriptive research called for by Holloway and Hosford (1983) as stage 1 of their model. Their second stage concerns the examination of relationships between and among supervision-related variables.

Testing Hypotheses and Building Theory: Stages 2 and 3.   Descriptive research provides an important source of hypotheses that then might be tested. There are particular methodological challenges to be met by supervision researchers who wish to undertake studies of the next type, that is, studies consistent with stages 2 or 3 of the Holloway and Hosford model. Eight of these challenges seem especially important.

I. Sample sizes: The first issue is the practical one of obtaining a sufficient number of subjects to conduct supervision research. This is a greater difficulty in supervision research than it is in research on counseling or psychotherapy. Whereas clients, or at least people who might be reasonably construed as potential clients, are readily accessible, the same is not true of supervisors and/or supervisees.

There *are* training programs that have large numbers of trainees spread across the various levels of preparation. But these are few in number, and the many researchers who are not in such settings must often consider such strategies as the following, each of which imposes certain constraints on the types of research questions that can be examined.

1. Researchers can extend the time of their work to enable them to perform their interventions over longer periods (in universities, for example, data can be gathered across two or more semesters). This, of course, can be a substantial hurdle for the doctoral student who is eager to complete dissertation research.

2. Researchers can employ mailed surveys or questionnaires. Although such studies have been the source of much of our empirical knowledge of supervision, they do not allow observation of actual supervision events. Also, return rates in typical studies of this sort pose interpretive problems. For example, if 40 percent of a sample does not respond to a survey, the investigator is left to speculate about the representativeness of the 60 percent who did return their materials. Did they, for example, return their materials because of a special investment in the issue being addressed (a type of investment that might bias results in particular ways)?

3. Researchers can develop analogue studies that employ nonsupervisors (or nonsupervisees) as subjects. An example of this is the study by Stone (1980), who used introductory psychology students as "inexperienced supervisors." Studies of this sort may be of special value in the preliminary stages of investigations of previously unexamined phenomena. They must of necessity, however, be analogue in nature.

II. Cross-sectional versus other designs: Researchers, especially those interested in investigations of developmental models, should consider alternatives to cross-sectional designs (see Holloway, 1987). The use of the (too infrequent) longitudinal study (e.g., Hill, Charles, & Reed, 1981) adds an important dimension. But it, too, has limitations, such as those associated with cohort effects. Ellis et al. (1988) recommended instead a sequential design that combines aspects of both cross-sectional and longitudinal designs.

III. Information about raters: "When using raters and rating procedures, provide sufficient information about the raters and their training for the reader to evaluate the raters' qualifications, potential for biases (e.g., whether they are blind to experimental conditions), standardization of ratings, and how rating materials were assigned to raters" (Ellis et al., 1988, p. 9). In fact, in their review of published studies, Goodyear, Ettelson, O'Neil, Sakai, and Smart (1996) found considerable variability in the extent and type of information that researchers provide about their coding procedures.

IV. Demographics report: "In case of nonrandomized studies, full reporting of participant demographics (e.g., age, sex, degree program) and other data germane to the study (e.g., amount of supervised counseling experience, theoretical orientation, types of clients seen) are needed to assess for differences among groups" (Ellis et al., 1988, p. 10).

V. Multiple roles for participants: "Avoid using participants in multiple roles (e.g., as both supervisor in one group and supervisee in another). If this is unavoidable, control for this confound methodologically and statistically" (Ellis et al., 1988, p. 11).

VI. Clear working definitions: Basic to social science is that phenomena being investigated have well-accepted and clear operational definitions. There are, however, a number of important concepts in supervision that have proved difficult to operationalize, at least in a consistent way. The concept of parallel processes, for example, is intuitively compelling to practitioners, but has proved difficult to define clearly for research purposes.

There are many other possible examples of other such supervision concepts that have been difficult to

operationalize. Two examples will suffice, though. The first of these is the notion of developmental level, which has been challenged on conceptual grounds (Holloway, 1987) and too often has been defined only in terms of the trainee's amount of experience or practicum level (one attempt to operationalize the developmental level for research purposes is the scale by McNeill et al., 1992, found in Appendix C). Also, the concept of level of structure, which is central to many discussions of supervisory relationships and interventions, is another that is difficult to actually operationalize.

But if a field is to advance, it is not sufficient that a researcher develop a clear working definition of a concept but one that no one else employs. Other researchers must use that definition as well if we are to make sense of the aggregated findings from multiple studies that purport to measure that concept. One example of this issue is with the definition of interpersonal power, or relational control, which Lichtenberg and Wetterson (1996) showed to have been operationalized in multiple ways in counseling and supervision research.

An inextricably related matter is that of the instruments used in supervision research. The particular measure used automatically becomes the de facto operational definition of the particular variable. Fortunately, as we discuss later in this chapter, supervision researchers have been giving increasing attention to instrument development.

VII. Self-reports of satisfaction: In her discussion of the future research agenda in supervision, Borders (1989a) called for a moratorium on the use of self-reports of supervisee satisfaction as an outcome measure. Satisfaction is imperfectly correlated with effectiveness. For example, during periods of confrontation by and conflict with the supervisor, the supervisee may find himself or herself very dissatisfied and even angry, even though the effects on his or her functioning as a therapist or practitioner may eventually be very positive.

We recently heard an analogy to illustrate the imperfect link between satisfaction and actual outcome. Consider persons who are just leaving a donut shop: If they were asked whether they liked the product and would return for more, they very likely would affirm that they would. This is very different, though, from evaluating the nutritional value of the donuts they had consumed.

On the other hand, Worthington (personal communication, 1990) made the point that satisfied supervisees might be expected to learn better than those who are dissatisfied. He argued that, as an alternative to imposing a moratorium on the use of satisfaction data, supervision researchers give more empirical attention to determining the actual link between supervisees' satisfaction and supervision outcome.

One alternative to satisfaction measures is to have the supervisee rate the quality of the supervision and the extent to which it met his or her expectations and needs. An example of that is the scale Ladany, Hill, Corbett, and Nutt (1996) developed (see Appendix C).

VIII. Analogue versus real-life studies: Analogue studies can provide high internal validity ["rigor" in Gelso's (1979) discussion of rigor–relevance tensions]. They can be of particular value in the first stages of attempting to extrapolate the implications of a particular theory (cf. Stone, 1984). Analogue designs can also be useful to safeguard clients or trainees when researchers are investigating phenomena that have the potential for harm. For example, one reasonable research question concerns the potential effects on clients of therapists' erotic disclosures to them (Goodyear & Shumate, 1996); whereas it might be possible to have potential clients give their perceptions of a tape depicting a therapist's erotic disclosure to a client, no responsible researcher actually would expose a real client to this as an experimental manipulation.

But useful as analogue studies can be, there comes a point in a program of counseling and supervision research when real-life situations must be employed. For example, the research on the social influence model (for recent discussions of its applications to supervision, see Dixon & Claiborn, 1987; Stoltenberg et al., 1995) has been based primarily on analogue research. In their review of this model, Heppner and Claiborn (1989) urged "researchers to move away from analogue methodologies . . . [it] seems absolutely essential that the social influence process be examined in realistic counseling situations" (p. 383).

We do not intend to suggest, though, an either–or, all-or-nothing situation with respect to analogue versus real-life studies. It is possible, in fact, to think of studies as varying in their degrees of "analogueness" or artificiality (Munley, 1974; Strong, 1971). Strong (1971) proposed useful criteria for gauging the degree of artificiality of a particular analogue study. Specifically, he suggested that researchers meet as many of five "boundary conditions" as possible in designing analogue research. These are that (1) counseling (and supervision) is a conversation between two or more people; (2) the interactants (supervisor and supervisee or supervisee and client) have clearly defined roles that constrain conversation; (3) supervision exists in varying (though usually extended) durations; (4) clients (and supervisees) are motivated to change; and (5) many clients are psychologically distressed and heavily invested in the behaviors they wish to change (the parallel here to supervisees should be obvious).

Significantly, though, there has been an increasing recent focus on realistic field studies in supervision. This was documented by Ellis, Ladany, Krengel, and Schult (1996).

Assessing Supervision Process and Outcome. We have discussed some methodological issues in conducting supervision research. Two additional issues are essential to consider as well. The first concerns the criteria to employ in assessing supervision processes and outcomes. The second revisits the discussion we already have had about the need to operationalize variables in a satisfactory manner. In this case, though, our interest specifically is on the instruments available to supervision researchers.

Choice of Variables and Criteria. Lambert and his colleagues (Lambert & Ogles, 1997; Stein & Lambert, 1995) have argued on the basis of their literature reviews that psychotherapy training and supervision are generally effective. They have asserted that studies that have compared training to a no-training control group have usually demonstrated the superiority of training, both in (1) level of skills and (2) greater personal adjustment.

These are important conclusions. But they have at least two significant caveats. The first concerns the distinctions we made early on in this book between training and clinical supervision. Training is more structured, limited in scope, and explicitly skills oriented; and it is *training* that seems to have demonstrated success. For example, Baker and his colleagues have conducted reviews of the research on specific training programs. Baker, Daniels, & Greeley (1990) examined the effectiveness of Ivey's microcounseling, Kagan's interpersonal process recall, and Carkhuff's human resource training. They concluded that all three were effective, though Kagan's had the smallest effect, whereas Carkhuff's had the largest. In another review, Baker and Daniels (1989) focused only on the microcounseling program. They found that across the 81 studies they reviewed the typical trainee moved from the 50th percentile of the control group to the 80th percentile.

With respect to the more specific domain of family therapy training, Avis and Sprenkle (1990) found that a small literature has gradually begun to develop that generally is supportive of the effectiveness of training. This was in contrast to Kniskern and Gurman's (1979) inability to locate any empirical study on that topic just a decade earlier.

The second significant caveat concerns the criteria for evaluating supervision's effectiveness. Unfortunately, it is not possible to separate this from the larger problem of establishing valid and meaningful criteria to demonstrate expertise in professional psychology (cf. Goodyear, 1997; Lichtenberg, 1997). Consider, for example, the commonsense notion that both level of training and amount of experience should be associated with expertise levels. Yet the cumulative evidence across multiple literature reviews (summarized by Dawes, 1994, and Wierzbicki, 1993) is that neither experience nor training predicts (1) better therapeutic outcomes or (2) more accurate clini-

cal judgment. This circumstance is dissonance producing for those of us who respect the cumulative weight of research outcomes, yet also have committed our professional lives to supervision and training in the belief that we *must* be having some desired effects!

The situation is more promising when the outcome criterion is change in trainees' specific skills, response modes (e.g., Hill et al., 1981), or within-session intentions (e.g., Kivlighan, 1989). These have been demonstrated as effects of training and supervision. But whereas these certainly are important products of training, it is safe to assert that the "gold standard" against which most of us would like to evaluate supervision's effectiveness is improved therapeutic outcomes for clients who are being treated by our supervisees.

This somewhat troubling situation underscores some of the criterion problems that face supervision theorists and researchers. Gelso (1979) noted that, whereas the selection of appropriate criteria has been a problem for researchers since the beginning of psychology, it has been especially troublesome for counseling and psychotherapy researchers. In supervision, this problem becomes yet more troublesome, as this discussion has already illustrated.

Gelso found promise in Strupp and Hadley's (1977) tripartite model of mental health whereby any assessment of therapy outcomes would include the perspectives of the *therapist,* the *client,* and *society* (including people significant in the life of the client). Strupp and Hadley suggested eight different outcome combinations that might be judged from the three vantage points. "The critical point for the present discussion is these researchers' demonstration of a variety of ways in which outcome criteria can be conflicting when the three vantage points are combined (as they need to be)" (Gelso, 1979, p. 19).

Compared to psychotherapy, supervision has both more people involved and more contexts in which the evaluations might be conducted. Holloway (1984) has argued that the traditional criteria of supervision effectiveness, supervisees' skill acquisition, and client change are overly restrictive. She stated also that "design for outcome evaluation in supervision has primarily grown out of isolated experimental needs" (p. 168). Analogous to Strupp and Hadley (1977), she recommended that researchers instead employ multiple criteria that evolve from the perspectives of the supervisor; the supervisee, the client (or client system), and an external observer; each of whom might evaluate the supervisor, the supervisee, and the client in the contexts of either counseling or supervision.

Table 12.1 depicts the 24 possible data points this would yield. As can be seen, 6 (marked with dashes) make no conceptual sense to employ. It is also noteworthy that Holloway was at that time able to locate no studies that employed 6 of the remaining 18 perspectives. Her suggested framework should be helpful both to researchers planning investigations of supervision and to those who attempt to make sense of that research.

An important point to underscore is the usefulness of obtaining more than one perspective when assessing effectiveness. Borders (1989a), for example, urged caution in relying on only self-reports of the perceptions of *either* supervisees or supervisors. For example, supervisors have an investment in perceiving positive change in their trainees; moreover, their perceptions can easily be colored by theoretical orientation or individual traits. To illustrate her point, Borders noted the observation Martin, Goodyear, and Newton (1987) had made. Specifically, when supervisees have been surveyed, they have reported that they perceived their super-

visors to be supportive (e.g., Rabinowitz, Heppner, & Roehkle, 1986; Worthington & Roehlke, 1979). Yet at least some studies that focused on actual verbalizations of supervisors have found supervisors to use relatively few supportive verbalizations (e.g., Holloway & Wampold, 1983; Martin et al., 1987). In short, the perspective and type of data obtained by the particular researcher affected the obtained finding.

But rather than argue against using self-reports as Borders did, we argue that self-reports should be used in conjunction with *other* sources of data. Contradictions that emerge between and among various perspectives (e.g., supervisees' perceptions of support versus what actually seems to be offered; Holloway & Wampold, 1983) are important to know of and can suggest directions for additional, second-generation research.

This last point bears underscoring, for researchers are not always clear about how to handle the multiple perspectives yielded when they conduct multivariate outcome investigations. Worthington (personal communication, 1990) argued that "simply trying to combine measures across raters (e.g., insider versus outsider perspectives) does not necessarily reveal *more* truth about what is going on. It may, in fact, obscure truth."

Measures of Supervision Process and Outcome. Ellis et al. (1988) made a number of recommendations based on their review of 7 years (1981–1987)

TABLE 12.1   Summary of Holloway's (1984) Survey of Studies Addressing Possible Measures of Supervision Outcome

	EVALUATION CONTEXT: SUPERVISION INTERVIEW			EVALUATION CONTEXT: COUNSELING INTERVIEW		
	Person Evaluated			*Person Evaluated*		
EVALUATOR	SUPERVISOR	TRAINEE	CLIENT	SUPERVISOR	TRAINEE	CLIENT
Supervisor	×	×	—	0	×	0
Trainee	×	×	—	0	×	0
Client	—	—	—	0	×	×
Observer	×	×	—	×	×	0

× signifies that studies addressing this type of outcome were cited; 0 signifies that no such studies were located;—signifies that these combinations would not be sensible to use in outcome research.

of published supervision research. One of those was "for psychometrically sound measures for supervision" (p. 9). Almost all instruments that have been used to assess supervision process and outcomes variables are ones that were originally developed for other purposes, such as psychotherapy or (occasionally) classroom instructional research. Lambert and Ogle's (1997) review of 50 different instruments that have been used in supervision research vividly illustrates the extent to which this is true.

When measures designed for counseling or instructional research have been used in supervision research, they have often been modified with minimal attention to possible changes in their meanings. One example of this has been the use of the Counselor Rating Form (CRF) in supervision research. Barak and LaCrosse (1975) designed the CRF to measure perceptions of counselors' expertness, attractiveness, and trustworthiness, but it has been used in supervision studies after simply substituting the word *supervision* or *supervisor* for *counseling* or *counselor* and retitling it the Supervision Rating Form.

There are at least two problems with this practice of adapting instruments from other domains for supervision research by simply changing some of the words. First, to tinker with an instrument through word changes, and so on, without then checking its psychometric properties results in an instrument that has been changed in unknown ways. Second, using such instruments can perpetuate the use of roles and metaphors from interventions *other* than supervision (e.g., therapy or teaching). Ellis et al. (1988) recommended that when using such measures the researcher should, at minimum, conduct a pilot study to examine the psychometric properties of the measure in the new setting and report internal consistency (e.g., Cronbach's alpha) based on the entire sample.

Importantly, though, there is a clear trend toward the development of instruments that are specifically for supervision and that have some established psychometric properties. Table 12.2 summarizes a sample of the small, but growing number of instruments that have been designed

specifically for supervision research. The list is not exhaustive, but does include measures for which some psychometric data are available [we are also less critical of some of these instruments than are Ellis & Ladany (1997), to which we refer readers who desire a more detailed analysis]. With each instrument is the primary citation or citations. Those marked with an asterisk are reprinted with the authors' permission in Appendix C.

We should note that we are not including here measures of the level and/or type of trainee performance, though some number are available to supervision researchers and practitioners. Some of these scales require third-party observers to rate individual trainee responses with respect to certain qualities such as empathy or other "facilitative conditions" (e.g., Carkhuff, 1969) or to categorize them as being of certain types (e.g., Hill, 1986). Still others have the supervisor rate the trainee's level of functioning (e.g., Jones, Krasner, & Howard, 1992; Robiner, Fuhrman, Ristvelt & Bobbitt, 1994). And some have been developed to assess very specific proficiencies. An example is LaFromboise, Coleman, and Hernandez's (1991) scale to assess trainees' cross-cultural competence.

Concluding Remark about Methodology

We conclude this portion of the chapter with the following statement by Russell et al. (1984):

> [A]s we see it, there have been four primary obstacles to progress in supervision research: (1) the failure of theory in most cases to offer clear-cut directions for supervisory research, (2) the small sample sizes of trainees and supervisors available at most training sites, (3) the difficulty, in both pragmatic and ethical terms, of manipulating independent variables in real-life training settings, and (4) the "criterion problem," which includes such issues as how best to measure change, from whose perspective, and on what dimensions.   (pp. 667–668)

Although some time has passed since they wrote this, their observations remain relevant. And equally relevant is their later observation that these obstacles are not insurmountable. Indeed,

TABLE 12.2 Selected Coding Systems and Scales to Assess Supervision Processes and Outcomes

Supervisory Feedback Rating System (Friedlander, Siegel, & Brenock, 1989). A coding system by which supervisor's feedback can be categorized according to (1) type (interpersonal or cognitive–behavioral), (2) specificity (global or specific), (3) valence (positive or negative), and (4) focus (counseling relationship or supervisory relationship).

Psychotherapy Supervisory Inventory (Shanfield, Mohl, Matthews, & Hetherly, 1989). Scales by which observers of supervision sessions can rate supervisors on such dimensions as degree of focus on the therapist and on the patient, intellectual and experiential orientation, number of clarifying and interpretive comments, intensity of confrontation, depth of exploration, verbal activity level of the supervisor, dominance of the supervisor and the therapist, comfort and tension levels, and empathy of the supervisor.

The Supervision Perception Form (Heppner & Roehlke, 1984). The SPF was developed to assess supervisor impact and consists of 25 items in two subscales (Supervisory Impact and Willingness to Learn). Two parallel forms exist, one for supervisors and one for supervisees.

Supervisory Styles Inventory* (Friedlander & Ward, 1984). A 33-item scale with parallel forms for supervisors and supervisees. Yields scores on three scales concerning the supervisor's style: (1) attractive, (2) interpersonally sensitive, (3) task oriented.

Supervisor Emphasis Rating Form—Revised (Lanning & Freeman, 1994; Lanning, Whiston, & Carey, 1994). A 60-item, ipsative measure to assess the relative degree of emphasis on four supervisory foci: (1) process, (2) professional behavior, (3) personalization skills, and (4) client conceptualization.

The Supervisory Focus and Style Questionnaire (Yager, Wilson, Brewer, & Kinnetz, 1989). A 60-item scale for supervisors that yields nine scores, three in each of three areas: personality (affection, inclusion, and control), supervisory focus (process, conceptualization, and personalization), and supervisory style (teaching, counseling, and consultation).

Supervision Questionnaire* (Ladany, Hill, Corbett, & Nutt, 1996). An eight-item scale to assess supervisees' perceptions of their supervision.

Psychotherapy Supervisor Development Scale (Watkins, Schneider, Haynes, & Nieberding, 1995). Supervisor self-report measure with 18 items that yield a single total score for level of supervisor development.

Counseling Self-estimate Inventory (Larson, Suzuki, Gillespie, Potenza, Bechtel, & Toulouse, 1992). Trainee self-report instrument with five factor analytically derived scales, reflecting counselor trainees' confidence in using (1) microskills, (2) attending to process, (3) dealing with difficult client behaviors, (4) behaving in a culturally competent way, and (5) being aware of one's values.

Role Conflict and Role Ambiguity Inventory (RCRAI)* (Olk & Friedlander, 1992). A 29-item self-report measure of trainees' perceptions of role difficulties they are having. It has two scales: (1) role conflict and (2) role ambiguity.

Supervisee Levels Questionnaire—Revised* (McNeill et al., 1992). A 30-item scale for trainees to complete. It yields scores on three scales: (1) self and other awareness; (2) motivation, and, (3) dependency–autonomy.

Supervisory Working Alliance Inventory* (Efstation, Patton, & Kardash, 1990). A 29-item scale for supervisors and trainees that measures (1) rapport, (2) client focus, and (3) identification.

This list of scales is not inclusive. The scales marked with an asterisk are reproduced in Appendix C. Otherwise, those interested in using these scales should contact the authors directly.

Continued

TABLE 12.2   Continued

Relationship Inventory (Schact, Howe, & Berman, 1988). Supervisees rate supervisors on one of two forms (L and M), based on the Barrett–Lennard Relationship Inventory, but specific to supervision. The five measures (1) regard, (2) empathy, (3) unconditionality, (4) willingness to be known, (5) total score (i.e., overall quality of relationship).

Congruence of Supervisory Expectations Scale* (Ellis et al., 1994). The CSES is still in development as we write this. It has parallel, 52-item forms for supervisor and supervisee. The three scales at this writing concern (1) role behaviors, (2) nature of the relationship, and (3) task focus and goals.

Supervision Questionnaire—Revised (Worthington, 1984b). This scale is based on Worthington and Roehlke (1979). Trainees rate 3 items measuring satisfaction, perception of supervisor competence, and rating of contribution of the supervisor to improvement, as well as 46 items measuring perceptions of a supervisor's behaviors. The SQ—R has been used by beginning counselors through postdoctoral interns to rate their supervisors.

The Critical Incidents Questionnaire. The CIQ asks supervisees to describe events related to critical incidents, or major turning points, within the supervision process that resulted in change in the supervisee's effectiveness as a counselor. The original instrument (Heppner & Roehlke, 1984) consisted of three open-ended questions; Rabinowitz, Heppner, and Roehlke (1986) provided a rank order format of the 13 most frequently reported critical incidents.

---

the research literature on supervision that has developed in the years since they made that observation shows just how prescient they were.

CONCLUSION

Raimy (1950) once stated with some irony that "[p]sychotherapy is an undefined technique applied to unspecified problems with unpredictable outcomes. For this technique we recommend rigorous training" (p. 93). Fortunately, though, circumstances now are much different. We have a substantial empirical literature to undergird the practice of counseling and therapy; and the literature to undergird the "rigorous training" of which Raimy spoke is also evolving at a healthy rate.

The recent growth in the quantity and quality of supervision research is heartening to those concerned with improving the practice of supervision. But, though growing, the empirical foundation for supervisory practice is still relatively small. Moreover, it is also not uniform across the various supervision modalities and models. The body of research on family therapy training and supervision, for example, remains especially small. But this very unevenness in the literature is an opportunity for those interested in conducting supervision research. Because supervision is a young field, practitioners and researchers alike have much yet to learn. It is our hope that this book will play a small role in contributing to this discovery process.

In concluding this chapter, we also conclude the book. In doing this, we want to borrow from Keith, Connell, and Whitaker (1992), who ended their article by expressing the worry that they had not accomplished exactly what they set out to do. But they then invited readers to think of them as cooks who were offering elements of a recipe that other cooks might follow to produce a "uniquely flavored result" (p. 109).

This useful metaphor characterizes our intentions as well. In this book, we have tried as best we could within space and other constraints to characterize the existing practical, theoretical, and empirical literature concerning supervision. Moreover, we have attempted to do so by drawing from the literature of the various mental health professions. We conclude, then, by expressing our hope that in reading this book you have found some essential recipe(s) that can help you to concoct your own, unique perspectives on the nature and practice of supervision.

Abadie, P. D. (1985). *A study of interpersonal communication processes in the supervision of counseling.* Unpublished doctoral dissertation, Kansas State University.

Abroms, G. M. (1977). Supervision as metatherapy. In F. W. Kaslow (Ed.), *Supervision, consultation, and staff training in the helping professions.* San Francisco: Jossey–Bass, 81–99.

Acker, M. (July, 1992). *The relationship in clinical supervision.* Paper presented at the B.A.S.P.R. International Conference on Supervision, London, England.

Adamek, M. S. (1994). Audio-cueing and immediate feedback to improve group leadership skills: A live supervision model. *Journal of Music Therapy, 31,* 135–164.

Adams, J. (1995). Perspectives on live supervision: Working live. *The Supervision Bulletin, 8*(2), 4.

Adamson, L. A. (1993). Psychological separation and the working alliance in the supervisory relationship. *Dissertation Abstracts International, 54* (5-A), 1673 (Abstract 1995-75098).

Akamatsu, T. J. (1980). The use of role-play and simulation technique in the training of psychotherapy. In A. K. Hess (Ed.), *Psychotherapy supervision: Theory, research and practice.* New York: Wiley, 209–225.

Albee, G. W. (1970). The uncertain future of clinical psychology. *American Psychologist, 25,* 1071–1080.

Albott, W. L. (1984). Supervisory characteristics and other sources of supervision variance. *Clinical Supervisor, 2*(4), 27–41.

Alderfer, C. (1983). *The supervision of the therapeutic system in family therapy.* Unpublished manuscript.

Allen, D. W. (Ed.) (1967). *Mictroteaching: A description.* Stanford, CA: Stanford Teacher Education Program.

Allen, G. J., Szollos, S. J., & Williams, B. E. (1986). Doctoral students' comparative evaluations of best and worst psychotherapy supervision. *Professional Psychology: Research and Practice, 17,* 91–99.

Allen, J. (1976). Peer group supervision in family therapy. *Child Welfare, 55,* 183–189.

Allphin, C. (1987). Perplexing or distressing episodes in supervision: How they can help in the teaching and learning of psychotherapy. *Clinical Social Work Journal, 15,* 236–245.

Alonso, A. (1983). A developmental theory of psychodynamic supervision. *Clinical Supervisor, 1*(3), 23–26.

Alonso, A., & Rutan, J. S. (1988). Shame and guilt in supervision. *Psychotherapy, 25,* 576–581.

Alpher, V. S. (1991). Interdependence and parallel processes: A case study of structural analysis of social behavior in supervision and short-term dynamic psychotherapy. *Psychotherapy, 28,* 218–231.

American Association for Marriage and Family Therapy (1991). *Code of ethics* (rev. ed.). Washington, DC: Author.

American Association for Marriage and Family Therapy (1993). *Approved supervisor designation: Standards and responsibilities.* Washington, DC: Author.

American Counseling Association (1995). *Code of ethics* (rev. ed.). Alexandria, VA: Author.

American Psychological Association Ethics Committee (1992). Ethical principles of psychologists and code of conduct. *American Psychologist, 47,* 1597–1611.

Anderson, J. R. (1996). ACT: A simple theory of complex cognition. *American Psychologist, 51,* 355–365.

Anderson, T. (1987). The reflecting team: Dialogue and meta-dialogue in clinical work. *Family Process, 26,* 415–428.

Andrews, J. D. W. (1989). Integrating visions of reality: Interpersonal diagnosis and the existential vision. *American Psychologist, 44,* 803–817.

Anonymous (1991). Sexual harassment: A female counseling student's experience. *Journal of Counseling and Development, 69,* 502–506.

Anonymous (1995). Perspectives on live supervision: A client's voice. *Supervision Bulletin, 8*(2), 5.

Ansbacher, H., & Ansbacher, R. (1956). *The individual psychology of Alfred Adler.* New York: Basic Books.

Aponte, H. J. (1994). How personal can training get? *Journal of Marital and Family Therapy, 20,* 3–15.

Appelbaum, P. S. (1993). Legal liability and managed care. *American Psychologist, 48,* 251–257.

Aronson, M. L. (1990). A group therapist's perspectives on the use of supervisory groups in the training of psychotherapists. *Psychoanalysis and psychotherapy, 8,* 88–94.

Atwood, J. D. (1986). Self-awareness in supervision. *Clinical Supervisor, 4*(3), 79–96.

Ault-Riche, M. (1988). Teaching an integrated model of family therapy: Women as students, women as supervisors. *Journal of Psychotherapy and the Family, 3,* 175–192.

Aveline, M. (1992). The use of audio and videotape recordings of therapy sessions in the supervision and practice of dynamic psychotherapy. *British Journal of Psychotherapy, 8,* 347–358.

Avis, J. M., & Sprenkle, D. H. (1990). Outcome research on family therapy training: A substantive and methodological review. *Journal of Marital and Family Therapy, 16,* 241–264.

Bahrick, A. S. (1990). Role induction for counselor trainees: Effects on the supervisory working alliance. *Dissertation Abstracts International, 51* (3-B), 1484 (Abstract 1991-51645).

Bahrick, A. S., Russell, R. K., & Salmi, S. W. (1991). The effects of role induction on trainees' perceptions of supervision. *Journal of Counseling and Development, 69,* 434–438.

Baker, D. E. (1990). The relationship of the supervisory working alliance to supervisor and supervisee narcissism, gender, and theoretical orientation. *Dissertation Abstracts International, 51*(7-B), 3602–3603 (Abstract 1991-54991).

Baker, S. D., & Daniels, T. G. (1989). Integrating research on the microcounseling program. *Journal of Counseling Psychology, 36,* 213–222.

Baker, S. D., Daniels, T. G., & Greeley, A. T. (1990). Systematic training of graduate-level counselors: Narrative and meta-analytic reviews of three major programs. *Counseling Psychologist, 18,* 355–321.

Balint, E. (1985). The history of training and research in Balint groups. *Psychoanalytic Psychotherapy, 1,* 1–9.

Bandura, A. (1982). Self-efficacy mechanism in human agency. *American Psychologist, 37,* 122–147.

Bandura, A. (1986). Self-efficacy. In A. Bandura (Ed.), *Social foundations of thought and action: A social cognitive theory.* Upper Saddle River, NJ: Prentice Hall.

Barak, A., & LaCrosse, M. B. (1975). Multidimensional perception of counselor behavior. *Journal of Counseling Psychology, 22,* 471–476.

Barlow, D. H. (Ed.) (1993). *Clinical handbook of psychological disorders: A step-by-step treatment manual* (2nd Ed.). New York: Guilford Press.

Barnat, M. R. (1977). Spontaneous supervisory metaphor in the resolution of trainee anxiety. *Professional Psychology, 8,* 307–315.

Bartell, P. A., & Rubin, L. J. (1990). Dangerous liaisons: Sexual intimacies in supervision. *Professional Psychology: Research & Practice, 21,* 442–450.

Bartlett, W. E., Goodyear, R. K., & Bradley, F. O. (Eds.) (1983). Supervision in counseling II (Special issue). *Counseling Psychologist, 11*(1).

Bateson, G. (1972). *Steps to an ecology of mind.* New York: Ballantine Books.

Batten, C. (1990). Dilemmas of "crosscultural psychotherapy supervision." *British Journal of Psychotherapy, 7,* 129–140.

Baum, L. E. (1956). *The wizard of Oz.* Chicago: Reilly & Lee Co.

Bauman, W. F. (1972). Games counselor trainees play: Dealing with trainee resistance. *Counselor Education and Supervision, 11,* 251–256.

Bear, T. M., & Kivlighan, D. M., Jr. (1994). Single-subject examination of the process of supervision of beginning and advanced supervisees. *Professional Psychology: Research and Practice, 25,* 450–457.

Beavers, W. R. (1986). Family therapy supervision: An introduction and consumer's guide. *Family Therapy Education and Supervision, 1*(4), 15–24.

Beck, A. T., Rush, J. A., Shaw, B. F., & Emery, G. (1979). *Cognitive therapy of depression.* New York: Guilford.

Beck, T. D., Yager, G. G., Williams, G. T., Williams, B. R., & Morris, J. R. (March, 1989). *Training field supervisors for adult counseling situations.* A paper presented at the Annual Meeting of the American Association for Counseling and Development, Boston.

Behling, J., Curtis, C., Foster, S. A. (1988). Impact of sex-role combinations on student performance in field instruction. *Clinical Supervisor, 6*(3), 161–168.

Beis, E. (1984). *Mental health and the law.* Rockville, MD: Aspen.

Belar, C. D., Bieliauskas, L. A., Klepac, R. K., Larsen, K. G., Stigall, T. T., & Zimet, C. N. (1993). National conference on postdoctural training in professional psychology. *American Psychologist, 48,* 1284–1289.

Benshoff, J. M. (1993). Peer supervision in counselor training. *Clinical Supervisor, 11*(2), 89–102.

Berg, K. S., & Stone, G. L. (1980). Effects of conceptual level and supervision structure on counselor development. *Journal of Counseling Psychology, 27,* 500–509.

Berger, M., & Dammann, C. (1982). Live supervision as context, treatment, and training. *Family Process, 21,* 337–344.

Bergin, A. E. (1991). Values and religious issues in psychotherapy and mental health. *American Psychologist, 46,* 394–413.

Bernard, J. L. (1975). Due process in dropping the unsuitable clinical student. *Professional Psychology, 6,* 275–278.

Bernard, J. L., & Jara, C. S. (1986). The failure of clinical psychology graduate students to apply understood ethical principles. *Professional Psychology: Research and Practice, 17,* 313–315.

Bernard, J. M. (1979). Supervisor training: A discrimination model. *Counselor Education and Supervision, 19,* 60–68.

Bernard, J. M. (1981). Inservice training for clinical supervisors. *Professional Psychology, 12,* 740–748.

Bernard, J. M. (1982). *Laboratory training for clinical supervisors: An update.* Paper presented at the annual meeting of the American Psychological Association, Washington, DC.

Bernard, J. M. (1987). Ethical and legal considerations for supervisors. In L. D. Borders & G. R. Leddick, *Handbook of counseling supervision.* Alexandria, VA: Association for Counselor Education and Supervision, 52–57.

Bernard, J. M. (1989). Training supervisors to examine relationship variables using IPR. *Clinical Supervisor, 7*(1), 103–112.

Bernard, J. M. (1992). The challenge of psychotherapy-based supervision: Making the pieces fit. *Counselor Education and Supervision, 31,* 232–237.

Bernard, J. M. (1994a). Multicultural supervision: A reaction to Leong and Wagner, Cook, Priest, and Fukuyama. *Counselor Education and Supervision, 34,* 159–171.

Bernard, J. M. (1994b). Reaction: On-campus training of doctoral-level supervisors. In J. E. Myers (Ed.), *Developing and directing counselor education laboratories.* Alexandria, VA: American Counseling Association, 141–144.

Bernard, J. M. (1997). The discrimination model. In C. E. Watkins, *Handbook of psychotherapy supervision.* New York: Wiley, 310–327.

Berne, E. (1964). *Games people play.* New York: Grove Press.

Berne, E. (1972). *What do you say after you say hello? The psychology of human destiny.* New York: Grove Press.

Bernstein, B. L. (1993). Promoting gender equity in counselor supervision: Challenges and opportunities. *Counselor Education and Supervision, 32,* 198–202.

Bernstein, B. L., & Lecomte, C. (1979). Self-critique technique training in a competency-based practicum. *Counselor Education and Supervision, 19,* 69–76.

Bernstein, R. M., Brown, E. M., & Ferrier, M. J. (1984). A model for collaborative team processing in brief systemic family therapy. *Journal of Marital and Family Therapy, 10,* 151–156.

Betcher, R. W., & Zinberg, N. E. (1988). Supervision and privacy in psychotherapy training. *American Journal of Psychiatry, 145,* 796–803.

Beutler, L. E. (1988). Introduction: Training to competency in psychotherapy. *Journal of Consulting and Clinical Psychology, 56,* 651–652.

Bierig, J. R. (1983). Whatever happened to professional self-regulation? *American Bar Association Journal, 69,* 616–619.

Biggs, D. A. (1988). The case presentation approach in clinical supervision. *Counselor Education and Supervision, 27,* 240–248.

Bion, W. (1961). *Experience in groups.* New York: Basic Books.

Birk, J. M., & Mahalik, J. R. (1996). The influence of trainee conceptual level, trainee anxiety, and supervision evaluation on counselor developmental level. *Clinical Supervisor, 14*(1), 123–137.

Blocher, D. (1983). Toward a cognitive developmental approach to counseling supervision. *Counseling Psychologist, 11,* 27–34.

Blocher, D. H. (1987). On the uses and misuses of the term theory. *Journal of Counseling and Development, 66,* 67–68.

Blocher, D. H., Christensen, E. W., Hale-Fiske, R., Neren, S. H., Spencer, T., & Fowles, S. (1985). Development and preliminary validation of an instrument to measure cognitive growth. *Counselor Education and Supervision, 25,* 21–30.

Blodgett, E. G., Schmidt, J. F., & Scudder, R. R. (1987). Clinical session evaluation: The effect of familiarity with the supervisee. *Clinical Supervisor, 5*(1), 33–43.

Bonney, W. (1994). Teaching supervision: Some practical issues for beginning supervisors. *Psychotherapy Bulletin, 29*(2), 31–36.

Bonosky, N. (1995). Boundary violations in social work supervision: Clinical, educational and legal implications. *Clinical Supervisor, 13*(2), 79–95.

Borders, L. D. (1989). A pragmatic agenda for developmental supervision research. *Counselor Education and Supervision, 29,* 16–24.

Borders, L. D. (1989a). *Learning to think like a supervisor.* Paper presented at the American Psychological Association Annual convention, New Orleans, LA.

Borders, L. D. (1989b). Developmental cognitions of first practicum supervisees. *Journal of Counseling Psychology, 36,* 163–169.

Borders, L. D. (1989c, March). *Structured peer supervision.* Paper presented at the annual convention of the American Association for Counseling and Development, Boston.

Borders, L. D. (1990). Developmental changes during supervisees' first practicum. *Clinical Supervisor, 8*(2), 157–167.

Borders, L. D. (1991). Supervisors' in-session behaviors and cognitions. *Counselor Education and Supervision, 31,* 32–47.

Borders, L. D. (1992). Learning to think like a supervisor. *Clinical Supervisor, 10*(2), 135–148.

Borders, L. D., Bernard, J. M., Dye, H. A., Fong, M. L., Henderson, P., & Nance, D. W. (1991). Curriculum guide for training counseling supervisors: Rationale, development, and implementation. *Counselor Education and Supervision, 31,* 58–82.

Borders, L. D., & Cashwell, C. S. (1992). Supervision regulations in counselor licensure legislation. *Counselor Education and Supervision, 31,* 209–218.

Borders, L. D., Cashwell, C. S., & Rotter, J. C. (1995). Supervision of counselor licensure applicants: A comparative study. *Counselor Education and Supervision, 35,* 54–69.

Borders, L. D., & Fong, M. L. (1984). Sex-role orientation research: Review and implications for counselor education. *Counselor Education and Supervision, 24*(1), 58–69.

Borders, L. D., & Fong, M. L. (1989). Ego development and counseling ability during training. *Counselor Education and Supervision, 29,* 71–83.

Borders, L. D., & Fong, M. L. (1991). Evaluations of supervisees: Brief commentary and research report. *Clinical Supervisor, 9*(2), 43–51.

Borders, L. D., & Fong, M. L. (1994). Cognitions of supervisors-in-training: An exploratory study. *Counselor Education and Supervision, 33,* 280–293.

Borders, L. D., Fong, M. L., & Neimeyer, G. J. (1986). Counseling students' level of ego development and perceptions of clients. *Counselor Education and Supervision, 26,* 36–49.

Borders, L. D., & Leddick, G. R. (1987). *Handbook of counseling supervision.* Alexandria, VA: Association for Counselor Education and Supervision.

Borders, L. D. & Leddick, G. R. (1988). A nationwide survey of supervision training. *Counselor Education and Supervision, 27*(3), 271–283.

Borders, L. D., & Usher, C. H. (1992). Post-degree supervision: Existing and preferred practices. *Journal of Counseling and Development, 70,* 594–599.

Bordin, E. S. (1979). The generalizability of the psychodynamic concept of the working alliance. *Psychotherapy: Theory, Research, and Practice, 16,* 252–260.

Bordin, E. S. (1983). A working alliance model of supervision. *Counseling Psychologist, 11,* 35–42.

Bowen, M. (1978). *Family therapy in clinical practice.* New York: Aronson.

Bowlby, J. (1969). *Attachment and loss: Attachment* (Vol.1). New York: Basic Books.

Bowlby, J. (1977). The making and breaking of affectional bonds. I. Aetiology and psychopathology in the light of attachment theory. *British Journal of Psychiatry, 130,* 201–210.

Bowlby, J. (1978). Attachment theory and its therapeutic implications. In S. C. Feinstein & P. L. Giovacchini (Eds.), *Adolescent psychiatry* (Vol. VI: Development and clinical studies). Chicago: University of Chicago Press, 5–33.

Bowman, J. T., & Roberts, G. T. (1979). Effects of tape-recording and supervisory evaluation on counselor trainee anxiety levels. *Counselor Education and Supervision, 19,* 20–26.

Bownan, V. E., Hatley, L. D., & Bownan, R. L. (1995). Faculty–student relationships: The dual role controversy. *Counselor Education and Supervision, 34,* 232–242.

Boxley, R., Drew, C., & Rangel, D. (1986). Clinical trainee impairment in APA approved internship programs. *Clinical Psychologist, 39,* 49–52.

Boyd, J. (1978). *Counselor supervision: Approaches, preparation, practices.* Muncie, IN: Accelerated Development.

Bradey, J., & Post, P. (1991). Impaired students: Do we eliminate them from counselor education programs? *Counselor Education and Supervision, 31,* 100–108.

Bradley, J. R., & Olson, J. K. (1980). Training factors influencing felt psychotherapeutic competence of psychology trainees. *Professional Psychology, 11,* 930–934.

Bradley, L. J. (1989). *Counselor supervision: Principles, process, practice.* Muncie, IN: Accelerated Press.

Bradshaw, W. H., Jr. (1982). *Supervision in black and white: Race as a factor in supervision.* In M. Blumenfield (Ed.), Applied supervision in psychotherapy. New York: Grune & Stratton, 199–220.

Brandell, J. R. (1992). Focal conflict analysis: A method of supervision in psychoanalytic psychotherapy. *Clinical Supervisor, 10*(1), 51–69.

Brashears, F. (1995). Supervision as social work practice: A reconceptualization. *Social Work, 40,* 692–699.

Brehm, J. (1966). *A theory of psychological reactance.* New York: Academic Press.

Breunlin, D., Karrer, B., McGuire, D., & Cimmarusti, R. (1988). Cybernetics of videotape supervision. In H. Liddle, D. Breunlin, & R. Schwartz (Eds.), *Handbook of family therapy training and supervision.* New York: Guilford, 194–206.

Bridge, P., & Bascue, L. O. (1990). Documentation of psychotherapy supervision. *Psychotherapy in Private Practice, 8,* 79–86.

Brill, R., Wolkin, J., McKeel, N. (1987). Strategies for selecting and securing the predoctoral clinical internship of choice. In R. H. Dana & W. T. May (Eds.), *Internship training in professions psychology.* New York: Hemisphere, 220–226.

Brock, C. D., & Stock, R. D. (1990). A survey of Balint group activities in U.S. family practice residency programs. *Family Medicine, 22,* 33–37.

Broder, E., & Sloman, L. (1982). A contextual comparison of three training programmes. In R. Whiffen & F. Byng-Hall (Eds.), *Family therapy supervision: Recent developments in practice.* London: Academic Press, 229–242.

Brodsky, A. (1980). Sex role issues in the supervision of therapy. In A. K. Hess (Ed.), *Psychotherapy supervision: Theory, research and practice.* New York: Wiley, 509–524.

Brodsky, S., & Myers, H. H. (1986). In vivo rotation: An alternative model for psychotherapy supervision. *Clinical Supervisor, 4*(1), 95–104.

Brown, L. M., & Gilligan, C. (August, 1990). *Listening for self and relational voices: A responsive/resisting reader's guide.* Paper presented at the Annual Meeting of the American Psychological Association, Boston.

Brown, R. W., & Otto, M. L. (1986). Field supervision: A collaborative model. *Michigan Journal of Counseling and Development, 17*(2), 48–51.

Brownstein, C. (1981). Practicum issues: A placement planning model. *Journal of Education for Social Work, 17*(3), 52–58.

Bruce, M. A. (1995). Mentoring women doctoral students: What counselor educators and supervisors can do. *Counselor Education and Supervision, (35),* 139–149.

Bubenzer, D. L., Mahrle, C., & West, J. D. (1987). *Live counselor supervision: Trainee acculturation and supervisor interventions.* Paper presented at the American Association for Counseling and Development Annual Convention, New Orleans, LA.

Bubenzer, D. L., West, J. D., & Gold, J. M. (1991). Use of live supervision in counselor preparation. *Counselor Education and Supervision, 30,* 301–308.

Buhrke, R. A. (1989). Incorporating lesbian and gay issues into counselor training: A resource guide. *Journal of Counseling and Development, 68,* 77–80.

Buhrke, R. A., & Douce, L. A. (1991). Training issues for counseling psychologists in working with lesbian women and gay men. *Counseling Psychologist, 19,* 216–234.

Burke, W. R. (1992). Weakenings and repairs of the working alliance in counselor supervision. *Dissertation Abstracts International, 52*(7-B), 3899 (Abstract 1992-75221).

Burke, W. R., Goodyear, R. K., & Guzzard, C. (March, 1997). *Weakenings/Repairs in the Supervisory Alliance: A Multiple-case Study.* Paper presented at the American Educational Research Association, Chicago.

Burns, C. I., & Holloway, E. L. (1990). Therapy in supervision: An unresolved issue. *Clinical Supervisor, 7*(4), 47–60.

Butler, K. (1990). Spirituality reconsidered. *Family Therapy Networker, 14*(5), 26–37.

Byng-Hall, J. (1982). The use of the earphone in supervision. In R. Whiffen & J. Byng-Hall (Eds.), *Family therapy supervision: Recent developments in practice.* London: Academic Press, 47–56.

Cacioppo, J. T., & Petty, R. E. (1981). Social psychological procedures for cognitive response measurement: The thought listing technique. In T. V. Merluzzi, C. R. Glass, & M. Genest (Eds.), *Cognitive assessment.* New York: Guilford, 309–342.

Cade, B. W., Speed, B., & Seligman, P. (1986). Working in teams: The pros and cons. *Clinical Supervisor, 4,* 105–117.

Caligor, L. (1984). Parallel and reciprocal processes in psychoanalytic supervision. In L. Caligor, P. M. Bromberg, & J. D. Meltzer (Eds.), *Clinical perspectives on the supervision of psychoanalysis and psychotherapy.* New York: Plenum.

Campbell, T. W. (1994). Psychotherapy and malpractice exposure. *American Journal of Forensic Psychology, 12,* 5–41.

Caplan, G. (1970). *The theory and practice of mental health consultation.* New York: Basic Books.

Caplow, T. (1968). *Two against one: Coalitions in triads.* Upper Saddle River, NJ: Prentice Hall.

Carey, J. C., & Lanning, W. L. (1993). Supervisors' emphases in the master's practicum. *Clinical Supervisor, 11*(1), 203–215.

Carkhuff, R. R. (1969). *Helping and human relations* (Vol. 2). New York: Holt, Rinehart and Winston.

Carroll, M. (1996). *Counseling supervision: Theory, skills, and practice.* London: Cassell.

Cartwright, D., & Zander, A. (1968). *Group dynamics: Research and theory* (3rd ed.). New York: Harper & Row.

Casey, J. A., Bloom, J. W., & Moan, E. R. (1994). Use of technology in counselor supervision. In L. D. Borders (Ed.), *Supervision: Exploring the effective components.* Greensboro, NC: ERIC/CASS, EDO-CG-94-25.

Cashwell, C. S., Looby, E. J., & Housley, W. F. (1997). Appreciating cultural diversity through clinical supervision. *Clinical Supervisor, 15*(1), 75–85.

Chagnon, J., & Russell, R. K. (1995). Assessment of supervisee developmental level and supervision environment across supervisor experience. *Journal of Counseling and Development, 73,* 553–558.

Chaiklin, H., & Munson, C. E. (1983). Peer consultation in social work. *Clinical Supervisor, 1,* 21–34.

Chambers, W. V., & Grice, J. W. (1986). Behavior research methods, instruments, & computers. *Circumgrids: A Repertory Grid Package for Personal Computers, 18,* 468.

Cheng, L. Y. (1993). Psychotherapy supervision in Hong Kong. *Australian and New Zealand Journal of Psychiatry, 27,* 127–132.

Chessick, R. D. (1971). How the resident and supervisor disappoint each other. *American Journal of Psychotherapy, 25,* 272–283.

Chickering, A. W. (1969). *Education and identity.* San Francisco: Jossey–Bass.

Claiborn, C. D., Etringer, B. D., & Hillerbrand, E. T. (1995). Influence processes in supervision. *Counselor Education and Supervision, 35,* 43–53.

Claiborn, C. D., & Lichtenberg, J. W. (1989). Interactional counseling. *Counseling Psychologist, 17,* 355–453.

Clarkson, P. (1994). In recognition of dual relationships. *Transactional Analysis Journal, 24,* 32–38.

Clifton, D., Doan, R., & Mitchell, D. (1990). The reauthoring of therapist's stories: Taking doses of our own medicine. *Journal of Strategic & Systemic Therapies, 9*(4), 61–66.

Cohen, B. Z. (1987). The ethics of social work supervision revisited. *Social Work, 32,* 194–196.

Cohen, M., Gross, S., & Turner, M. (1976). A note on a developmental model for training family therapists through group supervision. *Journal of Marriage and Family Counseling, 2,* 48–56.

Cohen, R. J. (1979). *Malpractice: A guide for mental health professionals.* New York: Free Press.

Coll, K. M. (1995). Clinical supervision of community college counselors: Current and preferred practices. *Counselor Education and Supervision, 35,* 111–117.

Collins, D., & Bogo, M. (1986). Competency-based field instruction: Bridging the gap between laboratory and field learning. *Clinical Supervisor, 4*(3), 39–52.

Congress, E. P. (1992). Ethical decision making of social work supervisors. *Clinical Supervisor, 10*(1), 157–169.

Conn, J., & Conn, W. E. (1990). Christian spiritual growth and developmental psychology. *The Way, 69,* 3–13.

Connell, G. M., & Russell, L. A. (1986). In-therapy consultation: A supervision and therapy technique of symbolic–experiential family therapy. *American Journal of Family Therapy, 14,* 313–323.

Constantine, J. A., Piercy, F. P., & Sprenkle, D. H. (1984). Live supervision-of-supervision in family therapy. *Journal of Marital & Family Therapy, 10,* 95–97.

Cook, D. A. (1994). Racial identity in supervision. *Counselor Education and Supervision, 34,* 132–141.

Cook, D. A., & Helms, J. E. (1988). Visible racial/ethnic group supervisees' satisfaction with cross-cultural supervision as predicted by relationship characteristics. *Journal of Counseling Psychology, 35,* 268–274.

Cooper, L., & Gustafson, J. P. (1985). Supervision in a group: An application of group theory. *Clinical Supervisor, 3,* 7–25.

Corey, G. (1986). *Theory and practice of counseling and psychotherapy* (3rd ed.). Monterey, CA: Brooks/Cole.

Corey, G., Corey, M. S., & Callanan, P. (1993). *Issues and ethics in the helping professions* (4th ed.). Pacific Grove, CA: Brooks/Cole.

Cormier, L. S., & Bernard, J. M. (1982). Ethical and legal responsibilities of clinical supervisors. *Personnel and Guidance Journal, 60,* 486–491.

Cornell, W. F. (1994). Dual relationships in transactional analysis: Training, supervision, and therapy. *Transactional Analysis Journal, 24,* 21–30.

Corrigan, J. D., Dell, D. M., Lewis, K. N., & Schmidt, L. D. (1980). Counseling as a social influence process: A review [Monograph]. *Journal of Counseling Psychology 27,* 395–441.

Costa, L. (1994). Reducing anxiety in live supervision. *Counselor Education and Supervision, 34,* 30–40.

Couchon, W. D., & Bernard, J. M. (1984). Effects of timing of supervision on supervisor and counselor performance. *Clinical Supervisor, 2*(3), 3–20.

Council for the Accreditation of Counseling and Related Educational Programs (1994). *CACREP accreditation standards and procedures manual.* Alexandria, VA: Author.

Counselman, E. F., & Gumpert, P. (1993). Psychotherapy supervision in small leader-led groups. *Group, 17,* 25–32.

Covey, S. R., Merrill, A. R., & Merrill, R. R. (1994). *First things first.* New York: Simon & Schuster.

Covner, B. J. (1942a). Studies in phonographic recordings of verbal material: 1. The use of phonographic recordings in counseling practice and research. *Journal of Consulting Psychology, 6,* 105–113.

Covner, B. J. (1942b). Studies in phonographic recordings of verbal material: II. A device for transcribing phonographic recordings of verbal material. *Journal of Consulting Psychology, 6,* 149–151.

Craig, C. H., & Sleight, C. C. (1990). Personality relationships between supervisors and students in communication disorders as determined by the Myers–Briggs Type Indicator. *Clinical Supervisor, 8*(1), 41–51.

Craske, M. G., & Barlow, D. H. (1990). *Therapist's guide for the Mastery of Your Anxiety and Panic (MAP) program.* Delmar, NY: Graywind.

Crits-Christoph, P., Chambless, D. L., Frank, E., Brody, C., & Karp, J. F. (1995). Training in empirically validated treatments: What are clinical psychology students learning? *Professional Psychology: Research & Practice, 26,* 514–522.

Cross, E. G., & Brown, D. (1983). Counselor supervision as a function of trainee experience: Analysis of specific behaviors. *Counselor Education and Supervision, 22,* 333–341.

Cummings, A. L., Hallberg, E. T., Martin, J., Slemon, A., & Hiebert, B. (1990). Implications of counselor conceptualizations for counselor education. *Counselor Education and Supervision, 30,* 120–134.

Daniels, T. G., Rigazio-Digilio, S. A., & Ivey, A. E. (1997). Microcounseling: A training and supervision paradigm for the helping professions. In C. E. Watkins, Jr. (Ed). *Handbook of psychotherapy supervision.* New York: Wiley, 277–295.

Danskin, D. G. (1957). A role-ing counselor gathers no moss. *Journal of Counseling Psychology, 4,* 41–43.

Davison, G. C., Navarre, S. G., & Vogel, R. S. (1995). The articulated thoughts in simulated situations paradigm: A think-aloud approach to cognitive assessment. *Current Directions in Psychological Science, 4,* 29–33.

Dawes, R. M. (1994). *House of cards: Psychology and psychotherapy built on myth.* New York: Free Press.

Delaney, D. J. (1972). A behavioral model for the practicum supervision of counselor candidates. *Counselor Education and Supervision, 12,* 46–50.

Dickey, K. D., Housley, W. F., & Guest, C. (1993). Ethics in supervision of rehabilitation counselor trainees: A survey. *Rehabilitation Education, 7,* 195–201.

Disney, M. J., & Stephens, A. M. (1994). *Legal issues in clinical supervision.* Alexandria, VA: ACA Press.

Dixon, D. N., & Claiborn, C. D. (1987). A social influence approach to counselor supervision. In J. E. Maddux, C. D. Stoltenberg, & R. Rosenwein (Eds.), *Social processes in clinical and counseling psychology.* New York: Springer-Verlag, 83–93.

Dixon, D. N., & Kruczek, T. (August, 1989). *Attributions of counseling by counselor trainees and supervisors.* Paper presented at the annual meeting of the American Psychological Association, New Orleans, LA.

Dobson, K. S., & Shaw, B. F. (1993). The training of cognitive therapists: What have we learned from treatment manuals? *Psychotherapy, 30,* 573–577.

Dodds, J. B. (1986). Supervision of psychology trainees in field placements. *Professional Psychology: Research and Practice, 17,* 296–300.

Dodenhoff, J. T. (1981). Interpersonal attraction and direct–indirect supervisor influence as predictors of counselor trainee effectiveness. *Journal of Counseling Psychology, 28,* 47–52.

Doehrman, M. (1976). Parallel processes in supervision and psychotherapy. *Bulletin of the Menninger Clinic, 40,* 3–104.

Dole, A. A., Nissenfeld, M., Browers, C., Herzog, F., Levitt, D., McIntyre, P., Wedeman, S., & Woodburn, P. (April, 1984). *Counselor retrospections and supervisor cognitions: A case study.* Paper presented at the annual meeting of the American Educational Research Association, New Orleans, LA.

Dombeck, M. T., & Brody, S. L. (1995). Clinical supervision: A three-way mirror. *Archives of Psychiatric Nursing, 9,* 3–10.

Douce, L. (August, 1989). *Classroom and experiential training in supervision.* Paper presented at the annual meeting of the American Psychological Association, New Orleans, LA.

Dowling, S. (1984). Clinical evaluation: A comparison of self, self with videotape, peers, and supervisors. *Clinical Supervisor, 2*(3), 71–78.

Dryden, W. (1983a). *The use of audio-tapes in counselling and supervision.* Middlesex, UK: Institute for RET.

Dryden, W. (1983b). Audiotape supervision by mail: A rational–emotive perspective. *British Journal of Cognitive Psychotherapy, 1,* 57–64.

Dryden, W., & Thorne, B. (Eds.) (1991). *Training and supervision for counselling in action.* Newbury Park, CA: Sage.

Dubin, W. (1991). The use of meditative techniques in psychotherapy supervision. *Journal of Transpersonal Psychology, 23,* 65–80.

Dye, A. (1994). Training doctoral student supervisors at Purdue University. In J. E. Myers (Ed.), *Developing and directing counselor education laboratories.* Alexandria, VA: American Counseling Association, 121–130.

Efstation, J. F., Patton, M. J., & Kardash, C. M. (1990). Measuring the working alliance in counselor supervision. *Journal of Counseling Psychology, 37,* 322–329.

Eisenberg, S. (1956). *Supervision in the changing field of social work.* Philadelphia: Jewish Family Service of Philadelphia.

Eisikovits, Z., Meier, R., Guttman, E., Shurka, E., & Levinstein, A. (1986). Supervision in ecological context: The relationship between the quality of supervision and the work and treatment environment. *Journal of Social Service Research, 8*(4), 37–58.

Ekstein, R. (1964). Supervision of psychotherapy: Is it teaching? Is it administration? Or is it therapy? *Psychotherapy, Research, and Practice, 1,* 137–138.

Ekstein, R., & Wallerstein, R. S. (1972). *The teaching and learning of psychotherapy* (2nd ed.). New York: International Universities Press.

Elizur, J. (1990). "Stuckness" in live supervision: Expanding the therapist's style. *Journal of Family Therapy, 12,* 267–280.

Elks, M. A., & Kirkhart, K. E. (1993). Evaluating effectiveness from the practitioner perspective. *Social Work, 38,* 554–563.

Ellis, A. (1974). *The techniques of Disputing Irrational Beliefs (DIBS).* New York: Institute for Rational Living.

Ellis, A. (1989). Thoughts on supervising counselors and therapists. *Psychology: A Journal of Human Behavior, 26,* 3–5.

Ellis, M. V. (1991a). Critical incidents in clinical supervision and in supervisor supervision: Assessing supervisory issues. *Journal of Counseling Psychology,* 342–349.

Ellis, M. V. (1991b). Research in clinical supervision: Revitalizing a scientific agenda. *Counselor Education and Supervision, 30,* 238–251.

Ellis, M. V., Anderson-Hanley, C. M., Dennin, M. K., Anderson, J. J., Chapin, J. L., & Polstri, S. M. (August, 1994). *Congruence of expectation in clinical supervision: Scale development and validity data.* Paper presented at the American Psychological Association, Los Angeles.

Ellis, M. V., Chapin, J. L., Dennin, M. K., & Anderson-Hanley, C. (August, 1996). *Role induction for clinical supervision: Impact on neophyte supervisees.* Paper presented at the American Psychological Association, Toronto, Canada.

Ellis, M. V., & Dell, D. M. (1986). Dimensionality of supervisor roles: Supervisors' perceptions of supervision. *Journal of Counseling Psychology, 33,* 282–291.

Ellis, M. V., Dell, D. M., & Good, G. E. (1988). Counselor trainees' perceptions of supervisor roles: Two studies testing the dimensionality of supervision. *Journal of Counseling Psychology, 35,* 315–322.

Ellis, M. V., & Douce, L. A. (1994). Group supervision of novice clinical supervisors: Eight recurring issues. *Journal of Counseling & Development, 72,* 520–525.

Ellis, M. V., & Ladany, N. (1997). Inferences concerning supervisees and clients in clinical supervision: An integrative review. In C. E. Watkins, Jr. (Ed.), *Handbook of psychotherapy supervision.* New York: Wiley, 467–507.

Ellis, M. V., Ladany, N., Krengel, M., & Schult, D. (August, 1988). *An investigation of supervision research methodology: Where have we gone wrong?* Paper presented at the annual meeting of the American Psychological Association, Atlanta, GA.

Ellis, M. V., Ladany, N., Krengel, M., & Schult, D. (1996). Clinical supervision research from 1981 to 1993: A methodological critique. *Journal of Counseling Psychology, 43,* 35–50.

Ellis, M. V., & Robbins, E. S. (1993). Voices of care and justice in clinical supervision: Issues and interventions. *Counselor Education and Supervision, 32,* 203–212.

Erera, I. P., & Lazar, A. (1994). The administrative and educational functions in supervision: Indications of incompatibility. *Clinical Supervisor, 12*(2), 39–55.

Ericcson, K. A., & Lehmann, A. C. (1996). Expert and exceptional performance: Evidence of maximal adaptation to task constraints. *Annual Review of Psychology, 47,* 273–305.

Everctt, C. A., & Koerpel, B. J. (1986). Family therapy supervision: A review and critique of the literature. *Contemporary Family Therapy: An International Journal, 8,* 62–74.

Eysenck, M. W., & Calvo, M. G. (1992). Anxiety and performance: The processing efficiency theory. *Cognition & Emotion, 6,* 409–434.

Falvey, J. E. (1987). *Handbook of administrative supervision.* Alexandria, VA: Association for Counselor Education and Supervision.

Falvey, J. E., Caldwell, C. F., & Cohen, C. R. (1996). *Focused Risk Management Supervisory System (FoRMSS).* Unpublished document.

Feiner, A. H. (1994). Comments on contradictions in the supervisory process. *Contemporary Psychoanalysis, 30,* 57–75.

Fennell, D. L., Hovestadt, A. J., & Harvey, S. J. (1986). A comparison of delayed feedback and live supervision models of marriage and family therapist clinical training. *Journal of Marital and Family Therapy, 12,* 181–186.

Fine, M., & Fenell, D. (1985). Supervising the supervisor-of-supervision: A supervision-of-supervision technique or an hierarchical blurring? *Journal of Strategic & Systemic Therapies, 4,* 55–59.

Fiscalini, J. (1985). On supervisory parataxis and dialogue. *Contemporary Psychoanalysis, 21,* 591–608.

Fisher, B. (1989). Differences between supervision of beginning and advanced therapists: Hogan's hypothesis empirically revisited. *Clinical Supervisor, 7*(1), 57–74.

Fitzgerald, L. E, & Osipow, S. H. (1986). An occupational analysis of counseling psychology: How special is the specialty? *American Psychologist, 41,* 535–544.

Fleming, J. (1953). The role of supervision in psychiatric training. *Bulletin of the Menninger Clinic, 17,* 157–159.

Fong, M. L., Borders, L. D., & Neimeyer, G. J. (1986). Sex role orientation and self-disclosure flexibility in counselor training. *Counselor Education and Supervision, 25*(3), 210–221.

Fong, M. L. & Lease, S. H. (in press). Cross-cultural supervision: Issues for the white supervisor. Newbury Park, CA: Sage.

Forsyth, D. R., & Ivey, A. E. (1980). Micro-training: An approach to differential supervision. In A. K. Hess (Ed.), *Psychotherapy supervision: Theory, research and practice.* New York: Wiley, 242–261.

Fox, R. (1983). Contracting in supervision: A goal oriented process. *Clinical Supervisor, 1*(1), 37–49.

Frame, M. W., & Stevens-Smith, P. (1995). Out of harm's way: Enhancing monitoring and dismissal processes in counselor education programs. *Counselor Education and Supervision, 35,* 118–129.

Frank, A. D. (1961). *Persuasion and healing.* Baltimore, MD: Johns Hopkins University Press.

Frank, J. (1973). *Persuasion and healing* (2nd ed.). Baltimore, MD: Johns Hopkins University Press.

Frankel, B. R. (1990). Process of family therapy live supervision: A brief report. *Commission on Supervision Bulletin, 3*(1), 5–6.

Frankel, B. R., & Piercy, F. P. (1990). The relationship among selected supervisor, therapist, and client behaviors. *Journal of Marital and Family Therapy, 16,* 407–421.

Frayn, D. H. (1991). Supervising the supervisors: The evolution of a psychotherapy supervisors' group. *American Journal of Psychotherapy, 45,* 31–42.

Freeman, B., & McHenry, S. (1996). Clinical supervision of counselors-in-training: A nationwide survey of ideal delivery, goals, and theoretical influences. *Counselor Education and Supervision, 36,* 144–158.

French, J. R. P., Jr., & Raven, B. (1959). The bases of social power. In D. Cartwright (Ed.), *Studies in social power.* Ann Arbor, MI: Institute for Social Research.

Frick, D. E., McCartney, C. F., & Lazarus, J. A. (1995). Supervision of sexually exploitive psychiatrists: APA district branch experience. *Psychiatric Annals, 25,* 113–117.

Fried, L. (1991). Becoming a psychotherapist. *Journal of College Student Psychotherapy, 5,* 71–79.

Fried, Y., Tiegs, R. B., & Bellamy, A. R. (1992). Personal and interpersonal predictors of supervisors' avoidance of evaluating subordinates. *Journal of Applied Psychology, 77,* 462–468.

Friedberg, R. D., & Taylor, L. A. (1994). Perspectives on supervision in cognitive therapy. *Journal of Rational–Emotive & Cognitive Behavior Therapy, 12*(3), 147–161.

Friedlander, M. L., Keller, K. E., Peca-Baker, T. A., & Olk, M. E. (1986). Effects of role conflict on counselor trainees' self-statements, anxiety level, and performance. *Journal of Counseling Psychology,* 73–77.

Friedlander, M. L., & Schwartz, G. S. (1985). Toward a theory of strategic self-presentation in counseling and psychotherapy. *Journal of Counseling Psychology, 32,* 483–501.

Friedlander, M. L., Siegel, S. M., & Brenock, K. (1989). Parallel process in counseling and supervision: A case study. *Journal of Counseling Psychology, 36,* 149–157.

Friedlander, M. L., & Snyder, J. (1983). Trainees' expectations for the supervisory process: Testing a developmental model. *Counselor Education and Supervision, 22,* 342–348.

Friedlander, M. L., & Ward, L. G. (1984). Development and validation of the Supervisory Styles Inventory. *Journal of Counseling Psychology, 31,* 542–558.

Friedman, D., & Kaslow, N. J. (1986). The development of professional identity in psychotherapists: Six stages in the supervision process. *Clinical Supervisor, 4*(1–2), 29–49.

Friedman, R. (1983). Aspects of the parallel process and counter-transference issues in student supervision. *School Social Work Journal, 8*(1), 3–15.

Froehle, T. C. (1984). Computer-assisted feedback in counseling supervision. *Counselor Education and Supervision, 24,* 168–175.

Fukuyama, M. A. (1994). Critical incidents in multicultural counseling supervision: A phenomenological approach to supervision. *Counselor Education and Supervision, 34,* 142–151.

Fulero, S. M. (1988). Tarasoff: 10 years later. *Professional Psychology: Research and Practice, 19,* 184–190.

Fuller, F. F., & Manning, B. A. (1973). Self-confrontation reviewed: A conceptualization for video playback in teacher education. *Review of Educational Research, 43,* 469–528.

Galassi, J. P., & Brooks, L. (1992). Integrating scientist and practitioner training in counseling psychology: Practicum is the key. *Counselling Psychology Quarterly, 5,* 57–65.

Gallant, J. P., & Thyer, B. A. (1989). The "bug-in-the-ear" in clinical supervision: A review. *Clinical Supervisor, 7*(2), 43–58.

Gallant, J. P., Thyer, B. A., & Bailey, J. S. (1991). Using bug-in-the-ear feedback in clinical supervision. *Research on Social Work Practice, 1,* 175–187.

Garfield, S. L. (1983). Effectiveness of psychotherapy: The perennial controversy. *Professional Psychology: Theory, Research, and Practice, 14,* 35–43.

Garfield, S. L. (1986). Research on client variables in psychotherapy. In S. L. Garfield & A. E. Bergin (Eds.), *Handbook of psychotherapy and behavior change* (3rd ed.). New York: Wiley.

Garfield, S. L. (1996). Some problems associated with "validated" forms of psychotherapy. *Clinical Psychology: Science & Practice, 3,* 218–229.

Garfield, S. L., & Kurtz, R. M. (1976). Clinical psychologists in the 1970s. *American Psychologist, 31,* 1–9.

Gautney, K. (1994). What if they ask me if I am married? *Supervisor Bulletin, 7*(1), 3, 7.

Gelso, C. J. (1974). Effects of recording on counselors and clients. *Counselor Education and Supervision, 13,* 5–12.

Gelso, C. J. (1979). Research in counseling: Methodological and professional issues. *Counseling Psychologist, 8*(3), 7–36.

Gelso, C. J. (1985). Rigor, relevance, and counseling research: On the need to maintain our course between Scylla and Charybdis. *Journal of Counseling and Development, 63,* 551–553.

Gelso, C. J., & Carter, A. (1985). The relationship in counseling and psychotherapy. *Counseling Psychologist, 13,* 155–243.

Gelso, C. J., & Carter, J. A. (1994). Components of the psychotherapy relationship: Their interaction and unfolding during treatment. *Journal of Counseling Psychology, 41,* 296–306.

Genest, M., and Turk, D. C. (1981). Think-aloud approaches to cognitive assessment. In T. V. Merluzzi, C. R. Glass, & M. Genest (Eds.), *Cognitive Assessment.* New York: Guilford, 233–269.

Gergen, K. J. (1982). *Towards transformation in social knowledge.* New York: Springer-Verlag.

Gershenson, J., & Cohen, M. (1978). Through the looking glass: The experiences of two family therapy trainees with live supervision. *Family Process, 17,* 225–230.

Getzel, G. S., & Salmon, R. (1985). Group supervision: An organizational approach. *Clinical Supervisor, 3*(1), 27–43.

Gilbert, L. A., & Rossman, K. M. (1992). Gender and the mentoring process for women: Implications for professional development. *Professional Psychology: Research and Practice, 23,* 233–238.

Gilligan, C. (1982). *In a different voice.* Cambridge, MA: Harvard University Press.

Gizynski, M. (1978). Self awareness of the supervisor in supervision. *Clinical Social Work Journal, 6,* 203–210.

Glaser, R. D., & Thorpe, J. S. (1986). Unethical intimacy. *American Psychologist, 41,* 43–51.

Glenn, E., & Serovich, J. M. (1994). Documentation of family therapy supervision: A rationale and method. *American Journal of Family Therapy, 22,* 345–355.

Glickauf-Hughes, C., & Campbell, L. F. (1991). Experiential supervision: Applied techniques for a case presentation approach. *Psychotherapy, 28,* 625–635.

Glidden, C. E., & Tracey, T. J. (1992). A multidimensional scaling analysis of supervisory dimensions and their perceived relevance across trainee experience levels. *Professional Psychology: Research and Practice, 23,* 151–157.

Gloria, A. M., & Robinson, S. E. (1994). The internship application process: A survey of program training directors and intern candidates. *Counseling Psychologist, 22,* 474–488.

Goffman, E. (1959). *The presentation of self in everyday life.* Garden City, NY: Doubleday.

Goin, M. K., & Kline, F. (1976). Countertransference: A neglected subject in clinical supervision. *American Journal of Psychiatry, 133,* 41–44.

Goldberg, D. A. (1985). Process notes, audio, and videotape: Modes of presentation in psychotherapy training. *Clinical Supervisor, 3,* 3–13.

Goldstein, A. P., Heller, K., & Sechrest, L. B. (1966). *Psychotherapy and the psychology of behavior change.* New York: Wiley.

Gonccalves, O. F. (1994). Cognitive narrative psychotherapy: The hermeneutic construction of alternative meanings. *Journal of Cognitive Psychotherapy, 8,* 105–125.

Good, G. E., & Mintz, L. B. (1990). Gender role conflict and depression in college men: Evidence for compounded risk. *Journal of Counseling and Development, 69,* 17–21.

Goodman, R. W. (1985). The live supervision model in clinical training. *Clinical Supervisor, 3* (2), 43–49.

Goodyear, R. K. (1982). *Psychotherapy supervision by major theorists* [Videotape series]. Manhattan, KS: Kansas State University Instructional Media Center (for further information, contact the author at the University of Southern California.)

Goodyear, R. K. (1990). Gender configurations in supervisory dyads: Their relation to supervisee influence strategies and to skill evaluations of the supervisee. *Clinical Supervisor, 8*(2), 67–79.

Goodyear, R. K. (August, 1994). Toward a science of graduate education in professional psychology. Paper presented at the annual meeting of the American Psychological Association, Los Angeles.

Goodyear, R. K. (1997). Psychological expertise and the role of individual differences: An exploration of issues. *Educational Psychology Review, 9,* 251–265.

Goodyear, R. K., Abadie, P. D., & Efros, F. (1984). Supervisory theory into practice: Differential perceptions of supervision by Ekstein, Ellis, Polster, and Rogers. *Journal of Counseling Psychology, 31,* 228–237.

Goodyear, R. K., Ettelson, D. M., O'Neil, S. H., Sakai, P., & Smart, R. (August, 1996). *Training and deploying process research coders: A review of practices.* Paper presented at the American Psychological Association, Toronto, Canada.

Goodyear, R. K., & Nelson, M. L. (1997). The major supervision formats. In C. E. Watkins, Jr. (Ed), *Handbook of psychotherapy supervision.* New York: Wiley.

Goodyear, R. K., & Robyak, J. E. (1982). Supervisors theory and experience in supervisory focus. *Psychological Reports, 51,* 978.

Goodyear, R. K., & Shumate, J. (1996). Perceived effects of therapist self-disclosure of attraction to clients. *Professional Psychology: Research and Practice, 27,* 613–616.

Goodyear, R. K., & Sinnett, E. D. (1984). Current and emerging ethical issues for counseling psychologists. *Counseling Psychologist, 12*(3), 87–98.

Gordon, S. P. (1990). Developmental supervision: An exploratory study of a promising model. *Journal of Curriculum and Supervision, 5,* 293–307.

Gorely, T., Gordon, S., & Ford, I. (1994). NUDIST: A qualitative data analysis system for sport psychology research. *Sport Psychologist, 8,* 319–320.

Grace, W. C. (1985). Evaluating a prospective clinical internship: Tips for the applicant. *Professional Psychology: Research and Practice, 16,* 475–480.

Granello, D. H. (1996). Gender and power in the supervisory dyad. *Clinical Supervisor, 14*(2), 53–67.

Greben, S. E., & Ruskin, R. (Eds.). (1994). *Clinical perspectives on psychotherapy supervision.* Washington, DC: American Psychiatric Press.

Green, S. L., & Hansen, J. C. (1986). Ethical dilemmas in family therapy. *Journal of Marital and Family Therapy, 12,* 225–230.

Gregorc, A. (1979). Learning/teaching styles: Potent forces behind them. *Educational Leadership,* January, 234–236.

Grey, A. L., & Fiscalini, J. (1987). Parallel process as transference–countertransference interaction. *Psychoanalytic Psychology, 4,* 131–144.

Grimm, D. W. (1994). Therapist spiritual and religious values in psychotherapy. *Counseling and Values, 38,* 154–164.

Guest, P. D., & Beutler, L. E. (1988). Impact of psychotherapy supervision on therapist orientation and values. *Journal of Consulting & Clinical Psychology, 56,* 653–658.

Gurk, M. D., & Wicas, E. A. (1979). Generic models of counselor supervision: Counseling/instruction dichotomy and consultation metamodel. *Personnel and Guidance Journal, 57,* 402–407.

Haas, L. J. (1991). Hide-and-seek or show-and-tell? Emerging issues of informed consent. *Ethics and Behavior, 1,* 175–189.

Haas, L. J. & Cummings, N. A. (1991). Managed outpatient mental health plans: Clinical, ethical and practical guidelines for participation. *Professional Psychology: Research and Practice, 22,* 45–51.

Haas, L. J., Malouf, J. L., & Mayerson, N. H. (1986). Ethical dilemmas in psychological practice: Results of a national survey. *Professional Psychology: Research and Practice, 17,* 316–321.

Hackney, H. L., & Cormier, L. S. (1996). *The professional counselor: A process guide to helping.* Boston: Allyn and Bacon.

Hackney, H. L., & Goodyear, R. K. (1984). Carl Rogers' client-centered supervision. In R. F. Levant and J. M. Schlien (Eds.), *Client-centered therapy and the person-centered approach.* New York: Praeger.

Haferkamp, C. J. (1989). Implications of self-monitoring theory for counseling supervision. *Counselor Education and Supervision, 28,* 290–298.

Hahn, W. K., & Molnar, S. (1991). Intern evaluation in university counseling centers: Process, problems, and recommendations. *Counseling Psychologist, 19,* 414–430.

Hale, K. K., & Stoltenberg, C. D. (1988). The effects of self-awareness and evaluation apprehension on counselor trainee anxiety. *Clinical Supervisor, 6,* 49–69.

Haley, J. (1976). *Problem solving therapy.* San Francisco: Jossey–Bass.

Haley, J. (1987). *Problem solving therapy,* (2nd ed.) San Francisco: Jossey–Bass.

Haley, J. (1993). How to be a therapy supervisor without knowing how to change anyone. *Journal of Systemic Therapies, 12*(4), 41–42.

Halgin, R. P. (1985–86). Pragmatic blending of clinical models in the supervisory relationship, *Clinical Supervisor, 3*(4), 23–46.

Hall, J. E. (1988a). Protection in supervision. *Register Report, 14*(4), 3–4.

Hall, J. E. (1988b). Dual relationships in supervision. *Register Report, 15*(1), 5–6.

Hamilton, N., & Else, J. F. (1983). *Designing field education: Philosophy, structure and process.* Springfield, IL: Charles C Thomas.

Hamlin, E. R., II, & Timberlake, E. M. (1982). Peer group supervision for supervisors. *Social Casework, 67,* 82–87.

Handley, P. (1982). Relationship between supervisors' and trainees' cognitive styles and the supervision process. *Journal of Counseling Psychology, 25,* 508–515.

Hansen, J., & Stevic, R. (1967). Practicum in supervision: A proposal. *Counselor Education and Supervision, 7,* 205–206.

Hardcastle, D. A. (1991). Toward a model for supervision: A peer supervision pilot project. *Clinical Supervisor, 9*(2), 63–76.

Hardy, K. V. (1993). Live supervision in the postmodern era of family therapy: Issues, reflections, and questions. *Contemporary Family Therapy: An International Journal, 15,* 9–20.

Harkness, D., & Poertner, A. (1989). Research and social work supervision: A conceptual review. *Social Work, 34,* 115–119.

Harmon, L. W. (1989). The scientist/practitioner model and choice of research paradigm. *Counseling Psychologist, 17*(1), 86–89.

Harrar, W. R., VandeCreek, L., & Knapp, S. (1990). Ethical and legal aspects of clinical supervision. *Professional Psychology: Research and Practice, 21,* 37–41.

Harris, M. B. C. (1994). Supervisory evaluation and feedback. In L. D. Broders (Ed.), *Supervision: Exploring the Effective Components.* Greensboro, NC: ERIC/CASS.

Harris, S., & Goodyear, R. K. (April, 1990). *The circumplex model in four supervisory dyads: A study of interaction.* Paper presented at the annual meeting of the American Educational Research Association, Boston.

Hart, G. (1982). *The process of clinical supervision.* Baltimore, MD: University Park Press.

Hartman, C., & Brieger, K. (1992). Cross-gender supervision and sexuality. *Clinical Supervisor, 10*(1), 71–81.

Harvey, C., & Katz, C. (1985). *If I'm so successful, why do I feel like a fake? The impostor phenonenon.* New York: St. Martin's Press.

Harvey, O. J., Hunt, D. E., & Schroeder, H. M. (1961). *Conceptual systems and personality organization.* New York: Holt, Rinehart and Winston.

Haverkamp, B. E. (1994). Using assessment in counseling supervision: Individual differences in self-monitoring. *Measurement & Evaluation in Counseling & Development, 27,* 316–324.

Hawkins, P., & Shohet, R. (1989). *Supervision in the helping professions.* Milton Keynes, UK: Open University Press.

Hawthorne, L. S. (1987). Teaching from recordings in field instruction. *Clinical Supervisor, 5*(2), 7–22.

Hayes, J. R. (1981). *The complete problem solver.* Philadelphia: Franklin Institute Press.

Hayes, J. R. (1985). Three problems in teaching general skills. In S. Chipman, J. Segal, & R. Glaser (Eds.), *Thinking and learning skills.* Hillsdale, NJ: Erlbaum, 391–406.

Hayes, R. L. (1989). Group supervision. In L. J. Bradley & J. D. Boyd (Eds.), *Counselor supervision* (2nd ed.). Muncie, IN: Accelerated Development, 399–421.

Hayes, S. C., Follette, V. M., Dawes, R. M., & Grady, K. E. (Eds.). (1995). *Scientific standards of practice: Issues and recommendations.* Reno, NV: Context Press.

Heath, A. (1982). Team family therapy training: Conceptual and pragmatic considerations. *Family Process, 21,* 187–194.

Helms, J. E. (1994). Racial identity and career assessment. *Journal of Career Assessment, 2,* 199–209.

Helms, J. E., & Piper R. E. (1994). Implications of racial identity theory for vocational psychology. *Journal of Vocational Behavior, 44,* 124–138.

Henderson, P. (1994). Administrative skills in counseling supervision. In L. D. Borders (Ed). *Supervision: Exploring the effective components.* Greensboro, NC: ERIC/CASS, EDO–CG-94–25.

Henry, W. P., Strupp, H. H., Butler, S. F., Schacht, T. E., & Binder, J. L. (1993). Effects of training in time-limited dynamic psychotherapy: Changes in therapist behavior. *Journal of Consulting and Clinical Psychology, 61,* 434–440.

Heppner, P. P., & Claiborn, C. D. (1989). Social influence research in counseling: A review and critique [Monograph]. *Journal of Counseling Psychology, 36,* 365–387.

Heppner, P. P., & Dixon, D. N. (1981). A review of the interpersonal influence process in counseling. *Personnel and Guidance Journal, 59,* 542–550.

Heppner, P. P., & Handley, P. G. (1982). A study of the interpersonal influence process in supervision. *Journal of Counseling Psychologist, 28,* 437–444.

Heppner, P. P., Kivlighan, D. M., Burnett, J. W., Berry, T. R., Goedinghaus, M., Doxsee, D. J., Hendricks, F. M., Krull, L. A., Wright, G. E., Bellatin, A. M., Durham, R. J., Tharp, A., Kim, H., Brossart, D. F., Wang, L., Witty, T. E., Kinder, M. H., Hertel, J. B., & Wallace, D. L. (1994). Dimensions that characterize supervisor interventions delivered in the context of live supervision of practicum counselors. *Journal of Counseling Psychology, 41,* 227–235.

Heppner, P. P., & Krauskopf, C. J. (1987). An information-processing approach to personal problem solving. *Counseling Psychologist, 15,* 371–447.

Heppner, P. P., & Roehlke, H. J. (1984). Differences among supervisees at different levels of training: Implications for a developmental model of supervision. *Journal of Counseling Psychology, 31,* 76–90.

Herman, K. C. (1993). Reassessing predictors of therapist competence. *Journal of Counseling and Development, 72,* 29–32.

Herzberg, G. L. (1994). The successful fieldwork student: Supervisor perceptions. *American Journal of Occupational Therapy, 48,* 817–823.

Hess, A. K. (1980). Training models and the nature of psychotherapy supervision. In A. K. Hess (Ed.), *Psychotherapy supervision: Theory, research, and practice.* New York: Wiley, 15–28.

Hess, A. K. (1986). Growth in supervision: Stages of supervisee and supervisor development. *Clinical Supervisor, 4*(1–2), 51–67.

Hess, A. K. (1987). Psychotherapy supervision: Stages, Buber, and a theory of relationship. *Professional Psychology: Research and Practice, 18,* 251–259.

Hess, A. K., & Hess, K. A. (1983). Psychotherapy supervision: A survey of internship training practices. *Professional Psychology: Research and Practice, 14,* 504–513.

Hill, C. E. (1986). An overview of the Hill counselor and client verbal response category systems. In L. Greenberg & W. Pinsof (Eds.), *The psychotherapeutic process: A research handbook.* New York: Guilford, 131–160.

Hill, C. E. (1989). *Therapist techniques and client outcomes: Eight cases of psychotherapy.* Newbury Park, CA: Sage.

Hill, C. E., Carter, J. A., & O'Farrell, M. K. (1981). A case-study of the process and outcome of time-limited counseling. *Journal of Counseling Psychology, 30,* 428–436.

Hill, C. E., Charles, D., & Reed, K. G. (1981). A longitudinal analysis of changes in counseling skills during doctoral training in counseling psychology. *Journal of Counseling Psychology, 28,* 428–436.

Hill, C. E., O'Grady, K. E., Balenger, V., Busse, W., Falk, D. R., Hill, M., Rios, P., & Taffe, R. (1994). Methodological examination of videotape-assisted reviews in brief therapy: Helpfulness ratings, therapist intentions, client reactions, mood, and session evaluation. *Journal of Counseling Psychology, 41,* 236–247.

Hill, R. (1958). Genetic features of families under stress. *Social Casework, 39,* 139–150.

Hillerbrand, E. T. (1989). Cognitive differences between experts and novices: Implications for group supervision. *Journal of Counseling and Development, 67,* 293–296.

Hillerbrand, E. T., & Claiborn, C. D. (1990). Examining reasoning skill differences between expert and novice counselors. *Journal of Counseling and Development, 68,* 684–691.

Hills, H. I., & Strozier, A. L. (1992). Multicultural training in APA-approved counseling psychology programs: A survey. *Professional Psychology Research and Practice, 23,* 43–51.

Hilton, D. B., Russell, R. K., & Salmi, S. W. (1995). The effects of supervisor's race and level of support on perceptions of supervision. *Journal of Counseling and Development, 73,* 559–563.

Hines, P. M., & Hare-Hustin, R. T. (1978). Ethical concerns in family therapy. *Professional Psychology, 9,* 165–171.

Hinterkopf, E. (1994). Integrating spiritual experiences in counseling. *Counseling and Values, 38,* 165–175.

Hipp, J. L., & Munson, C. E. (1995). The partnership model: A feminist supervision/consultation perspective. *Clinical Supervisor, 13*(1), 23–38.

Hoffman, L. W. (1990). *Old scapes, new maps: A training program for psychotherapy supervisors.* Cambridge, MA: Milusik Press.

Hoffman, L. W. (1994). The training of psychotherapy supervisors: A barren scape. *Psychotherapy in private practice, 13,* 23–42.

Hofstadter, D. (1979). *Godel, Escher, Bach: An eternal golden brain.* New York: Basic Books.

Hogan, R. (1964). Issues and approaches in supervision. *Psychotherapy: Theory, Research, and Practice, 1,* 139–141.

Holiman, M., & Lauver, P. J. (1987). The counselor culture and client-centered practice. *Counselor Education and Supervision, 26,* 184–191.

Hollingsworth, D. K., & Witten, J. (1983). Clarification of the counselor-trainee and supervisor roles in clinical education. *Clinical Supervisor, 1,* 47–56.

Holloway, E. L. (1982). Interactional structure of the supervision interview. *Journal of Counseling Psychology, 29,* 309–317.

Holloway, E. L. (1984). Outcome evaluation in supervision research. *Counseling Psychologist, 12,* 167–174.

Holloway, E. L. (1987). Developmental models of supervision: Is it supervision? *Professional Psychology: Research and Practice, 18,* 209–216.

Holloway, E. L. (1988). Instruction beyond the facilitative conditions: A response to Biggs. *Counselor Education and Supervision, 27,* 252–258.

Holloway, E. L. (1992). Supervision: A way of teaching and learning. In S. D. Brown & R. W. Lent (Eds.), *Handbook of Counseling Psychology.* New York: Wiley, 177–214.

Holloway, E. L. (1995). *Clinical supervision: A systems approach.* Thousand Oaks, CA: Sage.

Holloway, E. L. (1997). Structures for the analysis and teaching of psychotherapy. In C. E. Watkins, Jr. (Ed.), *Handbook of psychotherapy supervision.* New York: Wiley, 249–276.

Holloway, E. L., & Carroll, M. (1996). Reaction to the special section on supervision research: Comment on Ellis et al. (1996), Ladany et al. (1996), Neufeldt et al. (1996), and Worthen and McNeill (1996). *Journal of Counseling Psychology, 43,* 51–55.

Holloway, E. L., Freund, R. D., Gardner, S. L., Nelson, M. L., & Walker, B. R. (1989). Relation of power and involvement to theoretical orientation in supervision: An analysis of discourse. *Journal of Counseling Psychology, 36,* 88–102.

Holloway, E. L., & Hosford, R. E. (1983). Toward developing a prescriptive technology of counselor supervision. *Counseling Psychologist, 11,* 73–77.

Holloway, E. L., & Johnston, R. (1985). Group supervision: Widely practiced but poorly understood. *Counselor Education and Supervision, 24,* 332–340.

Holloway, E. L., & Neufeldt, S. A. (1995). Supervision: Its contributions to treatment efficacy. *Journal of Consulting and Clinical Psychology, 63,* 207–213.

Holloway, E. L., & Roehlke, H. J. (1987). Internship: The applied training of a counseling psychologist. *Counseling Psychologist, 15,* 205–260.

Holloway, E. L., & Wampold, B. E. (1983). Patterns of verbal behavior and judgments of satisfaction in the supervision interview. *Journal of Counseling Psychology, 30,* 227–234.

Holloway, E. L., & Wampold, B. E. (1986). Relationship between conceptual level and counseling-related tasks: A meta-analysis. *Journal of Counseling Psychology, 33,* 310–319.

Holloway, E. L., & Wolleat, P. L. (1980). Relationships of counselor conceptual level to clinical hypothesis formation. *Journal of Counseling Psychology, 27,* 539–545.

Holloway, E. L., & Wolleat, P. L. (1981). Style differences of beginning supervisors: An interactional analysis. *Journal of Counseling Psychology, 28,* 373–376.

Holloway, E. L., & Wolleat, P. (1994). Supervision: The pragmatics of empowerment. *Journal of Educational and Psychological Consultation, 5,* 23–43.

Holloway, S., & Brager, G. (1989). *Supervising in the human services: The politics of practice.* New York: Free Press.

Holtzman, R. F., & Raskin, M. S. (1988). Why field placements fail: Study results. *Clinical Supervisor, 6*(3), 123–136.

Horvath, A. O., & Greenburg, L. S. (1989). Development and validation of the working alliance inventory. *Journal of Counseling Psychology, 36,* 223–233.

Hosford, R. (1981). Self-as-a-model: A cognitive social learning technique. *Counseling Psychologist, 9,* 45–62.

Hoshmand, L. L. (1989). Alternative research paradigms: A review and teaching proposal. *Counseling Psychologist, 17,* 3–79.

Hotelling, K., & Forrest, L. (1985). Gilligan's theory of sex-role development: A perspective for counseling. *Journal of Counseling and Development, 64,* 183–186.

Hoyt, M. F., & Goulding, R. (1989). Resolution of a transference–countertransference impasse: Using Gestalt techniques in supervision. *Transactional Analysis Journal, 19,* 201–211.

Huber, C. H. (1994). *Ethical, legal, and professional issues in the practice of marriage and family therapy* (2nd ed.). New York: Macmillan.

Hurt, D. J., & Mattox, R. J. (1990). Supervisor feedback using a dual-cassette recorder. *Clinical Supervisor, 8*(2), 169–172.

Hutt, C. H., Scott, J., & King, M. (1983). A phenomenological study of supervisee's positive and negative experiences in supervision. *Psychotherapy: Theory, Research, and Practice, 20,* 118–123.

Ing, C. (1990). The application of learning style research in the supervisory process. *Child and Youth Services, 13,* 143–155.

Ivey, A. E. (1971). *Microcounseling: Innovations in interviewing training.* Springfield, IL: Charles C Thomas.

Ivey, A. E. (1986). *Developmental therapy: Theory into practice.* San Francisco: Jossey–Bass.

Ivey, A. E., & Authier, J. (1978). Microcounseling: Innovations in interviewing, counseling, psychotherapy, and psychoeducation. Springfield, IL: Charles C Thomas.

Jackson, J. M. & Stricker, G. (1989). Supervision and the problem of grandiosity in novice therapists. *Psychotherapy Patient, 5*(3–4), 113–124.

Jacobson, N. S., & Margolin, G. (1979). *Marital therapy: Strategies based on social learning and behavior exchange principles.* New York: Brunner/Mazel.

Jakubowski-Spector, P., Dustin, R., & George, R. L. (1971). Toward developing a behavioral counselor education model. *Counselor Education and Supervision, 11,* 242–250.

Johnson, E., Baker, S. B., Kopala, M., Kiselica, M. S., & Thompson, E. C. (1989). Counseling self-efficacy and counseling competence in prepracticum training. *Counselor Education & Supervision, 28,* 205–218.

Johnson, E., & Moses, N. C. (August, 1988). *The dynamic developmental model of supervision.* Paper presented at the annual convention of the American Psychological Association, Atlanta, GA.

Johnson, E., & Seem, S. R. (August, 1989). *The dynamic development of self-efficacy in counselor training.* Paper presented at the annual meeting of the American Psychological Association, New Orleans, LA.

Johnson, M. K., Searight, H. R., Handal, P. J., & Gibbons, J. L. (1993). Survey of clinical psychology graduate students' gender attitudes and knowledge: Toward gender-sensitive psychotherapy training. *Journal of Contemporary Psychotherapy, 23,* 233–249.

Jones, E. E. (1979). The rocky road from acts to dispositions. *American Psychologist, 34,* 107–117.

Jones, S. H., Krasner, R. F., & Howard, K. I. (1992). Components of supervisors' ratings of therapists' skillfulness. *Academic Psychiatry, 16,* 29–36.

Kadushin, A. (1968). Games people play in supervision. *Social Work, 13,* 23–32.

Kadushin, A. (1976). *Supervision in social work.* New York: Columbia University Press.

Kadushin, A. (1985). *Supervision in social work* (2nd ed.). New York: Columbia University Press.

Kadushin, A. (1992). *Supervision in social work* (3rd ed.). New York: Columbia University Press.

Kadushin, A. (1992a). What's wrong, what's right with social work supervision. *Clinical Supervisor, 10*(1), 3–19.

Kadushin, A. (1992b). Social work supervision: An updated survey. *Clinical Supervisor, 10*(2), 9–27.

Kagan, H. K., & Kagan, N. I. (1997). Interpersonal process recall: Influencing human interaction. In C. E. Watkins, Jr. (Ed.), *Handbook of Psychotherapy Supervision.* New York: Wiley, 296–309.

Kagan, N. (1976). *Influencing human interaction.* Mason, MI: Mason Media, Inc.; Or Washington, DC: American Association for Counseling and Development.

Kagan, N. (1980). Influencing human interaction—eighteen years with IPR. In A. K. Hess (Ed.), *Psychotherapy supervision: Theory, research and practice.* New York: Wiley, 262–286.

Kagan, N., & Krathwohl, D. R. (1967). *Studies in human interaction: Interpersonal process recall stimulated by videotape.* East Lansing, MI: Michigan State University.

Kagan, N., Kratwohl, D. R., & Farquahar, W. W. (1965). *IPR—Interpersonal process recall by videotape: Stimulated recall by videotape.* East Lansing, MI: Michigan State University.

Kagan, N., Krathwohl, D. R., & Miller, R. (1963). Stimulated recall in therapy using videotape—a case study. *Journal of Counseling Psychology, 10,* 237–243.

Kaplan, M. (1983). A woman's view of DSM–III. *American Psychologist, 38,* 786–792.

Kaplan, R. (1987). The current use of live supervision within marriage and family therapy training programs. *Clinical Supervisor, 5*(3), 43–52.

Kaslow, N. J., & Deering, C. G. (1994). A developmental approach to psychotherapy supervision of interns and postdoctoral fellows. *Psychotherapy Bulletin, 28*(4), 20–23.

Kaslow, N. J., McCarthy, S. M., Rogers, J. H., & Summerville, M. B. (1992). Psychology postdoctoral training: A developmental perspective. *Professional Psychology: Research and Practice, 23,* 369–375.

Kaslow, N.J., & Rice, D. G. (1985). Developmental stresses of psychology internship training: What training staff can do to help. *Professional Psychology: Research and Practice, 16,* 253–261.

Katz, J. H. (1985). The sociopolitical nature of counseling. *Counseling Psychologist, 13,* 615–624.

Kaul, T. J., & Bednar, R. L. (1986). Research on group and related therapies. In S. L. Garfield & A. E. Bergin (Eds.), *Handbook of psychotherapy and behavior change* (3rd ed.). New York: Wiley, 671–714.

Keeney, B. P. (1990). Supervising client conversation: A note on a contextual structure for evoking therapeutic creativity. *Journal of Family Psychotherapy, 1,* 51–56.

Keith, D. V., Connell, G., & Whitaker, C. A. (1992). Group supervision in symbolic experiential family therapy. *Journal of Family Psychotherapy, 3*(1), 93–109.

Keith-Spiegel, P., & Koocher, G. P. (1985). *Ethics in psychology: Professional standards and cases.* New York: Random House.

Kell, B. L., & Burow, J. M. (1970). *Developmental counseling and therapy.* Boston: Houghton Mifflin.

Kell, B. L., Morse, J., & Grater, H. (undated). *The supervision and training of counselors and psychotherapists: An instance of ego-evaluation, support and development.* Unpublished paper.

Kell, B. L., & Mueller, W. J. (1966). *Impact and change: A study of counseling relationships.* New York: Appleton-Century-Crofts.

Kelly, E. W., Jr. (1994). The role of religion and spirituality in counselor education: A national survey. *Counselor Education and Supervision, 33,* 227–237.

Kelly, E. W., Jr. (1995). *Spirituality and religion in counseling and psycho-therapy: Diversity in theory and practice.* Alexandria, VA: ACA Press.

Kennard, B. D., Stewart, S. M., & Gluck, M. R. (1987). The supervision relationship: Variables contributing to positive versus negative experiences. *Professional Psychology: Research and Practice, 18,* 172–175.

Kitchener, K. S. (1984). Intuition, critical evaluation and ethical principles: The foundation for ethical decisions in counseling psychology. *Counseling Psychologist, 12,* 43–55.

Kitchener, K. S. (1988). Dual role relationships: What makes them so problematic? *Journal of Counseling and Development, 67,* 217–221.

Kivlighan, D. M. (1989). Changes in counselor intentions and response modes and in client reactions and session evaluation after training. *Journal of Counseling Psychology, 36,* 471–476.

Kivlighan, D. M., & Angelone, E. O. (1991). Helpee social introversion, novice counselor intention use, and helpee rated session impact. *Journal of Counseling Psychology, 36,* 471–476.

Kivlighan, D. M., Angelone, E. O., & Swafford, K. G. (1991). Live supervision in individual psychotherapy: Effects on therapist's intention use and client's evaluation of session effect and working alliance. *Journal of Counseling Psychology, 22,* 489–495.

Kleintjes, S., & Swartz, L. (1996). Black clinical psychology trainees at a "white" South African University: Issues for clinical supervision. *Clinical Supervisor, 14*(1), 87–109.

Klerman, G. L., Weissman, M. M., Rounsaville, B. J., & Chevron, E. S. (1984). *Interpersonal psychotherapy of depression.* New York: Basic Books.

Klitzke, M. J., & Lombardo, T. W. (1991). A "bug-in-the-eye" can be better than a "bug-in-the-ear": A teleprompter technique for on-line therapy skills training. *Behavior Modification, 15,* 113–117.

Knapp, S., & VandeCreek, L. (1997). Ethical and legal aspects of clinical supervision. In C. E. Watkins, Jr. (Ed.), *Handbook of psychotherapy supervision.* New York: Wiley, 589–602.

Kniskern, D. P., & Gurman, A. S. (1979). Research on training in marriage and family therapy: Status, issues, and directions. *Journal of Marital and Family Therapy, 5,* 83–92.

Knoff, H. M., & Prout, H. T. (1985). Terminating students from professional psychology programs: Criteria, procedures and legal issues. *Professional Psychology: Research and Practice, 16,* 789–797.

Koerin, B., & Miller, J. (1995). Gate-keeping policies: Terminating students for nonacademic reasons. *Journal of Social Work Education, 31,* 247–260.

Kolb, D. (1984). *Experiential learning: Experiences as the source of learning and development.* Upper Saddle River, NJ: Prentice Hall.

Kollock, P., Blumstein, P., & Schwartz, P. (1985). Sex and power in interaction: Conversational privileges and duties. *American Sociological Review, 50,* 34–46.

Kopp, R. R., & Robles, L. (1989). A single-session, therapist-focused model of supervision of resistance based on Adlerian psychology. Individual Psychology: Journal of Adlerian Theory, *Research & Practice, 45,* 212–219.

Kopp, S. (1971). *Guru: Metaphors from a psychotherapist.* Palo Alto, CA: Science and Behavior Books.

Krause, A. A., & Allen, G. J. (1988). Perceptions of counselor supervision: An examination of Stoltenberg's model from the perspectives of supervisor and supervisee. *Journal of Counseling Psychology, 35,* 77–80.

Kruger, L. J., Cherniss, C., Maher, C. A., & Leichtman, H. M. (1988). A behavioral observation system for group supervision. *Counselor Education and Supervision, 27,* 331–343.

Kugler, P. (1995). *Jungian perspectives on clinical supervision.* Einsiedeln, Switzerland: Daimon.

Kuhn, T. S. (1970). *The structure of scientific revolutions* (2nd ed.). Chicago: University of Chicago Press.

Kurpius, D. J., Benjamin, D., & Morran, D. K. (1985). Effects of teaching a cognitive strategy on counselor trainee internal dialogue and clinical hypothesis formulation. *Journal of Counseling Psychology, 32,* 263–271.

Ladany, N., & Friedlander, M. L. (1995). The relationship between the supervisory working alliance and trainees' experience of role conflict and role ambiguity. *Counselor Education and Supervision, 34,* 220–231.

Ladany, N., Hill, C. E., Corbett, M. M., & Nutt, E. A. (1996). Nature, extent, and importance of what psychotherapy trainees do not disclose to their supervisors. *Journal of Counseling Psychology, 43,* 10–24.

Ladany, N., Inman, A. G., Constantine, M. G., & Hofheinz, E. W. (1997). Supervisee multicultural case conceptualization ability and self-reported multicultural competence as functions of supervisee racial identity and supervisor focus. *Journal of Counseling Psychology, 44,* 284–293.

Ladany, N., Lehrman-Waterman, D., Molina, M. Wolgast, B., & Laney, N. (August, 1996). *Supervisor ethical practices as perceived by the supervisees they train.* Poster session presented at the American Psychological Association annual meeting, Toronto, Ontario, Canada.

LaFromboise, T. D., Coleman, H. L., Hernandez, A. (1991). Development and factor structure of the Cross-Cultural Counseling Inventory—Revised. *Professional Psychology: Research and Practice, 22,* 380–388.

Lamb, D. H., Cochran, D. J., & Jackson, V. R. (1991). Training and organizational issues associated with identifying and responding to intern impairment. *Professional Psychology: Research and Practice, 22,* 291–296.

Lamb, D., Presser, N., Pfost, K., Baum, M., Jackson, R., & Jarvis, P. (1987). Confronting professional impairment during the internship: Identification, due process, and remediation. *Professional Psychology: Research and Practice, 18,* 597–603.

Lambert, M. E., & Meier, S. T. (1992). Utility of computerized case simulations in therapist training and evaluation. *Journal of Behavioral Education, 2,* 73–84.

Lambert, M. J. (1974). Supervisory and counseling process: A comparative study. *Counselor Education and Supervision, 14,* 54–60.

Lambert, M. J. (1980). Research and the supervisory process. In A. K. Hess (Ed.), *Psychotherapy supervision: Theory, research, and practice.* New York: Wiley, 423–450.

Lambert, M. J., & Arnold, R. C. (1987). Research and the supervision process. *Professional Psychology: Research and Practice, 18*(3), 217–224.

Lambert, M. J., & Ogles, B. M. (1988). Treatment manuals: Problems and promise. *Journal of Integrative & Eclectic Psychotherapy, 7,* 187–220.

Lambert, M. J., & Ogles, B. M. (1997). The effectiveness of psychotherapy supervision. In C. E. Watkins, Jr. (Ed.), *Handbook of psychotherapy supervision.* New York: Wiley, 421–446.

Landau, J., & Stratton, M. D. (1983). Aspects of supervision with the "Pick-a-Dali-Circus" model. *Journal of Strategic and Systemic Therapies, 2,* 31–89.

Landis, L. L., & Young, M. E. (1994). The reflecting team in counselor education. Special section: Marriage and family training methods. *Counselor Education & Supervision, 33,* 210–218.

Lane, R. C. (1986). The recalcitrant supervisee: The negative supervisory reaction. *Current Issues in Psychoanalytic Practice, 2,* 65–81.

Lanning, W., & Freeman, B. (1994). The Supervisor Emphasis Rating Form—Revised. *Counselor Education & Supervision, 33,* 294–304.

Lanning, W. L., Whiston, S., & Carey, J. C. (1994). Factor structure of the Supervisor Emphasis Rating Form. *Counselor Education & Supervision, 34,* 41–51.

Larrabee, M. J., & Miller, G. M. (1993). An examination of sexual intimacy in supervision. *Clinical Supervisor, 11*(2), 103–126.

Larson, L. M. (in press). The social cognitive model of counselor training. *Counseling Psychologist.*

Larson, L. M., & Daniels, J. A. (in press). Review of the counseling self-efficacy literature. *Counseling Psychologist.*

Larson, L. M., Suzuki, L. A., Gillespie, K. N., Potenza, M. T., Bechtel, M. A., & Toulouse, A. (1992). Development and validation of the Counseling Self-Estimate Inventory. *Journal of Counseling Psychology, 39,* 105–120.

Lazar, A., & Mosek, A. (1993). The influence of the field instructor–student relationship on evaluation of students' practice. *Clinical Supervisor, 11*(1), 111–120.

Lazarus, A. A. (1993). Theory, subjectivity and bias: Can there be a future? *Psychotherapy, 30,* 674–677.

Lazarus, J. A. (1995). Ethical issues in doctor–patient sexual relationships. Special issue: Clinical sexuality. *Psychiatric Clinics of North America, 18,* 55–70.

Leary, M. R., & Kowalski, R. M. (1990). Impression management: A literature review and two-component model. *Psychological Bulletin, 107,* 34–47.

Leary, T. (1957). *Interpersonal diagnosis of personality: A theory and a methodology for personality evaluation.* New York: Ronald Press.

Leddick, G. R. (1994). Counselor education clinics as community resources. In J. E. Myers (Ed.), *Developing and directing counselor education laboratories.* Alexandria, VA: ACA Press, 147–152.

Leddick, G. R., & Dye, H. A. (1987). Effective supervision as portrayed by trainee expectations and preferences. *Counselor Education and Supervision, 27,* 139–154.

Leonardelli, C. A., & Gratz, R. R. (1985). Roles and responsibilities in fieldwork experience: A social systems approach. *Clinical Supervisor, 3*(3), 15–24.

Leong, F. T. L., & Wagner, N. S. (1994). Cross-cultural counseling supervision: What do we know? What do we need to know? *Counselor Education and Supervision, 34,* 117–131.

Lesser, R. M. (1983). Supervision: Illusions, anxieties, and questions. *Contemporary Psychoanalysis, 19,* 120–129.

Levenson, E. A. (1984). Follow the fox. In L. Caligor, P. M. Bromberg, & J. D. Meltzer (Eds.), *Clinical perspectives on the supervision of psychoanalysis and psychotherapy.* New York: Plenum Press, 153–167.

Levine, F. M. & Tilker, H. A. (1974). A behavior modification approach to supervision and psychotherapy. *Psychotherapy: Theory, Research and Practice, 11,* 182–188.

Levinson, D. J. (1978). *The seasons of a man's life.* New York: Knopf.

Levy, L. H. (1983). Evaluation of students in clinical psychology programs: A program evaluation perspective. *Professional Psychology: Research and Practice, 14,* 497–503.

Lewis, G. J., Greenburg, S. L., & Hatch, D. B. (1988). Peer consultation groups for psychologists in private practice: A national survey. *Professional Psychology: Research and Practice, 9,* 81–86.

Lewis, W. (1988). A supervision model for public agencies. *Clinical Supervisor, 6*(2), 85–91.

Lewis, W., & Rohrbaugh, M. (1989). Live supervision by family therapists: A Virginia survey. *Journal of Marital and Family Therapy, 15,* 323–326.

Lichtenberg, J. W. (1997). Can we define expertise in counseling psychology? *Educational Psychology Review, 9,* 221–238.

Lichtenberg, J. W., & Heck, E. J. (1986). Analysis of sequence and pattern in process research. *Journal of Counseling Psychology, 33,* 170–181.

Lichtenberg, J. W., & Wettersten, K. B. (August, 1996). *Relational control: Historical perspective and current empirical status.* Paper presented at the American Psychological Association, Toronto, Canada.

Liddle, H. A. (1988). Systemic supervision: Conceptual overlays and pragmatic guidelines. In H. A. Liddle, D. C. Breunlin, & R. C. Schwartz (Eds.), *Handbook of Family Therapy Training and Supervision.* New York: Guilford, 153–171.

Liddle, H. A., Becker, D., & Diamond, G. M. (1997). Family therapy supervision. In C. E. Watkins, Jr. (Ed.), *Handbook of psychotherapy supervision.* New York: Wiley, 400–421.

Liddle, H. A., Breulin, D. C., & Schwartz, R. C. (Eds.). (1988). *Handbook of family therapy training and supervision.* New York: Guilford Press.

Liddle, H. A., Breunlin, D. C., Schwartz, R. C., & Constantine, J. A. (1984). Training family therapy supervisors: Issues of content, form and context. *Journal of Marital and Family Therapy, 10,* 139–150.

Liddle, H., Davidson, G., & Barrett, M. (1988). Outcomes in live supervision: Trainee perspectives. In H. Liddle, D. Breunlin, & R. Schwartz (Eds.), *Handbook of family therapy training and supervision.* New York: Guilford Press, 183–193.

Liddle, H., & Halpin, R. (1978). Family therapy training and supervision literature: A comparative review. *Journal of Marriage and Family Counseling, 4,* 77–98.

Liddle, H. A., & Saba, G. W. (1982). Teaching family therapy at the introductory level: A conceptual model emphasizing a pattern which connects training and therapy. *Journal of Marital and Family Therapy, 8,* 63–72.

Liddle, H. A., & Saba, G. W. (1983). On context replication: The isomorphic relationship of family therapy and family therapy training. *Journal of Strategic and Systemic Therapies, 2*(2), 3–11.

Liddle, H. A., & Schwartz, R. C. (1983). Live supervision/consultation: Conceptual and pragmatic guidelines for family therapy trainers. *Family Process, 22,* 477–490.

Liese, B. S., & Beck, J. S. (1997). Cognitive therapy supervision. In C. E. Watkins, Jr. (Ed.), *Handbook of psychotherapy supervision.* New York: Wiley, 114–133.

Linehan, M. M. (1980). Supervision of behavior therapy. In A. K. Hess (Ed.), *Psychotherapy supervision: Theory, research and practice.* New York: Wiley.

Linchan, M. (1993). *Cognitive–behavioral treatment of borderline personality disorder.* New York: Guilford Press.

Lipovsky, J. A. (1988). Internship year in clinical psychology training as a professional adolescence. *Professional Psychology: Research and Practice, 19,* 606–608.

Littrell, J. M., Lee-Borden, N., & Lorenz, J. A. (1979). A developmental framework for counseling supervision. *Counselor Education and Supervision, 19,* 119–136.

Lloyd, A. P. (1992). Dual relationship problems in counselor education. In B. Herlihy and G. Corey (Eds.), *Dual relationships in counseling.* Alexandria, VA: AACD, 59–64.

Loevinger, J. (1976). *Ego development.* San Francisco: Jossey–Bass.

Loganbill, C., Hardy, E., & Delworth, U. (1982). Supervision: A conceptual model. *Counseling Psychologist, 10,* 3–42.

Lower, R. B. (1972). Countertransference resistances in the supervisory relationship. *American Journal of Psychiatry, 129,* 156–160.

Lowy, L. (1983). Social work supervision: From models to theory. *Journal of Education for Social Work, 19*(2), 55–62.

Luborsky, L. (1984). *Principles of psychoanalytic psychotherapy: A manual for supportive–expressive treatment.* New York: Basic Books.

Luborsky, L., & DeRubeis, R. (1984). The use of psychotherapy treatment manuals: A small revolution in psychotherapy research style. *Clinical Psychology Review, 4,* 5–14.

Luborsky, L., Singer, B., & Luborsky, L. (1975). Comparative studies of psychotherapy: Is it true that "Everyone has won and all must have prizes?" *Archives of General Psychiatry, 32,* 995–1008.

Mabe, A. R., & Rollin, S. A. (1986). The role of a code of ethical standards in counseling. *Journal of Counseling and Development, 64,* 294–297.

Mack, M. L. (1994). Understanding spirituality in counseling psychology: Considerations for research, training, and practice. *Counseling and Values, 39,* 15–31.

Magnuson, S. (1995). *Supervision of prelicensed counselors: A study of educators, supervisors, and supervisees.* Unpublished doctoral dissertation, University of Alabama.

Maher, M. F., & Hunt, T. K. (1993). Spirituality reconsidered. *Counseling and Values, 38,* 21–28.

Mahoney, M. (1974). *Cognition and behavior modification.* Cambridge, MA: Ballinger.

Mahoney, M. J. (1977). Reflections on the cognitive-learning trend in psychotherapy. *American Psychologist, 32,* 5–13.

Mahrer, A. R. (1988). Discovery-oriented psychotherapy research: Rationale, aims, and methods. *American Psychologist, 43,* 694–702.

Mallinckrodt, B., & Nelson, M. L. (1991). Counselor training level and the formation of the psychotherapeutic working alliance. *Journal of Counseling Psychology, 38,* 133–138.

Malouf, J. L., Haas, L. J., & Farah, M. J. (1983). Issues in the preparation of interns: Views of trainers and trainees. *Professional Psychology: Research and Practice, 14,* 624–631.

Marek, L. I., Sandifer, D. M., Beach, A., Coward, R. L., & Protinsky, H. O. (1994). Supervision without the problem: A model of solution-focused supervision. *Journal of Family Psychotherapy, 5,* 57–64.

Margolin, G. (1982). Ethical and legal considerations in marital and family therapy. *American Psychologist, 37,* 788–801.

Marikis, D. A., Russell, R. K., & Dell, D. M. (1985). Effects of supervisor experience level on planning and in-session supervisor verbal behavior. *Journal of Counseling Psychology, 32,* 410–416.

Markowski, E. M., & Cain, H. I. (1983). Live marital and family therapy supervision. *Clinical Supervisor, 1*(3), 37–46.

Marks, J. L., & Hixon, D. F. (1986). Training agency staff through peer group supervision. *Social Casework, 67,* 418–423.

Markus, H. (1977). Self-schemata and processing information about the self. *Journal of Personality and Social Psychology, 35,* 63–78.

Marrow, A. J. (1969). *The practical theorist: The life and work of Kurt Lewin.* New York: Basic Books.

Martin, J. M. (1985). Measuring clients' cognitive competence in research on counseling. *Journal of Counseling and Development, 63,* 556–560.

Martin, J. M. (1988). A proposal for researching possible relationships between scientific theories and the personal theories of counselors and clients. *Journal of Counseling and Development, 66,* 261–265.

Martin, J. M. (1990). Confusions in psychological skills training. *Journal of Counseling and Development, 68,* 402–407.

Martin, J. M., Slemon, A. G., Hiebert, B., Hallberg, E. T., & Cummings, A. L. (1989). Conceptualizations of novice and experienced counselors. *Journal of Counseling Psychology, 36,* 395–400.

Martin, J. S., Goodyear, R. K., & Newton, F. B. (1987). Clinical supervision: An intensive case study. *Professional Psychology: Research and Practice, 18,* 225–235.

Matarazzo, R. G., & Patterson, D. R. (1986). Methods of teaching therapeutic skill. In S. L. Garfield & A. E. Bergin (Eds.), *Handbook of psychotherapy and behavior change* (3rd ed.). New York: Wiley, 821–843.

Mathews, G. (1986). Performance appraisal in the human services: A survey. *Clinical Supervisor, 3*(4), 47–61.

McCarthy, P., DeBell, C., Kanuha, V., & McLeod, J. (1988). Myths of supervision: Identifying the gaps between theory and practice. *Counselor Education and Supervision, 28,* 22–28.

McCarthy, P., Kulakowski, D., & Kenfield, J. A. (1994). Clinical supervision practices of licensed psychologists. *Professional Psychology: Research and Practice, 25,* 177–181.

McCarthy, P., Sugden, S., Koker, M., Lamendola, F., Maurer, S., & Renninger, S. (1995). A practical guide to informed consent in clinical supervision. *Counselor Education and Supervision, 35,* 130–138.

McColley, S. H., & Baker, E. L. (1982). Training activities and styles of beginning supervisors: A survey. *Professional Psychology, 13,* 283–292.

McCollum, E. (1995). Perspectives on live supervision: The supervisor's view. *Supervision Bulletin, 8*(2), 4.

McCubbin, J., & Patterson, J. (1983). The family stress process: The double ABCX model of adjustment and adaptation. *Marriage and Family Review, 6,* 7–38.

McDaniel, S., Weber, T., & McKeever, J. (1983). Multiple theoretical approaches to supervision: Choices in family therapy training, *Family Process, 22,* 491–500.

McKenzie, P. N., Atkinson, B. J., Quinn, W. H., & Heath, A. W. (1986). Training and supervision in marriage and family therapy: A national survey. *American Journal of Family Therapy, 14,* 293–303.

McNeill, B. W., Hom, K. L., & Perez, J. A. (1995). The training and supervisory needs of racial and ethnic minority students. *Journal of Multicultural Counseling and Development, 23,* 246–258.

McNeill, B. W., & Stoltenberg, C. D. (1992). Agendas for developmental supervision research: A response to Borders. *Counselor Education and Supervision, 31,* 179–183.

McNeill, B. W., Stoltenberg, C. D., & Pierce, R. A. (1985). Supervisee's perceptions of their development: A test of the counselor complexity model. *Journal of Counseling Psychology, 32,* 630–633.

McNeill, B. W., Stoltenberg, C. D., & Romans, J. S. (1992). The Integrated Developmental Model of supervison: Scale development and validation procedures. *Professional Psychology: Research & Practice, 23,* 504–508.

McNeill, B. W., & Worthen, V. (1989). The parallel process in psychotherapy supervision. *Professional Psychology: Research & Practice, 20,* 329–333.

McRae, M. B., & Johnson, S. D., Jr. (1991). Toward training for competence in multicultural counselor education. *Journal of Counseling and Development, 70,* 131–135.

McRoy, R. G., Freeman, E. M., Logan, S. L., & Blackmon, B. (1986). Cross cultural field supervision: Implications for social work education. *Journal of Social Work Education, 22,* 50–56.

McWilliams, N. (1994). *Psychoanalytic diagnosis: Understanding personality structure in the clinical process.* New York: Guilford.

Mead, D. E. (1990). *Effective supervision: A task-oriented model for the mental health professions.* New York: Brunner/Mazel.

Meichenbaum, D. (1977). *Cognitive-behavior modification.* New York: Plenum.

Merluzzi, T. V., Glass, C. R., & Genest, M. (Eds.) (1981). *Cognitive assessment.* New York: Guilford.

Meyer, R. G. (1980). Legal and procedural issues in the evaluation of clinical graduate students. *Clinical Psychologist, 33,* 15–17.

Meyer, R. G., Landis, E. R., & Hays, J. R. (1988). *Law for the psychotherapist.* New York: W. W. Norton.

Miars, R. D., Tracey, T. J., Ray, P. B., Cornfield, L., O'Farrell, M., & Gelso, C. J. (1983). Variation in supervision process across trainee experience levels. *Journal of Counseling Psychology, 30,* 403–412.

Middleman, R. R., & Rhodes, G. B. (1985). *Competent supervision: Making imaginative judgments.* Upper Saddle River, NJ: Prentice Hall.

Mill, J. (1984). High and low seif-monitoring individuals: Their decoding skills and empathic expression. *Journal of Personality, 52,* 372–388.

Miller, G. M., & Larrabee, M. J. (1995). Sexual intimacy in counselor education and supervision: A national survey. *Counselor Education and Supervision, 34,* 332–343.

Miller, G. R. (1976). *Explorations in interpersonal communication.* Beverly Hills, CA: Sage.

Miller, H. L., & Rickard, H. C. (1983). Procedures and students' rights in the evaluation process. *Professional Psychology: Research and Practice, 14,* 830–836.

Miller, M. J. (1989). A few thoughts on the relationship between counseling techniques and empathy. *Counselor Education and Supervision, 67,* 350–351.

Miller, N., & Crago, M. (1989). The supervision of two isolated practitioners: It's supervision Jim, but not as you know it. ANZJ *Family Therapy, 10,* 21–25.

Milne, D. L. (1989). A multidimensional evaluation of therapist behaviour. *Behavioral Psychotherapy, 17,* 253–266.

Minuchin, S., & Fishman, C. (1981). *Family therapy techniques.* Cambridge, MA: Harvard University Press.

Mitchell, R. W. (1991). *Documentation in counseling records.* Alexandria, VA: American Counseling Association Press.

Mohl, P. C., Sadler, J. Z., & Miller, D. A. (1994). What components should be evaluated in a psychiatry residency. *Academic Psychiatry, 18,* 22–29.

Moldawsky, S. (1980). Psychoanalytic psychotherapy supervision. In A. K. Hess (Ed.), *Psychotherapy supervision: Theory, research, and practice.* New York: Wiley.

Moncher, F. J., & Prinz, R. J. (1991). Treatment fidelity in outcome studies. *Clinical Psychology Review, 11,* 247–266.

Montalvo, B. (1973). Aspects of live supervision. *Family Process, 12,* 343–359.

Moore, H. B., & Nelson, E. S. (1981). A workshop model for developing awareness of sex-role bias in counseling students. *Counselor Education and Supervision, 20,* 312–316.

Moras, K. (1993). The use of treatment manuals to train psychotherapists: Observations and recommendations. *Psychotherapy, 30,* 581–585.

Moy, C. T., & Goodman, E. O. (1984). A model for evaluating supervisory interactions in family therapy training. *Clinical Supervisor, 2*(3), 21–29.

Mueller, W. J. (1982). Issues in the application of "Supervision: A conceptual model" to dynamically oriented supervision: A reaction paper. *Counseling Psychologist, 10,* 43–46.

Mueller, W. J., & Kell, B. L. (1972). *Coping with conflict: Supervising counselors and therapists.* New York: Appleton-Century-Crofts.

Multon, K. D., Kivlighan, D. M., & Gold, P. B. (1996). Changes in counselor adherence over the course of training. *Journal of Counseling Psychology, 43,* 356–363.

Munley, P. H. (1974). A review of counseling analogue research methods. *Journal of Counseling Psychology, 21,* 320–330.

Munson, C. E. (1983). *An introduction to clinical social work supervision.* New York: Haworth Press.

Munson, C. E. (1987). Sex roles and power in supervision. *Professional Psychology: Research and Practice, 18,* 236–243.

Munson, C. E. (1991). Duty to warn and the role of the supervisor. *Clinical Supervisor, 9*(2), 1–6.

Munson, C. E. (1993). *Clinical social work supervision* (2nd ed.). New York: Haworth Press.

Murphy, J. W., & Pardeck, J. T. (1986). The "burnout syndrome" and management style. *Clinical Supervisor, 4,* 35–44.

Muslin, H. L., Singer, P. R., Meusea, M. F., & Leahy, J. P. (1968). Research and learning in psychiatric interviewing. *Journal of Medical Education, 43,* 398–404.

Muslin, H. L., Thurnblad, R. J., & Meschel, G. (1981). The fate of the clinical interview: An observational study. *American Journal of Psychiatry, 138,* 823–825.

Myers, I. B. (1962). *The Myers–Briggs Type Indicator.* Palo Alto, CA: Consulting Psychologist Press.

Myers, I. B., & McCaulley, M. H. (1985). *Manual: A guide to the development and use of the Myers–Briggs Type Indicator.* Palo Alto, CA: Consulting Psychologists Press.

Myers, J. E. (1994) (Ed.) *Developing and directing counselor education laboratories.* Alexandria, VA: ACA Press.

Myers, J. E., & Hutchinson, G. H. (1994). Dual role or conflict of interest? Clinics as mental health providers. In J. E. Myers (Ed.), *Developing and directing counselor education laboratories.* Alexandria, VA: ACA Press.

National Association of Social Workers. (1990). *Code of ethics* (rev. ed.). Washington, DC: Author.

National Board for Certified Counselors (1993). *A work behavior analysis of professional counselors.* Greensboro, NC: Author.

Navin, S., Beamish, P., & Johanson, G. (1995). Ethical practices of field-based mental health counselor supervisors. *Journal of Mental Health Counseling, 17,* 243–253.

Neiss, R. (1988). Reconceptualizing arousal: Psychobiological states in motor performance. *Psychological Bulletin, 103,* 345–366.

Nelson, M. L., & Holloway, E. L. (1990). Relation of gender to power and involvement in supervision. *Journal of Counseling Psychology, 37,* 473–481.

Nelson, T. S. (1991). Gender in family therapy supervision. *Contemporary Family Therapy: An International Journal, 13,* 357–369.

Neufeldt, S. A. (1994). Use of a manual to train supervisors. *Counselor Education and Supervision, 33,* 327–336.

Neufeldt, S. A. (in press). A social constructivist approach to counseling supervision. In T. E. Sexton & B. Griffin (Eds.), *Constructivist thinking in counseling research, practice, and supervision.* New York: Teachers' College Press.

Neufeldt, S. A., Iverson, J. N., & Juntunen, C. L. (1995). *Supervision strategies for the first practicum.* Alexandria, VA: American Counseling Association.

Neufeldt, S. A., Karno, M. P., & Nelson, M. L. (1996). A qualitative analysis of experts' conceptualization of supervisee reflectivity. *Journal of Counseling Psychology, 43,* 3–9.

Neukrug, E. S. (1991). Computer-assisted live supervision in counselor skills training. *Counselor Education and Supervision, 31,* 132–138.

Nicholas, M. W. (1989). A systemic perspective of group therapy supervision: Use of energy in the supervisor–therapist–group system. *Journal of Independent Social Work, 3*(4), 27–39.

Nichols, M. (1984). *Family therapy: Concepts and methods.* New York: Gardner Press.

Nichols, W. C., Nichols, D. P., & Hardy, K. V. (1990). Supervision in family therapy: A decade restudy. *Journal of Marital and Family Therapy, 16,* 275–285.

Norcross, J. C., & Halgin, R. P. (1997). Integrative approaches to psychotherapy supervision. In J. C. E. Watkins (Ed.), *Handbook of psychotherapy supervision.* New York: Wiley, 203–222.

Norcross, J. C., & Napolitano, G. (1986). Defining our journal and ourselves. *International Journal of Eclectic Psychotherapy, 5,* 249–255.

Norcross, J. C., Prochaska, J. O., & Farber, J. A. (1993). Psychologists conducting psychotherapy: New findings and historical comparisons on the psychotherapy division membership. *Psychotherapy,* 692–697.

Norcross, J. C., Prochaska, J. O., & Gallager, K. M. (1989). Clinical psychologists in the 1980's: II. Theory, research, and practice. *Clinical Psychologist, 42,* 45–53.

Norell, J. (1991). The International Balint Federation: Past, present, and future. *Family Practice, 8,* 378–381.

Oetting, E. R., & Michaels, L. (1982). *OMART: Oetting/Michaels Anchored Ratings for Therapists.* Fort Collins, CO: Rocky Mountain Behavioral Science Institute.

Olk, M., & Friedlander, M. L. (1992). Trainees' experiences of role conflict and role ambiguity in supervisory relationships. *Journal of Counseling Psychology, 39,* 389–397.

Olsen, D. C., & Stern, S. B. (1990). Issues in the development of a family therapy supervision model. *Clinical Supervisor, 8*(2), 49–65.

Olson, U. J., & Pegg, P. F. (1979). Direct open supervision: A team approach. *Family Process, 18,* 463–470.

Orlinski, D. E., Grawe, K., & Parks, B. K. (1994). Process and outcome in psychotherapy—noch einmal. In A. E. Bergin & S. L. Garfield (Eds.), *Handbook of psychotherapy and behavior change* (3rd ed.). New York: Wiley, 270–376.

Orlinsky, D. E., & Howard, K. I. (1986). Process and outcome in psychotherapy. In S. L. Garfield & A. E. Bergin (Eds.), *Handbook of psychotherapy and behavior change.* New York: Wiley, 311–384.

Osborn, C. J., & Davis, T. E. (1996). The supervision contract: Making it perfectly clear. *Clinical Supervisor, 14*(2), 121–134.

Osterberg, M. J. (1996). Gender in supervision: Exaggerating the differences between men and women. *Clinical Supervisor, 14*(2), 69–83.

O'Sullivan, J. J., & Quevillon, R. P. (1992). 40 years later: Is the Boulder Model still alive? *American Psychologist, 47,* 67–70.

Overholser, J. C. (1991). The Socratic method as a technique in psychotherapy supervision. *Professional Psychology: Research and Practice, 22,* 68–74.

Overholser, J. C., & Fine, M. A. (1990). Defining the boundaries of professional competence: Managing subtle cases of clinical incompetence. *Professional Psychology: Research and Practice, 21,* 462–469.

Page, S., & Wosket, V. (1994). *Supervising the counsellor: A cyclical model.* London: Routledge, 1994.

Paisley, P. O. (1994). *Gender issues in supervision.* ERIC Digest. Greensboro, NC: ERIC/CASS.

Parihar, B. (1983). Group supervision: A naturalistic field study in a specialty unit. *Clinical Supervisor, 1*(4), 3–14.

Parker, W. M. (1987). Flexibility: A primer for multicultural counseling. *Counselor Education and Supervision, 26,* 176–180.

Parker, W. M., Bingham, R. P., & Fukuyama, M. (1985). Improving cross-cultural effectiveness in counselor training. *Counselor Education and Supervision, 24,* 349–352.

Parker, W. M., Valley, M. M., & Geary, C. A. (1986). Acquiring cultural knowledge for counselors in training: A multifaceted approach. *Counselor Education and Supervision, 26,* 61–71.

Parry, A. (1991). A universe of stories. *Family Process, 30,* 37–50.

Parry, A., & Doan, R. E. (1994). *Story re-visions: Narrative therapy in the postmodern world.* New York: Guilford.

Pate, R. H., & Bondi, A. M. (1992). Religious beliefs and practice: An integral aspect of multicultural awareness. *Counselor Education and Supervision, 32,* 108–115.

Pate, R. H., Jr., & High, H. J. (1995). The importance of client religious beliefs and practices in the education of counselors in CACREP-accredited programs. *Counseling and Values, 40,* 2–5.

Patrick, K. D. (1989). Unique ethical dilemmas in counselor training. *Counselor Education and Supervision, 28,* 337–341.

Patterson, C. H. (1964). Supervising students in the counseling practicum. *Journal of Counseling Psychology, 11,* 47–53.

Patterson, C. H. (1983). Supervision in counseling: II. Contemporary models of supervision: A client-centered approach to supervision. *Counseling Psychologist, 11*(1), 21–25.

Patterson, C. H. (1986). *Theories of counseling and psychotherapy* (4th ed.). New York: Harper & Row.

Pedersen, P. B. (1991). Multiculturalism as a generic approach to counseling. *Journal of Counseling and Development, 70,* 6–12.

Penman, R. (1980). *Communication processes and relationships.* London: Academic Press.

Perlesz, A. J., Stolk, Y., & Firestone, A. F. (1990). Patterns of learning in family therapy training. *Family Process, 29,* 29–44.

Perris, C. (1994). Supervising cognitive psychotherapy and training supervisors. *Journal of Cognitive Psychotherapy, 8,* 83–103.

Perry, W. G., Jr. (1970). *Forms of intellectual and ethical development in the college years.* New York: Holt, Rinehart and Winston.

Peterson, F. K. (1991). Issue of race and ethnicity in supervision: Emphasizing who you are, not what you know. *Clinical Supervisor, 9*(1), 15–31.

Peterson, M. (1993). Covert agendas in supervision. *Supervision Bulletin, 6*(1), 1, 7–8.

Petty, M. M., & Odewahn, C. A. (1983). Supervisory behavior and sex role stereotypes in human service organizations. *Clinical Supervisor, 1*(2), 13–20.

Petty, R. E., & Cacioppo, J. T. (1986). *Communication and persuasion: Central and peripheral routes to attitude change.* New York: Springer-Verlag.

Piaget, J., & Inhelder, B. (1969). *The psychology of the child.* New York: Basic Books.

Pierce, R. M., & Schauble, P. G. (1970). Graduate training of facilitative counselors: The effects of individual supervision. *Journal of Counseling Psychology, 17,* 210–215.

Pierce, R. M., & Schauble, P. G. (1971). Toward the development of facilitative counselors: The effects of practicum instruction and individual supervision. *Journal of Counseling Psychology, 17,* 210–215.

Piercy, F. P., Sprenkle, D. H., & Constantine, J. A. (1986). Family members' perceptions of live, observation/supervision: An exploratory study. *Contemporary Family Therapy, 8,* 171–187.

Pilkington, N. W., & Cantor, J. M. (1996). Perceptions of heterosexual bias in professional psychology programs. *Professional Psychology: Research and Practice, 27,* 604–612.

Pinsof, W. M., & Wynne, L. C. (1995). The efficacy of marital and family therapy: An empirical overview, conclusions, and recommendations. *Journal of Marital and Family Therapy, 21,* 585–613.

Pistole, M. C., & Watkins, C. E. (1995). Attachment theory, counseling process, and supervision. *Counseling Psychologist, 23,* 457–478.

Poertner, J. (1986). The use of client feedback to improve practice: Defining the supervisor's role. *Clinical Supervisor, 4*(4), 57–67.

Polkinghorne, D. (1988). *Narrative knowing and the human sciences.* Albany, NY: State University of New York Press.

Ponterotto, J. G. (1987). Client hospitalization: Issues and considerations for the counselor. *Journal of Counseling and Development, 65,* 542–546.

Ponterotto, J. G., Alexander, C. M., & Grieger, I. (1995). A multicultural competency checklist for counseling training programs. *Journal of Multicultural Counseling and Development, 23,* 11–20.

Ponterotto, J. G., & Casas, J. M. (1987). In search of multicultural competence within counselor education programs. *Journal of Counseling and Development, 65,* 430–434.

Pope, K. S., Levenson, H., & Schover, L. R. (1979). Sexual intimacy in psychology training: Results and implications of a national survey. *American Psychologist, 34,* 682–689.

Pope, K. S., Spiegel, K. P., & Tabachnik, B. G. (1986). Sexual attraction to clients: The human therapist and the sometimes inhuman training system. *American Psychologist, 41,* 147–158.

Pope, K. S., Tabachnick, B. G., & Keith-Spiegel, P. (1988). Good and poor practices in psychotherapy: National survey of beliefs of psychologists. *Professional Psychology: Research and Practice, 19,* 547–552.

Pope, K. S., Tabachnik, B. G., & Spiegel, P. K. (1987). Ethics of practice: The beliefs and behaviors of psychologists and therapists. *American Psychologist, 42,* 993–1006.

Pope, K. S., & Vasquez, M. J. T. (1991). *Ethics in psychotherapy and counseling: A practical guide for psychologists.* San Francisco: Jossey–Bass.

Pope, K. S., & Vetter, V. A. (1992). Ethical dilemmas encountered by members of the American Psychological Association. *American Psychologist, 47,* 397–411.

Popper, K. (1959). *The logic of scientific discovery.* London: Hutchinson (original work published 1935).

Popper, K. (1968). Predicting overt behavior versus predicting hidden states. *Behavioral & Brain Sciences, 9,* 254.

Porter, N. (1994). Empowering supervisees to empower others: A culturally responsive supervision model. *Hispanic Journal of Behavioral Sciences, 16,* 43–56.

Powell, D. J. (1993). "She said . . . he said" gender differences in supervision. *Alcoholism Treatment Quarterly, 10,* 187–201.

Preli, R., & Bernard, J. M. (1993). Making multiculturalism relevant for majority culture graduate students. *Journal of Marital and Family Therapy, 19,* 5–16.

Prest, L. A., Darden, E. C., & Keller, J. F. (1990). "The fly on the wall" reflecting team supervision. *Journal of Marital and Family Therapy, 16,* 265–273.

Prest, L. A., Schindler-Zimmerman, T., & Sporakowski, M. J. (1992). The initial supervision session checklist (ISSC): A guide for the MFT supervision process. *Clinical Supervisor, 10*(2), 117–133.

Price, D. (1963). *Little Science, Big Science.* New York: Columbia University Press.

Priest, R. (1994). Minority supervisor and majority supervisee: Another perspective of reality. *Counselor Education and Supervision, 34,* 152–158.

Prieto, L. R. (1996). Group supervision: Still widely practiced but poorly understood. *Counselor Education and Supervision, 35,* 295–307.

Proctor, B. (1991). On being a trainer. In W. Dryden & B. Thorne (Eds.), *Training and supervision for counselling in action.* London: Sage, 49–73.

Protinsky, H., & Preli, R. (1987). Interventions in strategic supervision. *Journal of Strategic and Systemic Therapies, 6*(3), 18–23.

Putney, M. W., Worthington, E. L., & McCulloughy, M. E. (1992). Effects of supervisor and supervisee theoretical orientation and supervisor–supervisee matching on interns' perceptions of supervision. *Journal of Counseling Psychology, 39,* 258–265.

Quarto, C. J., & Tracey, T. J. (August, 1989). *Factor structure of the supervision level scale.* Paper presented at the annual meeting of the American Psychological Association, New Orleans, LA.

Quinn, W. H., Atkinson, B. J., & Hood, C. J. (1985). The stuck-case clinic as a group supervision model. *Journal of Marital and Family Therapy, 11,* 67–73.

Rabinowitz, F. E., Heppner, P. P., & Roehlke, H. J. (1986). Descriptive study of process and outcome variables of supervision over time. *Journal of Counseling Psychology,* 292–300.

Raimy, V. C. (Ed.) (1950). *Training in clinical psychology.* Upper Saddle River, NJ: Prentice Hall.

Raphael, R. D. (1982). *Supervisee experience: The effect on supervisor verbal responses.* Paper presented at the annual meeting of the American Psychological Association, Washington, DC.

Raskin, M. S. (1985). Field placement decisions: Art, science or guesswork? *Clinical Supervisor, 3*(3), 55–67.

Ravets, P., Goodyear, R. K., & Halon, A. M. (August, 1994). *Group supervision: An intensive, multiple case study.* Paper presented at the annual meeting of the American Psychological Association, Los Angeles.

Reed, J. R. (1990). *What group practicum events do students relate to their development as counselors?* Paper presented at the American Educational Research Association, Boston.

Reid, E., McDaniel, S., Donaldson, C., & Tollers, M. (1987). Taking it personally: Issues of personal authority and competence for the female in family therapy training. *Journal of Marital and Family Therapy, 13,* 157–165.

Reising, G. N., & Daniels, M. H. (1983). A study of Hogan's model of counselor development and supervision. *Journal of Counseling Psychology, 30,* 235–244.

Remington, G., & DaCosta, G. (1989). Ethnocultural factors in resident supervision: Black supervisor and white supervisees. *American Journal of Psychotherapy, 43,* 398–404.

Resnikoff, R. D. (1981). Teaching family therapy: Ten key questions for understanding the family as patient. *Journal of Marital and Family Therapy, 7,* 135–142.

Rice, L. N. (1980). A client-centered approach to the supervision of psychotherapy. In A. K. Hess (Ed.), *Psychotherapy supervision: Theory, research and practice.* New York: Wiley.

Rich, P. (1993). The form, function, and content of clinical supervision: An integrated model. *Clinical Supervisor, 11,* 137–178.

Richardson, B. K., & Bradley, L. J. (1984). Microsupervision: A skill development model for training clinical supervisors. *Clinical Supervisor, 2*(3), 43–54.

Richman, J. M., Aitken, D., & Prather, D. L. (1990). Intherapy consultation: A supervisory and therapeutic experience from practice. *Clinical Supervisor, 8*(2), 81–89.

Rickards, L. D. (1984). Verbal interaction and supervisor perception in counselor supervision. *Journal of Counseling Psychology, 31,* 262–265.

Rickert, V. L., & Turner, J. E. (1978). Through the looking glass: Supervision in family therapy. *Social Casework, 59,* 131–137.

Rigazio-DiGilio, S. A. (1997). Integrative supervision: Pathways to tailoring the supervisory process. In T. C. Todd and C. L. Storm (Eds.), *The complete systemic supervisor: Context, philosophy, and pragmatics.* Boston: Allyn & Bacon.

Rigazio-DiGilio, S. A., & Anderson, S. A. (1994). A cognitive–developmental model for marital and family therapy supervision. *Clinical Supervisor, 12*(2), 93–118.

Rigazio-Digilio, S. A., Anderson, S. A., & Kunkler, K. P. (1995). Gender-aware supervision in marriage and family counseling and therapy: How far have we actually come? *Counselor Education and Supervision, 34,* 344–355.

Rinas, J., & Clyne-Jackson, S. (1988). *Professional conduct and legal concerns in mental health practice.* Norwalk, CT: Appleton & Lange.

Rioch, M. J., Coulter, W. R., & Weinberger, D. M. (1976). *Dialogues for therapists: Dynamics of learning and supervision.* San Francisco: Jossey–Bass.

Riva, M. T., & Cornish, J. A. E. (1995). Group supervision practices at psychology predoctoral internship programs: A national survey. *Professional Psychology: Research and Practice, 26,* 523–525.

Roberts, J. (1983). Two models of live supervision: Collaborative team and supervisor guided. *Journal of Strategic and Systemic Therapies, 2,* 68–78.

Roberts, J. (1997). Reflecting processes and "supervision": Looking at ourselves as we work with others. In T. C. Todd and C. L. Storm (Eds.), *The complete systemic supervisor: Context, philosophy, and pragmatics.* Boston: Allyn and Bacon, 334–348.

Robiner, W. N. (1982). Role diffusion in the supervisory relationship. *Professional Psychology, 13,* 258–267.

Robiner, W. N., Fuhrman, M. J., & Bobbitt, B. L. (1990). Supervision in the practice of psychology: Toward the development of a supervisory instrument. *Psychotherapy in Private Practice, 8,* 87–98.

Robiner, W. N., Fuhrman, M., & Ristvedt, S. (1993). Evaluation difficulties in supervising psychology interns. *Clinical Psychologist, 46,* 3–13.

Robiner, W. N., Fuhrman, M. J., Ristvelt, S., & Bobbitt, B. L. (1994). The Minnesota Supervisory Inventory (MSI): Development, psychometric characteristics, and supervisory evaluation issues. *Clinical Psychologist, 47,* 4–17.

Robiner, W. N., Fuhrman, M. J., Ristvedt, S., Bobbitt, B. L., & Schirvar, J. (1991). *Minnesota Supervisory Instrument.* Minneapolis, MN: University of Minnesota.

Robinson, W. L., & Reid, P. T. (1985). Sexual intimacies in psychology revisited. *Professional Psychology: Research and Practice, 16,* 512–520.

Robyak, J. E., Goodyear, R. K., & Prange, M. (1987). Effects of supervisor's sex, focus, and experience on preferences for interpersonal power bases. *Counselor Education and Supervision, 26,* 299–309.

Rodenhauser, P. (1992). Psychiatry residency programs: Trends in psychotherapy supervision. *American Journal of Psychotherapy, 46,* 240–249.

Rodenhauser, P. (1994). Toward a multidimensional model for psychotherapy supervision based on developmental stages. *Journal of Psychotherapy Practice and Research, 3,* 1–15.

Rodenhauser, P., Rudisill, J. R., & Painter, A. F. (1989). Attributes conducive to learning in psychotherapy supervision. *American Journal of Psychotherapy, 43,* 368–377.

Rodolfa, E., Rowen, H., Steier, D., Nicassio, T., & Gordon, J. (1994). Sexual dilemmas in internship training: What's a good training director to do? *APPIC Newsletter, 19*(2), 1, 22–24.

Rodway, M. R. (1991). Motivation and team building of supervisors in a multi-service setting. *Clinical Supervisor, 9*(2), 161–169.

Rogers, C. R. (1942). The use of electrically recorded interviews in improving psychotherapeutic techniques. *American Journal of Orthopsychiatry, 12,* 429–434.

Rogers, C. R. (1951). *Client-centered therapy.* Boston: Houghton Mifflin.

Rogers, C. R. (1957). The necessary and sufficient conditions of therapeutic personality change. *Journal of Consulting Psychology, 21,* 95–103.

Rogers, G., & McDonald, P. L. (1995). Expedience over education: Teaching methods used by field instructors. *Clinical Supervisor, 13*(2), 41–65.

Romans, J. S. C., Boswell, D. L., Carlozzi, A. F., & Ferguson, D. B. (1995). Training and supervision practices in clinical, counseling, and school psychology programs. *Professional Psychology: Research and Practice, 26,* 407–412.

Ronnestad, M. H., & Skovholt, T. M. (1993). Supervision of beginning and advanced graduate students of counseling and psychotherapy. *Journal of Counseling and Development, 71,* 396–405.

Rosenberg, M. J. (1979). *Conceiving the self.* New York: Basic Books.

Rosenblatt, A., & Mayer, J. E. (1975). Objectionable supervisory styles: Students' views. *Social Work, 20,* 184–189.

Rosenblum, A. F., & Raphael, F. B. (1987). Students at risk in the field practicum and implications for field teaching. *Clinical Supervisor, 5*(3), 53–63.

Rosenzweig, S. (1936). Some implicit common factors in diverse methods in psychotherapy. *American Journal of Orthopsychiatry, 6,* 412–415.

Ross, L. (1977). The intuitive psychologist and his shortcomings: Distortions in the attribution process. In L. Berkowitz (Ed.), *Advances in experimental social psychology, 10,* 174–220.

Ross, R. P., & Goh, D. S. (1993). Participating in supervision in school psychology: A national survey of practices and training. *School Psychology Review, 22,* 63–80.

Roth, A., & Fonagy, P. (1996). *What works for whom? A critical review of psychotherapy research.* New York: Guilford.

Royal, E., & Golden, S. (1981). Attitude similarity and attraction to an employee group. *Psychological Reports, 48,* 251–254.

Rubinstein, M., & Hammond, D. (1982). The use of videotape in psychotherapy supervision. In M. Blumenfield (Ed.), *Applied supervision in psychotherapy.* New York: Grune & Stratton, 143–164.

Russell, P. A., Lankford, M. W., & Grinnell, Jr., R. M. (1983). Attitudes toward supervisors in a human service agency. *Clinical Supervisor, 1*(3), 57–71.

Russell, R. K., Crimmings, A. M., & Lent, R. W. (1984). Counselor training and supervision: Theory and research. In S. D. Brown & R. W. Lent (Ed.), *Handbook of counseling psychology.* New York: Wiley, 625–681.

Russell, R. K., & Petrie, T. (1994). Issues in training effective supervisors. *Applied and Preventive Psychology, 3,* 27–42.

Ryan, A. S., & Hendricks, C. O. (1989). Culture and communication: Supervising the Asian and Hispanic social worker. *Clinical Supervisor, 7*(1), 27–40.

Ryder, R., & Hepworth, J. (1990). AAMFT ethical code: "Dual relationships." *Journal of Marital and Family Therapy, 16,* 127–132.

Sagrestano, L. M. (1992). Power strategies in interpersonal relationships. *Psychology of Women Quarterly, 16,* 439–447.

Sakinofsky, I. (1979). Evaluating the competence of psychotherapists. *Canadian Journal of Psychiatry, 24,* 193–205.

Sansbury, D. L. (1982). Developmental supervision from a skill perspective. *Counseling Psychologist, 10*(1), 53–57.

Sanville, J. (1989). The play in supervision. *Smith College Studies in Social Work, 59,* 157–159.

Sawatzky, D. D., Jevne, R. F., & Clark, G. T. (1994). Becoming empowered: A study of counsellor development. *Canadian Journal of Counselling, 28,* 177–192.

Scanlon, C. R., & Gold, J. M. (1996). The balance between the missions of training and service at a university counseling center. *Clinical Supervisor, 14*(1), 163–173.

Schacht, A. J., Howe, H. E., & Berman, J. J. (1988). A short form of the Barrett–Lennard Inventory for supervisor relationships. *Psychological Reports, 63,* 699–703.

Schacht, A. J., Howe, H. E., & Berman, J. J. (1989). Supervisor facilitative conditions and effectiveness as perceived by thinking- and feeling-type supervisees. *Psychotherapy, 26,* 475–483.

Schauer, A. H., Seymour, W. R., & Geen, R. G. (1985). Effects of observation and evaluation on anxiety in beginning counselors: A social facilitiation analysis. *Journal of Counseling and Development, 63,* 279–285.

Schiavone, D. D., & Jessell, J. C. (1988). Influence of attribute expertness and gender in counselor supervision. *Counselor Education and Supervision, 28,* 28–42.

Schimel, J. L. (1984). In pursuit of truth: An essay on an epistemological approach to psychoanalytic supervision. In L. Caligor, P. M. Bromberg, & J. D. Meltzer (Eds.), *Clinical perspectives on the supervision of psychoanlysis and psychotherapy.* New York: Plenum Press, 231–241.

Schlenker, B. R. (1980). *Impression management: The self-concept, social identity, and interpersonal relations.* Monterey, CA: Brooks/Cole.

Schlenker, B. R., & Leary, M. R. (1982). Social anxiety and self-presentation: A conceptualization and model. *Psychological Bulletin, 92,* 641–669.

Schmidt, J. P. (1979). Psychotherapy supervision: A cognitive–behavioral model. *Professional Psychology, 10,* 278–284.

Schneider, S. (1992). Transference, counter-transference, projective identification and role responsiveness in the supervisory process. *Clinical Supervisor, 10*(2), 71–84.

Schön, D. A. (1983). *The reflective practitioner: How professionals think in action.* New York: Basic Books.

Schön, D. A. (1987). *Educating the reflective practitioner.* San Francisco: Jossey–Bass.

Schrag, K. (1994). Disclosing homosexuality. *Supervisor Bulletin, 7*(1), 3, 7.

Schreiber, P., & Frank, E. (1983). The use of a peer supervision group by social work clinicians. *Clinical Supersivor, 1*(1), 29–36.

Schutz, B. M. (1982). *Legal liability in psychotherapy.* San Francisco, CA: Jossey–Bass.

Schwartz, R. (1981). The conceptual development of family therapy trainees. *American Journal of Family Therapy, 2,* 89–90.

Schwartz, R. C., Liddle, H. A., & Breunlin, D. C. (1988). Muddles in live supervision. In A. A. Liddle, D. C. Breunlin, & R. C. Schwartz (Eds.), *Handbook of family therapy training and supervision* New York: Guilford, 183–193.

Searles, H. (1955). The informational value of the supervisor's emotional experiences. *Psychiatry, 18,* 135–146.

Sells, J., Goodyear, R., Lichtenberg, J., & Polkinghorne, D. (1997). Relationship of supervisor and trainee gender to in-session verbal behavior and ratings of trainee skills, *Journal of Counseling Psychology, 44,* 1–7.

Shafranske, E. P., & Malony, H. N. (1990). Clinical psychologists' religious and spiritual orientation and their practice of psychotherapy. *Psychotherapy, 27,* 72–78.

Shanfield, W. B., Mohl, P. C., Matthews, K., & Hetherly, V. (1989). A reliability assessment of the Psychotherapy Supervisory Inventory. *American Journal of Psychiatry, 146,* 1447–1450.

Shapiro, C. H. (1988). Burnout in social work field instructors. *Clinical Supervisor, 6*(4), 237–248.

Sharon, D. (1986). The ABCX model—implications for supervision. *Clinical Supervisor, 6*(4), 237–248.

Sharpe, M. (1995). *The third eye: Supervision of analytic groups.* New York: Routledge.

Shaw, B. F., & Dobson, K. S. (1988). Competency judgments in the training and evaluation of psychotherapists. *Journal of Consulting and Clinical Psychology, 56,* 666–672.

Shechter, R. A. (1990). Becoming a supervisor: A phase in professional development. *Psychoanalysis & Psychotherapy, 8,* 23–28.

Sherry, P. (1991). Ethical issues in the conduct of supervision. *Counseling Psychologist, 19,* 566–584.

Shilts, L., Rudes, J., & Madigan, S. (1993). The use of a solution-focused interview with a reflecting team format: Evolving thoughts from clinical practice. *Journal of Systemic Therapies, 12*(1), 1–10.

Shoben, E. J. (1962). The counselor's theory as personal trait. *Personnel and Guidance Journal, 40,* 617–621.

Shulman, L. (1982). *Skills of supervision and staff management.* Itasca, IL: F. E. Peacock.

Siegel, M. (1979). Privacy, ethics and confidentiality. *Professional Psychology, 10,* 249–258.

Simon, R. (1982). Beyond the one-way mirror. *Family Therapy Networker, 26*(5), 19, 28–29, 58–59.

Simonton, D. K. (1994). *Greatness: Who makes history and why.* New York: Guilford.

Skolnik, L. (1988). Field instruction in the 1980s—Realities, issues, and problem-solving strategies. *Clinical Supervisor, 6*(3), 47–75.

Skovholt, T. M., & Ronnestad, M. H. (1992a). *The evolving professional self: Stages and themes in therapist and counselor development.* Chichester, England: Wiley.

Skovholt, T. M., & Ronnestad, M. H. (1992b). Themes in therapist and counselor development. *Journal of Counseling and Development, 70,* 505–515.

Slimp, P. A. O., & Burian, B. K. (1994). Multiple role relationships during internship: Consequences and recommendations. *Professional Psychology: Research and Practice, 25,* 39–45.

Sluzki, C. E., Beavin, J., Tarnopolski, A., & Vernon, E. (1967). Transactional disqualifications: Research on the double-bind. *Archives of General Psychiatry, 16,* 494–504.

Smadi, A. A., & Landreth, G. G. (1988). Reality therapy supervision with a counselor from a different theoretical orientation. *Journal of Reality Therapy, 7*(2), 18–26.

Smith, H. D. (1984). Moment-to moment counseling process feedback using a dual-channel audiotape recording. *Counselor Education and Supervision, 23,* 346–349.

Smith, J., Staudinger, U. M., & Baltes, P. B. (1994). Occupational settings facilitating wisdom-related knowledge: The sample case of clinical psychologists. *Journal of Consulting & Clinical Psychology, 62,* 989–999.

Smith, M. L., & Glass, G. V. (1977). Meta-analysis of psychotherapy outcome studies. *American Psychologist, 32,* 752–760.

Smith, T. E., Winton, M., & Yoshioka, M. (1992). A qualitative understanding of reflective teams: II. Therapists' perspectives. *Contemporary Family Therapy: An International Journal, 14,* 419–432.

Smith, T. E., Yoshioka, M., & Winton, M. (1993). A qualitative understanding of reflecting teams: I. Client perspectives. *Journal of Systemic Therapies, 12,* 28–43.

Snider, P. D. (1985). The duty to warn: A potential issue of litigation for the counseling supervisor. *Counselor Education and Supervision, 25,* 66–73.

Snider, P. D. (1987). Client records: Inexpensive liability protection for mental health counselors. *Journal of Mental Health Counseling, 9,* 134–141.

Snyder, M. (1987). *Public appearances, private realities: The psychology of self-monitoring.* New York: W. H. Freeman.

Snyder, M., & Gangestad, S. (1986). On the nature of self-monitoring: Matters of assessment, matters of validity. *Journal of Personality and Social Psychology, 51,* 125–139.

Soisson, E. L., Vandecreek, L., & Knapp, S. (1987). Thorough record keeping: A good defense in a litigious era. *Professional Psychology: Research and Practice, 18,* 498–502.

Sonne, J. L. (1994). Multiple relationships: Does the new ethics code answer the right questions? *Professional Psychology: Research and Practice, 25,* 336–343.

Sparks, D., & Loucks-Horsley, S. (1989). Five models of staff development for teachers. *Journal of Staff Development, 10*(4), 40–57.

Speed, B., Seligman, P. M., Kingston, P., & Cade, B. W. (1982). A team approach to therapy. *Journal of Family Therapy, 4,* 271–284.

Sperling, M. B., Pirrotta, S., Handen, B. L., Simons, L. A., Miller, D., Lysiak, G., Schumm, P., & Terry, L. (1986). The collaborative team as a training and therapeutic tool. *Counselor Education and Supervision, 25,* 183–190.

Stalans, L. J. (1995). Multidimensional scaling. In L. G. Grimm & P. R. Yarnold (Eds.), *Reading and understanding multivariate statistics.* Washington, DC: American Psychological Association, 137–168.

Stander, V., Piercy, F. P., MacKinnon, D., & Helmeke, K. (1994). Spirituality, religion and family therapy: Competing or complementary worlds? *American Journal of Family Therapy, 22,* 27–41.

Stanton, J. L., & Stanton, M. D. (1986). Family therapy and systems supervision with the "Pick-a-Dali Circus" model. *Clinical Supervisor, 4,* 169–182.

Starling, P. V., Baker, S. B., & Campbell, L. M. (August, 1996). *The impact of structured peer supervision on practicum supervisees.* Paper presented at the American Psychological Association, Toronto, Canada.

Stein, D. M., & Lambert, M. J. (1995). Graduate training in psychotherapy: Are therapy outcomes enhanced? *Journal of Consulting and Clinical Psychology, 63,* 182–196.

Stein, M., & Stone, G. L. (1978). Effects of conceptual level and structure on initial interview behavior. *Journal of Counseling Psychology, 25,* 96–102.

Stenack, R. J., & Dye, H. A. (1982). Behavioral descriptions of counseling supervision roles. *Counselor Education and Supervision, 22,* 295–304.

Sterling, M. M., & Bugental, J. F. (1993). The meld experience in psychotherapy supervision. *Journal of Humanistic Psychology, 33,* 38–48.

Sternberg, R. J. (Ed.) (1990). *Wisdom: Its nature, origins, and development.* Cambridge: Cambridge University Press.

Sternitzke, M. E., Dixon, D. N., & Ponterotto, J. G. (1988). An attributional approach to counselor supervision. *Counselor Education and Supervision, 28,* 5–14.

Stevens, D. T. (1995). Changes in supervisor response and focus with experience and training. Unpublished doctoral dissertation, University of Southern California.

Stevens, D. T., Goodyear, R. K., & Robertson, P. (in press). Supervisor development: An exploratory study in changes in stance and emphasis. *Clinical Supervisor.*

Stevens-Smith, P. (1995). Gender issues in counselor education: Current status and challenges. *Counselor Education and Supervision, 34*(4), 283–293.

Stewart, A. E., & Stewart, E. A. (1996). Personal and practical considerations in selecting a psychology internship. *Professional Psychology: Research and Practice, 27,* 295–303.

Stigall, T. T., Bourg, E. F., Bricklin, P. M., Kovacs, A. L., Larsen, K. G., Lorion, R. P., Nelson, P. D., Nurse, A. R., Pugh, R. W., & Wiens, A. N. (Eds.) (1990). *Report of the Joint Council on Professional Education in Psychology.* Baton Rouge, LA: Joint Council on Professional Education in Psychology.

Stiles, W. B., Shapiro, D. A., & Elliott, R. (1986). "Are all psychotherapies equivalent?" *American Psychologist, 41,* 165–180.

Stiles, W. B., Shapiro, D. A., & Firth-Cozens, J. A. (1988). Do sessions of different treatments have different impacts? *Journal of Counseling Psychology, 35,* 391–396.

Stiles, W. B., & Snow, J. S. (1984). Counseling session impact as viewed by novice counselors and their clients. *Journal of Counseling Psychology, 31,* 3–12.

Stoltenberg, C. (1981) Approaching supervision from a developmental perspective: The counselor-complexity model. *Journal of Counseling Psychologists, 28,* 59–65.

Stoltenberg, C., & Delworth, U. (1987). *Supervising counselors and therapists.* San Francisco: Jossey–Bass.

Stoltenberg, C. D., & Delworth, U. (1988). Developmental models of supervision: It is development—Response to Holloway. *Professional Psychology: Research and Practice, 19,* 134–137.

Stoltenberg, C. D., McNeill, B. W., & Crethar, H. C. (1994). Changes in supervision as counselors and therapists gain experience: A review. *Professional Psychology: Research & Practice, 25,* 416–449.

Stoltenberg, C. D., McNeill, B. W., & Crethar, H. C. (1995). Persuasion and development in counselor supervision. *Counseling Psychologist, 23,* 633–648.

Stoltenberg, C. D., Pierce, R. A., & McNeill, B. W. (1987). Effects of experience on counselors' needs. *Clinical Supervisor, 5,* 23–32.

Stone, D., & Amundson, N. (1989). Counselor supervision: An exploratory study of the metaphoric case drawing method of case presentation in a clinical setting. *Canadian Journal of Counseling, 23,* 360–371.

Stone, G. L. (1980). Effects of experience on supervision planning. *Journal of Counseling Psychology, 27,* 84–88.

Stone, G. L. (1984). Reaction: In defense of the "artificial." *Journal of Counseling Psychology, 31,* 108–110.

Stone, G. L. (August, 1988). *Clinical supervision: An occasion for cognitive research.* Paper presented at the annual meeting of the American Psychological Association, Atlanta, GA.

Storm, C. L. (1997). Back to the future: A review through time. In T. C. Todd & C. L. Storm (Eds.), *The complete systemic supervisor: Context, philosophy, and pragmatics.* Boston: Allyn and Bacon, 283–287.

Storm, C. L., & Haug, I. E. (1997). Ethical issues: Where do you draw the line? In T. C. Todd & C. L. Storm (Eds.), *The complete systemic supervisor: Context, philosophy, and pragmatics.* Boston: Allyn and Bacon, 26–40.

Storm, C. L., & Heath, A. W. (1982). Strategic supervision: The danger lies in discovery. *Journal of Strategic and Systemic Therapies, 1,* 71–72.

Storm, C. L. & Heath, A. W. (1985). Models of supervision: Using therapy as a guide. *Clinical Supervisor, 5,* 87–95.

Storm, H. A. (1994). *Enhancing the acquisition of psychotherapy skills through live supervision.* Paper presented at the annual meeting of the American Psychological Association, Los Angeles.

Stout, C. E. (1987). The role of ethical standards in the supervision of psychotherapy. *Clinical Supervisor, 5*(1), 89–97.

Strein, W., & Hershenson, D. B. (1991). Confidentiality in nondyadic counseling situations. *Journal of Counseling and Development, 69,* 312–316.

Strong, S. R. (1968). Counseling: An interpersonal influence process. *Journal of Counseling Psychology, 15,* 215–224.

Strong, S. R. (1971). Experimental laboratory research in counseling. *Journal of Counseling Psychology, 18,* 106–110.

Strong, S. R., & Claiborn, C. D. (1982). *Change through interaction: Social psychological processes of counseling and psychotherapy.* New York: Wiley–Interscience.

Strong, S. R., & Matross, R. P. (1973). Change process in counseling and psychotherapy. *Journal of Counseling Psychology, 20,* 25–37.

Strong, S. R., Hills, H. I., Kilmartin, C. T., DeVries, H., Lanier, K., Nelson, B. N., Strickland, D., & Meyer III, C. W. (1988). The dynamic relations among interpersonal behaviors: A test of complementarity and anticomplementarity. *Journal of Personality and Social Psychology, 54,* 798–810.

Strozier, A. L., Kivlighan, D. M., & Thoreson, R. W. (1993). Supervisor intentions, supervisee reactions, and helpfulness: A case study of the process of supervision. *Professional Psychology: Research & Practice, 24,* 13–19.

Strupp, H. H., & Binder, J. (1984). *Psychotherapy in a new key: A guide to time-limited dynamic psychotherapy.* New York: Basic Books.

Strupp, H. H., & Hadley, S. W. (1977). A tripartite model of mental health and therapeutic outcomes. *American Psychologist, 32,* 187–196.

Strupp, H. H., & Hadley, S. W. (1979). Specific versus nonspecific factors in psychotherapy. *Archives of General Psychiatry, 36,* 1125–1136.

Sue, S., Akutsu, F. O., & Higashi, C. (1985). Training issues in conducting therapy with ethnic-minority-group clients. In P. Pedersen (Ed.), *Handbook of cross-cultural counseling and therapy.* Westport, CT: Greenwood Press, 275–280.

Sullivan, H. S. (1953). *The interpersonal theory of psychiatry.* New York: W. W. Norton.

Supervision Interest Network, Association for Counselor Education and Supervision (1990). Standards for counseling supervisors. *Journal of Counseling and Development, 69,* 30–32.

Supervision Interest Network, Association for Counselor Education and Supervision (Summer, 1993). ACES ethical guidelines for counseling supervisors. *ACES Spectrum, 53*(4), 5–8.

Swanson, J. L., & O'Saben, C. L. (1993). Differences in supervisory needs and expectations by trainee experience, cognitive style, and program membership. *Journal of Counseling and Development, 71,* 457–464.

Tabachnick, B. G., Keith-Spiegel, P., & Pope, K. S. (1991). Ethics of teaching beliefs and behaviors of psychologists as educators. *American Psychologist, 46,* 506–515.

Talen, M. R., & Schindler, N. (1993). Goal-directed supervision plans: A model for trainee supervision and evaluation. *Clinical Supervisor, 11* (2), 77–88.

Tarasoff v. *Regents of the University of California.* 118 Cal. Rptr. 129, 529 P 2d 533 (1974).

Tarico, V. S., VanZelzen, D. R., & Altmaier, E. M. (1986). Comparison of thought-listing rating methods. *Journal of Counseling Psychology, 33,* 81–83.

Tarvydas, V. M. (1995). Ethics and the practice of rehabilitation counselor supervision. *Rehabilitation Counseling Bulletin, 38,* 294–306.

Task Force on Promotion and Dissemination of Psychological Procedures (1995, 1996). Training in and dissemination of empirically validated treatments: Report and recommendations. *Clinical Psychologist, 48,* 3–23.

Teitelbaum, S. H. (1990). Supertransference: The role of the supervisor's blind spots. *Psychoanalytic Psychology, 7,* 243–258.

Teitelbaum, S. H. (1995). The changing scene in psychoanalytic supervision. *Psychoanalysis & Psychotherapy, 12,* 183–192.

Tennen, H. (1988). Supervision of integrative psychotherapy: A critique. *Journal of Integrative & Eclectic Psychotherapy, 7,* 167–175.

Tetlock, P. E., & Hannum, K. (1984). *The Berkeley Integrative Complexity Scoring Manual.* Unpublished manuscript, Department of Psychology, University of California, Berkeley.

Tetlock, P. E., & Tyler, A. (1996). Churchill's cognitive and rhetorical style: The debates over Nazi intentions and self-government for India. *Political Psychology, 17,* 149–170.

Thoreson, R. W., Shaughnessy, P., Heppner, P. P., & Cook, S. W. (1993). Sexual contact during and after the professional relationship: Attitudes and practices of male counselors. *Journal of Counseling and Development, 71,* 429–434.

Thyer, B. A., Sowers-Hoag, K., & Love, J. P. (1988). The influence of field instructor–student gender combinations on student perceptions of field instruction quality. *Clinical Supervisor, 6*(3), 169–179.

Tinsley, H. E. A., Bowman, S. L., & Ray, S. B. (1988). Manipulation of expectancies about counseling and psychotherapy: A review and analysis of expectancy manipulation strategies and results. *Journal of Counseling Psychology, 35,* 99–108.

Tinsley, H. E. A., Workman, K. R., & Kass, R. A. (1980). Factor analysis of the domain of client expectancies about counseling. *Journal of Counseling Psychology, 27,* 561–570.

Todd, T. C. (1997). Purposive systemic supervision models. In T. C. Todd & C. L. Storm (Eds.), *The complete systemic supervisor: Context, philosophy and pragmatics.* Boston: Allyn and Bacon, 173–194.

Todd, T. C., & Storm, C. L. (Eds.). (1997). *The complete systemic supervisor: Context, philosophy, and pragmatics.* Boston: Allyn and Bacon.

Todtman, D. A., Bobele, M., & Strano, J. D. (1988). An inexpensive system for communication across the one-way mirror. *Journal of Marital and Family Therapy, 14,* 201–203.

Tracey, T. J., Ellickson, J. L., & Sherry, P. (1989). Reactance in relation to different supervisory environments and counselor development. *Journal of Counseling Psychology, 36,* 336–344.

Tracey, T. J., Hays, K. A., Malone, J., & Herman, B. (1988). *Journal of Counseling Psychology, 35,* 119–126.

Tracey, J., & Sherry, P. (1993). Complementary interaction over time in successful and less successful supervision. *Professional Psychology: Research and Practice, 24,* 304–311.

Truax, C. B., & Carkhuff, R. R. (1967). *Toward effective counseling and psychotherapy: Training and practice.* Chicago: Aldine.

Tuckman, B. W. (1965). Developmental sequence in small groups. *Psychological Bulletin, 63,* 384–399.

Tuckman, B. W., & Jensen, M. A. C. (1977). Stages of small group development revisited. *Group and Organizational Studies, 2,* 419–427.

Turban, D. B., & Jones, A. P. (1988). Supervisor–subordinate similarity: Types, effects, and mechanisms. *Journal of Applied Psychology, 73,* 228–234.

Turban, D. B., Jones, A. P., & Rozelle, R. M. (1990). Influences of supervisor liking of a subordinate and the reward context on the treatment and evaluation of that subordinate. *Motivation and Emotion, 14,* 215–233.

Turner, J. (1993). Males supervising females: The risk of gender-power blindness. *Supervisor Bulletin, 6,* 4, 6.

Turner, J., & Fine, M. (1997). Gener and supervision: Evolving debates. In T. C. Todd and C. L. Storm (Eds.), *The complete systemic supervisor: Context, philosophy, and pragmatics.* Boston: Allyn and Bacon, 72–82.

Twohey, D., & Volker, J. (1993). Listening for the voices of care and justice in counselor supervision. *Counselor Education and Supervision, 32,* 189–197.

Upchurch, D. W. (1985). Ethical standards and the supervisory process. *Counselor Education and Supervision, 25,* 90–98.

Usher, C. H., & Borders, L. D. (1993). Practicing counselors' preferences for supervisory style and supervisory emphasis. *Counselor Education and Supervision, 33,* 66–79.

VanderKolk, C. (1974). The relationship of personality, values, and race to anticipation of the supervisory relationship. *Rehabilitation Counseling Bulletin, 18,* 41–46.

Vargas, L. A. (August, 1989). *Training psychologists to be culturally responsive: Issues in supervision.* Paper presented at the Annual Convention of the American Psychological Association, New Orleans, LA.

Vasquez, M. J. T. (1988). Counselor–client sexual contact: Implications for ethics training. *Journal of Counseling and Development, 67,* 238–241.

Vasquez, M. J. T. (1992). Psychologist as clinical supervisor: Promoting ethical practice. *Professional Psychology: Research and Practice, 23,* 196–202.

Vogel, D. (1994). Narrative perspectives in theory and therapy. *Journal of Constructivist Psychology,* 243–261.

Vygotsky, L. S. (1978). *Mind in society: The development of higher psychological processes.* (M. Cole, V. John-Steiner, S. Scribner, & Souberman, Eds. and Trans.) Cambridge, MA: Harvard University Press.

Wallach, M. A., Kogan, N., & Bem, D. J. (1962). Group influence on individual risk taking. *Journal of Abnormal and Social Psychology, 65,* 75–86.

Wampold, B. E. (1986). State of the art in sequential analysis: Comment on Lichtenberg and Heck. *Journal of Counseling Psychology, 33,* 182–185.

Wampold, B. E., & Holloway, E. L. (in press). Methodology, design, and evaluation in psychotherapy supervision research. In C. E. Watkins (Ed.), *Handbook of psychotherapy supervision.* New York: Wiley.

Wampold, B. E., Mondin, G. W., Moody, M., Stich, F., Benson, K., & Ahn, H. (in press). A meta-analysis of outcome studies comparing bonafide psychotherapies: Empiricaly, "all must have prizes," *Psychological Bulletin.*

Warburton, J. R., Newberry, A., & Alexander, J. (1989). Women as therapists, trainees, and supervisors. In M. McGoldrick, C. Anderson, & F. Walsh (Eds.), *Women in families: A framework for family therapy.* New York: W. W. Norton, 152–165.

Ward, G. R., Kagan, H., & Krathwohl, D. R. (1972). An attempt to measure and facilitate counselor effectiveness. *Counselor Education and Supervision, 11,* 179–186.

Ward, L. G., Friendlander, M. L., Schoen, L. G., & Klein, J. G. (1985). Strategic self-presentation in supervision. *Journal of Counseling Psychology, 32,* 111–118.

Wark, L. (1995). Defining the territory of live supervision in family therapy training: A qualitative study and theoretical discussion. *Clinical Supervisor, 13*(1), 145–162.

Watkins, C. E., Jr. (1990a). Development of the psychotherapy supervisor. *Psychotherapy, 27,* 553–560.

Watkins, C. E., Jr. (1990b). The separation–individuation process in psychotherapy supervision. *Psychotherapy, 27,* 202–209.

Watkins, C. E., Jr. (1993). Development of the psychotherapy supervisor: Concepts, assumptions, and hypotheses of the supervisor complexity model. *American Journal of Psychotherapy, 47,* 58–74.

Watkins, C. E. (1994). The supervision of psychotherapy supervisor trainees. *American Journal of Psychotherapy, 48,* 417–431.

Watkins, C. E. (1995a). Pathological attachment styles in psychotherapy supervision. *Psychotherapy, 32,* 333–340.

Watkins, C. E., Jr. (1995b). Considering psychotherapy supervisor development: A status report. *Psychotherapy Bulletin, 29*(4), 32–34.

Watkins, C. E., Jr. (1995c). Psychotherapy supervisor and supervisee: Developmental models and research nine years later. *Clinical Psychology Review, 15,* 647–680.

Watkins, C. E. (1995d). Psychotherapy supervisor development: On musings, models, and metaphor. *Journal of Psychotherapy Practice & Research, 4,* 150–158.

Watkins, C. E., Jr. (1995e). Researching psychotherapy supervisor development: Four key considerations. *Clinical Supervisor, 13*(2), 111–118.

Watkins, C. E., Jr. (Ed.) (1997). *Handbook of psychotherapy supervision.* New York: Wiley.

Watkins, C. E., Lopez, F. G., Campbell, V. L., & Himmell, C. D. (1986). Contemporary counseling psychology: Results of a national survey. *Journal of Counseling Psychology, 33,* 301–309.

Watkins, C. E., Schneider, L. J., Haynes, J., & Nieberding, R. (1995). Measuring psychotherapy supervisor development: An initial effort at scale development and validation. *Clinical Supervisor, 13*(1), 77–90.

Watson, M. F. (1993). Supervising the person of the therapist: Issues, challenges and dilemmas. Special Issue: Critical issues in marital and family therapy education. *Contemporary Family Therapy: An International Journal, 15,* 21–31.

Watzlawick, P., & Beavin, J. (1976). Some formal aspects of communication. In P. Watzlawick & J. H. Weakland (Eds.), *The interactional view.* New York: Norton, 56–67

Watzlawick, P., Beavin, J. H., & Jackson, D. D. (1967). *Pragmatics of human communication: A study of interactional patterns, pathologies, and paradoxes.* New York: W. W. Norton.

Webb, N. B. (1983). Developing competent clinical practitioners: A model with guidelines for supervisors. *Clinical Supervisor, 1* (4), 41–51.

Webster's New World Dictionary of the American Language (1966). New York: World Publishing.

Weisinger, H., & Lobsenz, N. M. (1981). *Nobody's perfect: How to give criticism and get results.* Los Angeles: Stratford.

Weiss, D. S., & Marmar, C. R. (1993). Teaching time-limited dynamic psychotherapy for post-traumatic stress disorder and pathological grief. *Psychotherapy, 30,* 587–591.

Wendorf, D. J. (1984). A model for training practicing professionals in family therapy. *Journal of Marital and Family Therapy, 10,* 31–41.

Wendorf, D. J., Wendorf, R. J., & Bond, O. (1985). Growth behind the mirror: The family therapy consortiums' group process. *Journal of Marriage & Family Therapy, 11,* 245–255.

Wessler, R. L., & Ellis, A. (1983). Supervision in counseling: Rational–emotive therapy. *Counseling Psychologist, 11*(1), 43–49.

West, J. D., Bubenzer, D. L., & Delmonico, D. L. (1994). Preparation of doctoral-level supervisors. In J. E. Myers (Ed.), *Developing and directing counselor education laboratories.* Alexandria, VA: ACA Press.

West, J. D., Bubenzer, D. L., Pinsoneault, T., & Holeman, V. (1993). Three supervision modalities for training marital and family counselors. Special Section: Marriage and family counselor training. *Counselor Education and Supervision, 33,* 127–138.

West, J. D., Bubenzer, D. L., & Zarski, J. J. (1989). Live supervision in family therapy: An interview with Barbara Oken and Fred Piercy. *Counselor Education and Supervision, 29,* 25–34.

Wetchler, J. L. (1989). Supervisors' and supervisees' perceptions of the effectiveness of family therapy supervisor interpersonal skills. *American Journal of Family Therapy, 17,* 244–256.

Wetchler, J. L. (1990). Solution-focused supervision. *Family Therapy, 17,* 129–138.

Wetchler, J. L., & Vaughn, K. A. (1992). Perceptions of primary family therapy supervisory techniques: A critical incident analysis. *Contemporary Family Therapy: An International Journal, 14,* 127–136.

Wetchler, J. L., Piercy, F. P., & Sprenkle, D. H. (1989). Supervisors' and supervisees' perceptions of the effectiveness of family therapy supervisory techniques. *American Journal of Family Therapy, 17,* 35–47.

Whiffen, R. (1982). The use of videotape in supervision. In R. Whiffen and J. Byng-Hall (Eds.). *Family therapy supervision: Recent developments in practice.* London: Academic Press.

Whiston, S. C., & Emerson, S. (1989). Ethical implications for supervisors in counseling of trainees. *Counselor Education and Supervision, 28,* 318–325.

White, L. J., Rosenthal, D. M., & Fleuridas, C. L. (1993). Accountable supervision through systematic data collection: Using single-case designs. *Counselor Education and Supervision, 33,* 32–46.

White, R. W. (1959). Motivation reconsidered: The concept of competence. *Psychological Review, 66,* 297–323.

Wierzbicki, M. (1993). *Issues in clinical psychology: Subjective versus objective approaches.* Boston: Allyn & Bacon.

Wilbur, M. P., & Roberts-Wilbur, J. (1983). *Schemata of the steps of the SGS model.* Unpublished table.

Wilbur, M. P., Roberts-Wilbur, J., M., Hart, G., Morris, J. R., & Betz, R. L. (1994). Structured group supervision (SGS): A pilot study. *Counselor Education and Supervision, 33,* 262–279.

Wilbur, M. P., Roberts-Wilbur, J. M., Morris, J., Betz, R., & Hart, G. M. (1991). Structured group supervision: Theory into practice. *Journal for Specialists in Group Work, 16,* 91–100.

Wilcoxon, S. A. (1992). Videotape review of supervision-of-supervision in concurrent training: Allowing trainees to peer through the door. *Family Therapy, 19,* 143–153.

Wiley, M., & Ray, P. (1986) Counseling supervision by developmental level. *Journal of Counseling Psychology, 33,* 439–445.

Wiley, M. O. (August, 1982). *Developmental counseling supervision: Person–environment congruency, satisfaction, and learning.* Paper presented at the annual meeting of the American Psychological Association. Washington, DC.

Wiley, M. O. (August, 1994). *Supervising oneself in independent practice: From student to solo practitioner.* Paper presented at the American Psychological Association, Los Angeles.

Willbach, D. (1989). Ethics and family therapy: The case management of family violence. *Journal of Marital and Family Therapy, 15,* 43–52.

Williams, A. (1995). *Visual and active supervision: Roles, focus, technique.* New York: W. W. Norton.

Williams, L. (1994). A tool for training supervisors: Using the Supervision Feedback Form (SFF). *Journal of Marital & Family Therapy, 20,* 311–315.

Williams, S., & Halgin, R. P. (1995). Issues in psychotherapy supervision between the white supervisor and the black supervisee. *Clinical Supervisor, 13*(1), 39–61.

Wilson, G. T. (1996). Manual-based treatments: The clinical application of research findings. *Behavior Research and Therapy, 34,* 295–314.

Wilson, S. (1981). *Field instruction techniques for supervisors.* New York: Free Press.

Winter, M., & Holloway, E. L. (1991). Relation of trainee experience, conceptual level, and supervisor approach to selection of audiotaped counseling passages. *Clinical Supervisor, 9*(2), 87–103.

Wise, P. S., Lowery, S., & Silverglade, L. (1989). Personal counseling for counselors in training: Guidelines for supervisors. *Counselor Education and Supervision, 28,* 326–336.

Wolpe, J. (1972a). Supervision transcripts: I - Fear of success. *Journal of Behavior Therapy and Experimental Psychiatry, 3,* 107–110.

Wolpe, J. (1972b). Supervision transcripts: II - Problems of a novice. *Journal of Behavior Therapy and Experimental Psychiatry, 3,* 199–203.

Wolpe, J. (1972c). Supervision transcripts: III - Some problems in a claustrophobic case. *Journal of Behavior Therapy and Experimental Psychiatry, 3,* 301–305.

Wolpe, J. (1973a). Supervision transcripts: IV - Planning therapeutic tactics. *Journal of Behavior Therapy and Experimental Psychiatry, 4,* 41–46.

Wolpe, J. (1973b). Supervision transcripts: V - Mainly about assertive training. *Journal of Behavior Therapy and Experimental Psychiatry, 4,* 141–146.

Wolpe, J. (1973c). Supervision transcripts: VI - Hypochondriacal neurosis. *Journal of Behavior Therapy and Experimental Psychiatry, 4,* 249–255.

Wolpe, J. (1973d). Supervision transcripts: VII - Neglecting the case history and other elementary errors. *Journal of Behavior Therapy and Experimental Psychiatry, 4,* 365–370.

Wolpe, J., Knopp, W., & Garfield, Z. (1966). *Post-graduate training in behavior therapy.* Exerta Medica International Congress Series, No. 150. Proceedings of the Fourth World Congress of Psychiatry, Madrid, Spain.

Wong, Y-L. S. (1997). Live supervision in family therapy: Trainee perspectives. *The Clinical Supervisor, 15*(1), 145–157.

Wood, B., Klein, S., Cross, H., Lammers, C., & Elliot, J. (1985). Impaired practitioners: Psychologists' opinions about prevalence, and proposals for intervention. *Professional Psychology: Research and Practice, 16,* 843–850.

Woods, P. J., & Ellis, A. (1996). Supervision in rational emotive behavior therapy. *Journal of Rational–Emotive & Cognitive Behavior Therapy, 14,* 135–152.

Woodside, D. B. (1994). Reverse live supervision: Leveling the supervisory playing field. *Supervision Bulletin, 7*(2), 6.

Woody, R. H. and Associates (1984). *The law and the practice of human services.* San Francisco: Jossey–Bass.

Woolley, G. (1991). Beware the well-intentioned therapist. *Family Therapy Networker,* Jan/Feb, *15,* 30.

Worthen, V., & McNeill, B. W. (1996). A phenomenological investigation of "good" supervision events. *Journal of Counseling Psychology, 43,* 25–34.

Worthington, E. L. (1984). Empirical investigation of supervision of counselors as they gain experience. *Journal of Counseling Psychology, 31,* 63–75.

Worthington, E. L., Jr. (1984). Use of trait labels in counseling supervision by experienced and inexperienced supervisors. *Professional Psychology: Research and Practice, 15,* 457–461.

Worthington, E. L., Jr. (1987). Changes in supervision as counselors and supervisors gain experience: A review. *Professional Psychology: Research and Practice, 18,* 189–208.

Worthington, E. L., Jr., & Roehlke, H. J. (1979). Effective supervision as perceived by beginning counselors-in-training. *Journal of Counseling Psychology, 26,* 64–73.

Worthington, E. L., Jr., & Stern, A. (1985). Effects of supervisor and supervisee degree level and gender on the supervisory relationship. *Journal of Counseling Psychology, 32,* 252–262.

Wright, L. M. (1986). An analysis of live supervision "phone-ins" in family therapy. *Journal of Marital and Family Therapy, 12,* 187–191.

Wynne, M. E., Susman, M., Ries, S., Birringer, J., & Katz, L. (1994). A method for assessing therapists' recall of in-session events. *Journal of Counseling Psychology, 41,* 53–57.

Yager, G. G., Wilson, F. R., Brewer, D., & Kinnetz, P. (1989). *The development and validation of an instrument to measure counseling supervisor focus and style.* Paper presented at the American Educational Research Association, San Francisco.

Yalom, I. D. (1985). *The theory and practice of group psychotherapy* (3rd ed.). New York: Basic Books.

Yenawine, G. G., & Arbuckle, D. (1971). Study of the use of video-tape and audio-tape as techniques in counselor education. *Journal of Counseling Psychology, 28,* 1–6.

Yerkes, R. M., & Dodson, J. D. (1908). The relation of strength of stimulus to rapidity of habit formation. *Journal of Comparative Neurology and Psychology, 18,* 459–482.

Yerushalmi, H. (1992). Psychoanalytic supervision and the need to be alone. *Psychotherapy, 29,* 262–268.

Yogev, S. (1982). An eclectic model of supervision: A developmental sequence for beginning psychotherapy students. *Professional Psychology, 13,* 236–243.

York, R. O. (1985). Applying the exception principle to the field instruction program. *Clinical Supervisor, 3,* 77–86.

Young, J., Perlesz, A., Paterson, R., O'Hanlon, B., Newbold, A., Chaplin, R., & Bridge, S. (1989). The reflecting team process in training. *Australia and New Zealand Journal of Family Therapy, 10,* 69–74.

Zajonc, R. B. (1980). Compresence. In P. B. Paulus (Ed.), *Psychology of group influence.* Hillsdale, NJ: Erlbaum, 35–60.

Zarski, J. J., Sand-Pringle, C., Pannell, L., & Lindon, C. (1995). Critical issues in supervision: Marital and family violence. *The Family Journal: Counseling and Therapy for Couples and Families, 3*(1), 18–26.

Zucker, P. J., & Worthington, E. L., Jr. (1986). Supervision of interns and postdoctoral applicants for licensure in university counseling centers. *Journal of Counseling Psychology, 33,* 87–89.

Zuniga, M. E. (1987). Mexican-American clinical training: A pilot project. *Journal of Social Work Education, 23,* 11–20.

Standards for Preparation and Practice
of Counseling Supervisors

STANDARDS FOR
COUNSELING SUPERVISORS*

**Supervision Interest Network, Association
for Counselor Education and Supervision**

The Standards for Counseling Supervisors consist of 11 core areas of knowledge, competencies, and personal traits that characterize effective supervisors.

Standards for Counseling Supervisors
(As Adopted by the AACD Governing Council,
July 13–16, 1989)

The Standards include a description of eleven core areas of personal traits, knowledge and competencies that are characteristic of effective supervisors. The level of preparation and experience of the counselor, the particular work setting of the supervisor and counselor and client variables will influence the relative emphasis of each competency in practice.

The core areas and their related competencies have been consistently identified in supervision research and, in addition, have been judged to have face validity as determined by supervisor practitioners, based on both select and widespread peer review.

1. Professional counseling supervisors are effective counselors whose knowledge and

competencies have been acquired through training, education, and supervised employment experience.

The counseling supervisor:
1.1 demonstrates knowledge of various counseling theories, systems, and their related methods;
1.2 demonstrates knowledge of his/her personal philosophical, theoretical and methodological approach to counseling;
1.3 demonstrates knowledge of his/her assumptions about human behavior; and
1.4 demonstrates skill in the application of counseling theory and methods (individual, group, or marital and family and specialized areas such as substance abuse, career-life rehabilitation) that are appropriate for the supervisory setting.

2. Professional counseling supervisors demonstrate personal traits and characteristics that are consistent with the role.

The counseling supervisor:
2.1 is committed to updating his/her own counseling and supervisory skills;
2.2 is sensitive to individual differences;
2.3 recognizes his/her own limits through self-evaluation and feedback from others;
2.4 is encouraging, optimistic and motivational;
2.5 possesses a sense of humor;
2.6 is comfortable with the authority inherent in the role of supervisor;
2.7 demonstrates a commitment to the role of supervisor;

*From Supervision Interest Network, Association for Counselor Education and Supervision (1990). Standards for counselor supervisors, *Journal of Counseling and Development, 69* 30–32. Copyright © (1990) by the American Counseling Association. Reprinted by permission.

2.8 can identify his/her own strengths and weaknesses as a supervisor; and

2.9 can describe his/her own pattern in interpersonal relationships.

3. Professional counseling supervisors are knowledgeable regarding ethical, legal and regulatory aspects of the profession, and are skilled in applying this knowledge.

The counseling supervisor:

3.1 communicates to the counselor a knowledge of professional codes of ethics (e.g., AACD, APA;

3.2 demonstrates and enforces ethical and professional standards;

3.3 communicates to the counselor an understanding of legal and regulatory documents and their impact on the profession (e.g., certification, licensure, duty to warn, parents' rights to children's records, third party payments, etc.);

3.4 provides current information regarding professional standards (NCC, CCMHC, CRC, CCC, licensure, certification, etc.);

3.5 can communicate a knowledge of counselor rights and appeal procedures specific to the work setting; and

3.6 communicates to the counselor a knowledge of ethical considerations that pertain to the supervisory process, including dual relationships, due process, evaluation, informed consent, confidentiality, and vicarious liability.

4. Professional counseling supervisors demonstrate conceptual knowledge of the personal and professional nature of the supervisory relationship and are skilled in applying this knowledge.

The counseling supervisor:

4.1 demonstrates knowledge of individual differences with respect to gender, race, ethnicity, culture and age and understands the importance of these characteristics in supervisory relationships;

4.2 is sensitive to the counselor's personal and professional needs;

4.3 expects counselors to own the consequences of their actions;

4.4 is sensitive to the evaluative nature of supervision and effectively responds to the counselor's anxiety relative to performance evaluation;

4.5 conducts self-evaluations, as appropriate, as a means of modeling professional growth;

4.6 provides facilitative conditions (empathy, concreteness, respect, congruence, genuineness, and immediacy);

4.7 establishes a mutually trusting relationship with the counselor;

4.8 provides an appropriate balance of challenge and support; and

4.9 elicits counselor thoughts and feelings during counseling or consultation sessions, and responds in a manner that enhances the supervision process.

5. Professional counseling supervisors demonstrate conceptual knowledge of supervision methods and techniques, and are skilled in using this knowledge to promote counselor development.

The counseling supervisor:

5.1 states the purposes of supervision and explains the procedures to be used;

5.2 negotiates mutual decisions regarding the needed direction of learning experiences for the counselor;

5.3 engages in appropriate supervisory interventions, including role-play, role-reversal, live supervision, modeling, interpersonal process recall, micro-training, suggestions and advice, reviewing audio and video tapes, etc.;

5.4 can perform the supervisor's functions in the role of teacher, counselor, or consultant as appropriate;

5.5 elicits new alternatives from counselors for identifying solutions, techniques, responses to clients;

5.6 integrates knowledge of supervision with his/her style of interpersonal relations;
5.7 clarifies his/her role in supervision;
5.8 uses media aids (print material, electronic recording) to enhance learning; and
5.9 interacts with the counselor in a manner that facilitates the counselor's self-exploration and problem solving.

6. Professional counseling supervisors demonstrate conceptual knowledge of the counselor developmental process and are skilled in applying this knowledge.

The counseling supervisor:
6.1 understands the developmental nature of supervision;
6.2 demonstrates knowledge of various theoretical models of supervision;
6.3 understands the counselor's roles and functions in particular work settings;
6.4 understands the supervisor's roles and functions in particular work settings;
6.5 can identify the learning needs of the counselor;
6.6 adjusts conference content based on the counselor's personal traits, conceptual development, training, and experience; and
6.7 uses supervisory methods appropriate to the counselor's level of conceptual development, training and experience.

7. Professional counseling supervisors demonstrate knowledge and competency in case conceptualization and management.

The counseling supervisor:
7.1 recognizes that a primary goal of supervision is helping the client of the counselor;
7.2 understands the roles of other professionals (e.g., psychologists, physicians, social workers) and assists with the referral process, when appropriate;
7.3 elicits counselor perceptions of counseling dynamics;
7.4 assists the counselor in selecting and executing data collection procedures;

7.5 assists the counselor in analyzing and interpreting data objectively;
7.6 assists the counselor in planning effective client goals and objectives;
7.7 assists the counselor in using observation and assessment in preparation of client goals and objectives;
7.8 assists the counselor in synthesizing client psychological and behavioral characteristics into an integrated conceptualization;
7.9 assists the counselor in assigning priorities to counseling goals and objectives;
7.10 assists the counselor in providing rationale for counseling procedures; and
7.11 assists the counselor in adjusting steps in the progression toward a goal based on ongoing assessment and evaluation.

8. Professional counseling supervisors demonstrate knowledge and competency in client assessment and evaluation.

The counseling supervisor:
8.1 monitors the use of tests and test interpretations;
8.2 assists the counselor in providing rationale for assessment procedures;
8.3 assists the counselor in communicating assessment procedures and rationales;
8.4 assists the counselor in the description, measurement, and documentation of client and counselor change; and
8.5 assists the counselor in integrating findings and observations to make appropriate recommendations.

9. Professional counseling supervisors demonstrate knowledge and competency in oral and written reporting and recording.

The counseling supervisor:
9.1 understands the meaning of accountability and the supervisor's responsibility in promoting it;
9.2 assists the counselor in effectively documenting supervisory and counseling-related interactions;

9.3 assists the counselor in establishing and following policies and procedures to protect the confidentiality of client and supervisory records;

9.4 assists the counselor in identifying appropriate information to be included in a verbal or written report;

9.5 assists the counselor in presenting information in a logical, concise, and sequential manner; and

9.6 assists the counselor in adapting verbal and written reports to the work environment and communication situation.

10. Professional counseling supervisors demonstrate knowledge and competency in the evaluation of counseling performance.

The counseling supervisor:

10.1 can interact with the counselor from the perspective of evaluator;

10.2 can identify the counselor's professional and personal strengths, as well as weaknesses;

10.3 provides specific feedback about such performance as conceptualization, use of methods and techniques, relationship skills, and assessment;

10.4 determines the extent to which the counselor has developed and applied his/her own personal theory of counseling;

10.5 develops evaluation procedures and instruments to determine program and counselor goal attainment;

10.6 assists the counselor in the description and measurement of his/her progress and achievement; and

10.7 can evaluate counseling skills for purposes of grade assignment, completion of internship requirements, professional advancement, and so on.

11. Professional counseling supervisors are knowledgeable regarding research in counseling and counselor supervision and consistently incorporate this knowledge into the supervision process.

The counseling supervisor:

11.1 facilitates and monitors research to determine the effectiveness of programs, services and techniques;

11.2 reads, interprets, and applies counseling and supervisory research;

11.3 can formulate counseling or supervisory research questions;

11.4 reports results of counseling or supervisory research and disseminates as appropriate (e.g., inservice, conferences, publications); and

11.5 facilitates an integration of research findings in individual case management.

The Education and Training of Supervisors

Counseling supervision is a distinct field of preparation and practice. Knowledge and competencies necessary for effective performance are acquired through a sequence of training and experience which ordinarily includes the following:

1. Graduate training in counseling;
2. Successful supervised employment as a professional counselor;
3. Credentialing in one or more of the following areas: certification by a state department of education, licensure by a state as a professional counselor, and certification as a National Certified Counselor, Certifies Clinical Mental Health Counselor, Certified Rehabilitation Counselor, or Certified Career Counselor;
4. Graduate training in counseling supervision including didactic courses, seminars, laboratory courses, and supervision practica;
5. Continuing educational experiences specific to supervision theory and practice (e.g., conferences, workshops, self-study); and
6. Research activities related to supervision theory and practice.

The supervisor's primary functions are to teach the inexperienced and to foster their professional development, to serve as consultants to experienced counselors, and to assist at all levels in the provision of effective counseling services. These responsibilities require personal and professional maturity accompanied by a broad perspective on counseling that is gained by extensive, supervised counseling experience. Therefore, training for supervision generally occurs during advanced graduate study or continuing professional development. This is not to say, however, that supervisor training in the pre-service stage is without merit. The presentation of basic methods and procedures may enhance students' performance as counselors, enrich their participation in the supervision process, and provide a framework for later study.

Ethical Guidelines for Clinical Supervisors

The following are two codes of ethics specific to clinical supervision, that of the Association for Counselor Education and that of the British Association for Counselling.

ASSOCIATION FOR COUNSELING EDUCATION AND SUPERVISION
(Adopted: March, 1993)*

Preamble

The Association for Counselor Education and Supervision (ACES) is composed of people engaged in the professional preparation of counselors and people responsible for the ongoing supervision of counselors. ACES is a founding division of the American Counseling Association (ACA) and as such adheres to ACA's current ethical standards (AACD, 1988) and to general codes of competence adopted throughout the mental health community.

ACES believes that counselor educators and counseling supervisors in universities and in applied counseling settings, including the range of education and mental health delivery systems, carry responsibilities unique to their job roles. Such responsibilities may include administrative supervision, clinical supervision, or both. Administrative supervision refers to those supervisory activities which increase the efficiency of the delivery of counseling services; whereas, clinical supervision includes the supportive and educative activities of the supervisor designed to improve the application of counseling theory and technique directly to clients.

Counselor educators and counseling supervisors encounter situations which challenge the help given by general ethical standards of the profes-

*Supervision Interest Network, Association for Counselor Education and Supervision (1993, Summer). ACES ethical guidelines for counseling supervisors. *ACES Spectrum, 53*(4), 5–8. Copyright © (1993) by the Association for Counselor Education and Supervision. Reprinted by permission.

sion at large. These situations require more specific guidelines that provide appropriate guidance in everyday practice.

The Ethical Guidelines for Counseling Supervisors are intended to assist professionals by helping them:

1. observe ethical and legal protection of clients' and supervisees' rights;
2. meet the training and professional development needs of supervisees in ways consistent with clients' welfare and programmatic requirements; and
3. establish policies, procedures, and standards for implementing programs.

The specification of ethical guidelines enables ACES members to focus on and to clarify the ethical nature of responsibilities held in common. Such guidelines should be reviewed formally every five years, or more often if needed, to meet the needs of ACES members for guidance.

The Ethical Guidelines for Counselor Educators and Counseling Supervisors are meant to help ACES members in conducting supervision. ACES is not currently in a position to hear complaints about alleged noncompliance with these guidelines. Any complaints about the ethical behavior of any ACA member should be measured against the ACA Ethical Standards and a complaint lodged with ACA in accordance with their procedures for doing so.

One overriding assumption underlying this document is that supervision should be ongoing throughout a counselor's career and not stop when a particular level of education, certification, or membership in a professional organization is attained.

Definitions of Terms:

Applied Counseling Settings—Public or private organization of counselors such as community mental health centers, hospitals, schools, and group or individual private practice settings.

Supervisees—Counselors-in-training in university programs at any level who work with clients in applied settings as part of their university training program, and counselors who have completed their formal education and are employed in an applied counseling setting.

Supervisors—Counselors who have been designated within their university or agency to directly oversee the professional clinical work of counselors. Supervisors also may be persons who offer supervision to counselors seeking state licensure and so provide supervision outside of the administrative aegis of an applied counseling setting.

1. Client Welfare and Rights

1.01   The primary obligation of supervisors is to train counselors so that they respect the integrity and promote the welfare of their clients. Supervisors should have supervisees inform clients that they are being supervised and that observation and/or recordings of the session may be reviewed by the supervisor.

1.02   Supervisors who are licensed counselors and are conducting supervision to aid a supervisee to become licensed should instruct the supervisee not to communicate or in any way convey to the supervisee's clients or to other parties that the supervisee is himself/herself licensed.

1.03   Supervisors should make supervisees aware of clients' rights, including protecting clients' right to privacy and confidentiality in the counseling relationship and the information resulting from it. Clients also should be informed that their right to privacy and confidentiality will not be violated by the supervisory relationship.

1.04   Records of the counseling relationship, including interview notes, test data, correspondence, the electronic storage of these documents, and audio and videotape recordings, are considered to be confidential professional information. Supervisors should see that these materials are used in counseling, research, and training and supervision of counselors with the full knowledge of the client and that permission to use these materials is granted by the applied counseling setting offering service to the client. This professional information is to be used for the full protection of the client. Written consent from the client (or legal guardian, if a minor) should be secured prior to the use of such information for instructional, supervisory, and/or research purposes. Policies of the applied counseling setting regarding client records also should be followed.

1.05   Supervisors shall adhere to current professional and legal guidelines when conducting research with human participants such as section D-1 of the ACA Ethical Standards.

1.06   Counseling supervisors are responsible for making every effort to monitor both the professional actions, and failures to take action, of their supervisees.

2. Supervisory Role

Inherent and integral to the role of supervisor are responsibilities for:

a. monitoring client welfare;
b. encouraging compliance with relevant legal, ethical, and professional standards for clinical practice;
c. monitoring clinical performance and professional development of supervisees; and
d. evaluating and certifying current performance and potential of supervisees for academic, screening, selection, placement, employment, and credentialing purposes.

2.01   Supervisors should have had training in supervision prior to initiating their role as supervisors.

2.02   Supervisors should pursue professional and personal continuing education activities such as advanced courses, seminars, and professional conferences on a regular and ongoing basis. These activities should include both counseling and supervision topics and skills.

2.03 Supervisors should make their supervisees aware of professional and ethical standards and legal responsibilities of the counseling profession.

2.04 Supervisors of postdegree counselors who are seeking state licensure should encourage these counselors to adhere to the standards for practice established by the state licensure board of the state in which they practice.

2.05 Procedures for contacting the supervisor, or an alternative supervisor, to assist in handling crisis situations should be established and communicated to supervisees.

2.06 Actual work samples via audio and/or video tape or live observation in addition to case notes should be reviewed by the supervisor as a regular part of the ongoing supervisory process.

2.07 Supervisors of counselors should meet regularly in face-to-face sessions with their supervisees.

2.08 Supervisors should provide supervisees with ongoing feedback on their performance. This feedback should take a variety of forms, both formal and informal, and should include verbal and written evaluations. It should be formative during the supervisory experience and summative at the conclusion of the experience.

2.09 Supervisors who have multiple roles (e.g., teacher, clinical supervisor, administrative supervisor, etc.) with supervisees should minimize potential conflicts. Where possible, the roles should be divided among several supervisors. Where this is not possible, careful explanation should be conveyed to the supervises as to the expectations and responsibilities associated with each supervisory role.

2.10 Supervisors should not participate in any form of sexual contact with supervisees. Supervisors should not engage in any form of social contact or interaction which would compromise the supervisor–supervisee relationship. Dual relationships with supervisees that might impair the supervisor's objectivity and professional judg-

ment should be avoided and/or the supervisory relationship terminated.

2.11 Supervisors should not establish a psychotherapeutic relationship as a substitute for supervision. Personal issues should be addressed in supervision only in terms of the impact of these issues on clients and on professional functioning.

2.12 Supervisors, through ongoing supervisee assessment and evaluation, should be aware of any personal or professional limitations of supervisees which are likely to impede future professional performance. Supervisors have the responsibility of recommending remedial assistance to the supervisee and of screening from the training program, applied counseling setting, or state licensure those supervisees who are unable to provide competent professional services. These recommendations should be clearly and professionally explained in writing to the supervisees who are so evaluated.

2.13 Supervisors should not endorse a supervisee for certification, licensure, completion of an academic training program, or continued employment if the supervisor believes the supervisee is impaired in any way that would interfere with the performance of counseling duties. The presence of any such impairment should begin a process of feedback and remediation wherever possible so that the supervises understands the nature of the impairment and has the opportunity to remedy the problem and continue with his/her professional development.

2.14 Supervisors should incorporate the principles of informed consent and participation; clarity of requirements, expectations, roles and rules; and due process and appeal into the establishment of policies and procedures of their institution, program, courses, and individual supervisory relationships. Mechanisms for due process appeal of individual supervisory actions should be established and made available to all supervisees.

3. Program Administration Role

3.01 Supervisors should ensure that the programs conducted and experiences provided are in keeping with current guidelines and standards of ACA and its divisions.

3.02 Supervisors should teach courses and/or supervise clinical work only in areas where they are fully competent and experienced.

3.03 To achieve the highest quality of training and supervision, supervisors should be active participants in peer review and peer supervision procedures.

3.04 Supervisors should provide experiences that integrate theoretical knowledge and practical application. Supervisors also should provide opportunities in which supervisees are able to apply the knowledge they have learned and understand the rationale for the skills they have acquired. The knowledge and skills conveyed should reflect current practice, research findings, and available resources.

3.05 Professional competencies, specific courses, and/or required experiences expected of supervisees should be communicated to them in writing prior to admission to the training program or placement/employment by the applied counseling setting, and, in the case of continued employment, in a timely manner.

3.06 Supervisors should accept only those persons as supervisees who meet identified entry level requirements for admission to a program of counselor training or for placement in an applied counseling setting. In the case of private supervision in search of state licensure, supervisees should have completed all necessary prerequisites as determined by the state licensure board.

3.07 Supervisors should inform supervisees of the goals, policies, theoretical orientations toward counseling, training, and supervision model or approach on which the supervision is based.

3.08 Supervisees should be encouraged and assisted to define their own theoretical orientation toward counseling, to establish supervision goals for themselves and to monitor and evaluate their progress toward meeting these goals.

3.09 Supervisors should assess supervisees' skills and experience in order to establish standards for competent professional behavior. Super-

visors should restrict supervisees' activities to those that are commensurate with their current level of skills and experiences.

3.10 Supervisors should obtain practicum and fieldwork sites that meet minimum standards for preparing students to become effective counselors. No practicum or fieldwork setting should be approved unless it truly replicates a counseling work setting.

3.11 Practicum and fieldwork classes should be limited in size according to established professional standards to ensure that each student has ample opportunity for individual supervision and feedback. Supervisors in applied counseling settings should have a limited number of supervisees.

3.12 Supervisors in university settings should establish and communicate specific policies and procedures regarding field placement of students. The respective roles of the student counselor, the university supervisor, and the field supervisor should be clearly differentiated in areas such as evaluation, requirements, and confidentiality.

3.13 Supervisors in training programs should communicate regularly with supervisors in agencies used as practicum and/or fieldwork sites regarding current professional practices, expectations of students, and preferred models and modalities of supervision.

3.14 Supervisors at the university should establish clear lines of communication among themselves, the field supervisors, and the students/supervisees.

3.15 Supervisors should establish and communicate to supervisees and to field supervisors specific procedures regarding consultation, performance review, and evaluation of supervisees.

3.16 Evaluations of supervisee performance in universities and in applied counseling settings should be available to supervisees in ways consistent with the Family Rights and Privacy Act and the Buckley Amendment.

3.17 Forms of training that focus primarily on self-understanding and problem resolution (e.g., personal growth groups or individual counseling) should be voluntary. Those who conduct these forms of training should not serve simultaneously as supervisors of the supervisees involved in the training.

3.18 A supervisor may recommend participation in activities such as personal growth groups or personal counseling when it has been determined that a supervisee has deficits in the areas of self-understanding and problem resolution which impede his/her professional functioning. The supervisor should not be the direct provider of these activities for the supervisee.

3.19 When a training program conducts a personal growth or counseling experience involving relatively intimate self-disclosure, care should be taken to eliminate or minimize potential role conflicts for faculty and/or agency supervisors who may conduct these experiences and who also serve as teachers, group leaders, and clinical directors.

3.20 Supervisors should use the following prioritized sequence in resolving conflicts among the needs of the client, the needs of the supervisee, and the needs of the program or agency. Insofar as the client must be protected, it should be understood that client welfare is usually subsumed in federal and state laws such that these statutes should be the first point of reference. Where laws and ethical standards are not present or are unclear, the good judgment of the supervisor should be guided by the following list:

a. Relevant legal and ethical standards (e.g. duty to warn, state child abuse laws, etc.);
b. Client welfare;
c. Supervisee welfare;
d. Supervisor welfare; and
e. Program and/or agency service and administrative needs.

BRITISH ASSOCIATION FOR COUNSELLING CODE OF ETHICS AND PRACTICE FOR SUPERVISORS OF COUNSELLORS*

1. Status of the Code

1.1 In response to the experience of members of BAC, this Code is a revision of the 1988 Code of Ethics & Practice for the Supervision of Counsellors.

2. Introduction

2.1 The purpose of the Code is to establish and maintain standards for supervisors who are members of BAC and to inform and protect counsellors seeking supervision. Throughout this Code the terms Counsellor and Counselling are used in accordance with the definition of counselling in the Code of Ethics & Practice for Counselors.

2.2 All members of this Association are required to abide by existing Codes appropriate to them. They thereby accept a common frame of reference within which to manage their responsibilities to supervisees and their clients, colleagues, members of the Association and the wider community. Whilst this Code cannot resolve all ethical and practice related issues, it aims to provide a framework for addressing ethical issues and to encourage optimum levels of practice. Supervisors and supervisees (counsellors) will need to judge which parts of this Code apply to particular situations. They may have to decide between conflicting responsibilities.

2.3 Counselling Supervision is a formal and mutually agreed arrangement for counsellors to discuss their work regularly with someone who is normally an experienced and competent counsellor and familiar with the process of counselling supervision. The

*Copyright © (1996) by the British Association for Counselling, 1 Regent Place, Rugby, Warwickshire CV21 2PJ. The reader is advised to contact the BAC to confirm that this version of the Code is most current. Reprinted by permission.

task is to work together to ensure and develop the efficacy of the supervisees counselling practice.

Counselling Supervision is the term that will be used throughout this Code. It is also known as supervision, consultative support, clinical supervision or non-managerial supervision. It is an essential part of good practice for counselling. It is different from training, personal development and line management accountability.

2.4 This Association has a Complaints Procedure which can lead to the expulsion of members for breaches of its Codes of Ethics and Practice.

3. Nature of Counselling Supervision

3.1 Counselling supervision provides supervisees with the opportunity on a regular basis to discuss and monitor their work with clients. It should take account of the setting in which supervisees practise. Counselling supervision is intended to ensure that the needs of the clients are being addressed and to monitor the effectiveness of the therapeutic interventions.

3.2 Counselling supervision may contain some elements of training, personal development or line-management, but counselling supervision is not primarily intended for these purposes and appropriate management of these issues should be observed

3.3 Counselling supervision is a formal collaborative process intended to help supervisees maintain ethical and professional standards of practice and to enhance creativity.

3.4 It is essential that counsellor and supervisor are able to work together constructively as counselling supervision includes supportive and challenging elements.

3.5 There are several modes of counselling supervision (see 5), which vary in appropriateness according to the needs of supervisees. More than one mode of counselling supervision may be used concurrently. This Code applies to all counselling supervision arrangements.

3.6 The frequency of counselling supervision will vary according to the volume of counselling, the experience of supervisees and their work setting.

4. Anti-discriminatory Practice in Counselling Supervision

4.1 Anti-discriminatory practice underpins the basic values of counselling and counselling supervision as stated in this document and in the Code of Ethics & Practice for Counsellors. It also addresses the issue of the client's social context, B.2.7.3 of that Code (1993).

4.2 Supervisors have a responsibility to be aware of their own issues of prejudice and stereotyping, and particularly to consider ways in which this may be affecting the supervisory relationship. Discussion of this is part of the counselling supervision process.

4.3 Supervisors need to be alert to any prejudices and assumptions that counsellors reveal in their work with clients and to raise awareness of these so that the needs of clients may be met with more sensitivity. One purpose of counselling supervision is to enable supervisees to recognise and value difference. Supervisors have a responsibility to challenge the appropriateness of the work of a supervisee whose own belief system interferes with the acceptance of clients.

4.4 Attitudes, assumptions and prejudices can be identified by the language used, and by paying attention to the selectivity of material brought to counselling supervision.

5. Modes of Counselling Supervision

There are different modes of counselling supervision. The particular features of some of these modes are outlined below Some counsellors use combinations of these for their counselling supervision.

5.1 One to One, Supervisor–Supervisee

This involves a supervisor providing counselling supervision on an individual basis for an individual counsellor who is usually less experienced than the supervisor. This is the most widely used mode of counselling supervision.

5.2 Group Counselling Supervision with Identified Counselling Supervisor(s)

There are several ways of providing this form of counselling supervision. In one approach the supervisor acts as the leader, takes responsibility for organising the time equally between the supervisees, and concentrates on the work of each individual in turn. Using another approach the supervisees allocate counselling supervision time between themselves with the supervisor as a technical resource.

5.3 One to One Peer Counselling Supervision

This involves two participants providing counselling supervision for each other by alternating the roles of supervisor and supervisee. Typically, the time available for counselling supervision is divided equally between them. This mode on its own is not suitable for practitioners.

5.4 Peer Group Counselling Supervision

This takes place when three or more counsellors share the responsibility for providing each other's counselling supervision within the group. Typically, they will consider themselves to be of broadly equal status, training and/or experience. This mode on its own is unsuitable for inexperienced practitioners.

5.5 Particular issues of competence for each mode are detailed in the Code of Practice B.2.6.

6. The Structure of this Code

6.1 This Code has two sections. Section A, the Code of Ethics, outlines the fundamental values of counselling supervision and a number of general principles arising from these.

Section B, the Code of Practice, applies these principles to counselling supervision.

A   CODE OF ETHICS

A.1 Counselling supervision is a non-exploitative activity. Its basic values are integrity, responsibility, impartiality and respect. Supervisors must take the same degree of care to work ethically whether they are paid or work voluntarily and irrespective of the mode of counselling supervision used.

A.2 Confidentiality

The content of counselling supervision is highly confidential. Supervisors must clarify their limits of confidentiality.

A.3 Safety

All reasonable steps must be taken to ensure the safety of supervisees and their clients during their work together.

A.4 Effectiveness

All reasonable steps must be taken by supervisors to encourage optimum levels of practice by supervisees.

A.5 Contracts

The terms and conditions on which counselling supervision is offered must be made clear to supervisees at the outset. Subsequent revisions of these terms must be agreed in advance of any change.

A.6 Competence

Supervisors must take all reasonable steps to monitor and develop their own competence and to work within the limits of that competence. This includes having supervision of their supervision work.

B   CODE OF PRACTICE

B.1 Issues of Responsibility

B.1.1 Supervisors are responsible for ensuring that an individual contract is worked out with their supervisees which will allow them to present and explore their work as honestly as possible.

B.1.2 Within this contract supervisors are responsible for helping supervisees to reflect critically upon their work, while at the same time acknowledging that clinical responsibility remains with the counsellor.

B.1.3 Supervisors are responsible, together with their supervisees, for ensuring that the best use is made of counselling supervision time, in order to address the needs of clients.

B.1.4 Supervisors are responsible for setting and maintaining the boundaries between the counselling supervision relationship and other professional relationships, e.g. training and management

B.1.5 Supervisors and supervisees should take all reasonable steps to ensure that any personal or social contact between them does not adversely influence the effectiveness of the counselling supervision.

B.1.6 A supervisor must not have a counselling supervision and a personal counselling contract with the same supervisee over the same period of time.

B.1.7 Supervisors must not exploit their supervisees financially, sexually, emotionally or in any other way. It is unethical for supervisors to engage in sexual activity with their supervisee.

B.1.8 Supervisors have a responsibility to enquire about any other relationships which may exist between supervisees and their clients as these may impair the objectivity and professional judgement of supervisees.

B.1.9 Supervisors must recognise, and work in ways that respect, the value and dignity of supervisees and their clients with due regard to issues such as origin, status, race, gender, age, beliefs, sexual orientation and disability. This must include raising awareness of any discriminatory practices that may exist between supervisees and their clients, or between supervisor and supervisee.

B.1.10 Supervisors must ensure that together with their supervisees they consider their respective legal liabilities to each other, to the employing or training organisation, if any, and to clients.

B.1.11 Supervisors are responsible for taking action if they are aware that their supervisees' practice is not in accordance with BAC's Codes of Ethics & Practice for Counsellors.

B.1.12 Supervisors are responsible for helping their supervisees recognise when their functioning as counsellors is impaired due to personal or emotional difficulties, any condition that affects judgement, illness, the influence of alcohol or drugs, or for any other reason, and for ensuring that appropriate action is taken.

B.1.13 Supervisors must conduct themselves in their supervision-related activities in ways which do not undermine public confidence in either their role as a supervisor or in the work of other supervisors.

B.1.14 If a supervisor is aware of possible misconduct by another supervisor which cannot be resolved or remedied after discussion with the supervisor concerned, they should implement the Complaints Procedure, doing so within the boundaries of confidentiality required by the Complaints Procedure.

B.1.15 Supervisors are responsible for ensuring that their emotional needs are met outside the counselling supervision work and are not solely dependent on their relationship with supervisees.

3.1.16 Supervisors are responsible for consulting with their own supervisor before former clients are taken on as supervisees or former supervisees are taken on as clients.

B.2 Issues of Competence

B.2.1 Under all of the modes of counselling supervision listed above, supervisors should normally be practising and experienced counsellors.

B.2.2 Supervisors are responsible for seeking ways to further their own professional development.

B.2.3 Supervisors are responsible for making arrangements for their own supervision in order to support their counselling supervision work and to help them to evaluate their competence.

B.2.4 Supervisors are responsible for monitoring and working within the limits of their competence.

3.2.5 Supervisors are responsible for withdrawing from counselling supervision work either temporarily or permanently when their functioning is impaired due to personal or emotional difficulties, illness, the influence of alcohol or drugs, or for any other reason.

B.2.6 Some modes require extra consideration and these are detailed in this section.

	A	B	C	D	E	F	G	H
One to one supervisor supervisee	X							
Group counselling supervision with identified and more experienced supervisor	X	X		X	X			
One to one peer counselling supervision		X	X	X	X		X	X
Peer group counselling supervision		X	X	X	X		X	X	X

A. All points contained elsewhere within the Code of Practice should be considered.

B. Sufficient time must be allocated to each counsellor to ensure adequate supervision of their counselling work.

C. This method on its own is particularly unsuitable for trainees, recently trained or inexperienced counsellors.

D. Care needs to be taken to develop an atmosphere conducive to sharing, questioning and challenging each others' practice in a constructive and supportive way.

E. As well as having a background in counselling work, supervisors should have appropriate groupwork experience in order to facilitate this kind of group.

F.   All participants should have sufficient group-work experience to be able to engage the group process in ways which facilitate effective counselling supervision.

G.   Explicit consideration should be given to deciding who is responsible for providing the counselling supervision, and how the task of counselling supervision will be carried out.

H.   It is good practice to have an independent consultant to visit regularly to observe and monitor the process and quality of the counselling supervision.

B.3   Management of Work

B.3.1   The Counselling Supervision Contract

B.3.1.1   Where supervisors and supervisees work for the same agency or organisation the supervisor is responsible for clarifying all contractual obligations.

3.1.2   Supervisors must inform their supervisee, as appropriate, about their own training, philosophy and theoretical position, qualifications, approach to antidiscriminatory practice and the methods of counselling supervision they use.

3.1.3   Supervisors must be explicit regarding practical arrangements for counselling supervision, paying particular regard to the length of contact time, the frequency of contact, policy and practice regarding record keeping, and the privacy of the venue.

3.1.4   Fees and fee increases must be arranged and agreed in advance.

3.1.5   Supervisors and supervisees must make explicit the expectations and requirements they have of each other. This should include the manner in which any formal assessment of the supervisee's work will be conducted. Each party should assess the value of working with the other, and review this regularly.

3.1.6   Supervisors must discuss their policy regarding giving references and any fees that

may be charged for this or for any other work done outside counselling supervision time.

3.1.7   Before formalising a counselling supervision contract supervisors must ascertain what personal counselling the supervisee has or has had. This is in order to take into account any effect this may have on the supervisee's counselling work.

3.1.8   Supervisors working with trainee counsellors must clarify the boundaries of their responsibility and their accountability to their supervisee and to the training course and any agency/placement involved. This should include any formal assessment required.

B.3.2   Confidentiality

3.2.1   As a general principle, supervisors must not reveal confidential material concerning the supervisee or their clients to any other person without the express consent of all parties concerned. Exceptions to this general principle are contained within this Code.

3.2.2   When initial contracts are being made, agreements about the people to whom supervisors may speak about their supervisees' work must include those on whom the supervisors rely for support, supervision or consultancy. There must also be clarity at this stage about the boundaries of confidentiality having regard for the supervisor's own framework of accountability. This is particularly relevant when providing counselling supervision to a trainee counsellor.

3.2.3   Supervisors should take all reasonable steps to encourage supervisees to present their work in ways which protect the personal identity of clients, or to get their client's informed consent to present information which could lead to personal identification.

3.2.4   Supervisors must not reveal confidential information concerning supervisees or their clients to any person or through any public medium except:

a.   When it is clearly stated in the counselling supervision contract and it is in accordance with all BAC Codes of Ethics & Practice.

b. When the supervisor considers it necessary to prevent serious emotional or physical damage to the client, the supervisee or a third party. In such circumstances the supervisee's consent to a change in the agreement about confidentiality should be sought, unless there are good grounds for believing that the supervisee is no longer able to take responsibility for his/her own actions. Whenever possible, the decision to break confidentiality in any circumstances should be made after consultation with another experienced supervisor.

3.2.5 The disclosure of confidential information relating to supervisees is permissible when relevant to the following situations:

a. Recommendations concerning supervisees for professional purposes, e.g. references and assessments.

b. Pursuit of disciplinary action involving supervisees in matters pertaining to standards of ethics and practice.

In the latter instance, any breaking of confidentiality should be minimised by conveying only information pertinent to the immediate situation on a need-to-know basis. The ethical considerations needing to be taken into account are:

    i. Maintaining the best interests of the supervisee

    ii. Enabling the supervisee to take responsibility for their actions

    iii. Taking full account of the supervisor's responsibility to the client and to the wider community.

3.2.6 Information about work with a supervisee may be used for publication or in meetings only with the supervisee's permission and with anonymity preserved.

3.2.7 On occasions when it is necessary to consult with professional colleagues, supervisors ensure that their discussion is purposeful and not trivialising.

B.3.3 The Management of Counselling Supervision

3.3.1 Supervisors must encourage the supervisee to belong to an association or organisation with a Code of Ethics & Practice and a Complaints Procedure. This provides additional safeguards for the supervisor, supervisee and client in the event of a complaint.

3.3.2 If in the course of counselling supervision, it appears that personal counselling may be necessary for the supervisee to be able to continue working effectively, the supervisor should raise this issue with the supervisee.

3.3.3 Supervisors must monitor regularly how their supervisees engage in self-assessment and the self-evaluation of their work.

3.3.4 Supervisors must ensure that their supervisees acknowledge their individual responsibility for ongoing professional development and for participating in further training programmes.

3.3.5 Supervisors must ensure that their supervisees are aware of the distinction between counselling, accountability to management, counselling supervision and training.

3.3.6 Supervisors must ensure with a supervisee who works in an organisation or agency that the lines of accountability and responsibility are clearly defined: supervisee/client; supervisor/supervisee; supervisor/client; organisation/supervisor; organisation/supervisee; organisation/client. There is a distinction between line management supervision and counselling supervision.

3.3.7 Best practice is that the same person should not act as both line manager and counselling supervisor to the same supervisee. However, where the counselling supervisor is also the line manager, the supervisee should have access to independent counselling supervision.

3.3.8 Supervisors who become aware of a conflict between an obligation to a supervisee and an obligation to an employing agency must make explicit to the supervisee the nature of the loyalties and responsibilities involved.

3.3.9 Supervisors who have concerns about a supervisee's work with clients must be clear how they will pursue this if discussion in counselling supervision fails to resolve the issue.

3.3.10 Where disagreements cannot be resolved by discussions between supervisor and supervisee, the supervisor should consult with a fellow professional and, if appropriate, recommend that the supervisee be referred to another supervisor.

3.3.11 Supervisors must discuss with supervisees the need to have arrangements in place to take care of the immediate needs of clients in the event of a sudden and unplanned ending to the counselling relationship. It is good practice for the supervisor to be informed about these arrangements.

Supervision Instruments

The following instruments appear in this Appendix. They are described in Table 12.2.

Supervision Questionnaire (Ladany, Hill, & Nutt, 1996) [a measure of supervisee perceptions of the quality and outcomes of supervision].

Supervisory Styles Inventory (Friedlander & Ward, 1984).

Supervisory Working Alliance Inventory (Efstation, Patton, & Kardash, 1990).

Role Conflict and Role Ambiguity Inventory (called "Supervisor Perceptions of Supervision"; Olk & Friedlander, 1992).

Supervisee Levels Questionnaire—Revised (McNeill, Stoltenberg, & Romans, 1992).

SUPERVISION QUESTIONNAIRE*

1. How would you rate the quality of the supervision you have received?

1	2	3	4
Excellent	Good	Fair	Poor

2. Did you get the kind of supervision you wanted?

1	2	3	4
No, definitely not	No, not really	Yes, generally	Yes, definitely

3. To what extent has this supervision fit your needs?

4	3	2	1
Almost all of my needs have been met	Most of my needs have been met	Only a few of my needs have been met	None of my needs have been met

4. If a friend were in need of supervision, would you recommend this supervisor to him or her?

1	2	3	4
No, definitely not	No, I don't think so	Yes, I think so	Yes, definitely

5. How satisfied are you with the amount of supervision you have received?

1	2	3	4
Quite satisfied	Indifferent or mildly dissatisfied	Mostly satisfied	Very satisfied

6. Has the supervision you received helped you to deal more effectively in your role as a counselor or therapist?

4	3	2	1
Yes, definitely	Yes, generally	No, not really	No, definitely

7. In an overall, general sense, how satisfied are you with the supervision you have received?

4	3	2	1
Very satisfied	Mostly satisfied	Indifferent or mildly dissatisfied	Quite dissatisfied

8. If you were to seek supervision again, would you come back to this supervisor?

1	2	3	4
No, definitely not	No, I don't think so	Yes, I think so	Yes, definitely

*From Ladany, Hill, & Nutt (1996). Measures satisfaction with supervision. Score is sum of the items.

SUPERVISORY STYLES INVENTORY*

For trainees' form: Please indicate your perception of the style of your current or most recent supervisor of psychotherapy/counseling on each of the following descriptors. Circle the number on the scale, from 1 to 7, which best reflects your view of him or her.

For supervisors' form: Please indicate your perceptions of your style as a supervisor of psychotherapy/counseling on each of the following descriptors. Circle the number on the scale, from 1 to 7, which best reflects your view of yourself.

	1 not very	2	3	4	5	6	7 very
1. goal-oriented	1	2	3	4	5	6	7
2. perceptive	1	2	3	4	5	6	7
3. concrete	1	2	3	4	5	6	7
4. explicit	1	2	3	4	5	6	7
5. committed	1	2	3	4	5	6	7
6. affirming	1	2	3	4	5	6	7
7. practical	1	2	3	4	5	6	7
8. sensitive	1	2	3	4	5	6	7
9. collaborative	1	2	3	4	5	6	7
10. intuitive	1	2	3	4	5	6	7
11. reflective	1	2	3	4	5	6	7
12. responsive	1	2	3	4	5	6	7
13. structured	1	2	3	4	5	6	7
14. evaluative	1	2	3	4	5	6	7
15. friendly	1	2	3	4	5	6	7
16. flexible	1	2	3	4	5	6	7
17. prescriptive	1	2	3	4	5	6	7
18. didactic	1	2	3	4	5	6	7
19. thorough	1	2	3	4	5	6	7
20. focused	1	2	3	4	5	6	7
21. creative	1	2	3	4	5	6	7
22. supportive	1	2	3	4	5	6	7
23. open	1	2	3	4	5	6	7
24. realistic	1	2	3	4	5	6	7
25. resourceful	1	2	3	4	5	6	7
26. invested	1	2	3	4	5	6	7
27. facilitative	1	2	3	4	5	6	7
28. therapeutic	1	2	3	4	5	6	7
29. positive	1	2	3	4	5	6	7
30. trusting	1	2	3	4	5	6	7
31. informative	1	2	3	4	5	6	7
32. humorous	1	2	3	4	5	6	7
33. warm	1	2	3	4	5	6	7

Scoring Key for SSI

Attractive:	Sum items 15, 16, 22, 23, 29, 30, 33; divide by 7.
Interpersonally sensitive:	Sum items 2, 5, 10, 11, 21, 25, 26, 28; divide by 8.
Task oriented:	Sum items 1, 3, 4, 7, 13, 14, 17, 18, 19, 20; divide by 10
Filler items:	6, 8, 9, 12, 24, 27, 31, 32

*Developed by M.L. Friedlander & L. G. Ward (1984). Unpublished instrument.

SUPERVISORY WORKING ALLIANCE INVENTORY: SUPERVISOR FORM*

INSTRUCTIONS

Please indicate the frequency with which the behavior described in each of the following items seems characteristic of your work with your supervisee. After each item, check (X) the space over the number corresponding to the appropriate point of the following seven-point scale:

	1 Almost Never	2	3	4	5	6	7 Almost Always

1. I help my trainee work within a specific treatment plan with his/her client.

    1   2   3   4   5   6   7

2. I help my trainee stay on track during out meetings.

    1   2   3   4   5   6   7

3. My style is to carefully and systematically consider the material that my trainee brings to supervision.

    1   2   3   4   5   6   7

4. My trainee works with me on specific goals in the supervisory session.

    1   2   3   4   5   6   7

5. In supervision, I expect my trainee to think about or reflect on my comments to him or her.

    1   2   3   4   5   6   7

6. I teach my trainee through direct suggestion.

    1   2   3   4   5   6   7

7. In supervision, I place a high priority on our understanding the client's perspective.

    1   2   3   4   5   6   7

8. I encourage my trainee to take time to understand what the client is saying and doing.

    1   2   3   4   5   6   7

9. When correcting my trainee's errors with a client, I offer alternative ways of intervening.

    1   2   3   4   5   6   7

10. I encourage my trainee to formulate his/her own interventions with his/her clients.

    1   2   3   4   5   6   7

11. I encourage my trainee to talk about the work in ways that are comfortable for him/her.

    1   2   3   4   5   6   7

12. I welcome my trainee's explanations about his/her client's behavior.

    1   2   3   4   5   6   7

13. During supervision, my trainee talks more than I do.

    1   2   3   4   5   6   7

*The supervisor and supervisee forms of the Supervisory Working Alliance are reprinted with permission by the American Psychological Association. From: Efstation, J. F., Patton, M. J., & Kardash, C. M. (1990). Measuring the working alliance in counselor supervision. *Journal of Counseling Psychology, 37,* 322–329.

Continued

	1 Almost Never	2	3	4	5	6	7 Almost Always
14. I make an effort to understand my trainee.	1	2	3	4	5	6	7
15. I am tactful when commenting about my trainee's performance.	1	2	3	4	5	6	7
16. I facilitate my trainee's talking in our sessions.	1	2	3	4	5	6	7
17. In supervision, my trainee is more curious than anxious when discussing his/her difficulties with me.	1	2	3	4	5	6	7
18. My trainee appears to be comfortable working with me.	1	2	3	4	5	6	7
19. My trainee understands client behavior and treatment techniques similar to the way I do.	1	2	3	4	5	6	7
20. During supervision, my trainee seems able to stand back and reflect on what I am saying to him/her.	1	2	3	4	5	6	7
21. I stay in tune with my trainee during supervision.	1	2	3	4	5	6	7
22. My trainee identifies with me in the way he/she thinks and talks about his/her clients.	1	2	3	4	5	6	7
23. My trainee consistently implements suggestions made in supervision.	1	2	3	4	5	6	7

SCORING

The supervisor form of the SWAI has three scales. Rapport, Client Focus, and Identification. They are scored as follows.

Rapport: Sum items 10–16, then divide by 7.
Client Focus: Sum items 1–9, then divide by 9.
Identification: Sum items 17–23, then divide by 7.

SUPERVISORY WORKING ALLIANCE INVENTORY: TRAINEE FORM

INSTRUCTIONS

Please indicate the frequency with which the behavior described in each of the following items seems characteristic of your work with your supervisee. After each item, check (X) the space over the number corresponding to the appropriate point on the following seven-point scale:

	1 Almost Never	2	3	4	5	6	7 Almost Always

1. I feel comfortable working with my supervisor.

    1   2   3   4   5   6   7

2. My supervisor welcomes my explanations about the client's behavior.

    1   2   3   4   5   6   7

3. My supervisor makes the effort to understand me.

    1   2   3   4   5   6   7

4. My supervisor encourages me to talk about my work with clients in ways that are comfortable for me.

    1   2   3   4   5   6   7

5. My supervisor is tactful when commenting about my performance.

    1   2   3   4   5   6   7

6. My supervisor encourages me to formulate my own interventions with the client.

    1   2   3   4   5   6   7

7. My supervisor helps me talk freely in our sessions.

    1   2   3   4   5   6   7

8. My supervisor stays in tune with me during supervision.

    1   2   3   4   5   6   7

9. I understand client behavior and treatment technique similar to the way my supervisor does.

    1   2   3   4   5   6   7

10. I feel free to mention to my supervisor any troublesome feelings I might have about him/her.

    1   2   3   4   5   6   7

11. My supervisor treats me like a colleague in our supervisory sessions.

    1   2   3   4   5   6   7

12. In supervision, I am more curious than anxious when discussing my difficulties with clients.

    1   2   3   4   5   6   7

13. In supervision, my supervisor places a high priority on our understanding the client's perspective.

    1   2   3   4   5   6   7

Continued

	1 Almost Never	2	3	4	5	6	7 Almost Always

14. My supervisor encourages me to take time to understand what the client is saying and doing.

| 1 | 2 | 3 | 4 | 5 | 6 | 7 |

15. My supervisor's style is to carefully and systematically consider the material I bring to supervision.

| 1 | 2 | 3 | 4 | 5 | 6 | 7 |

16. When correcting my errors with a client, my supervisor offers alternative ways of intervening with that client.

| 1 | 2 | 3 | 4 | 5 | 6 | 7 |

17. My supervisor helps me work within a specific treatment plan with my clients.

| 1 | 2 | 3 | 4 | 5 | 6 | 7 |

18. My supervisor helps me stay on track during our meetings.

| 1 | 2 | 3 | 4 | 5 | 6 | 7 |

19. I work with my supervisor on specific goals in the supervisory session.

| 1 | 2 | 3 | 4 | 5 | 6 | 7 |

SCORING

The trainee form of the SWAI has two scales, Rapport and Client Focus. They are scored as follows.
   Rapport: Sum items 1–12, then divide by 12.
Client Focus: Sum items 13–19, then divide by 6.

SUPERVISEE PERCEPTIONS OF SUPERVISION*

INSTRUCTIONS

The following statements describe some problems that therapists-in-training may experience during the course of clinical supervision. Please read each statement and then rate the extent to which you have experienced difficulty in supervision in your most recent clinical training.

I HAVE EXPERIENCED DIFFICULTY IN MY CURRENT OR MOST RECENT SUPERVISION BECAUSE:

	Not at all				Very much so
1. I was not certain about what material to present to my supervisor	1	2	3	4	5
2. I have felt that my supervisor was incompetent or less competent than I. I often felt as though I was supervising him/her.	1	2	3	4	5
3. I have wanted to challenge the appropriateness of my supervisor's recommendations for using a technique with one of my clients, but I have thought it better to keep my opinions to myself.	1	2	3	4	5
4. I wasn't sure how best to use supervision as I became more experienced, although I was aware that I was undecided about whether to confront her/him.	1	2	3	4	5
5. I have believed that my supervisor's behavior in one or more situations was unethical or illegal and I was undecided about whether to confront him/her.	1	2	3	4	5
6. My orientation to therapy was different from that of my supervisor. She or he wanted me to work with clients using her or his framework, and I felt that I should be allowed to use my own approach.	1	2	3	4	5
7. I have wanted to intervene with one of my clients in a particular way and my supervisor has wanted me to approach the client in a very different way. I am expected both to judge what is appropriate for myself and also to do what I am told.	1	2	3	4	5
8. My supervisor expected to me to come prepared for supervision, but I had no idea what or how to prepare.	1	2	3	4	5
9. I wasn't sure how autonomous I should be in my work with clients.	1	2	3	4	5
10. My supervisor told me to do something I perceived to be illegal or unethical and I was expected to comply.	1	2	3	4	5
11. My supervisor's criteria for evaluating my work were not specific.	1	2	3	4	5
12. I was not sure that I had done what the supervisor expected me to do in a session with a client.	1	2	3	4	5
13. The criteria for evaluating my performance in supervision were not clear.	1	2	3	4	5
14. I got mixed signals from my supervisor and I was unsure of which signals to attend to.	1	2	3	4	5

*From M. Olk and M. L. Friedlander (1992).

Continued

	Not at all				Very much so
15. When using a new technique, I was unclear about the specific steps involved. As a result, I wasn't sure how my supervisor would evaluate my work.	1	2	3	4	5
16. I disagreed with my supervisor about how to introduce a specific issue to a client, but I also wanted to do what the supervisor recommended.	1	2	3	4	5
17. Part of me wanted to rely on my own instincts with clients, but I always knew that my supervisor would have the last word.	1	2	3	4	5
18. The feedback I got from my supervisor did not help me to know what was expected of me in my day to day work with clients.	1	2	3	4	5
19. I was not comfortable using a technique recommended by my supervisor; however, I felt that I should do what my supervisor recommended.	1	2	3	4	5
20. Everything was new and I wasn't sure what would be expected of me.	1	2	3	4	5
21. I was not sure if I should discuss my professional weaknesses in supervision because I was not sure how I would be evaluated.	1	2	3	4	5
22. I disagreed with my supervisor about implementing a specific technique, but I also wanted to do what the supervisor thought best.	1	2	3	4	5
23. My supervisor gave me no feedback and I felt lost.	1	2	3	4	5
24. My supervisor told me what to do with a client, but didn't give me very specific ideas about how to do it.	1	2	3	4	5
25. My supervisor wanted me to pursue an assessment technique that I considered inappropriate for a particular client.	1	2	3	4	5
26. There were no clear guidelines for my behavior in supervision.	1	2	3	4	5
27. The supervisor gave no constructive or negative feedback and as a result, I did not know how to address my weaknesses.	1	2	3	4	5
28. I didn't know how I was doing as a therapist and, as a result, I didn't know how my supervisor would evaluate me.	1	2	3	4	5
29. I was unsure of what to expect from my supervisor.	1	2	3	4	5

Scoring Key:
Role ambiguity items: 1, 4, 8, 9, 11, 12, 13, 18, 20, 21, 23, 24, 26, 27, 28, 29
Role conflict items: 2, 3, 5, 6, 7, 10, 14, 15, 16, 17, 19, 22, 25

SUPERVISEE LEVELS QUESTIONNAIRE—REVISED*

Please answer the items that follow in terms of your own *current* behavior. In responding to those items, use the following scale:

Never	Rarely	Sometimes	Half the Time	Often	Most of the Time	Always
1	2	3	4	5	6	7

	1	2	3	4	5	6	7
1. I feel genuinely relaxed and comfortable in my counseling or therapy sessions.	1	2	3	4	5	6	7
2. I am able to critique counseling tapes and gain insights with minimum help from my supervisor.	1	2	3	4	5	6	7
3. I am able to be spontaneous in counseling or therapy, yet my behavior is relevant.	1	2	3	4	5	6	7
4. I lack self-confidence in establishing counseling relationships with diverse client types.	1	2	3	4	5	6	7
5. I am able to apply a consistent personalized rationale of human behavior in working with my clients.	1	2	3	4	5	6	7
6. I tend to get confused when things don't go according to plan and lack confidence in the ability to handle the unexpected.	1	2	3	4	5	6	7
7. The overall quality of my work fluctuates; on some days I do well, on other days I do poorly.	1	2	3	4	5	6	7
8. I depend on my supervision considerably in figuring out how to deal with my clients.	1	2	3	4	5	6	7
9. I feel comfortable confronting my clients.	1	2	3	4	5	6	7
10. Much of the time in counseling or therapy I find myself thinking about my next response instead of fitting my intervention into the overall picture.	1	2	3	4	5	6	7
11. My motivation fluctuates from day to day.	1	2	3	4	5	6	7
12. At times, I wish my supervisor could be in the counseling or therapy session to lend a hand.	1	2	3	4	5	6	7
13. During counseling or therapy sessions, I find it difficult to concentrate because of my concern about my own performance.	1	2	3	4	5	6	7
14. Although at times I really want advice or feedback from my supervisor, at *other* times I really want to do things my own way.	1	2	3	4	5	6	7
15. Sometimes the client's situation seems so hopeless. I just don't know what to do.	1	2	3	4	5	6	7
16. It is important that my supervisor allow me to make my own mistakes.	1	2	3	4	5	6	7
17. Given my current state of professional development, I believe I know when I need consultation from my supervisor and when I don't.	1	2	3	4	5	6	7
18. Sometimes I question how suited I am to be a counselor or therapist.	1	2	3	4	5	6	7

*From B. W. McNeill, C. D. Stoltenberg, & J. S. Romans (1992).

Continued

19. Regarding counseling or therapy, I view my supervisor as a teacher or mentor.	1	2	3	4	5	6	7
20. Sometimes I feel that counseling or therapy is so complex I never will be able to learn it all.	1	2	3	4	5	6	7
21. I believe I know my strengths and weaknesses as a counselor sufficiently well to understand my professional potential and limitations.	1	2	3	4	5	6	7
22. Regarding my counseling or therapy, I view my supervisor as a peer or colleague.	1	2	3	4	5	6	7
23. I think I know myself well and am able to integrate that into my therapeutic style.	1	2	3	4	5	6	7
24. I find I am able to understand my clients' view of the world, yet help them objectively evaluate alternatives.	1	2	3	4	5	6	7
25. At my current level of professional development, my confidence in my abilities is such that my desire to do counseling or therapy doesn't change much from day to day.	1	2	3	4	5	6	7
26. I find I am able to empathize with my clients' feeling states, but still help them focus on problem resolution.	1	2	3	4	5	6	7
27. I am able to adequately assess my interpersonal impact on clients and use that knowledge therapeutically.	1	2	3	4	5	6	7
28. I am adequately able to assess the client's interpersonal impact on me and use that therapeutically.	1	2	3	4	5	6	7
29. I believe I exhibit a consistent professional objectivity and ability to work within my role as a counselor without *undue overinvolvement* with my clients.	1	2	3	4	5	6	7
30. I believe I exhibit a consistent professional objectivity and ability to work within my role as a counselor without *excessive distance* from my clients.	1	2	3	4	5	6	7

Scoring key for the three scales:

Self and Other Awareness: 1, 3, 5, 9, 10*, 13*, 24, 26, 27, 28, 29, 30

Motivation: 7, 11*, 15*, 18*, 20*, 21, 23, 25

Dependency–Autonomy: 2, 4*, 6*, 8, 12*, 14, 16, 17, 19*, 22

*Indicates reverse scoring. To score: sum the items in the scale and then divide by the number of items.

Structured Workshop in Clinical Supervision*

STRUCTURED WORKSHOP IN CLINICAL SUPERVISION

This workshop has been developed to give participants an opportunity to observe and practice distinct supervision approaches, as well as to consider primary supervision issues. The desired outcomes of the workshop are to equip the novice supervisor with some breadth of practice, as well as to instruct seasoned supervisors in alternatives to their present approach. Because of its brevity, the workshop only introduces the participants to relevant supervision models and issues. Therefore, in the optimal training situation the workshop is followed by extensive supervision-of-supervision.

Session 1

Topic: Obtaining baseline behavior on supervisor *focus*

Rationale and Assumptions: Counseling is a complex activity that weaves many different behaviors into its cloth. The observer (supervisor), however, must simplify this pattern into conceptual units that can be communicated back to the counselor or therapist for the purposes of supervision. Each super-

*Developed in 1980 by Janine M. Bernard. Revised 1989, 1996.

visor has an idiosyncratic style of observing based on his or her world view and will focus on certain behaviors to the exclusion of others. It is important for the supervisor to know his or her natural affinity to certain focus areas in order to compensate, if necessary. For this laboratory session, the three focus areas are defined as (1) intervention skills, (2) conceptualization skills, and (3) personalization skills (Bernard, 1979; Bernard, 1997).

Activities

1. Participants are shown a 30-minute counseling videotape and are asked to take notes on the counselor's performance as if they were the counselor's supervisor and would be giving feedback after the session.

2. When the tape is finished, participants are asked to study their notes and choose five items they would *most want* to cover in supervision. After the items have been identified, the participants rank order them by importance.

3. From the same observation notes, participants are also asked to choose three items they would use in the *first few minutes* of a supervision session (not necessarily from the list of five obtained above).

4. Referring to step 2, participants report their most important items to be covered in supervision (number 1 on their list of 5). These are written on a blackboard and the group discusses the focus of each item [intervention, conceptualization, or personalization using Bernard's (1979) discrimination model]. All participants are taught to discriminate between categories at this time.

5. The large group is broken down into groups of three or four. Each small group categorizes

each member's first five items. In addition, the items obtained in step 3 are categorized.

6. Back in the large group, each participant identifies his or her *primary* focus category (obtained from items the participant had deemed as most important) and his or her entry behavior (initial items). The implications of these for supervision are discussed.

Comments: Most supervisors are not aware of their baseline focus behaviors although they generally think that the results of the exercise are representative of their general style. They also find it interesting to consider the effect of their entry style on the process of supervision. (For instance, often supervisors want to focus on counselor feelings at the beginning of supervision, but then switch to intervention issues. Later they realize that this might leave the counselor at a disadvantage if the switch is done abruptly.) In addition to identifying baseline focus behavior, there are two additional advantages to this first session. First, participants are forced to condense their observation notes into five important feedback items. This is important since many supervisors attempt to give counselors too much feedback per session. Second, by comparing each supervisor's most important five items, participants become sensitized to the fact that any counseling session can be viewed in a variety of ways, again reflecting a variety of world views. This increases their motivation to move beyond their baseline focus behavior.

Session 2

Topic: Obtaining baseline behavior on supervisor *role*

Rationale and Assumptions: Once supervisors are aware of their primary focus, they superimpose role behavior in an attempt to communicate their perceptions to the counselor. As with focus behavior, there is a tendency for supervisors to favor certain roles over others when working with counselors. This baseline behavior becomes the target of Session 2 using the labels of teacher, counselor, and consultant (Bernard, 1979) as discriminate role cat-

egories. Again, the assumption is that if supervisors are made aware of their baseline role behavior, they will be in a more strategic position to choose other roles when appropriate.

Activities: The large group is divided into dyads for an exercise.

1. Using observation notes taken during Session 1, 30-minute role plays are conducted where one person plays the role of supervisor while the other is the counselor in the tape viewed earlier. These sessions are audiotaped.

2. A second round of simulations follows in order to give every participant an opportunity to perform in the role of supervisor. (However, dyads should be varied so that the same two participants are not in more than one role play with each other.)

3. The large group is reassembled. One of the participants' audiotapes is used as a demonstration tape. The group is instructed to focus on the supervisor only and to note the role the supervisor is using as the tape proceeds. The instructor monitors on a chalkboard or overhead projector so that participants can check their ability to identify each of the roles. The tape is stopped whenever there is a question about the role being used. At the end of this activity, participants should be able to identify the three different supervisor roles. If time permits, a second tape is reviewed. (Depending on the ability of the participants to recognize different supervisor roles, the audiotapes can be analyzed simultaneously for focus behaviors with a discussion of different combinations.)

4. An assignment is given for participants to analyze their own audiotapes for role behavior before Session 3.

   Note: If the training is being done as a two-day workshop, a 30-minute time slot is needed here for individual analysis of tapes.

Comments: Although some participants are not surprised with their baseline role behavior, others are. One participant had been pegged as a "counselor type"; his responses, however, were almost exclusively in the teacher category. This was important information for him in order to avoid confusion in his relationship with counselors. Some participants have made the comment that they were finding out as much about themselves as they had in their counselor training. This surprised them.

Session 3

Topic: The discrimination model
Rationale and Assumptions: A major assumption of this entire training workshop is that supervisors need practice in different supervisor behaviors before they can use them competently with counselors. Therefore, recognizing their baseline focus and role behaviors must be followed by practicing those behaviors which come less easily. Session 3 is designed to give supervisors practice in all three focus behaviors and all three role behaviors. As a result, their repertoire will be increased beyond their baseline abilities.
References: Bernard, 1979, 1997.

Activities

1. Participants are asked whether they had any difficulty in completing the assignment at the end of Session 2. Questions are answered and another audiotape is analyzed if necessary. Participants share the results of their tape analysis.
2. A different 30-minute counseling videotape is viewed by the group. Participants are asked to divide a piece of paper in thirds and take notes on the counselor's performance in the three different categories of intervention skills, conceptualization, and personalization. (By asking participants to take notes in this manner, they learn to discriminate among categories while viewing a counseling session.)
3. Using a fishbowl format, role plays follow with one participant playing the counselor in the videotape and the other playing the supervisor. The supervisor must give feedback in all three focus areas while being given role changes with flashcards (out of the counselor's view). Role plays are 10 to 15 minutes in length and are fol-

lowed by feedback from the counselor and discussion in the group.
4. More role plays follows until several participants have had an opportunity to use the discrimination model on cue.

Comments: As with prepracticum training for counselors, participants often complain at this point in the training that they are becoming overly conscious of their behavior to the detriment of the supervision process. It is important that the instructor support this reaction as an accurate reflection of the learning process. Participants are overlearning behaviors so that they can surface more naturally in the future. The comparison between counselor training and supervisor training is usually sufficient to handle this protest.

Session 4

Topic: Interpersonal process recall (IPR)
Rationale and Assumptions: IPR is an important supervision model, especially when there are interpersonal issues in the counselor–client relationship and the counselor has conceptual realizations that he or she is not translating into process. IPR is also important for the supervisor because it stresses the consultant and counselor roles, and most supervisors find it difficult to screen out the teacher role. Also, inherent in this model is a respect for the counselor as his or her own authority, which adds an important dimension to the supervisor–counselor relationship.
References: Kagan, 1980; Bernard, 1989.

Activities

1. Prior to this session, three volunteers must be used to make training videotapes. One 30-minute counseling session (simulated) is made using two of the volunteers, one as client and the other as counselor. Following this simulation, the third volunteer, who has observed the former videotape as it is being taped, acts as supervisor with the counselor in a 15-minute taped supervision session.
2. The first activity in the lab is an IPR demonstration with the counselor from the simulation,

the instructor taking the role of "inquirer." Once the role has been demonstrated, the supervisor volunteer from step 1 continues with the IPR session. Halfway through the tape, other participants are invited to take the role of observer.

3. Following the IPR segment is a discussion of the process, with the counselor and client giving feedback to the different inquirers and remarking on the learning involved in the IPR process.

4. The next activity is a supervisor–counselor IPR session using the 15-minute supervision tape made prior to the session. A volunteer from the group acts as inquirer. Similar relationship or conceptual issues between supervisor and counselor are targeted as was done between counselor and client.

5. A discussion similar to that in step 3 with feedback given by counselor and supervisor follows. The use of IPR for training counselors and supervisors is discussed.

Comments: Participants find it helpful to follow the usual counselor–client IPR session with the supervisor–counselor IPR session. Participants typically are of the opinion that IPR has the potential of magnifying a relationship and comment on the advantages and potential disadvantages of such a potential. Participants find it especially valuable to experience the model in the supervisor–counselor IPR session because it gives them insight as to how this model might be received by counselors. IPR is viewed as most helpful when interpersonal dynamics between counselor and client or between supervisor and counselor are subtle and thus need magnification. For more obvious relationship issues, the model is viewed as having potential drawbacks if magnification would result in distortion. Also, the role of inquirer is a good exercise for any supervisor who needs to do less teaching in supervision.

Note: If step 1 is not possible, the IPR demonstration can be done if one or two participants can bring an audiotape of one of their therapy session to the workshop. However, the supervisor–therapist dimensions will not occur using this option.

Session 5

Topic: Microtraining

Rationale and Assumptions: The microtraining (MT) model offers an excellent balance to IPR because it emphasizes the teacher role and stresses process skills. Thus, MT is an essential part of supervisor training since the supervisor is often put in the position of teaching new or more advanced skills or strategies to the counselor. Indeed, if teaching were not a component of supervision, professional growth for the counselor would be limited. Microtraining is the most direct and efficient form of teaching.

References: Akamatsu, 1980; Forsyth & Ivey, 1980.

Activities

1. A 30-minute counseling videotape is viewed by the group.

2. The large group is divided into smaller groups of three or four and these smaller groups decide on two or three strategies or skills that could be taught to the counselor in the videotape to improve the counseling session. It is important that suggestions be limited to *observable behaviors* that are very specific.

3. Back in the large group and using the MT format, a participant volunteers (as supervisor) to teach one of the skills or strategies, using modeling and practice, to another participant (counselor) from another small group. This MT session is videotaped. The counselor then attempts to use this learning in a 5-minute role play with yet another participant (client), and this is also videotaped.

4. The large group watches the videotape and feedback follows, which focuses on the supervisor's skills and clarity in teaching. The counselor's ability to translate the supervisor's teaching into behavior is the best feedback. If the original teaching was not complete, accurate, or skillful, the process is repeated. (Obviously, the last activity is more meaningful when the skill being taught is new to the "counselor." Although most participants are familiar with the techniques that are suggested, it is best if the "counselor" has not attempted

them in actual practice. When this is the case, this activity can offer some welcomed practice with unique therapeutic interventions.)

5. Steps 3 and 4 are repeated with a different pair or volunteers and different content.

Comments: Supervisors appreciate the immediate feedback they receive on their skills as teachers. They also find it very helpful to repeat the process until they have mastered teaching any one skill. For the purposes of the training session, it is assumed that if the volunteer counselor does not accurately perform the skill as the supervisor wished the supervisor did not instruct in a clear or concise enough manner. The videotape playback also gives supervisors information about assumptions they make in their instructions. Supervisors discover the value of taping their supervision sessions, as well as having counselors practice new skills in simulation, rather than attempting them initially in a subsequent counseling session. Although initially more time consuming, they feel this is more efficient in the long run.

Session 6

Topic: Live supervision
Reference: Haley, 1987.
Rationale and Assumptions: Live supervision is important for a variety of reasons. For training purposes, live supervision allows a counselor to work with a client that is too difficult for him or her to work with without live supervision. Another training advantage is that live supervision gives the supervisor an opportunity to pace the counselor through counseling strategies, which ultimately produces a more reinforcing and supportive atmosphere for learning. This eliminates a mutually frustrating situation where the supervisor sees major errors midway through a session but must wait until later to tell the counselor—when it is too late to do anything about it! One major condition and assumption for using live supervision is a positive relationship between supervisor and counselor. Live supervision is a delicate paradigm and will not be successful if the counselor feels criticized or threatened by the supervisor.

On another level, live supervision is important as an ethical safeguard for the supervisor. Most supervisors can remember a time when they wanted to, or should have, interrupted a counseling session for a number of reasons, most of which center around the well-being of the client. It is very disrupting for supervisor, counselor, and client if this kind of delicate or emergency situation is the first time a supervisor uses an active role as a supervisor during a counseling session. Therefore, training and regular, or even intermittent, use of a live supervision model allows for more flexibility, which tends to minimize the possibilities of ethical breaches occurring.

It is assumed also that the use of live supervision causes no major discomfort for clients if the counselor and supervisor are comfortable and competent in its use. Although there are several forms of live supervision (e.g., bug-in-the-ear, telephone systems, etc.), training is centered around calling the counselor out of the session by means of a light knock on the observation window, since this requires no additional facilities and allows for maximum application by the participants.

Finally, it should be noted that live supervision can look deceptively simple when, in fact, it is a complex model. Therefore, the following exercises take some components of live supervision out of context, more so than for other models. The participant should be alerted to the need for both additional training and follow-up if live supervision is to be used effectively.

Activities

1. A major skill in live supervision is the ability to give brief, clear, and helpful directives to the counselor. Although directives should have a sound rationale, they should be delivered in behavioral or intervention language so that the counselor can translate the directive into counseling behavior easily. In order to acquire skill in directive giving, participants watch a videotape of a counseling session, which is stopped at several predetermined times. Participants jot down a directive each time the tape is stopped. Several directives are then offered by members

of the group, and a discussion follows analyzing the directives for their precision, clarity, and helpfulness.

2. Practice in composing directives is followed by a simulated counseling session viewed by the participants on a TV monitor. During the counseling session, each participant is required to interrupt the session at least once with a directive. All directives are audiorecorded in the observation room. The counselor must attempt to implement each directive upon returning to the counseling room.

3. In addition to the immediate feedback that the participant receives by observing how the directive is translated by the counselor and received by the client, all directives are reviewed after the simulation is over and discussed by the entire group, with specific attention given to the counselor's feedback.

4. Because activities 2 and 3 serve almost as a caricature of live supervision (because of the frequency of the interruptions), rather than a typical live supervision session, they are followed by a simulation where observers are asked to be conservative and call for a directive only when they think one will be helpful to the therapist. This activity can be aided by giving the client a very resistant or manipulative role, one that would cause most therapists to welcome some help.

Comments: Of all the models taught in the lab, live supervision typically earns the strongest reaction. It is common for some participants to be very cautious, if not skeptical, about the possible gains in using this model. However, the workshop experience usually dispels such concerns. Those who volunteer to be counselors in the simulations remark that they felt a great deal of support in the form of directives, and not the criticism they had expected to experience. It is usually the general consensus that the team effort experience of live supervision and the potential of changing the direction of a session more than compensate for the interruption of the counseling process.

Session 7

Topic: Evaluation

Rationale and Assumptions: Evaluation is one of the most crucial responsibilities of the supervisor. It is important for the supervisor to be reacting to some objective criteria, while remaining sensitive to subjective issues. Without specific training in evaluation, this responsibility often is handled in a random fashion. Connecting this with Session 8, it is also important that the supervisor be a discriminating and clear evaluator for ethical reasons. This workshop session is based on three distinct evaluation skills: (1) identifying criteria for evaluation, (2) recognizing the relative strengths and deficits of the counselor, and (3) communicating these in clear, concrete language.

Activities

1. Prior to this session (or in the session in groups), participants are asked to identify 10 to 15 criteria they consider important for counselor effectiveness. In small groups they discuss their criteria and, perhaps, refine them.

2. In the large group, participants view a 20- to 30-minute counseling tape of a novice counselor. Participants then rate the counselor on their criteria (using a Likert scale). In addition, participants rate the counseling using the Evaluation of Therapist Performance: Short Form. (The short form has 15 items divided equally between intervention skills, conceptualization, and personalization.)

3. Participants return to small groups to discuss their evaluations. The instructor presents the key for the Short Form so that participants can see if they were more critical of intervention skills, for example, than for the other two areas of counselor performance. And differences among participants are discussed. Participants are also asked to discuss any difficulty in rating a counselor on the criteria they have chosen. It is at this point that participants may realize that they have selected too few criteria that lend themselves to observation.

4. Participants are then asked to take their criteria and translate them into behaviors that are observable. The instructor may need to take one participant's items and do this with the whole group. Once this is accomplished (this might be too time consuming to do in one session), participants can again rate the counselor seen on videotape using the revised criteria.

5. Depending on the time taken for steps 1 to 4, role plays can follow in which participants practice giving feedback (positive and negative) to volunteers who play the part of the counselor in the videotape. Feedback is given to the supervisor regarding the clarity and conciseness of the feedback by both the counselor and the larger group.

Comments: There are several insights that seem to develop from this workshop session. First, participants begin to appreciate the importance of selecting criteria that can be evaluated with some accuracy. This almost requires that the criteria (or some of them) be observable. Second, occasionally some of the information related to the first session emerges as a result of completing the Short Form. If a participant had a strong conceptualization theme in the first session, it is possible that he or she may be more critical of the counselor on this theme. If participants with other themes (e.g., intervention skills) are not as critical on the conceptualization items, this is important information. The instructor can help participants realize that their investment in part of the counseling process may compromise their ability to carry out objective (relatively speaking) evaluations. Finally, participants also find that receiving feedback on how they communicate their impressions to the counselors reveals new information for them. For instance, some participants are surprised that they receive more constructive feedback on their delivery of negative feedback than positive feedback. By this point in the workshop, participants are fairly confident and trust their critical perceptions. They can remain, however, somewhat ambiguous and unclear regarding positive impressions.

Session 8

Topic: Ethical and legal issues

References: Cormier & Bernard, 1982; Bernard, 1987.

Rationale and Assumptions: First, it must be noted that all of the above training is considered vital for avoiding ethical and legal problems. Assuming that the supervisor is able to evaluate counselors and clients accurately and perform in a variety of appropriate ways, ethical and legal situations most often arise as a result of avoidance, oversight, or discomfort on the part of the supervisor, rather than malice or a deliberate disregard of professional ethical guidelines. This workshop assumes that training must take two forms to adequately prepare the participant: (1) Because most supervisors in counseling or psychotherapy are primarily trained as practitioners, they are less apt to be prepared to accept the power and authority inherent in the role of supervisor. If they refuse to accept the responsibility to evaluate, they are more likely to find themselves in unethical situations. It is important that supervisor training not assume that this issue will work itself out naturally. Supervisors are much more comfortable and confident if they have had prior practice in asserting themselves in a direct and responsible manner. (2) Even if supervisors are generally comfortable with their roles, there might be particular situations that they are unprepared for and that they avoid because they make them uncomfortable. These particular situations tend to be those that can lead most often to ethical and legal problems. For instance, a supervisor might be neglectful in referring a client to another counselor even though she or he believes that the present counselor is not sufficiently skilled to handle the case. Supervisor training should include experiences in confronting uncomfortable situations so that supervisors have a repertoire of skills and alternatives that will enable them to be responsible and ethical without undue stress.

Activities

1. Participants view a videotape of a counseling session in which the counselor has performed

poorly. After about 20 minutes of viewing, the group divides into smaller units, and a volunteer in the role of supervisor gives direct, negative feedback to a volunteer in the role of counselor. The supervisor is instructed to be supportive when possible, but to be clear about what must take place for counseling to improve and the necessity of the latter. Observers and the counselor then give feedback to the supervisor.

2. In emergency situations, the supervisor is most likely to be the person called on to deal with a very distraught client. Using a fishbowl format, one participant assumes the stance of a client in need of hospitalization (the diagnosis can be agreed on by the group depending on the client population most participants serve). Another volunteer (as supervisor) works with this client to inform him or her that it is the supervisor's opinion that hospitalization is necessary. After a short while, feedback is given to the supervisor on his or her ability to communicate authority, caring, and important, specific information to the client.

3. Step 2 is followed by another brief simulation of the supervisor making contact with a professional in a discipline other than his or her own in order to make the referral. The instructor usually plays the part of the other professional. The purpose of this activity is to determine whether the supervisor obtained all necessary information from the client in order to make a referral and to tap stereotypes and difficulties in working with other professionals. A discussion follows.

4. The final exercise is designed around the particular needs of the group. Vignettes are presented that depict different ethical and/or legal dilemmas for the supervisor. Several vignettes are acted out in the following fashion. Each vignette has two roles. Depending on the situation, there is often missing information in each role. Although observers are given a description of both roles, those volunteering to be in the vignette are only given one of the roles. How each person communicates his or her in-

formation to the other is part of the exercise. The following is an example of a vignette.

COUNSELOR: You are seeing a woman as a client who has seen another therapist in town. When you ask her if she is currently seeing this person, she is vague. You inform her that you want to contact her former therapist before you can continue to see her. Having acquired the client's permission, you call the therapist, but she is not in. You make another attempt with the same result. Since then, you have made no further attempts to contact the former therapist. There has been no further mention of this therapist in your sessions with your client, and you assume that the issue is past. In your past counseling session with your client, she talks about being very depressed. You want to talk to your supervisor about the possibility of recommending her to a physician in conjunction with counseling, since you believe that her depression is interfering with counseling progress. She has not been sleeping or eating well. This is your major concern as you enter the upcoming supervision session. Your supervisor was not able to observe your last session, so she is dependent on your self-report for supervision.

SUPERVISOR: One of your counselors is seeing a female client, and there is some question whether the client is also seeing another therapist. The counselor informs the client that he must contact the other therapist, and the client agrees to this. Three weeks later you receive a very cold phone call from the therapist who was to be contacted. She has just learned that her client has been seeing your counselor. She makes it clear that professional courtesy (if not ethics) has been violated by your agency since she was not contacted by you or the counselor concerning his therapy with this client. You were not able to observe your supervisee's last session, so you will have to rely on self-report for supervision purposes. Your most urgent intent, however, is to discuss this breach of professional behavior.

Comments: This last session is particularly enjoyable because it involves a bit of drama. The best of some participants comes out as they work creatively through the role plays. Also, because of the type of information being covered, group cohesiveness usually occurs, which adds to the final session. The last activity has, at times, stimulated the use of constructive humor—a positive attribute for a supervisor. This last session should serve to integrate some of the concepts learned earlier in the lab. For instance, in the vignette given above, one supervisor was attempting to get the counselor to "fess up," relying heavily on the consultant role. However, he had a hidden, somewhat punitive alternative if the counselor did not share the critical information. In the feedback session that followed, the supervisor and the observers agreed that a much more straightforward teacher role as an initial style would have been more helpful and more honest. Several participants said that they became aware of how they hid behind the consultant role when uncomfortable and how this could develop into an ethical dilemma.

Evaluation of Counselor Behaviors: Long Form*

	POOR NEVER			GOOD OFTEN		EXCELLENT ALWAYS	
The Counseling Session							
Rate the counselor's ability to:							
1. Begin and end sessions smoothly	1	2	3	4	5	6	7
2. Convey warmth to the client	1	2	3	4	5	6	7
3. Convey competence to the client	1	2	3	4	5	6	7
4. Conduct a systematic and complete intake interview	1	2	3	4	5	6	7
5. Use a variety of counselor responses (reflection, summary, confrontation, ability potential, etc.)	1	2	3	4	5	6	7
6. Explain the nature and objectives of counseling when appropriate	1	2	3	4	5	6	7
7. Be flexible in the session	1	2	3	4	5	6	7
8. Focus on the client's primary concern	1	2	3	4	5	6	7
9. Integrate client's secondary concerns into counseling	1	2	3	4	5	6	7
10. Facilitate client expression of thought and feeling	1	2	3	4	5	6	7
11. Help the client set appropriate goals	1	2	3	4	5	6	7
12. Help the client work toward established goals	1	2	3	4	5	6	7
13. Follow client (nondirective) when client is working or needs some flexibility	1	2	3	4	5	6	7
14. Be directive and create a structured atmosphere when needed	1	2	3	4	5	6	7
15. Pace client to arrive at a good tempo	1	2	3	4	5	6	7
16. Interject counseling knowledge into the interview when appropriate (can teach the client)	1	2	3	4	5	6	7
17. Use different tests to enhance the counseling process	1	2	3	4	5	6	7
18. Arrive at a balance between implementing planned strategies and remaining spontaneous in the counseling session	1	2	3	4	5	6	7
19. Monitor reactions to client when appropriate	1	2	3	4	5	6	7
20. Resist client manipulation	1	2	3	4	5	6	7
21. Respond to client affect when appropriate	1	2	3	4	5	6	7
22. Address interpersonal dynamics between self and client	1	2	3	4	5	6	7

Developed by Janine M. Bernard, 1976. Revised 1981.

Continued

Evaluation of Counselor Behaviors: Long Form   **Continued**

	POOR NEVER				GOOD OFTEN		EXCELLENT ALWAYS	
23. React quickly to important developments in the counseling session	1	2	3	4	5	6	7
24. Keep control of the session	1	2	3	4	5	6	7
25. Be aware of client's nonverbal and verbal behaviors	1	2	3	4	5	6	7
26. Recognize and skillfully interpret client's covert messages	1	2	3	4	5	6	7

Supervision
Rate counselor's ability to:

27. Conceptualize a case accurately	1	2	3	4	5	6	7
28. Arrive at appropriate goals as a result of conceptualization	1	2	3	4	5	6	7
29. Understand interplay between strategies and goals	1	2	3	4	5	6	7
30. Plan a session to enhance overall goals	1	2	3	4	5	6	7
31. Understand the relationship between process goals and outcome goals	1	2	3	4	5	6	7
32. Implement a series of planned responses (strategy)	1	2	3	4	5	6	7
33. Be honest with self	1	2	3	4	5	6	7
34. Recognize his or her own defensive behavior	1	2	3	4	5	6	7
35. Accept feedback from supervisor	1	2	3	4	5	6	7
36. Use feedback in future session	1	2	3	4	5	6	7
37. Trust own insights and state these when they differ from supervisor's	1	2	3	4	5	6	7
38. Use supervision time to learn about counseling and himself or herself	1	2	3	4	5	6	7
39. Exhibit a balance between self-assuredness and awareness of the value of supervision	1	2	3	4	5	6	7
40. Write concise and complete intake and/or termination reports	1	2	3	4	5	6	7

Professional Development
Rate the counselor on the following criteria:

41. Is a reliable member of the staff	1	2	3	4	5	6	7
42. Turns in intake reports promptly	1	2	3	4	5	6	7
43. Behaves in a professional manner on site	1	2	3	4	5	6	7
44. Communicates responsibility for self	1	2	3	4	5	6	7
45. Exhibits professional values	1	2	3	4	5	6	7
46. Is a helpful colleague	1	2	3	4	5	6	7
47. Is sensitive to ethical issues and/or legal issues	1	2	3	4	5	6	7
48. Is respectful of differences among people	1	2	3	4	5	6	7
49. Conveys a respect for the power of counseling and an awareness of its limits	1	2	3	4	5	6	7
50. Overall, exhibits the behaviors and attitudes of a competent and professional counselor	1	2	3	4	5	6	7

Additional comments:

Evaluation of Therapist Performance: Short Form

	POOR NEVER		GOOD OFTEN			EXCELLENT ALWAYS	
Rate the therapist's ability to:							
1. Comprehend the client's issues	1	2	3	4	5	6	7
2. Facilitate client expression of thought and feeling	1	2	3	4	5	6	7
3. Keep control of the therapy session	1	2	3	4	5	6	7
4. Recognize and skillfully interpret client's covert messages	1	2	3	4	5	6	7
5. Identify relationship among conceptual themes as expressed by the client	1	2	3	4	5	6	7
6. Respond to important developments in the session	1	2	3	4	5	6	7
7. Trust his or her insights during therapy session	1	2	3	4	5	6	7
8. Appear comfortable in the role of therapist	1	2	3	4	5	6	7
9. Allow the client to see the *person* behind the *role* of therapist	1	2	3	4	5	6	7
10. Recognize the significance of client statements in relation to the presenting problem	1	2	3	4	5	6	7
11. Keep the session moving toward some therapeutic outcome	1	2	3	4	5	6	7
12. Help the client identify appropriate outcome and/or process goals	1	2	3	4	5	6	7
13. Convey competence to client	1	2	3	4	5	6	7
14. Resist being threatened by or defensive with the client	1	2	3	4	5	6	7
15. Convey warmth and caring to the client	1	2	3	4	5	6	7
16. Overall, the therapist seems to know what he or she is doing	1	2	3	4	5	6	7
17. Overall, the therapist seems to have conceptualized the case correctly	1	2	3	4	5	6	7
18. Overall, the therapist seems congruent as a therapist	1	2	3	4	5	6	7

Key:
Intervention skills items: 2, 3, 6, 10, and 13
Conceptualization skills items: 1, 4, 5, 11, and 12
Personalization skills items: 7, 8, 9, 14, and 15

Developed by Janine M. Bernard, 1982. Revised, 1997.

Name Index

AAMFT, 180, 194
Abadie, P. D., 16, 30, 72, 245, 256
Abroms, G.M., 66
ACA, 180
Acker, M., 88
Adamek, M.S., 132, 134, 141
Adams, J., 146
Adamson, L.A., 68
Ahn, H., 248
Aitken, D., 133
Akamatsu, T.J., 330
Akutsu, F.O., 39
Albee, G. W., 8
Albott, W.L., 61
Alderfer, C., 132
Alexander, J., 48
Allen, G. J., 26, 48, 56
Allen, J.. 112, 120, 129
Allphin, C., 83
Alonso, A., 23, 75, 83, 224, 225,
    226, 237
Alper, V.S., 64, 256
Altmaier, E.M., 254
American Psychological
    Association, 224
Amundson, N., 110
Anderson, C.M., 39
Anderson, J.J., 69, 244
Anderson, J.R., 240
Anderson, S.A., 46, 55, 91
Anderson, T., 142, 143
Anderson-Hanley, C.M., 69, 244
Andrews, J.D.W., 38
Angelone, E.O., 68, 131, 140, 141,
    148, 149
Ansbacher, H., 22
APA, 180
Aponte, H.J., 190
Appelbaum, P.S., 197
Arbuckle, D., 74
Arnold, R.C., 67, 108, 245
Aronson, M.L, 111, 113, 115
Atkinson, B.J., 147, 148
Atwood, J.D., 172
Ault-Riche, M., 46, 47
Authier, J., 107
Aveline, M., 96
Avis, J.M., 235, 260

Bahrick, A.S., 68, 69
Bailey, J.S., 132, 141, 148
Baker, D.E., 67, 68
Baker, E. L., 4
Baker, S.B., 113, 253

Baker, S.D., 260
Baldwin, N.F., 237
Balint, E., 118
Baltes, P.B., 10
Bandura, A., 253
Barak, A., 262
Barlow, D.H., 20, 247
Barnat, M.R., 83, 84
Barrett, M., 148
Bartell, P.A., 188, 189
Bartlett, W.E ., 16, 245
Bascue, L.O., 219, 220
Bateson, G., 143
Batten, C., 43
Baum, L.E, 11
Baum, M., 154
Bauman, W.F., 156
Beach, A., 17, 162
Beamish, P., 194
Bear, T.M., 56
Beavers, W.R., 203, 214
Beavin, J.H., 72, 79, 163
Bechtel, M.A., 263
Beck, A.T., 19, 247
Beck, J.S., 20
Beck, T.D., 213, 222
Becker, D., 21, 66
Bednar, R.L., 69
Behling, J., 50
Beis, E., 219
Belar, C.D., 167
Bellamy, A.R., 156, 172
Bem, D.J., 114
Benjamin, D., 254
Benshoff, J.M., 232
Benson, K., 248
Berg, K.S., 252
Berger, M.C., 139, 140
Bergin, A.E., 39
Berman, J.J., 38, 264
Bernard, J.L., 160, 178
Bernard, J.M., 20, 27, 28, 29, 30, 32,
    39, 42, 45, 47, 58, 60, 69, 90,
    101, 103, 104, 105, 107, 117,
    138, 140, 164, 172, 173, 197,
    203, 232, 233, 236, 238, 239,
    327, 328, 329, 333, 335, 337
Berne, E., 22, 81
Bernstein, B.L., 47, 166
Bernstein, R.M., 142
Betcher, R.W., 69, 80
Betz, R.L., 117, 122
Beutler, L.E., 2, 17, 38, 56, 245
Bierig, J.R., 178

Binder, J.L., 248
Bingham, R.P., 39
Bion, W., 116
Birk, J.M., 55
Birringer, J., 92
Blackmon, B., 44
Blanchette, M., 237
Blocher, D., 10, 23, 59, 78, 79, 116,
    250, 252
Blodgett, E.G., 166, 172
Bloom, J.W., 97, 100
Blumenfield, M., 237
Blumstein, P., 48
Bobbitt, B.L., 152, 262
Bobele, M., 134
Bogo, M., 161, 167
Bond, O., 120, 147
Bondi, A.M., 39
Bonney, W., 224, 232, 240
Bonosky, N., 189
Borders, L.D., 3, 13, 23, 26, 34, 46,
    52, 53, 54, 55, 56, 58, 60, 89, 90,
    91, 93, 95, 100, 105, 124, 125,
    156, 164, 166, 176, 194, 199,
    232, 233, 235, 237, 239, 240,
    245, 252, 258, 261
Bordin, E. S., 18, 67, 68, 69, 73
Boswell, D.L., 93, 98, 105
Bowen, M., 62
Bowlby, J., 35, 68
Bowman, S.L., 69
Bownan, R.L., 189
Bownan, V.E., 189
Boxley, R., 181
Boyd, J.D., 20, 237
Bradey, J., 181
Bradley, F. O., 16, 245
Bradley, J. R., 3
Bradley, L. J., 20, 237, 239
Bradshaw, W.H., Jr., 41
Brager, G., 236, 238
Brandell, J.R., 96, 97
Brashears, F., 3, 202
Braver, M., 53
Brehm, J., 54
Brenock, K., 63, 64, 163, 256, 263
Breunlin, D.C., 98, 99, 108, 141,
    236, 237
Brewer, D., 30, 263
Bridge, P.J., 219, 220
Brieger, K., 50
Brill, R., 208
British Association of Counselling, 310
Brock, C.D., 118

338